A STUDY OF HISTORY

Arnold Toynbee writes:

IN the first volume of *A Study of History,* I start by searching for a unit of historical study that is relatively self-contained and is therefore more or less intelligible in isolation from the rest of history. I was led into this quest by finding myself dissatisfied with the present-day habit of studying history in terms of national states. These seemed, and still seem, to me to be fragments of something larger, and I found this larger and more satisfying unit of study in a civilization. The history of the United States, for instance, or the history of Britain, is, as I see it, a fragment of the history of Western Christendom or the Western Christian World, and I believe I can put my finger on a number of other societies, living or extinct, that are of the same species. Examples of other living civilizations besides the Western Civilization are the Islamic and the Civilization of Eastern Asia, centring on China. Examples of extinct civilizations are the Greco-Roman and the Ancient Egyptian. This practice of dealing in civilizations instead of nations is taken for granted by orientalists, ancient-historians, archae-ologists, and anthropologists. The carving-up of a civilization into pieces labelled 'nations' is, I believe, something peculiar to students of modern Western history, and, with them too, this present practice of theirs is only recent. Down to the beginning of the eighteenth century, the classic works of Western historians took for their field the whole history of Western Christendom or even the whole history of the World from the Creation to the Last Judgement.

Having rounded up my horses, I set myself to put them through their paces. See how civilizations come into existence: that is the sub-ject of the rest of Volume 1. Here I am asking myself what it is that brings a civilization to birth. I first try Race and then try Environ-ment, and I find both these explanations unsatisfying, because they assume that living beings are subject to inexorable laws of nature, like dead matter. So I look for an explanation in terms of life, which in human affairs means in terms of free-will, and I find this in the Old Testament. Here we see human beings responding, or failing to re-spond, to challenges from God. In Volume 2, I try to discover the limits within which the interplay of challenge and response is effec-tively creative. I explore this by examining a number of test cases. In Volume 3, I go on to study the growth of a civilization that has suc-ceeded in coming to birth. After growth there comes breakdown and disintegration, but these are the subjects of the second group of vol-umes, which will follow these first three in the present paperback edition.

'Work . . . while it is day . . .'

JOHN IX. 4

'Nox ruit, Aenea . . .'

AENEID VI. 539

'Thought shall be the harder,
Heart the keener,
Mood shall be the more,
As our might lessens.'

THE LAY OF THE BATTLE OF MALDON

A STUDY OF HISTORY

2

The Geneses of Civilizations, Part Two

ARNOLD J. TOYNBEE

A Galaxy Book

New York   OXFORD UNIVERSITY PRESS   1962

A Study of History was first issued under the auspices of the Royal Institute of International Affairs, of which Arnold J. Toynbee was then Director of Studies.

First Edition, 1934
Second Edition, 1935
First published as a Galaxy Book, 1962

The illustration on the cover of this volume is a rendering by Charles Gottlieb of The Seated Scribe, *c.* 2500 B.C. [The Louvre].

PRINTED IN THE UNITED STATES OF AMERICA

CONTENTS

VOLUME II

D. THE RANGE OF CHALLENGE-AND-RESPONSE

I. ΧΑΛΕΠΑ ΤΑ ΚΑΛΑ

The Return of Nature

WE have now studied the action of Challenge-and-Response and have attempted to survey the role which challenges and responses have played in the geneses of civilizations. In embarking upon this survey, we have implicitly rejected the view that civilizations are apt to be generated in environments—physical or human —which offer unusually easy conditions of life to Man. This view is popularly held, or at any rate widely aired, in the modern Western World, though it is contradicted by the theory of our modern Western Physical Science as well as by the deeper intuition of Mankind which has found expression in the Mythology of various societies in various ages.[1] In the course of the survey which we have just concluded, we have ignored this false view; but we may find that, besides implicitly rejecting it, we have also indirectly refuted it by exposing the fallacy on which it is founded.

This fallacy springs from a failure to conceive the genesis of a civilization as an act of creation involving a process of change in Time. The final appearance of the scene, as it looks when the drama of genesis has been played to the finish, is thoughtlessly equated with the primitive appearance of the same scene in the prehistoric age before the site was taken in hand by Man to serve as the stage for a great human action. For example,

'we are accustomed to regard Egypt as a paradise, as the most fertile country in the World, where, if we but scratch the soil and scatter seed, we have only to await and gather the harvest. The Greeks spoke of Egypt as the most fit place for the first generations of men, for there, they said, food was always ready at hand, and it took no labour to secure an abundant supply.'[2]

The fallacy of this view is pointed out by the distinguished archaeologist who has formulated it in these sentences in order to refute it. His refutation is presented in the latter part of a passage which has already been quoted, in the preceding chapter of this Study, at greater length.

'There can be no doubt', he goes on to say, 'that the Egypt of to-day is a very different place from the Egypt of pre-agricultural times. . . .

[1] For this contrary scientific and mythological *Weltanschauung*, see above, II. C (ii) (b) 1, vol. i, *passim*.
[2] Newberry, op. cit. in II. C (ii) (b) 2, above, vol. i, p. 306.

The agricultural Egypt of modern times is as much a gift of Man as it is of the Nile.'[1]

In fact, the fallacious popular view entirely overlooks the stupendous human effort involved, not only in once transforming the prehistoric jungle-swamp of the Lower Nile Valley into the historical Land of Egypt, but also in perpetually preventing this magnificent but precarious work of men's hands from reverting to its primeval state of Nature.

What this state of Nature was, we have indicated, in the two instances of the Land of Egypt and the Land of Shinar, by citing[2] first-hand descriptions of the present state of certain other sections of the Nile Valley and the Tigris-Euphrates Valley which have remained, down to this day, in the primitive condition out of which Egypt was conjured up in the Lower Nile Valley by the fathers of the Egyptiac Civilization and Shinar by the fathers of the Sumeric Civilization in what used to be the Lower Tigris-Euphrates Valley before the present provinces of Basrah and 'Arabistan were built out into the Persian Gulf by the progressive deposit of alluvium during the last five or six thousand years. The present state of the Bahr-al-Jabal section of the Nile Valley[3] and of the 'Amārah-Nāsirīyah-Basrah triangle in the Tigris-Euphrates Valley[4] testifies to the feat which was performed by the pioneers who, some five or six thousand years ago, succeeded in transforming similar tracts of inhospitable jungle-swamp, out of all recognition, into an ordered network of dykes and fields, where soil and water are subject to human control for the service of human purposes. The view that civilizations are begotten in environments where the conditions are unusually easy is clearly shown to be untenable when we compare those howling wildernesses, which reproduce, in their virgin state to-day, the primeval state of Egypt and Shinar, with the actual state of Egypt and Shinar as we see it to-day side by side with the Bahr-al-Jabal and with the swamps in which the Tigris and Euphrates lose themselves below 'Amārah and Nāsirīyah. At the same time, just because the works of Man which have effaced the primeval state of Nature in the Lower Nile Valley and in the Lower Tigris-Euphrates Valley are still 'going concerns', we cannot observe the primeval state of Nature here directly. We have to be content with the reflections of it which we can discern in the watery mirrors of the Bahr-al-Jabal and the 'Amārah-Nāsirīyah-Basrah triangle; and though the scientific student may feel morally

[1] Newberry, op. cit., quoted in vol. i, pp. 306 and 308, above. For the celebrated aphorism of Herodotus, to which Professor Newberry takes exception in the second sentence here quoted, see footnote 2 on p. 252 in II. C (ii) (a) 2, in vol. i, above.

[2] In II. C (ii) (b) 2, vol. i, pp. 309-12 and 316-18, above.

[3] See vol. i, pp. 309-12, above.   [4] See vol. i, pp. 316-18, above.

certain, in his own mind, that these surviving reflections give a fair picture of the long-obliterated originals, he must be prepared to find the layman declaring, like doubting Thomas, that only direct observation will convince him.

Are there theatres of civilization, other than Egypt and Shinar, which can provide the layman with the direct evidence which he demands and which Egypt and Shinar cannot give him? Yes, there are, for the human feat of maintaining Egypt and Shinar as 'going concerns'—a feat only less remarkable than the original feat of creating them—is something exceptional. In general it is true that 'naturam expellas furca, tamen usque recurret'.[1] At various times and places, recalcitrant Nature, once broken in by human heroism, has broken loose again because later generations have ceased for some reason to keep up the constant exertions required of them in order to maintain the mastery which had been won for them and transmitted to them by the pioneers. In such cases of reversion, the primeval state of Nature, as it was before Man ever took it in hand, can be seen to-day—not merely in the mirror of some similar piece of Nature which has happened to remain in its virgin state— but by direct observation on the very spot which has temporarily been the scene of a signal human achievement. Such spectacles, in which the primeval state of Nature and the subsequent works of Man and the eventual reversion of Nature to her primeval state are all displayed together on one spot like geological strata, are certainly more striking, as visual demonstrations, than the spectacle —striking though this is—of the contrast between the present state of Egypt and the present state of the Bahr-al-Jabal, in which the two objects that have to be brought into simultaneous focus lie a thousand miles apart. Where Nature has actually reasserted her ascendancy over some spot that has once been the birth-place of a civilization or the scene of some other signal human achievement, it is impossible to behold Nature flaunting her ultimate triumph over these works of Man and still to doubt that here, at any rate, the conditions in which those human works were performed were not unusually easy but unusually difficult. We will therefore try to clinch our argument by passing a few instances of such reversions under review.

In Central America

One remarkable instance is the present state of the birth-place of the Mayan Civilization. Far different from the dykes and fields of Egypt and Shinar, which are still being kept in order by Man and

---

[1] Horace, *Epistles*, Book I, Ep. x, l. 24.

still duly serving his purpose in yielding him a livelihood, the works of the Mayas are no longer 'going concerns' to-day. Their sole surviving monuments are the ruins of the immense and magnificently decorated public buildings which now stand, far away from any present human habitations, in the depths of the tropical forest. The forest, like some sylvan boa-constrictor, has literally swallowed them up, and now it is dismembering them at its leisure: prising their fine-hewn, close-laid stones apart with its writhing roots and tendrils. The contrast between the present aspect of the country and the aspect which it must have worn when the Mayan Civilization was in being is so great that it is almost beyond imagination.[1] There must have been a time when these immense public buildings stood in the heart of large and populous cities, and when those cities lay in the midst of vast stretches of cultivated land which furnished them with their food-supplies. The masterpieces of Mayan architecture which are now being strangled by the forest must have been built as works of super-erogation with the surplus of an energy which, for leagues around, had already transformed the forest into fruitful fields. They were trophies of Man's victory over Nature; and, at the moment when they were raised, the retreating fringe of the vanquished and routed sylvan enemy was perhaps barely visible on the horizon, even from the highest platforms of the palaces or from the summits of the temple-pyramids. To the human beings who looked out over the World from those vantage-points then, the victory of Man over Nature must have seemed utterly secure; and the transitoriness of human achievements and the vanity of human wishes are poignantly exposed by the ultimate return of the forest, engulfing first the fields and then the houses, and finally the palaces and the temples themselves. Yet that is not the most significant or even the most obvious lesson to be learnt from the present state of Copan or Tikal or Palenque. The ruins speak still more eloquently of the intensity of the struggle with the physical environment which the creators of the Mayan Civilization must have waged victoriously in their day. In her very revenge, which reveals her in all her grue-some power, Tropical Nature testifies unwillingly to the courage and the vigour of the men who once, if only for a season, succeeded in putting her to flight and keeping her at bay.[2]

---

[1] The imaginative feat of conveying this contrast in words has been accomplished by Mr. Rudyard Kipling in his description of 'the Cold Lairs': a fictitious Hindu city which the Indian Jungle has swallowed up. (Read the story called 'Kaa's Hunting' in *The Jungle Book*.)

[2] Dr. Ellsworth Huntington suggests that the Nature whom the fathers of the Mayan Civilization once put to flight was a different (and less formidable) antagonist from the Nature who has since got the better of these men's descendants in the selfsame region. For Dr. Huntington's hypothesis of a periodic shifting of climatic zones, see II. D (vii), Annex I, below.

In Ceylon

With the same dumb eloquence, the creeper-covered ruins of Angkor Wat testify to the prowess of the men who once propagated the Hindu Civilization on soil conquered from the tropical forest of Cambodia; and the equally arduous feat of conquering the parched plains of Ceylon for agriculture is commemorated in the breached bunds and overgrown floors of the tanks which were once constructed on the wet side of the hill-country, on a colossal scale, by the Sinhalese converts to the Indic religion of the Hinayana.

'To realise how such tanks came into being one must know something of the history of Lanka. The idea underlying the system was simple but very great. It was intended by the tank-building kings that none of the rain which fell in such abundance in the mountains should reach the sea without paying tribute to Man on the way.

'In the middle of the southern half of Ceylon is a wide mountain zone, but to the east and north dry plains cover thousands of square miles, and at present are very sparsely populated. In the height of the monsoon, when armies of storm-swept clouds rush on day after day to match their strength against the hills, there is a line drawn by Nature that the rains are unable to pass. . . . There are points where the line of demarcation of the two zones, the wet and the dry, is so narrow that within a mile one seems to pass into a new country; for the whole character of the forest alters, and in size and kind and distribution the trees differ completely from those one can still see behind one. The wild flowers take new forms and colours; different birds sing in the bushes; cultivation changes abruptly; and wealth ends. The line curves from sea to sea and appears to be stable and unaffected by the operations of Man, such as felling forests.'[1]

Yet the missionaries of the Indic Civilization in Ceylon once achieved the *tour de force* of compelling the monsoon-smitten highlands—where 'rain pours down at a higher rate for the month than the rainfall of London for the whole of a very wet year'[2]—to give water and life and wealth to the plains which Nature had condemned to lie parched and desolate.

'Hill streams were tapped and their water guided into the giant storage-tanks below, some of them four thousand acres in extent; and, from those, channels ran on to other large tanks farther from the hills, and from them to others still more remote. And below each great tank and each great channel were hundreds of little tanks, each the nucleus of a village; all, in the long-run, fed from the wet mountain-zone. So gradually the ancient Sinhalese conquered all, or nearly all, of the plains that are now so empty of men.'[3]

The arduousness of the labour of first conquering and then

---

[1] Still, John: *The Jungle Tide* (Edinburgh 1930, Blackwood), pp. 74–5.
[2] Still, op. cit., p. 74.   [3] Still, op. cit., pp. 76–7.

holding for a man-made civilization these naturally barren and desolate plains is demonstrated by the two outstanding features in the
landscape of Ceylon at the present day. The first feature is the
relapse of that once irrigated and cultivated and populated country-
side into its primeval barrenness and desolation upon the stoppage
of the continuous human exertions which had been required in
order to produce and maintain this miraculous transformation of
the face of Nature.[1] The second feature is the avoidance of these
derelict plains, which were once the seat of a civilization, by our
modern Western coffee and tea and rubber planters who have
come to Ceylon to make their fortunes there in these latter days.

On the first of these two points, the following testimony is
borne by the modern Western eyewitness whom we have quoted
already:

'The tank age endured for more than fifteen centuries, and then the
jungle tide rose over it and all signs or memory of it became lost. . . . In
the forest which covers the ancient kingdom, far from the sounds of men,
one comes upon the bunds of tanks, now utterly forgotten, where the
banks have given way and the beds become like natural glades for deer
to graze in. . . .

'I know [a] city . . . [which] lies below the bund of an enormous tank
whose area may well have been thousands of acres, for the bund is miles
long. But now the very name of the tank is lost, for the bund burst
hundreds of years ago and its bed is but a low-lying region in the
unbroken forest, a deeper area amid the sea of trees. The only name it
now bears is a Tamil one meaning Tank of the Great Breach. At a
waterhole in a rock in the bed of that tank I saw a bear stoop and drink,
and it was curious to think how he sought for that small hole of stagnant
water, as for a rare treasure, in a place that for many centuries was at
the bottom of an inland sea where waves broke and pelicans sailed in
fleets. More than anything else, it brought home to me most vividly
how brief had been the age of tanks in the long history of the jungle.
For a million years animals drank from that narrow hole; then, for a
thousand years, the rock, hole and all, was underneath the waves; and
now the jungle drinks again where animals drank when Man used stone
arrowheads, and before he invented them, and before Nature invented
him.'[2]

The second feature in the present landscape of Ceylon which
demonstrates the arduousness of the feat which the ancient

---

[1] The cause of the breakdown of the ancient Sinhalese irrigation system was an incess-
ant civil war which was waged with alien mercenaries from Southern India. These
mercenaries deliberately cut the canals and breached the bunds as a short cut to military
decisions; and eventually this will to destroy overcame the will to repair. Therewith, the
plains not only went out of cultivation through the stoppage of the water-supply, but they
also became hot-beds of malaria when the running waters dwindled into stagnant pools
which were too shallow to harbour the fish that live by eating up the anopheles mosquito's
larvae. (Still, op. cit., pp. 88–92.) For the role of War in the breakdowns of civilizations,
see Part IV, *passim*, in vol. iv. and especially IV. C (iii) (*b*) 3; IV. C (iii) (*c*) 2 (γ); and
IV. C (iii) (*c*) 3 (α) and (β), below.

[2] Still, op. cit., pp. 77 and 79 and 111–12.

Sinhalese bund-builders temporarily accomplished is the avoidance of the derelict plains by our modern Western planters who have interested themselves in Ceylon not in order to propagate a civilization there but in order to get rich quick.

'It is a curious fact that ... the bulk of the population and most of the wealth have been found on the wet side of the line during the four centuries of European rule.... To make money, one stays as a rule on the wet side, but to see the ruins of temples or monasteries, of palaces or engineering works, one must go to the dry side of the line.[1] ... For the hills where we grow tea and rubber [the ancient Sinhalese] did not care. Few ancient remains are to be found among them, and the forests we found there, and destroyed, were of immense age and probably of true virgin growth.... Must one be ranked as opposed to civilization if one prefers the dry and thinly populated side of the monsoon's frontier to the prosperous and wet one? That is a question I find it impossible to answer without first settling what the word "civilization" means.'[2]

The irrefutable testimony of the return of Nature is repeated even where there are no stupendous ruins to work upon our imagination. We may perceive it in the last agonies of the poor village in the jungle—as witness the following passage from a modern Western work of fiction in which the scene of action is likewise Ceylon:

'The years had brought more evil, death and decay upon the village. ... Disease and hunger visited it year after year. It seemed, as the headman said, to have been forgotten by gods and men. Year after year, the rains from the north-east passed it by; only the sun beat down more pitilessly, and the wind roared over it across the jungle; the little patches of chena crop which the villagers tried to cultivate withered as soon as the young shoots showed above the ground. No man, traveller or headman or trader, ever came to the village now. No one troubled any longer to clear the track which led to it; the jungle covered it and cut the village off....

'They struggled hard against the fate that hung over them, clinging to the place where they had been born and lived, the compound they knew, and the sterile chenas which they had sown. No children were born to them now in their hut, their women were as sterile as the earth; the children that had been born to them died of want and fever. At last

---

[1] This geographical segregation of the fields of the ancient indigenous and the modern European enterprise in Ceylon has its analogue in Central America, where the modern Spanish colonists have similarly kept clear of the plains which were once the seat of the Mayan culture, and have established themselves in the highlands which were left unoccupied by both the fathers and the children of the Mayan Civilization. (See II. C (ii) (a) 2, vol. i, p. 267, above, and II. D (ii), pp. 34–6, below.) In this connexion, it is immaterial that, in contrast to the climatic conditions in Ceylon, the Central American plains are relatively wet and the Central American highlands relatively dry; for whereas, in Ceylon, an abundance of rain affords economic ease while a scarcity demands economic effort, in Central America the relations of economic effect to climatic cause are just the inverse, owing to the inverse correlation between climate and landscape.—A.J.T.

[2] Still, op. cit., pp. 75–6 and 77 and 92.

they yielded to the jungle. They packed up their few possessions and left the village for ever. . . .

'They tried to induce Punchi Menika to go with them, but she refused. . . . The only thing left to her was the compound and the jungle which she knew. She clung to it passionately, blindly. . . .

'The jungle surged forward over and blotted out the village up to the very walls of her hut. She no longer cleared the compound or mended the fence, the jungle closed over them as it had closed over the other huts and compounds, over the paths and tracks. Its breath was hot and heavy in the hut itself, which it imprisoned in its wall, stretching away unbroken for miles. Everything except the little hut with rotting walls and broken tattered roof had gone down before it. It closed with its shrubs and bushes and trees, with the impenetrable disorder of its thorns and creepers, over the rice-fields and the tanks. Only a little hollowing of the ground where the trees stood in water when rain fell, and a long little mound which the rains washed out and the elephants trampled down, marked the place where before had lain the tank and its land. The village was forgotten, it disappeared into the jungle from which it had sprung, and with it she was cut off, forgotten. It was as if she was the last person left in the World, a world of unending trees above which the wind roared always and the Sun blazed. . . .

'But life is very short in the jungle. Punchi Menika was a very old woman before she was forty. She no longer sowed grain, she lived only on the roots and leaves that she gathered. The perpetual hunger wasted her slowly, and when the rains came she lay shivering with fever in the hut. At last the time came when her strength failed her; she lay in the hut unable to drag herself out to search for food. The fire in the corner that had smouldered so long between the three great stones was out. In the day the hot air eddied through the hut, hot with the breath of the wind blowing over the vast parched jungle; at night she shivered in the chill dew. She was dying, and the jungle knew it; it is always waiting; can scarcely wait for death. When the end was close upon her a great black shadow glided into the doorway. Two little eyes twinkled at her steadily, two immense white tusks curled up gleaming against the darkness. She sat up, fear came upon her, the fear of the jungle, blind agonising fear.

' "Appochchi, Appochchi!" she screamed. "He has come, the devil from the bush. He has come for me as you said. Aiyo! save me, save me! Appochchi!"

'As she fell back, the great boar grunted softly, and glided like a shadow towards her into the hut.'[1]

As the reader closes the book, he speculates on the meaning of the tale which has this ending. Throughout the story, the writer has drawn in for us, stroke by stroke, his picture of the jungle as a sinister beast of prey which only lives its own life in order to

---

[1] Woolf, L. S.: *The Village in the Jungle* (London 1913, Edward Arnold), ch. ix, pp. 301–7.

bring human life to destruction—a sylvan counterpart to the
animated skeleton which is our image of Death.

> Haud igitur leti praeclusa est ianua caelo
> nec soli terraeque neque altis aequoris undis,
> sed patet immane et vasto respectat hiatu.[1]

Under the shadow of this inhuman monster, ever watching and
waiting with a leer on its obscene countenance till it finds its
opportunity to close in upon its victim, the human life of the poor
villagers seems unbearably wretched. The odds against them are
so heavy; the pressure upon them is so grinding; would it not have
been better for them never to have been born? And yet the story of
their lives, as it is told by the author in this painful setting, is
undoubtedly worth the telling. We read the tale to the end and
feel that these lives have not been lived for nothing, even though
at last the jungle overwhelms them. What is the significance and
the interest of them? Perhaps it is that the cruel and unceasing
struggle with the jungle, which at first sight seems almost to divest
them of their humanity—to degrade them to the level of the beasts
that perish[2] or of the creeping things that creep upon the earth[3]—
subtly reveals them in another light to the inward eye. If the jungle
is a malevolent beast of prey, then the villagers who have fought it
with their bare hands are heroes whose story is an epic. Without
the jungle the village could hardly have risen to be a theme for
literature. And when the jungle swallows the village up, we realize
in retrospect that we have been reading a tale of human prowess
which surpasses the tale told by the ruins of Angkor Wat.

In the North Arabian Desert

A celebrated and indeed almost hackneyed illustration of our
theme is the present state of Petra and Palmyra—a spectacle which
has inspired a whole series of modern Western essays in the
philosophy of history, from *Les Ruines*[4] onwards. To-day, these
former homes of the Syriac Civilization are in the same state as the
former homes of the Mayan Civilization at Copan and Tikal, and
their monuments astonish and confound the spectator for the same
reason. The parallel is indeed exact, except that hostile Nature is

---

[1] Lucretius, *De Rerum Natura*, Book V, ll. 373–5. [2] Psalm xlix, vv. 12 and 20.
[3] Leviticus xi. 29.
[4] Volney, C. F., Comte de: *Les Ruines, ou Méditation sur les Révolutions des Empires*
(1st edition, Paris 1791). For an attractive general acount of the caravan cities which
is based upon first-hand and recent archaeological research, especially at Dura, see
Rostovtzeff, M.: *Caravan Cities* (Oxford 1932, Clarendon Press). For Petra see also
Kammerer, A.: *Petra et la Nabatène* (Paris 1929–30, Geuthner, 1 vol.+atlas). For
Palmyra, see also Février, J. G.: *Essai sur l'Histoire Politique et Économique de Palmyre*
(Paris 1931, Vrin) and Partsch, J.: *Palmyra: Eine historisch-klimatische Studie*,
Sitzungsberichte Ak. Leipzig, lxxiv (1922).

represented here by the Afrasian Steppe instead of the tropical forest.[1] Here, too, we see the ruins of huge and splendid public buildings which are likewise desolate and likewise isolated from the nearest present human habitations by many leagues of surrounding wilderness—the Afrasian wilderness of dry rock and gravel and sand which is not less forbidding than the tropical wilderness of sodden and matted vegetation. The desert has swallowed up Petra and Palmyra, as the forest has swallowed up Tikal and Copan; and here, again, the ruins survive to point a contrast between present and past which is so great as to be almost unimaginable.

The ruins tell us that these elaborate temples and porticoes and tombs, at the time when they stood intact, must have been ornaments of cities which rivalled the Mayan cities in wealth and population; and here the deductions from the evidence of Archaeology, which are our sole means of composing a picture of the Mayan Civilization, are reinforced by the written testimony of historical records. The economic foundations on which the wealth and population of Petra and Palmyra were supported are not matters of conjecture. We know that the historical pioneers of the Syriac Civilization who conjured these cities up out of the desert were masters of the magic which the Syriac Mythology attributes to Moses.

These magicians knew how to bring water out of the dry rock and how to find their way across the untrodden wilderness. In their prime, Petra and Palmyra stood in the midst of irrigated gardens like those which still surround Damascus to-day or those which the Prophet Muhammad depicts in the Qur'an whenever he wishes to evoke in the minds of the faithful an image of Paradise; but Petra and Palmyra did not live then, any more than Damascus lives to-day, exclusively or even principally on the fruits of their narrow-verged oases.[2] Their rich men were not their market-gardeners but their merchants, who kept oasis in communion with oasis, and continent with continent, by a busy caravan-traffic from point to point across the intervening tracts of steppe and desert: gravelly hamād and sandy nafūd. The Nabataeans of Petra, operating the trans-desert route from the Mediterranean ports of Syria to the Ocean ports of the Yaman, competed with the Greek seamen of Alexandria for the trade between the Roman Empire and India;[3]

---

[1] Dr. Ellsworth Huntington seeks to explain the rise and fall of Petra and Palmyra, like the rise and fall of Copan and Tikal, by his hypothesis of a periodic shifting of climatic zones. For his application of the hypothesis to the case of Palmyra, see *Palestine and its Transformation* (London 1911, Constable), ch. xv. For a general discussion of Dr. Huntington's application of his hypothesis to the histories of civilizations, see II. D (vii), Annex I, below.

[2] The same point is made apropos of Jerash (Gerasa) by Rostovtzeff in op. cit., on pp. 67-8.   [3] See Rostovtzeff, op. cit., pp. 56-7.

the Palmyrenes, operating the trans-desert route from Syria to 'Irāq, virtually monopolized the trade between the Roman Empire and those regions lying east of it which were ruled successively by the Arsacids and the Sasanids.[1] The economic control of trade-routes brought political power in its train; and the Nabataean Kingdom, extending from Sinai to Damascus and from Taymā to Beersheba, ranked as one of the principal client-states of Rome before its annexation by Trajan.[2] As for Palmyra,[3] during those decades of the third century of the Christian Era when the Roman Empire was prostrated by a paralytic stroke premonitory of its coming dissolution, Queen Zenobia succeeded momentarily, before Aurelian carried her captive, in ruling from the Palmyrene oasis a premature and abortive 'successor-state' which anticipated, by four centuries, the principality of the Caliph Muʿāwīyah.[4]

Such were the achievements of the Syriac Civilization under the stimulus of the desert. And the ruins of Petra and Palmyra, in testifying, as they stand, to the final victory of the desert over Man, also testify, by the selfsame posture, to the previous victory of Man over the desert. Since the day when the Syriac Society— overcome by the pressure of the human environment in the shape of the Roman Empire[5]—relaxed its grip upon the physical environ-ment at these two points and allowed the desert to have its way with Petra and Palmyra again, no other society has ever attempted to repeat the achievement of the Syriac pioneers by recalling either of these dead cities to life. The attempt has not even been made up to the present by Western enterprise, though in our day we dispose

[1] See Rostovtzeff, op. cit., pp. 102-4.
[2] The Nabataean régime in this region lasted altogether for nearly three centuries, beginning *circa* 164 B.C. (Rostovtzeff, op. cit., p. 50).
[3] Palmyra is first heard of in 41 B.C. (Rostovtzeff, op. cit., p. 121). The earliest extant Palmyrene inscription was cut in 8 B.C. (Février, op. cit., p. 6).
[4] See vol. i, p. 74, above, footnote 4. It may be noted that while the Nabataean client-state of the Roman Empire was based on the single oasis of Petra and Zenobia's abortive 'successor-state' on the single oasis of Palmyra, the successful 'successor-state' which was established—or usurped—by Muʿāwiyah was based on a pair of oases: those of Medina and Mecca. The political union of these two oases was the supreme political achievement of Muhammad. In achieving it, he laid the foundations of a state which grew, first into a 'successor-state' of the Roman Empire in its Syriac provinces, and then into a reintegration or resumption of the Syriac universal state which had been built by the Achaemenids and overthrown by Alexander the Great. (See I. C (i) (b), vol. i, pp. 73-7, above.)
[5] Petra and Palmyra each rose in turn to greatness by finding places for themselves in the interstices between the dominions of mutually hostile Great Powers whose hostility was too great to admit of their coming to a direct understanding with each other, while it was not great enough to drive them into forgoing the advantage of doing business with one another indirectly through the agency of commercial go-betweens who would also serve as political buffers. Petra rose in this way in an interstice between the Seleucid and the Ptolemaic 'successor-state' of the Achaemenian Empire; Palmyra rose in an interstice between the Roman Empire and the Arsacid Power. Petra was doomed when the Roman Empire supplanted both the Seleucid and the Ptolemaic Power alike; Palmyra was doomed when the decay of the Arsacidae left Rome momentarily without a rival in this quarter likewise—pending the rise of the Sasanidae. (See further Rostovtzeff, op. cit., pp. 26-35.)

of technical facilities which the Nabataeans and the Aramaeans never dreamed of: artesian wells that can tap subterranean water-supplies quite beyond the reach of picks or the ken of divining-rods; and petrol-driven six-wheeled motor-cars which can traverse in a day a tract of desert which is a week's journey for a camel.[1] Thus the ruined monuments and the dried-up oases and the abandoned caravan-routes of Petra and Palmyra declare unmistakably, to the observer who considers them to-day, a fact which is not revealed in those lovely gardens that are still watered by the rivers of Damascus: the fact that the physical environment in which the Syriac Civilization came to birth was not unusually easy but, on the contrary, was unusually difficult for Man to master.

On Easter Island

In a different environment again, we may draw a corresponding conclusion concerning the origins of the Polynesian Civilization[2] from the present state of Easter Island.[3] At the time of its discovery by modern Western explorers, Easter Island was inhabited by two races: a race of flesh-and-blood and a race of stone; an apparently primitive human population of Polynesian physique, and a highly accomplished population of statues. The living inhabitants in that generation possessed neither the art of carving statues such as these nor the science of navigating the thousand miles of open sea that separate Easter Island from the nearest sister-island of the Polynesian Archipelago. Before its discovery by the seamen of the West, Easter Island had been isolated from the rest of the World for an unknown length of time. Yet its dual population of flesh and stone testifies, just as clearly as the ruins of Palmyra or Copan, to a vanished past which must have been utterly different from the visible present.

Those human beings must have been begotten, and those figures must have been carved, by Polynesian navigators who once found their way across the Pacific to Easter Island in flimsy open canoes,

---

[1] In the year 1930 of the Christian Era, the motor-car and the artesian well were being used by one great man who was not a Westerner but an Arab—King 'Abd-al-'Azīz Āl Saʻūd of the Najd-Ḥijāz—in order to reassert Man's ascendancy over Nature in one of the most forbidding tracts of the Afrasian Steppe, namely Central Arabia. With the aid of Western technique, Ibn Saʻūd was evoking, in a region which had previously been utilized for nothing better than the ranges of pastoral Nomads, a new world of irrigated oases, linked together by trans-desert routes which served the dual purpose of commerce and government. The empire ruled by the Wahhābī King from Riyāḍ promised, if it endured, to reproduce at last, in the twentieth century of the Christian Era, an image of the empires which had once been ruled by King Hārith from Petra and by Queen Zenobia from Palmyra. (See Rihani, Ameen: *Ibn Saʻoud of Arabia: His People and his Land* (London 1928, Constable); Philby, H. St. J. B.: *Arabia of the Wahhabis* (London 1928, Constable), and *Arabia* (London 1930, Benn).)

[2] For the arrested Polynesian Civilization, see further Part III. A, below.

[3] See Routledge, S.: *The Mystery of Easter Island* (London 1919, Sifton Praed); and Brown, J. Macmillan: *The Riddle of the Pacific* (London 1924, Fisher Unwin).

without chart, compass or chronometer and with no other motor-power than the wind behind their sails and the muscular force that plied their paddles. And this voyage can hardly have been an isolated adventure which brought one boat-load of Polynesian pioneers to Easter Island by a stroke of luck that was not repeated; for on that supposition it would really be impossible to account both for the presence of the population of statues and for the inability of the latter-day population of human beings to carve them. The art of sculpture must have been brought to Easter Island by the pioneers, and lost on Easter Island by their descendants, together with the art of navigation. The relapse of these distant colonists from the cultural level of the Polynesian Society elsewhere must have been due to the breaking of their contact with the rest of Polynesia. On the other hand, the population of statues is so numerous that it must have taken many generations to produce; and during those generations the art of sculpture, which has been lost in this latter-day age of isolation, must have been kept alive on Easter Island by continual transmarine intercourse. Taken together, these considerations point to a previous state of affairs in which the navigation across those thousand miles of open sea was carried on regularly over a long period of time. Eventually, for some reason which still remains a mystery to us, the sea, once traversed victoriously by Man, closed in round Easter Island, as the desert closed in round Palmyra and the forest round Copan. Yet, here again, Nature's reassertion of her power bears testimony to the prowess of Man in once overcoming her and thus indicates that there were certain features of unusual difficulty in the physical environment in which the Polynesian Civilization came to birth.

The truth thus proclaimed in unison by Past and Present on Easter Island is, of course, in flat contradiction to the popular Western view that the South Sea Islands are an earthly paradise and their inhabitants children of Nature in the legendary state of Adam and Eve before the Fall. Perhaps this view arises from a mistaken assumption that one portion of the Polynesian environment constitutes the whole of it. The physical environment of the Polynesian Society consists, in reality, of water as well as land: water which presents a formidable challenge to any human beings who propose to cross it without possessing any better means of navigation than those, described above, which were actually the only means at the Polynesian navigators' command. It was by responding boldly and successfully to this challenge of the estranging sea—by achieving, with their rudimentary means of navigation, the *tour de force* of establishing a regular maritime traffic across the open waters between island and island—that the Polynesian pioneers won their footing on the specks of dry land which are scattered through the vast watery wilderness of the Pacific Ocean almost as rarely as the stars are scattered through the depths of Space. Even granting that these beaching-places which constitute such an infinitesimally small fraction of the Polynesian environment do offer an earthly paradise to any human beings who may succeed in reaching them, it must be borne in mind that the Polynesians reached them by their own exertions, after hazarding their lives upon the waters, whereas the Adam and Eve of the Syriac Mythology were placed in the Garden of Eden by the act of their creator, and did not begin either to exert their minds and bodies or to hazard their lives until they had been driven out of the Garden, and kept out of it, by the angel with the flaming sword.[1]

It is possible that, in the environment where the Polynesian Civilization came to birth, there was an untoward degree of sharpness in the contrast between the difficulty of the first ordeal which had to be passed and the ease of the conditions of life with which the successful response to this first challenge was rewarded. The toils and dangers of Polynesian navigation on the Pacific were so formidable and the sweets of repose on the islands were so alluring that the children may well have been tempted to abandon that great Oceanic world of land and water which their fathers had opened up for them, in order to sink back—each on the island which he had inherited in virtue of his father's efforts—into a life of primitive ease and isolation. That seems to have been the history of the decline and fall of the Polynesian Civilization on Easter Island: the island which had to be won and held at the price of the longest sea-passage of all. The colonists of Easter Island must have been the flower of the Polynesian pioneers; and the virtue that was in them not only carried them across a thousand miles of open sea[2] but availed them—before it went out of them— to commemorate their achievement for ever by creating, at their distant journey's end, some of the finest masterpieces ever produced by Polynesian art. The history of the Polynesian Civilization on Easter Island may supply the clue to the history of the Polynesian Civilization as a whole. That is a problem which will demand our notice again hereafter.[3] In this place we are simply concerned to point out that the popular Western view of the Poly-

---

[1] For the significance of this myth of the Garden and the Fall, see above, II. C (ii) (*b*) 1, vol. i, pp. 290–3.
[2] 'The nearest land to Easter now inhabited, with the exception of Pitcairn Island, is in the Gambia Islands, about 1,200 miles to the westward; the little coral patch of Ducie Island, which lies between the two, is nearly 900 miles from Easter, and has no dwellers.' (Routledge, S.: *The Mystery of Easter Island* (London 1919, Sifton Praed), p. 292.)
[3] It is touched upon again in Part III. A, vol. iii, below.

nesian environment is mistaken and to explain how it has arisen; and the explanation turns out to be very simple. The Western observers who have given it currency have only had eyes for the land and have ignored the sea which covers all but a fraction of the area over which the Polynesian Civilization once ranged. Presumably they would not have ignored it if they had had to traverse it themselves in the craft of the Polynesian navigators, instead of travelling, as they have done, as passengers in modern Western ocean-going liners, leaving the responsibility of navigation to be borne by professional Western navigators with the assistance of compass and chart.

In New England

Before closing this review of reversions to a state of Nature, the writer may permit himself to cite two instances—one somewhat out of the way and the other exceedingly obvious—which happen to have come within his own personal observation.

I was once travelling in a rural part of the State of Connecticut in New England, when I came across a deserted village—a not uncommon spectacle, so I was told, in this section of the United States, yet a spectacle, nevertheless, which is inevitably surprising and even disconcerting to a European in America. This particular village—it was called Town Hill—had evidently been laid out much like other New England villages, still inhabited, in some of the more fertile districts of the same state through which I had already passed on my journey that very day. For some two centuries, perhaps, Town Hill had stood with its plank-built Georgian Church in the middle of the village green, and with the houses round the church, and with the orchards beyond the houses, and with the corn-fields stretching away beyond the fruit-trees. In 1925 the church still stood (it was being kept in repair by the State Archaeological Society as an ancient monument); the houses had vanished (though their former positions could still be traced by the remnants of their foundations); the fruit-trees had gone wild and had been swallowed up in the resurgent undergrowth. As for the fields, they had faded away altogether into the rocks and scrub of the barren hill-side.

Lingering on the spot and allowing my thoughts to play about the strange sights here presented to me, I marvelled first at an apparent paradox. Within the hundred years ending in this year 1925, those vanished New Englanders had wrested from Nature the whole breadth of a continent. In these few generations they had spread from the spot where I was standing, on the Atlantic slope, to the shores of the Pacific. Yet at the same time they had suffered Nature to recapture from them this village in the heart of their homeland—a village which their forefathers had founded almost as soon as they had set foot on American soil; a village where, for perhaps two hundred years before 'the Winning of the West', the ascendancy of Man over Nature had seemed to be established as securely as in any village in Europe. These were my first thoughts; but on second thoughts I began to understand the significance of what I was looking at. The rapidity, the thoroughness, the *abandon* with which Nature had reasserted her dominion over the site of Town Hill as soon as Man had relaxed his grip, surely gave the measure of the exertions which Man had formerly made, first to capture this position from Nature and then to hold it. Those exertions must have been extreme; and, when one came to think of it, only an energy as intense as the energy which the breaking-in of New England had called into play could have been sufficient for the Herculean labour of breaking-in a whole continent. Thus, so far from 'the Winning of the West' making the loss of Town Hill inexplicable, the truth was that, in the loss of Town Hill, the secret of 'the Winning of the West' was laid bare. The portent of this village in Connecticut, deserted to-day, explained the miracle of those great cities in Ohio and Illinois and Colorado and California which had sprung into existence overnight. In this hard environment of New England, an apprenticeship had been served for the hard task of building the United States. When the apprentice had felt himself fully trained in nerve and muscle and skill, he had simply left the place which had been his training-ground and had gone to the place where he was to do his work in life. The desertion of Town Hill was not a paradox after all; it was of one piece with the great human enterprise which had founded and peopled Cincinnati and Chicago and Denver and San Francisco.

On the Roman Campagna

Similar considerations resolve the apparent paradox in the present state of the Roman Campagna. It is beside the point to marvel, with Livy, that an innumerable multitude of yeoman-warriors should formerly have subsisted in a region which in his day, as in ours,[1] was a wilderness of barren gray fell and feverish

[1] In 1931, when the writer of this Study revisited the Roman Campagna after an interval of twenty years, he found that this statement required qualification. In 1911 the student who made the pilgrimage of the Via Appia Antica found himself walking through a wilderness almost from the moment when he passed beyond the City walls through the Porta San Sebastiano till the moment when he approached the outskirts of Albano. When he repeated the pilgrimage in 1931, he found that, in the interval, Man had been busily reasserting his mastery over the whole stretch of country that lies between Rome and the Castelli Romani. The Via Appia Antica itself was unchanged (being carefully preserved, like the church at Town Hill, by archaeological piety); but there was now no point along its course where the wayfarer was out of sight of modern motor-roads, aerodromes, wireless-masts and—more impressive than all these—newly cultivated fields. The tension of human energy on the Roman Campagna is now beginning to rise

green swamp where the only surviving vestiges of human habitation were the frail straw huts of a few miserable shepherds.[1] It is more apposite to reflect that this latter-day wilderness has reproduced the pristine state of the forbidding landscape which was once transformed by Latin or Volscian pioneers into a cultivated and populous countryside; and that the energy generated in the process of breaking-in this narrow plot of dour Italian soil was the energy which afterwards conquered the World in a radius extending from the Campagna to Britain and Egypt, and from the Alban Hills to the Atlas and the Caucasus.[2] If an energy which sufficed, in its diffusion, to build the Roman Empire was first generated and concentrated within the limits of the Campagna, this indicates the degree of human effort involved in first conquering the Campagna from the wilderness and then maintaining it against reversion. Is it any wonder that the cradle of the Roman Commonwealth did revert to its pristine state when the body politic which this cradle had nurtured eventually turned its energies outwards over all the kingdoms of the Earth? Surely it would have been more surprising if the Campagna had still continued to yield increase to the Roman husbandman and recruits to the Roman drill-sergeant in those latter days when the Roman Army was guarding the frontiers of the Empire, and tilling the *prata legionum,* far away on the fringe of the Afrasian Steppe and on the banks of the Rhine and the Danube?

We have now passed under review a number of sites—in the American and Asiatic Tropics, in the Afrasian Steppe, in the Pacific Archipelago, in North America, in the Mediterranean—which have reverted to their pristine state of Nature after having been the scene of signal human achievements that are now commemorated by deserted ruins. In this array, there is the utmost diversity both in the character of the local physical environment and in the shape of the yoke which Man has once laid upon it; yet all these sites agree in bearing unanimous witness to one essential condition of successful human activity:

> Nur der verdient sich Freiheit wie das Leben
> Der täglich sie erobern muss.[3]

Even when the efforts of the pioneers have succeeded in conquering some position from Nature, the conquered ground has to be

---

again for the first time since the end of the third century B.C., when, during the War of Hannibal, it began its great decline towards the zero point at which it has stood throughout the first nineteen centuries of the Christian Era.

[1] 'Innumerabilem multitudinem liberorum capitum in eis fuisse locis quae nunc, vix seminario militum exiguo relicto, servitia Romana ab solitudine vindicant' (Livy, Book VI, ch. 12). Compare the allusions in Horace, *Epistles*, Book I, Ep. xi, ll. 7–8 and 30.

[2] This is the theme of Professor Tenney Frank in *The Economic History of the Roman Republic* (2nd edition, Baltimore 1927, Johns Hopkins University Press).

[3] *Faust,* ll. 11575–6, quoted above in vol. i on p. 277.

held, by unremitting efforts on the part of the pioneers' successors, against Nature's unremitting counter-attacks. The fields of Egypt or the gardens of Damascus, which seem at first sight to yield their fruits automatically to any one who scratches the soil,[1] are really only maintained as 'going concerns' by constant and strenuous labour. How much greater, then, must have been the labour which it cost the fathers of the Egyptiac and the Syriac Civilization to bring the Land of Egypt and the Ghūtah of Damascus into existence out of the primeval jungle-swamp and the primeval desert? Perhaps we may now consider that we have proved the proposition which we first took for granted. It seems evident that the conditions offered to Man by the environments that have been the birth-places of civilizations have been not unusually easy but unusually difficult.

Perfida Capua

Having studied the character of certain environments which have actually been the scene of the geneses of civilizations or of other signal human achievements, and having found empirically that the conditions which they have offered to Man have been not easy but rather the contrary, let us pass on to a complementary study. Let us examine certain other environments in which the conditions offered to Man have in fact been easy, and study the effect on human life which such environments have produced. In attempting this study, we must distinguish between two different situations. The first is one in which people are introduced into an easy environment after having lived in some difficult environment of one of the kinds that we have examined above. The second situation is that of people in an easy environment who have never, so far as is known, been exposed to any other environment since their pre-human ancestors became men. In other words, we have to distinguish between the respective effects of exposure to an easy environment upon Mankind in process of civilization and upon Primitive Man. Let us deal with the two situations separately, in this order, and let us once more follow the empirical method of inquiry which we have employed so far.

Let us begin with a classic example of an easy environment which is suggested by the last example of a difficult environment that has occupied our attention. In Classical Italy, Rome found her antithesis in Capua—another great and famous city whose destinies were as different from those of Rome as her surroundings. The

---

[1] This seems to be the philosophy of Brazil, to judge by the following amiable saying which is reported to be current among the Brazilians: 'For twelve hours in the day we do our worst with the country; but for the other twelve hours we sleep, and then God and the country put things right again!'

Capuan Campagna was as kindly to Man as the Roman Campagna was dour;[1] and while the Romans went forth from their forbidding country to conquer one neighbour after another, the Campanians sat in their smiling country and allowed one neighbour after another to conquer them. From her last conquerors, the Samnites of the Abruzzi, Capua was delivered, at her own invitation, by the intervention of Rome herself; and then, at the most critical moment of the most critical war in Roman history, on the morrow of the Battle of Cannae, Capua repaid Rome by opening her gates to Hannibal, in the hope of recovering her freedom by exchanging one patron for another.[2] As far as Capua was concerned, the futility of this hope was written large in her previous history; but for Hannibal, in his war against the first city of Italy, the defection of the second city of Italy from Rome's side to his looked like a gain which was quite beyond question. In fact, Hannibal and his Roman opponents were of one mind in regarding Capua's change of sides as being the principal immediate consequence of the Battle of Cannae and perhaps the decisive event in the war. Hannibal responded to the Campanians' overtures by repairing to Capua and taking up his winter-quarters there—whereupon something happened which falsified everybody's expectations. A winter spent in Capua demoralized the troops who had just annihilated the greatest Roman army that had ever taken the field.

'The Carthaginian army, which [Hannibal] kept under cover there [in Capua] for the greater part of the winter, had been long and thoroughly hardened against all the ills that can afflict Mankind; but when it came to the good things of this life, the troops lacked both familiarity and experience. Accordingly these heroes who had resisted the utmost assaults of adversity were undone by an excess of prosperity and enjoyment; and they fell headlong, because their long abstinence made them plunge in head-over-ears. The round of sleeping, drinking, eating, whoring, bathing and taking their ease became sweeter to them as each passing day confirmed the habit, until they became so enervated by it, body and soul, that their safety came to rest in the prestige of their past victories rather than in the present strength of their right arms. It was

[1] The name Campagna, which clings to-day to the cradle of the Roman Commonwealth in the lowlands between the left bank of the Tiber and the Alban Hills, originally belonged (in its Latin spelling 'Campania') to the lowlands surrounding Capua, through which the Volturnus flows on its way from the Abruzzi to the sea, just north of Naples. The name was extended from the gates of Naples to the gates of Rome by Augustus, to designate one of the 'regions' into which he re-mapped Roman Italy; and the name has persisted in a territory to which it was thus artificially applied, after having died out (except as a pedantically applied archaism) in the territory where it was indigenous.

[2] It is noteworthy that while Capua, after Cannae, betrayed Rome who had fought the Samnites on her account, the Samnites, who had been fought and conquered by Rome on account of Capua, remained loyal to Rome, with the single exception of the south-easternmost canton of the former Samnite Confederation, the Hirpini. The loyalty of the Samnites to the Romans during the Hannibalic War was as remarkable as that of the Sikhs to the British during the Indian Mutiny.

the opinion of military experts that, in allowing them to come to this pass, their commander committed a still greater fault than in failing to march on Rome immediately after the Battle of Cannae. It might be argued that his dilatoriness after Cannae had merely postponed the hour of final victory, whereas his error at Capua had deprived him of the strength to win the war at all.'[1]

Hannibal's fatal error was never committed by the Roman Government to the end of its days. When Rome gave up the conscript army—exercised by the laborious husbandry of her Campagna—with which she had conquered the World, in order to place her conquests under the guard of an army of professionals, she did not make the mistake of stationing this new model army in Capua or even in any of those delectable places along the Riviera[2] where the spoilt children of our modern Western Society take up their winter-quarters nowadays. She took care that the soldiers of the Empire should be tempered by an environment which was not less severe than that which had produced the redoubtable soldiers of the Republic. The legionaries who were no longer to be exercised as yeomen in the Campagna by keeping its marshes in drainage and its fells under the plough were now stationed along the Rhine and the Danube among the Transalpine forests and rains and frosts, to be exercised by this new challenge from Physical Nature for their border warfare with the North-European barbarians. The avoidance of Hannibal's error by Augustus prolonged the life of the Roman Empire by some four hundred years.[3]

Augustus clearly divined the incompatibility between military efficiency and an easy environment, and he set himself to reform the spoilt and insubordinate soldiery which he inherited from the civil wars by banishing it to guard the frontiers on the bleaker side of the Alps. While the great Roman statesman was carrying this difficult policy through, was he ever confirmed in his resolution by any reminiscences of the Greek literature in which he had been educated?

The principle which governed the military policy of Augustus had been made the subject of a fable by the Greek historian Herodotus four centuries earlier. The fable was celebrated, since the great Greek writer had given it prominence by telling it as the tailpiece of his work;[4] and the fable was also apt, since it was told by

---

[1] Livy, Book XXIII, ch. 18.

[2] The Riviera—constituting, as it did at the time, the principal overland route between Italy and Transalpine Europe—would have offered a convenient station for the Imperial forces from a purely geographico-strategical point of view.

[3] Of course even the statesmanship of an Augustus was only able to delay the doom of Rome without being able permanently to avert it. For the eventual transference of the military and political power in the Roman Empire from the hands of the Romans themselves to the hands of the Transalpine barbarians, see II. D (v), pp. 164–5, below.

[4] Herodotus, Book IX, ch. 122.

Herodotus of the Persians—a military people who once upon a time had performed a feat which had afterwards proved to be beyond the genius of Hannibal and had barely been achieved by the staying-power of the Romans: the feat of establishing, by force of arms, a universal state.[1]

As Herodotus tells the story, it was a Persian grandee named Artembares, in the generation of the conquest,

'who first suggested to his Persian fellow-countrymen the proposition which they adopted and laid before Cyrus, to the following effect:

' "Now that Zeus has put down Astyages from his seat and has given the dominion to the Persians as a nation and to you, Sire, as an individual, why should we not emigrate from the confined and rocky territory which we at present possess, and occupy a better? There are many near at hand and many more at a distance, of which we have only to take our choice in order to make a greater impression on the World than we make as it is. This is a natural policy for an imperial people, and we shall never have a finer opportunity of realising it than now, when our Empire is established over vast populations and over the entire continent of Asia."

'Cyrus, who had listened and had not been impressed, told his petitioners to do as they wished, but he qualified his advice by telling them in the same breath to prepare their minds for exchanging positions with their present subjects. Soft countries, he informed them, invariably breed soft men, and it is impossible for one and the same country to produce splendid crops and good soldiers. The Persians capitulated to the superior intelligence of Cyrus, confessed their error, abandoned their proposition, and elected to live as an imperial people in a rough country rather than to cultivate the lowlands as some other nation's slaves.'[2]

---

[1] The Syriac universal state had taken the form of a Persian Empire. Whether the coming Hellenic universal state should take the form of a Carthaginian Empire or a Roman Empire was the real issue of the Hannibalic War,

> omnia cum belli trepido concussa tumultu
> horrida contremuere sub altis aetheris oris,
> in dubioque fuere utrorum ad regna cadendum
> omnibus humanis esset terraque marique.

(Lucretius, *De Rerum Natura*, Book III, ll. 834-7.)

[2] Whatever the historical value of this fable may be, it is certainly an historical fact that the rough country of Persis—the modern province of Fars and the ancient homeland of 'the Persians' in the original narrower sense of a name which was afterwards extended to cover all the kindred peoples of Iran—continued, unlike Latium, to be a breeding-ground for soldiers not only so long as its empire lasted but even after its fall. More than five centuries after the overthrow of the Empire of the Achaemenidae by Alexander the Great, the country which had bred the armies of Cyrus produced, in the Empire of the Sasanidae, a new military power which contended on equal terms with Rome and almost anticipated the Arabs in expelling an intrusive Hellenism from its last footholds in the Syriac World (see I. C (i) (b), vol. i, pp. 75–6, above). Thus the Persians, in their day, did better than either the Romans or the New Englanders. They managed to make use of their high energies in a great feat of expansion without at the same time losing their grip upon the rough country within whose confines those high energies had been generated. Though the Persian soldiers of the Great King served their time, in the garrisons of the Achaemenian Empire, as far afield as Egypt and Anatolia, their home-steads in the highlands of Fars did not go the way of Town Hill, Connecticut, or of Latin Ulubrae (Juvenal, *Satires*, x, l. 102). And so it was in vain that Alexander smirched his

The Temptations of Odysseus

This fable of the Persians' Choice, like the true story of Hannibal's Army at Capua, signifies that when human beings who have been living under pressure are set at ease, their energies are not released but are rather relaxed by this pleasurable change in their conditions of life. The same conception appears in a work of classical literature that is older and more famous than the histories of Herodotus and Livy. It is the theme of those four books of the *Odyssey*[1] in which the hero tells Alcinous the story of his wanderings from the day when he sailed with his companions from Troy to the day when he was washed up, the sole survivor, on the shores of Calypso's island.

In that long series of adventures, it is not when he is encountering his difficulties and dangers—running the gauntlet of the Laestrygons or confronting the Cyclops or making the passage between Scylla and Charybdis—that Odysseus comes nearest to failure in his struggle to make his way home to Ithaca. Rather, these ordeals speed him on his course towards the goal of his endeavours by calling his faculties of audacity and nimbleness of wit and endurance and ingenuity into action.[2] He comes nearest to failure when the resolution to persevere on the difficult and dangerous course towards the journey's end has to compete with the attractions of an assured and immediate ease.

Thus, when the three companions whom he sent out on a reconnaissance into the land of the lotus-eaters fell in with the inhabitants,

'the lotus-eaters did not bethink them to do our companions to death, but gave them of the lotus to taste. And which soever of them did eat that honey-sweet fruit, he no longer had the will to bring back tidings nor in any wise to return; but their will was to remain there with the lotus-eaters, feeding on lotus, and to think no more of the homeward voyage. So I took them to the ships weeping, under duress, and in the hollow ships I dragged them under the benches and bound them there. And then I bade the rest of my companions come aboard the swift ships

glory by burning the Great King's palace at Persepolis. The stony fields and bleak pastures amid which the ruined palace stood (and stands to-day) did not cease to breed warriors. Alexander himself was so deeply impressed by the military virtues of the Imperial People whom he had just overthrown that he enlisted the defeated Persians in his own army on equal terms with his victorious Macedonians. Had Herodotus lived a century later than he did, and carried his narrative of the secular conflict between the Syriac and Hellenic worlds down to the close of Alexander's dramatic contribution to the story, he might have capped his fable with a prophecy (in his ironic vein) that the rough country which had bred soldiers for Cyrus and soldiers for Alexander would continue to bear these formidable crops so long as the Persian peasant remained on his homestead to sow the dragon's-tooth seed.

[1] *Odyssey*, Books IX–XII.
[2]   Ἔνθεν δὲ προτέρω πλέομεν ἀκαχήμενοι ἦτορ,
      ἄσμενοι ἐκ θανάτοιο, φίλους ὀλέσαντες ἑταίρους.
                                    (*Odyssey*, IX, ll. 62–3 and 565–6.)

with all speed, lest any man should lose thought of the voyage home by eating of the lotus.'[1]

Again, when half his ship's company accepted Circe's invitation to come into her parlour,

'she led them in and gave them benches and chairs to sit on and mixed for them cheese and barley and yellow honey in Pramnean wine; and among the food she sprinkled baneful drugs, to make them utterly forget their native land. And then when she had given it to them and they had drunk it up, straightway she smote them with her staff and penned them in pig-styes. And, lo, they had the heads of swine and the voice and the bristles, yea and the body thereof,[2] albeit their understanding was steadfast as aforetime.'[3]

It needed not only Odysseus's human sword but Hermes' divine herb to rescue the poor fools from Circe's black magic.

Thereafter, Odysseus himself would have gone deliberately to his death, in the Sirens' clutches, when the enchantment of their singing fell upon his ears, had he not beforehand stopped his companions' ears with wax and made them bind him hand and foot to the mast and enjoined upon them only to multiply his bonds if he besought them to release him.[4]

Perhaps the hero is least heroic when, shipwrecked and alone, he is washed up on Calypso's island and is kindly entreated by the Goddess[5]—a fairer than Penelope[6]—who takes him to dwell with her in her earthly paradise[7] and promises him an immortality of perpetual youth.[8] He finds salvation when the nymph ceases to please him—when he begins to pass his nights as an unwilling lover in her willing arms and his days sitting on the sea-shore (as he is shown at his first appearance in the poem) with his eyes never dry of tears and his life ebbing away in his longing for home.[9] This revolt, in the eighth year of a passive captivity,[10] against a state of melancholy ease in which he might have continued for evermore, is the inward release which has its external counterpart in the intercession of Athene before the throne of Zeus and in the liberating mission of Hermes.[11] When Calypso pleads with him, at the last moment, to remain, Odysseus answers:

'"Lady Goddess, be not wroth with me for this. I, even I, know it all: I know that the prudent Penelope is not to be compared with thee, in

---

[1] Od. IX, ll. 92–102. An historical analogue to this legendary incident is the soporific effect upon the Polynesian navigators of the sweets of repose on the South Sea Islands. (See pp. 13–15, above.)
[2] Compare Plato's description of 'the City of Swine' in The Republic, 369 B–372 D, which is cited above in Part II. B, vol. i, p. 193, footnote 1.
[3] Od. X, ll. 233–40. [4] Od. XII, ll. 39–54 and 153–200.
[5] Od. VII, ll. 255–7. [6] Od. V, ll. 211–18.
[7] See the beautiful description of it, as Hermes saw it, in Od. V, ll. 63–74.
[8] Od. V, l. 209, and VII, l. 257. [9] Od. V, ll. 151–8.
[10] Od. VII, ll. 259–61. [11] Od. V, ll. 1–148.

figure nor in stature, face to face. She is a mortal woman, while thou art deathless and ageless. Yet none the less I long and pray daily to reach my home and to behold the day of my returning. Yea, and if some God shall wreck me in the wine-faced sea, I will endure it. For I have in my breast a spirit well schooled in enduring sorrows. Already have I suffered full many, and have borne the buffetings of wave and war. I care not if this other blow be added unto those."[1]

When Odysseus speaks these words, he is his clear-sighted and indomitable self again; and nothing—not even Poseidon's final stroke of malice, which the hero foresees—can prevent him from reaching Ithaca now. Moreover, as he knows already from the mouth of Teiresias' ghost, he will not rest on his oars, even when he has regained his home and slain Penelope's suitors. Another journey awaits him, in which he must bear his oar on his shoulder and exchange the toils and perils of the sea for those of the land.[2]

The Flesh Pots of Egypt

This *motif* in the Hellenic story of Odysseus' return from Troy to Ithaca appears, in a variant form, in the Syriac story of the Chosen People's exodus from Egypt to the Promised Land. The attraction which undermines the resolution of the Israelites during their wanderings in the wilderness is not the present delight of a Lotus Land or a Calypso's Isle, but a hankering after the flesh pots of Egypt,[3] which may perhaps be theirs again to-morrow if only they turn back now. They have no sooner crossed the sea dry-shod, and seen Pharaoh and his host perish in the returning waters, than they begin to murmur in the wilderness against Moses and Aaron:

'Would to God we had died by the hand of the Lord in the Land of Egypt, when we sat by the flesh pots and when we did eat bread to the full; for ye have brought us forth into this wilderness to kill this whole assembly with hunger.[4] . . .

'Wherefore is this that thou hast brought us up out of Egypt, to kill us and our children and our cattle with thirst?[5] . . .

'Who shall give us flesh to eat? We remember the fish which we did eat in Egypt freely—the cucumbers and the melons and the leeks and the onions and the garlic—but now our soul is dried away: there is nothing at all beside this manna before our eyes.'[6]

Even when they have crossed the wilderness as safely as they had crossed the sea, and stand at last on the threshold of Canaan, their

---

[1] *Od.* V, ll. 215–24.   [2] *Od.* XI, ll. 119–34.
[3] Egypt seems like an earthly paradise to the Israelites in retrospect, when the memory of their past sojourn there acts as a foil to the current experience of their present ordeal in the wilderness. Yet when they had been living and working in Egypt—making bricks without straw under the task-master's lash—they had realized as clearly as the Egyptian peasants themselves that in Egypt, as in other lands, it is ever in the sweat of his face that Man eats bread.
[4] Exodus xvi. 3.   [5] Exodus xvii. 3.   [6] Numbers xi. 4–6.

thoughts fly back to Egypt as they listen to the evil report of their spies—their sight of the Sons of Anak, the children of the giants, in whose presence the spies had seemed and felt like grasshoppers.

'And all the congregation lifted up their voice and cried; and the people wept that night. And all the children of Israel murmured against Moses and against Aaron, and the whole congregation said unto them: "Would God that we had died in the land of Egypt! Or would God we had died in this wilderness! And wherefore hath the Lord brought us unto this land, to fall by the sword, that our wives and our children should be a prey? Were it not better for us to return into Egypt?" And they said one to another: "Let us make a captain and let us return into Egypt." '[1]

The Chosen People are unable to enter into their inheritance until this haunting and enervating recollection of the flesh pots has been effaced; and it is not effaced until forty years of purgatory—spent in wandering over the face of the wilderness which they have just put behind them in one straight and rapid trek—have brought the older generation to the grave and the younger generation to manhood.[2]

The Doasyoulikes

These passages from myth and history surely demonstrate, between them, that when people are translated—whether in 'real life' or in imagination—from conditions of pressure into conditions of ease, the effect upon their behaviour is demoralizing. It may perhaps be retorted that this is a truism, and that we might have spared ourselves the trouble of demonstrating the fact and not have overlooked the obvious explanation. The ill effect, it may be argued, is a consequence of the process of transition and not a consequence of the condition in which the transition results. 'You infer, from the illustrations which you have put before us, that conditions of ease are inimical to civilization in themselves. You might as well argue that a full stomach is inimical to health on the ground that a heavy meal has been known to prove fatal to a starving man. You know very well that the proper treatment for starvation is neither to fill the patient's empty stomach at one sitting nor to keep him at starvation point in perpetuity, but to re-accustom him to taking a normal amount of nourishment by increasing his ration gradually. The disastrous effect of the heavy meal upon the health of the starving man was due not to any inherent fault in the quantity of the full ration, but solely to the rash abruptness with which it was administered.' In order to meet this

[1] Numbers xvi. 1–4.
[2] Numbers xiv. 26–35. On this point, see also II. C (ii) (*b*) 2, vol. i, pp. 334–5, above.

criticism, we must turn to the second of the two situations which
we have distinguished above—the situation of people in an easy
environment who have never, so far as is known, been exposed to
any other environment since their pre-human ancestors became
men. In this case, the factor of transition is eliminated and we are
enabled to study the effect of easy conditions in the absolute.

Here is an authentic picture of it from Nyasaland, as seen by a
Western observer, nearly half a century ago, in the early days of
'the opening-up of Africa':

'Hidden away in these endless forests, like birds' nests in a wood, in
terror of one another, and of their common foe, the slaver, are small
native villages; and here in his virgin simplicity dwells Primaeval Man,
without clothes, without civilisation, without learning, without religion
—the genuine child of Nature, thoughtless, careless, and contented.
This man is apparently quite happy; he has practically no wants. One
stick, pointed, makes him a spear; two sticks rubbed together make him
a fire; fifty sticks tied together make him a house. The bark he peels
from them makes his clothes; the fruits which hang on them form his
food. It is perfectly astonishing, when one thinks of it, what Nature can
do for the animal-man, to see with what small capital after all a human
being can get through the World. I once saw an African buried. According to the custom of his tribe, his entire earthly possessions—and he was
an average commoner—were buried with him. Into the grave, after the
body, was lowered the dead man's pipe, then a rough knife, then a
mud bowl, and last his bow and arrows—the bowstring cut through the
middle, a touching symbol that its work was done. That was all. Four
items, as an auctioneer would say, were the whole belongings for half a
century of this human being. No man knows what a man is till he has
seen what a man can be without, and be withal a man. That is to say, no
man knows how great Man is till he has seen how small he has been once.

'The African is often blamed for being lazy, but it is a misuse of words.
He does not need to work; with so bountiful a Nature round him it
would be gratuitous to work. And his indolence, therefore, as it is
called, is just as much a part of himself as his flat nose, and as little
blameworthy as slowness in a tortoise. The fact is, Africa is a nation of
the unemployed.

'This completeness, however, will be a sad drawback to development.
Already it is found difficult to create new wants; and when labour is
required, and you have already paid your man a yard of calico and a
string of beads, you have nothing in your possession to bribe him to
another hand's turn. Nothing almost that you have would be the
slightest use to him. . . .

'A fine-looking people, quiet and domestic, their life-history from the
cradle to the grave is of the utmost simplicity. Too ill armed to hunt,
they live all but exclusively on a vegetable diet. A small part of the year
they depend, like the monkeys, upon wild fruits and herbs; but the
staple food is a small tasteless millet-seed which they grow in gardens,

crush in a mortar, and stir with water into a thick porridge. Twice a day, nearly all the year round, each man stuffs himself with this coarse and tasteless dough, shovelling it into his mouth in handfuls, and consuming at a sitting a pile the size of an ant-heap. His one occupation is to grow this millet, and his gardening is a curiosity. Selecting a spot in the forest, he climbs a tree, and with a small home-made axe lops off the branches one by one. He then wades through the litter to the next tree, and hacks it to pieces also, leaving the trunk standing erect. Upon all the trees within a circle of thirty or forty yards' diameter his axe works similar havoc, till the ground stands breast-high in leaves and branches. Next, the whole is set on fire and burnt to ashes. Then, when the first rains moisten the hard ground and wash the fertile chemical constituents of the ash into the soil, he attacks it with his hoe, drops in a few handfuls of millet, and the year's work is over. But a few weeks off and on are required for these operations, and he may go to sleep till the rains are over, assured of a crop which never fails, which is never poor, and which will last him till the rains return again.

'Between the acts he does nothing but lounge and sleep; his wife, or wives, are the millers and bakers; they work hard to prepare his food, and are rewarded by having to take their own meals apart, for no African would ever demean himself by eating with a woman. I have tried to think of something else that these people habitually do, but their vacuous life leaves nothing more to tell.'[1]

This piece of first-hand testimony to the êthos and behaviour of Man in an easy environment has been chosen for quotation here because of the remarkable sharpness of vision and depth of insight which the witness displays; but of course his evidence does not stand alone. It could be supported, if that were necessary, by other modern Western evidence, ranging in Time over the four centuries that have elapsed since Western Man first began to take the whole World for his field, and ranging in Space over all parts of the World where he has found primitive societies still surviving.[2] From the opposite extremity of Tropical Africa, we could cite similar descriptions of the life of the Dinka and the Shilluk—a life which exhibits to-day, like some specimen in 'a living museum', the circumstances in which the fathers of the Egyptiac Civilization were living before they responded to the challenge of desiccation and plunged into the jungle-swamp of the Lower Nile Valley.[3]

[1] Drummond, H.: *Tropical Africa* (London 1888, Hodder and Stoughton), pp. 55–6 and 58–9.
[2] For a survey and classification of primitive societies that have come under the direct observation of our modern Western explorers and anthropologists, see *The Material Culture and Social Institutions of the Simpler Peoples: an essay in correlation,* by Hobhouse, L. T., Wheeler, G. C., and Ginsberg, M. (London 1915, Chapman and Hall; reprinted in 1930), which has been cited above in I. C (iii) (*a*), vol. i, p. 147, footnote 2.
[3] See the description of the social institutions of the Dinka and the Shilluk which has been quoted above in II. C (ii) (*b*) 2, vol. i, on p. 313, from Childe, V. G.: *The Most Ancient East* (London 1928, Kegan Paul), pp. 10–11. For a fuller account, see Seligman, C. G. and B. Z.: *Pagan Tribes of the Nilotic Sudan* (London 1932, Routledge).

Again, this Tropical African evidence could be reinforced by records of primitive tropical life in distant longitudes: in Amazonia[1] or in Melanesia.[2] All this modern Western evidence is readily accessible; and for this reason we will hold it in reserve and will close our review of the effect of easy conditions in the absolute (as distinct from the effect of easy conditions succeeding to difficult conditions, which we have examined already) by citing a description of Hellenic authorship, albeit this description is only given at second hand and has manifestly been enriched by certain legendary touches. Here is Herodotus's account of a people called the Argippaei who were to be found at the farthest extremity, as it stood in his day, of the trade-route leading from the Greek settlements on the north coast of the Black Sea north-eastward into the interior of the great Eurasian Steppe:[3]

'Up to this point, the whole of the country that I have described is plain-land with a deep soil, but from this point onwards it is broken country and the soil is stony. If you cross this broken country—and there is a great stretch of it—you come to the foothills of lofty mountains; and these foothills are inhabited by people who are all bald from birth, men and women alike. They also have snub noses and bushy beards, and a language of their own, though they wear Scythian clothes; and they live off trees. The tree off which they live is called the *Ponticum*. It is just about the size of a fig-tree, and it bears a fruit the size of a bean, with a stone in it. When the fruit ripens, they bag it in cloths, and then it exudes a thick black substance which is called *aschy*. This they either suck or drink mixed with milk, while from the thick dregs they make cakes and use these for solid food. They have not much livestock because there is not any good pastureland there; but every man lives under his tree. In the winter he covers in the tree with a tent of close white felt; in the summer he lives under the tree in the open. These people are not ill-treated by anybody. They are left in peace because they are regarded as holy, and they possess no arms. Their neighbours bring their disputes to them for arbitration, and anyone who takes asylum with them is safe from injury.'[4]

This Hellenic description of primitive life in Central Asia and the foregoing Western description of primitive life in Central Africa give, between them, a clear picture of how Man does live where he has never been exposed to a challenge either from the

---

[1] For the absence of response to any stimulus from the environment in the Amazon Basin (except, of course, on its Andean rim), see the allusions in Means, P. A.: *Ancient Civilisations of the Andes* (New York 1931, Scribner), p. 25, qualified by Nordenskiöld's observations which have been cited in II. C (ii) (a) 2, vol. i, on p. 259, footnote 1, above.

[2] See Malinowski, B.: *Argonauts of the Pacific* (London 1922, Routledge).

[3] The possibility that, a century or so before Herodotus's day, this trade-route may have extended right across the Eurasian Steppe, from the north-eastern extremity of the Hellenic World to the north-western extremity of the Sinic World, is examined by Hudson, G. F., in *Europe and China: A Survey of their Relations from the Earliest Times to 1800* (London 1931, Edward Arnold), ch. 1: 'Beyond the North Wind'.

[4] Herodotus, Book IV, ch. 23. See also chs. 24 and 25.

physical or from the human·environment. He vegetates, quite
comfortably and happily, in a state of lethargy; and, to all appearance, he might continue to vegetate in perpetuity, were he not on
the point of being exposed to a formidable challenge from the
human environment at last.

This imminent challenge is portended in the very fact that his
manner of life has come under the observation of one of those
energetic societies that are in process of civilization; for his
encounter with these importunate strangers will not end in a
mere platonic acquaintance. They observe in order to take action;
and, when once the explorer has crossed the primitive's threshold,
the trader and the missionary and the soldier are sure to follow in
quick succession at the explorer's heels. The primitive's isolation
is terminated, his peace is broken, his comfort and happiness are
replaced by a consciousness of pressure and a feeling of anxiety.
In fact, he is confronted by a challenge under which it is impossible
for his lethargy to persist. The lethargy may pass into death or it
may pass into action, but on either alternative it will pass away.

The possible alternative outcomes of collisions between primitive
societies and societies in process of civilization are examined in
later parts of this Study.[1] In this place we are concerned solely with
the state in which the primitive societies are found existing at the
moment when the first contact takes place. This state makes a profound impression upon the intruders because there is an extreme
contrast between the two colliding ways of life—between the êthos
of people who have been sheltered from challenges hitherto by an
easy environment and the êthos of people who have been challenged
and have responded victoriously. This impression works so powerfully upon the intruders' emotions and imagination that it issues in
mythology.

The classic Hellenic exposition of the myth is the fable of the
Lotus Eaters, which we have quoted already apropos of the effect
of the lotus fruit upon Odysseus' companions.[2] A classic Western
exposition is 'The History of the Great and Famous Nation of the
Doasyoulikes, who came away from the Country of Hardwork
because they wanted to play on the Jews' Harp all day long'. In
Charles Kingsley's fable, an improvident people who persist in
living a life of primitive ease in an earthly paradise overshadowed
by the eruptive crater of Etna, pay the penalty by degenerating
into Tropical African gorillas. This is the complement to another
Western fable which we have dealt with in an earlier chapter:[3]

---

[1] In a general way they are examined in V. C (i) (c) 3, vol. v, pp. 194–337, and in Part VIII;
the special case of the collisions between primitive societies and our Western Civilization
is further examined in Part XII.
[2] See pp. 22–3, above.   [3] See II. C (ii) (a) i, vol. i, pp. 216–21, above.

'The History of that Virtuous and Provident Creature Nordic Man, who followed the retreating Ice Cap because he wanted to harden his Moral Fibre.' In the Western version of the myth, which these two fables convey between them, the clear vision of the primitive êthos in an easy environment, which we find in the verse of Homer and the prose of Herodotus, is obscured by the mists of self-righteousness and self-interest. Yet these blemishes are irrelevant to our present purpose; and, if we consent for the moment to ignore them, we may perceive, underlying them, the philosophic truth which we have studied in the Syriac fable of the Garden of Eden.[1] The same philosophic truth is mirrored in the fable of the Lotus Eaters. In fact, the objective view of the primitive êthos in easy circumstances is found, when we abstract it,[2] to be substantially the same in the minds of the Western and the Hellenic observer. Alike, they see that the primitive environment presents the sharpest contrast to their own; they see that there is a corresponding contrast between the êthos which has been induced in the

[1] See II. C (ii) (b) 1, vol. i, pp. 290–3, above, for a discussion of the fable of the Garden of Eden and for the relevant quotations from Hesiod, Plato, Virgil, Origen, Volney, Huntington, and Myres. It will be noticed that the three passages quoted from the works of Western scholars are simply expurgated versions of the myth which the fable of Nordic Man renders so crudely.

[2] In all versions of the myth, the objective view—the purely intellectual perception of the facts—has to be disentangled from certain aesthetic and emotional concomitants. The difference between the turns which these concomitants take in the Western and Hellenic versions throws some interesting side-lights upon the difference of outlook which distinguishes the Hellenic from our Western Civilization. In the fable of the Lotus Eaters, the innocence and happiness of the primitive êthos in easy circumstances are appreciated at their full aesthetic value—appreciated so keenly that the Hellenic observer feels a lively fear of being captivated by this charming way of life and succumbing to its lethargy and so being beguiled into abandoning those practical ends on the pursuit of which his own civilization depends. The Hellene does not want to remake the Lotus Eater in his own image. Indeed, the idea never occurs to him. He is content to avoid turning into a Lotus Eater himself, and even on this point he is in two minds. As he sails away, he looks back on Lotus Land with a certain wistful regret. 'Perhaps', he thinks, 'I might have been happier as a Lotus Eater after all!' The Western observer's attitude is amusingly different. As a rule, he is blind to the beauty of the life which he is observing. A Malinowski's appreciation of the artistic and ritual and social refinements with which 'the Argonauts of the Pacific' occupy their vast leisure is the exception which proves the rule. The typical Western observer dismisses such primitive occupations as child's-play and triviality and waste of time. He is quite immune from the possibility of being captivated by them himself, and there is no shadow of this fear on his mind. The emotion which he feels is disgust—disgust that the Doasyoulikes should have played truant from the Country of Hardwork; disgust that the Shilluk and the Dinka should have evaded the challenge of desiccation to which the virtuous Egyptian has responded by becoming a fallāh. In the Westerner's view, this weak-minded malingering is so contemptible that it must bring the wretches who indulge in it to a bad end. A Doasyoulike, left to himself, is bound to degenerate into a gorilla. It follows that it is the duty of Nordic Man to intervene, in order to save the Doasyoulike, in spite of himself, from his natural and well-deserved fate. Fortunately, duty and self-interest coincide; for the Doasyoulike can only be saved by being remade in Nordic Man's image, and the first step in this transfiguration is to make him serve an apprenticeship as Nordic Man's hewer of wood and drawer of water. Nordic Man can do with any amount of cheap labour. 'And we know that all things work together for good to them that love God, to them who are the called according to His purpose' (Romans viii. 28). Fortified in his resolution by this oracle from the *Sortes Biblicae*, Nordic Man takes the poor Doasyoulike firmly in hand and—in the various roles of taskmaster, salesman, and evangelist—arouses him from his lethargy, with ultimate consequences which are not yet apparent but which may prove to be surprising.

primitive by his easy circumstances and the êthos which has been induced by a strenuous life in themselves; they see that the primitive will not and cannot ever join them in running the race of civilization[1] so long as an easy environment continues to shield him from the necessity; and finally they see that they themselves, if they succumb to this insidious environment, will cease to run with patience the race that is set before them.

II. THE STIMULUS OF HARD COUNTRIES

A Plan of Operations

We have now perhaps established decisively the truth that ease is inimical to civilization. The results of our investigation up to this point appear to warrant the proposition that, the greater the ease of the environment, the weaker the stimulus towards civilization which that environment administers to Man. Can we now proceed one step farther? Are we warranted in formulating, in equally simple and abstract terms, the inverse proposition that the stimulus towards civilization grows stronger in proportion as the environment grows more difficult? Let us put this second proposition to the test by our now well-tried empirical method. Let us review first the evidence in favour of the proposition and then the evidence against it, and see what inference emerges. Evidence indicating that the difficulty and the stimulus of an environment are apt to increase *pari passu* is not hard to lay hands upon. Rather, we are likely to be embarrassed by the wealth of illustrations that leap to the mind. Most of these illustrations present themselves in the form of comparisons. Let us begin by sorting out our illustrations into two groups in which the points of comparison relate to the physical environment and to the human environment respectively; and let us first consider the physical group. It subdivides itself into two categories: comparisons between the respective stimulating effects of physical environments which present different degrees of difficulty; and comparisons between the respective stimulating effects of old ground and new ground, apart from the intrinsic nature of the terrain.

The Yellow River and the Yangtse

Let us compare, for example, the different degrees of difficulty which are presented respectively by the lower valleys of the Yellow River and the Yangtse—starting in either case from the point where the river issues from its last gorge in order to flow the rest of its way through open country to the coast.

The primeval state of the lower section of the Yellow River

[1] For this metaphor, see II. C (ii) (a) 1, vol. i, pp. 233–4, above.

Valley is vividly described in a passage from the work of a distinguished Sinologist which has been quoted in an earlier chapter.[1] When Man first took this watery chaos in hand, the river was not navigable at any season; in the winter it was either frozen or choked with floating ice; the melting of this ice in the spring produced devastating annual floods which repeatedly changed the river's course by carving out new channels, while the old channels turned into jungle-covered swamps. This was the state of the river as Man first found it; and to-day, when some three or four thousand years of human effort have drained the swamps and have confined the main channel of the river between embankments, the devastating action of the floods has not been eliminated. The visitations have merely been reduced in frequency—only to ravage the works of Man with greater violence and over a wider range when they do occur.

The flood-waters of the Yellow River which, in the state of Nature, used to spread themselves annually over the plains, now in normal years travel harmlessly between embankments from the exit of the gorges to the sea; but, like Gods restrained by human impiety from satisfying their lust to destroy, these floods, in passing, prepare for a future revenge. They pile up trouble for Man in the literal sense by depositing the silt which they have brought down from the mountains as they slacken speed and move on sluggishly over the flat river-bed to which, in their lower course, the embankments now confine them. Year by year, as the deposits accumulate, the level of this river-bed rises above the level of the fields on either side; year by year, the people raise the height of the embankments, to prevent the flood-waters from spilling over. Yet at last there comes a point at which the level of the river-bed is so high above the level of the surrounding country that no heightening or thickening of the embankments avails any longer to lend them the requisite resisting power; and then, in some year of high flood, the imprisoned river savagely bursts its banks and engulfs a whole countryside, obliterating the fields and sweeping away the buildings and drowning the live stock and the population. Since the history of the region began to be recorded, these periodic inundations have occurred innumerable times; and on several occasions the river has changed its course completely. At the present moment it debouches into the Gulf of Chihli near the midpoint of its south-western coast, almost opposite the tip of the Liaotung Peninsula; in the prehistoric age it debouched at the north-west corner of the Gulf through the bed in which the Pei-ho River flows to-day;[2] but during the intervening three or four

---

[1] See II. C (ii) (b) 2, vol. i, pp. 318–20, above.   [2] Op. cit., loc. cit.

millennia it has played greater vagaries than this. Less than a century ago it was not debouching into the Gulf of Chihli at all. It was only the inundation of 1852 that diverted the river back into the Gulf from a channel debouching, south of the Shantung Peninsula, direct into the Yellow Sea; and this was not the first time on record that the Yellow River had switched its course from one side of the Shantung Peninsula to the other.

A remarkable contrast to this is presented by the lower valley of the Yangtse. The Lower Yangtse drains a basin where the land is potentially no less fertile than the northern plains and where agriculture has not to labour, as it labours there, under the twofold scourge of flood and drought. The Yangtse sometimes emulates his northern brother in inundating his human neighbours' fields,[1] but he never refuses to bear their craft upon his waters.[2]

Such are the respective characters of the two great rivers, as they were in the beginning and as they are to-day. And where did the Sinic Civilization come to birth? On the banks of the gracious Yangtse-kiang or on those of the demonic Hwang-ho? We know that it came to birth on the banks of the Hwang-ho, and that the Lower Yangtse Valley was not brought within the ambit of the Sinic Society until after the Sinic Civilization had broken down and had entered upon a Time of Troubles which was the first phase of its decline.

Chimu and Valparaiso

Again, on what section of the Pacific Coast of South America did the Andean Civilization come to birth? Not on that Central

[1] A week after these sentences had been written in the summer of the year 1931, the Yangtse produced, in the region of Hankow, a flood which, in scale and in destructiveness, is perhaps unsurpassed in the annals of the Yellow River itself. Nevertheless, the writer believes that on a long view, extending back to the local beginnings of recorded history in the middle of the last millennium B.C., the contrast here drawn between the characters displayed by the Yangtse and the Yellow River in their respective relations to Man is borne out on the whole by the facts.

[2] In the year 1926 of the Christian Era, 'the Yangtse was navigable' in 'the summer months, when the discharge of the river was augmented by the summer rainfall and by the melting of the snows in Tibet . . . as far up as Hankow (about 570 miles from its mouth) . . . for large ocean-going steamers'; and this point had been known to be reached by 'a foreign battleship of as much as 12,000 tons displacement. . . . Under the same conditions, steamers of ordinary construction, though not of heavy tonnage, could navigate likewise the next section of 367 nautical miles from Hankow to Ichang. The section of 400 nautical miles above this, between Ichang and Chungking, had been opened since 1919 to steam-navigation by specially constructed river-steamers of light draft and with engines sufficiently powerful to mount the rapids. This achievement had brought steam-navigation into Szechuan—the most populous Chinese province (with an estimated population of 50,000,000). For native junks, the passage of the rapids in the Ichang-Chungking section was a slow, laborious, and dangerous operation. On the other hand, they were able to ascend the river as far as Suifu, which was about 1,548 nautical miles from the mouth, or even as far as Pingshan, about 33 miles further, whereas Chungking, the limit of river-steamer navigation, was about 1,337 miles from the mouth, and Ichang, the limit of navigation for small steamers of ordinary build, about 937.' (Toynbee, A. J.: *Survey of International Affairs, 1926* (London 1928, Milford), pp. 302–3.)

Chilean section which enjoys such a generous rainfall that the Spanish explorers saluted an earthly paradise—Valparaiso—in the first of these green valleys which rejoiced their eyes after their long journey down the parched brown coast which they had to traverse farther north. The Andean Civilization came to birth on the North Peruvian section of the coast—described in a passage which has been quoted above[1]—where Man has to fight a perpetual battle with the desert and must water his fields, which the sky will not water for him, by his own hard labour: the spade-work of digging and maintaining innumerable irrigation-channels. Chile was not brought within the ambit of the Andean Society until the Andean Civilization had reached an advanced stage in its decline. Chile was one of the last conquests of the Empire of the Incas—the Andean universal state—and even then the Incas were content to leave the greater part of fertile Chile beyond their southern frontier, which they drew along the line of the River Maule. The Incas were at home on the Andean Plateau, to which the coastal civilization had spread at an early date in its growth. And on what section of the plateau did this civilization secure its first foothold? Neither on the section which was nearest to its primary home in the coastal valleys of Chimu, nor yet on the northerly section (in the territory of the modern Latin Republic of Colombia) where the altitudes are comparatively low and the valleys open and the climate genial. The ruins of Tiahuanaco testify that the first foothold of civilization on the plateau was in the upland basin of Lake Titicaca—a region which was hardly nearer to the primary home of the Andean Civilization in one direction than the upper basin of the Magdalena River was in the other, while in soil and climate it was manifestly less inviting.[2]

Lowlands and Highlands in Guatemala

Again, which face of Central America was it that saw the birth of the Mayan Civilization? Not the Pacific face, where a relatively high altitude co-operates with a relatively low rainfall to liberate a strip of country from the pall of tropical forest which smothers the Atlantic lowlands.[3]

[1] See II. C (ii) (b) 2, vol. i, pp. 322-3, above.
[2] See the description of the Titicaca Basin which has been quoted in vol. i, p. 322, above. For the birth-places of the Andean Civilization, and the course of its expansion during its growth, see II. C (i) (b), vol. i, pp. 120-3, above.
[3] For the contrast in climate and vegetation between the Pacific Highlands and the Atlantic Lowlands of Central America, see Huntington, E.: *The Climatic Factor as illustrated in Arid America* (Washington 1914, Carnegie Institution of Washington, Publication No. 192), chs. xvii and xviii. For the almost exact inversion of the relative degrees of civilization that have been prevalent respectively in the several different geographical zones of Central America in post-Columbian times, as contrasted with the situation in the age in which the Mayan Civilization came to birth and grew to maturity, see op. cit., pp. 218-19. For Dr. Huntington's hypothesis that this shift of social zones is to be accounted for by a shift of climatic zones, see II. D (vii), Annex I, below.

When the Spaniards arrived, they took to these open healthy Central American uplands overlooking the Pacific—an earthly paradise in the Tropics—as decidedly as they took to Chilean Valparaiso at the far extremity of their conquests in the New World. It was here that they planted their Central American settlements, working their way up the Pacific coast from the point where they bestrode the Isthmus of Panama as far as the present frontier between Guatemala and Mexico. On the other hand, they made no serious attempt to occupy the Atlantic coast of Central America between their settlements on the Isthmus and their settlements in Yucatan. The tropical forest in the hinterland deterred them, though this coast lay almost within sight of their island possessions in the Antilles and though the opening up of coast and hinterland would have shortened appreciably the length of the journey between the Spanish settlements on the Pacific face of Central America and the mother country. In spite of that, the Spaniards abandoned this Atlantic coast to indigenous Indians and to English interlopers,[1] and were content to leave the communications between Spain and the Spanish settlements on the Pacific coast to follow the round-about route across the Isthmus. The situation has not changed substantially since the Spanish Empire in the New World has disappeared. Though five out of the six republics which are its 'successor-states' in Central America possess Atlantic seaboards, the best-developed districts and the principal centres of population are still to be found on the uplands overlooking the Pacific where the Spaniards first made themselves at home. In 1933, there were still no more than two lines of railway spanning Central America from coast to coast between the Isthmus of Panama and the Isthmus of Tehuantepec; and in 1927 the capital city of at least one republic was still cut off from its Atlantic littoral by a barrier of virgin and virtually impassable jungle.[2]

The contrast between the eagerness and promptness with which the Spaniards took to the open highlands overlooking the Pacific coast of Central America and the almost complete failure of the colonists and their successors, over a period of more than four

---

[1] An unsuccessful attempt to found a Puritan colony on the islet of Santa Catalina or Providence, off 'the Mosquito Coast', was made in A.D. 1630 (see Newton, A. P.: *The Colonizing Activities of the English Puritans* (New Haven 1914, Yale University Press)), and the British Government continued to claim a protectorate over the Mosquito Indians till 1855. After the acquisition of Jamaica, the English secured a footing on another section of this coast which has now become the Crown Colony of British Honduras.

[2] The North American statesman, Mr. Henry L. Stimson, when he was at Managua, the capital of Nicaragua, in 1927, found that 'the Atlantic coast of Nicaragua was distant from us much less than 200 miles as the crow flies, but it takes longer to get there than to go from New York to San Francisco, and the only way of going was by sea through the Panama Canal, unless one was willing to travel on foot through the jungle or to follow down a tropical river in a canoe'. (Stimson, H. L.: *American Policy in Nicaragua* (New York 1927, Scribner), p. 47.)

centuries, to open up the Atlantic coast with its hinterland of tropical forest, gives some measure of the difference in the degree of the difficulty which these two neighbouring but very diverse regions oppose respectively to Man when he attempts to break them in. Where was it, then, that the oldest indigenous civilization of the New World came to birth? On the Central American uplands or in the Central American forests? We know that the Mayan Civilization came to birth in the forests and that, even when it spread, its line of expansion was not southwards into the adjoining uplands but northwards into the Yucatan Peninsula and on to the Mexican Plateau. It was in those quarters, and not on the southern uplands, that the two later civilizations which were related to the Mayan Civilization arose in their turn. Apparently the easily accessible Central American uplands were never occupied by any civilization until the Spaniards came to take possession of them from the other side of the Atlantic. The indigenous civilizations were as persistent in shunning the uplands as the intrusive civilization has been in shunning the forests. Then were the Mayas blind and the Spaniards sharp-sighted? We have only to compare the respective achievements in Central America of the Mayan Civilization on the one hand and of the Spanish version of our Western Civilization on the other in order to realize that the forests in which the Mayan Civilization came to birth surpass in two respects the uplands on which our Western Civilization has been propagated. They not only surpass them in the degree of the difficulty which they oppose to human efforts; they surpass them no less in the degree of the response which they have evoked from human beings who have made the effort to grapple with them.[1]

The Aegean Coasts and their Continental Hinterlands

Again, the unusual difficulty presented by the Aegean area, in which the Minoan and the Hellenic Civilization successively came to birth, becomes fully apparent only when the area is viewed in its geographical setting, against the foil provided by the regions round about. I can testify to this from personal experience. On my first visit to the Aegean, I came and went by sea; and, as always, the sea-voyage had the psychological effect of fixing a great mental gulf between its termini. The contrast between the physical features of Greece and those of England was of course obvious; but on both the journey out and the journey back the abrupt transition from the one country to the other made it impossible to

[1] This avoidance of the former theatre of the Mayan Civilization by the Spanish colonists in Central America may be compared with the avoidance of the former theatre of the Indic Civilization in Ceylon by the Scottish and English planters. (See II. D (i), pp. 6–7, above.) In both instances, the latter-day Western intruders chose the softer— and less stimulating—option.

appreciate this obvious matter of fact imaginatively. On my second visit to the Aegean, I again arrived by sea; but this time I broke my stay in Athens by making three reconnaissances into regions just outside the Aegean area. First I went to Smyrna and made expeditions from there by rail up country into the interior of Anatolia; next I went to Constantinople and made other expeditions into Anatolia from that quarter; and then, before coming home, I went to Salonica and made an expedition from there into the interior of Macedonia. Finally, I returned to England by the overland route, travelling in the same railway-carriage, without a change, from Constantinople to Calais. Thus, in the course of this visit, I travelled overland, out of the Aegean area into the regions round about, in four different directions; and each time, in every direction, I found myself travelling out of country that was bare, barren, rocky, mountainous, and broken into fragments by the estranging sea, into country that was greener and richer and softer—country in which mountain-ranges were replaced by rolling hills, and sea-filled gulfs and straits by broad cultivable river-valleys. The cumulative effect of these contrasts upon the observer's imagination was very powerful. On this comparative view, the Aegean area showed itself in its true colours as a region of unusual difficulty, not only by contrast with England or with the other Transalpine countries of Europe, but by contrast with every region adjoining it. In this light, I realized the deep meaning of the words which Herodotus puts into the mouth of the Spartan exile Dâmarâtus in a colloquy with the Great King Xerxes: 'Hellas has a foster-sister Poverty who never leaves her; but she has brought in a guest in the shape of Virtue, the child of Wisdom and Law; and by Virtue's aid Hellas keeps Poverty at bay and Servitude likewise.'[1]

Attica and Boeotia

Similar contrasts in the physical environment, capped by corresponding contrasts in the local variety of civilization, may be observed in the interior of the Aegean area itself. For instance, if one travels by train from Athens along the railway which eventually leads, through Salonica, out of the Aegean area into the heart of Europe, one passes, on the first stage of the journey, through a stretch of country which gives to Central or Western European eyes an anticipatory glimpse of familiar scenery. After the train has been climbing slowly for hours round the eastern flanks of Mount Parnes through a typical Aegean landscape of stunted pines and jagged limestone crags, the traveller is astonished to find himself

[1] Herodotus, Book VII, ch. 102. The Greek text is: Τῇ Ἑλλάδι πενίη μὲν αἰεί κοτε σύντροφός ἐστι, ἀρετὴ δὲ ἔπακτός ἐστι, ἀπό τε σοφίης κατεργασμένη καὶ νόμου ἰσχυροῦ· τῇ διαχρεωμένη ἡ Ἑλλὰς τήν τε πενίην ἀπαμύνεται καὶ τὴν δεσποσύνην.

being rattled down into a lowland country of gently undulating
deep-soiled ploughlands. He might imagine that he had just
crossed the Austro-German frontier on the railway between Inns-
bruck and Munich; the northern aspect of Parnes and Cithaerôn,
which he now views at a distance across this lowland foreground,
might be the northernmost range of the Tyrolese Alps. Of course
this landscape is a 'sport'. He will not see the like again until he
has put Nish behind him some thirty-six hours later and is
descending the Lower Valley of the Morava towards the Middle
Danube; and that makes this anticipatory patch of Bavaria-in-
Greece so much the more striking.

What was this odd piece of country called during the lifetime of
the Hellenic Civilization? It was called Boeotia; and in Hellenic
minds the word 'Boeotian' had a quite distinctive connotation. It
stood for an êthos which was rustic, stolid, unimaginative, brutal—
an êthos out of harmony with the prevailing genius of the Hellenic
culture. This discord between the Boeotian êthos and Hellenism
was accentuated by the fact that just behind the range of Cithaerôn,
and just round the corner of Parnes where the railway winds its way
nowadays, lay Attica 'the Hellas of Hellas': the country whose
êthos was the quintessence of Hellenism lying cheek by jowl with
the country whose êthos affected normal Hellenic sensibilities like
a jarring note. The contrast was summed up in piquant phrases:
'Boeotian Swine' and 'Attic Salt'.

The point of interest, for the purpose of our present study, is
that this cultural contrast, which impressed itself so vividly on the
ancient Hellenic consciousness, was geographically coincident with
an equally striking contrast in the physical environment which
already existed then and which still survives to-day to impress
the passing Western railway-traveller. For Attica is 'the Hellas of
Hellas' not only in her soul but in her physique. She stands to
the other countries of the Aegean as those Aegean countries stand
to the regions around. If you approach Greece by sea from the
west and enter through the avenue of the Corinthian Gulf, you may
flatter yourself that your eye has grown accustomed to the Greek
landscape—beautiful and forbidding at once—before the view is
shut out by the banks of the Corinth Canal. Yet when your
steamer emerges from the cutting through the Isthmus to plough
Aegean waters at last, you will still be shocked, in the Saronic Gulf,
by an austerity of landscape for which the scenery on the other
side of the Isthmus has not fully prepared you; and this austerity
attains its climax when you round the corner of Salamis and see the
land of Attica spread out before your eyes up to the summits of
Pentelicus and Hymettus.

In Attica, with her abnormally light and stony soil, the process
called denudation, which Boeotia has escaped down to this day,
was already complete in Plato's time, as witness the Attic philosopher's own graphic account of it.

'Contemporary Attica may accurately be described as a mere relic of
the original country, as I shall proceed to explain. In configuration,
Attica consists entirely of a long peninsula protruding from the mass of
the continent into the sea, and the surrounding marine basin is known
to shelve steeply round the whole coastline. In consequence of the
successive violent deluges which have occurred within the past 9,000
years (the interval which separates our own times from the period with
which we are dealing), there has been a constant movement of soil away
from the high altitudes; and, owing to the shelving relief of the coast,
this soil, instead of laying down alluvium, as it does elsewhere, to any
appreciable extent, has been perpetually deposited in the deep sea
round the periphery of the country or, in other words, lost; so that
Attica has undergone the process observable in small islands, and what
remains of her substance is like the skeleton of a body emaciated by
disease, as compared with her original relief. All the rich, soft soil has
moulted away, leaving a country of skin and bones. At the period,
however, with which we are dealing, when Attica was still intact, what
are now her mountains were lofty, soil-clad hills; her so-called shingle-
plains of the present day were full of rich soil; and her mountains were
heavily afforested—a fact of which there are still visible traces. There
are mountains in Attica which can now keep nothing but bees, but which
were clothed, not so very long ago, with fine trees producing timber
suitable for roofing the largest buildings; the roofs hewn from this
timber are still in existence. There were also many lofty cultivated
trees, while the country produced boundless pasture for cattle. The
annual supply of rainfall was not lost, as it is at present, through being
allowed to flow over the denuded surface into the sea, but was received
by the country, in all its abundance, into her bosom, where she stored it
in her impervious potter's earth and so was able to discharge the drainage
of the heights into the hollows in the form of springs and rivers with an
abundant volume and a wide territorial distribution. The shrines that
survive to the present day on the sites of extinct water-supplies are
evidence for the correctness of my present hypothesis.'[1]

What did the Athenians do with their poor country when she
lost the buxomness of her Boeotian youth? We know that they did
the things which made Athens 'the education of Hellas'.[2] When
the pastures of Attica dried up and her ploughlands wasted away,
her people turned from the common pursuits of stock-breeding and
grain-growing to devices that were all their own: olive-cultivation

[1] Plato, *Critias*, 111 A–D.
[2] The Athenian response to the challenge of the Attic environment has been touched
upon, by anticipation, in I. B (ii), vol. i, pp. 24–5, above.

and the exploitation of the subsoil. The gracious tree of Athena
not only keeps alive but flourishes on the bare rock. Yet Man
cannot live by olive-oil alone. To make a living from his olive-
groves, the Athenian must exchange Attic oil for Scythian grain.
To place his oil on the Scythian market, he must pack it in jars
and ship it overseas—necessities which called into existence the
Attic potteries and the Attic merchant-marine,[1] and also the Attic
silver-mines, since international trade demands a money economy
and thus stimulates an exploration of the subsoil for precious
metals as well as for potter's earth. Finally, all these things together—exports, industries, merchant ships, and money—required
the protection and defrayed the upkeep of a navy. Thus the
denudation of their soil in Attica stimulated the Athenians to
acquire the command of the sea from one end of the Aegean to the
other, and beyond; and therewith the riches which they had lost
were recovered a hundredfold. This effect of Athenian sea-power

[1] In the year 1921, the writer of this Study visited a modern Orthodox Christian
community in the Aegean area in whose life the olive was then playing the same part
as it had once played in Hellenic Attica. This modern Greek city-state of Ayvalyq (a
Turkish word meaning 'Quince Orchard') or Kydhoniés (the equivalent in modern
Greek) was situated on a little peninsula projecting into the Aegean from the west coast
of Anatolia opposite the Greek island of Mitylene (the ancient Lesbos). The soil of this
peninsula—which was as thin and stony and rock-ribbed as the soil of Attica itself—
made a striking impression of barrenness upon the traveller who came to Ayvalyq overland from the fertile valley of the Caicus and travelled on to Mitylene with its smiling
gardens and vineyards just across the water. From the citadel of Pergamum, which
commands the Caicus Valley, Macedonian Attalids and Turkish Qara 'Osmanoghlus
had sometimes extended their dominions over half Asia Minor. Yet barren Ayvalyq had
acquired an empire too: an overseas empire extracted from the olive. The Greek settlers
from all parts of the Aegean who had founded Ayvalyq during the last quarter of the
eighteenth century of the Christian Era had turned the barren soil, on which their lot was
cast, into a goodly heritage by planting it with two million olive trees; and, a century and
a half later, these plantations were supporting a community of thirty or forty thousand
people in a high degree of civilization. At Ayvalyq, the olive was at the bottom of everything. The community purchased its food supplies and other necessities of life by
exporting the produce of the olive in various forms: as fruit, as oil, and as soap (which
they manufactured out of the oil in their own factories). The waste product of the oil-
presses—skins and stones and dregs—was used as fuel for driving the oil-presses and
the soap-factories in Ayvalyq town, and also for driving the steamers (owned by local
capitalists and manned by local crews) which carried the produce of the olive-groves
from Ayvalyq port as far afield as Russia and America, in order to fetch the community's
foreign requirements as return cargoes. This olive-economy enabled Ayvalyq not only
to live but to live well. This community of fruit-growers and manufacturers and merchants and shippers did not neglect the things of the spirit. Its chief glory was an
academy which was one of the first places in which the literature of ancient Hellas and
the science of the modern West had been studied and taught together in the modern
Greek tongue.

This remarkable community at Ayvalyq was both brought into existence and wiped
out of existence by the process of Westernization, as this remorselessly worked itself
out in the Near East. After being twice destroyed and twice refounded in the struggle
for the heritage of the old Ottoman Empire—a struggle which the ferment of Westernization set on foot between the Greeks and the Turks and the other Near Eastern peoples—
Greek Ayvalyq was finally evacuated, this time presumably for good, in the great Greek
exodus from Anatolia after the *débâcle* of the Greek Army in 1922. To-day, modern
Greek Ayvalyq belongs to the past no less than ancient Greek Athens. The present
writer's glimpse of the place in 1921, on the eve of its extinction, has enabled him to
understand by analogy the part played in ancient Attic life by the miraculous tree which
was venerated and loved as the gift of Attica's tutelary Goddess.

has been vividly painted by an anonymous Athenian writer of the generation before Plato's:

'Bad harvests due to atmospheric conditions fall with crushing weight upon even the strongest land-powers, while sea-powers surmount them easily. Bad harvests are never of world-wide incidence, and therefore the masters of the sea are always able to draw upon regions in which the harvest has been abundant. If I may venture to descend to minor details, I may add that the command of the sea has enabled the Athenians . . . to discover refinements of luxury through their extensive foreign relations. Every delicacy of Sicily, Italy, Cyprus, Egypt, Lydia, the Black Sea, the Peloponnese or any other country has been accumulated on a single spot in virtue of the command of the sea. . . . Moreover, the Athenians are the only nation, Hellenic or non-Hellenic, that is in a position to accumulate wealth. If a country happens to be rich in ship-timber, what market is there for it, if it fails to conciliate the masters of the sea? Similarly, if a country happens to be rich in iron, copper or flax, what market is there for it, if it fails to find favour in the same quarter? But these are precisely the raw materials out of which I construct my ships—timber coming from one source, iron from a second, copper from a third, hemp from a fourth, flax from a fifth. In addition, they will refuse to licence the export of these commodities to other markets or—those who choose to oppose our wishes shall be excluded from the sea! Thus I, who produce not one of these commodities in my home territory, possess them all by way of the sea, while no other country possesses any two of them simultaneously.'[1]

But these riches of the sea—riches beyond the dream of the Boeotian ploughman whose deep-soiled fields had never failed him —were merely the economic foundation for a political and artistic and intellectual culture which made Athens 'the education of Hellas' and 'Attic Salt' the antithesis of Boeotian animality. On the political plane, the Athenian industrial and sea-faring population constituted the electorate of the Athenian democracy, while Attic trade and sea-power provided the framework for that international association of Aegean city-states which took shape in the Delian League under Athenian auspices. On the artistic plane, the prosperity of the Attic potteries gave the Attic vase-painter the opportunity which he used for creating a new form of beauty; and the extinction of the Attic forests compelled Athenian architects to translate their work from the medium of timber into the medium of stone and so led them on to create the Parthenon instead of resting content with the commonplace log-house which Man has always built in every place where tall trees grow.[2] On the

---

[1] Pseudo-Xenophon: *Athenaiōn Politeia* ('Athenian Institutions'), edited by Kalinka, E. (Leipzig 1913, Teubner), ch. 2.
[2] The translation of a commonplace architecture in timber into a unprecedentedly and unsurpassedly noble architecture in stone was of course not an exclusively Attic achievement. It was the general consequence of a general exhaustion of timber-supplies

intellectual plane, to quote our anonymous Athenian observer once again,

'their familiarity . . . with every language spoken under the Sun has enabled the Athenians to select this expression from that language and this from the other, with the result that—in contrast to other Hellenes, who, as a general rule, preserve their local dialect, life and costume— the Athenians rejoice in a cosmopolitan civilization for which the entire Hellenic and non-Hellenic worlds have been laid under contribution.[1]

This Attic culture did, indeed, gather the whole of the contemporary Hellenic culture into itself, in order to transmit it to posterity seasoned with the 'Attic Salt' and ennobled by the Attic impress.

Chalcidicê and Boeotia

The contrast between Boeotia and Attica is not the only illustration of our theme which the Aegean area has bequeathed from the age when it was the theatre of Hellenic history. Boeotia had another neighbour, Chalcis: a closer neighbour than Athens, though divided from Boeotia by the sea. The city of Chalcis stood on the Euboean shore of the Straits—so narrow that at times they have been spanned by a bridge—which run between the Island of Euboea and the Boeotian mainland. In the Euboean hinterland of Chalcis City, and within the frontiers of the Chalcidian State, lay the Lelantine Plain. And this Chalcidian campagna was not like the 'bad lands' of Latium or Attica. It was as good a ploughland as Boeotia itself; but, unfortunately—or fortunately—for the Chalcidians, the Lelantine Plain was narrow; and hence, while the Boeotian farmers were still finding land for the plough, enough and to spare, without looking beyond their borders, the Chalcidian farmers—brought up short, on their island, by the precipitous flanks of the towering peak of Dirphys—were stimulated to search for fresh ploughlands abroad. The salt waters of the Euripus Straits, which washed the foot of their city walls, offered the Chalcidians a sea-passage for their voyages of exploration. Sailing out into the Aegean and beyond it, they took to the land again wherever they found another Lelantine Plain awaiting the Chalcidian plough with a native population incompetent to hold its own against the Chalcidian colonist. Sailing north and east, they founded a new Chalcidicê on the coasts of Thrace; sailing south and west, they founded another in Sicily.

throughout the Aegean area. It was, however, on Athenian sites and in Athenian hands that the Hellenic architecture produced its masterpieces. We may note in passing that the absence of building timber had a profoundly stimulating effec⸴ not only upon the Hellenic architecture but upon the Sumeric. Here, however, the effect was of a different kind. While the Hellenic architect, in translating from timber into stone, was stimulated to create a new beauty, the Sumeric architect, in translating from timber into brick, was stimulated to invent a new technique. He discovered the principles of the arch and the vault.   [1] Op. cit., loc. cit.

Of course, this feat which the Chalcidians performed under the stimulus of land-shortage in Euboea is not to be compared with the feats to which the denudation of Attica stimulated the Athenians. While the Athenians responded to the Attic challenge by a qualitative change in their economy, the Chalcidians' response to the Euboean challenge was quantitative. They merely added field to field, instead of transforming fields into mines and olive-groves. The agricultural life of the Chalcidian colonies, each set in its arable plain—a Thracian Torone or a Sicilian Leontini—was a replica of the life which had been lived in the Lelantine Plain by the colonists' forefathers and which was still being lived there by their cousins whose forefathers had succeeded in staying at home. In other words, the expansion of Chalcis differed from the expansion of Athens in being extensive and not intensive.[1] Nevertheless, Chalcis too, in response to a less formidable challenge, made a mark—albeit a fainter mark than the Athenian—upon Hellenic history. It was through those Chalcidian farmer-settlers overseas that the barbarians of Macedonia and of Latium were drawn into the orbit of the Hellenic Civilization and were given their first tincture of the Hellenic culture.[2] The Chalcidians reacted, in their degree, to the prick of Necessity's spur, while comfortable Boeotia cared for none of these things.

Byzantium and Calchedon

The enlargement of the area of the Hellenic World *circa* 725–525 B.C., in which the Chalcidians played this prominent part, offers us some further Hellenic illustrations of our theme. Among the barbarians who came within range of the movement and who reacted to it by becoming converts to Hellenism instead of being supplanted by Greek settlers, the difference, in stimulating effect, between a hard and an easy environment is illustrated by the contrast between the careers of the two Italian city-states which arose respectively in the Roman and in the Capuan campagna. This contrast needs no more than a bare mention here, since we have examined it in another connexion already;[3] and we may pass on to the celebrated illustration which is afforded by the contrast between the two Greek colonies of Calchedon and Byzantium which were planted respectively on the Asiatic and on the European side of the entrance to the Bosphorus from the Sea of Marmara.

A century or so after the foundation of the two cities, the Persian

---

[1] This point has been noted, by anticipation, in I. B (ii), vol. i, pp. 24–5, above, and is taken up again in Part III. B, vol. iii, pp. 120–2, below.

[2] See further III. C (ii) (*b*), Annex IV, vol. iii.

[3] See pp. 18–21, above.

statesman Megabazus, who had been placed in charge of the European hinterland of the Straits by Darius,

'made a *mot* which won him immortal celebrity among the Hellespontine Greeks. At Byzantium he heard that the Calchedonians had planted their city seventeen years earlier than the Byzantines had planted theirs; and he had no sooner heard it than he remarked: "Then the Calchedonians must have been blind men all that time." He meant that they must have been blind to choose the worse site when the better was at their disposal.'[1]

Megabazus's famous observation was epigrammatic rather than acute; for it is not so difficult to be wise after the event, and in Megabazus's day the respective destinies of Calchedon and Byzantium were already manifest. Calchedon was still what she had been to begin with: an ordinary Greek transmarine agricultural settlement of the kind which Chalcis and Megara and half a dozen other agricultural communities in Old Greece had planted by the score round the coasts of the Mediterranean and its backwaters. Meanwhile, Byzantium was already growing into one of the busiest ports of the Hellenic World and was fairly launched on the career which was to culminate in her becoming the ultimate capital of a Hellenic universal state in the last phase of Hellenic history. Thus, by Megabazus's time, any comparison between the respective advantages of the sites of Byzantium and Calchedon would naturally turn upon their respective facilities as ports; and on this test the eligibility of Byzantium was no doubt incomparably greater than that of her neighbour over the water. Byzantium not only possessed the natural harbour of the Golden Horn which had no counterpart on the exposed and featureless section of the opposite Asiatic coastline where Calchedon stood. More than that, the set of the current which comes down the Bosphorus from the Black Sea into the Sea of Marmara is in favour of any vessel trying to make the Golden Horn from either direction, while it is adverse to any vessel heading for the open beach of Calchedon.[2] Thus every ship that plies between the Black Sea and the Mediterranean has a double incentive for passing by on the other side from Calchedon and making Byzantium its port of call. The founders of Calchedon would have been blind men indeed if, in face of this obvious fact, they had deliberately chosen Calchedon in preference to Byzantium as the site for a port.

In reality, of course, the founders of Calchedon made their historic choice on quite a different consideration. As they approached the southern entrance to the Bosphorus on their voyage

---

[1] Herodotus, Book IV, ch. 144.
[2] See the detailed account of this which is given by Polybius, Book IV, chs. 43 and 44.

of exploration, they looked at the landscape and chose their site with eyes that were not blind at all, but were simply farmers' eyes and not mariners'; and from the farmer's standpoint their choice was admirable. They planted their city on the Bithynian Riviera: a sheltered strip of fertile coast which seems like an enclave of Mediterranean scenery in a more northerly clime. On this favoured spot, the Greek farmer-prospectors who founded Calchedon settled down to raise the crops and plant the fruit-trees which they had always raised and planted at home. For their purpose, they could not have chosen better; and we may be sure that this was the judgement of the next company of Greek explorers, in search of fresh land for their ploughs, who came this way seventeen years later. We may picture the founders of Byzantium cursing the Calchedonians for their perspicacity and themselves for their tardiness as they turned their ships' prows away from the smiling Bithynian Riviera, now crowned by Calchedon's walls, towards the much less inviting opposite coast of Thrace. Some Hesiodic equivalent of the proverb that 'It is the early bird that gets the first worm' must have often been in the Byzantines' mouths when they tilled the soil of their little Thracian peninsula—only to see their crops carried off systematically, year after year, by the barbarians of the hinterland.

'The Byzantine territory is an enclave in Thrace, which marches with the entire Byzantine land-frontier and comes down to the sea on either side. In consequence, the Byzantines are afflicted with an interminable and insoluble war against the Thracians. Even when they make a military effort and get the better of the Thracians for the moment, they can never get rid of the Thracian war owing to the multitude of the Thracian hordes and Thracian princelings. If they overthrow one princeling, this simply clears the way for three others more formidable than the first. Even if the Byzantines give in and come to terms for paying a stipulated tribute, they find themselves no better off. For any concession which they make to one enemy has the direct effect of bringing five new enemies down upon them. So they are in the toils of this interminable and insoluble war, in which they are exposed to all the danger of being at close quarters with a bad neighbour and all the horror of warfare against a barbarian adversary. These, in a general way, are the evils against which they have to struggle on land; and, besides the ordinary evils attendant on war, they have to endure the legendary punishment of Tantalus. They possess a first-rate soil; they cultivate it intensively; they raise fine big crops—and then the barbarians arrive on the scene to gather in and carry off the crops and destroy what they do not take away! It is not only the loss of labour and money and the spectacle of devastation but the fineness of the crops that makes the business heartbreaking.'[1]

[1] Polybius, Book IV, ch. 45.

Thus Byzantium was subject, as a matter of course, throughout her history, to a recurrent calamity which Athens only experienced during fifteen out of the twenty-eight years of the Peloponnesian War[1] and Miletus only during her eleven years' war with Lydia in the reigns of Kings Sadyattes and Alyattes.[2] Her agriculture was at the mercy of an invader whom she was not strong enough to meet in the field and who therefore had a free hand to carry off or destroy her crops. After all, then, the Greek farmer-colonists who founded Calchedon were not blind men when, with both shores of the Bosphorus to choose between, they settled on the Bithynian Riviera and shunned the inhospitable Thracian shore; nor were the founders of Byzantium men of vision. They simply followed in the earlier prospectors' wake and took their leavings. However, a vindication of the Calchedonians' perspicacity is not the true moral of this story. The true moral is that when the Byzantines found themselves perpetually subject, on land, to a prohibitive handicap which the Athenians and the Milesians suffered only for a few critical years in the whole course of their respective histories, the Byzantines were thereby stimulated, even more powerfully than the Athenians and the Milesians were stimulated in their less desperate circumstances, to turn their attention from the land to the sea and to indemnify themselves for their ruinous losses as farmers by making handsome profits as merchants and mariners. Under this powerful stimulus, to which the prudent Calchedonian farmers on the opposite shore were never exposed, the Byzantines made the most of their straits and discovered—no doubt to their own surprise as well as to their neighbours'—that 'the Golden Horn' was a cornucopia. The wealth and influence which Byzantium was taught by Necessity to derive from her command of the Bosphorus are described in the second century B.C. by Polybius in terms which recall the passage already cited[3] from an anonymous Athenian writer of the fifth century who is describing the effects of his own country's wider but less durable sea-power.

'The Byzantines occupy a site which, from the twin standpoints of security and prosperity, is the most favourable of all sites in the Hellenic World to seaward and the most unprepossessing of all to landward. To

---

[1] During the first part of the War, the Peloponnesians invaded Attica in the years 431, 430, 428, 427, and 425 B.C. During the second part, they were in permanent occupation of a fortified position on Attic soil, at Decelea, during the years 413–404 B.C. inclusive.

[2] See the account of this war in Herodotus, Book I, chs. 17–22. The Lydian invaders of Milesia practised the same form of economic warfare as the Thracian invaders of the Byzantine territory and the Peloponnesian invaders of Attica. They destroyed or carried off the annual crops. On the other hand, the Lydians showed less barbarity—or at any rate more enlightened self-interest—than either the Thracians or the Peloponnesians in leaving the farm-buildings, out in the countryside, intact.

[3] On pp. 41–2, above.

seaward, Byzantium commands the mouth of the Black Sea so absolutely that it is impossible for any merchantman to pass either in or out
against the Byzantines' will; and thus the Byzantines control all the
numerous commodities originating in the Black Sea which are in general
demand. These commodities include both necessities—like the cattle
and slaves for which the hinterland of the Black Sea is notoriously a
prime source of supply, both for quantity and for quality—and luxuries
like honey, wax and caviar, which the same region provides in abundance. Moreover, the Black Sea hinterland offers a market for the
surplus of our Mediterranean products, such as olive oil and wines of
every vintage—grain being the medium of exchange in which the
balance of trade is adjusted periodically in either direction. The Hellenic
World would necessarily be debarred from all this trade completely, or
at any rate would lose all possibility of making a profit on it, if the
Byzantines chose to give up "playing the game" and went into partnership with the Celts (or, normally, with the Thracians), or again if
Byzantium itself were simply not on the map. The Straits are so narrow
and the adjoining hordes of barbarians so formidable that in those circumstances the Black Sea would unquestionably be closed to Hellenic
navigation. As a matter of fact, the Byzantines themselves probably
draw the greatest economic profit of all from their unique position,
which enables them to export all their surplus products, and import
all that they need, both easily and profitably, without any exertion or
danger. At the same time, many commodities which are in general
demand reach their destination through the Byzantines' agency, as has
been observed already. To this degree, the Byzantines are benefactors
of Society who fairly deserve not only gratitude but positive military
assistance, on an international basis, from the Hellenic World against the
standing menace of the barbarians.'[1]

The Byzantines were content to perform their service to Hellenic
Society without recompense so long as, on the landward side, they
only had to deal with their regular tormentors, the Thracians.[2]
When, however, in the course of the third century B.C., the local
Thracians were temporarily subjugated by a migratory horde of
Celts, the Byzantines suffered heavily from this change of masters
in their hinterland. Where the Thracians had chastised them with
whips, the Celts now chastised them with scorpions. They raised
the annual ransom for the Byzantine crops to an exorbitant figure;
and in this extremity the Byzantines met with hardly any response
when they appealed for financial assistance to the rest of the Hellenic World. Accordingly, the Byzantines were driven to raise
funds for ransoming their fields from the Celts by levying a toll
on all ships passing through the Bosphorus; and their action so
upset the Hellenic carrying-trade that the consequence was a war

---

[1] Polybius, Book IV, ch. 38.   [2] Polybius, Book IV, ch. 45.

between Byzantium and Rhodes, the leading maritime community in the Hellenic World of the day.[1]

Thus the vast divergence between the destinies of Byzantium and Calchedon is not explained by Megabazus's epigram. It was not the blindness of the Calchedonians but the barbarity of the Thracians and the Celts that made Byzantium's fortune. If the actual founders of Byzantium had arrived first on the scene, they would certainly have made the Calchedonians' choice; and if the actual founders of Calchedon had arrived second and had been left no choice but to found Byzantium, they, for their part, would inevitably have been confronted by the challenge of an intolerable situation on land, with the Byzantines' historic choice between starving as landsmen or making a fortune out of the sea.

Aegina and Argos

Another illustration of our theme from Hellenic history is the contrast between the careers of two city-states of the Argolid: Argos herself and Aegina. The Argives, being owners of one of the finest arable plains in the Peloponnese, had only one idea when they began to find their Argive plain too small for them. They set out, like the Chalcidians, to take possession of additional arable land beyond their borders; but, unfortunately for themselves, they did not look out to sea but lifted up their eyes unto the hills and coveted what lay beyond them. Taking up the spear before labouring at the oar, they sought their new fields in the quarter where it was hardest to acquire them: in the territory of their Hellenic neighbours, who were spearmen too. The Chalcidians had known better than to try conclusions with the sturdy Boeotians; they had reserved their steel for easy victories over ill-armed and ill-disciplined Thracians and Sicels. The Argives were less prudent. Fighting for the mastery of the Peloponnese, they collided with the Spartans, who had responded to the same challenge in the same way, but had faced the implications of their response by militarizing their life from top to bottom.[2] For spearmen such as these, the Argives were no match; and this was the end of their city's career. She never extricated herself from the role of being Sparta's discomfited rival until Hellenic history came to an end.

Meanwhile, the little Argolic island of Aegina had been playing an utterly different historical role, in conformity with the vastly poorer physical endowment which she had received from Nature. Aegina, raising her horn—a bare, solitary mountain-peak—above

---

[1] Polybius, Book IV, chs. 46 and 47.
[2] For Spartan militarism, see I. B (ii), vol. i, pp. 24–6, above, and III. A, vol. iii, pp. 50–79, below.

the waters of the Saronic Gulf within full view of Athens,[1] was no doubt one of those 'small islands' which were in the Athenian philosopher's mind[2] as signal examples of denudation at its worst. Aegina was, in fact, an Attica in miniature; and, under a still more severe pressure from the physical environment than that to which the Athenians were exposed, the Aeginetans anticipated, on a small scale, the Athenians' achievements. Aeginetan merchants were taking the lead in the activities of the Hellenic settlement at Naucratis in Egypt at a time when Athenian merchants were still rare visitors there;[3] and Aeginetan sculptors were carving statues to stand in the pediments of the temple which Aeginetan architects had built for the local goddess Aphaia, half a century before the Athenian Pheidias carved his masterpieces for the Parthenon.

Israelites, Phoenicians, and Philistines

If we turn now from Hellenic history to Syriac, we shall find that the various elements of population that entered Syria, or held their own there, at the time of the post-Minoan Völkerwanderung, distinguished themselves relatively thereafter in close proportion to the relative difficulty of the physical environment in the different districts in which they happened to have made themselves at home. In an earlier passage,[4] we have taken note of the difficulty which an immigrant population must have found in acquiring the art of irrigating the gardens of Damascus. Yet the Ghūtah—though a hard country compared with the fabulous Garden of Eden—was the choicest prize that offered itself in Syria to the incoming barbarians; and it is therefore remarkable that, in the subsequent progress of the Syriac Civilization, it was not the Aramaean occupants of Damascus that took the lead. Nor was the lead taken by those other Aramaeans who settled down at Hamath to irrigate the fertile banks of the Orontes with their water-wheels; nor again by those tribes of Israel who halted east of Jordan in order to fatten their cattle on the fine pasture-lands of Gilead.[5] Most remarkable of all, the primacy in the Syriac World was not retained by those refugees

---

[1] Aegina was execrated to an Athenian audience as λήμη Πειραιέως—'the eye-sore of the Peiraeus'—by the Athenian statesman Pericles when he was exhorting his countrymen to deal the maritime rival of Attica the knock-out blow at the culmination of a long and bitter struggle for the command of a sea which was too narrow to be shared between the barren island and the barren peninsula.

[2] See the quotation from Plato on p. 39, above.

[3] In the time of King Amasis of Egypt (*regnabat circa* 569–525 B.C.) the Aeginetans were one of three Hellenic communities—the other two being the Samians and the Milesians—that possessed separate religious precincts at Naucratis dedicated to their respective tutelary Gods. The other nine Hellenic communities which had a footing at Naucratis were content to share a common precinct: the Hellenion. At this time, Athens not only had no settlement of her own at Naucratis, but was not even one of the nine city-states that shared in the administration of the International Settlement. (Herodotus, Book II, ch. 178.)

[4] In II. C (ii) (b) 2, on pp. 334–5, above.   [5] Numbers, ch. xxxii.

from the Aegean who came to Syria not as barbarians but as the heirs of the Minoan Civilization and who took possession of the ports and cities and fields of the Shephelah: the maritime plain that extends from the south-western face of Mount Carmel to the north-eastern frontier of Egypt.

In the connotation which their name has acquired, the Philistines have fared still worse than the Boeotians. In our modern Western vocabulary, with its echoes of Syriac and Hellenic tradition, the word 'Boeotian' signifies nothing worse than a congenital obtuseness of vision, while 'Philistine' signifies a wilful blindness and a militant hostility towards 'the Chosen People' who see the light. Possibly, neither Philistines nor Boeotians fully deserve their bad name. It is probable, on the whole, that they have been misrepresented, considering that their reputation has been at the mercy of hostile neighbours. Yet this consideration in itself tells a tale. Why is it that the picture of these nations which has come down to us is a picture painted by their neighbours' hands and not by their own? It is because these neighbours and contemporaries of theirs were more active, more vocal, and more successful than they were, and hence were better able than they were to impress their own will and their own view upon the future. The Athenians and Chalcidians, who were the Boeotians' neighbours, have occupied our attention already. We have taken note of the feats accomplished by them which the Boeotians never attempted. Let us look now at the neighbours of the Philistines, and compare the Philistines' record with theirs.

The Syriac Civilization has three great feats to its credit.[1] It invented an alphabetic system of writing; it discovered the Atlantic Ocean; and it arrived at a particular conception of God which is common to Judaism, Zoroastrianism, Christianity, and Islam, but alien alike from the Egyptiac, Sumeric, Indic, and Hellenic veins of religious thought and feeling.[2] Which were the Syriac communities by whom these achievements were severally contributed? The Philistines may prove to have been the transmitters, if not the inventors, of the elements of the Alphabet, if the conjectured derivation of the Alphabet from some Minoan script[3] is substantiated in the future investigations of our Western archaeologists. Pending further archaeological research, the credit for the inven-

---

[1] See I. C (i) (b), vol. i, pp. 82 and 102, above.

[2] And equally alien, it would appear, from the Minoan and Hittite veins, as far as these are known to us. In this catalogue, the exception which proves the rule is the conception of God which was attained by Ikhnaton (see I. C (ii), vol. i, pp. 145–6. above, and V. C (i) (d) 6 (δ), Annex, vol. v, pp. 695–6, below). The abortive solar monotheism of Ikhnaton has a distinctly Syriac touch; but this flash of illumination in the soul of a single individual, who was repudiated by the society in which he happened to be born, can hardly be placed to the credit of the Egyptiac Civilization.

[3] See I. C (i) (b), vol. i, p. 102, footnote 3, above, and II. D (vii), p. 386, footnote 2, below.

tion of the Alphabet must at present be left unallocated. When we come, however, to the other two Syriac achievements, the history of which is a matter of common knowledge, we find that the Philistines have no part or lot in them.

Who were those Syriac seafarers who ventured to sail the whole length of the Mediterranean to the Pillars of Hercules and out beyond? Not the Philistines, whose Minoan ancestors had been the pioneers of long-distance seamanship in the Mediterranean.[1] In the Philistine communities of the maritime plain, the ancestral seafaring tradition was buried, with the sowing-corn, in the furrows of the broad ploughlands; and so, when the Philistines came to feel the need to expand, they took the same wrong turning as the Argives took in the Peloponnese. Turning their backs on the sea, the Philistines took up arms to conquer the arid lowlands of Beersheba and the well-watered valleys of Esdraelon and Jezreel; and they met the Argives' fate when, in fighting for the mastery of Palestine, they came into conflict with still better fighters: the tribesmen in the hill-country of Israel and Judah. The discovery of the Atlantic was achieved not by the Philistine Lords of the Shephelah, but by the Phoenician tenants of the rugged middle section of the Syrian coast.

These Phoenicians were a remnant of the Canaanites—the population which had been in occupation of Syria before the post-Minoan Völkerwanderung descended like a human flood upon the country. When the neighbours and kinsmen of the Phoenicians had been overwhelmed by the incoming Philistines and Teucrians from the sea and Israelites and Aramaeans from the desert, the Phoenicians had survived because their homes along the middle section of the Syrian coast were not sufficiently inviting to attract the invaders.

Phoenicia, which the Philistines left alone, presents a remarkable physical contrast to the Shephelah, in which the Philistines settled. On this section of the coast, there is no broad plain and no gradation between plain and hill-country. Instead, the mountain-range of Lebanon rises almost sheer out of the sea—grudging the coast-dwellers any plain of their own and cutting them off from the plains of the interior. Lebanon and Mediterranean lie in such a close embrace that they leave no easy passage between them for road or railway.[2] The Phoenicians communicated with each other

[1] See I. C (i) (b), vol. i, p. 102, footnote 4, above.
[2] In the year 1933 there was a continuous line of standard-gauge railway from Haydar Pasha, the Asiatic railway-terminus at Constantinople, all the way to Tarabulus at the northern end of the Phoenician section of the Syrian coast; there was also a continuous line of standard-gauge railway from Haifa, at the southern end of this section of coast, to Cairo; but the gap between Tarabulus and Haifa remained unbridged owing to the expense involved in the difficult engineering feat of building a standard-gauge coastal

and with the outer world by water, coastwise; and of the three
leading Phoenician cities—Tyre, Aradus, and Sidon—the two
first-mentioned were not even situated on the mainland but were
perched, like gulls' nests, on rocky off-shore islands. When the
Aramaeans drifted into Syria out of the desert, they silted up
against the eastern face of Lebanon without penetrating beyond it;
and when the Philistine Völkerwanderung passed that way *en
route* from Anatolia towards Egypt, we may presume that the ships
sailed southward straight past the forbidding Phoenician coast to
the farther side of 'the Ladder of Tyre', while the ox-carts took
the inland road, to the east of Lebanon, along which the modern
railway-traveller from Turkey to Egypt finds himself transported
to-day. Even when the Philistines and Teucrians were flung back
from the frontier of Egypt,[1] they did not fall upon Phoenicia in
their recoil. They fastened upon the Shephelah and made no
permanent settlements north of Mount Carmel. Thus, thanks to
Lebanon, the Phoenicians survived the Philistines' passage; and,
again thanks to Lebanon, they actually took over from their new
neighbours that Minoan tradition of long-distance navigation which
the Philistines themselves now discarded. While the Philistines
were browsing on the Shephelah like sheep in clover and were
moving inland, at their peril, in search of pastures new, the
Phoenicians, whose maritime horizon had hitherto been restricted
to the short range of the coastwise traffic between Byblos and the
Delta of the Nile,[2] now launched out, Minoan-fashion, into the
open sea and won a second home for the Syriac Civilization in
the western basin of the Mediterranean and on the coasts of the
Ocean beyond.

Thus the maritime achievement of the Syriac Civilization was
contributed not by the Philistines but by the Phoenicians. The
physical discovery of the Atlantic, however, is surpassed, as a feat
of human prowess, by the spiritual discovery of Monotheism; and
this achievement was contributed by a Syriac community that had
been stranded by the Völkerwanderung in a physical environment
which was still less inviting than the Phoenician coast: namely, the

railway to link Tarabulus and Haifa together. Thus the railway-traveller who, between
London and Aleppo, had only been required to change carriages twice—at the Straits of
Dover and at the Bosphorus—had to change four times more in order to complete his
railway-journey to Cairo. At Homs he had to leave his through-carriage, bound for
railhead at Tarabulus, in order to proceed along the branch line leading to the inland
junction of Rayāq. At Rayāq he had to change trains from the standard-gauge railway
on to a narrow-gauge railway which carried him (by rack-and-pinion over Anti-Lebanon)
to Damascus. At Damascus he had to change again on to another narrow-gauge railway.
And finally he had to change a fourth time in order to board a train running on the
standard-guage railway between Haifa and Cairo. In A.D. 1941–3 the missing stretch
of standard-gauge line between Haifa and Tarabulus was built at last under the un-
economic stimulus of military necessity.
    [1] See I. C (i) (b), vol. i, pp. 93 and 100–1, above.
    [2] See I. C (i) (b), vol. i, p. 102, footnote 4, above.

hill-country of Ephraim and Judah. This country was indeed so extremely uninviting that—in spite of its position in the heart of Syria, overlooking the high road between Egypt and Shinar—it appears to have remained (like the rift-valley of the Jordan)[1] a virgin wilderness throughout the thousand years and more during which the rest of Syria had been incorporated successively first in the Empire of Sumer and Akkad, which was the Sumeric universal state, and then in the Hyksos 'successor-state' of that empire, and then in 'the New Empire' of Egypt. Apparently, this patch of thin-soiled, forest-covered hill-country remained literally a no-man's-land until 'the New Empire' began to lose its grip upon Syria and the post-Minoan Völkerwanderung set in; and then, at last, it was populated by the adventurous vanguard of the Hebrew Nomads who had drifted into the fringes of Syria out of the North Arabian Steppe.[2] These Hebrews were content, for the most part, to halt in the pasture-lands east of Jordan and south of Hebron. The hill-country beyond was the farthest bourne of their migration; and here the Israelite pioneers transformed themselves from Nomadic stock-breeders into sedentary tillers of a stony ground which they laboriously cleared of its forests[3] only to see the soil which they had won from the trees washed away by the rains to deepen the Philistine ploughlands on the Shephelah. The hardness of the life which has to be lived by the husbandman whose lot is cast in this hill-country of Ephraim and Judah is conveyed in the following passages from the report of an experienced British investigator who, in the year 1930, observed on the spot the life of the Israelite husbandmen's modern Arab successors.[4]

'The cultivated land in the Hills varies very largely both in depth and quality of the soil. In the valleys there are stretches of fertile land, which will grow sesame as a summer crop. On the hillsides the soil is shallow and infertile, and the extent of land-hunger is evident from the fact that every available plot of soil is cultivated, even when it is so small that the plough cannot be employed. There cultivation is carried on with the mattock and the hoe. The harvest of such plots, even in a favourable year, is exceedingly small—in general it seems doubtful whether such

---

[1] See the quotation from Eduard Meyer in II. C (ii) (a) 2, vol. i, p. 257, above.
[2] These statements likewise are made on the authority of Eduard Meyer: *Geschichte des Altertums*, vol. ii (i), 2nd edition (Stuttgart and Berlin 1928, Cotta), p. 96.
[3] See Joshua xvii. 14-18, for the mark made upon the Israelites' folk-memory by the labour of deforesting this hill-country in order to find room for an ex-Nomadic people that had been driven off the North Arabian Steppe yet was deterred by its fear of the iron chariots of the Canaanites from descending into the fertile valley of Jezreel.
[4] The modern Arab peasantry of Palestine, like their Israelite predecessors, are descended partly from Nomadic intruders off the North Arabian Steppe, who in physical race were Afrasian 'long-heads', and partly from 'broad-headed' denizens of the highland zone of folded mountains (see vol. i, p. 328, above), who worked their way down to the Palestinian highlands from the Anatolian Plateau. Anthropometric studies of the modern population of Palestine indicate that, in the repeated mixture of two races which has here taken place, the 'Alpine' strain has prevailed over the 'Mediterranean'.

cultivation can pay. On the other hand, even the most rocky hillsides support trees, especially olives; and, if capital were available, many of the cultivators of these exiguous and infertile plots would be able to gain a livelihood by cultivation of fruit trees and of olives. These cultivators have, however, no capital, and cannot afford to forgo even the meagre crops obtained, for the four or five years which are required before fruit-trees render a return. In the case of the olive, the period before a return may be expected is much longer.

'There is little irrigation in the Hill Country. Here and there are springs which afford a supply for the irrigation of a small area; but, taken as a whole, the country is arid and the crops depend on rain. . . .

'In the best case . . . it is impossible that the general character of the cultivation in the Hill Country can be radically changed, except in so far as fruit can be made to replace grain. . . . From the point of view of agriculture, the Hill Country will always remain an unsatisfactory proposition. . . .

'The life of the fallāh is one of great struggle and privation. . . .

'It is a common impression that the fallāh's cultivation is entirely inadequate, and a good deal of ridicule has been and is poured upon the nail-plough which he uses. In the stony country of the Hills, no other plough would be able to do the work at all. With regard to the use of that plough, Dr. Wilkansky [a modern Zionist agricultural expert] writes:—"The Arab plough is like the ancient Hebrew plough. . . . It performs—very slowly, it is true, but very thoroughly—all the functions for which a combination of modern machines is required. . . . The ploughing of the fallāh is above reproach. His field, prepared for sowing, is never inferior to that prepared by the most perfect implements, and sometimes it even surpasses all others." '[1]

In such a country, and under such conditions, the Israelites continued to live in obscurity until the Syriac Civilization had passed its zenith. As late as the fifth century before Christ, at a date when all the great prophets of Israel had already said their say, the name of Israel was still unknown to the great Greek historian Herodotus and the Land of Israel was still masked by the Land of the Philistines in the Herodotean panorama of the Syriac World. When Herodotus wishes to designate the peoples of Syria as a whole, he calls them 'the Phoenicians and the Syrians in the Land of the Philistines';[2] and 'the Land of the Philistines'—Filastin or Palestine —is the name by which Erez Israel has continued to be known among the Gentiles down to this day.[3] Yet in these barren land-locked highlands, which were not of sufficient worldly importance to acquire even a recognized name of their own, there was immanent

[1] Simpson, Sir J. H.: *Palestine: Report on Immigration, Land Settlement and Development* (British Parliamentary Paper Cmd. 3686 of 1930: London 1930, H.M. Stationery Office), pp. 14, 65, and 66.
[2] e.g. in Book II, ch. 104, and in Book VII, ch. 89.
[3] Παλαιστίνη is the Ancient Greek and فلسطين the modern Arabic for Philistia.

(to paraphrase Plato's language)[1] a divine inspiration which made this uninviting country a means of grace to those who came to settle there. A Syriac fable tells how this divinity once tested a king of Israel with the most searching test that a God can apply to a mortal.

'The Lord appeared to Solomon in a dream by night; and God said: "Ask what I shall give thee." And Solomon said: " . . . Give . . . thy servant an understanding heart." . . . And the speech pleased the Lord, that Solomon had asked this thing. And God said unto him: "Because thou hast asked this thing, and hast not asked for thyself long life; neither hast asked riches for thyself, nor hast asked the life of thine enemies; but hast asked for thyself understanding to discern judgment; behold, I have done according to thy words: lo, I have given thee a wise and an understanding heart, so that there was none like thee before thee, neither after thee shall any arise like unto thee. And I have also given thee that which thou hast not asked, both riches and honour, so that there shall not be any among the kings like unto thee all thy days." '[2]

This fable of Solomon's Choice is a parable of the history of the Chosen People. In the power of their spiritual understanding, the Israelites surpassed the military prowess of the Philistines and the maritime prowess of the Phoenicians. They had not sought after those things which the Gentiles seek, but had sought first the kingdom of God; and therefore all those things were added unto them.[3] As for the life of their enemies, the mighty men of the Philistines were delivered into Israel's hands to be smitten with the edge of the sword. As for riches, Jewry entered into the inheritance of Tyre and Carthage to conduct transactions on a scale beyond Phoenician dreams in continents beyond Phoenician knowledge. As for long life, the Jews live on—the same peculiar people—to-day, long ages after the Phoenicians and the Philistines have lost their identity like all the nations. The ancient Syriac neighbours of Israel have fallen into the melting-pot and have been re-minted, in the fullness of time, with new images and superscriptions, while Israel has proved impervious to this alchemy—performed by History in the crucibles of universal states and universal churches and wanderings of the nations—to which we Gentiles all in turn succumb.[4]

Lebanon and Jabal Ansariyah

The contrast between the roles of the Phoenicians and the Philistines in the history of the Syriac Civilization is reproduced, in

---

[1] See the passage quoted above in II. C (ii) (a) 2, vol. i, on p. 252, in footnote 2.
[2] I Kings iii. 5–13.   [3] Matt. vi. 31–3; Luke xii. 29–31.
[4] From the Gentile standpoint, modern Jewry is the 'fossil' remnant of a society that is extinct. For this phenomenon of 'fossilization', see I. B (iii), vol. i, p. 35, and I. C (i) (b), pp. 90–2, above; and II. D (vi) and Part IX, below.

the history of the affiliated Arabic Civilization, in a corresponding contrast—which can be studied in the life at the present day—between the enterprise of the Lebanese highlanders, in the hinterland of the former Phoenician ports of Sidon and Tyre and Byblus, and the stagnation of the Nusayrī highlanders who live on the northern side of the Nahr-al-Kabīr in the hinterland of Aradus.

In modern times the highlanders of the Lebanon have emulated the historic exploits of the Phoenician islanders of Tyre and Aradus by seeking their fortunes abroad and making a livelihood as traders and shopkeepers far and wide—in Egypt and in West Africa and in the New World.[1] The Nusayrī highlanders, on the other hand, have been as stay-at-home as the Philistine contemporaries of the Phoenicians.

The extreme degree and long continuance of the Nusayrīs' stagnation in their highland homes is attested by the antique aspect of their religion. The Lebanon, in its own degree, is a museum of religious survivals. The ex-Monothelete[2] Maronites and the Monophysite Jacobites and the Imāmī Shī'īs of the Jabal 'Āmil and the Druses are so many 'fossil' remnants of different phases in the long contact between the Syriac Civilization and the Hellenic.[3] The Nusayrīs, too, have acquired some tincture of Syriac religion in its latest phase. They have travestied the Ismā'īlī Shī'ism which forced an entry into their mountain fastness in the age of the Crusades[4] by deifying the Caliph 'Alī abī Tālib; but this worship of 'Alī is only an accretion;[5] and the core of their religion appears to be some local worship which is more ancient than either Islam or Christianity and is perhaps even prior to that impact of Hellenism on the Syriac World in which both Christianity and Islam have originated. The sharpness of the contrast, in every aspect of social life, between the Nusayrīs and the Lebanese is very striking; and there is also a striking contrast between the two peoples' respective physical environments.

While the native physical environment of the Lebanese is perhaps not quite so stimulating as the rocky islet of Tyre, which cannot be cultivated at all, it presents a severer challenge to the husbandman than the hill-country of Ephraim and Judah. On the stony flanks of Lebanon there is a rigid limit to the harvests that can be wrung out of a scanty soil, and this soil itself can only be

---

[1] See II. D (vi), p. 238, below.
[2] Ex-Monothelete, because the Maronites have been in full communion with the Roman Catholic Church since A.D. 1445, though they have retained their own Syriac liturgy and their own ecclesiastical discipline.
[3] See II. D (vi), pp. 234-6, and II. D (vii), pp. 285-8, below.
[4] See II. D (vi), p. 258, below.
[5] On the strength of it, the French mandatory authorities have dubbed the Nusayrīs (Arabic plural 'Ansarīyah') 'Alouites', which is a Gallicism for the Arabic 'Alawīyin.

conserved and kept under cultivation by laborious terracing.[1] By contrast, the Jabal Ansarīyah, though it 'has been described as a barren region', is in reality 'an extremely agreeable and fertile tract. Being lower and less rocky, it is naturally much more fertile than the Lebanon'.[2] In the light of the local precedents, it looks as though the Lebanese had been stimulated to emulate the Phoenicians by the barrenness of their native mountain, while the agreeableness of the Jabal Ansarīyah has inveigled the Nusayrīs into vegetating in a Philistine sloth.

Brandenburg and the Rhineland

When we turn from the Aegean and from Syria[3] to the scenes of our own Western history, similar contrasts strike the eye.

Suppose, for example, that one finds oneself in the capital city of either of the two great Central European Empires of the modern age: the Hohenzollern Empire of Brandenburg-Prussia-Germany and the Danubian Hapsburg Monarchy. One has only to board an outgoing train at any railway terminus in either Berlin or Vienna in order to receive the same impression that a traveller receives when he goes by train from the Aegean area into the interior of Anatolia or into the interior of Europe.[4] In whichever direction you may happen to be travelling outwards from the nucleus of the Hohenzollern or of the Hapsburg Empire into its fringes and outskirts, you find yourself passing out of an unusually difficult physical environment into environments where the difficulties are less formidable.

[1] See II. D (vi), p. 258, below.
[2] British Admiralty: *A Handbook of Syria* (London 1920, H.M. Stationery Office), p. 339.
[3] We cannot take leave of the Syriac World without observing that, in the penultimate phase of Syriac history, the contrast which we have brought out between Phoenicia and Philistia was reproduced, in the Hijāz (a region which is a southward extension of Syria into Arabia), in the similar contrast between the two oases of Mecca and Medina. 'The community which had settled in the valley of Mecca . . . cannot, when they selected this spot, have hoped to live by its produce; for that the soil is incapable of producing anything is attested by all who know it, from the author of the Qur'ān to the present day. . . . Unlike Mecca, Yathrib [Medina] lies in a fruitful plain. "Walled habitations, green fields, running water, every blessing the Eastern mind can desire, are there." And indeed the richness of the soil finds expression in the name Tā'ibah, "the pleasing".' (Margoliouth, D. S.: *Mohammed*, 3rd edition (London 1905, Putnam), pp. 7–8 and 185.) In consequence, we find that the Yathribis, like the Philistines, were content to cultivate their garden without turning their hands or minds to other things or betaking themselves beyond their own borders, whereas the Meccans were stimulated by the challenge of a barren home to take to the Steppe as the Phoenicians, in similar circumstances, had taken to the sea, and to earn their livings as camel-caravaners. It is significant that Mecca, and not Medina, was the oasis in which the Hijāzī Prophet Muhammad was born and brought up. It was the stimulus of his contact with the great world in his caravan expeditions to the Syrian desert-ports of the Roman Empire, *circa* A.D. 594 seqq., that gave Muhammad the mental stimulus which impelled him to embark upon the career of a religious revolutionary. (For the career of Muhammad, see III. C (ii) (*b*), vol. iii, pp. 276–8, with Annex II, below.)
[4] For this impression, as experienced by the writer of this Study, see pp. 36–7, above.

Take the nucleus of the Hohenzollern dominions : the territories which Frederick the Great inherited from his father when he came to the Prussian throne : Brandenburg, Pomerania, East Prussia. As you travel through this unprepossessing country between the Havel and the Masurian Lakes, with its starveling pine-plantations and its sandy fields, you might fancy that you were traversing some outlying corner of the Eurasian Steppe, where the aggressive desert was thrusting its dry bones up and out through the skin of the European landscape. Then travel on westward from Brandenburg into the Rhineland or eastward from Prussia into Lithuania or northward from Pomerania into Scandinavia : whichever way you go, you will experience a new sensation. As the pastures and beech-woods of Denmark or the black earth of Lithuania or the vineyards of the Rhineland greet your eyes, you will breathe a sigh of relief at your passage into a normal European landscape out of a land-scape which was an offence to your aesthetic sensibilities. 'So this repulsive Ostelbisches Land is, after all, something exceptional in the European physical environment!' True enough; yet it is no less true that the descendants of the medieval Western colonists whose lot was cast in these 'bad lands' have played an exceptional role in the modern history of the Western World. The legendary 'Prussian' may be as unprepossessing as his homeland. (There is always a flicker of flame behind a screen of smoke and always a grain of truth beneath the most hostile caricature.) Be that as it may, he has managed to make his unpromising kingdom 'the education of Europe' in certain matters which no good European can affect to despise. The Prussian has taught his neighbours how to make sand produce cereals by enriching it with artificial manures; and he has taught us how to raise a whole population to an unprecedented standard of social efficiency by a system of universal compulsory state education and to an unprecedented standard of social security by a similar system of health and unemployment insurance. In these responses to his physical environ-ment, the Prussian has performed a greater service to Mankind and has established a more lasting memorial for himself than in his more notorious achievements : the training of the Prussian Army and the building of the German Reich.

Austria and Lombardy

Take, again, the nucleus of the Danubian Hapsburg dominions : those Danubian territories which the Emperor Charles V inherited from the Emperor Maximilian before the Danubian Monarchy took shape in the sixteenth century of the Christian Era, and which the Austrian Republic inherited again from the last Austrian

Emperor Charles when the Monarchy broke up in 1918. On the aesthetic scale of values, the heart of Austria and the heart of Prussia are of course at opposite extremes. The Alps in the Tyrol and the Salzkammergut, and the Danube in Upper and Lower Austria, are as beautiful as the sands and pine woods of Brandenburg and Pomerania are ugly. Yet, if the observant traveller is not an artist but an economist, his prosaic eye will register the same impression when he travels outwards from Vienna as when he travels outwards from Berlin. Whether his journey carries him out of the Tyrolese or Styrian mountains into the plains of Bavaria or Lombardy or Croatia or Hungary, or from the banks of the Austrian Danube to the banks of the Bohemian Elbe, the economist, as he observes the changes in the landscape, will ignore the transition from variety to monotony which the artist perceives, and will take note that he has left a lean land, flowing with nothing better than milk and honey, and has entered fat lands where the plains are covered with hop-fields or vineyards or wheat-fields or beet-fields, and where the mountains are loaded with mineral ores. Yet that lean land of Austria bred the dynasty[1] which gathered together the fat lands round about and held them united for four centuries against a host of enemies without and within.

The contrast between the relative poverty of the nucleus of the Hapsburg Monarchy and the relative riches of the appended crownlands gives the physical explanation of the genesis of the Danubian Monarchy.[2] A dynasty bred in a difficult environment supplanted the more softly nurtured dynasties round about. The same contrast explains the economic straits to which the City of Vienna has been reduced since the Danubian Monarchy's dissolution. A stranger, visiting Vienna after 1918 without any knowledge of modern Western history and witnessing Vienna's plight to-day, would be at a loss to understand how a magnificent city of some two million souls could ever have come into existence in a poorly endowed country of some six million souls all told. Actually, of course, the present size and magnificence of Vienna are explained by the city's *ci-devant* status as the capital of an empire with fifty million inhabitants and with abundant natural resources, while the location of Vienna is explained by the Danubian Empire's origin. The capital of the Hapsburg Monarchy was never moved from the

[1] As a matter of strict historical accuracy, the Hapsburg Dynasty was bred in the castle of Hapsburg, in the present Swiss Canton of Aargau, before it came to rule over Austria. This, however, only gives additional point to our present argument; for, compared with the Aargau, even Austria is a land of plenty.

[2] For the human explanation, see II. D (v), pp. 177–90, below. In particular, see p. 181, footnote 1, where a distinction is drawn between the êthos of the Tyrolese highlander, which once made Austria an Imperial Power, and the êthos of the Viennese bourgeois, which reflects the demoralizing influence of an empire upon the inhabitants of its capital city.

Austrian homeland of the Hapsburg Dynasty—a land which was
the most venerable but least valuable jewel in the Hapsburg Crown.

'The Black Country' and 'The Home Counties'

When we turn from Central Europe to Great Britain, the apparent law of correspondence between the difficulty and the stimulus
of a physical environment—the law illustrated by the geographical
situations of Vienna and Berlin—seems at first sight to be put in
question by the geographical situation of London. While the
capitals of the *ci-devant* Hapsburg and Hohenzollern Empires lie
in the leanest districts of Central Europe, the Thames Valley, in
which London lies, is one of the most well-favoured districts of the
United Kingdom. This superficial anomaly disappears, however,
as soon as we look deeper. For one thing, we shall find that,
although the so-called 'home counties' certainly were the choicest
portion of the English physical environment in the age when the
capital of England came to be established at London, it is also true
that London did not win her position without having to respond
to any challenge at all. In that very age, she responded victoriously
to a challenge from the human environment which we shall
examine further on in this Part.[1] This, however, is by the way.
For our present purpose, it is more to the point to notice that, in
the modern social geography of the United Kingdom, London has
not remained the capital of the country in every sense.

While London has retained her status in the Kingdom as the
focus of politics and finance, the economic centre of gravity
shifted, during the Industrial Revolution, from the south-east
towards the north-west, until, on the eve of the General War of
1914–18, it had come to rest on the farther side of a line drawn
diagonally across the island from the estuary of the Severn through
Coventry and Leicester to the estuary of the Humber. If we now
fix our attention upon the region north-west of this line and pick
out the districts which shared between them the industrial primacy
in 'pre-war' Great Britain, we shall see at once that they conform
to our law conspicuously. The midland manufacturing cities—
Birmingham and Coventry, Leicester and Northampton—which
almost bestride our dividing line are the only group situated in
good arable or grazing country; and this is the exception that
proves the rule. In each of the other industrial districts of 'pre-
war' Great Britain, the physical environment is one which, judged
by the average standard of the island, offers unusually difficult
conditions to Man. This is true alike of the valleys of South Wales;
of Tyneside and Teesside; and of the neck of Scotland where

[1] See II. D (v), p. 199, with the Annex, below.

Clydeside now harbours, in Glasgow, the second largest city of Great Britain after London herself. The most striking illustration of all is the gigantic industrial zone which embraces the southern end of the Pennines in the shape of a magnet with its tips at Preston and Leeds and its curve skirting the upper course of the Trent—a zone which includes the Lancashire cotton-mills and the Staffordshire potteries and collieries and the multiple industries of Nottingham and the steel-works of Sheffield and the wool-mills of the North Riding.

The forbidding character of the physical environment in which this Pennine industrial zone is set was brought home to the writer of this Study once when he had occasion to travel by road from the rural spot in the east of Yorkshire, in which he is writing these lines at this moment, to a place in Shropshire within sight of the Wrekin. After traversing York—a city not less reminiscent than Canterbury of medieval England—we drove on south-westwards across a fertile plain still innocent of other products than crops and cattle, till we reached the frontier of the industrial zone at a village which is celebrated for a legend. The legend is that, a century ago, a certain Anglican prelate whose diocese extended over the West Riding used to appoint the church of this village as his trysting-place with West Riding candidates for confirmation, because, he declared, this was the farthest point west, towards the new *terra incognita* of industrial squalor, to which any gentleman—in orders or out of them—could be expected to ride! And indeed, when we passed that prelate's legendary bourne now that the squalor beyond it, on which he had refused ever to set eyes, had had a hundred years longer to grow, the aesthetic side of our nature protested in sympathy with the prelate's scandalous ultimatum to the lost souls in his industrial cure. Beyond this village, the fertile lowlands came to an end and at the same point the fells and the factories began.

In their outward aspect, the 'dark satanic mills' seemed a fitting match for the bleak grey landscape; and at the same time the *tour de force* of these monstrous works of Man, erected in defiance of the wilderness, had all the moral incongruity of an abomination of desolation standing in the place where it ought not. In this pullulating, throbbing, squalid life in a forbidding landscape, there was something portentously unnatural; and the acme of unnaturalness was reached when we paused on the summit of the Pennine Range itself—a hand's-breadth of fell-country that had been left still inviolate in its state of Nature—and looked down, this way and that, towards Leeds just behind us and Manchester just ahead. When, at nightfall, we found ourselves passing through

Shrewsbury—such another mellow city as York in such another pleasant countryside—our glimpse of the West Riding and South Lancashire already began to fade into the unreality of an evil dream.

Yet this industrial *tour de force* that has been accomplished in the Pennine Zone is of course not just a hideous blemish on the landscape. The portent has also an import which the legendary prelate who deplored its appearance never divined. The Pennine Zone is indeed a magnet, not only in a fanciful geographical conceit, but in sober economic reality. It is a magnet which has drawn to itself the productivity and the population of a great country so potently that it has actually succeeded in shifting that country's economic centre of gravity—shifting it from the fertile basin of the Thames to the barren skirts of the Pennine fells. The uncompromising prelate himself, if he could return to life to-day, would almost be constrained by curiosity to ride on into his *terra incognita* in order to explore the ugly wonderland into which the ugly wilderness has been transformed. And what is the agency which has produced these astonishing effects? When we look into it, we find ourselves, here again, in presence of a now familiar social phenomenon: the stronger stimulus of a more difficult environment prevailing over the weaker stimulus of an environment in which the difficulty is less.

In this psychological aspect, the contrast between the rural south-east and the industrial north-west of modern Britain since the Industrial Revolution reproduces that contrast between Boeotia and Attica, in ancient Greece, which struck the imagination of Hellenic observers after the great Athenian statesmen and economists —a Solon and a Peisistratus and a Cleisthenes and a Themistocles —had done their work. In our so-called Middle Ages, the inhabitants of 'the home counties' of England, south-east of our line, held economic assets comparable to those which the Boeotians held in the first age of Hellenic history. Indeed, they not only possessed the best arable and pasture lands in the Kingdom, but in Surrey and Sussex they also had command of easily workable iron ores, with the woods of the Weald to supply fuel for their forges and with a near and accessible market for their products in London. Blessed with these rich but wasting assets, the Southerners, like the Foolish Virgins in the parable, improvidently burnt up their fuel till it was all consumed away. The iron railings round St. Paul's are said to be the last substantial piece of work that was produced by the Southern iron-masters. By the time when these railings were forged, the Weald was bare, and thereupon the Southern iron industry came to a dead halt. The stagnant reed-choked hammer-ponds upon which the latter-day 'hiker' stumbles in the middle of the Surrey heaths are no more to-day than this dead industry's funeral monument.[1] Meanwhile, the medieval inhabitants of the Welsh and Scottish and Northern English 'bad lands' had been stimulated by the poverty of their environment to exercise their ingenuity in making the most of it. In South Wales and in Durham, they probed the sub-soil, in the spirit of the ancient inhabitants of Attica, to see whether Nature might prove to be less niggardly below than she was on the surface; and their inquisitiveness was rewarded by the discovery of a new kind of fuel. In the Pennine Zone, they took to supplementing the meagre livelihood obtainable from fell-farms by spinning and weaving; and they turned to human profit fell-sides that were too steep and barren for the plough by harnessing the water-power of the falling beck. And so, under the constant prick of Necessity, they equipped themselves, unwittingly, for exchanging roles with their Southern neighbours as soon as their neighbours' improvidence gave them their opportunity. When the oil in these Foolish Virgins' lamps gave out, the Wise Virgins of the North were ready to step into their places and to astonish the World with the mighty—though sadly vulgar—illumination which they were able to produce. In the Industrial Revolution, the Northern coal-fuel with its unheard-of potency and the Northern mechanical processes with their unheard-of productivity replaced and eclipsed the commonplace wood-fuel and the traditional hand-work of the South.[2] The modern industrial Britain which arose, like a jinn of the desert, out of the 'bad lands' beyond the Severn–Humber line, surpassed the medieval agrarian Britain of 'the home counties' as Solomon—the king of the hill-country of Ephraim and Judah—surpassed in all his glory the oasis-queen of Sheba.[3]

[1] For the history of the Southern iron industry, see Straker, E.: *Wealden Iron* (London 1931, Bell).
[2] It is amusing to notice that the dearth of wood, which stimulated the ancient Greeks into creating the beauties of Hellenic architecture, and the ancient Sumerians into inventing the arch and the vault (see footnote 2 on p. 41, above), has stimulated the modern British into burning coal.
[3] The shifting of the economic centre of gravity of Great Britain at the time of the Industrial Revolution is sometimes attributed in large measure to the change in the flow of international trade which followed the discovery of the New World. Since the Western explorers who made this discovery were not natives of the British Isles, the effect of their discovery upon the economic life of Great Britain must be regarded, from the British standpoint, as the accidental effect of an extraneous cause. So far, therefore, as this extraneous cause contributed to the shift in the economic centre of gravity of Britain, it tells against our explanation of the shift as an incident in the internal history of Britain and as a consequence of the different relations between Man and his physical environment which respectively obtained, during the Middle Ages, in the South and in the North of the island. Admittedly, of course, the effect of the discovery of the New World upon the economic geography of Great Britain was considerable. Accentuating, as it did, the effect of the foregoing decay of the Hansa trade, it worked for the benefit of the ports on the west coast and of their economic hinterlands, and to the prejudice of the ports on the east coast. This dividing line between the eastern and the western faces of Great Britain by no means coincides, however, with the line, running diagonally across the country from Severn to Humber, which came eventually—some two or three centuries after the discovery of America had taken place—to divide the agrarian section

In the present 'post-war' age, this glory is perhaps departing. Since about the year 1920 there have been indications that the economic centre of gravity of Great Britain is tending to shift back again, south-eastward, towards its medieval locus,[1] and simultaneous indications that the economic centre of gravity of the World is shifting away from the British Isles, and indeed from Europe, altogether, and is passing over to North America. It may be that, if these symptoms become more sharply pronounced, the *ci-devant* industrial focus of Britain, marooned among the barren Pennine fells, will come to present as melancholy a spectacle as the *ci-devant* political capital of the Danubian Monarchy, imprisoned within the frontiers of the little Alpine Republic of Austria. The drama of Industrial Britain, which opened in a busy squalor and culminated in a grim magnificence, may be transfigured in its third act into an austere tragedy with a cruel end.[2]

The economic contrast between the two sections into which Great Britain is divided by the Severn–Humber line is not the only illustration of our theme which the island provides. Still more familiar is the cultural contrast between England and Scotland, which has survived the union of the two kingdoms and which still lends reality to a Border which has lost its political and has never possessed any economic significance. The notorious difference of temperament and habit between the legendary Scotchman—solemn, parsimonious, precise, persistent, cautious, conscientious, and thoroughly well educated—and the legendary Englishman—frivolous, extravagant, vague, spasmodic, careless, free-and-easy, and ill-grounded in book-learning—follows the same lines, and corre-

---

of Great Britain from the industrial. For instance, the discovery of America, as was to be expected, brought prosperity in the sixteenth century to the seamen of Devonshire and to the merchants of Bristol: the western maritime districts which were least distant from 'the home counties' and from London. Yet it has still to be explained why Bristol afterwards lost the primacy in the American trade to Liverpool and Glasgow: west-coast ports which were geographically handicapped, in competition with Bristol, by being separated from the open Atlantic by a longer stretch of narrow dangerous waters. It has also to be explained why, in the Industrial Revolution, the new life showed itself not only in the Lancashire and Lanarkshire hinterlands of Merseyside and Clydeside but equally in Tyneside and Teesside and in the West Riding of Yorkshire, which was served by the port of Hull. Newcastle and Middlesbrough and Hull, like the extinct hearths of medieval English trade and industry in East Anglia, all face away from the Atlantic and from America. If the accessibility of the American market and of the American source of supply was really the determining factor in the shift of the economic centre of gravity of Great Britain at the time of the Industrial Revolution, it would be impossible to explain why at this very time Bristol decayed and Newcastle began to flourish. On the other hand, the phenomena are all explicable if it is conceded that the geographical relation to America was no more than a secondary factor and that the governing factor in the shift was the difference, examined above, in the degree of the respective stimuli which were administered to human activities by the two sections of the island, as demarcated by our diagonal dividing line.

[1] These symptoms are discussed, in another connexion, in III. C (i) (*d*), vol. iii, p. 207, below.

[2] These lines were written a few weeks before the 21st September, 1931, which, at the time of revision, seemed likely to be a momentous date in English economic and financial history.

sponds to the same contrast in the local physical environment, as the similar difference, which has likewise been elaborated and caricatured on both sides, between the legendary Prussian and the legendary Bavarian.

The Struggle for North America

The classic illustration of our present theme in our Western history is the outcome of the competition between half a dozen different groups of Western colonists for the mastery of North America. The victors in this contest were the New Englanders; and at an earlier point in this chapter, apropos of the reversion of Town Hill, Connecticut, to its pristine state of Nature, we have taken note of the unusual difficulty of the local American environment which first fell to the lot of the ultimate masters of the whole continent. Let us now compare this New England environment, of which the site of Town Hill is a specimen, with the earliest American environments of the New Englanders' unsuccessful competitors: the Dutch, the French, the Spaniards, and the New Englanders' own kinsmen and neighbours from England who established themselves along the southern section of the Atlantic seaboard.

In the middle of the seventeenth century of the Christian Era, when all these settlers had already found their first footing on the fringes of the North American mainland, it would have been quite easy to predict the coming conflict between them for the possession of the interior; but the most acute and far-sighted observer then alive would hardly have been likely to hit the mark if he had been asked, at the time, to designate the ultimate victor. He might conceivably have had the acumen to rule out the Spaniards in spite of their two obvious assets: their ownership, in Mexico, of the only region in or adjoining North America which had been broken-in and developed economically, before the European colonists' arrival, by an indigenous civilization; and the primacy of Spain, in our hypothetical observer's own day, among the Great Powers of the Western World. Our observer might have discounted the high development of Mexico in view of its outlying position—cut off, as it was, from the main body of North America by a broad belt of inhospitable plateau and desert; and have discounted the political strength of Spain by reading the political signs of the times as they were written between the lines of the Treaty of Westphalia.

'The Spanish Empire', he might have pronounced, 'is already a carcass round which the vultures are gathering. France will succeed to the military hegemony of Spain in Europe, Holland and England will succeed to her naval and commercial supremacy on the seas. The competition for North America lies now between these three countries. Let us estimate their respective chances in the double light of their general positions in the World and of their local holdings in America. On a short view, Holland's chances might appear to be the most promising. She is mistress of the seas (England being no match for her on this element, and France not seriously competing); and in America she holds a splendid watergate opening into the interior: the valley of the Hudson. On a longer view, however, France seems more likely to be the winner; for the French St. Lawrence offers still better means of access to the interior of North America than the Dutch Hudson, while it is in the power of the French to immobilize and exhaust the Dutch by bringing to bear against them the overwhelming military superiority of France on the Continent of Europe. All the same, as between French and Dutch prospects, I hesitate' (we hear him saying) 'to decide. The one prophecy that I make with confidence is that the English are not in the running. Possibly the more southerly of the English colonies, with their relatively genial soil and climate, will manage to survive—though at best they will find themselves hemmed in between the Dutch along the Hudson in the north and the Spaniards in Florida on the south and the Dutch or the French, whichever it may be that cuts off their hinterland on the west by securing the control of the Mississippi. One thing, however, is certain. The little group of settlements in the bleak and barren country which the colonists have christened "New England" is bound to disappear. They are cut off from the other English settlements by the Dutch in the Hudson Valley, while the French in the St. Lawrence Valley press them close on the opposite flank. The destinies of these New Englanders, at any rate, are not in doubt!'

Let us now suppose that our hypothetical observer lives to see the turn of the century. By the year 1701 he will be congratulating himself on his discernment, fifty years earlier, in rating French prospects higher than Dutch; for in the course of these last fifty years the St. Lawrence has vanquished the Hudson. The French explorers have pushed up the St. Lawrence on to the Great Lakes, and over the portage into the Basin of the Mississippi, and down these Western Waters to the delta of the great river, where they have established the new French colony of Louisiana to match the older French colony of Canada at the other end of the trans-continental waterway. As for the Dutch, our observer must admit that he had rated their prospects much too high. They might have made themselves masters of the Great Lakes before the French arrived there. Indeed, for the ocean-going vessels of the century, the head of navigation was rather less distant up the Hudson than it was up the St. Lawrence from the shores of Lake Ontario. Yet, far from that, the Dutch have tamely allowed the Hudson Valley itself to be taken from them by their weaker maritime rivals the English. Well, the Dutch are out of the running now in North America, and the French and the English are left there *tête à tête*; but the English can hardly be regarded as serious competitors. The events of the last half-century assuredly do not call for any revision of forecasts on this head—notwithstanding the unlooked-for success which the English have gained in the Hudson Valley. Certainly the New Englanders are making the most of this windfall. Already they are colonizing the back-country of the Dutch province and are linking New England up with the rest of the English settlements on the Atlantic coast. Possibly the New Englanders have been saved from extinction—but this only to share the modest prospects of their southern kinsfolk. For the English feat of conquering the Hudson Valley from the facile Dutch has been utterly surpassed by the simultaneous French feat of conquering from the formidable virgin wilderness the whole extent of the magnificent inland water-way between Quebec and New Orleans. While the English colonies have been consolidated, the French colonies have effectively hemmed them in. The future of the Continent is decided! The victors are the French!

Shall we endow our observer with superhuman length of life, in order that he may review the situation once more in the year 1803? If we do preserve him alive till then, he will be forced to confess that his wits have not been worthy of his longevity. By the end of 1803, the French flag has actually disappeared off the political map of North America altogether. For forty years past, Canada has been a possession of the British Crown, while Louisiana, after being ceded by France to Spain and retroceded again, has just been sold on the 20th December, 1803, by Napoleon to the United States—the new Great Power which has emerged out of the thirteen English colonies by a most extraordinary metamorphosis.

'The United States of America!' Who would have prophesied it? Yet the ambitious title is justified by the accomplished facts. In this year 1803, the United States have the continent in their pockets, and the scope for prophecy is reduced. It only remains to forecast which section of these United States is going to pocket the larger share of this vast estate—the breadth of a continent—that has come into their joint possession. And surely this time there can be no mistake? The Southern States are the manifest masters of the Union and residuary legatees in North America of Great Britain and France. Look how the Southerners are leading in this final round of the competition—in this inter-American race for the Winning of the West. It is the backwoodsmen of Virginia who have founded Kentucky—the first new state to be established west of those mountains which have so long conspired with the French to keep the English-speaking settlers on the Atlantic coast from penetrating into the interior. And take note of the key-position which Kentucky occupies, extending right down the left bank of the Ohio to the confluence of the Mississippi's principal tributary with the Mississippi himself. The West is in the Southerners' grasp, and mark how all things work together for their good. The statesmanship of an English Chatham and a Pennsylvanian Franklin and a Corsican Buonaparte has endowed them with an immeasurable supply of land; and, as fast as they can put this new land under the hoe, the new-fangled mills of distant Lancashire are offering them an ever-expanding market for the cotton-crop which the soil and climate of the South enable them to raise. The Negro provides the labour and the Mississippi the means of transporting the produce to the quays of New Orleans, where the ships from Liverpool are waiting to bear it away. Even the New Englander is a useful auxiliary, as the Southerner superciliously points out.

'Our Yankee cousin', the Southerner observes in 1807, 'has just invented a "steam-boat" which will navigate our Mississippi upstream; and he has made a practical success of a machine for carding and cleaning our cotton-bolls. Those unlovable, unfortunate fellow-citizens of ours in that out-of-the-way corner, down east! Their "Yankee notions" are more profitable to us than they are to the ingenious inventors! For what are New England's prospects? Her prospects are no better in this year 1807 than they were a century since. To-day, when the wide West has been thrown open to Southern enterprise at last, it still remains closed to the New Englander. New England is still barred in on the landward side by the barrier of Canada, which has not ceased to be a foreign country in passing from the French to the British Crown. So there our poor relation still sits in his out-of-the-way corner, cooped up on the "bad lands" of Town Hill; and there, presumably, he will go on sitting till Doomsday! "Sedet, aeternumque sedebit!" '[1]

If our unlucky prophet takes Southern prospects on the morrow of the Louisiana Purchase at the Southerner's own valuation, he must indeed be in his dotage; for in the last round of the two-centuries-long contest for the mastery of the North American Continent, the Southerner is destined to meet a swifter and more crushing defeat than those that have been met heretofore by the Spaniard and the Dutchman and the Frenchman. To witness his

[1] Virgil: *Aeneid*, Book VI, l. 617.

discomfiture, we shall not have to wait as long as a century. We shall see the relative positions of South and North reversed in less than a lifetime.

In the year 1865, the situation is already transformed, out of all recognition, from what it was in 1807. In the Winning of the West, the Southern pioneer had been outstripped and outflanked by his Northern rival. After almost winning his way to the Great Lakes through Indiana and after getting the best of the bargain in Missouri, the Southerner has been decisively defeated in Kansas, and he has never reached the Pacific. The descendants of the men who mastered the difficulties of Town Hill, Connecticut, have now become masters of the Pacific coast along the whole front from Seattle to Los Angeles. Nor has the Southerner's command of the Mississippi much availed him. He had counted on the network of the Western Waters to draw the whole of the West into a Southern system of economic and political relations; and when the Yankee presented him with steam-boats to ply on the Western Waters, he imagined that the Yankee had delivered the West into his hands. But 'Yankee notions' have not ceased. The inventor of the steamer has gone on to invent the locomotive; and the locomotive has taken away more from the Southerner than the steamer ever gave him; for the potential function of the Hudson Valley in the human geography of North America as the main gateway from the Atlantic to the West—a potentiality which the Dutch had failed to turn to account in competition with the French—has been actualized at last in the railway age. The railway-traffic which now passes up the valley of the Hudson and the valley of the Mohawk and then along the lake-side to link New York with Chicago has superseded the river-traffic on the Mississippi between New Orleans and St. Louis. Therewith, the internal lines of communication of the North American Continent have been turned at right angles from south and north to east and west; and the North-West has been detached from the South, to be welded on to the North-East in interest and in sentiment. Indeed, the Easterner, who once made the South-West a present of the river-steamer, has now won the heart of the North-West with a double gift: he has come to the North-Western farmer with the locomotive in one hand and with the reaper-and-binder in the other, and so has provided him with solutions for both the problems with which the West is confronted. In order to develop its potential economic capacities, the whole West has need of two things: transport and labour; but the South-Western planter—believing that his labour-problem has been solved for ever by the institution of negro slavery—has sought a solution for his transport-problem, and for this only, from the Yankee's mechanical ingenuity. The North-Western farmer is in a different case. He disposes of no servile man-power, and his free-labour force is recruited by the casual process of immigration from Europe all too slowly to till his fast-expanding fields. So he finds the agricultural machinery which is turned out by the Eastern factories as great a godsend as the Eastern railways. By these two 'Yankee notions', together, the allegiance of the North-West has been decided; and thus the Civil War has been lost by the South before it has been fought. In taking up arms in the hope of redressing her economic reverses by a military counterstroke, the South has merely precipitated and consummated a *débâcle* that was already inevitable.

This ultimate victory of the New Englanders, in a competition for the mastery of North America in which their Spanish, Dutch, French, and Southern competitors were successively discomfited, is illuminating for the study of the question with which we are concerned at the moment: the question of the relative stimulating effects of different degrees of difficulty in the physical environment of human life. For, unusually difficult though the New Englanders' environment was, it is manifest that the rival colonists' environments were none of them easy. To begin with, all alike had undergone the initial ordeal of plucking up their social roots in Europe and crossing the Atlantic and striking fresh roots in the soil of a New World;[1] and, when they had succeeded in re-establishing themselves, it was not only the New Englanders who found permanent difficulties to contend with in their new American home. The French settlers in Canada had to contend with an almost arctic cold; and the French settlers in Louisiana had to break in a great river. The Mississippi was as wayward in changing his course, and as devastating in his inundations, as the Yellow River or the Nile or the Tigris; and the *levées* with which the Creoles protected their hard-won fields and villages cost no less human effort to build and maintain than the earthen bulwarks of the Egyptiac and the Sumeric and the Sinic Civilization. In fact, the difficulties presented by the physical environment in Canada and in Louisiana were only less formidable than those which the New Englanders encountered on Town Hill itself. Thus this North American illustration, as far as it goes, tells in favour of the proposition that the difficulty and the stimulus of an environment are apt to increase *pari passu*. It will tell the same tale if we push it even farther.

Can we push it farther? Can we venture, in 1933, to prophesy

---

[1] The stimulus of transmarine colonization and migration is examined further on pp. 84–100, below.

in whose hands the mastery of North America will lie a century
hence? Can we hope to come any nearer to the mark ourselves
than our imaginary prophet in 1650 and 1701 and 1803? Can we
do more than ring down the curtain on the present scene, in which
the offspring of the New Englanders dominates the stage? Difficult though divination may be, there are already certain signs that
the drama is not yet played out and the final victory in the struggle
not yet decided. One small sign once came to the notice of the
author of this Study.

A few days after the occasion, mentioned above,[1] when I passed
by the deserted site of Town Hill, Connecticut, I found myself with
an hour to spend between trains in one of the small back-country
manufacturing towns of New England, on the Massachusetts side
of the Connecticut–Massachusetts state-line. Since the General
War of 1914–18, the industrial districts of New England have fared
as badly as those of the mother country. They have fallen on evil
days, and they show it in their aspect. In this town, however, on
this day, the atmosphere was not at all forlorn or lifeless. The town
was in fête, and the whole population was abroad in the streets.
Threading my way through the crowds I noticed that one person
out of every two was wearing a special badge, and I inquired what
the colours signified. I was told that they were the colours of the local
French Canadian club; and I ascertained that my rough impression
of their frequency in the streets was borne out by statistics. In that
year 1925, in that New England manufacturing town, the French
Canadians were by far the strongest contingent in the local labour-
force. The indigenous New Englanders had left these factories, as
they had left the fields of Town Hill, to find their fortunes in the
West; but the town, unlike the village, had not been deserted. As
fast as the indigenous population had ebbed out, a tide of French
Canadian immigrants had flooded in. Conditions of work and life
which had ceased to be attractive to the descendants of the Pilgrim
Fathers seemed luxurious to these Norman peasants' children from
the sub-arctic hinterland of Quebec. Moreover, I was told, the
French Canadian immigrants were spreading from the towns of
New England on to the land, where, as peasants, they found themselves truly at home. On their frugal standard of living, American
rates of industrial wages left them with a surplus which quickly
mounted up to the purchase-price of a derelict New England farm.
The immigrants were actually re-populating the deserted country-
side. Perhaps, on my next visit, I should find Town Hill itself no
longer desolate. Yet if, on that forbidding spot, the works of Man
overcame the wilderness for the second time, it could be foreseen

[1] See pp. 15–16, above.

that history would repeat itself with a difference. The fields and orchards and even the houses might wear again in 1950 the aspect which they had worn two centuries before; but this time the blood in the veins of the farmers would be French and not English, and divine worship in the antique wooden church would be conducted no longer by a Presbyterian minister but by a Catholic priest!

Thus it seems possible that the contest between the French Canadian and the New Englander for the mastery of North America may not, after all, have been concluded and disposed of finally by the outcome of the Seven Years' War. For, when the French flag was hauled down, the French peasant did not disappear with the emblem of the French Government's sovereignty. Under the tutelage of the Roman Catholic Church, this peasantry continued, undisturbed, to be fruitful and multiply and replenish the Earth; and now in the fullness of time the French Canadian is making a counter-offensive into the heart of his old rival's homeland. He is conquering New England in the peasant's way—by slower but surer methods than those which Governments have at their command. He is conducting his operations with the ploughshare and not with the sword, and he is asserting his ownership by the positive act of colonizing the countryside and not by the cartographical conceit of painting colours and drawing lines on a scrap of paper. Meanwhile, law and religion and environment are combining to assist him. The environment of a harsh countryside keeps him exposed to a stimulus which no longer invigorates his rival in the softer atmosphere of the distant Western cities. His religion forbids him to restrict the size of his family by contraceptive methods of birth-control. And United States legislation, which has restricted immigration from countries overseas but not from countries on the American Continent, has left the French Canadian immigrant in a privileged position which is shared with him by none but the Mexican.[1] Perhaps the present act in the drama of North American history may end, after a century of peaceful penetration, in a triumphal meeting between the two resurgent Latin peasantries in the neighbourhood of the Federal Capital of the United States! Is this the denouement that our great-grandchildren are destined to witness in A.D. 2033? There

---

[1] This restriction of immigration into the United States has been effected by the Immigration (Restriction) Acts of 1921 and 1924. It should be noted that the wide door left open for immigration into the United States across the land-frontiers is only open for native-born inhabitants of the adjoining American countries. A European or Asiatic who attempts to enter the United States through Canada or Mexico, without having secured a place in the annual quota of immigrants assigned to his own country of origin, finds himself excluded. In this matter, the United States Bureau of Immigration has adopted the British Admiralty's doctrine of 'continuous voyage'.

have been reversals of fortune every bit as strange as this in North
American history before.

III. THE STIMULUS OF NEW GROUND

The Testimony of Philosophy, Mythology, and Religion

So much for comparisons between the respective stimulating
effects of physical environments which present different degrees of
difficulty. Let us now approach the same question from a different
angle by comparing the respective stimulating effects of old ground
and new ground, apart from the intrinsic nature of the terrain.

Does the effort of breaking new ground act as a stimulus in itself?
The question is answered in the affirmative by the critical empiri-
cism of an eighteenth-century Western philosopher as well as by the
wider spontaneous human experience which has found a cumulative expression in Mythology. David Hume concludes his essay
Of the Rise and Progress of the Arts and Sciences with the observation that 'the arts and sciences, like some plants, require a fresh
soil; and, however rich the land may be, and however you may
recruit it by art or care, it will never, when once exhausted, produce anything that is perfect or finished in the kind'. The same
affirmative answer is conveyed in the myth of the Expulsion from
Eden and in the myth of the Exodus from Egypt. In their removal
out of the magic garden into the workaday world, Adam and Eve
transcend the food-gathering economy of Primitive Mankind and
give birth to the fathers of an agricultural and a pastoral civilization.[1] In their exodus from Egypt, the Children of Israel—though
they hanker in the wilderness after the flesh pots of the house of
bondage[2]—give birth to a generation which helps to lay the
foundations of the Syriac Civilization in taking possession of
the Promised Land.[3] When we turn from myths to records, we
find these intuitions confirmed by the evidence of empirical
observation.

In the histories of religions, we find that—to the consternation of
those who ask the scornful question: 'Can any good thing come
out of Nazareth?'[4]—the Messiah of Jewry does come out of that
obscure village in 'Galilee of the Gentiles':[5] an outlying piece of
new ground which had been captured for Jewry by the Maccabees rather less than a century before the date of Jesus's birth.[6]
And when the indomitable growth of this Galilaean grain of

[1] See II. C (ii) (*b*) 1, vol. i, p. 290, above.   [2] See pp. 24–5, above.
[3] See the passage quoted in II. B, vol. i, p. 198, above.
[4] John i. 46. Compare John vii. 41 and 52, and Matt. iv. 14–16, which is a reminiscence
of Isaiah ix. 1–2.
[5] Matt. iv. 15.   [6] *Regnante Alexandro Jannaeo*, 102–76 B.C.

mustard-seed turns the consternation of Orthodox Jewry into active hostility, and this not only in Judaea itself but among the Jewish diasporà, then the propagators of the new faith deliberately 'turn to the Gentiles'[1] and proceed to conquer new worlds for Christianity on ground which had lain wholly beyond the range of the strong right arm of an Alexander Jannaeus. In the history of Buddhism it is the same story, for the decisive victories of this Indic faith are not won on the old ground of the Indic World. The Hinayana first finds an open road in Ceylon, which was a colonial annex of the Indic Civilization. And the Mahayana starts its long and roundabout journey towards its future domain in the Far East by capturing the Syriacized and Hellenized Indic province of the Panjab. It is on the new ground of these alien worlds that the highest expressions of the Indic and the Syriac religious genius eventually bear their fruit—in witness to the truth that 'a prophet is not without honour save in his own country and in his own house'.[2]

The Testimony of the 'Related' Civilizations

A convenient empirical test of this social 'law' is offered by those civilizations of the 'related' class that have arisen partly on ground already occupied by the respective antecedent civilization and partly on ground which the 'related' civilization has taken over—either from primitive societies or from other civilizations—on its own account, without the antecedent civilization having here preceded it and prepared the way. We can test the respective stimulating effects of old ground and new ground by surveying the career of any one of these 'related' civilizations, marking the point or points within its domain at which its achievements in any line of social activity have been most signal, and then observing whether the ground on which such points are located is new ground or old.

Let us begin with the extreme case of the Babylonic Civilization, whose original home has been found to be wholly coincident with that of the 'apparented' civilization: the Sumeric.[3] In which of its three foci—Babylonia, Elam, Assyria[4]—did the Babylonic Civilization most distinguish itself? Undoubtedly in Assyria. Whether we judge by prowess in arms or by constructive ability in politics or by creative genius in art, we must pronounce that the Babylonic Civilization reached a higher level in Assyria than in either of the other two Babylonic countries. And was Assyria old ground or

---

[1] Acts xiii. 46.
[2] Matthew xiii. 57. Compare Mark vi. 4; Luke iv. 24; John iv. 44.
[3] See the table and the footnote in vol. i, p. 132, above.
[4] See I. C (i) (b), vol. i, pp. 116–17, above.

new? It turns out, on further examination, that Assyria was the one portion of the original home of the antecedent Sumeric Civilization which possibly might be regarded as new ground—at any rate by comparison with Sumer and Akkad and Elam; for when we probe the local history of Assyria as deep as the present state of our archaeological knowledge allows us to penetrate, we find some reason for supposing that Assyria was not one of the original communities into which the Sumeric Society articulated itself after its birth, but was in some sense a colony—albeit a colony that was almost coeval with the mother country. Perhaps it is not altogether fantastic to surmise that the stimulus derived from this breaking of new ground in Assyria at some early stage in the growth of the Sumeric Civilization may account in part for the special vigour which was afterwards displayed by the 'affiliated' Babylonic Civilization on this Assyrian ground.[1]

Turning next to the Hindu Civilization, let us mark the local sources of the new creative elements in Hindu life—particularly in religion, which has always been the central and supreme activity of the Hindu Society. We find these sources in the South. It was here that all the distinctive features of Hinduism took shape:[2] the cult of Gods represented by material objects or images and housed in temples; the emotional personal relation between the worshipper and the particular God to whose worship he has devoted himself; the metaphysical sublimation of image-worship and emotionalism in an intellectually sophisticated theology (Šankara, the father of Hindu Theology, was born, *circa* A.D. 788, in Southern Malabar).[3] All these features of Hinduism bear a Southern stamp. And was the South of India old ground or new? It was new ground, inasmuch as it had not been incorporated into the domain of the 'apparented' Indic Civilization until the time of the Maurya Empire (*circa* 323–185 B.C.),[4] when the Indic Society, after having first broken down and then passed through a Time of Troubles, at length entered upon that advanced stage in the disintegration of a civilization which we have learnt to recognize as a 'universal state'.

Let us look now at the two civilizations that are 'affiliated' to the Syriac, namely the Arabic and the Iranic.[5]

Where, during the short life of the Arabic Society, did its rather feeble pulse beat least feebly? Assuredly in Egypt, where a ghost of the ʿAbbasid Caliphate (a ghost, that is to say, of the 'reintegrated' Syriac universal state) was evoked in the thirteenth century of the

[1] For another explanation of Assyria's rise as a reaction to the stimulus of pressure from the human environment, see the present volume, pp. 133–7, below.
[2] See Eliot, Sir Charles: *Hinduism and Buddhism* (London 1921, Arnold, 3 vols.), vol. i, Introduction, p. xli.
[3] See Eliot, op. cit., vol. ii, p. 207.   [4] See I. C (i) (*b*), vol. i, pp. 86–7, above.
[5] See I. C (i) (*b*), vol. i, pp. 67–72, with Annex I, above.

Christian Era by the Mamlūks.[1] It was in Egypt that the Arabic literature and the Arabic architecture kept themselves alive during the quarter of a millennium that elapsed between the inauguration of the Cairene Caliphate and the Ottoman conquest. And was Egypt old ground or new? It was new ground inasmuch as it had not begun to be incorporated into the domain of the Syriac Civilization, to which the Arabic Civilization was 'affiliated', before the entry of this Syriac Civilization into its universal state; and even then the 'dead trunk' of the indigenous Egyptiac Civilization, which still cumbered the ground in Egypt, was only absorbed into the tissues of the Syriac Civilization slowly and arduously.

The conquest of Egypt by the Achaemenian Empire, which was the original Syriac universal state,[2] was a mere external annexation. The Egyptians were simply subdued politically by force of arms and even this only intermittently. The Achaemenian régime made no progress whatever towards converting their souls; and, when the Syriac universal state was interrupted by the intrusion of Hellenism, 'Hellenization' seemed a more likely destiny for the residue of the Egyptiac Society than a merger with the Syriac Society which had been submerged, quite as deeply as the Egyptiac Society itself, under the Hellenic flood. It was not until both the Hellenic and the Egyptiac Society were *in extremis* that, in the competition for spiritual dominion over Egypt, the Hellenic Society lost and the Syriac Society gained the upper hand. The ultimate victory of the Syriac Civilization in Egypt was first fore-shadowed when Egypt was captivated by Monophysitism—a version of Christianity in which the Syriac reaction against Hellenism expressed itself before the dissolution of the Roman Empire and the re-integration of the Syriac universal state in the 'Abbasid Caliphate.[3] The victory of the Syriac Civilization in Egypt was only consummated when the population of Egypt—after having successively abandoned their ancient Egyptiac religion for Primitive Christianity and Primitive Christianity for Monophysitism—were converted *en masse* from Monophysitism to Islam; and this did not happen until the 'Abbasid Caliphate itself had dissolved into the interregnum (*circa* A.D. 975–1275)[4] out of which the Arabic Civilization afterwards emerged. Thus, in Egypt, the Arabic Civilization was occupying ground which the 'apparented' Syriac civilization had not completely made its own until the Arabic Civilization was on the point of coming to birth. Yet it was on this new ground in

---

[1] See vol. i, p. 70, above.   [2] See vol. i, pp. 75–9, above.
[3] The reaction of the Syrian Civilization against the intrusion of Hellenism, of which this Monophysite version of Christianity was one symptom in one phase, is discussed further in II. D (vi), on p. 236, and II. D (vii), on pp. 286–7, as well as in Part IX, below.
[4] See vol. i, pp. 67–8, above.

Egypt that the Arabic Civilization displayed such vigour as it did display before its career was prematurely closed by incorporation into the body social of its lustier Iranic sister. This is noteworthy, considering that the original home of the Arabic Civilization included not only the new ground of Egypt but also the old ground of Syria—the very region in which the 'apparented' Syriac Civilization had taken its rise. Yet, in the history of the 'affiliated' Arabic Civilization, Syria always played the subordinate and Egypt the leading part.

Again, in what areas did the Iranic Civilization—the sister of the Syriac—most conspicuously flourish? Almost all the great achievements of the Iranic Civilization in the principal spheres of social activity—not only in war and in politics, but even in architecture and in literature[1]—were accomplished at one or other of the two extremities of the Iranic World: either in Hindustan, at one end, or in Anatolia, at the other;[2] and they culminated respectively, in these two areas, in the Mughal and in the Ottoman Empire. Were these two Iranic empires erected on old ground or on new ground? The ground was new in both cases. The Ottoman Empire was erected on the domain of the Orthodox Christian Civilization; and indeed it occupied this domain so effectively that it actually performed, for the main body of Orthodox Christendom, the function of a universal state.[3] Similarly, the Mughal Empire was erected on the domain of the Hindu Civilization and performed the function of a universal state in the Hindu World.[4] Thus the Iranic Civilization

[1] Persian literature—which in the early age of Iranic history continued to flourish, and this in the heart of the Iranic World, in Iran itself—is a conspicuous apparent exception to the general rule here formulated. This Persian literature, however, is to be regarded as a creation not of the Iranic but of the 'apparented' Syriac Civilization (as Latin literature is a creation of the Hellenic Civilization and not of the 'affiliated' Western or Latin Christendom). The genesis of Persian literature was an event of the 'Abbasid age, when the Syriac Civilization was enjoying a kind of 'Indian Summer' after the reintegration of its universal state. It is to this age of the Syriac Civilization that Persian literature genetically belongs, although chronologically the lifetime of one of its great masters, Sa'dī of Shīrāz (*vivebat circa* A.D. 1184–1291), falls within the post-Syriac interregnum, and the lifetimes of two others—Hāfiz of Shīrāz and Jāmī of Khurāsān—fall respectively within the fourteenth and the fifteenth century of the Christian Era: that is to say, within a time when the Iranic Civilization had already emerged. Hāfiz and the other Persian poets of his generation flourished under social conditions curiously resembling those which produced both the Scandinavian skalds and the Ionian Homeridae. 'It would seem that the existence of numerous small courts, rivals to one another, and each striving to outshine the others, was singularly favourable to the encouragement of poets and other men of letters, who, if disappointed or slighted in one city, could generally find in another a more favourable reception.' (Browne, E. G.: *A Literary History of Persia*, vol. iii (Cambridge 1928, University Press), pp. 160–1.) Thereafter, however, from the beginning of the sixteenth century of the Christian Era, Persian literature wilted in Iran under the régime of the Safawis. (For a discussion of this last-mentioned phenomenon, see Browne, E. G.: *A Literary History of Persia*, vol. iv (Cambridge 1928, University Press), pp. 24–31; and the present Study, I. C (i) (*b*), Annex I, in vol. i, above.)

[2] For the area covered by the original domain of the Iranic Civilization, see I. C (i) (*b*), vol. i, pp. 68–9, above.

[3] For this role of the Ottoman Empire, see further Part III. A, vol. iii, pp. 26–7, and IV. C (ii) (*b*) 1, vol. iv, p. 68, below.   [4] See IV. C (ii) (*b*) 2, vol. iv, p. 97, below.

displayed, at two points which were remote from one another, the identical idiosyncrasy of flourishing best on foreign soil. Moreover, it is to be noted that, in both cases, the acquisition of this foreign soil had not started until after the beginning of the interregnum (*circa* A.D. 975–1275) into which the universal state of the 'apparented' Syriac Civilization dissolved and out of which the 'affiliated' Iranic Civilization itself emerged. The first permanent conquests of Hindu territory in the Kābul Valley and in the Panjab were made (*circa* A.D. 975–1025)[1] by Sebuktegin and his more celebrated successor Mahmūd of Ghaznah; the first permanent conquests of Orthodox Christian territory were made (*circa* A.D. 1070–5) by the Saljūqs.

Accordingly, it was on sites acquired piecemeal from alien civilizations at recent dates that the Iranic Civilization eventually erected its most imposing monuments. On the other hand, the second home which the 'apparented' Syriac Civilization had once found on the Iranian Plateau and in the Oxus-Jaxartes Basin[2] never became the most active focus of the 'affiliated' Iranic Civilization, in spite of the fact that these two regions lay in the heart of the zone in which the Iranic Civilization originally emerged. During the age when, in the new territories conquered from Orthodox Christendom and Hinduism, the Iranic Civilization was going from strength to strength, it succumbed in Iran and in Transoxania to a series of local misdevelopments.[3] In the first place, during the post-Syriac interregnum, these regions bore the brunt of the Mongol invasion—the last and most destructive avalanche of the post-Syriac Völkerwanderung. Thereafter, they lay torpid under the dead weight of the two local Mongol 'successor-states' of the 'Abbasid Caliphate—the appanage of the Il-Khans and the appanage of the House of Chaghatāy; and these disorderly and sluggish régimes only disappeared to make way for the devouring militarism of Timur. The final blows, by which the two regions were prostrated simultaneously at the beginning of the sixteenth century of the Christian Era, were the establishment of the Shī'ī Power in Iran and the conquest of the Oxus-Jaxartes Basin by the Uzbeg barbarians off the Eurasian Steppe: two violent political transformations which had the identic effect of fixing a great religious and cultural gulf between the geographical heart of the

---

Sebuktegin established his suzerainty over the Kābul Valley in A.D. 975; and Mahmūd conquered it and forcibly converted the population to Islam in A.D. 1021. (Vaidya, C. V.: *A History of Mediaeval India* (Poona 1921–4, Oriental Book-Supplying Agency, 2 vols.), vol. i, p. 193.) Sebuktegin's raids on the Panjab began in A.D. 986–7; Mahmūd raided Kanauj in A.D. 1019 (Smith, V.: *The Early History of India*, 3rd edition (Oxford 1914, Clarendon Press), p. 382).   [2] See I. C (i) (*b*), vol. i, pp. 80–2, above.
   [3] See I. C (i) (*b*), Annex I, in vol. i; II. D (v), pp. 144–8 of the present volume; and IV. C (iii) (*c*) 3 (α), vol. iv, pp. 491–501, below.

Iranic World and either of its extremities. Thus it was in the extremities and not at the heart of the Iranic body social that the blood pulsated most vigorously; or, in terms of our original metaphor, it was on new ground and not on old ground that the seed of the Iranic culture produced its finest harvests.

In what regions has the greatest vigour been displayed by the Orthodox Christian Civilization? A glance at its history shows that its social centre of gravity has lain in different regions at different times. In the first age after its emergence out of the post-Hellenic interregnum, the life of Orthodox Christendom was most vigorous on the Asiatic side of the Bosphorus and Dardanelles—in the central and north-eastern parts of the Anatolian Plateau or, in the administrative terminology of the day, in the Anatolic and Armeniac army corps districts (*themata*) of the East Roman Empire. Thereafter, in the course of the two centuries which elapsed between the conversion of Bulgaria to Orthodox Christianity in A.D. 865–70 and the occupation of the interior of Anatolia by the Saljūq Turkish converts to Islam in A.D. 1070–5, the centre of gravity of Orthodox Christendom shifted from the Asiatic to the European side of the Straits; and, as far as the main body of Orthodox Christian Society is concerned, it has remained in the Balkan Peninsula ever since. In modern times, however, that portion of Orthodox Christendom which constitutes the main body of the society from an historical standpoint has been far outstripped in growth and overshadowed in importance by the mighty offshoot of Orthodox Christendom in Russia.[1]

Are these three areas in which the Orthodox Christian Civilization has successively raised its head to be regarded as old ground or as new? Central and North-Eastern Anatolia was certainly new ground as far as the Orthodox Christian Civilization was concerned. It was the former domain of the Hittite Civilization; and although the Hittite Civilization had died a premature death by violence during the Völkerwanderung in which the Hellenic Civilization was brought to birth,[2] its Anatolian homeland was not penetrated by Hellenism until after the destruction of the Achaemenian Empire by Alexander the Great. Even then, this region remained unhellenized much longer than many places that were far more distant from the Aegean. The process did not set in vigorously here until after the last of the local 'successor-states' of the Achaemenian Empire had been converted into Roman provinces; and the first positive local contributions to the Hellenic culture

---

[1] An offshoot which has neither lost its importance nor ceased to be recognizable through being draped twice over—first by Peter the Great and then by Lenin—in an exotic fancy dress of the momentarily fashionable Western cut.

[2] See I. C (i) (*b*), vol. i, pp. 93 and 100–1, above.

were made as late as the fourth century of the Christian Era by the Cappadocian Fathers of the Church. Thus the earliest centre of gravity of the Orthodox Christian Civilization in the interior of Anatolia lay in a region which had not been completely incorporated into the domain of the 'apparented' Hellenic Civilization until Hellenism was *in articulo mortis*.

The second centre of gravity in the interior of the Balkan Peninsula was established on new ground likewise. For the veneer of Hellenic Civilization in a Latin medium, with which this region had been thinly overlaid, in the lifetime of the Roman Empire, during a span of some five centuries, had been destroyed without leaving a trace[1] during the interregnum into which the Empire had eventually dissolved. The destruction was more thoroughgoing here than it was in any of the western provinces with the single exception of Britain. In the Balkan Peninsula, as in Britain, the superficial change of régime was accompanied by a radical change of population and religion. The Christian Roman provincials were not simply conquered but were practically exterminated by the pagan barbarian invaders; and these barbarians eradicated all elements of local culture so effectively that when their descendants repented of the evil which their fathers had done they had to obtain fresh seed from outside in order to start cultivation again. By the time when Orthodox Christianity was re-sown in the Balkan Peninsula in the ninth century of the Christian Era, the soil had been lying fallow for more than three centuries: that is to say, for about twice as long as the soil of Britain had been lying fallow at the time when Augustine was sent on his mission by Gregory the Great. Thus the region in which the Orthodox Christian Civilization established its second centre of gravity was ground which had recently been reclaimed *de novo* from the wilderness.

As for the third centre of gravity in Russia, there is no need to labour the point. The offshoot of Orthodox Christendom which was transplanted to Russia in the tenth century of the Christian Era was propagated there in virgin soil on which no civilization had ever grown before; and this new Russian offshoot of Orthodox Christendom was separated from the main body by a double barrier of sea and steppe.[2] Russia was new ground with a

[1] The survival of a Romance language among the mountains of South-Eastern Europe, from the Carpathians to the Pindus, cannot properly be regarded as a trace of the Latin version of the Hellenic Civilization in the Balkan Peninsula; for the survival of the language did not carry with it any survival of the culture of which this language had once been the vehicle. The still Latin-speaking and still nominally Christian Vlachs and Rumans had to be converted, in 'the Middle Ages', to the Orthodox Christian Civilization *de novo*, just like the contemporary Bulgars and Jugoslavs, who were pagan barbarians speaking outlandish tongues.

[2] At the present time, the domain of Orthodox Christendom in Russia and its domain in the Balkan Peninsula are geographically isolated from one another no longer. The

vengeance; and it is noteworthy that, in Russia, the Orthodox Christian Civilization has flourished with an exuberance which stands out in contrast to its strained and stunted growth elsewhere.

It is still more remarkable to observe that while the centre of gravity of the Orthodox Christian Civilization has shifted twice in the course of Orthodox Christian history, it has never lain in the homeland of the 'apparented' Hellenic Civilization in the Aegean area, although this area has been included in the domain of Orthodox Christendom from first to last. In the early age of the Orthodox Christian Civilization, when its centre of gravity lay on the Anatolian Plateau, the Aegean frontage of Anatolia, which had played a leading role in the early age of the Hellenic Civilization, was perhaps the least important district in the Asiatic peninsula.[1] Again, since the centre of gravity of the main body of Orthodox Christendom has shifted to the European side of the Straits, it has normally lain on the landward and not on the seaward side of Salonica. In fact, peninsular Greece, which was the hub of the Hellenic universe after the primacy had once passed from Ionia, has never played a prominent part in Orthodox Christian history except on two occasions—one in the 'medieval' and the other in the 'modern' age of Western history—when Greece has served as a

---

Rumanian Orthodox Christians of the Balkan area now march with their Ukrainian co-religionists of the Russian area along a line extending from the Central Carpathians through the Bukovina and Bessarabia to the Black Sea coast. This geographical continuity between the Russian and the Balkan domains of Orthodox Christendom does not, however, date back farther than the eighteenth century. The two domains were separated from one another by an outlying strip of the Eurasian Steppe until after the Russo-Turkish War of A.D. 1768–74. It was only in the sequel to this war, when the north coast of the Black Sea and its whole hinterland were annexed to the Russian Empire, that this insulating strip of steppe was cleared of the last of its Nomadic pastoral tenants and was colonized with an agricultural population of Orthodox Christian peasants. This was the final stage in a gradual converging encroachment of the Orthodox Christian peasant's ploughland upon the Muslim or pagan herdsman's cattle-range which had been in progress since the Ruman pioneers had descended into the plains of Wallachia and Moldavia, and since the Zaporogian Cossacks had established themselves—as they did at about the same date —on their island-fortress in the River Dniepr. (See II. D (v), pp. 154–7, below.) In the tenth century, however, this encroachment had not yet begun. At that time, the pagan Turkish Pechenegs were pasturing their flocks on virgin steppe-land from the banks of the Don to the Iron Gates of the Danube without interruption. The Orthodox Christian missionaries who carried the seeds of their civilization to Russia could only reach this new field by facing the perils of sea and steppe in succession. They had first to travel by ship from Constantinople to the Crimea, and thence to pick their way across the open prairie, where they were at the mercy of the Pechenegs until they found safety at last in the southern outskirts of the Russian forests.

[1] When the East Roman Army was concentrated in Anatolia during the military crisis produced by the Persian and Arab invasions in the seventh century of the Christian Era, this district was assigned to the Thracensian Army Corps, which was permanently withdrawn from the European district from which it derived its name and was stationed here in Western Anatolia in order to support the Anatolic Army Corps, which had been withdrawn from Syria on to the Anatolian Plateau. The Anatolici were the front-line troops; the Thracenses were mere reserves. Accordingly, the Thracensian district was little accounted of, whereas the Anatolic district, in conjunction with the Armeniac, swayed the destinies of the East Roman Empire.

watergate through which Western influence has forced an entry into the Orthodox Christian World.[1]

Turning now to Hellenic history, let us ask our question apropos of the two regions which (as we have just observed in passing) successively held the primacy in the Hellenic World. When the Hellenic Civilization flowered on the Anatolian coast of the Aegean and afterwards on the European Greek peninsula, was it on new ground or on old ground that this flowering took place? It was on new ground, here again; for neither of these regions had lain within the original home of the antecedent Minoan Civilization, to which the Hellenic Civilization was related. On the European Greek peninsula, the Minoan Civilization, even at its widest extension in its latest age, had held no more than a chain of fortified positions along the southern and eastern coast-lines.[2] On the Anatolian coast of the Aegean, the failure of our modern Western archaeologists to find traces of the presence, or even influence, of the Minoan Civilization has been so signal that it can hardly be attributed to chance, but seems rather to indicate that for some reason this coast actually did not come within the Minoans' range.[3] As far as we know, the first settlers from the Aegean to occupy the west coast of Anatolia effectively were those refugees of Minoan culture and Greek speech who were driven thither, as late as the twelfth century B.C., in the same final convulsion of the post-Minoan Völkerwanderung that drove the Philistines on to the coast of Syria.[4] These were the founders of Aeolis and Ionia; and thus Hellenism flowered first on soil which the antecedent civilization had never seriously cultivated. Moreover, when the seeds were scattered abroad from Ionia into other parts of the Hellenic World, the Ionic soil on which they flowered next was the stony ground of Attica on the opposite side of the Aegean. They did not germinate in the Cyclades: the Ionic islands which stood, like stepping-stones, between the Ionic mainlands in Asia and in Europe. Through the whole course of Hellenic history the Cycladic islanders played a subordinate role as humble servants of the successive masters of the sea. This is remarkable, since the Cyclades had been one of the two foci of the antecedent Minoan Civilization. The other Minoan focus, of course, was Crete; and the role played in Hellenic history by Crete is even more surprising.

[1] The first of these two forcible entries was the military conquest of peninsular Greece by the Latins, during and after the so-called 'Fourth Crusade'. The second was the infiltration of modern Western ideas which began towards the end of the seventeenth century and came to a head politically, some hundred and fifty years later, in the Greek War of Independence which broke out in A.D. 1821.

[2] See I. C (i) (b), Annex II, vol. i, above.

[3] On this point, see I. C (i) (b), vol. i, p. 95, above.

[4] See I. C (i) (b), vol. i, pp. 100–2, above.

Crete might have been expected to retain its social importance not only for historical reasons, as the place in which the Minoan Civilization had attained its culmination, but for geographical reasons as well. Crete was by far the largest island in the Aegean Archipelago, and it lay athwart two of the most important sea-routes in the Hellenic World. Every ship that sailed from the Peiraeus for Sicily had to pass between the western end of Crete and Laconia; every ship that sailed from the Peiraeus for Egypt had to pass between the eastern end of Crete and Rhodes. Yet, whereas Laconia and Rhodes each played a leading part in Hellenic history, Crete remained aloof, obscure and benighted from first to last. While Hellas all around was giving birth to statesmen and poets and artists and philosophers, the island which had once been the home of the Minoan Civilization now bred nothing more reputable than medicine-men and mercenaries and pirates; and though the greatness of Minoan Crete had left its impress upon the Hellenic Mythology in the fables of Minos the thalassocrat and his brother Rhadamanthys, the judge of the dead, this did not save the latter-day Cretan scapegrace from becoming a Hellenic byword. Indeed, he has passed judgement on himself in the song of Hybrias[1] and in a hexameter which has been embedded, like a fly in amber, in the canon of Christian Scripture. 'One of themselves, even a prophet of their own, said: "The Cretians are always liars, evil beasts, slow bellies." '[2] Thus even the Apostle of the Gentiles excepted the Hellenes of Crete from the charity which he bestowed upon Hellenes in general.[3]

Let us ask our question once again—this time in regard to the Far Eastern Civilization which is 'affiliated' to the Sinic Civilization. At what points in its domain has this Far Eastern Civilization shown the greatest vigour? The Japanese and the Cantonese stand out unmistakably as its most vigorous representatives to-day; and both these peoples have sprung from soil which is new ground and not old ground from the standpoint of Far Eastern history. As regards the south-eastern seaboard of China, we have noticed in an earlier chapter[4] that it was not incorporated into the domain of the

---

[1] An English translation of the Song of Hybrias, by Gilbert Murray, will be found below in Part III. A, vol. iii, on p. 87, footnote 1.

[2] The Epistle of Paul to Titus, ch. i, v. 12. The hexameter here quoted runs in Greek:

Κρῆτες ἀεὶ ψεῦσται, κακὰ θηρία, γαστέρες ἀργοί.

For the original context of this verse in the poem called 'Minos' which was attributed to the Cretan 'prophet' Epimenides, see I. C (i) (b), vol. i, p. 99, footnote 2.

[3] The Cretans have not forgiven St. Paul for immortalizing their ill repute, and they have racked their brains to turn the passage of Scripture in which they are pilloried to the Apostle's own discredit. When the present writer was travelling in Crete in the year 1912, a Cretan peasant adjured him in all seriousness to discount Paul's testimony on the ground that Paul was a biased witness. On being asked what had given Paul his anti-Cretan bias, the peasant explained that a Cretan had once got the better of Paul in a business transaction!   [4] In I. C (i) (b), vol. i, p. 90, footnote 2.

'apparented' Sinic Society until the last phase of Sinic history, and
even then only on the superficial plane of politics, as a frontier
province of the Empire of the Han, which was the Sinic universal
state. Its inhabitants remained barbarians; and their successors
in the four modern Chinese provinces of Kwangtung, Kwangsi,
Fukien, and Chekiang testify, in the nomenclature which they
employ, that they claim no part or lot in the chapter of history
which the Han Dynasty brought to a close. They resign the
glorious name of 'Han people' to their neighbours in the basins of
the Yangtse and the Yellow River, and use the name of 'T'ang
people' to designate themselves. In this designation they signify
that their own history did not begin until the Far Eastern Civilization had already emerged from the post-Sinic interregnum; for the
lineaments of the Far Eastern Civilization had taken shape before
the close of the fifth century of the Christian Era, whereas the T'ang
Dynasty was not founded until A.D. 618. Thus the four provinces
of China Proper which are now the most vigorous and progressive
are the four in which the Far Eastern Civilization has broken new
ground. As for the Japanese Archipelago, the offshoot of the Far
Eastern Civilization which was transplanted thither, by way of
Korea, in the sixth and seventh centuries of the Christian Era was
propagated there on ground where there was no trace of any previous culture. The strong growth of this offshoot of the Far Eastern
Civilization on the virgin soil of Japan is comparable to the growth
of the offshoot of the Orthodox Christian Civilization which was
transplanted from the Anatolian Plateau to the virgin soil of Russia.[1]

The Special Stimulus of Migration Overseas

This survey of the relative fertility of old ground and new
ground, as exemplified in the histories of seven 'related' civilizations, has given us a certain empirical support[2] for the doctrine
which is implicit in the myths of the Exodus and the Expulsion:
the doctrine that the ordeal of breaking new ground has an intrinsic
stimulating effect. Before passing on from the physical to the
human environment, let us pause to glance at certain illustrations
by which the foregoing empirical evidence may be reinforced.
These additional illustrations confirm the view—which is suggested by the unusual vitality of the Orthodox Christian Civilization in Russia and of the Far Eastern Civilization in Japan—that
the stimulating effect of breaking new ground is greatest of all when
the new ground can only be reached by crossing the sea.

The special stimulus inherent in transmarine colonization appears

[1] See pp. 80-1, above.
[2] For a defence of this empirical evidence against a possible criticism, see II. D (iii),
Annex, below.

very clearly in the history of the Mediterranean during the first half
of the last millennium B.C., when the Western Basin of the Mediterranean was being colonized competitively by maritime pioneers
representing three different civilizations in the Levant. It appears,
for instance, in the degree to which the two greatest of these
colonial foundations—Syriac Carthage and Hellenic Syracuse—
each outstripped its parent-city.[1] Carthage dwarfed Tyre in the
volume and value of her commerce, and on this economic basis she
built up a political empire to which the parent-city did not and
could not aspire. Syracuse likewise dwarfed her parent Corinth in
political power, and perhaps even more signally in the contribution
which she made to Hellenic culture. Again, the Achaean colonies
in Magna Graecia became busy seats of Hellenic commerce and
industry, and brilliant centres of Hellenic thought, as early as the
sixth century B.C., whereas the parent Achaean communities along
the northern coast of the Peloponnese remained in a backwater—
outside the main stream of Hellenic history—for three more
centuries, and only emerged from this long obscurity after the
Hellenic Civilization had passed its zenith. As for the Locrians,
who were the Achaeans' neighbours on both sides of the Ionian
Sea, it was only the Epizephyrian Locrians, in their transmarine
settlement in Italy, who ever distinguished themselves at all. The
Locrians of Continental Greece remained obscure from first to last.

The most striking case of all is that of the Etruscans,[2] who were
the third party competing with the Greeks and the Phoenicians
for the colonization of the Western Mediterranean. In this competition, the Etruscans effectively held their own. Their colonies on
the west coast of Italy were comparable, in size and number, to the
Greek colonies in Magna Graecia and Sicily and to the Phoenician
colonies in Africa and Spain; and the Etruscan colonists, unlike
either the Phoenicians or the Greeks, were not content to remain
within sight of the sea across which they had come. They pushed
forward from the west coast of Italy into the interior with an *élan*
which carried them on across the Appennines and across the Po,
until their outposts halted at last at the foot of the Alps. At the
same time, these colonial Etruscans remained in close contact with
their Greek and Phoenician rivals; and though this contact gradually drew them into the ambit of the Hellenic Society and eventually
resulted in their being incorporated into the Hellenic body social,
this cultural 'conversion' increased rather than diminished the
importance of their position in the Mediterranean World. Thus

[1] As, in the modern European colonization of North America, Boston in Massachusetts has outstripped its parent-town in Lincolnshire, and New York and New Orleans
have outstripped the two cities in England and France after which they are respectively
named.   [2] See I. C (i) (*b*), vol. i, p. 114, footnote 3, with Annex II, above.

the Etruscan colonies in Italy are illuminated by the full light of
history; and we are also not without evidence of an abortive
Etruscan colonial enterprise in another quarter: a daring but unsuccessful attempt to compete with the Greeks, in Greek home waters,
for the mastery of the Dardanelles and for the command of the
Black Sea.[1] It is the more remarkable that the Etruscan homeland
in the Levant, which sent out overseas the Etruscan colonists of
Italy and the Etruscan colonists of Lemnos, should be an historical
terra incognita. No historical record of its exact location survives;
and nothing can be built on the Hellenic legend that the Etruscans
came from Lydia.[2] We have to be content with the knowledge,
supplied by the records of 'the New Empire' of Egypt, that the
ancestors of the Etruscans, like the ancestors of the Achaeans, took
part in the post-Minoan Völkerwanderung; and in the presumption
that the ports from which the descendants of those older Etruscan
sea-raiders afterwards set sail to make their fortunes in the west lay
somewhere on the Asiatic coast of the Levant in the no-man's-land
between Greek Sidê and Phoenician Aradus. This surprising gap
in the historical record can only mean one thing:[3] namely, that the
Etruscans who stayed at home never did anything worth recording.
The astonishing contrast between the nonentity of the Etruscans at
home and their eminence overseas gives the measure of the stimulus
which they must have received in the process of transmarine
colonization.

The stimulating effect of crossing the sea is perhaps greatest of
all in a transmarine migration which occurs in the course of a
Völkerwanderung.

Such occurrences seem to be uncommon. The only instances
which the writer of this Study can call to mind are the migration of
the Teucrians, Aeolians, Ionians, and Dorians across the Aegean to
the west coast of Anatolia and the migration of the Teucrians and
Philistines round the eastern end of the Mediterranean to the coast
of Syria in the course of the post-Minoan Völkerwanderung; the
migration of the Angles and Jutes across the North Sea to Britain in
the course of the post-Hellenic Völkerwanderung; the consequent
migration of the Cornavii and other Britons across the Channel to
the Armorican Peninsula of Gaul; the contemporary migration of
the Irish Scots across the North Channel to the corner of North
Britain that is now called Argyll;[4] and the migrations of the

---

[1] See I. C (i) (*b*), Annex II, in vol. i, above.
[2] This legend may have no better basis than the not very close resemblance between
two proper names: Tyrrhenoi and Torrheboi.
[3] *Pace* those modern Western scholars who take this to mean that the Etruscans of
Italy were either 'autochthonous' Italians or else immigrants, by an overland route,
from the interior of the European Continent.
[4] See II. D (v), p. 194, and II. D (vii), pp. 323-4, below.

Scandinavians in the course of the Völkerwanderung which followed the abortive evocation of a ghost of the Roman Empire by the Carolingians.[1] This Scandinavian Völkerwanderung took place almost entirely by sea, and this in several directions: from Norway across the North Atlantic to the Shetlands and Orkneys and thence by way of the Hebrides to Ireland and by way of the Faroes to Iceland; from Denmark across the North Sea to England; from either Norway or Denmark down the English Channel to Normandy; and from Sweden across the Baltic to Russia.

The Philistine migration, as we have observed at an earlier point in this chapter,[2] came to a standstill in an easy environment which produced a soporific effect upon the immigrants after they had settled down; and this sequel would appear to have neutralized any stimulating effect that may have been produced by the previous sea-passage.[3] The British migration, likewise, appears to have produced no appreciable stimulating effect—to judge by the rather undistinguished subsequent history of the Bretons—and this in spite of the facts that the new Continental Brittany was decidedly a hard country, and that the new-comers from overseas did not establish their footing there without having to encounter and overcome a considerable resistance, both from the Roman Church and from the Frankish 'successor-state' of the Roman Empire.[4] In the other four instances, however—that is to say, in the transmarine migrations of the Ionians, the Angles, the Scots, and the Scandinavians—we can discern certain striking phenomena which have an inner connexion with one another and which appear in conjunction, in each instance, with singular uniformity, while they are not to be found in the far more numerous instances of migration overland. Considering that the four migrations in question have occurred quite independently of one another at wide intervals of time and place,[5] we may venture, perhaps, to generalize from them

[1] For the abortive Scandinavian Civilization, see II. D (vii), pp. 340–60, below. For the Scandinavian Heroic Age, out of which the abortive Scandinavian Civilization failed to come to birth, see Part VIII, below. For the abortive Carolingian ghost of the Roman Empire, see Part X, below.

[2] See pp. 49–51, above.

[3] Moreover, the Philistine migration was only maritime in part. The flotilla which skirted the Asiatic coast was accompanied by a train of ox-carts in which the women and children and goods of the migrant horde were transported overland.

[4] The failure of the Bretons to distinguish themselves is the more remarkable when we consider that their migration across the Channel in the post-Hellenic Völkerwanderung is the exact analogue of the migration of the Aeolians and Ionians across the Aegean in the post-Minoan Völkerwanderung. The Continental Bretons, like the Asiatic Aeolians and Ionians, are the overseas descendants of refugee representatives of the antecedent civilization who have been dislodged by the incoming barbarians. They are not the overseas descendants of the barbarians themselves, like the Angles and the Dorians. In the history of the Aeolians and Ionians, the combination of the stimulus of transmarine migration with the asset of an inherited culture has, of course, shown itself particularly potent.

[5] With the exception of the English and the Scottish migrations, which were contemporary in date though geographically isolated from one another.

to the extent of regarding those phenomena which are common to all four as being inherent features of a Völkerwanderung when this takes place not in the usual fashion overland but in this exceptional fashion over the water.

The distinctiveness of these phenomena and their inner connexion with one another are both explained by one and the same simple fact: In transmarine migration, the social apparatus of the migrants has to be packed on board ship before they can leave the shores of the old country and then unpacked again at the end of the voyage before they can make themselves at home on new ground. All kinds of apparatus—persons and property, techniques and institutions and ideas—are equally subject to this law. Anything that cannot stand the sea voyage at all has simply to be left behind; and many things—and these not only material objects—which the migrants do manage to take with them can only be shipped after they have been taken to pieces—never, perhaps, to be reassembled in their original form.

This law governs all transmarine movements whatsoever. It has governed, for example, the ancient Greek and Phoenician and Etruscan colonization of the Western Basin of the Mediterranean and the modern European colonization of America; and the challenge which, in virtue of this law, is inherent in a sea-passage accounts for the intrinsic stimulus of crossing the sea which we have observed already in these two cases. In these particular cases, however, the colonists happen to have belonged to societies which were already in process of civilization at the time when the sea was crossed. When a transmarine migration occurs in the course of a Völkerwanderung, the challenge is much more formidable and the stimulus proportionately more intense because the impact here falls upon a society which is not socially progressive at the time but is overtaken by the challenge while it is still in that static condition which is the last state of Primitive Man.[1] The transition, in the Völkerwanderung, from this passivity to a sudden paroxysm of storm and stress produces a dynamic effect upon the life of any community which undergoes the experience;[2] but this effect is naturally more intense when the migrants take ship than when they keep their feet on solid ground throughout their trek. The driver of an ox-cart has a greater command than the master of a ship over the circumstances of his journey. He can maintain an unbroken

---

[1] For the Yin-state in which we find Primitive Man as we know him, see I. C (iii) (e), vol. i, pp. 179–80, and II. B, vol. i, pp. 192–5. In essentials, every society which takes part in a Völkerwanderung is still in that static condition—even though, ex hypothesi, it has been irradiated by certain elements of the civilization into whose ambit it has been attracted and in whose 'external proletariat' it has been enrolled and whose former domain it is now invading. (See Part II. A, vol. i, pp. 187–8, above, and Part VIII, below.)   [2] See further Part VIII, below.

contact with his base of operations; he can pitch camp and strike camp where and when he chooses; he can set his own pace; and in these circumstances he can carry with him much of the social apparatus which has to be discarded by his seafaring comrade. Thus we can measure the stimulating effect of transmarine migration in the course of a Völkerwanderung by comparing the phenomena with the effect of migration overland, and *a fortiori* with the effect of staying at home and letting the paroxysm pass without being moved to follow either the swan-path or the cart-track.

'When the Scandinavians went beyond the sea, their migration meant more than a change of place. At home, the World, large as it was, could be surveyed from the homestead with the eyes of the mind; but, as one horizon burst on the view and another closed in . . . the ancient Middlegarth lost its definiteness and made way for something more akin to our Universe. This change of outlook gave birth to a new conception of gods and men. The local deities whose power was coextensive with the territory of their worshippers were replaced by a corporate body of gods ruling the World. The holy place with its blot-house which had formed the centre of Middlegarth was raised on high and turned into a divine mansion. Time-honoured myths setting forth the doings of mutually independent deities were worked up into a poetical mythology, a divine saga, on the same lines that had been followed by an earlier race of Vikings, the Homeric Greeks. This religion brought a new god to birth: Odin, the leader of men, the lord of the battlefield.'[1]

In somewhat similar fashion, the overseas migration of the Scots from Ireland to North Britain prepared the way for the entry of a new religion. It is no accident that the transmarine Dalriada became the head-quarters of St. Columba's missionary movement which not only achieved the conversion of the Picts and the Northumbrians but also exercised a profound retroactive influence upon Christianity in Ireland itself through the *Familia Columbae*: a cluster of federated monasteries, mostly situated on Irish soil, which all recognized the supremacy of Iona.[2]

One distinctive phenomenon of transmarine migration is the intermingling and interbreeding of diverse racial strains; for the first piece of social apparatus that has to be abandoned is the primitive tribe or horde. No ship will hold more than one ship's company, and the primitive ship is small. At the same time, the primitive ship is relatively mobile compared with the ox-cart or other primitive means of transport on land. Moreover, in transmarine migration, no less than in overland migration, there is safety in numbers. For these reasons, a new community founded

---

[1] Grönbech, V.: *The Culture of the Teutons* (London 1931, Milford, 3 parts in 2 vols.), Part II, pp. 306-7.
[2] For the *Familia Columbae*, see further II. D (vii), p. 325, below.

by migrants across the sea is apt to be established by the concerted efforts of a number of crews which have joined forces from different quarters—in contrast to the ordinary process of migration overland, in which a whole tribe is apt to pack its women and children and seed-corn and household gods and household utensils into its ox-carts and move off *en masse*, at a foot's pace, over the face of the Earth. We catch a glimpse of this phenomenon of maritime race-mixture in the foundation-legends of Hellenic Aeolis and Ionia—whatever these legends may be worth in the form in which they have been transmitted by Herodotus and Pausanias. In almost every Greek city-state along the west coast of Anatolia, the latter-day inhabitants traced their ancestry back to more places than one in the European Greek peninsula—not to speak of the strains introduced by intermarriage with the native women whom the pioneers took captive. We are on surer ground when we turn from the case of Ionia to that of Iceland, where an exact and detailed oral record survived to be perpetuated in the *Landnamabok*.

'Among the peculiarly favourable conditions for mental development in Iceland, the most important was the selection of the human stock that settled the island. It included all those families of petty kings and peasant chieftains from Western Norway who refused to yield to the autocratic rule of Harold Fairhair, preferring to seek a new home on the distant island which had recently been discovered. At the same time it was impossible for the society of Iceland to become a mere repetition of the old Norwegian community; the racial mixture was too pronounced for that. There came Norwegians from various parts of the country, stragglers from Sweden, vikings from the West, including even some semi-Celtic elements.'[1]

This distinctive phenomenon of unusually far-going racial mix-ture is closely connected with another: the unusually rapid dis-integration of the kin-group which is the basis of social organization in a primitive society. The comparative efficacy of transmarine migration and of overland migration as solvents of the kin-group is appraised as follows, at the conclusion of an exhaustive inquiry, by a distinguished modern student of Scandinavian antiquities:

'The analogy of the Icelandic settlers will incline us to accept the idea that a migration involving transport by sea was especially liable to impair the sense of kin-solidarity among those who venture on it, though the organization of those who remained behind might not be appreciably affected. It is extremely unlikely that each group of kindred would build a vessel and man it exclusively, or even mainly, with their own kinsmen; on the contrary, all analogies show us that any individuals wishing to join an expedition would rally to the first ship that was sailing and

[1] Olrik, A.: *Viking Civilisation* (English translation: London 1930, Allen and Unwin), pp. 175–6. Cp. p. 112.

probably remain permanently associated with its crew in the new country. . . .

'A classic example is afforded by the sons of Earl Hrollaug of Norway, one of whom, Göngu-Hrolf, is declared by Snorri to have founded the Duchy of Normandy; one lost his life in the Western Isles of Scotland on an expedition with Harald Hairfair; another became Earl of the Orkneys, while yet another settled in Iceland. It seems more than probable that the peoples of Schleswig-Holstein lived under similar conditions in the 5th century, with viking expeditions, and finally the permanent conquest of England, as the result. The settlers in England might therefore be almost as lacking in full kindreds as the settlers in Iceland a few centuries later. Before we make certain that the invaders must have come over *en masse*, in full kindreds, in order to achieve such a vast result as the conquest of England, we shall do well to remind ourselves that the feat was all but paralleled, in a much shorter time and in the teeth of a resistance at least equally obstinate, by the vikings of a later period; yet that no one thinks it necessary to assume a wholesale emigration of kindreds in this case, or to postulate that the organization of the Vikings, when they arrived in England, was on a basis of kindreds.

'If we are to adopt the Danish theory that the Normans are mainly of Danish and not Norwegian origin, we can point to Normandy also as affording corroborative evidence for the disintegrating influence on the kindred of a settlement by sea. According to this theory the invaders of Normandy came from the highly cohesive kindreds of Denmark. Yet the traces of kinship-solidarity in thirteenth-century Normandy are far fainter than in other districts of Northern France, which the Teutons reached by land.

'So far as it goes, too, the evidence available for the easternmost and westernmost of Teutonic settlements bears out our contention. The laws of the Swedish kingdom in Russia, won by naval expeditions, show but a feeble conception of kinship: the slayer alone pays for his deed, and the right of vengeance is limited to brother, father, son and nephew. On the other hand, West Gothic custumals in Spain show division of wergild between kinsmen, definitely organized blood-feuds between kindreds, and oath-helpers of the kindred. . . . The West Goths travelled a long way, but they travelled by land.

'Thus we are driven to the conclusion that the main disintegrating factor in the case of the Teutonic kindreds was migration, and especially migration by sea. Denmark and Schleswig are the strongholds of the kindreds: those of Friesland, the Netherlands and Northern France had vitality enough to withstand centuries of highly adverse influences, whereas the Icelander stood alone from the moment he set foot on Icelandic soil; and it may be questioned whether the Anglo-Saxon settler was in much better case in this respect. Here, too, we should find an explanation of the weakness of the kindreds in Norway, for much of the settlement of that country must have been accomplished by sea, and at a very late period.'[1]

[1] Phillpotts, B. S.: *Kindred and Clan* (Cambridge 1913, University Press), pp. 257-65.

Another distinctive phenomenon of transmarine migration is the atrophy of a primitive institution which is perhaps the supreme expression of undifferentiated social life before this is refracted, by a clarifying social consciousness, on to the separate planes of economics and politics and religion and art: the institution of the ἐνιαυτὸς δαίμων and his cycle.[1] On this point we may quote another work by the same authority:

'In Iceland the May Day game, the ritual wedding, and the wooing scene seem hardly to have survived the settlement, partly, no doubt, because the settlers were mainly of a travelled and enlightened class, and partly because these rural observances are connected with agriculture, which could not be an important branch of activity in Iceland.'[2]

If we wish to see the ritual of the ἐνιαυτὸς δαίμων in its glory in the Scandinavian World, we must study its development among Scandinavian peoples who did not leave their homes:

'It seems that at Lejre and Salhaugar in Sjaelland, at Upsala in Sweden, and possibly at the old Skiringssal in South Norway, the fertility-drama was presented in ancient sanctuaries consecrated by the tombs of kings or gods. There is some reason for believing that it was the central rite of a religious confederacy. This drama was apparently performed only once every nine years, by actors of royal birth, and there was a tradition of an actual slaying. Such stately drama as this was bound by immemorial tradition to one locality. The sanctuary, the goddess, the priest-king[3] could not migrate with the members of the confederate tribes. There is therefore no trace of what we may call literary drama, or of such highly developed tragic drama, outside Southern Scandinavia, where Teutonic peoples had been settled for several thousand years.'[4]

The thesis of the work from which these two last passages are quoted is that the Scandinavian poems which have been preserved by Icelandic tradition and committed to writing in the Icelandic compilation called the Elder Edda are derived from the spoken words of the primitive Scandinavian fertility-drama—the only element in the traditional ritual which the migrants were able to cut away from its deeply-embedded local roots and to take on board ship with them. According to this theory, the development of a primitive ritual into a Scandinavian drama was arrested among

---

[1] See Part II. B, vol. i, p. 189. The undifferentiated unity of Art and Religion and Life itself in a primitive human society is pointed out, apropos of the Scandinavian case, by Grönbech, V.: *The Culture of the Teutons* (London 1931, Milford, 3 parts in 2 vols.), Part II, pp. 239–41 and 269.

[2] Phillpotts, B. S.: *The Elder Edda and Ancient Scandinavian Drama* (Cambridge 1920, University Press), p. 204. On the same subject, see further Grönbech, V.: *The Culture of the Teutons* (London 1931, Milford, 3 parts in 2 vols.), Part II, ch. xiv: 'The Creative Festival' (pp. 216–45), and ch. xv: 'Essay on Ritual Drama' (pp. 260–340).

[3] 'As a matter of fact the priest-king did survive migration among the Franks. But the migrations of the Franks did not last long and affected their customs very little.'

[4] Phillpotts, op. cit., p. 207.

those Scandinavians who migrated across the sea; and the theory is supported by an analogy from Hellenic history. For it is a well-established fact that, although the Hellenic Civilization came to flower in transmarine Ionia first, the Hellenic drama, which was one of the highest creations of Hellenic culture, sprang from the continental soil of the European Greek peninsula. The counterpart, in Hellas, of the sanctuary at Upsala was the theatre of Dionysus at Athens. Neither Ionia nor Iceland could show the like.

The distinctive phenomena of transmarine migration which we have noticed so far are all negative; but the challenge implicit in these negative phenomena has evoked a remarkable positive response which must now engage our attention.

At an earlier point in this Study we have found reason to believe that race-mixture, by setting up a physical disturbance, administers a stimulus to the psyche which is conducive to the genesis of a civilization—so much so, that the geneses of civilizations may actually prove to require contributions from more races than one.[1] This indirect physical stimulus may be assumed to reinforce the direct psychic stimulus which is administered by 'a sea change'; and the two factors in combination shatter the 'cake of custom' in which primitive societies, as we know them, are fast bound.[2] Thereupon, in long-imprisoned and suddenly liberated souls there emerges a rudimentary social consciousness which reveals itself in two closely connected forms: an awareness of strong individual personalities and an awareness of momentous public events. The circumstances and spirit of this mental awakening are forcibly conveyed in the following description of it, as it came to pass in Iceland, from the pen of one of the three modern Western scholars whom we have quoted already.

'The largest part of the population came from the districts of Hordaland and Rogaland in Western Norway, [and] it was these regions that had contributed most to the great Viking Age and the period of discoveries. Many families had spent years in the western colonies. They had acquired a wide horizon and an insight into political conditions in near and distant places; for all these scattered habitations were closely connected with each other by family ties and common enterprises. The numerous merchant-ships constantly brought news, which was received, scrutinised and judged. The experiences of contemporaries naturally became transformed into sagas.

'These aristocratic and talented persons settled in Iceland under more severe conditions of life than they had formerly known. Instead of being a petty king, the peasant had at most a very limited chieftain authority as the *godi* (sacrificial priest and *thing* leader) of his district; many a man

[1] See II. C (ii) (a) 1, vol. i, pp. 239–243, and II. C (ii) (b) 1, vol. i, p. 278, above.
[2] For this 'cake of custom' see Part II. B, vol. i, p. 192, above.

of noble origin had to settle as a peasant in the *godord* (*godi* district) of another man. Instead of proud raftered halls, they built houses with walls of earth several yards thick, a continuous row or group of such houses constituting the farm buildings. Cattle-breeding, bird-hunting, fishing required an extreme degree of attention if they were to yield foodstuffs for all the housecarls and servants; a man who once had traded in the most precious commodities of foreign countries had now only the home-woven frieze to export. The external circumstances of life were narrowing down. The only earmark of nobility that was still retained from the forefathers was the mental culture, the ability to pass in review a succession of events, to form a judicious estimate of situations.'[1]

In the strenuous and stimulating mental atmosphere here described, the void resulting from the absence of the primitive social apparatus that has been left behind in crossing the sea is filled by new acts of social creation. The energies released by the breaking of the 'cake of custom' crystallize, in the new transmarine environment, into new activities which are definite in their forms and are limited in their scope, in each case, to some single plane of social life. In the field left clear by the atrophy of the fertility-ritual there arises a narrative form of literary art: the Saga or the Epic. In the field left clear by the disintegration of the kin-group there arises a polity in the likeness of a ship's company on an enlarged scale and on a permanent basis: a commonwealth in which the binding element is not community of blood but that common obedience to a freely chosen leader and common respect for a freely accepted law which has been called 'the social contract' in the figurative language of our modern Western Political Mythology.

The Saga and the Epic both alike arise in response to the same new mental need. In both, the new awareness of strong individual personalities and of momentous public events, which the storm and stress of the Völkerwanderung has brought into consciousness, finds an expression through art.[2]

'The Icelandic Saga . . . grew out of reports of contemporary happenings. A man who had recently returned home would sit at the *Althing*

---

[1] Olrik, op. cit., pp. 176-7.

[2] The difference between the Saga and the Epic lies not in the nature of the stimulus by which they are evoked nor in the nature of the interests and feelings and ideas which are expressed in them, but merely in the method and origin of their respective techniques. In the Icelandic Saga, the new interest in personalities and events finds expression in a technique which is new likewise. The form and matter of the dialogues and soliloquies that grew out of the continental Scandinavian fertility-ritual are religiously preserved in the Elder Edda; but, having once been torn away from their roots in order to be transported across the sea, they are not put to new uses in the new country nor developed any further. They are preserved, as it were, as fossils; and when the Icelanders fashion 'the Saga, the true Icelandic counterpart of the Epic, out of the stories current in the country-side', they create, to convey it, 'a new prose form' in which they are 'hampered by no fossilised tradition' (Phillpotts: *The Elder Edda*, p. 205). The sagas only indirectly reveal the existence of an older dramatic technique in a certain dramatic sense and dramatic detachment which are characteristic of their style (op. cit., loc. cit.). On the othe hand the makers of the Epic—in Ionia or in England—solve the same problem of

and tell his story—a connected account—of all that had taken place during the year at well-known scenes of action. . . . Probably many a saga originated in this way. The story was related to an attentively listening circle of hearers by one who had himself been taking part in the events; and while the first scene is being thus reported, Life itself continues the destinies of the acting persons.'[1]

Thus, one day at the *Althing*, Thormod listens to a saga that is being told by Thorgrim and slays the teller after the tale is done because an incident in the story has been the slaying, by Thorgrim himself, of Thormod's own foster-brother.[2] Thus, likewise, during the siege of Troy, when Achilles is sulking in his tent, he is there found entertaining himself by singing 'the tales of warriors'[3]—such tales as 'the wrath of Achilles' itself is destined to become in the mouths of Homeric minstrels. Already, in the tenth year after the fall of Troy, the tales of the siege and of the victors' homeward voyages are ever in the mouths of the minstrel Phemius in Ithaca and the minstrel Demodocus in the land of the Phaeacians.[4]

'That lay is praised of men the most which ringeth newest in their ears.'[5] Yet there is one thing in an epic lay that is still more highly prized than its novelty by the hearers, and that is the intrinsic human interest of the story. The interest in the present predominates just so long as the storm and stress of the Heroic Age continues; but this social paroxysm is essentially transitory; and,

finding an artistic expression for the new interest in personalities and events by 'making over' both the form and the matter of the continental fertility-ritual to fit the new demand. Thus, in the Greek and English Epic we find the tale of Troy's fall or Achilles' wrath or Odysseus' wanderings or Beowulf's exploits grafted on to myths in which the stuff of primitive ritual has been reshaped and projected into heroic narrative. The amalgamation of these two elements in the Epic is so thorough, and the artistic perfection of the finished product is so complete, that it needs all the paraphernalia of 'the Higher Criticism' to analyse the process which has taken place. Nevertheless, such analysis reveals not only the presence of these two once separate elements in the Epic but also the extreme diversity of their nature and origin. The Epic, unlike the Saga, has a ritual root, and it shares this root with the Drama. The continental Ionic Drama of Attica and the transmarine Ionic Epic of Ionia are two flowers of art which have sprung from a single religious stem. By contrast, the poetry of the Elder Edda and the prose of the Sagas are two flowers that have sprung from different stems out of roots bedded in different soils. The Elder Edda is a flower which has wilted, before it has been able to unfold itself in its full perfection, because its root has been cut in order to transport it across the sea. The Saga is a flower which has blossomed because it has grown up from new roots in the new ground.

[1] Olrik, op. cit., pp. 177-8.

[2] This illustration is cited at greater length in op. cit., loc. cit., in the passage here omitted in the foregoing quotation.

[3]
τὸν δ' εὗρον φρένα τερπόμενον φόρμιγγι λιγείῃ. . . .
τῇ ὅ γε θυμὸν ἔτερπεν, ἄειδε δ' ἄρα κλέα ἀνδρῶν.

(*Iliad*, IX, ll. 186-9.)

[4] Of the four lays sung by Phemius and Demodocus in the *Odyssey*, no less than three are taken from the Trojan Cycle, while only one is a tale of the Gods. Phemius sings of the homeward voyage of the Achaeans (*Od.* I, ll. 325-7), Demodocus of a quarrel between Odysseus and Achilles (*Od.* VIII, ll. 73-82), and of the Wooden Horse (*Od.* VIII, ll. 499-520).

[5]
τὴν γὰρ ἀοιδὴν μᾶλλον ἐπικλείουσ' ἄνθρωποι
ἥ τις ἀκουόντεσσι νεωτάτη ἀμφιπέληται.

(*Od.* I, ll. 351-2.)

as the storm abates, the lovers of the Epic and the Saga come to feel that life in their time has grown tamer than it was in the time of their heroic predecessors. Therewith, they cease to prefer new lays to old; and the latter-day minstrel or saga-man, responding to his hearers' change of mood, repeats, like Nestor, the tales of the older generation. When the storm abated in Iceland, 'now that the present moment was less eventful and exciting, attention was fixed on the deeds of the past; they were again brought forth and shaped artistically into connected accounts. . . . And only then did the sagas in the proper sense of the term begin to take shape.'[1] When the storm abated in Ionia, the latter-day epic poet still harped upon Phemius's and Demodocus's Trojan theme:

'Tell me, Muse, of a man; a man of many shifts; a man who wandered much when he had sacked Troy's sacred fastness. O, many were the folk whose cities he beheld and knew their thoughts beside; and many were the sorrows that he suffered in his heart; sorrows of the sea, in striving for his life and striving therewithal to bring his comrades homeward.'[2]

Thus the art of the Homeric Epic and the Icelandic Saga continued to live and flourish when the stimulus which had first evoked it was no longer at work. It ultimately attained its literary zenith in the altered circumstances of a later age. The literary history of the English Epic—as exemplified in *Beowulf*—is the same. Nevertheless, these mighty works of art would never have come into being if that original stimulus had not been exerted; and it was produced, as we have seen, by the ordeal of migration across the sea. This explains why the Hellenic Epic developed in transmarine Ionia and not, like the Hellenic Drama, in the European Greek peninsula; the Teutonic Epic on the island of Britain and not on the European Continent;[3] and the Scandinavian Saga on the island of Iceland and not, like the Scandinavian Drama, in Denmark or Sweden. This contrast between the transmarine and the continental artistic phenomena appears with such regularity in such widely different times and places that one of the authorities whom we have cited formulates it as a law. 'Drama . . . develops in the home country, Epic among migrating peoples, whether they migrate to France or England or Germany—or to Ionia, for the analogy with Greek Drama holds good here too.'[4]

---

[1] Olrik, op. cit., p. 179.   [2] *Od.* I, ll. 1–5.

[3] Of the Teutonic peoples who took part in the post-Hellenic Völkerwanderung, the majority migrated overland on the European Continent and only the Angles and the Jutes overseas from the Continent to Britain. Yet, of the extant epic poetry that has sprung from the Teutonic migrations of that age, all the mature and complete specimens are of English make, while the Continental School is represented by a handful of rather rudimentary original fragments and some Latin versions.

[4] Phillpotts, B. S.: *The Elder Edda* (Cambridge 1920, University Press), p. 207.

The other positive creation that emerges from the ordeal of transmarine migration in the course of a Völkerwanderung is not artistic, like the Epic and the Saga, but political. This new kind of polity is a commonwealth in which the binding element is contract and not kinship. We have noted its nature already by anticipation, and examples of it leap to the mind.

The most famous examples, perhaps, are those city-states which were founded by seafaring Greek migrants in the last convulsion of the post-Minoan Völkerwanderung along the west coast of Anatolia, in the districts which subsequently came to be known as Aeolis and Ionia and Doris. The scanty surviving records of Hellenic constitutional history seem to indicate that the principle of political organization by law and locality instead of by custom and kinship asserted itself first in these Greek settlements overseas and was afterwards adopted in the European Greek peninsula by mimesis. In the act of establishing their foothold on the Anatolian coast in the face of opposition from the previous occupants of the country, the Greek seafarers would proceed upon the new principle spontaneously. A number of ship's companies—each hailing from a different district and recruited from members of many different kin-groups—would join forces to conquer a new home for themselves overseas and to secure their common conquest by building a common citadel. In the city-state thus founded, the 'cells' of the new political organization would be, not kindreds held together by the tie of common descent, but 'tribes'[1] representing ship's companies; and these ship's-companies, in taking to the land, would still be held together by the ties which had held them on shipboard. Having co-operated at sea as men do co-operate when they are 'all in the same boat' in the midst of the perils of the deep, they would continue to feel and act in the same way ashore when they had to hold a strip of hardly-won coast against the menace of a hostile hinterland. On shore, as at sea, comradeship would count for more than kin, and the orders of a chosen and trusted leader would override the promptings of habit and custom. In fact, a bevy of ship's-companies joining forces to conquer a new home for themselves overseas in a strange land would turn spontaneously into a city-state articulated into local 'tribes' and governed by an elective magistracy.

There are no corresponding circumstances to account for the evolution of the Hellenic city-state in European Greece; and indeed our scanty records indicate that the Greeks who had stayed at home in Europe came into line politically with the Greeks who had migrated across the sea to Asia by imitating, artificially and

---

[1] The conventional English translation of the Greek word φυλαί.

belatedly, an act which, in the settlement of Aeolis and Ionia and Doris, had been something immediate and spontaneous. On the coast of Anatolia, the city-state was a new creation evoked by the stimulus of transmarine migration. In European Greece it was the second-hand product of a deliberate 'synoecism'—a revolutionary aggregation of village-communities into city-states, which was accompanied or followed by the substitution of locality for kin as the basis of political organization. There is no reason to suppose that any such 'synoecism' would ever have been carried out or even thought of in 'the old country' if the spontaneous generation of the city-state in 'the new country' overseas had not provided the Hellenic Society with a model polity—a model which was commended not only by its own obvious intrinsic merits but also by the prestige of its creators, the Hellenes of Aeolis and Ionia, who were in the forefront of the Hellenic Civilization in this first age of Hellenic history.[1]

When we turn from the post-Minoan Völkerwanderung to the Scandinavian, we can discern the rudiments of a similar political development in certain new Scandinavian communities which arose out of transmarine migrations likewise.[2] If the abortive Scandinavian Civilization had actually come to birth, the part once played in Hellenic history by the city-states of Aeolis and Ionia might have been played in Scandinavian history by the five city-states of the Ostmen along the Irish coast[3] or by the five boroughs which were organized by the Danes to guard the landward border of their conquests in Mercia.[4] Even as it was, the stimulus of transmarine

[1] The artificial character of the process of 'synoecism' in Continental Greece, as a deliberate imitation of an overseas pattern, is indicated by the fact that the four 'Ionic' φυλαί, into which the Athenian body politic was articulated before the Cleisthenic reorganization of 508 B.C., were a selection from a larger number of φυλαί into which we know that the body politic was articulated at Miletus. (See Wilamowitz-Moellendorff, U. von: *Aristoteles und Athen* (Berlin 1893, Weidmann, 2 vols.), vol. ii, pp. 138–42.) On this analogy, we may conjecture that the three 'Doric' φυλαί likewise originated spontaneously in some city-state of the overseas Doris and were reproduced artificially in some of the 'Dorian' city-states of Continental Greece (there is no evidence for their reproduction in Sparta). So much for the overseas origin of the 'Ionic' and 'Doric' φυλαί in the city-states of Continental Greece. We may attribute the same origin to the 'Dorian', 'Ionian', and 'Aeolian' races into which the Greek-speaking World as a whole was conventionally articulated. The Greek transmarine settlements on the Anatolian coast fell into three distinct geographical groups speaking three different dialects of the Greek language. The local names of these groups were Aeolis, Ionia, and Doris; and we may conjecture that the same names were subsequently applied to communities in other parts of the Greek-speaking World on grounds of linguistic affinity or of accidental similarity of name. (See Beloch, K. J.: *Griechische Geschichte*, 2nd edition, vol. i (i) (Strassburg 1912, Trübner), pp. 139–42.)
[2] See Olrik, A.: *Viking Civilisation* (London 1930, Allen and Unwin), pp. 98–9.
[3] These city-states were Dublin, Wexford, Waterford, Cork, and Limerick. (For their history, see Kendrick, T. D.: *A History of the Vikings* (London 1930, Methuen), pp. 277 and 299.)
[4] These five boroughs were Lincoln, Stamford, Leicester, Derby, and Nottingham (see Kendrick, op. cit., p. 236). Compare the four similar boroughs which were established, after the conclusion of the Treaty of Wedmore, at Northampton, Huntingdon, Cambridge, and Bedford, in order to guard the landward borders of Danish East Anglia (Kendrick, op. cit., p. 240).

migration produced several Scandinavian polities that did attain a high degree of development. On the south coast of the Baltic, in Wendland, the short-lived fraternity of the Jomsvikings developed a standard of asceticism, discipline, and prowess which won for Jomsborg, in its day, the same reputation in the Scandinavian World that Sparta had once enjoyed in Hellas.[1] The older Scandinavian settlement of Aldeigjuborg—established by vikings who had crossed the Baltic from west to east and had pushed on up the Gulf of Finland and up the River Neva into Lake Ladoga—made an impression of political efficiency upon the minds of the Northern Slavs which is reflected in the foundation-legend of the Scandinavian empire in Russia. The legend relates that the Slavs who had fallen under the yoke of these intruders from beyond the sea succeeded in driving their new masters out; but that, having once experienced, under duress, the benefits of Scandinavian rule, they found the reversion to their native anarchy so intolerable that they invited the Scandinavians to return and receive their willing obedience. This legendary 'social contract' between a primitive Slavonic population and a Scandinavian ruling class which had acquired its political education in crossing the sea is the traditional explanation of the origin of the Russian State. Yet the creation of Russia was not the greatest political feat that was achieved by Scandinavians who migrated overseas. It was surpassed by the creation of the Republic of Iceland—a Scandinavian polity whose foundation is not veiled in legend but is illuminated by the full light of history. On the apparently unpromising soil of this barren arctic island, which could only be reached from the nearest Scandinavian *point d'appui* in the Faroes by crossing some five hundred miles of open Atlantic, the political as well as the literary genius of the Scandinavian Civilization produced its finest flower.

As for the political consequences of the transmarine migration of the Angles and Jutes to Britain in the course of the post-Hellenic Völkerwanderung, it is perhaps something more than a coincidence that an island which was occupied at the dawn of Western history by immigrants who had shaken off the shackles of the primitive kin-group in crossing the sea should afterwards have been the

---

[1] 'Jomsborg . . . was inhabited by a . . . viking garrison; and legend tells that this society within the fortress was governed by strict rules. There were no women at all allowed inside, and each one of the men was a warrior of tested valour, not older than fifty years of age nor younger than eighteen. Courage, and courage alone, won admission to their company, and in that company a self-sacrificing loyalty to each and all one's fellows was demanded of the Jomsvikings, slander of any kind was prohibited, and the private retention of booty forbidden. Military efficiency was the sole object of their organization and regulations, and though no single man might be away from the fortress for more than three days without special licence, each summer the Jomsvikings were abroad together fighting, and so widespread did their fame become that soon they were counted as the greatest warriors of the North.' (Kendrick, op. cit., pp. 181–2.)

country in which our Western Civilization achieved some of the most important steps in its political progress. The Danish and Norman invaders who followed on the heels of the Angles, and who share the credit for subsequent English political achievements, likewise came over the element that has to be traversed by all who set foot on the shores of an island; and the sea-passage had the same liberating effect upon their social organization as upon that of their seafaring predecessors. A people thus fruitfully diversified in its racial composition, and at the same time uniformly freed from the encumbrance of a hampering primitive institution, offered an unusually favourable field for political cultivation. It is not surprising that our Western Civilization should have succeeded, in England, in creating first 'the King's Peace' and thereafter 'Parliamentary Government', while, on the Continent, our Western political development was retarded by the survival of the kin-group among the descendants of Franks and Lombards who had not been relieved of that social incubus at the outset by a liberating transit of the sea.

Finally, we may observe, in this political connexion, the curious fact that one of the two enduring political entities that have eventually emerged out of the struggle for existence between the ephemeral barbarian 'successor-states' of the Roman Empire in Britain has been the Kingdom of Scotland;[1] and that the founders and eponyms of this Scotland in Britain were an overseas offshoot of those original Scots of Ireland who, in their native island, are a byword for their prolonged failure to create an effective united Irish state—even under the pressure of the most formidable foreign aggression from the Scandinavians and thereafter from the English.[2]

IV. THE STIMULUS OF BLOWS

Having now examined the relative stimulating effects of a less and a more difficult environment in cases in which the environments are physical, we may complete this part of our study by surveying the field of human environments on the same comparative method.

For convenience, we may divide this field into sections. We may distinguish, first, between those human environments that are geographically external to the societies upon which they act, and

---

[1] For the creation of the Kingdom of Scotland, see further II. D (v), pp. 190–2 and 194–5, below.

[2] It is one of the curiosities of history that even in these latter days, when the Irish have to some extent retrieved their political reputation by their success in establishing an Irish Free State, this political achievement in Ireland itself has been forestalled by the success of the Irish emigrants across the Atlantic in playing the game of 'machine politics' in the United States!

those that are geographically intermingled with them. The former category will cover the action of societies, peoples, states, cities, and other social organizations that are in exclusive occupation, at any given time, of particular portions of the habitable world, upon neighbouring social organizations of the same kind. From the standpoint of the organizations which play the passive role in such social intercourse, the human environment with which they are confronted here is 'external' or 'foreign'. The second of our two categories will cover the action of one social 'class' upon another, where the two 'classes' are in joint occupation of the same geographical area, and where the term 'class' is employed in its widest meaning. From the standpoint of a 'class' which plays the passive role, the human environment constituted by the other 'classes' that are acting upon it is 'internal' or 'domestic'. Leaving this 'internal human environment' for later examination, and starting with the 'external human environment', we may begin by making a further subdivision between the impact of the 'external human environment' when it takes the form of a sudden blow and its impact in the form of a continuous pressure.

What is the effect of sudden blows from the external human environment? Does our proposition 'The greater the challenge the greater the stimulus' hold good here? Let us seek light, once more, from our well-tried empirical method of inquiry.

The first test-cases that naturally occur to our minds are certain sensational instances in which a military and militant Power has first been stimulated by successive contests with its neighbours, and has then suddenly been prostrated in an encounter with some adversary against whom it has never measured its strength before. What usually happens when incipient empire-builders are thus dramatically overthrown in mid-career? Do they usually remain lying, like Sisera, where they have fallen, while their half-built empire collapses like a house of cards? Or, on the contrary, do they rise again from their Mother Earth, like the giant Antaeus of the Hellenic Mythology,[1] with their strength and vigour and *moral* redoubled? Do they succumb? Or do they react to an unprecedentedly heavy blow by an unprecedented outburst of purposeful energy? The historic examples indicate that the second and not the former alternative reaction is the normal outcome.

What, for example, was the effect of the *Clades Alliensis* upon the fortunes of Rome? The catastrophe overtook her only five years after her victory in her long and arduous duel with Veii had placed her, at last, in a posture to assert her hegemony over Latium. The overthrow of the Roman Army at the Allia and the occupation of

---

[1] For the myth of Antaeus, see further Part X, below.

Rome herself by barbarians from the back of beyond might have been expected to wipe out, at one stroke, once and for all, the power and prestige which Rome had won, just before, by the overthrow and annexation of her Etruscan neighbour. Instead, Rome recovered from the Gallic disaster so rapidly that, within less than half a century after the Gauls had been ignominiously bought off, the Roman State was able to engage in a longer and more arduous duel with a mightier neighbour than Veii for higher stakes. The Roman State was able to fight the Samnite Confederacy for the prize of a hegemony over all Italy, and eventually to emerge victorious from a fifty-years' war which far surpassed, in scale and severity, any previous war which Rome had ever ventured to wage.[1]

What, again, was the effect on the fortunes of the 'Osmanlis when Timur Lenk took Bāyezīd Yilderim captive on the field of Angora? This catastrophe overtook the 'Osmanlis just when they were on the point of completing their conquest of the main body of Orthodox Christendom in the Balkan Peninsula. The 'Osmanlis had planted their military colonies in Thrace and Macedonia; they had overthrown the latest masters of the interior—the Serbs—on the field of Kosovo; and they were beleaguering the last remnant of the East Roman Empire in Constantinople. At the moment when they were thus on the verge of consolidating the results of fifty years' labours in Europe, they were prostrated, on the Asiatic side of the Straits, by a thunderbolt from Transoxania. A collapse of the Ottoman Empire in the Balkans might have been expected to follow the disaster at Angora—the more so, inasmuch as Timur, being rather more provident if not much more persevering than Brennus, had taken steps to paralyse the Ottoman Power in its Anatolian homeland by liberating and re-establishing the rival Anatolian Turkish principalities. So far from that, however, Mehmed the Conquerer, who succeeded to the Ottoman throne just half a century after his ancestor Bāyezīd had been carried away captive to Samarqand, was able to place the coping-stone on Bāyezīd's building by taking possession of Constantinople and rounding off the Ottoman Empire until, from Trebizond to the gates of Belgrade and from the Crimea to the Morea, it comprised the whole domain of Orthodox Christendom except its transmarine annex in Russia.[2]

In the third place, we may take notice of the fortunes of the Incas after their passage of arms with the Chancas towards the middle of the fourteenth century of the Christian Era. When the Chancas

---

[1] The traditional initial and terminal dates of the first three Romano-Samnite Wars are 343–290 B.C.; the traditional date of the Battle of the Allia is 390 B.C.

[2] Mehmed Fātih *imperabat* A.D. 1451–81; the Battle of Angora had been fought in A.D. 1402.

marched on Cuzco and the reigning Inca Yahuar Huaccac evacuated his capital in a panic, it looked as though the Incas had lost the empire which had been founded a hundred years before when their ancestors had conquered the Collao and Nazca.[1] The battle on the plain of Sacsahuana, in which Prince Hatun Tupac—the future Inca Viracocha—just succeeded in staying the Chancas' onslaught and saving Cuzco from fire and sword, was the hardest battle that the Incas had yet had to fight. Nevertheless, the great work of expanding and elevating the Empire into an Andean universal state was taken up and completed by Viracocha's son and successor the Inca Pachacutec, who came to the throne at Cuzco some fifty years after the Battle of Sacsahuana had been fought.[2]

Other illustrations of the same 'law'—the stronger stimulus of the heavier blow—will meet our eyes if we reopen the book of Roman history at a later page and study the course of those wars between Rome and the rival Great Powers of the Hellenic World which cleared the ground for the eventual conversion of the Roman Empire into a Hellenic universal state. In this phase of Roman and Hellenic history—which began with the outbreak of the first Romano-Punic War in 264 B.C. and ended with the simultaneous destruction of Carthage and annexation of Macedonia in the year 146—Rome had to fight three rounds with Carthage and four with Macedonia before she was able to deliver two 'knock-out blows' which brought the titanic struggle to a close. No doubt, the poet Virgil had these two series of wars in mind when he bade his countrymen ever remember 'to battle down the stiff-necked': *debellare superbos*.[3] Yet the historical facts surely indicate that the method of attrition was not a masterly choice but a costly and dangerous necessity; for, though the Romans managed to beat the Carthaginians and the Macedonians in every war that they fought with either Power, nevertheless, at each successive renewal of the combat, the prowess displayed by the vanquished and the exertions required of the victors were both conspicuously greater than they had been each time before.

The defeat of Carthage in the first Romano-Punic War stimu-lated Hamilcar Barca to conquer for his country an empire in Spain which far surpassed her lost empire in Sicily, and Hamilcar's son Hannibal to strike at the heart of the Roman Power in Italy. Even after the Hannibalic War had ended in the defeat of Hannibal's

---

[1] For the foundation of the Inca Empire, see I. C (i) (b), vol. i, pp. 121–2, above.
[2] The elevation of the Empire of the Incas into an Andean universal state may be said to have been accomplished through the incorporation of the states along the seaboard of the Pacific, from Ica to Chimu inclusive, which covered, between them, the original home of the Andean Society. The Inca Pachacutec, who achieved this, *imperabat circa* A.D. 1400–48; the Battle of Sacsahuana had been fought *circa* A.D. 1347.
[3] *Aeneid*, Book VI, l. 853.

last army at Zama, in the home territory of Carthage, the Carthaginians twice astonished the World during the half century that was still to run before their name was blotted out of the Book of Life. Under the stimulus of this appalling situation, when they lay at the mercy of an implacable enemy, with their impending doom ever present to their minds, they displayed an energy and a fortitude which had not distinguished them in the days of their power and their security. They showed their mettle first in the rapidity with which they paid off their war indemnity to Rome and recovered their commercial prosperity;[1] and they showed it again in the heroism with which the whole population of the doomed city—men, women, and children—fought and died in the last struggle, when the Romans were avowedly bent upon destroying them utterly, and when it was certain that nothing now could save them from their fate.

Again, King Philip V of Macedon had been content during the Hannibalic War, when he might have saved his country by joining forces with Hannibal himself in Italy, to engage in desultory and ineffective 'side-shows' on his own side of the Adriatic. It was the blow of Cynoscephalae, which cost him his hegemony in Greece, that stimulated him to show that 'his last sun had not yet set'[2] and to transform Macedonia into so formidable a power that, a quarter of a century after Cynoscephalae had been fought, Philip's son Perseus was able to challenge Rome single-handed and almost to defeat her utmost efforts to overcome him. Even when Perseus' stubborn resistance was finally broken at Pydna, the Macedonian people were so far from losing their spirit that, some twenty years later, it only needed the appearance of an adventurer impersonating Perseus' son Philip to make the nation rise in arms again in a last struggle for liberty which was a forlorn hope from the start.

In our own Western history, similar reactions were evoked by Napoleon I's premature and abortive attempt, during the General War of 1792–1815, to establish a Western universal state in the form of a French Empire.[3]

For example, the Austrians, who in 1792 had scarcely lifted a finger to support their Prussian allies in an invasion of France

---

[1] As early as 191 B.C., only ten years after the restoration of peace, the Carthaginians offered to pay off the whole outstanding amount of the indemnity forthwith in a single lump sum, in anticipation of the stipulated succession of instalments. This offer was not accepted by the Romans. (Livy, Book XXXVI, ch. 4.)

[2] See the account given by Livy (Book XXXIX, ch. 26) of an interview in the year 185 B.C. (the eleventh year after Cynoscephalae) between Philip and a Roman commissioner. After stating his case, Philip 'elatus deinde ira adiecit nondum omnium dierum solem occidisse'. The Macedonian king's outburst was a reminiscence of a line of Theocritus: Ἤδη γὰρ φράσδηι πάνθ' ἅλιον ἄμμι δεδυκεῖν; (Theocritus: Thyrsis, l. 102).

[3] This aspect of the Napoleonic Empire is examined further in V. C (i) (d) 6 (γ), Annex I, vol. v, pp. 619–42, below.

which might have nipped the Revolution in the bud, and had allowed themselves thereafter to be ejected by the French twice over from Italy, were aroused at last by the blow of 1805, when in a single campaign Napoleon captured half the Austrian Army at Ulm and occupied Vienna and destroyed the rest of the Austrian Army at Austerlitz. Austria after Austerlitz prepared for a renewal of the contest with the same grim energy that Macedonia had displayed after Cynoscephalae; and in 1809, when she tried conclusions with the conqueror again, and this time single-handed, without an ally, she made him pay as much more dearly for a second victory as Macedonia made the Romans pay in 171–168 B.C. If Austerlitz was Austria's Cynoscephalae, Wagram was her Pydna. Moreover, the Austrians, like the Macedonians, still had the spirit, after suffering two signal defeats, to take up arms once again; and, more fortunate than the Macedonians, they marched this time to victory. The intervention of Austria on the side of Russia and Prussia in 1813 was the decisive act which made the overthrow of Napoleon inevitable and brought his ephemeral empire to the ground.

Again, the Prussians played the same ineffective part in 1805 as the Macedonians played during the Hannibalic War, and they paid the penalty by meeting their Cynoscephalae at Jena; but the effects of Jena upon Prussia were dynamic. The remnant of the Prussian Army which had marched out so ingloriously in the autumn to an ignominious defeat had the hardihood to fight a winter campaign and to exact a Pyrrhic victory from Napoleon at Eylau and after that to go on fighting still, in the farthest corner of Prussian territory beyond the Memel. In the year after Jena, the Prussians only accepted the French conqueror's terms because they were virtually coerced into surrender by their own Russian allies; and the severity of the terms only added to the stimulus which the shock of Jena had first administered. The energy evoked in Prussia by this stimulus was extraordinary. It not only regenerated the Prussian Army (and this through the instrumentality of the very restrictions which Napoleon had imposed upon the Prussian Army in order to reduce it to impotence); it regenerated, into the bargain, the Prussian Administrative Service and the Prussian Education System. In fact, this new-found energy transformed the Prussian State into a chosen vessel for holding the new wine of German Nationalism; and simultaneously it performed the miracle of conjuring this strong German wine out of a watery cosmopolitanism. The first-fruits of this titanic Prussian response to the challenge of Jena were the acts of faith which decided the issue of the Befreiungskrieg; the final harvest was gathered in by Bismarck in that calculated combination of diplomacy and war which produced its intended result in the establishment of a new polity: Prussia-Germany.

As for the role of the Russians in the General War of 1792–1815, it is notorious that they fought indifferently so long as they were fighting the French on foreign ground. In 1812 the national energies of the Russian people were evoked, in successively higher degrees, as the French invaders crossed the political frontier and as they passed, at Smolensk, out of the insensitive fringe of alien territories, recently incorporated in the Russian Empire, into the quick of Holy Russia. At last, in the burning of Moscow, Russia found herself; and then she turned upon her invader in a counter-attack that did not come to a standstill until the tide of war had ebbed back right across the Continent from Moscow to Paris.

When we turn to the next chapter of Western history, in which the roles of France and Germany are reversed, exactly the same phenomena present themselves *mutatis mutandis*. In 1870, when the French, in their turn, played the vainglorious and ignominious role of the Prussians in 1806, the Prussian General Staff, who this time had calculated and provided for everything down to the last button, were half-surprised at the ease with which they were able to invade France and destroy the French armies in the field and lay siege to Paris.[1] On the other hand, in 1914 the Prussian General Staff of the day, who were obsessed by the memory of what had happened forty-four years before, were astonished at what happened this time when they repeated the invasion of France with apparently greater odds in their favour than their predecessors had been able to count upon in 1870. In 1914 the Germans encountered a French resistance for which the campaign of 1870 offered no precedent; and their under-estimate of French *moral* in 1914 was one of several psychological miscalculations which, cumulatively, were responsible in large measure for Germany's final defeat in the War of 1914–18. The Germans fell into this particular error of judgement because they neglected to take into account the momentous effect of the stimulus which their own fathers had administered to France in dealing her the blow of 1870. This stimulus had revealed itself already, before the War of 1870 was over, in the contrast between the *débâcles* at Sedan and

[1] It was the glamour of Napoleon I's victories that blinded the French to realities in 1870, just as, in 1806, the Prussians had been blinded to realities by the glamour of the victories of Frederick the Great. Among neutral spectators, the expectation of a French victory in 1870 was widespread when war broke out. The writer of this Study possesses a map, published at that moment by *The Illustrated London News*, in which the section covered by the German Rhineland is printed in red in order to pick it out on the assumption that it is destined to be the war-zone. The French Army itself is said to have been supplied with maps of Germany but not with maps of France.

Metz and the stubborn resistance of the people of Paris in a siege from which they had no hope of being delivered. The same stimulus revealed itself again at a later date and in a sublimated form in the Affaire Dreyfus, when a moral issue stirred millions of French hearts to the depths. For those who had eyes to see, it was evident that this was the turning-point at which the shock of defeat, still working in French souls, had translated itself into the stirrings of regeneration; and so, to properly instructed observers, the extreme difference between the successive French reactions to successive German invasions in 1870 and in 1914 did not come altogether as a surprise.

The tenacity of the French resistance during the War of 1914–18—a tenacity which was symbolized by the defence of Verdun—was one of the principal factors in the victory of the Allied and Associated Powers. Perhaps the most impressive feature in the behaviour of the French during those war-years was the fortitude with which they endured the devastation of some of the wealthiest and most valuable parts of their national territory; and the sequel is still more remarkable. A sympathetic and admiring witness of French national heroism during this war might have imagined, at the time, that he was witnessing the death of a nation on the field of honour. 'France', he might have prophesied, 'may possibly emerge victorious, but her victory will certainly be the death of her. This long-drawn-out devastation of the war-zone must have inflicted a mortal wound upon the French national economy. These terrible casualties must have doomed the population of France to an irretrievable decline. A magnificent euthanasia! Yet death is still death of the body, even when it has been robbed of its spiritual sting.' Such prophets never dreamed that the ghastly wound which was being inflicted on France would actually rejuvenate her. Yet so it has turned out. In the reconstruction of the devastated areas, the whole material apparatus of life has had to be renewed. The debris of the old equipment has naturally been replaced by new equipment of the latest pattern; and, as the work of renovation has proceeded, the French have come to congratulate themselves on the accident—which they lamented so bitterly while the devastation was taking place—that the war-zone happened to include the majority of their industrial districts. Whether the cost of reconstruction actually has been, or ever will be, defrayed by German Reparations payments is a secondary question. In the fifteenth year after the Armistice, it is already evident that it has profited France handsomely to have had her hand forced by devastation, even if the consequent reconstruction has had to be carried out almost entirely at French expense. In this compulsory renovation of her industrial plant, France has been compelled to make an inestimably valuable capital investment. Moreover, her gain is not to be measured in crude terms of iron and steel and bricks and mortar. A new apparatus involves a new technique; and a new technique involves a new spirit. It is no paradox to say that, in the reconstruction of the devastated areas, France herself has renewed her youth.[1]

As for Germany, the miracle which a military devastation has accomplished in one fashion for victorious France has been accomplished in another fashion for the defeated rival of France by a financial inflation. It is already evident that the blows which have been rained upon Germany since the Armistice of 1918 are having the same stimulating effect as the blows inflicted on Prussia a century ago in 1806–7.[2] In fact, the unfriendly service which the Germans did to the French before the Armistice has been done by the French to the Germans during these post-war years; so that an observer who perceived only the outward actions and their effects, without being aware of the motives behind them or the temper informing them, might almost imagine that France and Germany were two flagellants who had gone into a partnership in asceticism under a mutual vow to wield the lash for one another in turn.

'These are they which came out of great tribulation';[3] and certainly, in the autumn of 1931, when the first draft of this chapter was written, both France and Germany seemed to be less far from salvation than Great Britain: the one Great Power in Europe which had succeeded for more than seventeen years after the outbreak of the Great War in turning the blows of Fortune aside and avoiding both the two calamities of invasion and inflation. An Englishman, communing with his own soul in the autumn of the year 1931 after the collapse of the Pound Sterling on the 21st September, might well ask himself whether this British *tour de force* had not really been a perverse evasion of 'things that accompany salvation'[4]—a perversity whereby Great Britain had simply condemned herself to 'work out' her 'own salvation' belatedly 'with

[1] In the autumn of 1931, some thirteen years after the Armistice, on the morrow of the fall of the Pound Sterling from the Gold Standard, France momentarily found herself in a position in the World which, even at the time of the Peace Conference, it had seemed inconceivable that she should ever occupy again. At that moment, she possessed and exercised an effective military supremacy and political hegemony on the European Continent; she was predominant over the whole of Europe in the air; she was second only to the United States in her holding of gold; and she was in a conspicuously better economic position than any other great country in the World in virtue of her relative immunity, for the time being, from the incidence of the world-wide economic depression. It was as if, when Zeus hurled the thunder-bolt which was to annihilate Semele, his defenceless victim had been transfigured, at the stroke, into Athene radiant in her shining armour.

[2] This passage was written in the summer of 1931, and it still holds good—with a vengeance—at the moment of revision on the 23rd March, 1935.

[3] Revelation vii. 14.   [4] Hebrews vi. 9.

fear and trembling',[1] instead of having salvation thrust upon her betimes. 'For whosoever will save his life shall lose it.'[2]

The classic example of the stimulating effect of a blow is the reaction of Hellas in general, and Athens in particular, to the onslaught of the Achaemenian Power—the Syriac universal state— in 480–479 B.C.

'The vastness of the forces employed in the expedition of Xerxes King of Persia against Hellas cast the shadow of a terrible danger over the Hellenic Society. The stakes for which the Hellenes were called upon to fight were slavery or freedom, while the fact that the Hellenic communities in Asia had already been enslaved created a presumption in every mind that the communities in Hellas itself would experience the same fate. When, however, the war resulted, contrary to expectation, in its amazing issue, the inhabitants of Hellas found themselves not only relieved from the dangers which had threatened them but possessed, in addition, of honour and glory, while every Hellenic community was filled with such affluence that the whole World was astonished at the completeness with which the situation had been reversed.

'During the half century that followed this epoch, Hellas made vast strides in prosperity. During this period, the effects of the new affluence showed themselves in the progress of the arts; and artists as great as any recorded in history, including the sculptor Pheidias, flourished at the time. There was an equally signal advance in the intellectual field, in which philosophy and public-speaking were singled out for special honour throughout the Hellenic World and particularly at Athens. In philosophy there was the school of Socrates, Plato, and Aristotle; in public-speaking there were such figures as Pericles, Isocrates and Isocrates' pupils; and these were balanced by men of action with great military reputations like Miltiades, Themistocles, Aristides, Cimon, Myronides and a long array of other names too numerous to mention.

'In the forefront of all, Athens achieved such triumphs of glory and prowess that her name won almost world-wide renown. She increased her ascendancy to such a point that, with her own resources, unsupported by the Lacedaemonians and Peloponnesians, she broke the resistance of powerful Persian forces on land and sea and so humbled the pride of the famous Persian Empire that she compelled it to liberate by treaty all the Hellenic communities in Asia.'[3]

The pre-eminence of Athenian vitality in this outburst of Hellenic life which followed the repulse of Xerxes' onslaught is comparable with the rejuvenation of France after the War of 1914–18; for Athens on that occasion, like France on this, bore the brunt of the stimulating blow. While the fertile fields of Boeotia were saved from devastation by the treachery of their owners to the Hellenic cause, and the fertile fields of Lacedaemon by the presence and the

---

[1] Philippians ii. 12. [2] Matthew xvi. 25.
[3] Diodorus of Agyrium: *A Library of Universal History*, Book XII, chs. 1–2[1].

prowess of the Athenian fleet at Salamis, the poor land of Attica
was devastated systematically by the invaders in two successive
seasons. Indeed, Attica suffered more in 480–479 B.C. than France
in A.D. 1914–18; for the Germans only succeeded in occupying a
fraction, albeit an especially valuable fraction, of the French
national territory, whereas the Persians occupied and devastated
the whole of Attica, including Athens itself and the Acropolis and
the temple of Athene, on the summit of the rock, which was the
Attic holy of holies. The whole population of Attica—men,
women, and children—had to evacuate the country and cross the
sea to the Peloponnese as refugees; and it was in this situation that
the Athenian fleet fought and won the Battle of Salamis, within
sight of the victors' abandoned fields and ruined homes and altars.
It is no wonder that a blow which aroused this indomitable spirit
in the Athenian people should have been the prelude to achievements which are perhaps unique in the history of Mankind for
their brilliance and multitude and variety. In the material reconstruction of Attica, the new equipment of the farmsteads surpassed
the old as conspicuously as the new equipment of the French
factories has surpassed the plant destroyed by German shell-fire.
Half a century later, this new apparatus of agriculture in Attica was
still so far superior to anything that was to be found in other parts
of Hellas that when Athens—betrayed into folly by excess of good
fortune—at last conjured up against herself an overwhelming
counter-coalition of other Powers, the Boeotian contingent in the
Allied and Associated Armies found it worth while to carry off the
woodwork of the Attic farm-buildings bodily across the mountains.[1] Yet, in the reconstruction of Attica, this imposing re-
equipment of the farmsteads was nothing accounted of. The work
which was regarded as truly symbolic of the country's glorious
resurrection was the rebuilding of the temples; and in this work
Periclean Athens displayed a vitality far superior to that of post-war
France. When the French recovered the battered shell of Rheims
Cathedral, they performed a pious restoration of each shattered
stone and splintered statue. When the Athenians found the Heka-

---

[1] This fact is recorded in the fragment of a history of Hellenic affairs, of unknown
authorship, which has come to light on the Oxyrhynchus Papyrus. The relevant passage
runs as follows:

'Thebes had enjoyed a great increase in general prosperity as an immediate result of
the outbreak of the Atheno-Peloponnesian War . . . she prospered still more after the
joint Thebano-Lacedaemonian occupation of Decelea. While the occupation lasted,
the Thebans bought up cheap the slaves and other prize of war; and the fact that they
were the Athenians' next-door neighbours enabled them to transport to the Thebaid
all the capital equipment of Attica, including the very timber and tiling of the buildings.
At that time the Attic countryside was more lavishly equipped than any other in Hellas.
It had suffered very little in the previous Lacedaemonian invasions, and an immense
amount of skill and labour had been invested in it by the Athenians. . . .' (*Hellenica
Oxyrhynchia* (Oxford 1909, University Press), xii. 3–4.)

tompedon burnt down to the foundations, they let the foundations lie and proceeded, on a new site, to create the Parthenon.

As for Sparta, she had to wait for the stimulus which she had been spared—or denied—by Destiny in 480–479 B.C. until it was accorded to her some fifteen years later by an act of God. It was the great earthquake of 464 B.C.—a catastrophe which laid the City of Sparta in ruins and raised all the Helots of Laconia in revolt against their stricken masters—that put the Spartans on their mettle again and nerved them first to check the expansion of the Athenian Empire and later to put an end to its existence. As for Thebes, she did not completely recover from the demoralization of her 'Medism' in 480 B.C., nor wholly efface its stigma, until almost a century later when, in the year 382, the Gods at last had mercy on her and inspired the Spartans to seize by fraud and hold by force the Theban citadel, the Cadmea. Under the stimulus of this heaven-sent blow, Thebes achieved, for a season, the miracle of adding a cubit to her stature. The liberation of the Cadmea in 378 B.C. was followed by the victory of Leuctra in 371 and the invasion of Laconia in 370. Thebes had not only fulfilled her ancient ambition of establishing an undisputed authority over the other city-states of Boeotia; she had actually defeated the invincible Spartans and raided their inviolable territory and wrested from them the hegemony of the Hellenic World.

In this series of examples from the military and political histories of sovereign states, the stimulus of blows is manifest. Yet if these examples warrant the inference that 'the heavier the blow the stronger the stimulus' is a genuine social law, we must beware of making the further inference that Militarism in itself is a source of creative energy; for the historic examples of our present law are not confined to the battle-field,[1] and there are other mediums besides those of war and politics in which these stimulating blows are dealt and received.

The classic example, which we have reserved until the end of this chapter, is presented on the field of religion in the Acts of the Apostles. These dynamic acts, which were to win the whole Hellenic World for Christianity as they worked themselves out in the fullness of time, were conceived at the moment when the Apostles were looking steadfastly toward Heaven as their Lord went

[1] One of the notorious deeds of Militarism in recent Western history—the burning of the city of Atlanta, Georgia, by General Sherman in A.D. 1864—has stimulated the stricken city to raise herself to an eminence in the arts of peace which she had never attained in her *ante-bellum* infancy. Sherman challenged Atlanta to show her destroyer that she was not a Persepolis but a phoenix; and he taught her the way by opening her eyes to the indestructible importance of her geographical position as a railway junction. On the morrow of her disaster, Atlanta took for her civic motto the Latin word *Resurgens*, and turned her strategic position to commercial account by making herself into a distributing centre for the whole of the south-eastern United States.

up out of their sight.[1] At the moment, it was a crushing blow for them to lose again the personal presence of a Master who had so lately returned to them from the dead. Yet the very heaviness of the blow evoked, in their souls, a proportionately powerful psychological reaction which is conveyed mythologically in the message of the two men in white apparel[2] and in the descent of the Pentecostal tongues of fire.[3] In the power of the Holy Ghost, they preached the divinity of the crucified and vanished Jesus not only to the Jewish populace but to the Sanhedrin ;[4] and, within three centuries, the Roman Government itself capitulated to the Church which the Apostles had founded at a moment of extreme spiritual prostration.

V. THE STIMULUS OF PRESSURES

'Marches' and 'Interiors'

So much for the stimulus of the human environment when its impact takes the form of a sudden external blow. We have next to examine the cases in which the impact takes the different form of a continuous external pressure.

In terms of political geography, the peoples, states, or cities which are exposed to such pressure fall, for the most part, within the general category of 'marches'; and the best way to study the effects of this particular kind of pressure empirically is to make some survey of the parts played by marches, in the histories of the societies or communities to which they belong, in comparison with the parts played by other territories that belong respectively to the same societies or communities but are situated geographically in their 'interiors'.[5]

In the Egyptiac World

In the history of the Egyptiac Civilization, for example, we have noticed already, in another connexion,[6] that, on no less than three momentous occasions, the course of Egyptiac history was directed by Powers originating in the south of Upper Egypt. The foundation of the United Kingdom circa 3200 B.C., the foundation of the universal state circa 2070/2060 B.C., and the restoration of the universal state circa 1580 B.C., were all accomplished by Powers that originated within this narrowly circumscribed district. We may observe now, apropos of our present inquiry, that this district is

---

[1] Acts i. 9–10.   [2] Acts i. 10–11.   [3] Acts ii. 1–4.   [4] Acts ii–v.

[5] In IV. C (iii) (c) 3 (α), vol. iv, pp. 501–4, below, we shall have occasion to recur to this survey of the parts played by marches, apropos of the pathological phenomenon of an excessive concentration of energy upon certain particular activities which are the responses to particular challenges. An example of this phenomenon which is conspicuous in the histories of marches is the social malady called Militarism.

[6] See I. C (ii), vol. i, p. 140, footnote 2, above, following Meyer, E.: Geschichte des Altertums, vol. ii (i), 2nd edition, pp. 60–1.

coincident with the Southern March of the Egyptiac World which was exposed to pressure from the barbarians of Nubia. And if we look further into Egyptiac history from our present angle of vision, we shall find other marches playing equivalent parts in reaction to pressures from barbarians or from alien civilizations which impinged upon the Egyptiac World from other quarters. In particular, a pressure from North-Western Africa or from South-Western Asia was apt to call into existence, in the Egyptiac World, a paramount Power with its seat in the corresponding marches on this or that fringe of the Delta.[1]

The polarization of political power at the two extremities of the Egyptiac domain was an early as well as a persistent phenomenon of Egyptiac history. A consolidation of the twenty or thirty once independent local states of the Lower Nile Valley[2] into two empires with the Northern and the Southern March as their respective nuclei was the prelude to the foundation of the United Kingdom; and after this dualism had been converted into unity through the triumph of the Southern over the Northern Power, the memory of it was still kept alive in the symbolism of the Double Crown, until at last, after the passage of some two thousand years, the Northern March succeeded in capturing in its turn, and thenceforth retaining, the primacy. In the thirteenth century B.C., new pressures from the Hittite Power on the Asiatic mainland and from the post-Minoan Völkerwanderung in the Levant caused the sceptre to pass from Thebes, the historic metropolis of the Southern March, to the City of Ramses: the new frontier-fortress on the eastern fringe of the Delta which now guarded this exposed extremity of the Egyptiac World as Thebes had guarded the frontier over against Nubia.[3] Thereafter, during the sixteen centuries of twilight which elapsed between the decline of 'the New Empire' and the ultimate extinction of the Egyptiac Society in the fifth century of the Christian Era, political power reverted to the Delta as persistently as it had been apt to revert to the Southern March during the preceding two thousand years. After being governed in the thirteenth and twelfth centuries B.C. from Deltaic Ramses, the Egyptiac

---

[1] e.g. at the City of Ramses and at Tanis and at Bubastis on the eastern fringe of the Delta; at Sais on the western fringe (see below).

[2] The historical 'nomes', i.e. provinces, as they were called after their 'mediatization'.

[3] For this transfer of the capital from Thebes to the City of Ramses, see Meyer, E.: *Geschichte des Altertums*, vol. ii (i), 2nd edition, pp. 453–4, 487–8, and 494–5. The City of Ramses was the first Deltaic capital of an oecumenical Egyptiac State with the exception of Avaris; and Avaris is the exception which proves the rule; for Avaris was the capital of the Hyksos; and the Hyksos were alien interlopers in the Egyptiac World who never felt themselves at home there. For this reason, the Hyksos did not attempt to establish themselves in the interior, but remained encamped at Avaris, on the edge of their Egyptian dominions, in order to keep open their line of retreat to their original settlements in Syria. Thus Avaris, under the Hyksos régime, was not really the capital of an Egyptiac State but rather the head-quarters of an alien military occupation.

World was governed in the eleventh century from Deltaic Tanis and in the tenth and ninth centuries from Deltaic Bubastis; and the classic instance of Deltaic paramountcy is the rise of the Twenty-Sixth Dynasty, which originated in the Delta in response to the challenge of the Assyrian occupation in the seventh century B.C. and came, after supplanting the intruders, to rule all Egypt, as far south as Elephantine, from Sais. The Saite Power, thus founded, endured until it failed to respond to another challenge from Asia in failing to save Egypt from political incorporation into the Achaemenian Empire. The subsequent successive attempts—some abortive and others temporarily successful—to throw off the Achaemenian yoke all emanated from the Delta likewise. During these centuries when the Delta was politically in the ascendant, the Thebaid was politically in eclipse. The position of post-Imperial Thebes in the latter-day Egyptiac World resembled that of post-Imperial Rome during the post-Hellenic interregnum and the early age of Western Christendom. The *ci-devant* Imperial City was perfunctorily compensated and consoled for the loss of its political power by the enjoyment of an ecclesiastical primacy which was a legacy from its previous greatness and a tribute to its enduring prestige.[1]

Can we discern why it was that, in the competition for political paramountcy between the Thebaid and the Delta, the Thebaid had the upper hand from the foundation of the United Kingdom until the decline of 'the New Empire', while the Delta had the upper hand thereafter? This permanent change in the balance of power is to be explained by certain permanent changes in the incidence of external pressure upon the Egyptiac World. From the fourteenth and thirteenth centuries B.C. onwards, the pressures from North-Western Africa and from South-Western Asia decidedly outweighed the pressures from other quarters; and accordingly, during these latter days, the stimulus derived from external pressure was felt in greatest measure by the Northern Marches in the Delta. Concurrently, the pressure from the Upper Nile Valley relaxed; and the classic Southern March, in the section of the valley immediately below the First Cataract, was relegated to the interior of the Egyptiac World by an extension of the Egyptiac domain ıp-river.

The classic Southern March was only a march so long as the First Cataract marked a sharp line of cultural division between the Egyptiac Civilization and a Nubian barbarism; and this condition

[1] See Meyer, E.: *Gottesstaat, Militärherrschaft und Ständewesen in Aegypten* = Berichten Berl. Akad. 1928, pp. 495 seqq.; eundem: *Geschichte des Altertums*, vol. ii (ii), 2nd edition (Stuttgart and Berlin 1931, Cotta), pp. 6–60.

did not prevail either in the evening or at the dawn of Egyptiac history. In the so-called pre-dynastic age, there had been no substantial difference in culture between the sections of the Nile Valley below the First Cataract and above it. The differentiation of a dynamic civilization in Egypt from a static primitive culture in Nubia declared itself on the eve of the foundation of the United Kingdom; and the stimulus of barbarian pressure upon the Egyptiac frontiersmen at the new dividing line perhaps accounts for the foundation of the United Kingdom by a dynasty whose seat was at Al Kāb. The new difference in cultural level between Egypt and Nubia was accentuated during the régime of the Egyptiac United Kingdom, as the Egyptiac Civilization soared to its zenith; and this cultural gulf remained fixed during the subsequent 'Time of Troubles'—when Nubia appears to have been occupied by Afrasian Nomads from the North-West—and also during the régime of the Egyptiac universal state, which was founded and maintained by the Theban emperors of the Eleventh and Twelfth Dynasties. Though Nubia was annexed to the Egyptiac universal state politically, its incorporation into the Egyptiac World remained superficial, like the incorporation of the southern seaboard of China into the Sinic World under the Han.[1] The Egyptiac Civilization was still exotic in Nubia; and such local interaction between the two cultures as took place in that age resulted in the barbarizing of the Egyptian garrison and not in the civilizing of the Nubian proletariat. On the other hand, Nubia was not only politically annexed but was also culturally assimilated by the restored Egyptiac universal state—'the New Empire'—and after the organization of the new dominion by Thothmes I (*imperabat circa* 1557–1505 B.C.) the southern boundary of the Egyptiac World stood near the foot of the Fourth Cataract, at the new frontier-fortress of Napata, instead of standing at the head of the First Cataract at the old frontier-fortress of Elephantine. In thus definitively incorporating Nubia into the Egyptiac World, the Theban emperors of the Eighteenth Dynasty cut the roots of their own country's greatness. They transferred from the Thebaid to Napata the military burden, and with it the political stimulus, of serving as the Southern March; and on the one occasion, during the last sixteen centuries of Egyptiac history, on which the now prevalent political paramountcy of the Northern Marches was contested by the South, the Southern Power which aspired to oecumenical authority had its roots in the new Southern March of Napata and not in the *ci-devant* Southern March of the Thebaid.

When the break-up of 'the New Empire' into successor-states,

[1] See pp. 83–4, above.

under the rule of local princelings descended from Libyan mercenaries, was followed by a re-polarization of political power at the
two extremities of the Egyptiac World, the two poles in the new
tension were not both coincident with those at which power had
been concentrated on the eve of the foundation of the United
Kingdom, some two thousand five hundred years earlier. In the
post-Imperial age, the capital of the Northern Power was duly
planted in the Delta, this time at Bubastis, by the Libyan princes of
Heracleopolis; while these latter-day Libyan Heracleopolites' Napatan kinsmen[1] and contemporaries, who established the Southern
Power, retained their capital at Napata, which was now the Southern
point of pressure and stimulus, and did not transfer it either to the
Thebaid or to any other point in the interior. In the fullness of
time, this Napatan Power attempted to emulate the thrice-repeated
feat of the Thebaid: the political unification of the whole Egyptiac
World under a single sovereignty. The new Southern March,
however, now failed to accomplish what the old Southern March
had achieved thrice over. The Napatan attempt to gain oecumenical power, which was initiated by Kashta when he annexed the
Thebaid *circa* 750 B.C. and was almost carried to completion by
Piankhi when he made his expedition down-Nile into the Delta *circa*
725, was frustrated first by the alien Assyrian invaders and finally
by the indigenous Deltaic Power of the Saites, who began as the
Assyrians' creatures and ended as their local residuary legatees. *Circa*
661–655 B.C., the frontier between the Saite and the Napatan Power
came to rest at Elephantine; and thereafter this obsolete boundary
between an Egyptiac Civilization and a Nubian barbarism acquired
a new function as the internal line of demarcation between the two
political units into which the enlarged Egyptiac World was thenceforth permanently divided.

Thus, in the post-Imperial age, the old Northern and the new
Southern March both failed to attain oecumenical power in the end;
and the resultant political dualism persisted during the remainder
of Egyptiac history. Yet though Napata fell short, in achievement,
of Al Kāb and Thebes, she was not altogether unresponsive to the
stimulus of external pressure to which, as the latter-day Southern
March of the Egyptiac World, she had come to be exposed in her
turn. The former frontier-fortress of 'the New Empire' on the
Upper Nile became the capital of a 'successor-state' which embraced
half, albeit the more backward half, of the latter-day expanded
Egyptiac World; and, unlike the Saites and their successors in the

---

[1] Reisner's view that these princes of Napata were Libyans is not accepted by Eduard
Meyer, who suggests that they were descended from Hrihor, the High Priest of Amon
who established the Theban theocracy *circa* 1075 B.C. (*Geschichte des Altertums*, vol. ii (ii),
2nd edition, p. 52).

Delta, the Napatans did not succumb to alien conquerors. During the long centuries when Egypt north of Elephantine was successively subject to the Achaemenids and the Ptolemies and the Romans, Ethiopia south of Elephantine remained an independent Egyptiac Power. Indeed, during these centuries the domain of the Egyptiac Culture was extended still farther up-river under this Ethiopian régime, until Napata herself, who had started her career as a frontier-fortress, was relegated to the interior as Thebes had been before her. Thereafter, *circa* 300 B.C., Napata was supplanted, as the capital of the Ethiopian state, by Meroe at the foot of the Sixth Cataract, midway between the junctions of the Atbara and the Blue Nile with the main river; and this Meroitic Power lived on, as a politically independent embodiment of the Egyptiac Society, until the third century of the Christian Era, when the Egyptiac Culture suffered a violent death in Ethiopia at the hands of barbarian invaders, some two centuries before it died peacefully in its sleep in Egypt itself.

Thus the political history of the Egyptiac World, from beginning to end, may be read as a tension between two poles of political power which, in every age, were located respectively in the Southern and in the Northern March of the day. One or other of these marches was the cradle of every successful or abortive oecumenical dynasty. On the other hand, there are no examples of oecumenical dynasties which originated at points in the interior of the Egyptiac World. The political creations of the interior were seldom more than parochial; and even when oecumenical dynasties whose roots lay in one of the marches—in the Delta or in the Thebaid—transferred their capitals to places in Middle Egypt for administrative convenience, political power was apt to ebb back to the marches as soon as times once more became critical. For instance, after the foundation of the United Kingdom, the capital was transferred from Al Kāb, in the Southern March, which had been the original seat of the founders, to Memphis on the border-line between the two lands of the Double Crown; yet the new task of founding the Egyptiac universal state after a time of troubles was accomplished by a dynasty from Thebes. Again, after the foundation of the universal state, the capital was transferred once more, this time from Thebes to a new central site just above Memphis;[1] yet the new task of restoring the universal state after the intrusion of the Hyksos was accomplished by a dynasty from Thebes, who thus asserted her political potency for the second

---

[1] This new central site, to which the capital was transferred by Amenemhat I from Thebes, was called Iz-Taui, which meant 'Conqueror of both Lands' (Meyer, E.: *Geschichte des Altertums*, vol. i (ii), 3rd edition, p. 267).

time. Finally, after the restoration of the universal state, the capital was transferred from Thebes by Ikhnaton to his new imperial city at Tell-el-Amarna, mid-way between Thebes and Memphis; yet this transfer was as ephemeral as the religious and artistic innovations with which it was bound up.[1] Upon the death of the imperial revolutionary, the capital reverted to Thebes and remained there until the Thebaid paid the inevitable penalty for having ceased to be a march by forfeiting, once for all, its ancient and long-enduring political paramountcy. Even then, the political heritage of the Thebaid did not fall to any district in the interior, but was divided, as we have seen, between the old Northern March in the Delta and the new Southern March of Nubian Napata.

In the Sinic World

The part played in the classical period of Egyptiac history by the Thebaid—the march which relieved the interior of the Egyptiac World from the pressure of the barbarians of Nubia—was played in Sinic history by the valleys of the Wei-ho and the Fen-ho, which were the marches of the Sinic World against the barbarian highlanders of Shensi and Shansi. The Chóu Dynasty, which founded the Sinic equivalent of the Egyptiac United Kingdom towards the close of the second millennium B.C., and the Ts'in Dynasty, which founded the Sinic universal state in the year 221 B.C., both originated in the Wei Valley, while the Fen Valley was the seat of the Tsin Dynasty, which was the rival of the Ts'in during the first phase of the Sinic Time of Troubles. In Sinic, as in Egyptiac, history, there was a tendency for Powers which originated in the marches and afterwards attained an oecumenical dominion to transfer their capitals from the periphery to the interior. The site in the Sinic World which corresponded to the Egyptiac Memphis was Loyang (the modern Honan-fu). It lay on the borderline between the western valleys and the eastern plain,[2] traversed by the Yellow River in its lower course, which was the geographical heart of the Sinic World.[3] The capital of the Chóu was transferred to the neighbourhood of Loyang from the Wei Valley after the dynasty

---

[1] For a discussion of Ikhnaton's role in Egyptiac history, see I. C (ii), vol. i, pp. 145–6, above.

[2] The exact location of Loyang was in the valley of the Lo-ho, a minor right-bank tributary of the Yellow River which debouches into the main stream just below the Yellow River's exit from the gorges that intervene between its Lower Basin in the eastern plain and its Upper Basin in the highlands where it receives the waters of the Wei and the Fen.

[3] The title of 'Middle Kingdom' (Chung Kuo), which was eventually taken over by the Sinic universal state as an alternative to 'All that is under Heaven' (T'ien-hia), appears to have been borne before that by the remnant of the Chóu Empire, in the middle of the eastern plain, on the borderline between the modern provinces of Honan and Shantung. (See Cordier, H.: Histoire Générale de la Chine (Paris 1920–1, Geuthner, 4 vols.), vol. i, p. 214.)

had fallen into decadence; and in a later age the capital of the
Sinic universal state, which had been located originally at Ch'ang
Ngan in the Wei Valley under the Prior Han, was transferred likewise to Loyang when the Posterior Han gave the Sinic universal
state a second lease of life. It is the more significant that, notwithstanding this repeated attraction of the capital of the Sinic
World from the periphery into the interior, the two Powers which
made Sinic history both originated in the Western March. The
only Power that is credited with an original seat in the eastern plain
is the semi-legendary Yin or Shang Dynasty, which was tradi-
tionally supposed to have been paramount before the Chóu united
the eastern plain with the Western March under their own sceptre.

In the Far Eastern World

When we turn to the history of the Far Eastern Civilization
which is 'affiliated' to the Sinic Civilization, we find that the
oscillation between a western capital and an eastern capital, which
had been characteristic of the political history of the 'apparented'
civilization, is reproduced, with a difference, in a new oscillation
between a southern capital and a northern.

In the Sinic World, there had been a tendency for oecumenical
Powers to originate in the Western March, under stimulus from
the pressure of the surrounding barbarian highlanders, and to
transfer their capitals to sites in the interior on the eastern plain.
In the Far Eastern World, the heaviest external pressure came
from a different source and a different quarter. The barbarian
highlanders of Shensi and Shansi had been subdued and assimilated
by the growing Powers of Ts'in and Tsin before the close of the
Sinic Time of Troubles; but this elimination of the barbarians of
the western highlands had merely removed a buffer which had
previously intervened between the Sinic World and the far more
formidable Nomadic peoples of the Eurasian Steppe; and the
simultaneous expansion of the two Sinic principalities of Chao and
Yen, at the northern end of the eastern plain, doubled the length of
the new front between the Sinic World and Eurasia. This front
now extended from the north-western coast of the Gulf of Liaotung
to the north-eastern escarpment of the Tibetan Plateau. The lines
of defence against Nomad inroads, which had been thrown up
piecemeal by the contending states of the Sinic World, with such
energies as they could spare from the last round in their own internecine struggle, were consolidated, after the 'knock-out blow' had
been delivered and the Sinic universal state founded by Ts'in She
Hwang-ti, into the Great Wall of China.[1] It was across the line of

[1] See Cordier, op. cit., vol. i, pp. 206–7.

the Wall, from north to south, that, some five centuries later, during the interregnum (*circa* A.D. 175–475) which followed the break-up of the Sinic universal state, the Eurasian Nomads came in, as barbarian invaders, in the post-Sinic Völkerwanderung; and the pressure from the north did not cease when the new Far Eastern Civilization emerged. Hence, in the Far Eastern World, there was a tendency, from the beginning, for oecumenical Powers either to originate in the Northern Marches or to transfer their capitals to the Northern Marches if they had originated in the southern interior.

For instance, the Power which evoked, in the Far Eastern World, a ghost of the Sinic universal state[1] in the first age of Far Eastern history, originated, like the Sinic universal state itself, in the Wei Valley; and in the new orientation of political geography the Wei Valley constituted the western section of those Northern Marches in which the pressure from the Eurasian Nomads was now making itself felt. It was here that the Sui Dynasty, which re-enacted the part of Ts'in She Hwang-ti by uniting the whole of Society under a single rule, established a new oecumenical capital at Si Ngan (the modern Sian-fu) in the neighbourhood of the ancient Ch'ang Ngan.[2] Si Ngan, under the Sui, drew to itself the power that had previously resided in Nanking, the capital of the South,[3] which the Sui had annexed to their dominions; and when the T'ang Dynasty reaped the fruits of the Sui Dynasty's labours, as their prototypes the Han had once entered into the heritage of Ts'in She Hwang-ti, the T'ang kept the seat of oecumenical power at Si Ngan, where they had found it.

Si Ngan, however, did not retain its primacy in perpetuity; for the incidence of the pressure from the Eurasian Nomads tended, in the course of Far Eastern history, to shift from the western sector of the Northern Marches to the east, and the seat of political power in the Far Eastern World shifted eastwards correspondingly. This shift was approximately contemporaneous with the momentary breakdown of the Far Eastern Oecumenical Power during the interval between the extinction of the T'ang Dynasty in A.D. 907 and the foundation of the Sung Dynasty in A.D. 960.

During the Sung Age, Far Eastern history consisted, for the main body of the Far Eastern Society on the Continent,[4] in a slow and

---

[1] See further the comparative study, in Part X, below, of the likenesses and differences between the evocation of the ghost of the Sinic universal state in the Far Eastern World and the evocation of ghosts of the Hellenic universal state in the Orthodox Christian and Western worlds.

[2] For Ch'ang Ngan, the capital of the Sinic universal state under the Prior Han, see p. 119, above.   [3] See p. 122, footnote 1, below.

[4] The different course taken by the history of the offshoot of the Far Eastern Society overseas, in Japan, is examined below in the present section, on pp. 158–9, as well as in IV. C (ii) (*b*) 2, vol. iv, pp. 93–4.

stubborn retreat of the Far Eastern Oecumenical Power from north to South under an ever increasing pressure from a succession of Nomad Powers operating from Manchuria. The Khitan had extorted the cession of sixteen districts along the northern border *circa* A.D. 927–37, before the oecumenical authority of the Sung had been established; the Khitans' successors, the Kin, conquered from the Sung, *circa* A.D. 1125–42, the whole of Northern China down to the watershed between the Yellow River and the Yangtse; and, when the Kin had been supplanted in their turn by the Mongols, the Mongol Great Khan Qubilay (*imperabat* A.D. 1259–94) completed the work of his Kin and Khitan predecessors by extinguishing the Sung altogether and reuniting the whole of the main body of the Far Eastern World under a barbarian dominion. The tide of barbarian conquest, however, had no sooner engulfed the last remnant of the Far Eastern Society on the mainland than it began to recede; and the point of interest, for our present purpose, lies in the sequel which followed the eviction of the Mongols from China in A.D. 1368[1] by a new thoroughbred Chinese Power: the Ming.

This new thoroughbred Chinese dynasty arose in the same quarter in which their last thoroughbred predecessors, the Sung, had held out longest, that is to say in the South; and the founder of the Ming, Hung Wu, signalized the expulsion of the barbarians from China and the restoration of a genuine Chinese régime by a solemn transfer of the capital.

When the Kin had conquered Northern China, they had established their capital on the site of the modern Peking ('the Northern Capital'), on the borderline between the barbarian portion of their dominions to the north of the Great Wall and the Chinese portion to the south of it.[2] The same site commended itself, for the same geographical reason, to Qubilay;[3] and in his reign Peking became the capital not merely of a reunited China but of a universal state which extended from the Pacific coasts of Asia right across the continent as far as the Persian Gulf and the Euphrates and the Carpathians and the Baltic and thus embraced the whole circumference of the Eurasian Steppe. This Kin and Mongol capital was naturally obnoxious to the Chinese as a reminder of the barbarian

---

[1] The insurrection against the Mongols which ended in their eviction began about the year 1351.

[2] Compare the location of the Hyksos' capital, Tanis, on the borderline between the non-Egyptiac portion of their dominions in Syria and the Egyptiac portion in the Lower Nile Valley. (See p. 113, footnote 3, above.)

[3] Qubilay began to recondition Peking in A.D. 1264 and transferred his capital thither in 1267 from Qaraqorum, which was his ancestral capital in the Basin of the Orkhon, in the heart of Eurasia. At the same time he kept a footing on the Steppe by building himself a subsidiary residence, within easy reach of Peking, at Chung-Tu (Coleridge's Xanadu) just outside the Great Wall.
'In Xanadu did Kubla Khan
A stately pleasure-dome decree. . . .

yoke which they had borne so long and had only just succeeded in throwing off. Accordingly, Hung Wu had no sooner driven the Nomads out again into their native steppes and re-established the frontier of a liberated China along the line of the Great Wall, than he transferred the capital from Qubilay's city to Nanking, which had been the 'Capital of the South' at the dawn of Far Eastern history.[1] Hung Wu laid out his new city at Nanking on a scale commensurate with the size of the greater empire of which it was designed to be the capital henceforward. Yet neither historical sentiment nor cultural *amour propre* nor administrative convenience nor a lavish outlay on public buildings availed to retain the capital of the Ming Empire on this site in the interior. For though the Nomads had been expelled from China for the moment by Hung Wu's prowess, he could not exorcize the danger of their possible return. On the morrow of their expulsion, as they began to recover from their momentary prostration and to rally their forces like Satan and his angels in the exordium of *Paradise Lost*, their pressure became perceptible once more at the point where it had been making itself felt for the past five centuries—that is, in the eastern sector of the Northern March—and, once again, the point which was bearing the brunt of the political pressure drew to itself the primacy in political power. In A.D. 1421, Hung Wu's son and second successor, Yung Lo (*regnabat* A.D. 1403–25), retransferred the capital of China from his own father's chosen city of Nanking to the very city of Peking which had first been raised to honour by the hereditary barbarian enemy.

Yung Lo's reversion from 'the Southern Capital' in the interior to 'the Northern Capital' in the Marches was justified by the event. Indeed, the renewed pressure from the north became so strong that, though the retransference of the capital to the danger-point postponed the day of fresh disaster for China, it could not for ever avert it. In A.D. 1619–44, rather more than two centuries after Yung Lo's statesmanlike move, the Great Wall was broken through and Peking captured and all China overrun by a new Power from the north-eastern no-man's-land in the shape of the Manchus;[2] and

[1] Nanking had been continuously the capital of the South, under five successive dynasties, from A.D. 317 (the date which saw the end of the ephemeral restoration of the Sinic universal state under the so-called 'United Tsin') down to A.D. 589 (the date which saw the evocation of a ghost of the Sinic universal state by the Sui). In A.D. 589 the Sui annexed the South to their own Northern dominions and thereby united the whole Far Eastern World of the day under a single rule. (See p. 120, above.)

[2] Unlike the Mongols, the Manchus were not stock-breeding Nomads but primitive hunters who were at home, not on the Eurasian Steppe, but in the highlands—clad in virgin forest—which bound, on the east, the easternmost enclave of the Eurasian Steppe in the common basin of the Rivers Liao and Sungari. The particular Manchu community which conquered China in the seventeenth century of the Christian Era came from the section of this highland-forest country that lies between Kirin and the Pacific coast. These Manchu conquerors of China, being still on the primitive level at

in the eighteenth century of the Christian Era the Manchu sovereign Ch'ien Lung ruled from Peking[1] an empire—uniting all China and half Eurasia under a common dominion—which could bear comparison with the empire that had once been ruled from Peking by the Mongol Great Khan Qubilay himself. From A.D. 1421 down to A.D. 1928, Peking remained the capital of China through all vicissitudes. The attempt of the T'aip'ing insurgents, in the middle of the nineteenth century,[2] to bring back the capital to Nanking collapsed with the failure of their endeavour, of which it was a part, to deal with the Manchus as the Ming had dealt with the Mongols. In 1928, however, the Emperor Yung Lo's historic act was reversed, at last, by President Chiang Kai-shek; and at the time of writing Nanking is the capital of the Chinese Republic, while Peking has been degraded to the rank of a provincial centre under the belittling title of Peping.

Is this change likely to be permanent? And, if it is, will it militate against the validity of our social 'law' that marches are apt to be stimulated, by the external pressure to which they are exposed, into developing a political power which gives them a predominance over the interior? In the writer's belief, the recent transfer of the Chinese capital from Peking to Nanking is likely to be perpetuated, and this just because, so far from invalidating our 'law', it actually illustrates and confirms it.

How are we to account for the success of the Kuomintang in retransferring the capital of China from Peking to Nanking some three-quarters of a century after the T'aip'ing's failure in their attempt to do this very thing? The explanation is to be found in certain far-reaching transformations of China's human environment which have taken place during the interval.

In 'the eighteen-fifties' of the Christian Era, the quarter from which China was subject to the heaviest external pressure was still the north, as it had been since the beginning of Far Eastern history. At that moment, China was under the rule of a dynasty of north-barbarian origin whose founder had forced his entry by breaking through the Great Wall, in its eastern sector, from north to south;

the time of the conquest, were much more readily assimilated to the Far Eastern culture, and absorbed into the Far Eastern body social, than their Mongol predecessors, who had entered China as full-fledged Eurasian Nomads with a tincture of the abortive Far Eastern Christian culture of the Nestorian Diasporà (see II. D (vi), pp. 237–8, below). For the primitive culture of the Manchus, see Lattimore, Owen: *Manchuria Cradle of Conflict* (New York 1932, Macmillan), pp. 44–5. It will be seen that the Manchu conquest of China differed from the Mongol conquest both in nature and in outcome, and bore a greater resemblance to the Chichimec conquest of Mexico.

[1] The Manchu rulers of China followed Qubilay's example by supplementing their capital at Peking, on Chinese soil, with a secondary residence—a glorified hunting lodge and summer retreat—outside the Great Wall. This Manchu counterpart of Qubilay's 'Xanadu' was Jehol in Eastern Inner Mongolia.

[2] The T'aip'ing insurrection lasted from A.D. 1850 to A.D. 1864.

and, according to our 'law', it was to be expected that the capital of China would remain in the zone of pressure—that is to say, at Peking, in the eastern sector of the Northern Marches—so long as this state of affairs continued. By 1928, however, a historic situation which had still been intact in 'the eighteen-fifties' had become entirely obsolete; and the Chinese Political Revolution of 1911, which overthrew the Manchu Dynasty and put an end to the Manchu ascendancy in China Proper, was by no means the most revolutionary event in this radical change. The Manchu Dynasty and the Manchu Bannermen who had transferred their residence from Manchuria to China at the time of the conquest had been converted to Chinese culture many generations before they were put down from their seat by Chinese Nationalism.[1] The really moment-ous change in the situation since the failure of the T'aip'ing has been not political but economic, and has consisted in a counter-offensive of the Chinese cultivator against the Nomad herdsman.[2] This Chinese colonization of the steppe country, which was well under way before 1911, has been facilitated by the lapse of the Manchu régime's migration-restrictions and has been stimulated by the subsequent ravages of civil war and banditry and famine and flood in the heart of China itself: a fourfold scourge which has been driving the Chinese peasantry of Shantung and Honan and Chihli to emigrate in their hundreds of thousands to the empty and unharassed virgin lands of Manchuria and Inner Mongolia. Thus, to-day, the Great Wall no longer marks the boundary between Chinese peasant and barbarian Nomad. The line across which the Nomad invader has trespassed so many times during the last two thousand years has been left far behind in the Chinese peasant's peaceful but potent counter-offensive, until now a broad zone of the steppe-land which the Mongol herdsman used to range has

[1] Indeed, it would hardly be an exaggeration to say that the Manchu Dynasty and Nobility, at any rate, had been Sinified before they crossed the Great Wall in A.D. 1619. For their previous extra-mural dominions had included not only their own original homeland in the forest-clad highlands east of Kirin but also the relatively well-watered portion of the lowlands in the Liao River basin which had been brought under the plough by Chinese peasant-colonists and had been shielded from Nomad incursions by the construction of the Willow Palisade: a north-eastern prolongation of the Great Wall which takes off from the Wall just above Shanhaikwan and runs down the eastern escarpment of the Central Asian Plateau and then across the South Manchurian plains until it strikes the left bank of the Upper Sungari after traversing the foot-hills of the eastern mountains between Changchun and Kirin. By the time when the Manchus descended from their highlands, these well-watered and colonized and cultivated and protected lowlands had become a Chinese country; and it was at Mukden, in this Chinese milieu, that the Manchus held their court before they crossed the Wall and moved to Peking. This residence at Mukden Sinified the Manchu princes as effectively as the Scottish kings were Anglicized by transferring their residence from the Highlands to Edinburgh, and the Achaemenidae Babylonicized by transferring theirs from Persis to Susa. Half the Bannermen who conquered intra-mural China for the Manchu Dynasty were not Manchus at all, but South-Manchurian Chinese; and the so-called Manchu conquest of China was, in effect, a Chinese civil war. (See Lattimore, op. cit., pp. 45–71.)   [2] For this, see further Part III. A, vol. iii, pp. 16–22, below.

been brought under the Chinese plough. Under the counter-attack of these ever advancing furrows, the Mongols have almost evacuated their former pasturelands south of the Gobi Desert, while the Manchus have become almost extinct in 'the Three Eastern Provinces' of the Chinese Republic which are still popularly known as Manchuria. In other words, the environs of Peking have ceased to be a march and have become assimilated to the interior for the first time in Far Eastern history; and it is in accordance with our law that in these new circumstances Peking itself should forfeit its long-maintained status of being the capital of China.[1]

But has Nanking undergone any converse change of circumstances which entitles it to re-acquire the status which Peking has now lost? If our law is to be vindicated completely, we must be able to demonstrate that, concurrently, the environs of Nanking have ceased to be part of the interior, as they have been hitherto since the beginning of Far Eastern history, and have become a march; and, as soon as we state the problem in these terms, we perceive that, in this quarter, there has in fact been a transformation of China's human environment which is not less far-reaching than the change in the north. While, along the northern land-frontiers of China, the old pressure from the Nomads of the Eurasian Steppe has gradually been reduced to vanishing point and has latterly given place to a counter-pressure upon the Nomads from the Chinese, China has been exposed contemporaneously to a new pressure, of steadily increasing intensity, along her eastern frontage, where she faces the sea. In earlier ages of Far Eastern history, the coast-line of China was the quarter on which the pressure upon her was least severe. Save for the desultory visits of Arab and Persian Muslim merchant-ships in the T'ang period and the desultory raids of Japanese pirates in the Ming period, the sea remained, from the Chinese standpoint, 'a perfect and absolute blank', until, some four centuries ago, it became the vehicle of the impact of our Western Civilization upon the Far East.

This impact of a human force from the opposite side of the globe was feeble at first; and it is less than a century ago that it began to acquire its present formidable momentum. At the date, for instance, when the T'aip'ing made their unsuccessful attempt to retransfer the capital of China to Nanking, the Western international settlement of Shanghai was still in its puny infancy: an unregarded bunch of 'godowns' planted on a mud-bank up a backwater of the Yangtse estuary. To-day Shanghai is not only the greatest of the treaty-ports that stud the coast of China from Canton at one end

[1] Compare the eclipse of Thebes after it had been relegated to the interior of the Egyptiac World through the incorporation of Nubia (see the present chapter, pp. 114–18, above).

to Tientsin at the other. She is also one of the greatest ports and greatest cities in the World, and, to all appearance, she commands a future that will quite eclipse her imposing present. In other words, as China's northern landward marches have fallen into atrophy with the cessation of pressure from the Nomads, a new eastern maritime march has been brought into existence by a new pressure from overseas which is being exerted upon China by the Westerners. This new maritime march has taken the place of the old landward march as the quarter from which the incidence of external pressure upon China is heaviest; and the sector in which it is now heaviest of all is the central sector containing Shanghai. Shanghai is the point of the spear which the West is thrusting into China's side; and accordingly, in the political geography of China, as it has come to be re-orientated during the last three-quarters of a century, the province of Kiangsu, in which Shanghai is embedded, has succeeded to the historic position of the province of Chihli, which used to lie athwart the war-paths of Nomad invaders from Mongolia and Manchuria.[1]

Now Nanking occupies in Kiangsu a position corresponding to

[1] The reader of this passage may demur to this implied relegation of Manchuria to a secondary role; for he can point out that Manchuria has never ceased to be a zone in which external pressure is being brought to bear upon China and that, since the 18th–19th September, 1931, the pressure upon China from this quarter has become so intense that it has come to be regarded as a matter of world-wide concern. This is quite true; but it should also be observed that, since the last decade of the nineteenth century of the Christian Era, the pressure which has been exerted upon China through Manchuria has not been the pressure either of Mongol Nomadism or of Manchu Barbarism. In these latter days, the pressure through Manchuria has been exerted by Russia and Japan; and it has been exerted by these two Powers as a consequence of the process of Westernization which each of them has previously undergone. In fact, Russia and Japan in Manchuria are acting as representatives of the West; and, in virtue of this, 'the importance of Manchuria as a channel conducting towards China the aggression of the West is at least as great' at the present day 'as its importance in bringing the expansive powers of China to bear on the frontier'. (Lattimore, op. cit., p. 259.) Under the shadow of the Sino-Russian conflict in Manchuria in 1929 and the more formidable Sino-Japanese conflict in Manchuria which came to a head in 1931, an observer might be inclined to judge that, while the personality of the aggressor in Manchuria has changed—the Japanese and the Russian having replaced the Mongol and the Manchu—Manchuria itself has not forfeited its historic role as the quarter from which the heaviest external pressure upon China is exerted. Yet on closer inspection it will be found that, in spite of superficial appearances, the Manchurian frontier, as a zone of entry for the Western impact upon China, is really secondary to the maritime frontier round the estuary of the Yangtse. This truth is borne out by the history of the Sino-Japanese conflict which broke out in Manchuria in 1931; for the conflagration which had first flared up at Mukden spread to Shanghai forthwith.

'There could have been no more conclusi⸱ ⸱ demonstration than this of the truth that the centre of gravity of China had indeed effectively shifted from the Province of Chihli and the Basin of the Peiho River and the port of Tientsin and the former political capital at Peking to the Province of Kiangsu and the basin of the Yangtse River and the port of Shanghai and the new political capital at Nanking. In effect, the new centre of energy with which Western enterprise had endowed—or encumbered—China at Shanghai had become so potent that, by the years 1931–2, it was virtually impossible for anything of major importance to happen to China at large without Shanghai becoming the principal scene of action. In this phase of Chinese history, Shanghai was a dominant magnetic point; and the magnetic power of this Western-made focus of modern Chinese economic life proved stronger than Japanese military dispositions.' (Toynbee, A. J.: Survey of International Affairs 1931 (London 1932, Milford), p. 461.)

In A.D. 1950 there was no ground for jumping to the conclusion that Shanghai's role was played out.

that of Peking in Chihli. Peking commands the Mongolian war-path down the Nankow defile and the Manchurian war-path through the passage of Shan-hai-kwan, where the Great Wall descends from the mountains to the sea. Similarly, Nanking commands the path by which Western men-o'-war penetrate into the heart of China up the waterway of the Yangtse. A Chinese Government established at Nanking can defend China against the most formidable of the external pressures to which she is subject to-day at the point where the pressure is the most intense; and, in keeping the intruder under surveillance and holding him in check from this post of vantage, the rulers of China can learn his arts as well. *Fas est et ab hoste doceri*;[1] and Nanking is only one short night's railway-journey distant from Shanghai: the den—and school—of thieves which Western enterprise has planted at China's eastern door.

'Military defeat from the seaward side, in spite of the history of the nineteenth century, is still novel and terrifying to the consciousness of the [Chinese] people at large. There is no buffer territory between the sea and the heart of China; there are no non-Chinese "reservoir" tribes to graduate the shock; and the tradition of the sea-going population itself is one of exploiting, not of being exploited. The impact of Western nations, the alien standards of the West, treaties dictated by the West, have always aroused a reaction of terror and hate far greater than any defeat in the vague buffer territories of the North. There is no under-lying tradition to prescribe a method of dealing with aggression from over the sea. The methods applied in the eighteenth and nineteenth centuries were, generally speaking, coloured by the traditions applying to the northern land-frontier barbarians. They did not work well; in fact, they tended to bring on disasters. Hence a feeling, which has now penetrated very deep, that the Western nations are incalculable, that they are always likely to spring a fresh surprise, something quite outside of experience and the "rules of the game".'[2]

It was in order to learn the outlandish rules of the new Western game of war and diplomacy and trade and industry and finance that the capital of China was transferred from Peking to Nanking in A.D. 1928. It will be seen that this transfer is a perfect illustration of our law that the external pressure of the human environment upon a march administers a stimulus which gives the march pre-dominance over the interior.

In the Hindu World

If we turn next from Far Eastern history to Hindu, we shall recognize certain corresponding phenomena. We shall notice, for instance, that in India, as in China, to-day the march which is

[1] Ovid, *Metamorphoses*, Book IV, l. 428.
[2] Lattimore, Owen: *Manchuria Cradle of Conflict* (New York 1932, Macmillan), pp. 297–8.

subject to the heaviest pressure is the seaboard, and that the pressure from overseas is being applied by the same Western force. In Bombay, 'the Gate of India', we shall identify the Indian analogue of Shanghai; and we shall observe that just as the vital elements of the Far Eastern Society in China have been concentrating themselves latterly in the immediate hinterland of Shanghai, so the vital elements of the Hindu Society in India seem to be concentrating themselves now in the immediate hinterland of Bombay. It is the Bombay Presidency, from Poona to Ahmadabad, that is producing the foremost politicians and industrialists and saints and thinkers in India in our generation.

We shall notice, again, that, in India as in China, this concentration of pressure and stimulus and response in the maritime march is of recent date; and indeed in India it is still far from being complete. If we pass, for instance, from the intellectual and economic indices of social vitality to the military, and inquire into the comparative contributions of the various subdivisions of contemporary India to the Indian Army, we shall find that nearly 58 per cent. of the personnel is supplied by the Panjab and by the adjoining North-West Frontier Province, and that, on this criterion, the Bombay Presidency is altogether outmatched by the Panjab in vitality, even though it holds its own in the military field, as in the civil, against all other provinces of British India.[1] Moreover, the capital of the Indian Empire, though it was transferred to a new site in A.D. 1912, as the capital of the Chinese Republic was transferred in 1928, has not been transplanted to the Bombay Presidency. It has been located at Delhi; and Delhi, though not appreciably nearer than the previous capital, Calcutta, to Bombay, is on the fringe of the Panjab. In fact, the special enclave containing the new imperial capital has been carved out of territory which previously belonged to the Panjab as delimited in British Indian administrative geography.

[1] In the year 1930, the total combatant strength of the British Indian Regular Army was 158,200. Of these troops, 91,600 had been recruited from the Panjab and the North-West Frontier Province; some 35,500 from the Himalayan Highlands (Garhwal, Kumaon, Nepal); some 31,100 from the rest of India, including the Bombay Presidency; and 7,000 from the Bombay Presidency itself. (See the *Report of the Indian Statutory Commission* = British Parliamentary Paper Cmd. 3568 of 1930 (London 1930, H.M. Stationery Office), vol. i, pp. 96–8. In the figures extracted from this source in the present footnote, the 16,500 troops recruited from the United Provinces have been credited to the Himalayan Highlands on the assumption that the majority of them came from the highland districts of Garhwal and Kumaon.) The above figures include recruitments outside as well as inside the limits of territory under British administration or control. In the year 1930, about one-seventh of the Indian Regular Army was recruited from territories beyond the limits of British administration or control: partly among the highlanders of the North-West Frontier in districts which were not under effective British rule though they were on the Indian side of the Indo-Afghan Frontier; and partly (to the strength of 19,000) among the highlanders of Nepal: an independent state hanging on the southern flanks of the Himalayas. For the tendency of civilizations, when they find themselves confronting barbarians along stationary artificial frontiers, to recruit their frontier defence-forces from among the trans-frontier barbarians themselves, see V. C (i) (d) 6 (α), vol. v, pp. 459–80, as well as Part VIII, below.

Why has the capital of India moved to Delhi and not to the hinterland of Bombay? And why do the Panjab and the North-West Frontier Province supply, between them, more recruits than all the rest of India together to the Indian Army?

The answer to the second question is, of course, that, in the Panjab and in the North-West Frontier Province, in contrast to the Maritime March and the interior alike, Indian vitality has been stimulated to express itself in military prowess by exposure to external military pressure. This pressure is being applied nowadays by the warlike highlanders who still preserve their independence *de facto* on the extreme edge of the Iranian Plateau, where its south-eastern escarpment descends upon the north-western flank of the Indus Valley. The proximity of these barbarian hill-men has the same stimulating effect upon the frontiersmen of the Hindu World, along the banks of 'the Five Rivers', that the proximity of similar barbarians in the highlands of Shensi and Shansi once had upon the frontiersmen of the Sinic World in the valleys of the Wei and the Fen.[1] And the parallel goes further. On the northern marches of China, the highland zone once occupied by barbarian hill-men eventually became, as we have observed,[2] a passage through which China was invaded by the more formidable Nomadic peoples from the Eurasian Steppe in the hinterland. Similarly, on the north-western marches of India, the pressure which is being exerted by the local highlanders at the present day was formerly far surpassed in severity by a pressure from the Nomads of the Eurasian Steppe, who found a passage into India across the highlands of Afghanistan, as their counterparts found a passage into China across the highlands of Shensi and Shansi and Jehol.

In Hindu history, as in Far Eastern, it is this pressure from Eurasian Nomads across an inland frontier that has been the heaviest external pressure until recently, and this ever since the time when Hindu history began. The Nomads' pressure was felt in full force during the interregnum, following the disintegration of the 'apparented' Indic Civilization, out of which the Hindu Civilization originally emerged. In the post-Indic Völkerwanderung after the break-up of the Gupta Empire—the Indic Power that had resumed and fulfilled the social functions of an Indic universal state[3]—India was invaded, across this north-west frontier, by the

---

[1] See the present section, pp. 118–19, above, and compare the relations between the Chinese frontiersmen and the Manchu barbarian hill-men in Manchuria, on the eve of their joint conquest of intra-mural China. (See p. 124, footnote 1, above.)

[2] See p. 119, above.

[3] For the role of the Gupta Empire in Indic history, as a resumption of the Indic universal state which had been first embodied in the Maurya Empire and had then been interrupted prematurely by a Hellenic intrusion upon the Indic World, see I. C (i) (b), vol. i, pp. 85–6, above.

Nomad Gurjaras and Huns. The invaders swamped the Indus Valley, made themselves at home in the Indian Desert beyond it, and swept on through Rājputāna into the Deccan.[1] The historic issue was whether these barbarians should or should not forestall the emergence of a new civilization, 'affiliated' to the defunct Indic Civilization, by engulfing the Ganges Valley as well; and this question was decided in the negative because, along the line of the River Jumna, a stand against their onslaughts was made with success. In the historical geography of the Hindu World, the cross-section of the great plain of Hindustan which contains the course of the Jumna, from the southern foot-hills of the Himalayas to the northern foot-hills of the Central Indian highlands, has had the same strategic importance as the passes from Manchuria and Mongolia into the Chinese province of Chihli in the historical geography of the Far East. Here was the gap through which the Nomad invaders must pass if they were to penetrate farther; and here was the point where they met with serious resistance. To this neighbourhood, accordingly, the capital of India has gravitated hitherto throughout the history of the Hindu Civilization.

Already, during the post-Indic interregnum, when Harsha (*imperabat* A.D. 606-47) momentarily restored the Indic universal state, he fixed his capital in this new north-western march at Sthanesvara, covering the approach from the Panjab to the Jumna, and not at Pataliputra in Magadha—the natural administrative centre of the Ganges Basin, at the junction of the Ganges with the Jumna and with two other tributaries, which had been the capital of both the Guptas and the Mauryas. Again, some two centuries later, when the new Hindu Civilization, which had emerged in the meanwhile, was threatened in its infancy by pressure from the Arabs, who had reached the delta of the Indus from the sea and were pushing their way inland up-river,[2] the Arabs' advance was arrested by the rise of a Hindu Power, the Prātihāra Rājputs, who ruled from Gujerat to the Jumna-Ganges Duab and fixed their capital in the Duab, on the west bank of the Ganges, at Kanauj.[3]

---

[1] In Vincent Smith's opinion, the Chalukyas, who founded a principality in the Deccan *circa* A.D. 550, were probably Gurjara invaders from Rājputāna. (Smith, Vincent: *The Early History of India*, 3rd edition (Oxford 1914, Clarendon Press), p. 424.)

[2] For the province of the Arab Caliphate in the Indus Valley, see I. C (i) (*b*), vol. i, pp. 105-6, above.

[3] The Prātihāras were Gurjara converts to Hinduism who defended the society of their adoption against the aggression of the Syriac universal state (now resumed, after the Hellenic intrusion, in the Arab Caliphate), just as, on the opposite edge of the Syriac World, another nascent society—in this case, Western Christendom—was defended against the same Arab aggressors by the Frankish converts to Christianity. The Eurasian Nomad origin of the Prātihāras is attested by their military technique. They were horse-archers and camel-men, not elephant-riders. (See Vaidya, C. V.: *The History of Mediaeval India* (Poona 1924, Oriental Book Supplying Agency), vol. ii, p. 105.) The Prātihāras made themselves masters of the Jumna-Ganges Duab definitively *circa* A.D. 810-16. It is remarkable that they fixed their capital at Kanauj, in this

Both Kanauj and Sthanesvara, however, were to be eclipsed by a later foundation in the same region. Delhi was built on the west bank of the Jumna, on a site intermediate between the sites of the two earlier capitals, in A.D. 993-4[1] by Hindu hands; but Delhi, like Peking, was first raised to honour by rulers who were alien intruders.

At this very juncture, the Nomads of the Eurasian Steppe broke their bounds again and began to make their way into India by the old route across the north-west frontier; but this time they appeared in a new guise. The Hun and Gurjara invaders of the post-Indic Völkerwanderung (*circa* A.D. 475-775) had come in as undifferentiated barbarians who were not immune from conversion to Hinduism. Their Turkish kinsmen who took the same road two centuries later arrived in India as converts to Islam—the Syriac universal church—and as apostles of a new Iranic Civilization to which the expiring Syriac Civilization was 'apparented'. By force of arms these latter-day Turkish invaders carried their alien religion and culture into the Ganges Valley, where their Gurjara predecessors had not secured a footing until after they had become Hindus. The Turks broke through the Jumna March, and conquered the Ganges Valley down to the coast of Bengal, in A.D. 1191-1204; they conquered the Deccan in A.D. 1294-1309; and eventually a great Turkish statesman, Akbar the Timurid (*imperabat* A.D. 1556-1605), reunited the Hindu World under an alien rule, as the Mongol Qubilay reunited the main body of the Far Eastern World,[2] by bringing together its motley fragments—Hindu and Muslim principalities alike—into an all-embracing empire which performed the functions of a Hindu universal state. For the Eurasian invaders of India, Delhi was the natural site for a capital—situated, as it was, on the borderline between the Indus Valley and the Ganges Valley, between the region in which Islamic religion and Iranic culture and Eurasian blood had become predominant and the region where Hinduism was still holding its own under an alien yoke. Accordingly, Delhi was the normal seat of Turkish Muslim rule in India from the thirteenth century of the Christian Era, when the 'Slave Kings' fixed their capital there, down to the eighteenth, when the descendants of Akbar, the maker of the Hindu universal state, were maintaining a shadow court at Delhi as protégés and pensioners of the British East India Company.[3]

newly acquired province at the extremity of their dominions, instead of retaining it at some site in Rājputāna, the country in which they had been at home for several centuries and which was still the geographical centre of their empire. In order to explain their choice, we must suppose that the strategic importance of the Jumna-Ganges Duab was already well recognized.

[1] Smith, V., op. cit., p. 384.   [2] See p. 121, above.

[3] While Delhi was normally the capital of India during the five or six centuries of Muslim Turkish rule, her enjoyment of this status was not uninterrupted. In the

Moreover, Delhi, like Peking, has succeeded in recovering her status after the downfall of the Power by which this status was first conferred upon her. The replacement of the Mughal Rāj in India by the British Rāj, like the expulsion of the Mongols from China by the Ming, was accompanied at the moment by a transfer of the capital from the principal landward march to a new site in the interior where the new rulers felt themselves at home and were sure of their authority. In the nineteenth century, Delhi had to yield her primacy to Calcutta, as, in the fourteenth century, Peking had to yield hers to Nanking. Yet in India, as in China, the old capital in the march eventually won back, from the new capital in the interior, the status which it had temporarily forfeited. In A.D. 1912, fifty-five years after the definitive extinction of the Mughal Rāj and confirmation of the British Rāj in the suppression of the Indian Mutiny, the British Government itself retransferred the capital of India to Delhi, as the Ming Emperor Yung Lo retransferred the capital of China to Peking fifty-three years after the expulsion of the Mongols from China by Yung Lo's own father Hung Wu.

It is noteworthy that, while the capital of India has perpetually gravitated to the environs of Delhi since the genesis of the Hindu Civilization, it has never established itself permanently anywhere in the Middle or Lower Ganges Valley, in Bihar or in Bengal. Before the advent of the British, it never established itself thereabouts at all; and no permanent change in the political geography of the Hindu World has been produced by the historical accident that the British rule began in Bengal a century before it was fully confirmed throughout India. This accident gave Bengal a double temporary advantage over other Indian provinces: she became the base of operations and seat of government of the new All-India rāj which was taking the place of the broken-down rāj of the Mughals; and her people were exposed to the process of intensive Westernization several generations earlier than their neighbours. Yet these accidental advantages, considerable though they are, have not availed against the permanent handicap to which Bengal is subject: the lack of stimulus which is the penalty of her situation in the interior. Even under the British Rāj, which has its source in sea-power, the capital of India has departed from Calcutta—a port

early days of the empire of the Great Mughals, the capital was at Agra; and Akbar, who unknowingly followed in Ikhnaton's footsteps in attempting to turn his autocratic political authority to account for the artificial creation and imposition of a new universal church (see V. C (i) (d) 6 (δ), Annex, vol. v, pp. 699–704, below), likewise followed Ikhnaton in building himself a brand-new capital city. After the founder's death, however, Fātihpur Sikri had the same fate as Tell-el-Amarna; the capital reverted to Agra and thence, under Shah Jahān, to Delhi; and so, in the latter days of the Mughal Empire, the Turkish Muslim rule in India ended at Delhi, where it had begun.

accessible to ocean-going vessels—and has shifted back to Delhi, where the Eurasian horseman is at home and the Western sea-farer is a stranger. As for the stimulus of the impact of our Western Civilization from across the sea—an impact which has given Bengal the character of a march for the first time in Hindu history—the Bengali response to this challenge seems to lack vitality and originality. In Bengali souls, the ferment of Westernization is apt to deteriorate into 'the leaven of the Scribes'. 'Where there is no vision, the people perish';[1] and, in the Indian National Movement, which the challenge of the West has evoked, the inspiration and the leadership have been passing, as we have observed already, from Bengal to the Bombay Presidency. We may observe further that this hinterland of Bombay, which has thus become the principal march of India *vis-à-vis* the West, has not now acquired the character of a march for the first time in Hindu history. From the beginning, it has been exposed to external pressure of various kinds from various quarters: military pressure from Gurjaras and Arabs by land; economic pressure from Arabs and Parsees by sea. 'The greater the pressure the greater the stimulus' is a maxim which is borne out by the phenomena of social geography in the Hindu World, as well as in the Far Eastern World and in the Sinic and in the Egyptiac.

In the Sumeric and Babylonic Worlds

In the Sumeric World, we find the same law illustrated in the history of the Sumeric universal state.[2] The Empire of Sumer and Akkad was founded by a Sumerian dynasty whose capital was at Ur, in the heart of the homeland of the Sumeric Civilization. The Empire was restored, after a temporary breakdown, by an Amorite dynasty whose capital was at Babylon: 'the Gate of the Gods' which was also the gate through which the Amorite Nomads of the North Arabian Steppe had forced an entry into the Land of Shinar. Thus, in the Sumeric universal state, political power passed from the interior to the march on which the heaviest external pressure was being exerted.

The same phenomena reappear in the history of the Babylonic Civilization which was 'affiliated' to the Sumeric. We have seen that, in Babylonic history, Babylonia was surpassed, in arms and arts alike, by Assyria; and we have attributed Assyria's superiority to the fact that, as compared with Babylonia, she was in a certain sense 'new ground'.[3] We shall now find a second and possibly more potent cause of Babylonia's failure to hold her own against Assyria

---

[1] Proverbs xxix. 18.
[2] See I. C (i) (*b*), vol. i, pp. 103 and 106, above.   [3] See pp. 74–5, above.

in the fact that Babylonia occupied a sheltered position in the interior of the Babylonic World, whereas Assyria was a march which bore the brunt of successive external pressures. In the post-Sumeric Völkerwanderung, Babylonia had suffered—and succumbed to—an invasion of barbarian Kassites at the time when Assyria was suffering—and repelling—an invasion of barbarian Mitannians; and thereafter the Assyrians experienced—and resisted —further pressures from which the Babylonians were exempt.

After being liberated, in the fourteenth century B.C., from the Mitannian pressure by the vicarious exertions of the Hittite Power,[1] Assyria was involved, throughout the eleventh and tenth centuries, in a new struggle for existence against a more formidable adversary than Mitanni in the shape of Aram. The Aramaeans were Nomads who had issued out of the Arabian Peninsula, in company with the Hebrews, during the Völkerwanderung which preceded the birth of the Syriac Civilization; and while the Hebrews had drifted into Southern Syria, the Aramaeans had drifted northwards in the ancient track of the Amorites. One wing of the migrant Aramaean horde had settled in the oases of east-central Syria, from Damascus to Hamah; another wing had lapped over the Middle Euphrates and had occupied the pasture-lands of Northern Mesopotamia; and it was this eastern wing that came into collision with Assyria. The situation, however, was not in all respects the same as when the Aramaeans' Amorite predecessors had forced an entry into the Sumeric World along this very track some twelve hundred years before.

The Amorites when they entered Akkad, like the Huns and Gurjaras when they entered India, had come in as undifferentiated barbarians and, as such, they had been converted easily and rapidly to the culture which they found in occupation of the ground on which they were trespassing. On the other hand, the Aramaeans, when they began to encroach upon the western borders of Assyria, had already come within the ambit of the nascent Syriac Civilization, just as the Turks who invaded India in the footsteps of the Huns had previously come within the ambit of the nascent Iranic Civilization and had been rendered immune to Hinduism by an anticipatory inoculation with Islam. Thus the Aramaean Syriac pressure upon the Babylonic World was as formidable a danger to the existence of the threatened civilization as the Turkish Muslim pressure upon the Hindu World; but, whereas the Rājputs failed to save India from being overrun by the Turks, the Assyrians not only checked the Aramaeans' eastward advance in two centuries of defensive warfare but passed over thereafter, in the ninth century

---

[1] See I. C (i) (b), vol. i, p. 113, above.

B.C., into a counter-offensive which carried the Assyrian arms to the shores of the Mediterranean and ground all Syria under the Assyrian heel. Thus, in this first round of the long and arduous struggle between the Syriac and Babylonic civilizations, Assyria bore the brunt and gained the victory for the Babylonic World. In the meantime Babylonia had the easy task of assimilating the Chaldaeans—a Nomadic people who had issued out of the Arabian Peninsula simultaneously with the Aramaeans and the Hebrews, but whose line of migration lay so far to the south-east that the influence of the nascent Syriac Civilization did not reach them. Thus the Chaldaeans—like the Amorites and unlike the Aramaeans —came in as undifferentiated barbarians who were open to assimilation; and their infiltration into Babylonia, during the centuries when Assyria was fighting the Aramaeans for her life, was a peaceful penetration instead of being a formidable ordeal.

Moreover, the Aramaean front was only one of the fronts on which Assyria had to fight. While she was resisting the pressure from the Syriac Civilization on the south-west, she had to defend her rear against the highlanders of the Iranian and Anatolian plateaux on the east and the north. In this quarter, again, Assyria performed the function of a march covering the interior of the Babylonic World; and, while she eventually gained the upper hand over her Syriac adversaries, the highlanders kept her perpetually on the defensive. Indeed, when, through this warlike intercourse, the highland principality of Urartu, in the basin of Lake Van, eventually became converted to the Babylonic Civilization, the struggle only became the more intense—like the struggle between the East Roman Empire and Bulgaria after the conversion of the Bulgarians to Orthodox Christianity.

Nevertheless Assyria, under this perpetual pressure from every quarter, developed a vitality which Babylonia could not match so long as Assyria's prowess gave her shelter. On the other hand, the positions were reversed when Assyria turned her arms against the interior of the Babylonic World and ceased to defend its frontiers.[1] During the seventh century B.C. she applied to her sister-country Babylonia the grinding pressure which she had applied in the ninth and eighth centuries to alien Syria; and this fearful challenge stimulated the Babylonians as potently as it stimulated the Syrians, though in a different way. In Syrian souls, it evoked the religious inspiration which found expression through the mouths of the Prophets of Israel; in Babylonian souls it evoked a dogged nationalism

[1] This change in the direction of Assyrian energies is examined further in IV. C (iii) (c) 3 (z), vol. iv, pp. 468-84, below, apropos of the pathological phenomenon of Militarism as a specific malady of the marches.

which proved more than a match for the *furor Assyriacus*. The Babylonians—fortified by Chaldaean infusions and steeled by Assyrian atrocities—were in at the death when, at the close of the seventh century B.C., the highlanders of the Iranian Plateau over-whelmed Assyria at last; and these Median allies of Babylon in the war of annihilation against Assyria were able now to achieve the destruction of the Power which had successfully resisted the pressure of Urartu and the earlier pressure of Mitanni because Assyria, by the time when she had to deal with the Medes, had ceased to perform her historic function as a march.

In the seventh century B.C., a wave of Eurasian Nomads—-the Cimmerians and the Scyths—broke over the north-western extremity of the Iranian Plateau and descended upon the Babylonic and Syriac worlds, as the Huns and Gurjaras broke over the north-eastern extremity of the same plateau and descended upon the Indic World in the fifth and sixth centuries of the Christian Era. Therewith, the challenge of Nomadic invasion was presented in South-Western Asia for the first time since the occasion when, more than a thousand years earlier, during the post-Sumeric Völker-wanderung, the Hyksos had broken out of the Eurasian Steppe and had swept across the derelict domain of the Empire of Sumer and Akkad to settle in Syria.[1] This time, Assyria was the South-West Asian Power whose proper task it was to take the Eurasian Nomads' challenge up; but, this time, Assyria failed to rise to the occasion for the first time in her history. Whether from impotence or from impolicy, she allowed the Nomads to raid South-Western Asia unchastised; and she even enlisted their services as mercenaries to fight for her in her Median and Babylonian wars. Thereby, she repudiated the function which she had made her own for the last five centuries; and the Medes seized the opportunity thus offered to them. They stepped into the breach; occupied the vacant post of danger and honour; exterminated or subdued or expelled the Scythian intruders; and inherited, as their reward, the hegemony previously exercised by Assyria over South-Western Asia.[2] For

---

[1] See I. C (i) (*b*), vol. i, pp. 104-5, above. In the seventh century B.C., the Scythians penetrated to Syria, like the Hyksos before them and the Turks after them; and the name Scythopolis, by which the Greeks afterwards knew the Biblical city of Bethshean (the modern Baisan) in the Valley of Jezreel, attests that at least one Scythian war-band made a permanent settlement in Palestine.

[2] Except in the western extremity of the Anatolian Peninsula, beyond the River Halys, where the local task of exterminating or subduing or expelling the intrusive Nomads was taken in hand, not by the Medes, but by the Lydians: a local people who were under the influence of the Hellenic and not the Babylonic or the Syriac Civilization. The local response of Lydia to the challenge from the Nomads won her a double reward. On the landward side, she shared with Media, Babylonia, and Egypt the dominion previously exercised by Assyria over South-Western Asia. On the seaward side, towards the Aegean, she imposed her suzerainty upon the Greek city-states along the seaboard, who had failed to save themselves from the Nomads and therefore forfeited their political independence to the Power in the hinterland which had performed the work of

Assyria was a march or nothing. As soon as she failed to respond to the challenge of external pressure from the human environment, she fell; and Media, who had taken up the Scythian challenge, was the Power that dealt Assyria her death-blow.

In the Syriac World

While the immediate consequence of the presentation of the Scythian challenge was the replacement of Assyria by Media, an ultimate consequence—which was of much greater historical importance—was the eventual victory of the Syriac Civilization in its long duel with the Babylonic—the duel which had begun in the eleventh century B.C. with the collision between Assyria and Aram. After the first round had been decided in favour of the Babylonic Civilization by the victorious Assyrian counter-offensive against Syria in the ninth and eighth centuries B.C., the struggle had shifted from the military to the cultural plane and had resolved itself into a competition between the two rival civilizations for the conversion of the highlanders on the Anatolian and Iranian plateaux. In this competition, the Babylonic Civilization gained an initial success, which has been mentioned above, in the conversion of Urartu; but this cultural 'Babylonicization' of one highland country on the north which did not succumb to Assyrian arms was counterbalanced by the 'Syriacization' of another highland country on the east which the Assyrians temporarily succeeded in subjugating; and here, in Media, the Assyrians—in applying their ruthless policy of breaking their victims' spirit by uprooting them from their homes and carrying them away captive—actually served as 'carriers' for the Syriac Civilization which they had trampled under foot.

When the Assyrians finally broke the resistance of the Syriac peoples in the latter half of the eighth century B.C., they deported part of the conquered population to 'the cities of the Medes';[1] but this extreme application of the maxim 'Divide and rule' had an unintended consequence. By the forcible introduction of Syriac deportees, the Medes were inoculated with the germs of the Syriac Civilization before they were stimulated, by the challenge of Scythian pressure, to step into Assyria's place. At the same time, the Scythian challenge, which called out this 'Syriacized' Media's energies, broke the 'Babylonicized' Urartu's back; and thus the fivefold interaction between Syria and Assyria and Media and the Scyths and Urartu worked together for the Syriac Civiliza-

salvation for them. The political subjection of the Asiatic Greeks to Lydia naturally expedited the cultural conversion of the Lydians to Hellenism. Indeed, this was perhaps the first of many instances in which 'Graecia capta ferum victorem cepit'. (Horace: *Epistolae*, Book II, Ep. 1, l. 156.) [1] 2 Kings xvii. 6 and xviii. 11.

tion's good. After the fall of Assyria, the remnant of the Babylonic World—now gathered together into 'the Neo-Babylonian Empire' of Nabopolassar and Nebuchadnezzar—found itself hemmed in and pressed upon by the Syriac World on both flanks: not only from the rival civilization's homeland in Syria itself but from the great new domain which the Syriac Civilization had now acquired for itself in Iran. From this encircling movement, the Babylonic Civilization had no more chance of escape than an antelope has from the toils of a boa-constrictor. The constriction and mastication of the Babylonic Civilization by its victorious rival was only a matter of time; and the process was completed before the beginning of the Christian Era.[1]

If we now turn our attention to the subsequent history of the Syriac Civilization, we shall find our law illustrated here again.

The enlarged Syriac World which had been brought into existence by the 'Syriacization' of Iran remained, from the seventh century B.C. onwards, in direct contact with the Eurasian Steppe; and it was from the Eurasian Nomads that it continued to receive the heaviest external pressure. In consonance with this, we find that, thenceforward, the primacy in the Syriac World passed, in succession, to the peoples who successively took over the burden of keeping the Eurasian Nomads at bay, and to the regions which successively served as anti-Nomad marches. The Median hegemony, for example, lasted just so long as the Medes held the front line in the defensive warfare against Nomad aggression. The hegemony was forfeited by the Medes to the Persians because the princes of Persis had succeeded in snatching from their Median neighbours the wardenship of the Eurasian Marches and thereby relegating Media to an unexposed and unstimulating position in the interior of the Syriac World. The Medes had been content to bar the passage of the Nomads at its narrowest point, where the Elbruz Range on one side and the Central Desert of Iran on the other side barely leave open, between them, 'the Caspian Gates'. The Achaemenidae masked this Median front line, and redeemed from Nomad occupation a vast additional zone of Iranian territory, by extending their own dominions north-eastwards from their home territory of Persis right up to the line of the Oxus; and it was their expansion in this direction that made their fortune by putting them in a position to supersede the Medes as the Medes had superseded the Assyrians.[2]

---

[1] For the attraction of Iran into the orbit of the Syriac Civilization, and the absorption of the dead body of the Babylonic Civilization into the Syriac Civilization's living tissues, see I. C (i) (b), vol. i, pp. 79–81, above.

[2] It may be noted that the Lydians as well as the Medes succumbed to the Achaemenidae, and that Lydia, like Media, had previously been 'relegated to the interior' by the Achaemenids' assumption of the wardenship of the Eurasian marches.

This Achaemenian enterprise in the north-east, which was the preliminary to the overthrow of the Median Astyages and to the foundation of a Syriac universal state in the form of an Achaemenian Empire, went almost unmarked among Hellenic observers, whose vision did not yet extend to such distant horizons. Yet the acquisition of Bactria was a more important step in the rise of the Achaemenian Power than the acquisition of Elam; and it was not for nothing that Cyrus met his death in fighting the Nomad Massagetae beyond the Jaxartes.[1] Under Cyrus's successors, the Achaemenian Empire held against the Nomads, with a strong hand, every oasis that could be created by irrigation along the courses of those rivers —Heri Rud and Murghab, Oxus and Jaxartes—which flow out from the northern foot of the Iranian Plateau and from the western foot of the Pamirs to reach the Caspian or the Sea of Aral or else to lose themselves in the desert. We may conjecture that the pressure of the Eurasian Nomads upon this North-Eastern March of the Syriac universal state always weighed more heavily on the minds of Achaemenian statesmen than the pressure of the Hellenes upon the opposite extremity of their dominions—and this even during the Athenian counter-offensive that was kept up intermittently for thirty years after the failure of Xerxes' expedition against Greece. It was assuredly not until Alexander had crossed the Dardanelles, and perhaps not until he had crossed the Euphrates, that the Hellenic peril became a greater anxiety than the Nomad peril to the last Darius.

Moreover, Alexander's own experience in the process of conquering the Achaemenian Empire indicates that, here as elsewhere, the march which was exposed to the heaviest external pressure had been stimulated into a greater vitality than any other region. It took Alexander not more than five years to conquer outright, without parley or compromise, the vast mass of the Achaemenian dominions, from the Dardanelles and the Libyan oases up to 'the Caspian Gates', where the Medes had halted in their pursuit of the routed Scyths and where Alexander overtook the dying Darius. Persis itself—the home territory of the imperial dynasty and the native land of the imperial people—quietly accepted the verdict of the Battle of Arbela, notwithstanding the stimulus which the Persians—having 'elected to live as an imperial people in a rough country rather than to cultivate the lowlands as some other nation's

[1] See the picturesque account of Cyrus's last campaign in Herodotus, Book I, chs. 202–15. Herodotus's accurate knowledge of geography did not extend much farther eastwards than a line drawn from Trebizond to Susa (i.e. a line roughly coincident with the present eastern frontiers of Turkey and 'Irāq); and his 'River Araxes'—on the crossing of which his story turns—appears to be a conflation of the actual river, still bearing that name, which flows from Armenia through Azerbaijan into the Caspian, with the actual Oxus and Jaxartes, into a single mighty and fabulous stream.

slaves'[1]—had never ceased to derive from their physical environment. Nevertheless, in this instance, the physical stimulus of a rough country upon the Persians showed itself less potent than the human stimulus of Nomad pressure upon their kinsmen in the north-eastern marches; for, whereas it had taken Alexander no more than five years to conquer the interior of the Achaemenian Empire up to 'the Caspian Gates', it took him two whole years more to complete his task by conquering the marches in the Oxus-Jaxartes Basin.

As soon as Alexander passed beyond the Caspian Gates, he experienced an entire change in the nature of the resistance which he encountered. Up to that point, he had secured the submission of vast provinces at the price of a few pitched battles against heterogeneous imperial field armies which showed little enthusiasm for defending territories where they felt themselves hardly more at home than the invader. Upon setting foot, however, in the Oxus-Jaxartes Basin after the last of the Achaemenian armies had been scattered to the winds, the Macedonian conqueror met with a spontaneous resistance from a feudal aristocracy with local roots. The border barons of Bactria and Sogdiana defended themselves against the Macedonians as they were accustomed to defend themselves against the Massagetae. Their resistance was not only spontaneous but energetic and protracted. Every castle stood a siege; and even when a baron had been brought to his knees he rose in revolt again the moment the conqueror's back was turned. At the end of two strenuous campaigns, Alexander had to win the allegiance which force could not exact by a policy of conciliation.

Thus, during the two centuries that had elapsed between the day when Cyrus met his death at the hands of the Massagetae on the far side of the Jaxartes and the day when Alexander gave the Nomads a lesson by bombarding them with his catapults without crossing the frontier river, the vitality of the Syriac universal state which was embodied in the Achaemenian Empire had come to be concentrated in these north-eastern marches, where the Syriac World was exposed to the severest external pressure. It is remarkable to find this phenomenon reappearing when the Syriac universal state, which had been prematurely cut short by the destruction of the Achaemenian Empire through Alexander's action, was reintegrated and resumed, after a Hellenic intrusion which had lasted a thousand years, in the 'Abbasid Caliphate.[2]

Though the 'Abbasid capital was fixed, on considerations of geo-

---

[1] See the passage quoted from Herodotus in II. D (i), on p. 21, above.
[2] For the historical relation between the 'Abbasid Caliphate and the Achaemenian Empire, see I. C (i) (b), vol. i, pp. 73–8, above.

graphical and administrative convenience, at Baghdad,[1] in the ancient homeland of the Babylonic Civilization which had long since been absorbed into the Syriac World, the political and military movement which completed the re-establishment of the Syriac universal state by setting up the 'Abbasids in the place of the Umayyads originated in Khurāsān: the province lying between 'the Caspian Gates' and the Murghab, which was the north-eastern march of the Syriac World in that age.[2] The stimulus which nerved Abu Muslim and his Khurāsānīs to overthrow the Umayyads was the selfsame stimulus that, in earlier ages of Syriac history, had nerved Cyrus and his Farsīs to overthrow Astyages and the Medes, and had nerved the dihkans of Balkh and Sughd to measure themselves against the invincible Iskandar Dhu'l-Qarnayn. The challenge of pressure from the Nomads of the Eurasian Steppe was as stimulating to the latter-day Syriac frontiersmen who were confronted by the Ephthalites and the Turks and the Türgesh as it had been to their predecessors who had had to deal with the Scyths and the Massagetae; and the Khurāsānīs' historic feat of re-establishing the Syriac universal state in A.D. 750 was led up to, during the years 705-41, by the more arduous, if less momentous, feat of reincorporating the Oxus-Jaxartes Basin into the Syriac World after a separation that had lasted some eight or nine centuries.[3]

[1] The 'Abbasids fixed their capital at Baghdad on the same considerations that had once led the Achaemenids to hold their court at Babylon for four months in the year (Herodotus, Book I, ch. 192). It lay in the most remunerative province in their dominions and at the mid-point between the Syrian and the Iranian half of the Empire.

[2] The destruction of the Achaemenian Empire had been followed, within two centuries, by the submergence of the former North-Eastern Marches in the Oxus-Jaxartes Basin under a flood of Nomad invasion; for the Seleucid Empire, which was the Hellenic 'successor-state' of the Achaemenian Empire in Asia, was too exactingly preoccupied by the task of holding its own against rival Hellenic Powers in the Levant to discharge efficiently those responsibilities on the distant borders of the Eurasian Steppe which it had inherited from its Achaemenian predecessor. (See pp. 143-4, below.) Thus, from the latter part of the second century B.C. to the beginning of the eighth century of the Christian Era, the Oxus-Jaxartes Basin had been lost to the Syriac World and had been living a separate life of its own under the dominion of successive Nomad intruders— Massagetae (= Sakas) and Yuechi and Ephthalites and Turks. Under this dispensation, the Oxus-Jaxartes Basin had often been in closer relations with India than with Iran; and in these conditions it had developed symptoms of a distinctive social individuality which promised, for a time, to take definite shape in the genesis of a new 'Far Eastern Christian' Civilization. (See II. D (vii), pp. 369-85, below.) During this long secession and estrangement of the Oxus-Jaxartes Basin from the Syriac World, the role of anti-Nomad march devolved upon the province of Khurāsān, which was saved for the Syriac World by the Arsacid prince Mithradates the Great (regnabat 123-88 B.C.) after a struggle between the Arsacid Power and the invading Sakas or Massagetae which had lasted for nearly half a century.

[3] Khurāsān—the frontier province over against the Eurasian Nomads which the Umayyads took over from the Sasanian successors of the Arsacidae—was the base of operations from which, under the Umayyad régime, the Oxus-Jaxartes Basin was eventually reincorporated into the Syriac World, by force of arms, in A.D. 705-41. (See Gibb, H. A. R.: The Arab Conquests in Central Asia (London 1923, Royal Asiatic Society).) The work was accomplished by the combined efforts of Arab garrisons which had been cantoned in Khurāsān after the Arab conquest of the Sasanian Empire, half a century before, and local levies which were raised, by the Arab authorities, from the

Thereby, the North-Eastern Marches of the Syriac World, over against the Nomads of Eurasia, were restored, on the eve of the reintegration of the Syriac universal state under the 'Abbasids, to the limits up to which they had been carried originally on the eve of the first establishment of the universal state under the Achaemenids. And thereafter history repeated itself yet again; for under the 'Abbasid, as under the Achaemenid, régime the vitality of the Empire concentrated itself in the North-Eastern Marches as it ebbed away from the interior. This became apparent at the break-up of the 'Abbasid Caliphate, as it had become apparent, once before, at the destruction of the Achaemenian Empire by Alexander; for the most powerful and effective and socially beneficent of the Caliphate's 'successor-states' arose one after another in this region. The Sāmānid régime at Balkh and Bukhārā (A.D. 819–999) fostered Persian literature in its infancy and accomplished something which the Caliphate had never achieved in propagating Islam among the Nomads of the Steppe;[1] and it was only as converts that it suffered them at last to trespass from the desert on to the sown. Thereafter, one horde of these trespassers, the Saljūqs, when they had penetrated to Baghdad in order to rescue the 'Abbasid Caliphs from the tyranny of the sectarian Buwayhids, turned back to supplant their fellow-converts, the Ilek Khans, as wardens of the North-Eastern Marches against their unconverted Nomadic kinsmen who still remained on the Steppe. Under this Saljūq régime at Merv (A.D. 1089–1141) the frontier of Dār-al-Islām was once more guarded as faithfully as it had been guarded by the Sāmānids; and even the Shahs of Khwārizm, who first rose to power by betraying their religion and allegiance when they joined forces (in A.D. 1141) with the pagan Nomad Qara Qitays in order to expel the Saljūq Sultan Sanjar from the Oxus-Jaxartes Basin, eventually redeemed their honour when (from A.D. 1220 to 1231) they bore the brunt of the Mongol avalanche which finally overwhelmed Dār-al-Islām in the last convulsion of the post-Syriac Völkerwanderung.[2]

---

indigenous Iranian Khurāsānīs. It is noteworthy that it was here, in the North-Eastern Marches, under the formative influence of a common pressure from beyond the frontier, that the vanquished Iranians and the victorious Arabs first fraternized with one another. And it was this Arab-Iranian frontier-force that completed the re-establishment of the Syriac universal state, by putting down the Umayyads and setting up the 'Abbasids, ten years after it had proved its mettle and acquired its *esprit de corps* by completing the re-conquest of Transoxania on the Syriac Society's account.

[1] The Saljūqs, who at that time were ranging over the steppe-country in the Oxus-Jaxartes Basin, were converted about A.D. 956; the followers of the Ilek Khans, who were ranging over the steppes adjoining the Oxus-Jaxartes Basin on the north-east, in the gap between the Tien Shan and the Altai Mountains (in the fourteenth-century 'Mughalistan' and the modern 'Zungaria'), were converted about A.D. 960.

[2] In A.D. 1209/1210, ten years before the Mongol avalanche descended upon them, the Khwārizm Shahs had partially counteracted the effects of their original act of treachery against the Saljūqs by similarly betraying the Qara Qitays. They partitioned the dominions of the Qara Qitays in conjunction with Gushluk the Naiman, another

Thus, over the course of some nineteen centuries of Syriac history, from the seventh century B.C. to the thirteenth century of the Christian Era, we can observe one constant phenomenon. We find the pressure from the Eurasian Nomads normally exceeding in severity the pressures from other neighbours of the Syriac World, and concurrently we find the North-Eastern Marches, upon which the brunt of this pressure fell, normally surpassing in vitality all the other marches as well as the interior.

The exception which proves the rule is the situation which prevailed, for some two centuries out of these nineteen, under the Seleucid Empire, which was the Achaemenian Empire's Hellenic 'successor-state' in Asia.[1] Under the Seleucid régime, as under the Achaemenid and the 'Abbasid, vitality and power tended to pass from the interior of the Empire to the periphery; but whereas they passed under the Achaemenids from Persepolis and Susa and Babylon and Ecbatana to Bactria and Sogdiana, and under the 'Abbasids from Baghdad to Khurāsān and to Transoxania, they flowed out, under the Seleucids, in the diametrically opposite direction: that is, from Seleucia-on-Tigris not to 'Alexandria on the Verge' of the Eurasian Steppe but to Antioch-on-Orontes. This gravitation of the Seleucid capital to a site which lay almost in view of the Mediterranean indicated that the Seleucid statesmen, unlike their Achaemenid predecessors, felt the pressure from the Hellenic World more acutely than the pressure from the Eurasian Nomads. The outcome, however, was to prove that the Seleucids' policy was ill-advised and the site of Antioch eccentric; for, notwithstanding the clever location of Antioch athwart the shortest portage between the Mediterranean and the Euphrates, the transfer of the capital from Seleucia to Antioch cost the Seleucidae their Empire and the Syriac World its North-Eastern Marches. The first consequence was that the Greek garrisons in the Oxus-Jaxartes Basin, finding themselves left to their own resources, seceded from the Seleucid Empire and constituted themselves into an independent Power: the Hellenic Kingdom of Bactria. The second consequence was that this Hellenic Bactria, which had responded with such spirit to the challenge of desertion by resorting to self-help, found herself unequal in the long run to the task of holding the

pagan Nomad Power, who took the Qara Qitays in the rear. In this unheroic manner, the whole of the Oxus-Jaxartes Basin was momentarily recovered again for Dār-al-Islām; but retribution quickly overtook the spoilers. The Naiman and the Khwārizm Shah were overwhelmed in turn by the Mongol Chingis Khan; and it was in response to this terrific Mongol challenge that the last of the Khwārizm Shahs, Jalāl-ad-Dīn Mankobirnī, redeemed the treacheries of his ancestors by the heroic rear-guard action in which he covered the interior of Dār-al-Islām from Mongol assault and battery for a whole decade after the Mongols had overrun his own home-territories on the banks of the Lower Oxus.

[1] See the second footnote on p. 141, above.

North-Eastern Marches against the Nomads without support from
the interior. In the second century B.C., Bactria succumbed to a
Nomad invasion;[1] and the ground then lost to the Nomads by the
Greeks was only recovered from the Nomads by the Arabs some
eight or nine centuries later.[2]

In the Iranic World over against Eurasia

The North-Eastern Marches over against the Eurasian Nomads,
which were thus reincorporated into the Syriac World on the eve of
the reintegration of the Syriac universal state, and which played a
part of steadily increasing importance under the 'Abbasid régime,[3]
produced their historic social effect once more in the first age of
the Iranic Civilization, 'affiliated' to the Syriac Civilization, which
emerged, after the interregnum following the break-up of the 'Abbasid Caliphate, when the waters of the Mongol cataclysm began
to subside.

We can discern this effect in the diversity between the respective
historical roles of the two Mongol 'successor-states' which were
deposited here—one in the borderland and the other in the interior.
As between these two appanages of the Mongol Empire in Dār-al-
Islām, nothing came of the principality of the House of Hulāgū,
the so-called Il-Khans, in Iran and 'Irāq. 'The lines' were 'fallen
unto' these barbarians 'in pleasant places; yea', they had 'a goodly
heritage'.[4] And yet, 'as the cloud is consumed and vanisheth away',
so the Il-Khans went down to the grave and came up no more.[5]
On the other hand, out of the principality of the House of Chaghatāy, which bestrode the borderline between the desert and the
sown, there came forth two Powers which made their mark, for
good or evil, on history: the Empire of Timur Lenk ('Tamerlane')
in Central Asia and the later Empire of the Timurids in India,
where Timur's great-great-great-grandson Bābur played the part
of David and Bābur's grandson Akbar the part of Solomon.
A glance at the careers of Timur and Bābur shows that both
were frontiersmen who were confronted by a challenge from
the Eurasian Nomads of their time, and that both rose to greatness by responding to this challenge successfully—each in his
own way.

Timur (imperabat A.D. 1369–1405) started life as a feudal baron
in the district of Kish in Transoxania: that is to say, in the sedentary
as opposed to the Nomad section of the Chaghatāy dominions.
The Chaghatāy principality had been compacted of two component

---

[1] See the second footnote on p. 141, above.
[2] See the third footnote on p. 141, above.
[3] See p. 142, above.   [4] Psalm xvi. 6.   [5] Job vii. 9.

parts: the oases of the Oxus-Jaxartes Basin,[1] where this pagan Mongol dynasty bore rule over a sedentary Muslim population; and the steppes of Zungaria, adjoining the Oxus-Jaxartes Basin on the north-east, where the Chaghatāy Khans were the leaders of pagan Nomads who were made in their own image. In A.D. 1321, however, a century after the Mongol conquest of the Oxus-Jaxartes Basin and forty years before the beginning of Timur's career, the two ill-assorted sections of the Chaghatāy principality had been separated from one another politically through the partition of Chaghatāy's appanage between two different branches of the eponym's descendants; and the prelude to Timur's career opened with this event. The political separation enabled the sedentary population in the Oxus-Jaxartes Basin to assert itself culturally against the Nomadic element after a century of subjection; and the first consequence was that here, as in contemporary Iran and Hindustan and Anatolia, the nascent Iranic Civilization began to make headway.

The partition was accompanied by, and was perhaps causally connected with, the conversion of the western branch of the Chaghatayids, who obtained the Oxus-Jaxartes Basin for their portion, from their primitive Mongol paganism to the Islamic faith of their subjects; while even the eastern branch of the House, whose portion was the Zungarian Steppe (now styled, *par excellence*, 'Mughalistan'), seem to have been converted likewise a generation later. The next consequence was a reaction of the Nomads against the rising power of the new sedentary civilization on their borders. In A.D. 1360 Tughluq Timur, the newly converted Eastern Chaghatāy Khan of 'Mughalistan', presented himself in the Oxus-Jaxartes country—perhaps at the instigation of the Nomad element there, who felt their old ascendancy slipping out of their hands—and claimed dominion over the western as well as the eastern portion of his ancestral appanage. By this time, the settled population of the oases, having enjoyed for some forty years the benefits of a milder and less barbarous régime, had come to regard the untamed Nomads of 'Mughalistan' as odious marauders[2] who —whether converted or not—were definitely beyond the pale of

---

[1] Excluding the oases along the lower course of the Oxus, in Khwārizm, which were included, not in Chaghatāy's appanage, but in his brother Jūjī's. (See further p. 147, below.)

[2] The mysterious word 'jātah', which the Turkī-speaking sedentary population of the Oxus-Jaxartes oases in Timur's day applied to the Nomads of 'Mughalistan' as a term of abuse, is perhaps identical with the Ottoman Turkish word 'cheteh', which means something between a brigand and a guerrilla. Is it perhaps derived from the tribal name of the Getae (Massagetae and Thyssagetae) or Jāts, who were the nearest Nomadic neighbours of the Oxus-Jaxartes oases in the Achaemenian Age, before they erupted out of the Steppe and poured over the Hindu Kush into the Panjab in the second century B.C.?

civilization. Thus, for them, the Eastern Khan's pretension carried with it the menace of a fresh bout of Nomad domination and a relapse into the barbarism from which they were just beginning to emerge. In this crisis, when Nomadism had returned to dispute with the young Iranic Civilization the possession of the borderland between the Iranic World and the Eurasian Steppe, Timur Lenk stood forth as the champion of the Iranic Civilization.

In A.D. 1360, when Timur Lenk's fellow-barons in Transoxania fled before the face of the Eastern Khan towards Khurāsān, Timur alone had the courage to turn back and make terms with the intruder; and two years later, when Tughluq Timur Khan returned to Mughalistan, he rewarded Timur Lenk by appointing him lieutenant, in the Oxus-Jaxartes Basin, to the Khan's son, who remained behind as his father's viceroy. This gave Timur his opportunity. He first organized a successful insurrection, in the Oxus-Jaxartes Basin, against the Eastern Khan's authority; and when, under his leadership, the people of the oases had defeated, in six years of defensive warfare (A.D. 1362–7), the efforts of the 'jātah' to subdue them,[1] Timur ventured upon the enterprise which had led Cyrus to his death beyond the Jaxartes and Darius to his discomfiture beyond the Danube. With the forces—military and religious—of the nascent Iranic Civilization at his back, Timur passed over to the offensive and attacked the Nomads on their own ground, in the heart of the Eurasian Steppe; and, as far as is known, he was the first sedentary Power before the Cossacks to attempt this *tour de force* with any success. In five campaigns in 'Mughali-stan' (*circa* A.D. 1369–80), he crushed the local Nomads of Chag-hatāy's appanage and broke their spirit; and he finally reduced them to submission after he had performed an even greater feat: the crushing of the Nomads of Jūjī's appanage, who ranged over the vast steppes of Qipchāq,[2] between the Altai Mountains and the Carpathians, and were the overlords of Khwārizm, along the Lower Oxus, on the one side and of Russia on the other.

The collision between Timur and the hordes of Qipchāq was brought on by an act of aggression on Timur's part. Not content with chastising the Chaghatāy Nomads for their attempt to reassert

---

[1] This war of defence was a popular movement, as was shown by the fact that, when Timur was momentarily routed by the 'jātah' in the open field at the Battle of the Mire in A.D. 1365, the oasis-city of Samarqand was successfully defended against the victorious Nomads by the townspeople under the leadership of their 'ulamā. Thus Timur's first and greatest achievement—the expulsion of the Nomads from the Oxus-Jaxartes Basin —was accomplished by him as the leader of a popular movement and not in his later character of a capricious militarist going forth conquering and to conquer for conquest's sake.

[2] So called after the name of the Turkish Nomad horde which, at the moment of the Mongol conquest, was in occupation of the region afterwards assigned, as an appanage, to Chingis Khan's eldest son Jūjī.

their mastery over the sedentary section of Chaghatāy's appanage, he set himself to liberate the oases of Khwārizm from the dominion of the Nomads of Qipchāq; and by A.D. 1380 he had attained this second objective as well, in a series of campaigns which alternated with his punitive expeditions into 'Mughalistan'. At the time, the Nomads of Qipchāq were impotent because they were a house divided against itself; and in 1378–80, when Timur was completing the liberation of Khwārizm, the Russians, in the opposite hinterland of the Qipchāq Steppe, momentarily succeeded in liberating themselves from these same Nomads' domination likewise. Immediately thereafter, however, the Nomads of Jūjī's appanage were all united politically—perhaps for the first and last time in their history[1]—by the definitive victory of one of their warring princes, Toqatmysh Khan, over his rivals. In 1382 Toqatmysh re-established the ascendancy of Qipchāq over Russia by taking and sacking Moscow. In 1388 he invaded the Oxus-Jaxartes Basin in order to re-establish the *status quo* which Timur's aggression had overthrown there.

Toqatmysh's attack was formidable, since he made it, not only at the head of the united forces of Qipchāq, but at a moment when Timur, at the head of his own forces, was absent on a campaign in the interior of the Iranic World, in Fars. The hordes of Qipchāq, like the hordes of 'Mughalistan' before them, overran the oases of the Oxus-Jaxartes Basin up to the walls of Samarqand; but on Timur's approach they withdrew into their steppes without accepting battle, and left it to him to seek them out at home. Two years later, he did so. In January 1391, in midwinter, Timur plunged into the Qipchāq steppes; and this time it was in vain that the Nomads resorted to the elusive tactics with which they were accustomed to frustrate the punitive expeditions of sedentary Powers. When Darius had invaded these selfsame steppes at their opposite extremity some nineteen centuries earlier, he had been first exasperated and finally intimidated by the perpetual retreat of his mobile adversaries ever farther into the interior of their wilderness. When Timur embarked on the same enterprise, he had the hardihood and the generalship to beat the Nomads at their own game. He did not cease to follow them up until he had traversed, at their heels, the whole breadth of the Eurasian Steppe and had forced them to give battle with their backs to the farther boundary of their vast ranges. Here, at Urtapa, in June 1391, he crushed the

---

[1] Jūjī had died before his father Chingis Khan, and consequently, when Chingis died himself and his dominions were distributed among his heirs, Jūjī's appanage was partitioned at the outset among Jūjī's sons. Thereafter, one of these sons, Bātū, enormously extended his portion of the appanage as a result of his famous campaigns of 1237–41, in which he subjugated Russia and raided the Central European Marches of Western Christendom. For these reasons, the appanage of Jūjī was both the largest and the most loosely knit of all the appanages of Chingis Khan's descendants.

hordes of Qipchāq, as he had once crushed those of 'Mughalistan',
and then retraversed the breadth of the Steppe in midwinter to
re-enter Samarqand twelve months after he had set out on this
extraordinary campaign.

In Timur's military prowess, the stimulating effect of pressure
from the external human environment upon the frontiersmen who
bear the brunt of it is eminently apparent. When Timur turned his
arms against the interior of the Iranic World, he met there no
Power that was able to withstand him. Indeed, when he traversed
his own world from east to west, as he had traversed the Eurasian
Steppe from south to north, he momentarily prostrated even his
redoubtable fellow-frontiersmen the 'Osmanlis.[1] The collapse of
the 'Osmanlis when they came into collision with Timur's Transoxanians may be taken as giving the measure of the difference in
strength between the stimuli which these two frontier-com-
munities of the Iranic World had derived respectively from their
warfare against the Nomads and their warfare against Orthodox
Christendom. It is not, of course, surprising that the challenge of
the Nomads should have evoked a supreme military prowess in the
frontier-community which nerved itself to take that challenge up.
Nor is it surprising that a community which was so violently
stimulated in this direction as were the Transoxanians in Timur's
day should have lost its social balance under the strain and have
been drawn into that pathological pursuit of war for war's sake
which constitutes the malady of Militarism. Timur's militarism,
which brought to naught almost the whole of his constructive work
and has justly given him as sinister a reputation as Sennacherib's,
is examined in a later part of this Study in another connexion.[2]
Considering the predominance of this militaristic expression of
Transoxanian vitality in Timur's generation, it is the more remarkable to find that, in the century immediately following Timur's
death, the North-Eastern Marches, after having demonstrated their
superiority to the interior of the Iranic World in arms, proceeded to
make their own distinctive contribution to the Iranic intellectual
culture.

While Timur's older contemporary Hāfiz, the last but one of the
great masters of Persian poetry,[3] lived and died in Fars, at Shīrāz,
the last great master, Jāmī (*vivebat* A.D. 1414–92), was a Khurāsānī
who lived at Herat, at the court of the Timurid Sultan Husayn b.
Mansūr b. Bayqarā (*regnabat* A.D. 1468–1506). At the same court

---

[1] For the reaction of the 'Osmanlis to the blow which Timur dealt them at Angora
in A.D. 1402, see p. 102, above.
[2] See IV. C (iii) (c) 3 (α), vol. iv, pp. 491–501, below.
[3] For the role of Persian Literature in the histories of the Syriac and Iranic civilizations,
see p. 77, footnote 1, in II. D (iii), above.

lived Mīr 'Alī Shīr Nawā'ī, a versatile genius who was not only Sultan Husayn's minister of state but was also the centre of a literary circle which gave birth to a new vernacular literature, on the Persian model, in the Turkī language.[1] Timur himself was a patron of men of letters; and personal contributions to the Iranic culture were made by several of his descendants. His grandson, Ulugh Beg (*regnabat* A.D. 1447–9) made his fame before he ascended the throne by building an observatory at Samarqand in A.D. 1421 and organizing the compilation of a set of astronomical tables which were completed in 1437/8.[2] Timur's great-great-great-grandson Zahīr-ad-Dīn Bābur (*vivebat* A.D. 1482–1530)—the Timurid prince of Farghāna who found a new field of action for his House in India—and Bābur's cousin and contemporary Mīrzā Haydar Dūghlāt (*vivebat* A.D. 1499/1500–51) each wrote, in Turkī and in Persian respectively, a noteworthy autobiographical history of his own times;[3] and the literary gifts which manifested themselves in Bābur's memoirs reappeared, among his descendants, in Gul Badan Begum's *Humāyūn Nāma* and in Jahāngīr's *Tūzuk*.

Still more impressive is the hold which the Iranic culture acquired, after Timur's harrying of the Steppes, over the hearts and minds of the Nomads, as illustrated by the career and personality of Yunus Khan: a common grandfather of Bābur and Haydar who ruled over 'Mughalistan' in the latter part of the fifteenth century of the Christian Era. Yunus had been handed over in his childhood as a hostage to the Timurids; studied for twelve years under Sharaf-ad-Dīn 'Alī Yazdī (the biographer of Timur); travelled in Fars and Azerbaijan; settled in Shīrāz, where he was known as 'ustād' or 'master of arts'; and had finally been reinstated in 'Mughalistan' by the Timurid Sultan Abu Sa'īd.[4] The following sketch of him is given by his grandson Haydar:[5]

'Yunus Khan was the greatest of all the Chaghatāy Khans, and before him there was, in many respects, no one like him in his family. None of the Chaghatāy Khans who preceded him had passed the age of forty; nay, most of them never reached that age; but this prosperous Khan attained to the age of seventy-four. Towards the end of his life, growing repentant and devout, he became a disciple of that Refuge of the Pious, Nāsir-ad-Dīn Khwāja 'Ubayd-allāh [in this history, wherever the term "His Holiness" is used, it refers to the Khwāja]; and him the Khan followed with piety. He was also acquainted with many other shaykhs,

[1] For Mīr 'Alī Shīr Nawā'ī, see Browne, E. G.: *A Literary History of Persia*, vol. iii (Cambridge 1928, University Press), pp. 390–1, 422–3, and other passages.
[2] Browne, op. cit., p. 386.
[3] Mīrzā Haydar had a musical as well as a literary bent. See Mīrzā Haydar Dūghlāt: *Tarīkh-i-Rashidī*, English translation by Ross, E. D., and Elias, N. (London 1895, Sampson Low and Marston), Introduction, p. 23.
[4] See op. cit., pp. 83–5.   [5] In op. cit., ed. cit., pp. 155–7.

and used to associate with them. His nature was adorned with many high qualities and virtues; he possessed also many acquirements, among which may be mentioned the reading of the Qur'ān. He was of an even temper, his conversation was charming, and he had a quick perception. He excelled in penmanship, painting, and other accomplishments conformable with a healthy nature, and was well-trained in singing and instrumental music. . . .

'At the beginning of the reign of Yunus Khan, all the Mughals dwelt, according to their custom, in Mughalistan; they avoided all towns and cultivated countries [and regarded them] with great repugnance. They were Musulmans in nothing but the name; in fact, not even in name, for they were carried off into countries round about, and sold as slaves like other infidels. After the Khan had had the happiness to kiss the feet of His Holiness, the latter wrote letters to all the surrounding Musulman rulers, saying: "We have seen Sultan Yunus Khan, and it is not lawful to molest a tribe whose chief is so good a Musulman."

'From that date no more Mughals who had been carried off were ever bought or sold as slaves in a Muhammadan country. The Mughals had always been this kind of Nomadic people. The Khan felt that until they settled down in cultivated countries and towns, they could never become true Musulmans. He therefore exerted himself to the utmost to bring their settlement about.'

Here we are shown the picture of a Khan of Mughalistan who was different indeed from that barbaric Tughluq Timur whose descent upon Transoxania a century earlier had been the starting-point of Timur Lenk's career. The Nomads themselves, who had formerly made the transit from the desert to the sown as conquerors or raiders, now only make it when they are sold into slavery to their sedentary neighbours. As a result of Timur's action, the Nomads and their former victims have exchanged their roles. Even when, a century after the death of the great Transoxanian harrier of the Steppes, his homeland was swamped once again by an influx of Nomad conquerors—this time the uncouth Uzbegs from the far northern ranges of Western Siberia[1]—the light of the Iranic culture in the Oxus-Jaxartes Basin was not quite put out. It communicated itself to the conquerors; and we have a history of the Mongols from the hand of a latter-day Uzbeg scholar-prince, Abu'l-Ghāzi Khan of Khiva[2] (*regnabat* A.D. 1643–63).

In the Iranic World over against Orthodox Christendom

So much for the effect of the pressure from the Eurasian Steppe upon the Iranic World in administering to the North-Eastern Marches a special stimulus which was not received by the interior. If we turn to the North-Western March, where the Iranic Society

---

[1] See I. C (i) (*b*), Annex I, in vol. i, above.   [2] i.e. Khwārizm.

was confronted by Orthodox Christendom, we shall find another illustration of the same phenomenon in the remarkable diversity between the fortunes of the 'Osmanlis and the Qaramanlis.

These two Turkish communities were both of them 'successor-states' of the Anatolian Saljūq Sultanate: a Muslim Turkish Power which had been established in the interior of Anatolia in the eleventh century of the Christian Era, during the post-Syriac Völkerwanderung, by Saljūq Turkish adventurers who made provision for themselves in this world and in the next by thus enlarging the borders of Dār-al-Islām at Orthodox Christendom's expense. When this Anatolian Saljūq Sultanate eventually broke up in the course of the thirteenth century, the Qaramanlis appeared to have the finest, and the 'Osmanlis the poorest, prospects of all the Saljūqs' heirs. The Qaramanlis inherited the kernel of the former Saljūq domain, including their predecessors' capital, Qonīyah, while the 'Osmanlis found themselves in possession of a piece of the husk.

In fact, the 'Osmanlis had received the leavings of the Saljūq estate in Anatolia because they were the latest comers of all the Anatolian Saljūq Sultans' Turkish feudatories and had arrived, when they did arrive, in humble circumstances. Their eponym, 'Osmān, was the son of a certain Ertoghrul who had led into Anatolia a nameless band of Turkish refugees: an insignificant fragment of the human wreckage which had been hurled to the farthest extremities of Dār-al-Islām by the tremendous impact of the Mongol wave when it broke upon the North-Eastern Marches out of the heart of the Eurasian Steppe. The last of the Anatolian Saljūqs had assigned to these refugee fathers of the 'Osmanlis a strip of territory on the north-western edge of the Anatolian Plateau, where the Saljūq dominions then marched with the Anatolian territories which were still held by the East Roman Empire along the Asiatic shores of the Sea of Marmara. This outlying and exposed position, where the 'Osmanlis at last found rest for the sole of their foot after a trek which had carried them from the Oxus to the Sangarius, was appropriately called *Sultan Önü*, the Saljūq Sultan's 'battle-front'. The refugees had broken contact with the Mongols, only to be thrown into action against the East Romans; and they must have envied the fortune of the Qaramanlis, whose lot had been cast in the sheltered interior of Anatolia. But beggars could not be choosers. 'Osmān submitted to the decree of Destiny which had condemned him, in a new and strange environment, to be a frontiersman like his fathers before him. He set himself to enlarge the borders at his Orthodox Christian neighbours' expense, and took as his first objective the East Roman city of

Brusa. The capture of Brusa took him nine years (A.D. 1317–26); but the 'Osmanlis have justly called themselves by his name, for 'Osmān was the true founder of the Ottoman Empire. He had determined the direction in which the Ottoman Power was thenceforth to expand without ever being brought to a halt until the day when it laid siege in vain to Vienna.[1]

Within thirty years of the fall of Brusa, the 'Osmanlis had gained a footing on the European shore of the Dardanelles; and it was in Europe and not in Asia that they made their fortunes. Through their conquests in the Balkan Peninsula, into which the centre of gravity of the Orthodox Christian World had already shifted from its earliest seat in Anatolia,[2] the 'Osmanlis acquired a prestige, as 'the Ghāzis of Rum',[3] which spread through the Iranic World to India and through the Arabic World to Morocco;[4] and at the same time these conquests beyond the borders of the Iranic World so increased their power by comparison with that of the other Turkish 'successor-states' of the Anatolian Saljūq Sultanate in the interior that, before Timur Lenk launched his lightning campaign in Anatolia,[5] they had subdued the Qaramanlis and the other Turkish communities in Anatolia with their left hand while they were subduing the Greeks and Serbs and Bulgars with their right.

Timur sought to give permanence to the effects of the blow which he had dealt the 'Osmanlis at Angora by restoring throughout Anatolia the *status quo ante* the establishment of the Ottoman ascendancy; but Timur's hasty revision of the local political map could not perform the miracle of instilling into the static Qaramanli Turk of the interior the qualities of energy and adaptability which he needed in order to hold his own against the dynamic 'Osmanli Turk of the marches. 'All the King's horses and all the King's men could not set up Caramania again.' The Transoxanians could only have changed the history of Anatolia if they had come to stay; and when, after a single campaign, they departed, never to return, the fate of Qaraman was sealed. She had merely obtained

---

[1] For the special adaptation of Nomadic institutions by means of which the 'Osmanlis brought Orthodox Christendom into subjection and kept Western Christendom at bay, see Part III. A, vol. iii, pp. 22–50, below.

[2] See II. D (iii), pp. 79–80, above.

[3] The title by which Bābur refers to the 'Osmanlis in his memoirs (English translation by Mrs. Beveridge: *The Bābur-nāma in English* (London 1922, Luzac, 2 vols.), vol. ii, p. 564).

[4] The earliest known first-hand description of the Ottoman community is from the hand of the Moroccan traveller Ibn Battūtah, who travelled through Asia Minor in the second quarter of the fourteenth century of the Christian Era. (See Ibn Battúta: *Travels in Asia and Africa 1325–1354*, translated and selected by H. A. R. Gibb (London 1929, Routledge).)

[5] See II. D (iv), p. 102, and the present chapter, p. 148, above. Timur made his onslaught upon the 'Osmanlis in February 1402, after having wintered in Qarabagh. The Battle of Angora was fought on the 20th July. In December 1402, Timur was at Smyrna. By the summer of 1403 he was far away again, in Georgia.

a reprieve; and, although she showed herself as stubborn as ever in defensive warfare, the Ottoman Sultan Mehmed the Conqueror, after rounding off his dominions in the Balkan Peninsula by taking Constantinople in A.D. 1453, was able to round them off in Anatolia also by annexing Qaraman to the Ottoman Empire, once and for all, in 1465.

The Turkish principality of Qaraman, which thus succumbed to the ʿOsmanlis after having existed for something less than two centuries from first to last, was almost coincident in area with the District of the Anatolic Army Corps which, in the earliest age of Orthodox Christian history, had held the primacy among all the army corps districts of the East Roman Empire.[1] In its cantonments here on the plateau, the Anatolic Corps had established its precedence over the Thracensian Corps, which was cantoned in the Anatolian hinterland of the Aegean, and over the Imperial Guard ('Obsequium'), which was cantoned in the Anatolian hinterland of the Marmara. On the other hand, the Qaramanlis, when they occupied the site of the Anatolic Army Corps District in a later age, failed to hold their own against the ʿOsmanlis, who in this later age were occupying the former cantonments of the East Roman Imperial Guard. It will be seen that, in terms of physical geography, the respective roles of these several regions of Anatolia in the earlier and the later of the two ages in question were precisely inverted. The region which had played the dominant role in the East Roman Empire as the District of the Anatolic Corps played a secondary role in Turkish Anatolia as the principality of Qaraman; and, conversely, the region which had played a secondary role as the District of the East Roman Imperial Guard played a dominant role as the nucleus of the Ottoman Empire. Why was it that these regions thus came to exchange roles within the span of a few centuries? It was because, in terms of human geography, Anatolia had been transferred, in the interval, from the domain of one civilization to that of another—and had been made, in the process, to turn right-about-face—as a result of the Saljūq conquest.

If the political geography of Anatolia is examined again in the light of this historic transformation, it will be seen that, in both

---

[1] See II. D (iii), p. 81, with footnote 1, above. The only trace of this primacy which survives to-day is the name 'Anatolia' itself, which has come to be extended to the whole peninsula from the district in the centre of the plateau which was once occupied by the Anatolic Army Corps. 'Anatolia' is a corruption of the Turkish 'Anadolu', which is itself a corruption of the Greek Ἀνατολή; and Ἀνατολή is a translation of the Latin 'Oriens', which, in the official nomenclature of the Roman Empire in the fourth to seventh centuries of the Christian Era, was the name of a *dioecesis* which corresponded, not to Anatolia, but to Syria (in the widest extension of the name Syria, from the Taurus Mountains to the North Arabian Steppe, and from the north-east frontier of Egypt to the north-west frontier of 'Irāq). The Anatolic Army Corps retired to the north-west side of Taurus in the seventh century of the Christian Era, when the Roman provinces south-east of Taurus were overrun by the Arabs.

periods alike, the respective roles of the several regions conform to and illustrate the law that a march enjoys a stimulus which does not reach the interior. During the eighth and ninth centuries of the Christian Era, when the Anatolic Corps was dominating the East Roman Empire, it was at the same time holding the front line on the front on which Orthodox Christendom was then being subjected to the heaviest external pressure—the south-eastern front, over against the Arab Caliphate—while the Thracensian Corps and the Imperial Guard, which were playing secondary parts, were standing relatively at ease, in the rear. On the other hand, during the fourteenth and fifteenth centuries, when the 'Osmanlis were establishing their ascendancy over the other Turkish successors of the Saljūqs, their domain in the former cantonments of the East Roman Imperial Guard had become the north-western march of the Iranic World against Orthodox Christendom, while the domain of the Qaramanlis, in the former cantonments of the Anatolic Corps, had ceased to be a march and had been relegated to the interior as a consequence of the transfer of this region from the Orthodox Christian World to the Iranic.

In Russian Orthodox Christendom

When we pass on from the main body of Orthodox Christendom to its offshoot in Russia, we find that here, as elsewhere, the vitality of the society has tended to concentrate itself, successively, in one march after another as the relative strengths of the respective external pressures upon the several marches have varied in the course of history.

The Russian region in which the Orthodox Christian Civilization first took root, at the time of its original transplantation across the Black Sea and across the Eurasian Steppe from Constantinople,[1] was the upper basin of the River Dniepr. From there, the centre of gravity of the Orthodox Christian Civilization in Russia was transferred, in the course of the twelfth century, to the upper basin of the Volga by the Russian frontiersmen who were enlarging the borders in this direction at the expense of the primitive pagan Finnish denizens of the north-eastern forests. Thereafter, the seat of vitality shifted again and passed, this time, from the Upper Volga to the lower Dniepr when the light pressure from the forest peoples was outweighed by a crushing pressure from the Nomads of the Eurasian Steppe. This pressure, which was suddenly imposed upon the Russians as a result of the Mongol Bātū Khan's famous campaign of A.D. 1237, was indeed extreme and prolonged; and it is interesting to observe that, in this instance as in others, a challenge

[1] See p. 80, footnote 2, above.

of unusual severity evoked a response which was remarkably original and creative.

This response was nothing less than the evolution of a new manner of life, and a new social organization, which enabled a sedentary society, for the first time in the history of civilizations, not merely to hold its own against the Eurasian Nomads (as the Transoxanian frontiersmen had once held their own in certain ages of Syriac history), and not merely to chastise the Nomads (as Timur had chastised them) by transitory punitive expeditions into the Steppes, but actually to make an enduring conquest of Nomad ground and to change the face of the landscape by transforming the Nomads' cattle-ranges into peasants' fields and replacing their mobile camps by permanent villages. The Cossacks, who performed this unprecedented feat, were frontiersmen of Russian Orthodox Christendom, over against the Eurasian Nomads, who were tempered in the furnace and fashioned on the anvil of border-warfare in the course of the two centuries following the first establishment of the Mongol domination.[1] The far-flung Cossack communities which—at the moment of their annihilation in the Russian Communist Revolution of 1917—were echeloned right across Asia from the banks of the Don to the banks of the Ussuri—were all derived from a single mother community, the Cossack Army of the Dniepr; and we find the characteristic Cossack institutions already fully developed here by the time when, in the fifteenth century, the Dniepr Cossacks first make their appearance in recorded history.

These original Cossacks were a semi-monastic military brotherhood, existing for a single purpose, which displays points of resemblance to the Scandinavian brotherhood of the Jomsborg Vikings[2] and to the Hellenic brotherhood of the Spartans[3] as well as to the Cossacks' own Western Christian contemporaries the Crusading Orders of Knighthood. The water-girt fortress of Jomsborg,

---

[1] The name Cossack describes the Cossacks as they appeared from their Nomad adversaries' point of view. 'Cossack' is simply the Turkish word 'Kazak'; and 'Kazaks', in the political terminology of the Eurasian Nomad World, mean people who live on the Steppe but live there beyond the pale of the organized Nomadic Society: contumacious outlaws who refuse to acknowledge the authority of the legitimate lords of the Steppe, and parasitic marauders who live by lifting the cattle of those productive Nomads who make the Steppe support life by pursuing their skilful and laborious avocation of stock-breeding. (For the nature, genesis, and fate of the Nomadic Civilization, see further Part III. A, vol. iii, pp. 7–22, below.)

[2] See p. 99, footnote 1, above. It may be recalled, in this connexion, that while one of the two constituent elements of the Russian Civilization was Orthodox Christian, the other was Scandinavian (see p. 99, above), and that in the tenth century of the Christian Era the Cataracts of the Dniepr, among which the original Cossacks planted their stronghold before the fifteenth century, had possessed a Scandinavian as well as a Slavonic set of names. (See Constantine Porphyrogenitus: *De Imperio Administrando*, ch. 9.)

[3] See Part III. A, vol. iii, pp. 50–79, below.

ensconced between sea and 'haff', is reproduced in 'the Sich': the river-girt fortress of the Cossacks on an island in the Dniepr. The Helot peasantry which tilled the Spartans' fields, in order that their masters might devote their whole time and energy to the practice of arms, is reproduced in the servile peasantry which laboured for the Cossacks in return for their protection. The devotion of the Templars and Hospitallers and Teutonic Knights to a single purpose is reproduced in the similar devotion of the Cossacks, whose avocation it was likewise to live and die as Crusaders against pagans and Muslims. The Cossacks, however, in their method of conducting their truceless warfare against the Eurasian Nomads, displayed a further characteristic in which they did not so much reproduce the past as anticipate the future. For they resembled the Colonial Powers of the modern Western World in their strategic outlook. They realized that, if a civilization is to wage war against barbarians with success, it must fight them with other weapons and other resources than their own.

Just as the modern Western 'empire-builders' have overwhelmed their primitive opponents by bringing to bear against them the superior resources of Industrialism, so the Cossacks overwhelmed the Nomads by availing themselves of the superior resources of agriculture. And as modern Western generalship has reduced the Nomads to military impotence, on the Nomads' own ground, by outmatching their mobility and overtaking their elusiveness through the employment of newfangled and bewildering and invincible technical devices like railways and motor-cars and aeroplanes, so the Cossacks reduced the Nomads to military impotence in their own way by seizing upon the rivers: the one natural feature on the Steppe which was not under the Nomads' control and which told against them instead of telling in their favour. The rivers were formidable as obstacles and useless as means of transport to the Nomad horseman, whereas the Russian peasant and lumberman, with a lingering trace of Scandinavian seamanship in his social tradition, was expert in river navigation. Accordingly the Cossacks, when they ventured out of the Russian forests in order to dispute with the Nomads the mastery of the Nomads' native Steppes, did not neglect, in their new environment, to take advantage of their own hereditary skill. In learning to vie with their Nomad adversaries in the art of horsemanship, they did not forget to be watermen; and it was by boat, and not on horseback, that they eventually won their way to the dominion of Eurasia.

Descending the Dniepr, the Cossacks held the river-line, maintaining their own communications upstream with Russia, and cutting the Nomads' communications from bank to bank, by their command of the water. Moreover, the tributary streams led the Cossack boatmen, by easy portages, from one river-basin to another; and before the end of the sixteenth century the parent Cossack community along the line of the Dniepr had given birth to two daughter communities: the Cossacks of the Don and the Cossacks of the Yaik.[1] Thereafter, in an unequal alliance with Muscovy which accelerated their expansion but ultimately cost them their independence, the Cossacks extended their range from the rivers which flow into the Black Sea and the Caspian across the Steppes to the rivers which flow into the Arctic Ocean across Siberia. In A.D. 1586 they crossed the watershed between the basins of the Volga and the Ob; by 1638 their exploration of Siberian inland waters had brought them to the shores of the Pacific on the Sea of Okhotsk.[2]

In the same century in which the Cossacks thus signalized their victorious reaction to the pressure of the Nomads on the south-eastern borders of Russian Orthodox Christendom, another frontier became the principal recipient of external pressure upon Russia and concurrently the principal focus of Russian vitality. In the seventeenth century, Russia experienced, for the first time in her history, a formidable pressure from the Western World. A Polish army penetrated to Moscow and remained in occupation of the Kremlin for over two years (20th September, 1610, to 22nd October, 1612), and soon afterwards Sweden barred out Russia from the Baltic by making herself mistress of the whole eastern coastline of that sea from Finland southwards to the Dvina, where she marched with the United Kingdom of Poland-Lithuania.[3] The century had barely closed when Peter the Great retorted to this Western pressure by founding Petersburg in A.D. 1703 and displaying the flag of a Russian Navy, in the Western style, on Baltic waters. As the capital of a Russian Empire which did not cease to expand towards the south and the east till it had pushed its frontiers across the Caucasus and on to the Pamirs, Petersburg was even more 'eccentric' in its situation than Antioch had been as the capital of the Seleucidae.[4] Nevertheless, the capital of the Russian Empire was retained in this fantastic city—founded by a political genius in a frozen swamp on the extreme northern verge of the habitable world—by the exigency of a pressure from the West which ever

[1] i.e. the Ural River—a name under which the Yaik has been given a curious notoriety by the caprice of our modern Western geographers, who have made this artery of the Eurasian Steppe into the conventional boundary between Europe and Asia.
[2] For a fuller account of the Cossacks, see an article entitled 'Russia, Germany and Asia' in *The Round Table*, issue of June 1918.
[3] Sweden conquered Livland from Poland-Lithuania in A.D. 1621–5, after having compelled Russia, in a peace-treaty concluded in A.D. 1617 at Stolbovo, to sign away her precious strip of coastline at the head of the Gulf of Finland.
[4] See pp. 143–4, above.

continued to rise until the steam was blown off at last in the great explosion of 1914–18. After that catastrophe, which shattered the pre-existent political structure of Europe and interposed a broad barrier of debris—the East-European 'successor-states'—between Russia and the surviving Great Powers of the Western World, the capital of the Russian Empire, in its latest metamorphosis the U.S.S.R., promptly swung back from the eccentric position on the Western March in which it had remained fixed for more than two centuries to the position of greatest administrative convenience in the interior: that is to say, from Leningrad to Moscow.[1]

In Japan

If we now take a comparative view of this history of the offshoot of the Orthodox Christian Civilization in Russia and the history of the offshoot of the Far Eastern Civilization in Japan, we shall observe, in Japanese history, an outflow of vitality and power from the interior into a march which closely corresponds to the first of the three movements in Russian history which we have just been examining. We have seen that the centre of gravity of the Orthodox Christian Civilization in Russia was transferred from the upper basin of the Dniepr—the region in which the offshoot first took root—to the upper basin of the Volga when this latter region was added to the domain of Russian Orthodox Christendom by the prowess of the Russian backwoodsmen. We may now observe that the centre of gravity of the Far Eastern Civilization in Japan likewise shifted from the region in which the offshoot first took root in this case—that is, from Yamato—to a region in the back-woods which was subsequently added to the domain of the Japanese Far Eastern Civilization: shifted, that is to say, from Yamato to the Kwanto. In the historical geography of Japan, Nara and Kyoto are the analogues of the Russian Kiev, while Kamakura and Yedo-Tokyo are the analogues, respectively, of the Russian Vladímir and the Russian Moscow. The contrast between 'the Kiev Period' and 'the Moscow Period' of Russian history reappears, with an accentuated sharpness, in the contrast between 'the Nara and

---

[1] By the time when the capital was retransferred from Leningrad to Moscow under the Russian Communist régime, Moscow, which had lain within the north-eastern marches of Russia from the thirteenth to the sixteenth century of the Christian Era, had long since been relegated to the interior by the eastward and southward expansion of the Russian Empire. In this retransfer, however, there was another force at work besides *vis inertiae*. If, in one aspect, the retransfer of the capital of the U.S.S.R. from Leningrad to Moscow by the Russian Communists was an almost automatic recoil, there was also another aspect in which this transfer, like the contemporary transfer of the capital of the Turkish Republic from Constantinople to Angora by the Turkish Nationalists, was a deliberate move in a systematic campaign of social revolution. This aspect is referred to again in Part III. C (i) (d), vol. iii, pp. 200–2, and is dealt with further in Part IX, apropos of contacts in the Space-dimension between different civilizations.

Kyoto Period' of Japanese history (sixth[1] to twelfth century of the Christian Era) on the one hand and 'the Kamakura and Ashikaga Period' (A.D. 1184–1597) on the other. The first precocious and sophisticated bloom of the Far Eastern Civilization on Japanese soil at Nara and Kyoto has that exotic air of a hot-house plant, keeping alive by a *tour de force* in an unfavourable climate, which is also characteristic, though in a less extreme degree, of the first bloom of the Orthodox Christian Civilization on Russian soil at Kiev. And the passing of the sceptre in the twelfth century of the Christian Era from sophisticated Kiev to rude Vladímir—the natural breakdown of an artificial state of affairs—is analogous to the more violent and dramatic revolution in Japan through which, in the course of the same century, the régime of 'the Cloistered Emperors' of Yamato was overthrown and was replaced by that of the feudal nobility of the Kwanto. The new masters of Japan, like those of Russia, were men of war who had acquired land and power and military spirit in the process of enlarging the borders at the expense of the primitive peoples of the north-eastern forests (the Ainu being the counterparts, in the Japanese hinterland, of the Finns in the Russian). Thus in Japan, as in Russia, vitality flowed away from the sheltered interior towards the exposed frontier until eventually power followed suit.[2]

In the Minoan and Hellenic Worlds

In the Minoan World, which we may consider next, the quarter in which the heaviest pressure was felt was the frontier over against the continental European barbarians; and, in the course of Minoan history, vitality and power duly passed from the maritime interior to the continental European marches. When 'the Thalassocracy of Minos' was in its hey-day, the cultivated inhabitants of the unwalled imperial capitals at Cnossos and Phaestus, on the island of Crete, doubtless looked down upon the wardens of the marches who had to live a ruder life—cribbed, cabined, and confined within the clumsily massive walls of Tiryns and Mycenae—for fear of the barbarians at their gates. How much more elegant and comfortable to be protected, as the Eteocretans were, by the shapely wooden

---

[1] Strictly, 'the Nara Period' did not begin till the laying out of the first fixed capital of the Japanese Empire at Nara in A.D. 710. From a broader point of view, however, this period may be taken as coeval with the introduction of the Far Eastern Civilization into Japan. In this process the two major events were the importation of Mahayanian Buddhism into the Japanese Archipelago, via Korea, during the second half of the sixth century of the Christian Era, and the reorganization of the Japanese Imperial Government on the Chinese model of the T'ang in A.D. 645.

[2] The breakdowns of the Far Eastern Civilization in Japan and of the Orthodox Christian Civilization in Russia, which accompanied these shifts of the centres of gravity in the course of the twelfth century of the Christian Era, are examined in IV. C (ii) (b) 2, vol. iv, pp. 95–6, below.

walls of an Imperial Navy which was in sole and complete command of the estranging sea! Yet, here again, pressure administered a stimulus which eventually gave Mycenae and Tiryns the mastery over Phaestus and Cnossos. The pioneers who had won for the Minoan Civilization a footing on the European mainland, in defiance of the continental barbarians, by building those gigantic fortifications, found energy and enterprise to spare, from their task of holding their own on land, to compete with their imperial cousins[1] in Crete for the control of the sea. While they kept the continental barbarians at bay with one hand, they launched a battle-fleet with the other; and our archaeologists conjecture that it was a Mycenaean Armada which put a sudden and catastrophic end to the Minoan Thalassocracy by breaking through the boasted wooden walls of Crete and sacking the open city of Cnossos towards the close of the fifteenth century B.C.

When we pass on to the history of the Hellenic Civilization which was 'affiliated' to the Minoan Civilization, we find that in the Hellenic World, likewise, the continental European marches were the zone of greatest external pressure and that the vitality and power of the Hellenic Society tended to concentrate themselves at different points in this zone successively as the incidence of the pressure shifted hither and thither in the course of Hellenic history.

In the Greek Peninsula, the hegemony which was first held by a city-state situated in 'the Island of Pelops' passed from Sparta to Athens, on the continental side of the Isthmus of Corinth, and then from both Athens and Sparta to Thebes, on the continental side of Mounts Cithaeron and Parnes, until it came to rest at the roots of the Peninsula in Macedonia: the frontier state of Greece over against the continental European barbarians.[2] Similarly, in the

---

[1] This language is not intended to imply that these Mycenaean pioneers of the Minoan Civilization were Eteocretan colonists, or even that they were akin to the Eteocretans in race or linked with them by the bond of a kindred language. It is possible and even probable that the majority of the exponents of the Minoan Civilization on the mainland of European Greece were not colonists but converts. (On this question, see II. C (i) (b), vol. i, p. 101, footnote 1, with Annex II.)

[2] The writer of this Study vividly remembers how the continental character of Macedonia impressed itself upon him at the first view. He first visited Macedonia in the summer of 1912, at the end of a visit to the Kingdom of Greece within the frontiers as they then stood. Since the standard-gauge railway which now links Athens with Salonica had not been completed at that date, he travelled from the Peiraeus to Salonica by sea. He had been looking forward with interest to observing the political aspect of the passage from territory under Greek to territory under Turkish rule; but, as the steamer entered Salonica harbour, his eye was caught, not by the Turkish flag flying above the custom house, but by Austrian and German railway-wagons standing along the quay, on rails which ran without a break from Salonica to Vienna and from Vienna to Berlin. He then realized in a flash that this economic solidarity with Central Europe was the distinctive and fundamental characteristic of Macedonia, and that the political connexion with Turkey-in-Asia, though picturesque, was accidental and superficial. (For the history of the question whether the Hellenic Great Power in Macedonia was to be a monarchy—as it actually came to be—or a confederacy of city-states of the kind that was built up in Italy by Rome, see III. C (ii) (b), Annex IV, in vol. iii, below.)

Italian Peninsula, the hegemony which had first been held by Syracuse in the island of Sicily (an island which, in terms of human geography, is only insular in the same degree as the Peloponnese) was afterwards contended for between two Powers which were both situated on the continental side of the Straits of Messina: Samnium and Rome. Moreover, this contest was won, not by Samnium, who h..d both hands free for fighting her duel with her Italian neighbour, but by Rome, who was constrained to fight Samnium with one hand while she was employing the other in keeping at arm's length the Celtic barbarians who were pressing upon Italy from the heart of Continental Europe. Yet Rome beat Samnium and won the hegemony of Italy, not in spite of, but because of, the fact that she had previously taken over the wardenship of the continental march of Italy when the Etruscans had shown themselves unequal to the task;[1] for the pressure which had thus fallen upon Rome acted as a stimulus and not as a handicap.

From the days of Camillus to the days of Caesar, during the four centuries which it took the Romans to build up their empire, the peril which was their bugbear—more trying to Roman nerves than Carthaginian galley-beaks or Macedonian pike-heads—was the barbarian avalanche: the 'Gallicus Tumultus'; and the genius of Hannibal showed itself in nothing so much as in his decision to attack Rome from the quarter from which, in Roman eyes, an aggressor ever appeared the most formidable. In making the passage of the Alps and bringing the Celtic avalanche down with him in full force in his descent of the Italian slope, Hannibal was seeking to reproduce artificially, for the undoing of the Romans, the natural catastrophe which, some two centuries earlier, had overwhelmed the Etruscans. He was seeking to bring upon the Romans the destruction which, in Mr. Kipling's story, Mowgli brought upon Shere Khan when he sent the herd of buffalo stampeding down from the head of the valley upon the tiger who stood trapped in the valley-bottom. But the strategy which succeeded so brilliantly in the hands of the fictitious Indian changeling failed in the hands of the historic Carthaginian man of genius, because Hannibal's human antagonists reacted, in this desperate situation, quite otherwise than Mowgli's bestial victim. Instead of losing nerve, like Shere Khan, and turning tail, the Romans refused to

---

[1] Before the collapse of the Etruscan Power, Rome had held the wardenship of the Etruscan marches of Latium and had finally reacted to Etruscan pressure by a victorious counter-attack in which she had conquered and incorporated the Etruscan city-state which had lain closest to the Latin border: that is, Veii. In virtue of this original wardenship of the Etruscan marches, Rome had captured the hegemony of Latium from Alba Longa—another example of the phenomenon of the frontier prevailing over the interior, since Alba, ensconced among the hills that bear her name, was shielded from Etruscan attack by the Roman watch on the Tiber.

'despair of the Republic' and turned at bay; and in defeating Hannibal and his Celtic allies they determined their own destinies. The general result of the victory of Rome in the Hannibalic War was that the Roman Empire grew—and merged—into a Hellenic universal state. One particular result was that Rome won—and lost—the hegemony over the whole Hellenic World by becoming the sole warden of the continental European marches.

This devolution upon Rome of the sole responsibility for the defence of Hellenism against the continental European barbarians was manifest to the World, and was acknowledged even by the Romans themselves, when Augustus organized the Roman frontier along the longest diameter of the Continent from the mouth of the Rhine to the mouth of the Danube; but this vast extension of Rome's commitments, as compared with the local wardenship of the Italian march which she had originally taken over from the Etruscans, had devolved upon the Romans against their will and had still been repudiated by them in theory long after it had become an accomplished fact. The advance of the Roman frontier from the line of the Po, where it had stood at the outbreak of the Hannibalic War, to the distant line of the Rhine was a direct, though long-delayed, consequence of the Hannibalic War itself, in which the western corner of Transalpine Europe had become both the prize of victory and the key to the retention of its fruits.[1] The parallel advance of the frontier from the Po to the Danube was a direct consequence of Rome's victory over Macedonia and therefore an indirect consequence of her victory over Hannibal, since it was the Hannibalic War that precipitated the collision between Rome and Macedonia and also predetermined the outcome.

In this trial of strength between the Power which had become the warden of the continental European marches of the Hellenic Civilization in Italy and the Power which was the warden of the corresponding marches in Greece, Macedonia did not succumb to Rome without a struggle;[2] for the Macedonians had been trained in the same school of border-warfare as the Romans, and they too were redoubtable frontiersmen and barbarian-fighters in their degree. The Hannibalic War, however, had been an unprecedented ordeal from which the Macedonians had held aloof, while the Romans had been made by their Punic adversaries to pass through the fire like the children offered to Molech;[3] and the burning fiery furnace had tempered the Roman steel to a cutting edge which clove the Macedonian buckler at one stroke and mercilessly shore through the living flesh. This figurative manner of speech is

---

[1] On this point see I. B (iv), vol. i, p. 40, above.
[2] For the increase in the vigour and effectiveness of the Macedonian resistance as the struggle proceeded, see II. D (iv), pp. 103–4, above.   [3] Lev. xviii. 21, xx. 2; Jer. xxxii. 35.

literally borne out by the following description[1] of the effect upon the Macedonians' *moral* when they first encountered a weapon which the Romans had just adopted, in the course of the Hannibalic War, from some of the European barbarians in Hannibal's service. The incident was the sequel to a cavalry skirmish in Illyria between the Roman and Macedonian outposts in the opening phase of the campaign of the year 200 B.C.

'Philip reckoned that it would conduce to his popularity with the troops, and would increase their readiness to risk their lives in his service, if he looked after the burial of the men who had fallen in this reconnaissance; so he gave orders for the bodies to be brought to camp and buried in the sight of the whole army with military honours. Nothing, however, is so uncertain and so unpredictable as the psychology of the crowd; for the spectacle which was to have fortified the troops' *moral* actually had the effect of shaking it. In hostilities with their usual Greek and Illyrian adversaries, the Macedonians were only familiar with spear-wounds and arrow-wounds and occasional lance-wounds. They now saw the execution done by the Spanish sword: mutilated trunks with the arms shorn away, heads severed from bodies by strokes that had cleft right through the neck, intestines laid bare, and other horrors; and this ocular demonstration of the type of weapon and type of fighting-man that they now had to face simply threw them into a panic. The King himself was terror-stricken at the thought that he had not yet faced the Romans in a pitched battle; and accordingly he recalled his son, with the garrison that was guarding the Pelagonian Pass, to reinforce his own army, and thus exposed Macedonia to invasion by Pleuratus and by the Dardanians.'

Thus the Macedonian frontiersman, when he came to grips with the Roman, found himself as hopelessly outmatched in armament as Hector when he faced Achilles in his last battle. Yet, in that legendary combat, it was not only Hector who was fey. It was Achilles' doom to meet his death from a Dardanian arrow when he had laid his Trojan rival low; and the drama of Achilles and Hector was re-enacted to the bitter end by Rome and Macedonia. The King of Macedonia, in the shock of his collision with the deadly power of Rome, had thrown up his wardenship of the continental European marches of the Hellenic World in that vital section, covering the Greek Peninsula, which Macedonia had guarded hitherto. By withdrawing the frontier guard, he had exposed not only his own Kingdom but the whole of Greece to invasion by the Dardanian barbarians of the Upper Vardar Valley and the Illyrian barbarians of Scodra. But the responsibility which King Philip had thrown off in his extremity, as he went out to meet defeat at Roman hands, could not be repudiated by Philip's conquerors.

[1] Livy, Book XXXI, ch. 34.

Inexorably, the burden of vanquished Macedonia became the burden of victorious Rome; and it was Philip's abandonment of the old Macedonian border in the Vardar Basin in the year 200 B.C. that compelled Augustus, two centuries later, to advance the Roman border up to the Danube, as well as up to the Rhine, from the Basin of the Po. Thus, in the event, the Illyrian and the Dardanian, as well as the Spaniard and the Gaul, were brought within the frontiers of the Hellenic universal state by Roman force of arms; and so it was that Rome, in winning the hegemony of the Hellenic World from Carthage and Macedon, set up a train of events which inevitably transferred the hegemony to other hands again in the fullness of time.

For Rome had no peculiar magic.

> The same arts that did gain
> A power, must it maintain—

and Rome was no more capable than her predecessors and victims of maintaining a hegemony which had been gained under the stimulus of barbarian pressure after she had deprived herself of that stimulus in obedience to the very necessities of her new situation.   In the last phase of Hellenic history, power and vitality flowed away once more from the interior to the marches; and this time the current left Rome stranded. The stimulus which had once nerved Rome to overcome Syracuse and Samnium and Carthage and Macedon now nerved Illyria and Gaul, in their turn, to dominate Rome herself.   Some three centuries after Augustus had organized the Danubian frontier, the dominion which the first Roman Emperor had gathered into his hands for transmission to Roman successors was being exercised by the Illyrian Diocletian[1] and by the Dardanian Constantine;[2] and the Roman Empire was being governed, not from the banks of the Tiber nor even from Milan beyond the farther bank of the Po, but from two cities in the immediate hinterlands of the two continental frontiers: from Constantinople behind the Lower Danube and from Trier behind the Middle Rhine.   In the last agony, when the Empire broke up and the Old Rome opened her gates to the Goths and Vandals, New Rome remained an impregnable city of refuge—never to be swamped by the barbarian waves that broke upon its walls from beyond the old front line.   As for the Rhineland, it played the same role in the break-up of the Roman Empire as Transoxania in the

---

[1] Diocletian came from Doclea, a village in the Basin of the Lake of Scodra which, in 200 B.C., had been the nucleus of the Illyrian principality of King Pleuratus.

[2] Constantine's father, Constantius Chlorus, came from Naissus (Nish) in the Morava Valley, which lay within the borders of Dardania; and the family traced their origin back to another Dardanian—Claudius Gothicus—who had anticipated Constantius Chlorus, by several generations, in attaining to the purple.

break-up of the 'Abbasid Caliphate. Under the Merovingian régime it became the seat of the least ineffective and least ephemeral of all the defunct empire's 'successor-states'.

In the break-up of the Hellenic universal state, we can observe the stimulus of exposure to external pressure at work, not only in its general social effect upon whole territories and populations, but also in its particular personal effect upon single individuals. On this plane, it produced, 'in real life', the astonishing results which Mr. G. K. Chesterton has imagined in his fantasy 'The Napoleon of Notting Hill'. It transformed pacific men of letters into warlike men of action. In order to perform this miracle, the stimulus had, of course, to be administered with extreme violence. Pausanias the antiquarian, for example, was not made a new man by the momentary appearance, in the Asopus Valley, of a stray band of trans-frontier barbarians. Pausanias was a contemporary of Marcus Aurelius, and in that generation, some two centuries after the establishment of the Danubian frontier, such mishaps as this passed off without stirring men's souls to the depths, because they were regarded as curiosities rather than as portents. Even so, the vagaries of the outlandish Costoboci caused at least one citizen of one city in Greece to take up arms and die in battle for hearth and home in the manner of the past which was also to be the manner of the future;[1] while the more formidable upheaval in the hinterland of the Danubian frontier —a wave in a new movement of barbarian unrest in which the Costobocan raid on Greece was a casual ripple—compelled the philosopher-emperor to devote his last years to the uncongenial business of punitive border warfare.

The emergency which gave a Mnêsibûlus or a Marcus the occasion for a noble gesture was felt in grim earnest in the days of Athenian Dexippus, and yet more in the days of Cyrenaean Synesius and Arvernian Sidonius Apollinaris. In those latter days, no man could blind himself to the fact that the barbarian enemy was now within the gates of the Hellenic World; and this challenge to the inner citadel of Hellenism transfigured the last custodians of the Hellenic cultural tradition. The Gothic threat to Athens nerved the historian Dexippus to take up the sword in order to resume the pen when the tyranny was overpast. The Gothic threat to Auvergne, and the Berber threat to Cyrenaica, which did not pass

---

[1] 'The marauding band of Costoboci which raided Greece in my lifetime appeared, in the course of their raid, before the walls of Elatea; whereupon, an Elatean gentleman, Mnêsibûlus, raised an armed force under his own command and succeeded in inflicting heavy casualties on the barbarians, though he himself was killed in action.' (Pausanias: *Descriptio Graeciae*, Book X, ch. 34.)

These Elateans who died for their country in the second century of the Christian Era were worthy of the epitaph in which the self-sacrifice of the Tegeatans had been commemorated in the fifth century B.C. by Simonides.

away, changed the whole course of Synesius's and Sidonius's lives.
It turned them from cultivated and lethargic country-gentlemen into
energetic barbarian-fighters and devoted shepherds of souls. By the
third generation, when the intrusive barbarism had become endemic,
the *ci-devant* heirs of the Hellenic culture in a derelict world had
adapted themselves so well to the monstrous conditions of their
new environment that when the Arvernian nobility answered the
summons of their Visigothic overlords to march against the Franks,
they acquitted themselves better than their barbarian comrades-in-
arms in this contest between two barbarian 'successor-states' for
the residuary legateeship of Rome in Gaul. At the decisive Battle
of Vouillé (A.D. 507), Sidonius's grandson died gallantly on the
battle-field with King Alaric when Alaric's own Visigoths ran away.

*In the Western World over against the Continental European
Barbarians*

When we pass on to the history of our own Western Civilization
which is 'affiliated' to the Hellenic Civilization, we find on the one
hand that, in the Western World, the heaviest external pressure was
felt, at first, in the same quarter in which it had been felt from first
to last in the Hellenic World and in the Minoan World—that is
to say, on the frontier over against the continental European barbarians. On the other hand we find that the Western, unlike either
the Hellenic or the Minoan, reaction to the barbarian pressure was
in the end definitively victorious. The barbarian frontier of Western
Christendom on the Continent of Europe eventually faded out;
and thereafter our Western Society found itself in contact here, no
longer with barbarians, but with alien civilizations. The incidence
of these new pressures stimulated the vitality of our Western
Society to new responses in new forms.

In the first phase of Western history on the European Continent,
the stimulating effect of the pressure from the continental barbarians declared itself in the emergence of a fresh social structure
for a nascent society out of the debris of one of the 'successor-
states' of the defunct Roman Empire: the barbarian principality of
the Franks. The Merovingian Frankish régime had been Epi-
methean: its face had been turned towards the Roman past. The
succeeding Carolingian Frankish régime was Promethean; for,
although it incidentally evoked a ghost of the Roman Empire, its
face was turned towards the Western future, and the ghost was only
evoked—in the spirit of the cry 'Debout les morts!'—in order to
assist the living in carrying out an almost superhuman task.[1] This

---

[1] See Part X, below, for the phenomenon of the Evocation of Ghosts in general, and
in particular for this Carolingian evocation of a ghost of the Roman Empire.

complete transformation of the social functions of the Frankish
Power—this transubstantiation of the Frankish body politic—was
nothing less than a fresh celebration of the perpetual mystery of Life.
'Out of the eater came forth meat, and out of the strong came forth
sweetness.'[1] And in what part of the Frankish domain was this
fresh act of creation accomplished? Not in the interior but on the
continental European March; not in Neustria, on soil fertilized by
ancient Roman culture and sheltered from fresh continental barbarian inroads, but in Austrasia,[2] in a territory which bestrode the
ancient Roman frontier and which was still exposed to constant
assaults from the Saxons of the North European forest and from
the Avars of the Eurasian Steppe. The measure of the stimulus
which was administered by this external pressure to the Franks in
Austrasia is given by the achievements of Charlemagne. Charlemagne's eighteen Saxon campaigns and his extirpation of the Avars
are not incomparable, as sheer military triumphs, to Timur Lenk's
steppe campaigns in which he crushed the Nomads of Mughalistān
and Qipchāq;[3] and Charlemagne's military and political achievements were followed by the first faint manifestations of intellectual
energy in the Western World—a feeble counterpart to the outburst of intellectual energy in Transoxania and Khurāsān under the
Timurids.[4]

This Austrasian reaction to the stimulus of pressure from the
continental European barbarians—the reaction which came to a
head in the career of Charlemagne—was not conclusive. For
reasons which are examined at later points in this Study,[5] it came
to a premature standstill and was followed by a relapse. Accordingly, we find the Austrasian reaction reduplicated in our Western
history by the Saxon reaction which came to a head, rather less than
two centuries later, in the career of Otto I. The enduring (though
exhausting) achievement of Charlemagne's career had been the incorporation of the domain of the continental Saxon barbarians into
Western Christendom; and by this very success he had prepared
the way for a transfer of the kingdom, the power and the glory from

---

[1] Judges xiv. 14.
[2] The very nomenclature 'Austria-Neustria', which makes its appearance in the
Lombard as well as in the Frankish 'successor-state' of the Roman Empire, tells its own
tale. 'Austria' is a new name for a new living commonwealth which has sprung from the
soil of the derelict 'successor-state' in its eastern—i.e. continental—marches. 'Neustria'
simply means 'Non-Austria': that is to say, the leavings of the debris which still cumber
the ground on the rest of the derelict site after the new growth in the marches has
manifested itself.
[3] See pp. 146–8, above. Charlemagne, like Timur, though in a lesser degree, succumbed to the malady of Militarism and was inveigled by it into misdirecting his military
energies from the periphery to the interior of his world; and Charlemagne's error, like
Timur's, resulted—though this, again, in a lesser degree—in the collapse of the structure
which he had built up. For the malady of Militarism, as illustrated in both Charlemagne's
career and Timur's, see further IV. C (iii) (c) 3 (α), vol. iv, pp. 488–501, below.
[4] For this, see pp. 148–50, above.
[5] In II. D (vii), pp. 344–5, and in IV. C (iii) (c) 3 (α), vol. iv, pp. 488–91, below.

his own victorious Austrasia to the homeland of the vanquished and forcibly converted barbarians by pushing forward the continental European march of Western Christendom from Austrasia into Saxony and thereby exposing Saxony, instead of Austrasia, to the stimulus of continental barbarian pressure from the hinterland. In Otto's day, the same stimulus evoked in Saxony the same reaction that had been evoked by it, in Charlemagne's day, in Austrasia; and this time the counter-offensive of the Western Civilization against the continental barbarians was sustained until it reached its final objective.

Otto smote the Wends as Charlemagne had smitten Otto's own Saxon ancestors; and thereafter the continental frontiers of Western Christendom were pushed steadily eastward, partly through the voluntary conversion of the barbarians to Christianity and partly through their subjection or extirpation by force of arms. The Magyars and the Poles and the Scandinavians were converted at the turn of the tenth and eleventh centuries of the Christian Era by the prestige of Western Christendom under the Ottonid régime, as the Bohemians had been converted, two centuries earlier, by the prestige of Western Christendom under the régime of Charlemagne. The barbarians along the continental coastline of the Baltic were more recalcitrant. On this sector of the frontier, the Saxon frontiersmen had to follow up Otto's counter-stroke against the Wends in a stubborn border warfare that lasted some two centuries before they succeeded in definitively advancing the bounds of Western Christendom from the line of the Elbe to the line of the Oder. This result was achieved by the conversion of the Wends in Mecklenburg in A.D. 1161, and by the contemporary extirpation of their kinsmen in Brandenburg and Meissen.

Thereafter, in the thirteenth and fourteenth centuries, the task of 'Westernizing' the last remaining continental barbarians was carried on by the Germans with still greater vigour and effect through the instrumentality of two new Western institutions: the city-state and the militant monastic order. The Hansa Towns and the Teutonic Knights, between them, advanced the bounds of Western Christendom from the line of the Oder to the line of the Dvina, while, farther north, the Scandinavian converts to Western Christianity were winning fresh ground for Western Christendom and for themselves—the Danes in Estonia and the Swedes in Finland. That was the last round in this secular conflict; for, before the close of the fourteenth century of the Christian Era, the continental European barbarians, who had been pressing upon the frontiers of three successive civilizations over a total span of some three thousand years, had been wiped off the face of the Earth. By

A.D. 1400, Western Christendom and Orthodox Christendom, which had been entirely isolated from one another on the Continent by intervening barbarians no longer than five hundred years before, had come to march with one another continuously along a line extending across the whole breadth of the Continent from the coast of the Adriatic Sea to the coast of the Arctic Ocean.

It is interesting to observe how, on this frontier between a youthful Western Christendom and a senile continental European barbarism, the reversal in the direction of the pressure, which became constant from the time when Otto I took up Charlemagne's work, was followed by a transference of stimulus as the Western counter-offensive proceeded.

For example, the original Duchy of Saxony, west of the Elbe, suffered the same eclipse as a result of Otto's victories over the Wends that Austrasia had suffered, two centuries earlier, as a result of Charlemagne's victories over the Saxons themselves. Like Austrasia, Saxony owed the hegemony over Western Christendom which she inherited from Austrasia to the *esprit de corps* that was instilled by pressure from barbarians at close quarters; and, again like Austrasia, she lost her *esprit de corps*, and with it her hegemony, when this pressure was removed. Saxony actually lost her hegemony over the Western World in A.D. 1024: that is, as soon as the Wends beyond the Elbe had been thrown upon the defensive. She broke into fragments in A.D. 1182–91: that is, as soon as the frontier of the Western World had been definitively advanced, on this sector, from the line of the Elbe to the line of the Oder. Thereafter, when, in a later age of Western history, a state bearing the name of Saxony once again became a power in the Western World, this latter-day Saxony arose in the March of Meissen: that is, on one portion of the new ground which had been won for Western Christendom at the expense of the Wends during the two centuries of border warfare along the old Saxon frontier which had followed the reign of Otto I.

Again, as the continental frontier of Western Christendom was pushed farther and farther forward into the barbarian hinterland, the seat of 'the Holy Roman Empire' receded deeper and deeper into the interior; and simultaneously, as the vigour of the Western counter-offensive against the continental barbarians increased, the authority of 'the Holy Roman Emperor' diminished. The similitude of the Imperial office, which had been revived at the end of the eighth century of the Christian Era for the benefit of an Austrasian prince and had then passed from Austrasia to Saxony, did not continue thereafter to follow the ever advancing frontier. When the office fell, in due course, from Saxon hands in A.D. 1024, it passed this time, not to the makers of the new marches of the Western World beyond the Elbe, but to a dynasty whose homeland lay in Rhenish Franconia. Moreover, from the advent of the Salian Dynasty to the Imperial throne in this year 1024 down to the formal extinction of 'the Holy Roman Empire', nearly eight centuries later, in A.D. 1806, each successive dynasty that held the office had its roots in the Rhine Basin—that ancient continental march of the Roman Empire which had been relegated to the innermost interior of the expanding Western World. The Franconians came from the valley of the Main, the Hohenstaufen from the valley of the Neckar, the Luxemburgers from the valley of the Meuse, the Hapsburgs from the valley of the Aar. At each successive transfer, the office passed to a dynasty which sprang from soil more remote from the continental frontiers of the Western World than the native soil of its predecessors; and concurrently, at each successive transfer, the Imperial authority grew weaker. It was less effective in Salian hands than in Saxon and in Hohenstaufen hands than in Salian, until the downfall of the House of Hohenstaufen was followed by 'the Great Interregnum' (A.D. 1254–73).

It is noteworthy that, during this practical break in the continuity of the Imperial succession to Charlemagne and to Otto I, the work of reacting against the pressure of the continental barbarians—a work which Charlemagne had first set on foot and which Otto had taken up again—was being carried on, and this with unprecedented energy and success, by other agencies than the Imperial authority: such agencies as the Hansa towns and the Teutonic Knights and the crowns of Denmark and Sweden. It is also noteworthy that the Hohenstaufen, who were seeking to preserve 'the Holy Roman Empire' *in extremis*, and the Hapsburgs and Luxemburgers, who were seeking to re-establish it after it had fallen into practical abeyance, all alike sought to restore some real function and importance and power to an office which had in fact become superfluous by combining it, once more, as it had been combined in the great days of the Carolingians and the Ottonids, with something in the nature of a wardenship of the marches. The Hohenstaufens sought a new basis for their power in the Kingdom of the Two Sicilies, which was a march of Western Christendom against both the Orthodox Christian World and the Arabic World. The Luxemburgers mounted to the throne of the Empire by way of the throne of Bohemia, and justified their tenure of the highest office in Western Christendom by their service in bringing the full light of Western Civilization into a region which had previously lain in the penumbra. Rudolf of Hapsburg made the fortunes of his family not by his acquisition of the Imperial office but by his seizure of the opportunity which this gave him for adding the Austrian March of the Empire to his ancestral possessions in Swabia.

It was thanks to this permanent addition to the Hapsburg family inheritance that the Imperial office, which Rudolf had held for his lifetime, was reacquired by his descendants not much less than two centuries later. Yet the office would assuredly not have remained in the hands of the Hapsburgs permanently the second time any more than the first, and would probably not have remained in existence at all now that the ancient pressure from the continental European barbarians had been completely removed by the complete extinction of the barbarians themselves, if the Western World had not suddenly been subjected at this juncture to a new and formidable continental pressure from an alien civilization. The life of 'the Holy Roman Empire' was unexpectedly prolonged for another three centuries, and was permanently vested during the whole of this period in the House of Hapsburg, in consequence of the impact of the Ottoman Power upon the Western World in the Basin of the Danube. 'The Great Interregnum' which virtually began at the death of Frederick II Hohenstaufen and was nominally brought to an end when Rudolf of Hapsburg assumed the Imperial office a quarter of a century later, really continued until A.D. 1526, when, on the morrow of the Battle of Mohacz, Rudolf's descendant Ferdinand added the crowns of Hungary and Bohemia to the wardenship of the Austrian and Styrian marches and thereby founded the Danubian Hapsburg Monarchy, with which the Imperial office thenceforth remained indissolubly associated until it was finally extinguished in 1806 by a formal merger of the shadow in the reality.[1]

Thus the vitality of 'the Holy Roman Empire' varied, during the course of the Empire's existence, in the same degree as the intensity of the external pressure that was being exerted from time to time, by barbarians or by alien civilizations, upon the continental frontiers of Western Christendom. The Empire lost vitality as the pressure from the continental European barbarians relaxed, and then recovered vitality when a new pressure came to be exerted by the 'Osmanlis. Conversely, we find that the vitality of the barbarians who had remained beyond the pale of the Western Civilization and the *ci-devant* barbarians who had been brought just within the pale by conversion tended to increase as the pressure

[1] In August 1806 the Holy Roman Emperor Francis II Hapsburg formally renounced the style and title of 'Roman Emperor' in order to style himself thenceforward 'Emperor of Austria'—a titular solecism which was at the same time a tardy recognition of long since accomplished historical facts. (See the passage quoted from Lord Bryce in Part I. B (iv), Annex, vol. i, on p. 343, above.)

exerted upon them by the Western counter-offensive came to be intensified.

The Lithuanians, for example, as the last surviving pagans in Europe, drew upon themselves, in the thirteenth and fourteenth centuries of the Christian Era, the last impetus of the Crusading spirit in the Western World that survived the decisive failure of the Crusading enterprise in Syria. The head-quarters of the Teutonic Knights, which had been established at Acre, on the Syrian coast, until the fall of this sole remaining stronghold of the Crusaders in the Holy Land in A.D. 1291, were transferred, in 1308, to Marienburg on the easternmost arm of the delta of the Vistula; and during the next hundred years the Teutonic Order pressed Lithuania hard. This formidable Western pressure upon the Lithuanians in their homeland had the effect of stimulating the Lithuanians themselves to achieve sweeping conquests at the expense of Russian Orthodox Christendom in the upper basin of the Dniepr, and at the expense of the Eurasian Nomads in the sector of the Qipchāq Steppe that lay between the lower courses of the Dniepr and the Dniestr; and, as their struggle with the Order approached its climax, the stimulus increased to such a pitch that in A.D. 1363, when the Lithuanians were being worsted in their resistance to the Order's strategy of barring them out from their ancestral seaboard on the Baltic, they actually acquired a new seaboard on the remote shores of the Black Sea. The social energy and the military technique in virtue of which the Lithuanians were able to establish this far-reaching ascendancy over their non-Western neighbours had been acquired in the process of reacting to the pressure of their Western adversaries; and eventually this reaction became so powerful that it enabled the Lithuanians to launch a counter-offensive against the Teutonic Knights themselves.

This explanation of Lithuania's temporary political greatness as a reaction to the Teutonic Knights' contemporary Crusade is aptly conveyed in the heraldic emblem of the Lithuanian State: a galloping horseman clad—man and horse—in the elaborate plate-armour which was brought to perfection by the technique of Western armourers in the fifteenth century. This horseman is the last of the barbarians in a new guise. It is the woodland warrior of Lithuania who has taken unto him the whole armour of his Western adversaries that he 'may be able to withstand in the evil day, and, having done all, to stand'.[1] To the astonishment and confusion of the Teutonic Knights, he is bearing down upon them in their own accoutrements in order to trample them under foot on the field of Tannenberg.

This *tour de force*, however, was only achieved by the Lithuanian

[1] Ephesians vi. 13.

barbarian after he had adopted the religion and the culture as well as the military technique of the Western Civilization from which he was under pressure; and this conversion—which was the true turning-point in his struggle with the Teutonic Order—was brought about on the initiative, and through the agency, of a Western Christian neighbour and ally who had likewise become a victim of the Order's aggression and was likewise being stimulated into unprecedented activity by the necessity of fighting for his life. The Lithuanian's ally was the Pole, who had been converted to Western Christianity himself before the close of the tenth century of the Christian Era and had actually called in the Teutonic Order in the thirteenth century in order to assist him in extending the bounds of Western Christendom, on this sector of the frontier, at the pagan Prussian's and Lithuanian's expense. The Polish prince of Cujavia who gave the Teutonic Knights their first footing on the Baltic unwittingly laid the foundations of Poland's subsequent greatness by exposing her to a new German pressure which was far more formidable than the old Prusso-Lithuanian pressure from which he had intended to bring her relief. For the Teutonic Knights treated their neophyte Christian Polish hosts in much the same fashion as they treated the unconverted pagans whom they had been called in to fight; and the Poles, who at this time were still only feebly illuminated by the penumbra of the Western Civilization, were at first little more competent than their pagan neighbours to withstand a militant power which emanated from the heart of the Western World and which had at its command the most highly developed technique and organization that the Western Society had yet evolved. Accordingly, in the thirteenth century, the Teutonic Knights unceremoniously deprived the Poles of their ancestral Baltic seaboard in Pomerania while they were religiously depriving the Lithuanians of theirs in Prussia and Samogitia; and thereafter, in the fourteenth century, this same pressure from the same quarter produced the same reaction in Poland as in Lithuania.

While the Polish principalities of Cujavia and Masovia were being devoured by the Order, the nucleus of a new Polish Kingdom was being formed by Casimir the Great (*regnabat* A.D. 1333–70), whose reign was contemporary with the south-eastward expansion of Lithuania. The ultimate object of Casimir's work was to bring the offensive of the Teutonic Knights to a standstill; but Casimir's successors realized that Poland was no match for the Teutonic Order by herself; and, before trying conclusions with their assailants, they cast about for possible comrades-in-arms. The first combination which was achieved by Polish diplomacy—the personal union of the crowns of Poland and Hungary from A.D. 1370 to A.D.

1382, in the person of the Angevin King of Hungary, Louis the Great—was ephemeral and abortive, since the interests of the two parties did not coincide. Hungary had no quarrel with Poland's enemies nor Poland with Hungary's. The master-stroke of Polish statesmanship was the personal union between the crowns of Poland and Lithuania, which was achieved in A.D. 1386 by the grant of the Polish Queen Jadwiga's hand to the Lithuanian King Jagellon in consideration of Jagellon's conversion from his primitive Lithuanian paganism to Western Christianity.

It was Jagellon who opened the counter-offensive against the Teutonic Order by leading the combined forces of Lithuania and Poland to victory over the Knights at Tannenberg in A.D. 1410; and the work thus begun was completed by Jagellon's second successor on the Polish-Lithuanian throne in A.D. 1466, when he imposed on the Teutonic Order the Second Peace of Thorn. The First Peace of Thorn, in the year following the Battle of Tannenberg, had secured the retrocession of Samogitia to Lithuania. The fruits of the Second Peace were the cession[1] to Poland of Eastern Pomerania and Ermeland and the reduction of the Teutonic Order's domain in Prussia to the position of a geographical enclave in Polish-Lithuanian territory and to the status of a political dependency of the Polish Crown. Thus, in little more than half a century, the situations of the combatants had been completely reversed as a result of the combined Polish-Lithuanian reaction to the Teutonic Order's pressure. Before the year 1410, the dominions of the Order had extended along the continental coastline of the Baltic in an un-broken belt from the eastern frontier of the Holy Roman Empire all the way to the southern shore of the Gulf of Finland; and both Poland and Lithuania had been excluded thereby from access to the Baltic altogether. After 1466, the ancestral seaboards of Poland and Lithuania on the Baltic were once again in the hands of their original owners, while the two remnants of the Teutonic Order's dominions were now both insulated—by the restored 'Lithuanian Corridor' from one another, and by the restored 'Polish Corridor' from the Empire.

In the Western World over against Muscovy

Why did not Poland and Lithuania fall apart again after the pressure from the Teutonic Knights, which had originally brought them together, had thus been effectually counteracted? The ques-

---

[1] 'Cession', not 'retrocession', since the Polish territories which were recovered from the Teutonic Order in A.D. 1466 had been lost to the Order originally, some two centuries earlier, not by the Kingdom of Poland but by the then independent Polish principalities of Cujavia and Masovia. Before the conclusion of the Second Peace of Thorn in A.D. 1466, the two Polish principalities—or, rather, the remnants of them which had escaped annexation by the Order—had been absorbed into the Polish Kingdom.

tion is suggested by the actual course of events in Scandinavia—a region which had first come within the pale of the Western Civilization, by conversion to Western Christianity, contemporaneously with Poland, and had then been subjected, again contemporaneously with Poland, to pressure from certain more progressive and more efficient members of the Western Society. During the thirteenth and fourteenth centuries, while Poland was under pressure from the Teutonic Order, Scandinavia was under pressure from the Hansa; and in Scandinavia, as in Poland, the backward members of the Western Society succeeded in holding their own against their progressive assailants by resorting to the expedient of political combination. The personal union of the three Scandinavian kingdoms under the Treaty of Calmar in A.D. 1397[1] was a retort to the aggression of the Hanseatic League, just as the personal union of Poland and Lithuania in 1386 was a retort to the aggression of the Teutonic Order. The two unions, however, had very different histories. The Scandinavian Union of Calmar dissolved in A.D. 1520, after the sinews of the Hansa had been cut by the diversion of trade from the Baltic and the North Sea to the Atlantic in consequence of the discovery of America. On the other hand, the crushing of the Teutonic Order in 1466 was not followed by any corresponding dissolution of the parallel union between Poland and Lithuania. On the contrary, the Polish-Lithuanian Union was drawn closer in 1501 and still closer, by the Treaty of Lublin, in 1569, and it only ceased with the complete extinction of the political independence of the united commonwealth in 1795.

Why was the life of the Polish-Lithuanian Union prolonged almost to the close of the eighteenth century? And why was it completely extinguished then? The answer to these two questions is to be found in the imposition and the subsequent remission of a fresh pressure upon Lithuania and Poland from a new quarter. The Poles and Lithuanians had no sooner won relief from the pressure of the Teutonic Knights than they began to feel the pressure of the rising power of Muscovy. The expansion of Lithuania at the expense of the offshoot of Orthodox Christendom in Russia reached its farthest limits about the middle of the fifteenth century. Within the next century, the multitude of mutually independent and hostile states, into which the remnant of the Russian Orthodox Christian World had previously been articulated, was consolidated, by Muscovite conquest, into a single Russian Orthodox Christian universal state;[2]

---

[1] The definitive union which was achieved in A.D. 1397 had been preceded by tentative experiments in the direction of an All-Scandinavian union in the course of the fourteenth century.

[2] This function of the Muscovite Empire as a Russian Orthodox Christian universal state is studied further in IV, C (ii) (b) 2, vol. iv, pp. 88–92, below.

and in 1563—that is, half a dozen years before the Polish-Lithuanian Union of Lublin—this newly formed Russian universal state impinged upon the Western World by pushing back the eastern frontier of Lithuania, which had once run east of Smolensk, to a line running west of Polotsk on the Dvina. Thus the united commonwealth of Poland-Lithuania acquired a new function—and, therewith, a new vitality—as one of the marches of the Western World against a new pressure from Orthodox Christendom in Russia.

Poland shared this new function with the Kingdom of Sweden, which had broken off from the Scandinavian Union in A.D. 1520;[1] and the reaction of the Western Society to the new Russian pressure took the form of simultaneous Polish and Swedish counter-offensives. The Poles recaptured Smolensk in 1582 and held Moscow itself from 1610 to 1612; while the terms of the peace-treaty which was concluded between Sweden and Muscovy at Stolbovo in 1617 excluded Russia, in her turn, from all access to the Baltic.[2] In pushing their counter-offensives thus far, however, the Poles and the Swedes were guilty of an excess of zeal which brought its own retribution. The temporary presence of a Polish garrison in Moscow and the permanent presence of Swedish garrisons on the banks of the Narev and the Neva produced a profound psychological effect in Russian souls; and this inward spiritual shock translated itself into an outward practical act of equivalent magnitude: the deliberate 'Westernization' of Russia by Peter the Great.[3] Through this portentous revolution, the continental frontier of the Western World was advanced, at one bound, from the eastern borders of Poland and Sweden to the distant lines along which the newly initiated Russian proselytes to the Western Civilization already marched with the Nomad occupants of the Eurasian Steppe and with the Manchu conquerors of China. Therewith, the wardenship of the marches of the Western Society, which Russia's Western neighbours and adversaries had been exercising somewhat too zealously at Russia's expense, was suddenly snatched out of their hands, as a result of Peter's astonishing counter-stroke, by Russia herself. The Poles and Swedes thus found the ground cut from under their feet. Their function in the Western body social was taken from them; and the loss of the stimulus which the exercise of this function had formerly administered was followed by a swift decay. Within little more than a century—reckoning from the beginning of Peter's

---

[1] See p. 175, above.

[2] For the effect produced upon the internal economy of Russian Orthodox Christendom by the application of this pressure from the Western Civilization in the seventeenth century through the agencies of Poland and Sweden, see pp. 157-8, above.

[3] This 'Westernization' of Russia is examined in greater detail in III. C (ii) (b), vol. ii, pp. 278-84, and in Part IX, below.

effective rule—Sweden had lost to Russia all her possessions east of the Baltic, including her ancient dominion of Finland, while Poland had been erased from the political map altogether.

In the Western World over against the Ottoman Empire

It will be seen that Polish and Swedish history, from the opening of the sixteenth century of the Christian Era until after the close of the eighteenth, is best expressed in terms of the history of a foreign body social: in terms, that is, of the history of Orthodox Christendom in Russia. Poland and Sweden both flourished so long as they fulfilled the functions of anti-Russian marches of the Western Society; they both began to decline towards their fall so soon as Russian Orthodox Christendom had achieved the *tour de force* of filching this function from them. Let us now turn our attention to the history of the Danubian Hapsburg Monarchy, which can be traced back to approximately the same date as the histories of modern Poland and modern Sweden. Sweden upset the Scandinavian union of 1397 by breaking away from Denmark and Norway in 1520; Poland consolidated the Polish-Lithuanian union of 1386 by entering into the closer unions of 1501 and 1569; the Danubian Hapsburg Monarchy was brought into existence by the union of the Hungarian and Bohemian crowns with the Austrian patrimony of the Hapsburgs in 1526. Thus the Danubian Hapsburg Monarchy was modern Poland's and modern Sweden's contemporary; and we shall find that its history, like their histories, is best expressed in foreign terms. Poland and Sweden had their *raisons d'être* in serving as marches of the Western Society against an Orthodox Christian universal state which had been established in Russia by the Muscovites. Similarly, the Danubian Hapsburg Monarchy existed in order to serve as a march of the Western Society against another universal state into which the main body of Orthodox Christendom, in the Balkan Peninsula, had been welded by the Osmanlis.[1] It was called into existence at a moment when the Ottoman pressure upon the Western World had suddenly become really formidable; it remained in the first rank of the Great Powers of Europe as long as the Ottoman pressure remained at its height; it began to decline as soon as the Ottoman pressure began to relax; and it finally fell to pieces in the same general war—the War of 1914–18—in which the Ottoman Empire received its *coup de grâce*.

The impact of the Ottoman Power upon the Western World began

---

[1] This function of the Danubian Hapsburg Monarchy as a carapace evolved by the Western Society, in order to protect it against the Ottoman impact, has been noticed already, by anticipation, in I. C (iii) (b), vol. i, on p. 156, footnote 1, above. The function of the Ottoman Empire as the universal state of the main body of Orthodox Christendom is discussed further below in Part III. A, vol. iii, on pp. 26–7, below.

with the hundred years' war between the 'Osmanlis and Hungary which culminated in the Battle of Mohacz (A.D. 1526). Before the opening of this long duel in A.D. 1433/4, the 'Osmanlis and the Westerners had only crossed one another's paths occasionally—and these occasions had arisen through the desultory interference of this or that Western Power in the distracted affairs of the Orthodox Christian Society with a half-hearted intention of preventing the 'Osmanlis from accomplishing their work of welding the main body of Orthodox Christendom together under Ottoman rule. This work, however, was substantially complete before the end of the fourteenth century of the Christian Era; it was not undone by the blow which Timur dealt the 'Osmanlis at Angora in A.D. 1402;[1] and, after a momentary pause, it was easily rounded off by Mehmed the Conqueror (*imperabat* A.D. 1452–81). It was not the annexation of Constantinople and the Morea and Trebizond and Qaraman, but the offensive against Hungary, that made the greatest demands upon Ottoman military energies in the fifteenth century.

Hungary, standing at bay under the leadership of John Hunyadi and his son Matthias Corvinus (*regnabat* A.D. 1458–90), was the most stubborn opponent whom the 'Osmanlis had yet encountered; and she was stimulated culturally as well as militarily by the tremendous effort involved in withstanding the Ottoman pressure almost single-handed. The disparity, however, between the respective forces of the two combatants was so great that the maintenance of the effort eventually proved to be beyond Hungary's strength; and the ultimate break-down of Hungary and formation of the Danubian Hapsburg Monarchy—in order to carry on Hungary's work with greater resources—were both portended in a number of preliminary and abortive attempts at political union between Hungary and several of her Western neighbours while the hundred years' war between Hungary and the 'Osmanlis was in progress. For instance, the Hungarian crown was fitfully united with the Bohemian during the years 1436–9 and 1453–7 and 1490–1526; both crowns were united with part of the Austrian patrimony of the Hapsburgs in 1438–9 and again in 1453–7; and Hungary alone was united with Austria from 1485 to 1490. Moreover, the crowns of Hungary and Poland were temporarily united for a second time from 1440 to 1444—this time in the person of a Polish and not a Hungarian sovereign, and with the object, not of bringing Hungarian reinforcements to Poland in her struggle with the Teutonic Order (the purpose of the previous Hungarian-Polish union in A.D. 1370–82),[2] but of bringing Polish reinforcements to Hungary in her struggle with the 'Osmanlis. These loose and ephemeral

---

[1] See II. D (iv), p. 102, above.   [2] See pp. 173–4, above.

unions were not enough to give Hungary the strong permanent reinforcement which she needed. They perhaps postponed but did not ultimately avert the crushing blow which the 'Osmanlis finally dealt Hungary at Mohacz; and it was only a disaster of this magnitude that could produce a sufficient psychological effect to bring the remnant of Hungary together with Bohemia and Austria into a close and enduring union under the Hapsburg Dynasty. This result was immediate. The triple union was accomplished before the end of the calendar year (A.D. 1526) in which the Battle of Mohacz had been fought; and it endured for nearly four hundred years—only to dissolve in the same calendar year (A.D. 1918) that saw the final break-up of the Ottoman Power which had delivered the dynamic blow at Mohacz four centuries back.

Indeed, from the moment of the Danubian Hapsburg Monarchy's foundation, its fortunes followed those of the hostile Power, whose pressure had called it into existence, in each successive phase. The heroic age of the Danubian Monarchy coincided chronologically with the period during which the Ottoman pressure was felt by the Western World most severely. This heroic age may be taken as beginning with the first abortive Ottoman siege of Vienna in A.D. 1529 and as ending with the second in A.D. 1682-3. In these two supreme ordeals, the Austrian capital played the same role—psychological as well as strategic—in the desperate resistance of the Western World to the Ottoman assault that Verdun played in the French resistance to the German assault in the War of 1914-18.[1] The two sieges were both turning-points in Ottoman military history. The failure of the first brought to a standstill the tide of Ottoman conquest which had been flooding up the Danube Valley for a century past. The failure of the second siege was followed by an ebb which continued thereafter—in a secular movement that persisted through all pauses and fluctuations—until the European frontiers of Turkey, which stood at the outskirts of Vienna from 1529 to 1683, have fallen back in our time to the outskirts of Adrianople. The Ottoman Empire's loss, however, has not been the Danubian Hapsburg Monarchy's gain; for the heroic age of the Danubian Monarchy did not survive the beginning of the Ottoman decline. The collapse of the Ottoman Power, which threw open a field in South-Eastern Europe for other forces to occupy, simultaneously released the Danubian Monarchy from the pressure which had been stimulating it into heroic activity hitherto; and the withdrawal of the former stimulus inhibited the Danubian Monarchy from taking advantage of the new opportunity. So far

[1] For the part played by sieges in making the fortunes of cities, see further II. D (v), Annex, pp. 400-1, below.

from entering into the heritage of the Ottoman Empire in South-Eastern Europe, the Danubian Monarchy now followed into decline the Power that had originally called it into existence, and eventually shared the Ottoman Empire's fate.

In the counter-offensive which drove the 'Osmanlis back from the walls of Vienna in 1683, the Hapsburgs found themselves at the head of an anti-Ottoman coalition which included Venice, Poland, and Russia; yet they never avenged the sieges of Vienna by laying siege to Constantinople. The peace-treaty of Carlowitz in 1699 restored to the Hungarian Crown the greater part of the Hungarian territory which had been lost to the 'Osmanlis in 1526; the peace-treaty of Passarowitz in 1718 actually carried the frontier considerably beyond the line along which it had stood on the eve of the campaign of Mohacz, two centuries earlier. The peace-treaty of Belgrade in 1739, however, revised the frontier of 1718 in the 'Osmanlis' favour and to the Hapsburgs' disadvantage. The fortress of Belgrade itself, which Hungary had always held against the 'Osmanlis during the fifteenth century and which Prince Eugene had wrested from Ottoman hands in 1717, was retroceded in 1739 by the Hapsburg Monarchy to the Ottoman Empire; and though Austrian armies momentarily re-occupied Belgrade in the Austro-Turkish War of 1788–91 and again in the General War of 1914–18, Belgrade had another destiny. It finally passed out of Ottoman hands in 1866 to become the capital of the Serbian 'successor-state' of the Ottoman Empire; and it was recovered by the Serbs from the Austrians in 1918 in order to become the capital of Jugoslavia, which is a 'successor-state' of the Hapsburg Power as well as of the Ottoman. As for the south-eastern frontier of the Danubian Monarchy, it remained virtually stationary, at the line fixed in 1739, for the remainder of the Monarchy's existence. During the hundred and eighty years which elapsed between the conclusion of the Peace of Belgrade and the moment when the Hapsburg Monarchy signed its own death-warrant in the Armistice of 1918, the Monarchy made only two further acquisitions of Ottoman or ex-Ottoman territory, and these were of trivial dimensions.[1] Between 1683 and 1739, however, the Hapsburg frontier in this quarter had been advanced sufficiently far to relegate Vienna from the situation of a frontier-fortress to that of an imperial capital in the interior; and this change made itself felt in the city's fortunes and character. The glory which Vienna had gained by keeping the Turks at bay in 1529 and 1682–3 was tarnished by the humiliation

[1] The first of the two was the acquisition of the Bukovina in 1774–7; the second was the acquisition of Bosnia-Herzegovina, which was occupied by Austria-Hungary in 1878 and annexed in 1908.

of French occupations in 1805 and 1809; and the Viennese, who had first made their name as the heroic defenders of Western Christendom, eventually became a by-word for an attractive but decidedly unheroic combination of fecklessness with amiability and softness with elegance.[1]

If we look more closely, we shall see that the fate of Austria-Hungary was analogous to that of Poland-Lithuania. Just as the Polish counter-offensive against Russia at the end of the first decade of the seventeenth century precipitated the 'Westernization' of Russian Orthodox Christendom and thereby rendered Poland's previous *raison d'être*, as an anti-Russian march of the Western Society, superfluous, so the Austrian counter-offensive against the 'Osmanlis in the last two decades of the seventeenth century precipitated the 'Westernization' of the main body of Orthodox Christendom in the Balkan Peninsula and thereby deprived the Danubian Hapsburg Monarchy of its *raison d'être* likewise.

The parallel extends to details. For example, when the 'Westernization' of Russia was taken in hand by Peter the Great, the Russian imperial revolutionary did not obtain his Western inspiration through the medium of his backward and hostile Western neighbour Poland. He addressed himself, by preference, to Germany and Holland and England: countries which were then leading the van in the progress of the Western Civilization and which were not alienated from Russia by any unneighbourly tradition of hostility. Similarly, in the main body of Orthodox Christendom, when the process of 'Westernization' was initiated—in a less deliberate and systematic way than Peter's—by the 'Osmanlis and their subjects under the stimulus of the Austrian counter-offensive, the 'Westernizers' did not address themselves to the Hapsburgs. The 'Osmanlis turned to France, who was their natural Western ally inasmuch as she was the House of Austria's principal Western rival.[2] As for the Orthodox Christian peoples of the Ottoman Empire, they welcomed the Austrians at first as Christian liberators, only to find that the status of barely tolerated 'heretics' under a

[1] In the long run, this relaxing effect of an abnormal exemption from the pressure of the human environment has counted for more, in the evolution of the Austrian êthos, than the stimulating effect of the physical environment in the shape of an abnormally rough country. (For the latter aspect of Austria, see II. D (ii), pp. 58–60, above.) For Vienna, as the capital of the entire Danubian Hapsburg Monarchy over a span of four centuries, has outweighed the rural and highland remainder of Austria. It is the Viennese and not the Tyrolese who has set the tone of Austria in these latter days.

[2] Francis I of France actually co-operated with Suleymān the Magnificent in naval operations against the Hapsburg Power in the Mediterranean in 1543. France had been rewarded for her friendship already in 1535 by receiving 'capitulations' (i.e. a charter of trading rights) from the Ottoman Government in advance of any other Western Power apart from the Italian republics. These 'capitulations' were confirmed and improved in 1740 as a reward for diplomatic services which the French Government had rendered to the Ottoman Government during the negotiation of the Belgrade peace-treaty between Turkey and Austria in 1739.

Roman Catholic régime was less to their liking than that of explicitly licensed 'unbelievers' under the Islamic dispensation. Tantalized, and at the same time disillusioned, by their brief spells of Austrian and Venetian rule in the early years of the eighteenth century, the Serbs and Greeks turned eagerly towards their Russian co-religionists when these demonstrated the advantages of 'Westernization' by their decisive victory over the 'Osmanlis in the Russo-Turkish War of 1768–74.[1] Yet the Orthodox Christians of the Balkan Peninsula were not long content to derive their Western inspiration through this circuitous and stagnant Russian channel. They soon learnt to draw the living waters from the fountain-head. They eagerly imbibed the ideas of the American and the French Revolution; and they profited by a personal intercourse with the leading nations of the West when Napoleon burst into the Levant, with his British adversaries in his wake, in the course of the General War of 1792–1815. Before the close of the Napoleonic Wars, the main body of Orthodox Christendom was in ferment with the leaven of Romantic Nationalism which was the Western spirit of the age;[2] and this was the beginning of the end of the Hapsburg Monarchy.

It was in vain that the Monarchy, under the stimulus of Napoleon's repeated blows, played a decisive part in the overthrow of Napoleon by its military intervention in 1813[3] and thereafter dominated the Congress of Vienna. While, to outward appearance, Metternich had skilfully taken advantage of the 'restoration' of the pre-revolutionary régime in Western Europe in order to secure for the Danubian Monarchy a European hegemony which it had never quite succeeded in exercising at any previous stage of its history, the underlying reality was something altogether different. In reality, the Danubian Monarchy, in the 'post-war' period which began in 1815, found itself encircled, for the first time in its history, by a single ubiquitous adversary in front and rear—in Western Europe on the one side and in South-Eastern Europe on the other[4] —and this adversary was the Zeitgeist of that very Western Society

---

[1] See Khrysanthópoulos, Ph.: Ἀπομνημονεύματα περὶ τῆς Ἑλληνικῆς Ἐπαναστάσεως, (Athens 1899, Sakellarios, 2 vols.), vol. i, pp. 16–18.
[2] See Kolokotrónis, Th.: Διήγησις Συμβάντων τῆς Ἑλληνικῆς Φυλῆς, 1770–1836 (Athens 1889, Estía, 2 vols.), vol. i, pp. 48–9.
[3] See II. D (iv), p. 105, above.
[4] The Janus-like physiognomy of the Danubian Hapsburg Monarchy is aptly symbolized in the double-headed eagle (a heraldic perversion of the Roman eagle), which the Hapsburg Monarchy shared, as its official emblem, with Prussia and Russia). While one head of the Austrian eagle was keeping watch eastward towards the Ottoman Empire, the other head was ever craning back westward into the interior of the Western World; and the Ottoman pressure had no sooner begun to slacken than the Danubian Monarchy began to divert its attention and energy disastrously from Near Eastern to Western affairs. This tendency, which first declared itself in the Thirty Years' War, is examined further in V. C (i) (c) 3, vol. v, pp. 325–7, below.

in which the Monarchy itself inextricably lived and moved and had its being.

Thus the situation of the Monarchy had really changed, in the course of a century, most profoundly to the Monarchy's disadvantage. A hundred years earlier, on the morrow of the Western General War of 1672–1713, the Danubian Monarchy had still been secure in front and rear alike. On its front, *vis-à-vis* the Orthodox Christian World, it was then already more than holding its own against the slackening pressure of the 'Osmanlis, while in its rear, *vis-à-vis* its fellow-members in the Western Society to which the Monarchy itself belonged, it was still performing the service and fulfilling the function which was its *raison d'être*, in its original capacity as the carapace which the Western body social had evolved from its own living substance in order to protect it against Ottoman sabre-strokes. On the other hand, in 1815, though the Danubian Monarchy had once again emerged from a general war even more triumphantly, to outward appearance, than in 1714, its *raison d'être*, and therewith its security, existed no longer. The sabre against whose strokes the West had sought protection under the Austrian carapace had fallen, by this time, out of the 'Osmanli's decrepit hands; and the osseous growth of the Danubian Monarchy, which could not be re-absorbed into the living tissues of the Western body social now that its function had become obsolete, was simply cramping the internal growth of the society whose life it had once preserved against a deadly attack from an external enemy. Since the foundation of the Danubian Hapsburg Monarchy in A.D. 1526, the cumulative effect of the Dutch, English, American, and French revolutions had called into existence in the Western World a new political order—a comity of nations—in which a dynastic state like the Hapsburg Monarchy was an anachronism and an anomaly. In attempting to restore the pre-revolutionary régime in Europe on the basis of the principle of Dynastic Legitimacy and in defiance of the principle of Nationality, Metternich provocatively transformed the Monarchy from 'King Log' into 'King Stork', from a passive incubus upon the life of the Western Society into an active internal enemy of Western progress—an enemy more harmful, in its own fashion, than the now decrepit external Ottoman enemy which the Hapsburg Monarchy had formerly kept at bay.

The Monarchy spent the last century of its existence in attempts —all doomed to failure before they were made—at hindering the inevitable revision of the political map of Europe on national lines; and in this futile endeavour there are two points of interest for our present purpose. The first point is that, from 1815 onwards, the new Western leaven of Nationalism was fermenting just as vigorously among the Orthodox Christian peoples within and beyond the south-eastern frontiers of the Danubian Monarchy as it was among the Western peoples within and beyond the frontiers of the Monarchy on the western side. The second point is that when the Monarchy reconciled itself at last, under the discipline of hard experience, to the necessity of making some concessions to the spirit of the age, it duly succeeded in arriving at an accommodation with the national aspirations of the Western peoples. By renouncing the hegemony over Germany and the possession of territory in Italy in 1866, the Hapsburg Monarchy rendered possible its own coexistence with the new German Empire and with the new Italian Kingdom; and by accepting the Austro-Hungarian Ausgleich of 1867 and its Austrian corollary in Galicia, the Hapsburg Dynasty succeeded in identifying its own interests with the national interests of the Polish and the Magyar as well as the German element in its dominions. The problem which the Hapsburg Monarchy never succeeded in solving was the problem of Nationalism in the Balkans; and it was its inability to arrive at an accommodation in this quarter that eventually brought the Monarchy to destruction. The Western weapons of Nationalism, which had not dealt the Hapsburg Monarchy any mortal blow when they were wielded by the Italian and German and Magyar hands that had forged them, proved deadly in the alien hands of the Serbs. The discarded Danubian carapace of the Western body social, which had withstood so many blows from the Ottoman sabre, was eventually pierced and shattered by Serbian bayonets.

Since 1918, the south-eastern frontier of the Danubian Hapsburg Monarchy—a frontier which for a hundred and eighty years was one of the abiding landmarks in the political landscape of Europe—has been effaced by the establishment of two new national states—Jugoslavia and Greater Rumania—which are symbolic of the triumph of the new order. Each of these new states is a 'successor-state' both of the *ci-devant* Hapsburg Monarchy and of the *ci-devant* Ottoman Empire; and each of them unites within its newly drawn frontiers not only territories acquired from two different dynastic states, but also—under the sign of the Western principle of nationality—populations that have been nurtured, hitherto, by two different civilizations. This audacious experiment in political chemistry may succeed or fail; these synthetically produced nations may become organic unions or may disintegrate into their constituent elements; but the mere fact that the experiment is being made is conclusive evidence that the Hapsburg Monarchy and the Ottoman Empire are both defunct and that they have been destroyed simultaneously by an identic hostile force.

It is curious in the present 'post-war' age, as one's train crosses the railway-bridge over the Save, between Semlin and Belgrade, to reread the opening passage of Kinglake's *Eothen*. When, less than a century ago, the English traveller was ferried across the frontier-river from the Hapsburg to the Ottoman bank, he felt as though he were passing out of one world into another; and the Austrian hussar who escorted him to the ferry-boat took leave of him as solemnly as though he were Hermes Psychopompus committing a soul to Charon's barque on the River of Hades. To the uninitiated English observer and to the unsophisticated Austrian soldier alike, the gulf there fixed between 'West' and 'East' seemed as great in the post-Napoleonic age as it had ever been; but this was not the view of the anxious-minded Rhenish statesman who at that moment, from his cabinet in Vienna, was pulling the strings of European diplomacy like a human spider spinning a political web. Metternich knew well enough, by that time, that the ancient gulf had been bridged and the ancient barriers thrown down; he knew that the spiritual leaven of Nationalism had already been carried from the 'West' into the 'East' across the obsolete dividing line; and he knew that the political miasma which was arising from the fermentation of this Western leaven in Orthodox Christian souls was more difficult to exclude from the sacrosanct dominions of his Imperial Master than the Plague itself.

Already, Metternich had taken alarm at the outbreak of the Greek insurrection against Ottoman rule in 1821. Clear-sighted as he was according to his own lights, he had divined at once that this repudiation of the Ottoman Pādishāh's authority by a handful of his Orthodox Christian subjects in the remote Morea was a menace to the authority of the Austrian Kaiser because the Greeks were claiming Western sympathy and assistance for their cause in the name of the Western principle of Nationality. Metternich represented to the Holy Alliance insistently, though without success, that if their own principle of Legitimacy was to be maintained intact, the Greek insurgents must be boycotted as outlaws and Sultan Mahmūd be supported, in maintaining his dynastic rights, as one of the Lord's Anointed. From the Legitimist standpoint, Metternich's attitude on this occasion was entirely justified by the event. For the triumphant success of the Greek insurgents—a success which they owed to the friendly intervention of France, Great Britain, and Russia as much as to their own exertions—was an event of far more than local importance. The erection of a sovereign independent national Greek State in 1829–31 made it inevitable that every people in South-Eastern Europe should insist upon attaining its own national independence and national unity sooner or later; and thus the Greek insurrection of 1821 incidentally preordained the erection of Jugoslavia and Greater Rumania in 1918–20. Truly, Metternich's senses had not deceived him when he heard the death-knell of the Danubian Hapsburg Monarchy in those reverberations from the clash of arms in the Morea which fell upon his ears in Vienna.

It is curious, too, in this present 'post-war' age, to compare the situation and the êthos of Austria with those of contemporary Turkey on the one hand and Bavaria on the other.

Out of the destruction which overtook the Hapsburg and the Ottoman Empire simultaneously in the General War of 1914–18, there have emerged an Austrian and a Turkish Republic; and these two republics bear a superficial resemblance to one another inasmuch as they both conform outwardly to the conventional type of modern parliamentary national state with which the Hapsburg and Ottoman empires remained fundamentally incompatible to the end of their histories. This formal resemblance, however, between the new Austria and the new Turkey is of little significance in the light of their profound present difference in êthos. The Austrians are at once the hardest hit and the least recalcitrant of the five peoples that have emerged from the War of 1914–18 on the losing side. They have accepted the new order passively, with supreme resignation as well as with supreme regret. By contrast, the Turks are the only people among the five who have taken up arms again, after the Armistice, against the victorious Powers and have successfully insisted upon negotiating their own peace-treaty freely and on a footing of equality with their late opponents, instead of having the victors' peace-terms imposed upon them. More than that, the Turks have seized upon the catastrophe of the Ottoman Empire as an opportunity for renewing their youth and changing their destiny. So far from accepting the new order passively, they have welcomed it with open arms, and have plunged into the path of Westernization, at the heels of their former subjects the Greeks and Serbs and Rumans and Bulgars, with the zeal of eleventh-hour converts who are taking the Kingdom of Heaven by storm.

How are we to explain these strangely diverse psychological phenomena? Examination shows that this êthos in Turkish souls is something quite new. For more than five centuries—from the close of their dynamic age at the beginning of the fifteenth century of the Christian Era down to A.D. 1919—the Turks, in all the vicissitudes of their history, invariably displayed the psychological reactions of Conservatism. In the days of their prosperity, they waxed fat and kicked, like Jeshurun;[1] and in the days of their ad-

---

[1] Deuteronomy xxxii. 15.

versity they either stood stock still or behaved like sullen, thick-skinned mules who will not move until they are belaboured, and then not more than one step at a time.

The former ruling minority of Turkish landlords, who found themselves left stranded among alien minorities and under alien rule by the ebb of the Ottoman tide in Europe between 1683 and 1913, used to accept their sudden and extreme reversal of fortune as passively as the Austrians have accepted theirs since 1918. They would either abandon their ancestral lands and migrate *en masse* to squat and flit and squat again within the ever contracting Ottoman frontiers; or if they were too phlegmatic to make even this negative response to the new human challenge confronting them, and were restrained from migrating by sheer inertia, then they would resign themselves to sinking from the top to the bottom of the social ladder in their old homes under the new conditions. As for their fellows who continued to rule the Ottoman Empire, they could only be induced to 'Westernize' their institutions under *force majeure*, and then always piecemeal and to the minimum degree that seemed necessary at the moment in order to keep the Empire just alive. This stricture fairly applies to all the Ottoman 'Westernizers' from Sultan Selīm III and Sultan Mahmūd II down to the Committee of Union and Progress inclusive, with one notable exception to prove the rule in the person of Midhat Pasha.[1] How, then, are we to explain the revolutionary change in the Turkish state of mind, from an ultra-Austrian passivity to an ultra-Jacobin activity, which has come to pass since 1919? And how, for that matter, are we to explain the converse change in the Austrian state of mind from the heroism of the defence of Vienna in 1682–3 to the 'defeatism' of the present day?

The explanation of both changes is to be found in the normal operation of Challenge-and-Response. The Viennese are showing, now, the cumulative psychological effects of having lived for more than two centuries as an 'imperial people' in the interior of the Haps-burg Dominions instead of sustaining their historic role as wardens of the marches of Western Christendom against the 'Osmanlis. In their unstimulating latter-day environment, they learnt to feed out of the Dynasty's hand; and when the Imperial Government's ulti-matum to Serbia had precipitated the General War of 1914–18, they obeyed the mobilization order, like sheep who follow their shepherd to the slaughter-house, with a blind faith in their Emperor Francis Joseph's assurance that, in doing what he had done, he had foreseen, and made provision for, all the eventualities that might befall his

[1] The process of 'Westernization' in the Ottoman Empire is examined in greater detail in IV. C (ii) (*b*) 2, vol. iv, pp. 76–8, as well as in Part IX, below.

trusty and well-beloved subjects. On the other hand, the Turks have responded, at this eleventh hour, to the challenge from the West—a challenge first presented by the triumphant defenders of Vienna in A.D. 1683—because, in 1919, they were simply unable to evade the issue any longer.

On the morrow of the Armistice of 1918, the Turks found themselves standing with their backs to the wall, in a situation in which they must either conquer or die. In this supreme hour, they were betrayed by the Ottoman Dynasty—a dynasty which had created not only the Ottoman Empire but the 'Osmanli Turks themselves, who were stamped, in the very name which they bore, with their creator's own image and superscription.[1] The Turks were forced by this betrayal to rely upon themselves—and this in a struggle for their existence. For in 1919–22 the Turks were no longer fighting in order to preserve an Ottoman province for their Pādishāh or a fragment of Dār-al-Islām for their Caliph. They were fighting to preserve their own homelands. The battle-field of In Önü, on which the decisive action in the Graeco-Turkish War of 1919–22 was fought, lies in that original patrimony on the north-western edge of the Anatolian Plateau which had been assigned to the fathers of the 'Osmanlis by the last of the Saljūqs more than six centuries back.[2] On the day of this decisive battle, the tide of Ottoman history, whose mighty flood had once spread from the neighbourhood of In Önü to the neighbourhood of Vienna, at length completed its mighty ebb by returning to its source. In this situation, the Ottoman Turkish people was faced with the momentous choice between two, and only two, alternatives: annihilation or metamorphosis. It will be seen that the final urgency of the challenge to which the Turks have responded has been fully sufficient to account for the potency of their eleventh-hour response. It will also be seen that the reversal in the direction of the pressure between the Western World and the main body of Orthodox Christendom—a reversal which first manifested itself under the walls of Vienna in A.D. 1683—has been followed in due course by a corresponding transfer of stimulus, which has manifested itself, in turn, in the situation and in the êthos of the two communities by whom the brunt of the pressure has been given and taken.

So much for the comparison between Austria and Turkey. As for the other comparison of Austria with Bavaria, the interest of this lies in the fact that Bavaria and Austria were originally of one substance. By origin, Austria is simply Bavaria's 'eastern march'—

[1] For the creation of the Osmanlis, see further Part III. A, vol. iii, pp. 22–44, below.
[2] See pp. 151–2, above.

or, rather, a cluster of Bavarian marches: Upper Austria, Lower Austria, and Steiermark or Styria—which was first evolved by the Bavarian body politic in order to protect its eastern flank against assaults from the Avars and Slovenes, and which afterwards became differentiated and consolidated, by a series of historical accidents, into a separate political entity. When we formulate the history of Austria in these genetic terms, we find ourselves enabled to measure once again, from a new angle, the extent of the change which has been produced in the Austrian êthos by the successive imposition and removal of external pressures.

During the last ten or twelve centuries, the country which began life as the eastern march of Bavaria has passed through a long series of experiences in which the Bavarian interior has had no share. Austria has been first stimulated by recurring waves of attack from Avars and Magyars and 'Osmanlis and then debilitated by the paternal despotism of the Hapsburgs; she has performed in turn the strangely different functions of carapace to a society in jeopardy and metropolitan province to a Great Power; and each phase in this varied and distinguished history has left some mark upon her, until the sum total has effaced her original Bavarian identity and has transformed her character, as well as her name, into something that is now entirely her own. During all this time, while the transfigured eastern march of Bavaria has been playing her great part in the life of our Western Society and in the life of the World, the Bavarian interior has remained one of those small countries which are 'happy in having no history'—as is signified in the fact that it has retained the original Bavarian name which Austria has discarded. During the ten or twelve centuries that have elapsed since Bavaria and Austria first parted company and began to go their different ways, the Bavarian êthos has remained parochial and exuberant and sanguine, whereas the Austrian êthos has become oecumenical and fastidious and sceptical. The contrast between the temperaments respectively prevalent in these two South German Catholic countries to-day cannot fail to strike the traveller who passes from one into the other at almost any point on their long common frontier; and it is not a contrast that can possibly be explained by any difference of racial endowment. There is no reason to suppose that, in the population of the original Bavaria, there was any difference of race between the Bavarians of the eastern marches and the Bavarians of the interior, nor is there any record of substantial changes in the racial composition of either population since their subsequent segregation into separate communities. The only tenable explanation—and it is a wholly adequate explanation—of the difference between the Bavarian and the

Austrian êthos at the present day is to be found in the operation of
the psychological force of Challenge-and-Response.

In the Western World over against the Far Western Christendom

Having now surveyed such illustrations of Challenge-and-Response as are offered by the various historic responses to external
pressures upon the continental European frontiers of Western
Christendom, let us glance at three other frontiers of the same
society: its land-frontier *vis-à-vis* the now extinct Far Western
Christendom[1] in the *alter orbis* of Britain; its maritime frontier,
vis-à-vis the abortive Scandinavian Civilization,[2] along the seaboards of England and France upon the North Sea and the Channel;
and its land-frontier *vis-à-vis* the Syriac Civilization in the Iberian
Peninsula.

What has been the genesis of the present British 'United Kingdom'? It is a union of the two kingdoms of England and Scotland
in Great Britain, together with the English and Scottish conquests
and plantations in Ireland;[3] and these two kingdoms, which cover
the whole area of Great Britain between them, are the products
of a struggle for existence between half a dozen 'successor-states'
of the Roman Empire which were established, during the post-
Hellenic Völkerwanderung, by Anglian and Jutish barbarians who
migrated across the North Sea from the western coast of the
continent to the eastern and southern coasts of the Roman island.[4]
An inquiry into the genesis of the United Kingdom thus resolves
itself into the prior question: How is it that the struggle for
existence between the primitive and ephemeral barbarian principalities of the so-called 'Heptarchy' in Great Britain has resulted
in the emergence of these two progressive and enduring states-
members of our Western Society? If we now glance at the historical
process by which the two kingdoms of England and Scotland have
eventually replaced 'the Heptarchy' on the political map, we shall
find that the determining factor at every stage has been a response
to some challenge which has been presented by the incidence of an
external pressure.

The genesis of the Kingdom of Scotland can be traced back to

---

[1] This abortive Far Western Christian Civilization has been referred to, by anticipation, in I. B (iii), vol. i, p. 29, above, and is dealt with further in II. D (vii), on pp. 322–40,
below.

[2] See II. D (iii), pp. 86–100, above, and II. D (vii), pp. 340–60, below.

[3] At the time of writing, some twelve years after the establishment of the Irish Free
State, the United Kingdom still included an enclave of territory in Northern Ireland,
where the Scottish plantations of the seventeenth century were most thickly sown, as a
memorial of the fact that it once embraced the whole of the British Isles save for the
Isle of Man, whose special status was a legacy from its Norwegian past.

[4] This migration has been touched upon already, on pp. 86–100, above, apropos of
the stimulus of migrations across the sea.

a challenge which was presented, some nine or ten centuries ago, to the outlying Anglian kingdom of Northumbria by the Picts and Scots, who were the representatives of the abortive Far Western Christian Civilization in an adjoining section of 'the Celtic Fringe'. The present capital of Scotland, Edinburgh, was founded by the Northumbrian prince whose name it bears[1] as the frontier-fortress of Northumbria over against the Picts; the political and cultural nucleus of medieval and modern Scotland has been the district called Lothian; and Lothian was originally the march of Northumbria against both the Picts beyond the Firth of Forth and the Britons in Strathclyde. The challenge was presented when the Picts and Scots conquered Edinburgh in A.D. 954 and thereafter compelled the principality of Northumbria to cede the whole of Lothian to them round about the turn of the tenth and eleventh centuries. This cession raised the following issue: Was this lost march of Northumbria, which had likewise been a march of Western Christendom, to retain its Western Christian culture in spite of the local change of political régime, or was it to succumb to the alien Far Western Christian culture of its Celtic conquerors? So far from succumbing, Lothian responded to the challenge by 'taking its conquerors captive'.

The culture of the conquered territory exercised such an attraction upon the Scottish kings that they made it the seat of their kingdom and came to feel and to behave as though Lothian were their ancestral homeland and as though their native Highlands were an outlying and alien part of their dominions. In consequence, by an historical paradox, the eastern seaboard of Scotland, from the northern shore of the Firth of Forth to the southern shore of the Moray Firth, was colonized, and 'the Highland Line' was pushed back steadily farther towards the north-west, by settlers of Anglian origin from Lothian under the auspices of rulers of Celtic origin and at the expense of a Celtic population who were the Scottish kings' original kinsmen and who had once conquered the Lowlanders under the leadership of these very kings' forefathers. By a consequential and not less paradoxical transference of nomenclature, 'the Scottish language' came to mean the Teutonic dialect spoken in Lothian, the *ci-devant* march of the Anglian principality of Northumbria, instead of meaning the Gaelic dialect spoken by the original Scots who had first brought the Scottish name into Britain in a migration from the north-west corner of Ireland to Argyll during the post-Hellenic Völkerwanderung.

Thus the ultimate result of the conquest of Lothian by the Scots

[1] This traditional etymology is challenged by J. A. Duke in *The Columban Church* (Oxford 1932, University Press), p. 13.

and Picts was not to set back the north-western boundary of Western Christendom from the Forth to the Tweed but to push the boundary forward until it embraced the whole north-western corner of the mainland of Britäin. The new Kingdom of Scotland, which was brought into existence by the union of Lothian with the domain of the Scots and Picts in the Highlands, took the impress of the Western Christian culture which Lothian contributed to the common stock of the new Scottish body politic. Scotland became a member of the Western instead of the Far Western Christian Society; so that the conquest of Lothian by the Scots and Picts, which had first had all the appearance of being a redistribution of territory between Western and Far Western Christendom to the advantage of the latter at the former's expense, was actually turned to the advantage of Western Christendom by the triumphant response which Lothian made to the challenge thus presented to her. In virtue of this response, her transfer from Anglian to Scottish rule ultimately caused Western Christendom to increase and Far Western Christendom to decrease on this sector of their frontier in the British Isles.[1]

Thus a conquered fragment of one of the principalities of the English 'Heptarchy' actually became the nucleus of one of the two commonwealths which have now come to divide between them the whole of Britain and to constitute by their union the present United Kingdom. This was an extraordinary feat; and it is pertinent to observe, once again, that the fragment of Northumbria

[1] The political union which brought the medieval and modern Kingdom of Scotland into existence towards the beginning of the eleventh century of the Christian Era has several points of symmetry with the union which brought into existence the Danubian Hapsburg Monarchy five centuries later. In the Scottish instance, Lothian plays the part that is played in the Danubian instance by Austria. Though it is the smallest of the component members of the union in mere territorial extent, it manages to dominate the rest by its superiority in culture and in political ability. Again, Edinburgh corresponds to Vienna. Either city finds its destiny in being the capital of a union between two states after having started life as the frontier-fortress of one of the two states against the other: Vienna as the frontier-fortress of Austria (or rather Bavaria) against Hungary, Edinburgh as the frontier-fortress of Lothian (or rather Northumbria) against the Picts. The symmetry extends even further; for the Danubian Hapsburg Monarchy sprang from the union not of two states but of three, and so did the Kingdom of Scotland likewise. If Lothian is the analogue of Austria and if the country of the Picts and Scots, north of the Forth–Clyde line, is the analogue of Hungary, we find that Bohemia has its counterpart in Strathclyde. By comparison with these substantial correspondences, it is not a material point of difference that the dynasty which brought about the Danubian union originated in Austria, whereas the dynasty which brought about the North British union originated not in Lothian—the analogue of Austria—but in the domain of the Picts and Scots, which is the analogue of Hungary. It was only an accident that the Danubian Monarchy was not brought into existence by the Hungarian conquest of Austria in A.D. 1485. If Matthias Corvinus's anticipation of Ferdinand Hapsburg's achievement had lasted not merely half a dozen years but four centuries—as it well might have lasted—and had so precluded an Austrian ruler from performing the achievement with enduring success forty years later, as it was actually performed by Ferdinand, then the Danubian Monarchy would have come to be known as 'the Hungarian Empire' and not as 'the Austrian Empire'. In that event, the symmetry between the political structures of the Danubian Monarchy and the Kingdom of Scotland would have been complete down to the very nomenclature.

which performed this feat was the march between Forth and Tweed and not the interior between Tweed or Tyne or Tees and Humber.

If some enlightened traveller from Constantinople or Cordova had visited Northumbria in the tenth or eleventh century of the Christian Era, on the eve of the cession of Lothian to the Scots and Picts, he would assuredly have pronounced that Lothian had no future, and that, if any Northumbrian town was to become the capital of a great country, the town marked out for this destiny was not Edinburgh but York. Here was a city situated at the mid-point of the largest and richest arable plain that was to be found in the whole northern half of the island of Britain; a city which had once been a *point d'appui* of the Roman Empire and had now become a *point d'appui* of the Roman Church. Already, for a moment at the turn of the ninth and tenth centuries, York had bade fair to become the capital of a great kingdom—not indeed, as a state-member of Western Christendom, but as an important structural element in the rising edifice of the Scandinavian World which was then threatening to drive Western Christendom to the wall and to usurp its place.[1] Yet this Scandinavian Kingdom of York rose and fell as swiftly as some solid-seeming mountain of thick-piled cloud which dissolves into wisps before the eyes of the astonished gazer. By the year A.D. 920, the Danish Kingdom of York, as well as the surviving remnant of English Northumbria north of Tees, had submitted to the suzerainty of the English King of Wessex; and, through all the subsequent vicissitudes of Danish and Norman conquest, Yorkshire came to be welded more and more closely into the fabric of the new Kingdom of England. Nothing but the abnormal size of Yorkshire among the counties of England and Scotland to-day remains to recall the fact that York once aspired to be the capital not of a county but of a kingdom. This aspiration came to naught in the collapse of the abortive Scandinavian Civilization which had momentarily translated it into a reality. In A.D. 920, when King Ragnvald of York acknowledged the suzerainty of King Edward of Wessex, York lost her prospect of becoming the capital of a kingdom thirty-five years before Edinburgh was assured of this prospect through being conquered from her Northumbrian founders by the Picts and Scots in A.D. 955.

The Northumbrian city which came nearest to emulating Edinburgh's political eminence was not York but Durham; and Durham became eminent by inheriting from Lothian the role of northern march against the Scots after the incorporation of Lothian

[1] For the conflict between Western Christendom and the abortive Scandinavian Civilization, see II. D (vii), pp. 340–60, below.

itself into Scotland. As the county palatine of the medieval Kingdom of England *vis-à-vis* the medieval Kingdom of Scotland, Durham acquired something of the status of an independent state and her prince-bishop some of the attributes of a sovereign.

In the Western World over against Scandinavia

In the foregoing analysis of the differentiation between the respective fortunes of several parts of the early English principality of Northumbria, we have just had occasion to notice certain incidents in the Scandinavian impact upon Western Christendom. This Scandinavian impact was the other external pressure, over and above the pressure from the Far Western Christians of 'the Celtic fringe', which went to the making of the Kingdom of Scotland; and it also went to the making of the kingdoms of England and France likewise.

In the making of Scotland, the union between Lothian and the domain of the Picts and Scots was not the first stage. By the time when the Picts and Scots conquered Lothian, they were already united with one another; but this union was not of old standing. Before the Völkerwanderung that followed the break-up of the Roman Empire, the Picts had had the northern extremity of Britain to themselves. During the Völkerwanderung the Scots had migrated across the sea from Ireland and had settled in Argyll as hostile intruders on Pictish ground.[1] The hostility between the two peoples had only given place to a friendly political union between them in A.D. 843. What was the cause of this remarkable change in their relations? The date speaks for itself. The Picto-Scottish union was effected one year after the first Viking raid on London and two years before the first Viking raid on Paris; and while some of the Scandinavian sea-raiders were sailing down the North Sea into the English Channel, others had been finding their way round the north-west coasts of Britain into Ireland. Thus the date of the Picto-Scottish union seems to tell its own tale; and we may hazard the conjecture that the two peoples who before the advent of the Vikings had been contending with one another for possession of the northern extremity of Britain, now brought themselves to compose their feud and unite their forces in response to the challenge of this formidable new pressure which had suddenly descended upon both alike from Scandinavia.

If this conjecture is right, the genesis of the Kingdom of Scotland may be expressed in terms of the responses to two successive challenges: first, a Picto-Scottish response to a Scandinavian challenge, and, second, a response on the part of the Northumbrian

[1] See II. D (iii), p. 86, above, and II. D (vii), pp. 323-4, below.

frontiersmen in the march of Lothian to a challenge from the united Picts and Scots.

In the genesis of the Kingdom of England we can discern the operation of responses to the same two challenges, but we find that the challenges were delivered here in the inverse chronological order. In this case, the first pressure—corresponding chronologically to the impact of the Scandinavians upon the Picts and Scots—was the pressure of certain sections of 'the Celtic Fringe' upon the English principalities of 'the Heptarchy'; the second pressure—corresponding chronologically to the Picto-Scottish conquest of Lothian—was the impact of the Scandinavians upon the two English principalities which had previously marked themselves out as the two alternative candidates for the hegemony of Southern Britain by their respective responses to the challenge of Celtic pressure upon the western borders of the English settlements in the island.

Just as, in North Britain, it was not Yorkshire in the interior of the principality of Northumbria but Lothian on the local border of 'the Celtic Fringe' that became the nucleus of an enduring kingdom, so, in South Britain, this destiny did not await the principality of Kent, in the corner of the island which lay nearest to the focus of the Western Christian Civilization on the Continent, nor again the principality of Essex, just across the estuary of the Thames. Thanks to its geographical situation, Kent did indeed become the first *point d'appui* of the Roman Church in Britain, as York became the second. Yet the very geographical circumstances which told in favour of Canterbury and York becoming archbishops' sees at the same time militated against their becoming the capitals of kingdoms. On the political plane, Canterbury never rose to be anything more than the capital of the principality of Kent. Political power in South Britain accrued not to Kent and Essex in the interior, at the point of junction between the insular outpost of Western Christendom and its continental main body, but to Mercia and Wessex, the two English principalities which were 'up against' the two southerly sectors of 'the Celtic Fringe' on the main island of the British Archipelago.

Moreover, the relative strength of Mercia and Wessex, in the first phase of their histories, showed itself proportionate to the relative strength of the external pressure from 'the Celtic Fringe' to which these two English principalities were subject. The pressure exerted upon Mercia from Wales was stronger than that exerted upon Wessex from the Welsh communities south of the Bristol Channel. Though the resistance of these 'West Welsh' to the English invaders has left an undying echo in the legend of King

Arthur, this resistance seems nevertheless to have been overcome with comparative ease and rapidity. The Arthurian legend ends on a note of heroic disaster; and the front line of the 'West Welsh' defences, which the legend locates in the neighbourhood of Glastonbury, was driven back by the founders of the English border principality of Wessex, advancing up the Valley of the River Thames, from the western watershed of the Thames to the distant line of the River Tamar which now constitutes the boundary between the counties of Devon and Cornwall. Confined, as they thus were, to a by no means impregnable patch of territory in the extreme south-western corner of the island, the 'West Welsh' ceased to be formidable to the English principality of Wessex, whereas the Welsh of Wales, from their relatively extensive and defensible mountain fastnesses, continued to press upon the western frontier of the adjoining English principality of Mercia.

The severity of this pressure is attested philologically by the name Mercia itself ('The March' *par excellence*) and archaeologically by the vestiges of the great earthwork called 'Offa's Dyke' which once covered the Welsh frontier of Mercia from the estuary of the Severn to the estuary of the Dee; and the military and political energy generated in Mercia, in response to this external pressure, enabled this same Mercian King Offa, when he turned his arms from the frontier towards the interior, to come within an ace of establishing a Mercian hegemony over South Britain. At the time when Mercia was stimulated, by her reaction to the pressure from Wales, into indulging these great ambitions, Wessex was prompted, by the less powerful stimulus from her 'West Welsh' frontier, to achieve, in the interior, the less ambitious feat of absorbing Kent and Essex into her body politic. Thus, in the eighth century of the Christian Era, it looked as though Mercia rather than Wessex were marked out, by the greater energy of her response to the pressure from 'the Celtic Fringe', as the destined nucleus of a future Kingdom of England. In the ninth century, however, when the challenge from 'the Celtic Fringe' was eclipsed by the challenge from Scandinavia, these prospects were falsified. In face of this new challenge, Mercia forfeited her prospects of greatness by failing to respond this time,[1] while Wessex, under the leadership and inspiration of Alfred, responded triumphantly and thereby became the nucleus of the historic Kingdom of England as it exists at the present day.

The Scandinavian pressure upon the Oceanic (as contrasted with the Mediterranean) seaboards of Western Christendom evoked

---

[1] Before the close of the eighth century, Mercia had sapped her own strength by succumbing to the malady of Militarism (see IV. C (iii) (c) 3 (α), vol. iv, p. 501, below).

responses which resulted not only in the coalescence of the Kingdom of England out of the insular 'Heptarchy', but also in the
articulation of the Kingdom of France out of the continental mass
of Western Christendom which had once been embraced in
Charlemagne's Empire.

We have already observed that, in the tenth century, 'the Holy
Roman Empire' passed from the Carolingian Dynasty to the Ottonids; and we have explained[1] this transfer of power by the circumstance that, as a result of Charlemagne's conquest of Saxony, the
stimulus of serving as the march of Western Christendom against
the continental European barbarians had been inherited by conquered Saxony from her conqueror Austrasia. We may now consider the notorious historical fact that, when the Ottonids succeeded
the Carolingians in the Imperial office, they did not enter into the
whole of the Carolingian territorial inheritance. Of the three portions into which the Carolingian dominions had been partitioned in
A.D. 843,[2] only the eastern and the central portion were reunited,
rather more than a century later, under the rule of Otto I (*imperabat* A.D. 962–73).[3] In the western portion, the Carolingians were
succeeded, not by the Ottonids but by the Capetians (in A.D. 987);[4]
and this change of dynasty was the outward visible sign of an inward psychological change which was the genesis of 'France' in the
present meaning of the name. The West Frankish crown became
the French crown when it was transferred from the head of the last
Carolingian at Laon to Hugh Capet's head at Rheims. Out of the
old undifferentiated substance of the Carolingian Empire there had
emerged, in the west, a new kingdom which thenceforward was not
only recognized juridically as being independent of 'the Holy Roman
Empire' but was also felt to be a distinct body politic, within the
larger but more rudimentary body social of Western Christendom,
in the consciousness of the French people themselves. In fact, the
birth of France in the tenth century of the Christian Era was the
first—and has ever remained one of the most definite—of those
inner geographical articulations of our Western Society which in
our day have been carried to extremes in the name of 'the principle
of nationality'.

Why was it that, when 'the Holy Roman Empire' was rescued
from disintegration by the Ottonids, it failed to reunite the western
portion of the Carolingian Empire with the central and the eastern

---

[1] See pp. 167–8, above.   [2] See I. B (iv), vol. i, p. 37, above.
[3] Otto became German king (i.e. ruler of the easternmost of the three portions into
which the heritage of Charlemagne had been partitioned in A.D. 843) in A.D. 936, twenty-
six years before he assumed the Imperial title. The claim, implicit in this assumption, to
sovereignty over the entire Carolingian heritage was never, of course, made good either
by Otto or by his successors.
[4] The date of Hugh Capet's coronation at Rheims.

portion under its aegis? We have remarked above that the defence and extension of the continental European frontiers of Western Christendom was the original function of 'the Holy Roman Empire' and continued to be its function—in face of diverse pressures from barbarians and from alien civilizations—through all its subsequent metamorphoses. Thus the secession of France from 'the Empire' was not due to any failure, on 'the Empire's' part, to perform its own special duty. The emergence of the Kingdom of France, like that of the Kingdom of England, in the tenth century is rather to be explained as the response to a new external pressure upon a different frontier of Western Christendom: the Scandinavian pressure upon the Atlantic seaboards. From the continental pressures which it was 'the Holy Roman Empire's' task to meet, Britain was exempt by nature and Gaul by circumstance after Charlemagne had carried the continental frontier of Western Christendom forward from the right bank of the Rhine to the left bank of the Elbe. On the other hand, the impact of the Vikings subjected Western Christendom to a maritime pressure from which the central and eastern portions of the Carolingian dominions were exempt, but which fell with its full weight upon the western portion—that is, upon Western Gaul— together with Britain. The line of the original frontier between France and 'the Empire'—a frontier which bisected ancient Gaul longitudinally from the mouth of the Scheldt to the mouth of the Rhône—is explicable as the line along which, in the ninth and tenth centuries of the Christian Era, there was a substantial equilibrium between two simultaneous external pressures. East of this line, the continental pressure from Slavs and Nomads was still felt more severely than any other, while west of the same line this continental pressure was exceeded by the maritime pressure from the Vikings—a pressure which overbore all others in its zone of heaviest incidence within range of the Atlantic coast and up the navigable channels of the rivers which gave the Viking ships an entry from the coast into the interior.

The local responses to the maritime challenge from Scandinavia which were made by the Western Christian Society on the Atlantic slope of the European Continent and in the British Archipelago were literally the making of France and England as we know them to-day.[1] These responses not only brought the two kingdoms into

[1] In the subsequent course of Western history, the making of France and England was completed by the mutual pressure which the two kingdoms exerted in turn upon one another. In particular, the grinding pressure to which France was subjected by England in the last phase of 'the Hundred Years' War' evoked the tremendous French response which was inspired by and incarnated in Joan of Arc. The military energy generated by this French reaction against English aggression was so powerful that, after it had driven the English into the sea, sufficient impetus remained to carry French arms —in the opposite direction—right over the Alps and down the Italian Peninsula before the close of the fifteenth century. The work which the Vikings had begun and the

existence but determined their centres of gravity and assigned them
their historic capitals. The Kingdom of England coalesced, not
round Mercia, which failed to respond to the Scandinavian challenge, but round Wessex, which rose to the occasion. The old
capital of Wessex, however, did not become the capital of the new
English Kingdom; for Winchester, which had once lain within
range of the frontier of Wessex over against the 'West Welsh', did
not lie in the principal danger-zone in the struggle between the
English and the Danes. In the Danish ordeal, Winchester enjoyed
a comparative security for which it had afterwards to pay by an
irreparable loss of prestige and power. When Wessex had mastered
the Danes and had grown into England in the process of performing
the feat, the capital of the new kingdom soon passed from Winchester, in the inglorious interior, to London, the city which had
borne the heat and burden of the day and which had perhaps given
the long battle its decisive turn in A.D. 895 by repelling the attempt
of a Danish Armada to ascend the Thames. Similarly, the Kingdom of France found its centre of gravity, not in Provence or
Languedoc, whose Mediterranean coastline was rarely visited by
Viking raiders, but in the Langue d'Oïl, which felt the full force of
the storm from Scandinavia. Again, within the area of the Langue
d'Oïl, the capital passed away from Carolingian Laon—a city set
safely on a hill overlooking the sources of the Oise, far above the
highest point up to which the river was navigable for Viking craft.
The inevitable capital of the new French Kingdom was Paris in the
Île de France, a city which had stood in the breach and had brought
the Vikings to a halt in their ascent of the Seine as London had
brought them to a halt in their ascent of the Thames.[1]

Thus the response of Western Christendom to the Scandinavian
maritime challenge manifested itself in a new Kingdom of France
with its capital at Paris, as well as in a new Kingdom of England
with its capital at London; and at the same time it is to be observed
that these manifestations of new creative power on the face of the
political map, imposing though they are, do not reveal the actual
vigour and versatility of the response in its full measure. In order
to take its measure, we must add that, in the process of gaining the
upper hand over their Scandinavian adversaries, the French and
English peoples forged the potent military and social instrument of
the Feudal System, and that they also gave aesthetic expression to
the emotional experience of the ordeal in national epics.

English King Henry V continued was consummated by all the neighbours of France in
unison when they fell upon Revolutionary France in 1792, and provoked an eruption of
national energy which astonished the World.
    [1] For details of the rise of Paris and London through their heroic responses to the
Scandinavian challenge, see the Annex to the present chapter, pp. 400-1, below.

The English national Epic is represented by one notable work of art: the *Lay of the Battle of Maldon*. The French Epic, which is represented by the *Chanson de Roland* and the other *Chansons de Geste*, is the stem from which has sprung the mighty tree of our Western vernacular literature: a literature which has branched into an infinite variety of *genres* and which has learnt to operate with as many tongues as there are living languages in Western Christendom.[1]

With regard to the origins of the Feudal System, it will suffice to quote the following account of its emergence in England, before the Norman Conquest, from the work of a scholar who is one of the acknowledged masters of the subject:

'It became impossible to perform the ordinary *fyrd* service, in frequent expeditions and in proper equipment, on the basis of a tenement of one hide, without help from outside. The coat of mail and the horse acquired more and more value from a military point of view—one as a means of defence in the hard struggles with the Danes, the other as a means of quick locomotion. Well-forged helmets and swords were scarce and very expensive. Altogether, the difference between a well-armed warrior and a militiaman grew more and more important. This led ultimately to the formation of a professional force of knights and sergeants-at-arms. . . .

'The outfit of 1066 was more elaborate and costly than that of 800. Although horses were employed in Charlemagne's armies, especially in his *scarae* or picked troops, the decisive turn towards horsemanship was taken in the Danish wars, when the "horsed" Vikings had to be caught up and pursued by riding divisions, and the five-hide unit probably included provision for one or two horses. . . . The social foundation of the old army establishment—the status of the small free householder, provided on the average with a hide—was entirely inadequate to meet the altered requirements of the art of war and of military organisation. A unit five times as large grew up as the natural basis for the man-at-arms in the national array of the tenth and eleventh centuries. One might say —using political expressions with some caution—that the more ancient democratic arrangement had to be replaced by an aristocratic one.'[2]

---

[1] The author of the *Lay of Maldon* has derived his technique and style from the tradition of *Beowulf*, but his inspiration has quite a different source and character. The older epic poetry in the English tongue was inspired by the experience of barbarians who were overrunning the Roman Empire in the Völkerwanderung which occupied the interregnum between the submergence of the Hellenic Civilization and the emergence of the 'affiliated' Western Civilization. The *Lay of Maldon* is part of a response which was made by this Western Civilization, after its emergence, to one of the first great challenges with which it was confronted. Whereas *Beowulf* is an expression of barbarism on the war-path, the *Lay of Maldon* is the expression of a civilization fighting for its life. Thus, genetically, the true affinity of the *Lay of Maldon* is not with the previous English epic poetry but with the contemporary French epic poetry which was evoked in an adjoining province of Western Christendom by the same ordeal of the impact of the Vikings. The *Lay of Maldon* and the *Chansons de Geste*, between them, are the outcome, in the artistic sphere, of the collision between Western Christendom and the abortive Scandinavian Civilization in one of the two opposing camps. In the other camp, the outcome in the same sphere is the Icelandic Saga. (For the part played in the genesis of the Icelandic Saga by the stimulus of transmarine migration, see II. D (iii), pp. 86–100, above.)

[2] Vinogradoff, Paul: *English Society in the Eleventh Century* (Oxford 1908, Clarendon Press), pp. 30 and 34.

Thus the Feudal System, like the *Lay of Maldon* and the *Chanson de Roland*, and like the kingdoms of England and France with their new capitals in London and Paris, was an outcome of the reaction of Western Christendom to Scandinavian pressure upon her Atlantic seaboards; and these manifold creations testify to the versatility and the vigour of the Western response which the Scandinavian challenge evoked. The most cogent testimony of all is afforded by the actual outcome of the collision between Western Christendom and its Scandinavian adversaries. Western Christendom successfully defended herself, by force of arms, against the first fury of the Scandinavian onslaught which had threatened to overwhelm her; she then passed over to the offensive by rapidly converting to her religion and culture the invaders who had made a forcible lodgement on her soil in the Danelaw and in Normandy; and she reaped the fruits of this moral victory when she sent forth the converted Normans, as her knights errant, to fight in her service not less valiantly, and at the same time far more effectively, than their pagan ancestors had fought against her.

Little more than a century after Rollo and his companions had made with Charles the Simple the pact which secured them a permanent settlement on the Atlantic seaboard of France as newly initiated members of the Western Christian fraternity, their descendants were extending the bounds of Western Christendom in the Mediterranean at the expense of Orthodox Christendom and Islam, and were spreading the full light of the Western Civilization, as it now shone on the Continent in France, into the insular kingdoms of England and Scotland which still lay in the penumbra. Physiologically, the Norman Conquest of England might perhaps be regarded as the final achievement of an enterprise which adventurers of Scandinavian blood had been perpetually striving to accomplish for more than two centuries. From the cultural standpoint, however, this interpretation of the Norman Conquest makes nonsense; for the Normans came to England in the eleventh century on a mission which was the very contrary of the Danish mission in the ninth century. The Normans repudiated their Scandinavian pagan past by coming, not to destroy the law of Western Christendom in England, but to fulfil it. On the field of Senlac, when the Norman warrior-minstrel Taillefer rode singing into battle in the van of the Norman knights, the language on his lips was not Norse but French, and the matter of which he was inditing was not the tale of Sigurd but the tale of Roland. When the Western Christian Civilization had thus captivated the Scandinavian invaders of its own domain, it is no wonder that it was able to set the seal upon its victory by supplanting the abortive Scandinavian Civilization in

Scandinavia itself and in the uttermost parts of the Earth to which Scandinavian seafarers had penetrated. We shall have occasion to examine this impact of the Western Christian Civilization upon Scandinavia and Iceland and Greenland at a later point in this volume, when we shall be considering the collision between Christendom and the abortive Scandinavian Civilization from the Scandinavian standpoint.[1]

In the Western World over against the Syriac World in the Iberian Peninsula

The last frontier of Western Christendom that calls for consideration here is the land-frontier in the Iberian Peninsula *vis-à-vis* the Syriac Society in its latest phase—a phase which began when the Arabs reintegrated the Syriac universal state in the seventh century of the Christian Era. In the history of this frontier there are two outstanding features. In the first place, Western Christendom came under pressure from an alien civilization at a far earlier stage in this quarter than in any other. In the second place, the Powers which came into being, in response to this pressure, on the Iberian marches of Western Christendom eventually came to play a leading role, which was all their own, in the propagation of the Western Civilization.

As regards the first of these two points, we have seen that on the North European continental land-frontier Western Christendom was confronted at the outset solely by barbarians. In that quarter, the Western World did not become subject to pressure from the main body of Orthodox Christendom before the Ottoman impact upon Hungary in the fifteenth century of the Christian Era,[2] while it was not until the sixteenth century that the Russian offshoot of Orthodox Christendom exerted pressure upon the West in the form of a Muscovite impact upon Lithuania.[3] On the other hand, on the Iberian land-frontier, Western Christendom found itself under pressure from the Syriac Civilization at the dawn of Western history. Indeed, this Syriac menace to the existence of Western Christendom in its infancy was still more formidable than the contemporary menace from the North European barbarians;[4] and our Western Society was awakened to its first glimmer of self-consciousness by the ordeal of wrestling simultaneously with these two deadly foes—like the infant Hêraklês when he rose in his cradle to wrestle with the two serpents that had been sent by a malevolent

---

[1] See II. D (vii), pp. 340–60, below.
[2] See pp. 177–9, above.   [3] See pp. 175–6, above.
[4] See the passage cited in I. B (iii), vol. i, p. 30, footnote 1, above, from Edward Gibbon: *The History of the Decline and Fall of the Roman Empire*, ch. xlii.

goddess to take his life, and saved himself alive by strangling both monsters, each single-handed.

The Arab onslaught upon the infant civilization of the West was an incident in the final Syriac reaction against the long Hellenic intrusion upon the Syriac domain; for when the Arabs, in the strength of Islam, took up and completed the task which had proved to be beyond the strength of Zoroastrians and Jews and Nestorians and Monophysites, they did not rest until they had recovered for the Syriac Society the whole of its former domain at its widest extension. Not content with reconstituting as an Arab Empire the Syriac universal state which had originally been embodied in the Persian Empire of the Achaemenidae, the Arabs went on to reconquer the ancient Phoenician colonial domain in the Western Mediterranean which, in the Achaemenian age, had been welded into a unity of its own—an overseas counterpart of the Persian Empire—under the hegemony of Carthage. For a moment in the eighth century of the Christian Era an Arab Caliph fulfilled the ambition which a Persian King of Kings had found himself unable to fulfil in the sixth century B.C.[1] The last Umayyad who reigned at Damascus was at least nominally master of the whole compass of the Syriac World, from the farthest limits ever attained by the Achaemenian Empire in the east to the farthest attained by the Carthaginian Empire in the west.[2] In the latter direction, the Arab commanders had crossed not only the straits of Gibraltar but the Pyrenees in the footsteps of Hannibal in A.D. 713; and thereafter, though they had not emulated their great Carthaginian predecessor's passage of the Rhône and the Alps, they had broken ground which Hannibal never trod when they carried their arms to the Loire in A.D. 732. At the Battle of Tours, the Arabs were attacking Western Christendom in its cradle.

The discomfiture of the Arabs by the Franks on this occasion has assuredly been one of the decisive events in history; for the Western

---

[1] According to Herodotus, Cambyses, after his conquest of Egypt, aspired to round off the Achaemenian Empire in North Africa by conquering the Napatan Kingdom up the Nile and the oases of the Libyan Desert and the Carthaginian Empire beyond the Syrtes. Operations against Napata and the Oasis of Ammon were actually attempted with disastrous results. Simultaneously, Cambyses 'ordered the fleet to sail against Carthage; but the Phoenicians declined to carry the order out. They explained that they were bound to the Carthaginians by solemn pledges, and that they would be committing an atrocity if they made war upon their own colonists. The Phoenicians' refusal was decisive, since the remainder of the fleet by itself was no match for the Carthaginian forces. Accordingly, the Carthaginians escaped the Persian yoke; for Cambyses shrank from coercing the Phoenicians, who had become members of the Persian Empire of their own free will and were the mainstay of the Persian Navy.' (Herodotus: Book III, ch. 19.)

[2] On the eastern front, the Oxus-Jaxartes Basin was definitively incorporated into the Arab Empire in the years A.D. 737–41 (see p. 141, with footnote 3, above) by Nasr, while on the western front Musa had completed the Arab conquest of the Visigothic 'successor-state' of the Roman Empire as early as A.D. 713 by occupying the Transpyrenaean province of Septimania along the Gallic coast between the Pyrenees and the Rhône.

reaction to Syriac pressure which declared itself on the battle-field of Tours in A.D. 732 continued in force and increased in momentum on this front until, some eight centuries later, its impetus was carrying the Portuguese vanguard of Western Christendom right out of the Iberian Peninsula and onward overseas round Africa to Goa and Malacca and Macao, and the Castilian vanguard onward across the Atlantic to Mexico and thence across the Pacific to Manila.[1] These Iberian pioneers of Western Christendom per-formed an unparalleled service for the civilization which they represented. They expanded the horizon, and thereby potentially the domain, of our Western Society from an obscure corner of the Old World until it came to embrace all the habitable lands and navigable seas on the surface of the planet. It is owing to this Iberian energy and enterprise that Western Christendom has grown, like the grain of mustard seed in the parable,[2] until it has become 'the Great Society': a tree in whose branches all the nations of the Earth have come and lodged. This latter-day Westernized World is the peculiar achievement of Western Christendom's Iberian pioneers; and the Western energy which performed this feat was evoked and sustained and wrought up to its high intensity by the challenge of Syriac pressure on the Iberian front.

The Portuguese and Castilian seafarers who made their presence felt throughout the World in the first century of our modern age (*circa* A.D. 1475–1575) were the heirs of frontiersmen whose spirit had been tempered by thirty generations of strenuous border warfare against the Moors on the Iberian marches. On this frontier, the Franks first turned back the tide of Arab conquest from the heart of Gaul; thereafter, under Charlemagne's leadership, they carried their counter-offensive to the Iberian side of the Pyrenees, where they joined forces with the remnant of the Visigoths in the fastness of Asturia; and eventually, during the post-Syriac inter-regnum (*circa* A.D. 975–1275), when the Umayyad Caliphate in Andalusia broke up,[3] these Christian barbarians of the Pyrenaean hinterland contended victoriously for the possession of the Umay-yads' Peninsular heritage with the Muslim Berbers from the opposite hinterlands in Africa: the wild Murābit Nomads from the Sahara and the still wilder Muwahhid highlanders from the Atlas.

The dependence of Iberian Christian energy upon the stimulus administered by pressure from the Moors is demonstrated by the fact that this energy gave out as soon as the Moorish pressure

---

1 The expansion of Frankdom in this direction has been mentioned by anticipation in I. B (iv), vol. i, p. 38, above.
2 Matthew xiii. 31–2; Mark iv. 31–2; Luke xiii. 19.
3 When the Umayyad Caliphs who had ruled the whole Syriac World from Damascus were overthrown in A.D. 750 by the 'Abbasids, a branch of the Umayyad House succeeded in establishing itself in Andalusia, where it ruled at Cordova from A.D. 755 to 1028.

ceased to be exerted. In the seventeenth century of the Christian Era the Portuguese and Castilians were supplanted in the new world which they had called into existence overseas by interlopers from the Transpyrenaean parts of Western Christendom—the Dutch and the English and the French—and this discomfiture overseas coincided in date with the removal of the historic stimulus at home through the extirpation (by massacre, expulsion, or forcible conversion) of the remaining 'Moriscos' in the Peninsula.

Again, if we look farther back, we shall observe that Portugal and Castile were only two out of the three Christian 'successor-states' of the Umayyad Caliphate which had divided the Iberian Peninsula between them. Why did not Aragon take her part, side by side with Castile and Portugal, in the vaster enterprises of discovery and commerce and conquest on which the two sister kingdoms embarked at the turn of the fifteenth and the sixteenth century? In the immediate past, during the later 'Middle Ages', Aragon had played a more brilliant role than either Castile or Portugal in the life of the Western Society. She had shared in the brilliance of the North Italian city-states and had made certain original contributions of her own—in the fields of cartography and of international law—to the North Italian medieval culture. Why was it, then, that, just when Portugal and Castile both entered upon the brilliant phase of their careers, Aragon allowed herself to be dominated and effaced by her Castilian neighbour?[1] The explanation perhaps lies in the fact that the stimulus of Moorish pressure had been lost by Aragon several centuries before it was lost by either of the other two Peninsular kingdoms. In the days of da Gama and Columbus, both Portugal and Castile were still serving as marches of Western Christendom against the Moors. Castile then still marched in the Peninsula with the surviving Moorish kingdom of Granada, while Portugal marched with Morocco in her Tangerine province on the African side of the Straits of Gibraltar; and the Portuguese and Castilian exploits overseas, which began in that age, were simply diversions, to a new and wider field, of energies which had hitherto been employed assiduously against the Moors at home. On the

[1] The Aragonese themselves submitted passively to 'Castilianization'; the Catalans, who had been the active and progressive element in the medieval Kingdom of Aragon, kicked against the pricks. Yet this Catalan resistance to Castilian domination has been feeble and ineffective compared with the Portuguese. The Crown of Portugal was united with the Crown of Castile in A.D. 1581, only 102 years after the Catalans had been yoked with the Castilians by the union of the Crowns of Castile and Aragon which came about in 1479 through the marriage of Ferdinand and Isabella ten years earlier. The sequels to these two unions were very different. The Portuguese revolted against the Castilian yoke in 1640 and compelled the Government at Madrid to recognize the independence of Portugal in 1663. On the other hand, the Catalans failed in their belated attempt to recover their independence from Madrid during the War of the Spanish Succession, with the result that Catalonia disappeared altogether off the political map from the fall of Barcelona in 1714 down to the Spanish Revolution of 1931.

other hand, Aragon had been relegated to the interior of Western Christendom since A.D. 1235, when the overthrow of the Muwahhid Berbers by the Iberian Christians at the Battle of Las Navas had confined the Moors in the Peninsula to the Granadan enclave. Since that time, Aragon had been insulated from the Moors on land by the intervening Castilian province of Murcia, while in the Mediterranean her Moorish warfare had been brought to an end in A.D. 1229–32 by her conquest of the Balearic Islands.[1] Thus the stimulus which was the common source of Iberian Christian energies had ceased to play upon the Aragonese at least two-and-a-half centuries before it ceased to play upon their Castilian and Portuguese neighbours; and this may partly[2] explain why it was that Aragon fell out of the running before the great opportunity of overseas expansion offered itself to the Peninsular Powers, while Castile and Portugal did not finally succeed in cutting off the source of their own energies by extirpating the 'Moriscos' in their midst until the stimulus of Moorish pressure at home had carried the Portuguese and Castilian pioneers to the four corners of the World.

It will be seen that the relation of the Iberian marches of Western Christendom to the Moors resembles the relation of the Danubian Hapsburg Monarchy to the 'Osmanlis.[3] The Peninsular Powers, likewise, had their *raisons d'être* in serving as marches of the Western Society against an alien civilization; and their energies were responses to the pressure of this alien force. They were vigorous just so long as this pressure was formidable, and as soon as the pressure slackened they petered out.

In the Andean and Central American Worlds

We may conclude our present survey of the stimulus of pressures by making the historic passage from the Iberian Peninsula to 'the New World'. When the Spaniards broke in upon the Andean and Central American worlds in the sixteenth century of the Christian Era, they found the Andean Society already in a universal state and the Mexic Society on the point of falling into one. The Andean universal state had been established by the Incas of Cuzco;

---

[1] This conquest was not, of course, the end of Aragonese enterprise in the Mediterranean; for the Balearic Islands were stepping-stones to Sardinia and the Two Sicilies, and these to Greece; and, by the beginning of the fourteenth century, Catalan adventurers were harrying both their Latin predecessors and these predecessors' Greek victims on the shores of the Aegean. Yet these latter-day Catalan filibustering expeditions into the Levant were no substitute for the ancient border warfare with the Moors at close quarters. The Catalan victories in the fourteenth century over Greek East Roman Emperors and Burgundian Dukes of Athens were as facile, and therefore as barren of stimulus, as the Castilian victories in the sixteenth century over Aztecs and Incas.

[2] Some part of the explanation evidently lies in the fact that Aragon, alone of the three fifteenth-century Peninsular kingdoms, possessed no seaboard on the Atlantic, and was thus at the same disadvantage as Columbus's native city of Genoa for participating in the exploitation of a Transatlantic New World.

[3] For this relation, see pp. 177–90, above.

the Central American universal state was being established by the Aztecs of Tenochtitlan. To what did Cuzco and Tenochtitlan owe their imperial greatness? Or, to ask the same question, in regard to the Andean World, in other terms: Why was it that the Andean universal state found its nucleus on a previously obscure corner of the Andean Plateau, in the upper valley of the River Urubamba, and not in the Basin of Lake Titicaca, where the earliest and greatest development of civilization on the plateau has left its monument in the ruins of Tiahuanaco? Or, for that matter, why did not the Andean universal state find its nucleus somewhere within the original home of the Andean Civilization among the oases of the Pacific coast-land?

In the light of our foregoing survey, the answer to these questions becomes apparent when we notice the geographical fact that Cuzco in the Andean and Tenochtitlan in the Central American World were situated, like Rome and Macedonia in the Hellenic World,[1] in marches which were exposed to external pressure from formidable barbarians. Cuzco guarded the gate of the Andean World against the wild tribes of the Amazonian tropical forest; Tenochtitlan similarly guarded the gate of the Central American World against the Chichimecs: the vagrant hunting tribes of the North American arid zone, whence the Aztecs themselves were recent immigrants. Tenochtitlan always remained within close range of the northern frontier of the Central American Society over against the Chichimecs, and Cuzco within close range of the north-eastern frontier of the Andean Society over against the Amazonian savages, even when the conquests of the Aztecs in the interior of the Central American World and the conquests of the Incas in the interior of the Andean World had reached their greatest respective extents. This extreme difference in the range of Aztec and Inca expansion towards the outer darkness in the one direction and towards the interior of their own worlds in the other might seem at first sight to call for explanation; but reflexion shows that, on the contrary, this permanent proximity of both the Inca and the Aztec capital to a dangerous barbarian frontier, so far from requiring to be explained, itself explains why it was that the Andean and the Central American universal state actually grew out of precisely these two nuclei. It was the stimulus of perpetual reaction to external pressure that evoked in the Aztecs and in the Incas alike the energy which was required in order to perform a great feat of political construction at home.

Why did not either Tlaxcala or Cholula, rather than Tenochtitlan, become the nucleus of the incipient Central American universal

[1] See pp. 160–1, above.

state? Because these cities of the interior lacked the stimulus of external pressure from the Chichimecs of the outer darkness—a stimulus which never ceased to act upon Tenochtitlan on the frontier. And why did the Collas of the Titicaca Basin go down before the Incas of the Urubamba Valley in that trial of strength between two neighbouring Andean highland confederacies which was the beginning of the Incas' imperial career? The answer to this latter question may be given in terms of physical geography. 'Cuzco, the ancient capital of Ttahua-ntin-suyu, the Land of the Four Sections, otherwise the Inca Empire, lies in the drainage of the Amazon river-system. . . . The small torrential streams that flow through Cuzco pour themselves into the Urubamba, which is a tributary of the Ucayali, which in turn empties into the Marañon, just as that does into the Amazon.'[1] In other words, the physiography of the Inca section of the frontier between the Andean Civilization and an Amazonian barbarism facilitated and even invited barbarian incursions into the Andean domain and therefore kept the Andean wardens of the marches in this sector for ever on the *qui vive*. On the other hand, the Collao, in the Basin of Lake Titicaca, was safely insulated from the Amazonian savages by those 'snow-clad peaks of the Eastern Cordillera—Sorata, Huayna Potosi, and Illampu'—which 'bite into the sky with glittering white teeth'[2] on the horizon that unfolds itself before the gaze of the visitor to Tiahuanaco. The grimness of the physical environment in this rough country, from which the ancient builders of Tiahuanaco had perhaps derived their stimulus,[3] may have been the undoing of their latter-day successors the Collas—not because it presented the Collas, any more than their local predecessors, with a physical challenge beyond their strength, but, on the contrary, because it shielded them from a stimulating human pressure to which their neighbours and contemporaries the Incas, were exposed. The absence of this potent human stimulus in the Collao may have been the handicap which brought defeat upon the Collas when they had to meet the Incas in battle.

VI. THE STIMULUS OF PENALIZATIONS

The Nature of the Stimulus

We have now concluded our survey of the stimulus of the human environment when it takes the form of continuous external pressure. Let us next examine its effect when it takes the form of social penalization.

[1] Means, P. A.: *Ancient Civilisations of the Andes* (New York 1931, Scribner), p. 17.
[2] Means, op. cit., p. 130.
[3] See the fuller quotation from Means, op. cit., loc. cit., in II. C (ii) (*b*) 2, vol. i p. 322, above.

The nature of this effect may be indicated by an analogy between social phenomena and physical. It is a well-known fact that when a living organism is penalized, by comparison with other representatives of its species, through losing the use of a particular organ or faculty, it is apt to respond to this challenge by specializing in the use of some other organ or faculty until it has secured an advantage over its fellows in this second field of activity to offset its handicap in the first. The blind, for example, are apt to develop a more delicate sense of touch than is usually possessed by people who have not been deprived of the normal human sense of sight; and this enhancement of one faculty to offset the atrophy of another seems to occur in some degree universally and as it were spontaneously, apart from the special cases in which individuals of eminent character—a Henry Fawcett or a Helen Keller—are stimulated by their personal physical handicap into making some deliberate and sustained effort of will and ingenuity.[1] Somewhat similarly, we find that, in a body social, any section or group or class which is socially penalized—either by accident or by its own act or by the act of other members of the society in which it lives—is apt to respond to the challenge of being handicapped in, or altogether excluded from, certain fields of social activity by concentrating its social energies upon other fields and excelling in these.

We may remind ourselves, once again, of our simile of 'the pollarded willow'.[2] The more ruthless the execution that is done by the pruner among the shoots that he finds sprouting in springtime out of the willow's head, the more abundant will be the vitality that the tree will concentrate into the shoots which are spared, and the more vigorous, therefore, will be the growth of these surviving shoots in the course of the season

We may find an alternative simile, within the social sphere, in a famous incident in the history of the Hellenic Society. When the rising religion of the internal proletariat of the Hellenic World in its universal state was persecuted by the dominant minority, the Roman Imperial authorities were able to suppress the public practice of Christianity, but they failed to suppress Christianity itself: they merely drove it underground. The prohibition of Christian worship on the surface of pagan Rome stimulated the Christians to create for themselves a new Christian Rome in the Catacombs below the surface of the Campagna; and the City of the Catacombs

---

[1] Such purposive efforts are apt to carry those who make them to greater achievements than are accomplished by ordinary people who are in full possession of all their faculties, and perhaps even to greater achievements than the afflicted persons themselves would actually have accomplished if the challenge of physical penalization had not evoked in them a spiritual response that made the utmost demands upon their moral and intellectual as well as their physical energies.

[2] See I. C (iii) (b), vol. i, p. 168, above.

eventually triumphed over the City of the Seven Hills. The Church rose again from the bowels of the earth in order to raise in the City of the Vatican a dome which towers at this day above the Capitol;[1] and the early Latin peasant, who responded to the challenge of his physical environment by breaking in the intractable surface of the Campagna with his plough,[2] was emulated by the latter-day Christian denizen of the Roman slums, who responded to the challenge from his human environment by visiting the Campagna in the secrecy of the night-watches in order to carve a labyrinthine subterranean world of his own out of the solid tufa. The monument of the Latin peasant's feat is the Roman Empire; the monument of the Christian proletarian's feat is the Roman Catholic Church.

In surveying the effects of the stimulus of social penalizations, it may be convenient to start with the simplest case: a situation in which certain physical handicaps inhibit the individuals who are subject to them from following the ordinary avocations of the society in which they live. Let us remind ourselves, for example, of the predicament in which a blind man or a lame man finds himself in a barbarian society when the ordinary male member of society is a warrior—a situation which is apt to arise in 'the external proletariat' on the fringe of a decadent civilization on the eve of a Völkerwanderung.[3] How does the lame barbarian react? Though his feet cannot carry him into battle in the company of his fellows, his hands can forge weapons and armour for other men to wield and wear; and therefore, since he cannot use all his limbs to good effect in the normal activities of Man in the human environment into which he has been born, he counteracts his handicap by using those limbs in which he is sound to better effect than his fellows know how to use them—in a sleight of hand that is all his own. So he becomes the skilled artificer who is the workaday prototype of lame Hephaestus and lame Weland in the World of Mythology. And how does the blind barbarian react? His predicament is still worse than his lame brother's, for he cannot use his hands in the smithy to any better purpose than on the battle-field; yet he can use them to strike the harp in harmony with a voice that rings as clear and sweet as any other man's, and he can use his mind to make poetry out of the human life in which he cannot take an active part.

---

[1] Gibbon, sitting among the ruins of Ancient Rome on the Palatine, and listening to the friars singing Vespers among the ruins of Ancient Rome on the Capitol, was inspired to write The History of the Decline and Fall of the Roman Empire. (See Part XIII, below.)

[2] See II. D (i), pp. 16–17, above.

[3] This predicament has been touched upon in II. B, vol. i, p. 190, above, apropos of the phenomenon of the Division of Labour. For the blind bard as an institution, see the survey of examples that is given by Subotić, D., in Yugoslav Popular Ballads (Cambridge 1932, University Press), pp. 22–3.

Nor seeks nor finds he mortal blisses,
But feeds on the aërial kisses
Of shapes that haunt thought's wildernesses.

.   .   .

But from these create he can
Forms more real than living man,
Nurslings of Immortality.[1]

The deeds of god-like Achilles and Agamemnon only live on in the
verses of 'blind Thamyras and blind Maeonides'. The fame which
the barbarian warrior desires above all things, and in quest of
which he wanders over the face of the Earth 'like as a lion that is
greedy of his prey',[2] is in the barbarian poet's hand and voice and
mind to give or to withhold.

Vixere fortes ante Agamemnona
Multi, sed omnes illacrimabiles
Urgentur ignotique longa
Nocte, carent quia vate sacro.[3]

In the barbarian's universe, the blind bard, who cannot wield
either warrior's sword or blacksmith's hammer, is yet as potent as
the Galilaean fisherman who ranks as a proletarian in the Roman
census but as Prince of the Apostles in the Christian dispensation.
Homer, like Peter, is an arbiter of human destinies.[4] 'So the last
shall be first and the first last.'[5]

So much for the stimulus of social penalizations when these are
the automatic consequence of physical disabilities. When we pass
on to the penalization which is imposed by poverty, we may observe,
for example, in an English 'public school', that the 'commoners',
who have been born in well-to-do homes and have come to be
where they are, without exertions of their own, by reason of their
parents' capacity to pass muster and to pay the school fees, are less
apt to do hard work at school than their schoolfellows of the same
social class and social—but not personal—background who are
'scholars'. The 'scholars' know that their parents could not have
afforded to send them to a school of this kind if the boys themselves
had not won 'scholarships' by their own endeavours; and they
realize that, as it has been in their childhood, so it will continue to be
when they are grown up. They will have to make their way by their
own efforts; they will have to set off the handicap of starting life
with smaller material means than the average of their class by rising
above the average in intelligence and efficiency and application.

[1] Shelley: *Prometheus Unbound.*   [2] Psalm xvii. 12.
[3] Horace: *Carmina*, Bk. IV, Ode 9, vv. 25–8.
[4] 'And I say unto thee that thou art Peter, and upon this rock I will build my Church;
and the gates of Hell shall not prevail against it. And I will give unto thee the keys of the
Kingdom of Heaven; and whatsoever thou shalt bind on Earth shall be bound in Heaven;
and whatsoever thou shalt loose on Earth shall be loosed in Heaven.' Matthew xvi. 18–19.
[5] Matthew xx. 16.

Thus the penalization of poverty gives the 'scholar' a perpetual stimulus which the 'commoner' lacks except in the rare cases in which the soporific effect of 'independent means' is counteracted by personal ambition or by public spirit or by intellectual curiosity—and these are rare gifts of the Gods. Again, in an English university, we may observe that the County Council scholar, who is penalized not only by poverty but by a certain inferiority in social class, is apt to exert himself still more than the scholar from a 'public school', whose social, if not his economic, position is assured. And in general we may observe—not only in contemporary England but in every society in every age—that each class on the social ladder is apt to maintain its numerical strength, not by natural increase, but by recruitment from the classes below it, and that the topmost class, which cannot go up higher, is always making room for its recruits from below by a perpetual process of extinction in the third and fourth generation. In fact, the climber who reaches the topmost rung of the social ladder has arrived at the edge of a social abyss and has condemned his descendants—unintentionally and unwittingly—to 'walk the plank'. This social phenomenon is so manifest and so notorious that it has become proverbial. The Maghribī philosopher Ibn Khaldūn's generalization that the average duration of a dynasty is three generations[1] is an exact equivalent of the North American saying that 'It's three generations from shirt-sleeves to shirt-sleeves.'

Migration

An aptitude for rising in the social scale may also be observed among immigrants who have been impelled by the stimulus of poverty or persecution at home to seek their fortunes in a foreign country. The social handicap of finding himself in a new human environment, where he is unfamiliar with the prevailing manners and customs and language and where he has to contend with the instinctive prejudice of the native-born citizen against the immigrant alien, commonly stimulates the new-comer to put forth his energies and to keep a sharp look-out for opportunities of advancement until he has 'made good' in the country of his adoption. This is the common history of the Scotsman in modern England (and the Scottish engineer all over the World); the Flemish weaver in medieval England; the German miner in medieval Hungary; the French-Canadian factory-hand and farmer[2] and the Polish market-

---

[1] Ibn Khaldūn: *Muqaddamāt* (Prolegomena): translation by de Slane, Baron McG. (Paris 1863–8, Imprimerie Impériale, 3 vols.), vol. i, pp. 343–59. Compare the same volume, pp. 286–90, where Ibn Khaldūn suggests that it takes four generations for a family to reach its zenith.

[2] See II. D (ii), pp. 71–2, above.

gardener[1] in New England; the Huguenot silk-weaver in Spital-
fields and his fellow exiles whose descendants have distinguished
themselves in every walk and circumstance of life in almost every
Protestant country: England, Württemberg, Prussia, South Africa.[2]
In the Arabic World, it is the history of the Hadramī trader in Java.

Slavery

Perhaps the most extraordinary illustration on record of the
immigrant's aptitude for social efficiency is the history of the vast
concourse of immigrants from all the countries round the Mediterranean who were brought to Italy as slaves during those two
terrible centuries between the outbreak of the Hannibalic War and
the establishment of the Augustan Peace which were the climax of
the Hellenic 'Time of Troubles'.

The handicap under which these slave-immigrants began their
new life is almost beyond imagination. Some of them were heirs to
the cultural heritage of the Hellenic Civilization; and these had seen
their whole spiritual and material universe tumble about their ears
when their beautiful cities, which Gods had guarded and men
respected from of old, had been put to the sack and the citizens
sold into slavery against all laws human and divine and all precedents in Hellenic history. The Coronaean captives on the Delian
slave-market in the year 171 B.C. might have cried out to their
Haliartian companions in misfortune[3] in the words of the last
messenger who brought tidings of evil to Job: 'Behold, there came
a great wind from the wilderness and smote the four corners of the
house, and it fell upon the young men and they are dead; and I
only am escaped alone to tell thee.'[4] Indeed, the calamity was
overwhelming, even for those slave-immigrants to Italy who had
been taken, not from the dominant Hellenic minority in the Hellenic

---

[1] The writer of this Study once drove through a string of villages in the Connecticut
Valley in which all the houses were the handiwork of eighteenth-century colonists of
English origin, while all the present inhabitants (in A.D. 1925) were immigrant Poles who
were making a good living by growing onions on land which had ceased to yield a profit in
native-born American hands. The Polish immigrant prospered here because he worked
longer hours than his native-born American predecessor and because every member of
the Pole's large family laboured in the fields side by side with the head of the household.
The children of the original Polish immigrants were already beginning to attend the local
American high schools, and it was evident that the third generation would win their
way into the universities with the ultimate result that the fourth generation would cease
to benefit by the stimulus which had impelled their elders to climb towards the top of
the social tree!

[2] 'One drop of Huguenot blood in the veins is worth a thousand a year' is a saying that
is attributed to T. H. Huxley. The observation is acute; but of course the Huguenot's
money-making power is not an attribute of his race. In race, the Huguenot is no different
from his kinsmen who still remain in France. And, if it is true that the Huguenot shows
a greater aptitude for making money than the Catholic or agnostic Frenchman who has
stayed at home, his eminent business ability is to be interpreted as a response to the
challenge of having been driven into exile without resources—a challenge to which the
majority of the French nation has not been exposed.

[3] See Livy xlii. 63, and xliii. 4.   [4] Job i. 19.

World, but from the Oriental 'internal proletariat' which had lost its social heritage already, or from the barbarian 'external proletariat' which had none to lose; for there were other grievous losses of a personal kind that were inherent in enslavement. All these slave-immigrants alike had lost their personal liberty; they had been branded as human chattels instead of human beings with human rights; they had been uprooted from their homes and separated for ever from their families; and they had been subjected to new conditions of life which were almost beyond bearing. Their Roman masters, who had purchased their bodies wholesale as a speculative investment, thought only of wringing the utmost possible profit from their labour. The Roman law treated slaves with a harshness that reflected the apprehensions of a Roman governing class which was ever conscious of the volcanic stirrings of a servile under-world. Some of the recruits to the Roman servile labour-force had to spend their days working in chain-gangs on the plantations and their nights in semi-subterranean prisons; others were condemned to mines and quarries in which no worker's life was worth more than a few years' purchase. The minority whose lot was the relative independence of the slave-herdsman or the relative amenity of domestic service were fortunate; and it might have seemed that even this fortunate minority had no future. There was an ancient Greek saying that 'The day of enslavement deprives Man of half of his Manhood';[1] and this saying was terribly fulfilled in the debasement of the slave-descended urban proletariat of Rome which lived—not by bread alone, but by 'bread and shows'[2]—from the second century B.C. to the sixth century of the Christian Era until the flesh pots failed and the people perished off the face of the Earth. This long-drawn-out life-in-death was the penalty of failure to respond to the challenge of enslavement; and no doubt that broad path of destruction was trodden by a majority of those human beings of many different origins and antecedents who were enslaved en masse in the most evil age of Hellenic history. Yet some there were, nevertheless, who did respond to the challenge and did succeed in 'making good' in one fashion or anotner.

Some rose in their Roman masters' service until they became the responsible administrators of great estates; and Caesar's estate itself, when it had grown into the universal state of the Hellenic World, continued to be administered by Caesar's freedmen. Others,

---

[1] The lines are placed in the mouth of the slave-swineherd Eumaeus in the *Odyssey*:
ἥμισυ γάρ τ' ἀρετῆς ἀποαίνυται εὐρύοπα Ζεύς
ἀνέρος, εὖτ' ἄν μιν κατὰ δούλιον ἦμαρ ἕλῃσιν.   (*Od.* XVII, ll. 322–3.)
[2] 'Panem et circenses' (Juvenal, *Satire* x, l. 81).

whom their masters established in petty business, succeeded in
purchasing their freedom out of savings which they made on the
share of the profits that their masters allowed them; and some of
these afterwards rose to eminence and affluence in the Roman
business-world. Others remained slaves in this world to become
philosopher-kings or fathers of churches in another; and of such
was the Kingdom of Heaven. The true-born Roman who might
justly and sincerely contemn the illegitimate power of a Narcissus
or the ostentatious wealth of a Trimalchio would delight to honour
the wisdom and serenity of the lame slave Epictetus; and he could
not but admire—though he might not approve—the enthusiasm of
that nameless multitude of slaves and freedmen whose faith was
moving mountains.[1] During the five centuries which intervened
between the Hannibalic War and the Conversion of Constantine,
the Roman authorities saw this miracle of servile faith being performed under their eyes and being repeated—in defiance of their
utmost efforts to arrest it by physical force—until eventually they
themselves succumbed to it. For the slave-immigrants who had
lost their homes and their families and their property still kept
their religion and handed it down to their descendants in Italy.
The Greeks brought the Bacchanalia, the Anatolians the worship
of Cybele (a goddess who long outlived the Hittite Society in whose
womb she had been conceived); the Egyptians brought the worship
of Isis, the Babylonians the worship of the Stars, the Iranians the
worship of Mithra, the Syrians Christianity. *Syrus in Tiberim
defluxit Orontes;*[2] and the confluence of these waters raised a social
issue which revealed the limitations of a slave's subjection to his
master.

The issue was whether an immigrant religion of the internal
proletariat was to swamp the indigenous religion of the dominant
minority of the Hellenic Society. For, when once the waters had
met, it was impossible that they should not mingle; and, when once
they had mingled, there was little doubt as to which current would
prevail if Nature were not counteracted by Art or by Force. The
tutelary Gods of the Hellenic World—Attic Athene the Keeper of
the City and Spartan Athana of the Brazen House; Tyche of the
Antiochenes and Fortuna Praenestina; and even the omnipotent
Dea Roma and the Saviour Divus Caesar[3]—had already withdrawn

[1] Marcus Aurelius was impressed by the readiness of the Christians at any moment to
die for their faith, though he disapproved of its psychological basis, which he describes
as παράταξις (? 'mass suggestion' or 'esprit de corps') in contrast to what seems to the
philosopher the right basis: that is to say, rational judgement (Marcus Aurelius:
Meditations, xi. 3).

[2] Juvenal: *Satire* iii, l. 62. It was at Antioch-on-Orontes that the followers of Jesus
were first called Christians (Acts xi. 26).

[3] See I. C (iii) (*e*), Annex, vol. i, p. 443, above.

from the intimate life-giving communion in which they had once lived with their worshippers.

> Excessere omnes, adytis arisque relictis,
> Di quibus imperium hoc steterat.[1]

On the other hand, the Gods of the internal proletariat had proved themselves to be in truth their worshippers' 'refuge and strength, a very present help in trouble'.[2] If these Gods and those, who now divided the allegiance of Society between them, were left to contend with one another for the allegiance of the whole, the battle would assuredly go as it had gone in Israel when Elijah had challenged the prophets of Baal;[3] and in face of this prospect the Roman authorities halted for five centuries between two opinions. Should they take the offensive against these foreign religions which were making their way, by peaceful penetration, into Roman hearts? Should they attempt to stamp them out by pitting against their uncanny other-worldly power the Roman World-State's irresistible concentration of mundane force? Or should they rather welcome these new Gods who were offering to fill a spiritual void—unacknowledged but not unfelt—that had been left in the Roman universe by the old Gods' departure? Every one of the new Gods appealed to some section of the Roman governing class. Mithra appealed to the soldiers, Isis to the women, the Heavenly Bodies to the intellectuals, Dionysus to the Philhellenes, Cybele to the fetish-worshippers. In the year 205 B.C., in the crisis of the Hannibalic War, the Roman Senate anticipated Constantine's reception of Christianity by receiving, with official honours, the magic stone, fallen from Heaven and charged with the divinity of Cybele, which was the talisman of Anatolian Pessinus.[4] In the year 186 B.C., during the brief breathing-space between the Hannibalic affliction and the Gracchan, they anticipated Diocletian's persecution by suppressing the Bacchanalia.[5] The long Battle of the Gods, which thus began and ended, was the counterpart of an earthly contest between the slave-immigrants and their Roman masters; and, in this dual conflict, the slaves and the slaves' Gods won.

Caste

The same stimulus of penalization which is administered by poverty and by class-inferiority and by slavery is also administered by racial discrimination in a state of society in which two or more

---

[1] Virgil: Aeneid, Bk. II, ll. 351–2 (already quoted in I. C (i) (a), vol. i, on p. 57, in footnote 2, above).
[2] Psalm xlvi. 1.   [3] 1 Kings xviii.
[4] See the account of the translation of Cybele from Pessinus to Rome which is given by Livy in Book XXIX, chs. 10–14.
[5] See the account of this persecution which is given by Livy in Book XXXIX, chs. 8–19.

races live intermingled without merging into one. Such states of society are apt to arise by immigration in two alternative ways. An indigenous population may be conquered by invaders who forbear to exterminate it and disdain to coalesce with it and are therefore constrained to tolerate it in the status of a depressed caste.[1] Alternatively, an indigenous population may admit peaceful immigrants to live on sufferance as perpetual strangers in its midst on more or less disadvantageous and humiliating conditions. In both these varieties of what is ultimately the same situation, the dominant race is apt to reserve certain statuses and certain avocations as its own exclusive preserves, and to impose upon the penalized race the necessity of cultivating other fields of social activity if it is to find a living at all. The 'reserved' occupations usually include all those which have high social prestige—the priesthood, the business of government, the ownership of land, the bearing of arms, and the civilian 'liberal professions'—as well as the fundamental economic activity of Society, which has usually been agriculture in the social economies of societies in process of civilization down to recent times. By a process of exhaustion the penalized race is apt to find itself virtually confined to the field of trade and handicraft; and, just because the field is narrow, the penalized race is stimulated to make this field all its own and to conjure out of it, by a *tour de force* which fills the dominant race with astonishment and resentment, a harvest of wealth and power which this Naboth's vineyard would hardly have yielded to hands not debarred from other handiwork.

The classic example of this effect of racial discrimination is the strongly marked tendency in the Hindu Society for castes to become coincident with occupations; but this tendency in India is not without parallels elsewhere. In Europe, tinkering and fortune-telling have been monopolized by the Gipsies,[2] and in Arabia metal-working by the Sunnāʿ;[3] and other examples are to be found in the New World which has been called into existence, since the close of the fifteenth century of the Christian Era, by the expansion of Western Christendom over all the habitable lands and navigable seas of the planet. Round the shores of the Pacific—an ocean which has been transformed from an insulator into a medium of communication by Western maritime enterprise within the last century —the Chinese immigrant who has been admitted on sufferance

---

[1] The three possible alternative outcomes of the impact of one society upon another— that is, extermination, assimilation, and caste—are examined further in Parts VIII and IX, below.

[2] Strictly, perhaps, the occupational specialization of the Gipsies in Europe is not so much a parallel to, as a derivative from, the convergence between caste and occupation in India, since the Gipsies are by origin a vagrant Hindu caste which has happened to spread beyond the boundaries of the Hindu World.

[3] For this metal-working caste in Arabia, see The British Admiralty: *Handbook of Arabia*, vol. i (London, no date, H.M. Stationery Office), pp. 92, 94, and 610.

into countries under Western control has succeeded, as coolie and laundryman and shopkeeper, in making his fortune out of those meagre patches of the economic field which have been grudgingly thrown open to him. In British Malaya and Netherlands India to-day, there are Chinese millionaires who emulate Trimalchio's wealth without displaying his vulgarity; and if Petronius Arbiter's fictitious portrait of the penalized proletarian immigrant who has 'made good' in this world is reproduced in these authentic Chinese counterparts in 'the real life' of our modern society, we can also detect a counterpart to the historic figure of the ancient slave-philosopher in Harriet Beecher Stowe's fictitious portrait of 'Uncle Tom': a character who emulates the serenity of Epictetus without aspiring to his mental power.

The Negro slave-immigrant into modern North America has been subject to the twofold penalization of legal servitude and racial discrimination; and at this day, some seventy years after the first of these two handicaps has been removed, the second still weighs as heavily as ever upon the coloured freedman. From first to last, the Negro's sufferings at the hands of the English-speaking peoples of the Western World have probably been still greater in the aggregate than those of the Greeks and Orientals and barbarians who were enslaved by the Romans. The horrors of the Delian slave-market in the second century B.C. are hardly to be compared with those of 'the middle passage' on a Transatlantic slave-ship in the eighteenth century of the Christian Era; and even if we allow that, in the next stage of the slave's career, the conditions of servile life and labour on the plantations of modern America may not have been so bad as they were on those of ancient Italy, we must add that the Roman slave who had once landed alive on Italian soil saw his horizon faintly yet distinctly illuminated by a gleam of light which has never been vouchsafed to the Negro survivor of the Transatlantic voyage nor to any of his descendants even in the third or fourth generation.

The harshness of the Roman Law in its treatment of the slave, so long as he remained in servitude, was mitigated by its facility in the procedure of manumission and by its liberality in making the personal act of manumission carry with it automatically the political consequence of enfranchisement; and these legal provisions for the mitigation of the Roman slave's lot were implemented by social custom. The Roman masters who were merciless in exploiting their slaves were generous in granting them their freedom; and when once the legal formality had been accomplished, the social stigma of servile origin was extinguished in a few generations. In the third generation the poet Horace could afford to remind his readers that he was *libertino patre natus*[1] in order to point the contrast between what he had once been and what he had since become in virtue of his own genius and his intimacy with Maecenas. How different from the agony with which a modern American citizen who knows that there is a tincture of Negro blood in his veins[2] keeps watch and ward over his secret when he has surreptitiously violated 'the colour bar' by 'passing' from the black to the white side of the caste-line. The Roman freedman was wholly free from the doom of perpetual racial ostracism to which the American Negro freedman has been condemned without any prospect of reprieve even for his remotest posterity; and it is not surprising to observe that the Negro, finding the scales thus permanently and overwhelmingly weighted against him in this world, has turned to another world for consolation.

The Negro appears to be answering our tremendous challenge with a religious response which may prove in the event, when it can be seen in retrospect, to bear comparison with the ancient Oriental's response to the challenge from his Roman masters. The Negro has not indeed brought any ancestral religion of his own from Africa to captivate the hearts of his White fellow citizens on the American Continent. His primitive social heritage was of so frail a texture that every shred of it was scattered to the winds at the first impact of our Western Civilization. Thus he came to America spiritually as well as physically naked; and he has met the emergency by covering his nakedness with his enslaver's cast-off clothes. The Negro has been adapting himself to the rigours of his new social environment by rediscovering, in Christianity, certain original meanings and values which Western Christendom has long ignored. Opening a simple and impressionable mind to the Gospels, he has divined the true nature of Jesus's mission. He has understood that this was a prophet who came into the World not to confirm the mighty in their seat but to exalt the meek and the humble.[3] 'At that time Jesus answered and said: "I thank thee, O Father, Lord of Heaven and Earth, because thou hast hid these things from the wise and prudent and hast revealed them unto babes." '[4] The Syrian slave-immigrants who once brought Christianity into Roman Italy performed the miracle of establishing a new religion which was alive in the place of an old religion which was already dead. It is possible that the Negro slave-immigrants who have found Christianity in America may perform the greater miracle of raising the dead to life. With their childlike spiritual intuition and their genius for

---

[1] Horace: *Satires*, Bk. I, Sat. 6; *Epistles*, Bk. I, Ep. 20.
[2] 'A touch of the tar-brush' is the colloquial phrase.
[3] Luke i. 52.   [4] Matthew xi. 25; cp. Psalm viii. 2.

giving spontaneous aesthetic expression to emotional religious experience, they may perhaps be capable of rekindling the cold grey ashes of Christianity which have been transmitted to them by us, until in their hearts the divine fire glows again. It is thus, perhaps, if at all, that Christianity may conceivably become the living faith of a dying civilization for the second time. If this miracle were indeed to be performed by an American Negro Church, that would be the most dynamic response to the challenge of social penalization that had yet been made by Man.

Religious Discrimination

When we pass from racial to religious discrimination, we find that, *mutatis mutandis*, the phenomena are the same. A religious denomination which is penalized on account of its persuasion by being debarred from engaging in agriculture or in 'the liberal professions', is apt to respond, like a penalized caste, by developing an exceptional proficiency in trade or handicraft. The Hindu Banya has his analogue in the Jew; the Arabian Sunnā' have theirs in the otherwise obscure North American religious fraternity at Oneida, in New York State, whose members have made a name for themselves in the business-world as the manufacturers of 'Community Plate'.

The results of religious discrimination may be studied in three different situations: first, where the adherents of the penalized denomination are members of the same society and heirs of the same civilization as the adherents of the privileged denomination among whom they live; second, where the respective adherents of the penalized and of the privileged denomination belong to two different civilizations which are both still 'going concerns'; third, where the adherents of the privileged denomination belong to a civilization which is still a 'going concern', while the adherents of the penalized denomination represent a civilization which only survives as a 'fossil'.[1]

The first of these situations may be illustrated from the history of the English-speaking peoples of the Western World. In England, the re-establishment of the Anglican Church and the galling but not intolerable penalization of other Protestant religious denominations after the Restoration of A.D. 1660—a penalization which did not altogether cease at the Revolution of A.D. 1688—had the effect of stimulating the members of the Society of Friends to distinguish themselves in industry and banking,[2] and other Protestant Dis-

---

[1] For a list of the still extant 'fossils' of extinct civilizations, see above, I. B (iii), vol. i, pp. 34–5, and I. C (i) (b), vol. i, pp. 90–2. The psychological phenomena of the contact between 'fossils' and living societies are examined in Part IX, below.

[2] The Quakers, who appear to have been largely recruited from the agricultural population, found themselves in a more difficult position than the Nonconformists, owing to their conscientious objection to the payment of tithes.

senters and Nonconformists to prosper in various forms of retail trade.[1] *A fortiori*, the positive persecution to which the Puritans were exposed in England in the earlier decades of the seventeenth century, before the English Civil War, and again the Mormons in the United States some two centuries later, stimulated each of these persecuted sects into reacting with proportionate vigour. While the Quakers and the Nonconformists in eighteenth-century England were able to exist and even to prosper in that state of life to which it had pleased the Establishment to confine them, both the Puritans in early seventeenth-century England and the Latter-Day Saints in early nineteenth-century America made up their minds that there was no room in the same country for themselves and for their persecutors; and accordingly they each, in their day, went out into the wilderness in order to found ideal commonwealths, after their own heart, on virgin soil where they had only to contend with Physical Nature and not with stronger human powers.

The achievement of the Pilgrim Fathers in breaking-in the rough country of New England has been reviewed in this Study already.[2] It was fully equalled, in its own kind, by the achievement of the Latter-Day Saints. In the early nineteenth century, it needed no less courage to venture out in wagons into the unexplored hinterland of the North American Continent than it had needed in the early seventeenth century to set sail from the shores of Europe in the *Mayflower* for an uncharted American coast. Moreover, at the journey's end, the desert basin of Utah, with the Salt Lake at its core, offered an even more forbidding landscape for a Promised Land than the site of Town Hill, Connecticut. Indeed, it may be doubted whether the Mormons would ever have 'made good' in Utah if they had not been governed by the practical genius of Brigham Young. Happily for Joseph Smith's disciples, the first khalīfah of the Mormon prophet[3] played Joshua's as well as Moses' part in this latter-day American exodus. Brigham Young had the vision to perceive that the salt desert could be fertilized by the sweet waters descending from its mountain rim, and he also had the power of organization and command to carry through a great co-operative scheme of irrigation. These daring and romantic foundations of new commonwealths in the virgin wildernesses of Utah and New England have their place, beside the more passive and prosaic performance of the English Nonconformists in adapting themselves to their disabilities at home, as examples of the response which the

[1] For the movement in which the English Protestant Nonconformists withdrew from public life in the seventeenth century and returned in the nineteenth, see further III. C (ii) (*b*), vol. iii, p. 334, below.
[2] See II. D (i), pp. 15–16, above.
[3] For the analogy between the histories of Mormonism and of Islam, see Meyer, Eduard: *Ursprung und Geschichte der Mormonen* (Halle 1912, Niemeyer).

challenge of religious discrimination is apt to evoke from those who are exposed to it in diverse degrees.[1]

The Mormon response in the United States has a parallel in Russia in the history of the Old Believers and other dissenters from the established practice of Russian Orthodox Christendom. These Russian Orthodox Christian sectaries have won freedom to follow the devices of their own hearts by going out, beyond the advancing borders of the Russian Empire, into the wildernesses of Siberia and the Caucasus and the Eurasian Steppe. These sectarian pioneer settlements in no-man's-land have eventually been incorporated into the Russian body politic, as Utah has been incorporated into the United States; but the latter-day Czardom, in its treatment of schismatics, exercised a politic form of discrimination which was already customary in Western monarchies in the seventeenth century. While penalizing its Nonconformists in the interior, it tolerated and even encouraged them in the marches as unorthodox messengers of Holy Russia who could serve to prepare her way before her, just because they were officially beyond her pale.

The Phanariots

The situation arising when the respective adherents of the penalized and the privileged denomination belong to two different civilizations which are both 'going concerns' may be illustrated from the *ancien régime* of the Ottoman Empire as it existed down to the Revolution of A.D. 1908. In the Ottoman Empire, the main body of Orthodox Christendom had been endowed, by intruders of alien faith and culture, with a universal state which the Orthodox Christian Society could not do without yet was unable to establish for itself;[2] and the Orthodox Christians had paid for their social incompetence by ceasing to be masters in their own house. The Muslim conquerors who established and maintained the *Pax Ottomanica* in the Orthodox Christian World exacted payment, in the form of religious discrimination, for the services which they were rendering to their Christian subjects willy-nilly; and here, as elsewhere, the adherents of the penalized denomination responded to

---

[1] We may observe that while the sedentary Nonconformists of England learnt the lesson of toleration and eventually imparted it to their Anglican fellow countrymen, the Pilgrim Fathers and the Mormons both justified their persecutors in retrospect by persecuting others as soon as they had the power and the occasion. The ideal commonwealth which they went forth to found in the wilderness was not to be a place where every sect and every individual would be free to worship according to private conscience, but a place in which the pioneers would be able to do unto others what their persecutors had done unto them. The Quakers discovered this to their cost when they came out to Massachusetts at the Pilgrim Fathers' heels. An honourable and remarkable exception to the general spirit and practice of early New England was to be found in the State of Rhode Island, which from the outset granted freedom of conscience to all who settled on its diminutive territory.

[2] On this point, see further, Part III. A, vol. iii, pp. 26–7, below.

the challenge of discrimination by becoming past-masters in those pursuits to which their activities were now confined.

In the old Ottoman Empire, none who were not 'Osmanlis might govern or bear arms; and in large tracts of the Empire even the ownership and cultivation of the land passed out of the hands of the subject Christians into those of their Muslim masters. In these circumstances, the several Orthodox Christian peoples who found themselves forcibly united under a common Ottoman rule now came —for the first and last time in their histories—to a tacit but effective mutual understanding. They were inhibited by the 'Osmanlis' monopoly of sovereign power from carrying on their habitual internecine warfare with one another for the local mastery of cities and provinces. They were stimulated, by the 'Osmanlis' monopoly of 'the liberal professions', into parcelling out among themselves the humbler trades, which remained open for Christian practitioners, and learning each to excel in some special occupation of their own. By this road, the Orthodox Christian subjects of the Ottoman Pādishāh gradually regained a footing within the walls of the Imperial capital, from which they had been deliberately evicted wholesale by Mehmed the Conqueror. The Turkish-speaking Orthodox Christian Qaramanlis from the interior of Anatolia and the Romance-speaking Orthodox Christian Vlachs from the highlands of the Balkan Peninsula succeeded in establishing themselves in Constantinople as grocers; their Greek-speaking co-religionists from the islands of the Aegean Archipelago set up in business on a more ambitious scale; the Orthodox Christian Albanians came to Constantinople as masons; the Orthodox Christian Montenegrins as hall-porters and commissionaires. Even the bucolic Bulgars, who had managed to keep a firmer grip upon the land than the Greeks, came to find a livelihood in the suburbs of Constantinople as grooms and market-gardeners. In Ottoman Syria, likewise, the Arabic-speaking Orthodox Christians gravitated towards the towns and tended to specialize in trades and handicrafts, while the Arabic-speaking Muslims remained cultivators of the soil in the countryside.

Among the Orthodox Christian re-occupants of Constantinople, there was one coterie—the so-called Phanariots—who were stimulated by the challenge of penalization to such a degree that they actually rose to be the virtual partners and potential supplanters of the 'Osmanlis themselves in the political administration and control of the Ottoman Empire. The Phanar, from which the Phanariots derived their name,[1] was the extreme north-western corner of

---

[1] The word Phanar itself is the modern Greek for 'lighthouse'—the quarter being called after a lighthouse which stood here in the angle between the land-walls of Constantinople and the south shore of the Golden Horn.

Stamboul, which the Ottoman Government had grudgingly abandoned to its Orthodox Christian subjects as the equivalent of a
ghetto. The Oecumenical Patriarchate made its new head-quarters
here after the Church of the Holy Wisdom had been converted into
the Mosque of Aya Sofia and the Church of the Apostles demolished
to make way for the Mosque of the Conqueror. In this apparently
unpromising retreat, the Patriarchate became the rallying-point
and the preserve of the Greek-speaking Orthodox Christians from
the Aegean Archipelago who had found their way to Constantinople
and had prospered there in trade; and these 'Phanariots' developed
two special accomplishments. As merchants on the grand scale,
they entered into commercial relations with the Western World
and acquired a first-hand knowledge of Western manners and customs and Western languages. As managers of the Oecumenical
Patriarchate's affairs, they acquired a wide practice and close understanding of Ottoman administration, since, under the old Ottoman
régime, the Oecumenical Patriarch was the official intermediary
between the Pādishāh and his Orthodox Christian subjects throughout the Empire and was invested, in this capacity, by delegation,
with many of the functions of sovereignty over his co-religionists.
These two accomplishments, together, made the fortunes of the
Phanariots when, in the secular conflict between the Ottoman
Empire and the Western World, the tide definitely turned against
the 'Osmanlis after their second unsuccessful siege of Vienna in
A.D. 1682–3.[1]

The change introduced certain formidable complications into
Ottoman affairs of state. Before the reverse of 1683, the 'Osmanlis
had always been able to count upon settling their relations with
their Western Christian adversaries and with their Orthodox
Christian subjects to their own satisfaction by the simple application of force. Their military decline confronted them with two
new problems. They had now to negotiate at the conference-table
with Western Powers whom they could no longer defeat in the
field; and they had to consider the feelings of Orthodox Christian
subjects whom they could no longer be sure of holding down. In
other words, the Ottoman Empire could no longer dispense with
skilled diplomatists and skilled administrators; and the necessary
fund of experience, of which the 'Osmanlis found themselves
destitute in their hour of need, was opportunely placed at their
disposal by the Phanariots. In consequence, the 'Osmanlis were
constrained to disregard the precedents and tamper with the
principles of their own régime by conferring upon the Phanariots

---

[1] For this turn of the tide and its eventual effects upon the Turkish and the Austrian
éthos, see II. D (v), pp. 179–88, above.

the monopoly of four high offices of state which were key-positions in the new political situation of the Ottoman Empire.[1] In the course of the eighteenth century of the Christian Era, the political power of the Phanariots was steadily enhanced by the specific influence and patronage which these offices carried with them, and still more potently by the general effect of the steady increase in the political pressure from the West—an increase which was inevitably accompanied by a corresponding appreciation in the political value of the one element inside the Ottoman Empire which was capable, at the time, of coping with 'the Western Question'. A hundred years after the turn of the tide under the walls of Vienna in 1683, it looked as though the result of Western pressure might be to endow the old Ottoman Empire with a new governing class by first forcing the 'Osmanlis to take the Phanariots into partnership and then enabling the Phanariots to make themselves, in effect, the senior partners in the Ottoman firm.[2]

[1] These four offices were the Dragomanship of the Porte, the Dragomanship of the Fleet, and the hospodarships of the autonomous principalities of Wallachia and Moldavia. The two dragomanships were new creations; the two hospodarships were existing offices which were now placed in Phanariot hands.
    The importance of the dragomanships is not to be measured by the literal meaning of the title. The 'Osmanlis sought to 'save their faces' by giving the modest title of 'inter-preters' ('dragoman'= terjümen) to Phanariot officials who, in effect, discharged the functions of a Secretary of State for Foreign Affairs and a Secretary of State for the Navy and whose power and patronage, ex officio were not much less extensive than they would have been in any Western monarchy of the day.
    As for the principalities of Wallachia and Moldavia, these had been founded by Ortho-dox Christian pioneers of Rumanian nationality who had descended from the Tran-sylvanian highlands in the fourteenth century of the Christian Era and had wrested the extreme south-western corner of the great Eurasian Steppe from the Nomads. The two principalities had recognized the suzerainty of a paramount Power from the beginning of their existence, but their original suzerain had been the King of Hungary, from whose dominions their founders had come. The transference of their allegiance to the Ottoman Pädishäh had been one of the incidents in the long duel between Hungary and the Otto-man Power which ended on the field of Mohacz; and since the political orientation of these principalities was one of the factors on which the issue of the struggle between Hungary and Turkey depended, the Wallachian and Moldavian Rumans had been able to come to far more favourable terms with the 'Osmanlis than any of their co-religionists on the south side of the Danube. They had secured from the Pädishäh a pledge that, under his suzerainty, they should always be governed by princes of their own faith, and that no Muslim places of worship and no Turkish military fiefs or colonies should ever be established on their territories. The Ottoman Government faithfully observed these undertakings and implemented the first of them, to begin with, by placing the two Ruman principalities under local Ruman princes. This practice was abandoned after the turn of the tide in A.D. 1683, when the principalities acquired a new strategic and political importance as marches of the Ottoman Empire over against the Danubian Hapsburg Monarchy on the one hand and the Russian Empire on the other. When Peter the Great invaded Moldavia in 1711, the reigning prince, Demetrius Cantemir, went over to his side; and this danger-signal moved the Ottoman Government to strengthen its control over the principalities, without violating the letter of its bond, by thenceforth appointing Orthodox Christian princes who were not of Rumanian nationality and who had no heredi-tary local influence or attachments. Accordingly, from A.D. 1711 to 1821, the incum-bencies of the two principalities became a perquisite of the Phanariots—an arrangement which safeguarded Ottoman interests and lined Phanariot pockets at the local Rumanian population's expense.
[2] It was in this expectation that the Empress Catherine II of Russia played with the idea of re-establishing the East Roman Empire after the great Russian victory over the 'Osmanlis in the Russo-Turkish War of A.D. 1768–74.

In the event, the Phanariots failed to achieve their 'manifest destiny' because, towards the end of the eighteenth century, the Western pressure attained a degree of intensity at which its nature underwent a sudden transformation. The purely external pressure, of a military and diplomatic kind, which began to be exerted upon the Ottoman Empire by the great Powers of the Western World after the Second Siege of Vienna, was reinforced, after the American and French revolutions, by a far more penetrating and pervasive and disruptive pressure which was exerted, from within, by the Ottoman peoples themselves through that process of cultural fermentation and social metabolism for which we have coined the name 'Westernization'. The general operation of this process in the Ottoman Empire has been touched upon already;[1] and in this place we need only recall the two facts that the political gospel of 'Westernization' was Nationalism and that the Greeks, being the first of the Ottoman peoples to enter into intimate relations with the West, were also the first whom the virus of Western Nationalism infected. Between the outbreak of the French Revolution and the outbreak of the Greek War of Independence, the Greeks were under the spell of two incompatible aspirations. They had not given up the Phanariot ambition of entering into the whole heritage of the 'Osmanlis and keeping the Ottoman Empire intact as a 'going concern' under Greek instead of Turkish management; and at the same time they had conceived the new ambition of establishing a sovereign independent national state of their own—a Greece which should be as Greek as France was French—in order that the Greeks 'also' might 'be like all the nations'[2] of the Western World.

In their quest for this 'pound of flesh' the Greek nationalists eventually overreached themselves; but their miscalculation was not the same as Shylock's. The legendary Jew desired his victim's death, but forgot to stipulate for shedding his blood; the Greeks failed to foresee that the death of the Ottoman Empire must result from the bloodshed which they contemplated, and that therefore the new Greece of their dreams could be nothing but a gobbet of the old Empire's dismembered carcass. Their discomfiture was even more ironic than their Shakespearian prototype's; for fate permitted them to draw and use the knife in order to expose their miscalculation by an experiment which could never be undone. The incompatibility of the two Greek aspirations was demonstrated conclusively in 1821 when the Greeks attempted to realize both of them simultaneously.

When the Phanariot Prince Hypsilanti crossed the Pruth, from his 'jumping-off ground' in Russia, in order to make himself master

---

[1] See II. D (v), pp. 181–6, above.   [2] 1 Samuel viii. 20.

of the Ottoman Empire, and the Maniot chieftain Petro Bey Mavromikhális descended from his mountain-fastness in the Morea in order to carve out an independent Greece, the outcome of both enterprises was a foregone conclusion. The resort to arms, in itself, spelt the ruin of Phanariot aspirations, since the Phanariot ascendancy in the Ottoman Empire could only have been consummated by an uninterrupted process of 'peaceful penetration'. Prince Hypsilanti's armed incursion into the Danubian Principalities produced an electric effect upon the 'Osmanlis. The reed on which they had been leaning for more than a century had pierced their hand;[1] and their fury at this betrayal nerved them to break the treacherous staff in pieces and to stand again at all costs on their own feet. In 1821, the 'Osmanlis retorted to Prince Hypsilanti's act of war by destroying at one blow the fabric of power which the Phanariots had been peacefully building up for themselves since 1683; and this was the first step in a process of eradicating all non-Turkish elements from the remnant of the 'Osmanlis' heritage—a process which reached its climax in the eviction of the Orthodox Christian minority from Anatolia in 1922.

Thus the first explosion of Greek nationalism kindled the first spark of Turkish nationalism; but the effect of Prince Hypsilanti's act upon the non-Greek Christian peoples of the Ottoman Empire was, if possible, still more untoward, from the Greek standpoint, than its effect upon the Turks. The Greek Prince's appearance in the Danubian Principalities at the head of an armed force of Greek filibusters made the local Rumanian population realize that they were in imminent danger of exchanging 'King Log' for 'King Stork'. If the Muslim 'Osmanlis had chastised their Christian subjects with whips, the Christian Phanariots showed every intention of chastising their co-religionists with scorpions. The Rumans turned Hypsilanti's raid into a fiasco by passively but effectively taking the Turkish side; and not only the Rumans but the Bulgars and the Serbs and all the other Orthodox Christian peoples of the Ottoman Empire made up their minds forthwith that it was expedient for them to remain under Turkish rule until they could be sure of exchanging it for their own national independence. Therewith, it was decided that the Ottoman Empire should not have its unity maintained and its life prolonged by a peaceful transference of control from the 'Osmanlis to the Phanariots, but should be broken up by violence into a mosaic of sovereign independent national states on the Western pattern. This procrustean operation, by which an association of occupational castes was cruelly rough-hewn into a congeries of territorial nations, began with the

2 Kings xviii. 21.

extermination of the Turkish Muslim landowners in the Morea in 1821 by massacre or eviction at the hands of the local Greek insurgents, and was carried on—by the same 'methods of barbarism'—to the bitter end, until it reached its term, a hundred years later, in the massacre or eviction of the Greek and other Christian tradesmen and artisans in Anatolia in 1922 at the hands of the Turkish nationalists.

The Qāzānlis

Thus, after all, the Phanariots just failed to secure that 'senior partnership' in the Ottoman Empire which had seemed, in the eighteenth century, to be their 'manifest destiny'. Yet the fact that they came within an ace of success is sufficient evidence of the vigour with which they had responded to the challenge of penalization. Indeed, the history of their relations with the 'Osmanlis is an excellent illustration of the general social 'law' of Challenge-and-Response; and the antithesis between Greek and Turk, which has attracted so much interest and excited so much animus,[1] is explicable only in these terms and not in the racial and religious terms which have been in fashion on both sides in the popular polemics. Turcophils and Graecophils agree in attributing the historical differences in êthos between Greek Christians and Turkish Muslims to some ineradicable quality of race or indelible imprint of religion. They disagree simply in inverting the social values which they assign to these unknown quantities in the two cases. The Graecophil postulates an inherent virtue in Greek blood and in Orthodox Christianity and an inherent vice in Turkish blood and in Islam to make the Greek the angel and the Turk the devil that he alleges them to be. The Turcophil transposes his postulates and thereby proves the Turk an angel and the Greek a devil to his own satisfaction. Actually, the common assumption which underlies both these special pleadings is contradicted by unquestionable matters of fact.

It is unquestionable, for instance, in the matter of physical race, that the blood of Ertoghrul's Central Asian Turkish followers which flows in the veins of the Ottoman Turkish people to-day is no more than an infinitesimal tincture. The Ottoman Turkish people has grown into a nation out of a handful of refugees, not by natural increase, but by assimilating the Orthodox Christian population[2] in whose midst the 'Osmanlis have been living ever since the original settlement in Sultan Önü.[3] The process was in full swing in the second generation, under Ertoghrul's son 'Osmān,

---

[1] It is perhaps worth remarking that the animus of the Greeks and Turks against one another has been surpassed by that of their respective partisans in the Western World, who have shown still greater fanaticism than their protégés.

[2] For the method of assimilation, see Part III. A, vol. iii, pp. 28-44, below.

[3] For the challenge presented to the fathers of the 'Osmanlis by the geographical location of this settlement, see II. D (v), pp. 151-2, above.

whom the new community adopted as its eponymous hero when it
had to coin itself a new name. There is every reason to believe that
the blood of the indigenous Greek and other Orthodox Christian
recruits had swamped the blood of the immigrant Turkish Muslim
nucleus in the racial composition of the 'Osmanlis well before the
end of the first century of their existence as a distinctive community with a name of its own. If this sufficiently refutes the
a priori racial explanation of the Graeco-Turkish antithesis, we
may refute the *a priori* religious explanation by citing the following
description of one of the other Turkish Muslim peoples that are in
existence, side by side with the Ottoman Turks, at the present day:[1]

'The Volga Turks are, on the whole, distinguished by their sobriety,
honesty, thrift, and industry. By their assiduity they often acquire considerable wealth. They live on the best of terms with their Russian
peasant neighbours. The chief occupation of the Qāzān Turk is trade, to
which he turns at once when he has acquired a small capital by agriculture.
On his commercial journeys he is always a propagandist of Islam. His
chief industries are soap-boiling, spinning, and weaving. He is sometimes
a worker in gold. He makes a good shoemaker and coachman. . . . These
Turks are more cleanly in their houses than the Russian peasantry. . . .

'Till the end of the sixteenth century, no mosques were tolerated in
Qāzān, and the Tatars were compelled to live in a separate quarter. But
the predominance of the Muslims gradually prevailed, so that in the
second half of the eighteenth century there were as many as 250 mosques
in the Government of Qāzān. A ukase of tolerance promulgated in 1773[2]
helped the cause of Islam among these Turks. Far from being won by
Russian tolerance, the Muslims of the Volga have in modern times
become more closely united than ever with the Muhammadan world. . . .

'There has been a rapid increase in the number of mosques and a
steady improvement in the status of Muslim schools in the Government
of Qāzān. . . . These schools have not been affected in the least by the
Russian educational system. . . .

'In consequence of the attention paid to education, the percentage of
Qāzān Turks who cannot read and write is extremely low. The production
of printed books has also been considerable among these Muslims. . . .

'Thus, during a period of 360 years of Russian rule, the Asiatic conservatism of these Qāzān Muslims has in no way been weakened or
influenced by Russian culture. . . . No conversion except among their
ruling families takes place, and only the quite uneducated element is
liable to be absorbed in the Russian population. . . .'[3]

[1] At the present day there are approximately twice as many Turkish Muslims within
the frontiers of the U.S.S.R. as there are in Turkey.
[2] In the same year, the Ottoman Government granted its charter to the Greek Orthodox Christian community at Ayvalyq (see II. D (ii), footnote 1 on p. 40, above). The
Russian and Ottoman Empires, being engaged at the time in a formidable war with one
another, each found it advisable to make concessions to subject minorities which were of
the same civilization as the enemy Power.—A. J. T.
[3] The British Admiralty: *Manual on the Turanians and Pan-Turanianism* (London, no
date, H.M. Stationery Office), ch. vi (iii), 1, pp. 181–4.

It will be seen that, if the proper names in the foregoing passage were left blank, the text might serve, as it stands, to describe the Orthodox Christian Greeks of Constantinople under the old Ottoman régime just as well as the Muslim Turks of Qāzān under the Russian Czardom. This coincidence defies explanation on the hypothesis that Turks and Greeks or Muslims and Christians are what they are by reason of certain absolute racial characteristics or indelible religious hall-marks. On the other hand, it is just what we should expect on the hypothesis of Challenge-and-Response. For what has been the history of the Qāzānlī Turks? Qāzān was a Muslim city which was conquered by the Orthodox Christian Muscovites within a century of the conquest of Christian Constantinople by the 'Osmanlis; and under Muscovite rule the Qāzānlī Turks have had to adapt themselves, like the Stambouli Greeks under Ottoman rule, to a régime of religious discrimination. So far from being surprising, it is eminently natural that the Greek in Turkey and the Turk in Russia should have met the same challenge of religious discrimination with the same response. Both communities have concentrated their energies with success upon trade and handicraft because both have been debarred from following other walks of life as a penalty for their nonconformity with the religion of the Power under whose ascendancy they have each respectively had to live. In this connexion, the incidental fact that the Greeks in Turkey happen to have been penalized for being Christians and the Turks in Russia for being Muslims has made no difference. The common experience of being penalized on account of religion has been the governing factor in the development of both communities; and in the course of four or five centuries their identic reaction to this common experience has bred them into a 'family likeness' with each other which has quite effaced the diversity between the original imprints of Orthodox Christianity and Islam.

The Levantines

This 'family likeness' is shared by adherents of certain other religious denominations who have likewise been penalized on account of their religious allegiance and who have responded in the same way. Without extending our survey beyond the bounds of the old Ottoman Empire and the old Russian Czardom, we may observe that the distinctive characteristics of the Orthodox Christian Phanariots and the Muslim Qāzānlīs reappear unmistakably both in the Roman Catholic 'Levantines' and in the Protestant inhabitants of the seventeenth-century suburb of Moscow which was known as 'the Svoboda'.

These Catholics and Protestants were immigrants from Western

Christendom who were permitted to reside in the Ottoman and
Russian Empires on sufferance, under certain disabilities, as in our
day the Chinese are permitted to reside in countries under Western
control round the shores of the Pacific.[1] These Western residents
in a bygone Russia and a bygone Turkey were, indeed, in a less
unfortunate position than that of the Chinese residents in California or Australia at the present time, since the Chinese are the
victims of a racial discrimination from which they cannot escape by
any action which it lies with them to take, whereas the Levantines
could, and sometimes did, escape from the religious discrimination
to which they were subject by becoming 'renegades'—a step which
not only raised them from the degradation of being treated as
pariahs, but threw open to them the highest positions in the Ottoman State. The same avenue of escape was open to the 'Osmanlis'
Orthodox Christian subjects; and the Ottoman governing class
was actually recruited, by preference and on principle, from
Christian 'renegades', Christian prisoners-of-war and Christian
'tribute children' from the time of 'Osmān himself down to the turn
of the tide in A.D. 1682–3.[2] In this respect, the Levantines were
in the same position as the Phanariots; but in both communities
religious apostasy, notwithstanding the strength of the induce-
ments to it, remained the exception and did not become the rule;
and the Levantine Catholics who were unwilling to renounce their
religion were subject to the same disabilities under the old Ottoman
régime as the indigenous Orthodox Christians. In Galata on the
north shore of the Golden Horn, and in the Frankish quarters in
the other 'Échelles du Levant', the Catholic ra'īyeh[3] lived a ghetto-
life which was not very different from the life of the Orthodox
Christian ra'īyeh in the Phanar or the life of the Jews in the West
down to the time of the French Revolution; and the Levantines duly
developed the specific virtues and vices which the ghetto demands.[4]
It made no difference that they happened to be descended, in
physical race, from some of the most warlike and imperious and
high-spirited peoples of Western Christendom: from the medieval
Venetians and Genoese and the modern French and Dutch and
English. In the stifling atmosphere of their Ottoman ghetto, they
must either respond to the challenge of religious penalization in the

[1] See pp. 217–18, above.
[2] See further Part III. A, vol. iii, pp. 28–44, below.
[3] Ra'īyeh means literally 'the flock' of which the Ottoman Pādishāh was the shepherd.
The term was not applied exclusively to his non-Muslim subjects. The Muslim peasantry
of Anatolia were called ra'īyeh as well as the Christian merchants and ecclesiastics of
Constantinople.
[4] 'Nos négocians dans les diverses échelles . . . renfermés dans leurs kans comme dans
des prisons, ne s'embarrassent que peu de tout ce qui est étranger à leur commerce.'
(Volney, C. F.: Voyage en Syrie et en Egypte pendant les Années 1783, 1784 et 1785, 2nd
ed. (Paris 1787, Desenne et Volland, 2 vols.), vol. i, p. 142.)

same manner as other men, or else succumb. Again, the 'Nordic'
physique and Protestant tradition of the Dutch and Scottish and
German residents in 'the Svoboda' did not prevent the Christian
denizens of this Muscovite ghetto[1] from acquiring a strong 'family
likeness' to their Muslim neighbours and contemporaries and equals
in status: the Turks of Qāzān.

Moreover, if we let our eyes range farther afield over the world of
that day, we shall observe that, in the latter part of the seventeenth
century of the Christian Era, the life of the ghetto was being lived
by traders and handicraftsmen of Catholic or Protestant religion
and Western origin, not only under an Ottoman régime in Galata
and under a Muscovite régime in 'the Svoboda', but likewise under
the Mughal rulers of India on the island of Bombay and under the
Manchu rulers of China in the 'factories' at Canton[2] and under the
Shoguns of Japan on the island of Deshima.

The ingenuity and the severity with which the Japanese penalized
the Dutch have probably never been exceeded in the whole history
of religious and racial discrimination. At Japanese hands, Dutch
traders endured, for more than two centuries, humiliations worse
than any that have been inflicted by Turk on Greek or by Gentile on

---

[1] 'Svoboda' means literally 'free-town'; yet, at the accession of Peter the Great, the
social atmosphere of 'the Svoboda' was essentially the same as that of Galata or the Phanar
in the same age.

[2] For a description of the conditions under which the Western merchants lived and
traded, before their 'emancipation', in the 'factories' at Canton, see Morse, H. B.: *The
International Relations of the Chinese Empire* (London 1910, Longmans Green), vol. i,
chs. iv and xiv, esp. pp. 67-72:
'In 1757 an Imperial edict was issued making Canton the sole staple, and prohibiting
all foreign trade at any other port. . . .
'Regulations were made for the control of the foreigner, his ships and his trade. . . . The
more important among them may be summarised as follows:—
'1°. Ships of war must remain outside the river, and must not enter the Bogue.
'2°. Women must not be brought to the factories; nor could guns, spears, or other
arms.
'3°. Hong merchants must not be in debt to foreigners.
'4°. Foreign traders must not engage Chinese servants.
'5°. Foreigners must not use sedan chairs.
'6°. Foreigners must not row for pleasure on the river. Three days in the month (on
the 8th, 18th, and 28th) they might take the air at Fati (the flower gardens across the
river) in small parties, under the escort of an interpreter, who was held, literally and
personally, responsible for all their misdeeds.
'7°. Foreigners must not present petitions; if they have anything to represent, it must
be done through the Hong Merchants.
'8°. "In the Hong merchants' factories where foreigners live, let them be under the
restraint and control of the Hong merchants. The purchase of goods by them must pass
through the hands of a Hong merchant; this was originally designed to guard against
traitorous natives misleading them and teaching them. Hereafter the foreign merchants
dwelling in the Hong merchants' factories must not be allowed to presume of their own
accord to go out and in, lest they should trade and carry on clandestine transactions with
traitorous natives."
'9°. Foreigners must not remain at Canton out of season, but, their goods sold and
ships laden, must return home or go to Macao. . . .
'These factories provided palatial accommodation for the foreign visitors, guests of the
Empire, but they constituted in effect a gilded cage. The only ground for exercise available for the greater number was a square in front of the six factories in the middle,
measuring about 500 feet by 300 feet.'

Jew; and the reader of the story is left at a loss between admiration
for the tenacity and disgust at the servility with which these
'Nordic' Protestant Occidentals held their ground and made their
money, year in and year out, under conditions which were deliberately intended to make their residence in Japan intolerable.
From A.D. 1641 to 1858,[1] the Dutch in Japan were rigorously 'kept
in Coventry' on Deshima, a tiny island off the Japanese port of
Nagasaki; and the privilege of being allowed to do their business in
this insular ghetto, which was accorded to the Dutch alone among
the Western nations, had to be purchased at the price of periodic
self-abasement. One condition of the Hollanders' tenure of Deshima was that they should trample annually upon the Cross in the
presence of a Japanese official: a ceremony which was only allowed
to lapse in A.D. 1853 and was only abolished formally in 1856–7.[2]
Another condition was that they should pay an annual visit of
respect to the Shogun's capital at Yedo[3] and should make themselves objects of public derision by cutting capers for the enter-
tainment of the Court.[4] This was the only occasion in the year on
which the Dutch were permitted to stir outside their island prison-
house. Yet the Dutch became so well resigned to these odious
conditions of their residence in Japan that they left it to others to
take the initiative in bringing the relations between Westerners and
Japanese on to a footing of equality; and they showed no haste to
follow, even after the Americans had led the way.[5]

The relations in which the Dutch lived with the Japanese, from
the date of their confinement on Deshima in A.D. 1641 down to the

[1] On the 18th August, 1858, a Dutch-Japanese Treaty was concluded on the pattern
of the American-Japanese Treaty which had been signed on the 31st March, 1854.
[2] See Murdoch, J.: A History of Japan, vol. iii (London 1926, Kegan Paul), pp. 616–17.
[3] The present Tokyo.
[4] In compelling the Dutch residents in Japan to demean themselves periodically in
this public manner, the Japanese authorities were deliberately seeking to make the
Western peoples and the Western Civilization ridiculous and contemptible in Japanese
eyes. Without knowing it, they were adopting one of the expedients of Spartan statecraft. In ancient Lacedaemon, the Helots were periodically compelled to exhibit themselves to their Spartan masters in a maudlin condition, in order to confirm on both sides
the impression that the Helots were an inferior race who were born to be the slaves of the
Spartiates.

'Aristotle (I think it is) says that the Overseers (ἔφοροι) [the chief executive officers of
the Lacedaemonian Government, who were elected annually], when they take office,
formally declare war on the Helots, in order to keep a free hand for killing Helots without
blood-guiltiness. Altogether, the Spartans' treatment of the Helots was harsh and inhuman. For instance, they used to force them to drink quantities of neat wine and then
bring them into the military messes, in order to give the young Spartiates an ocular
demonstration of what drunkenness looks like. And they used to give them orders to sing
songs and dance dances that were low and ludicrous, and not to sing or dance anything
classical. On this account they say that in the sequel, during the Theban invasion of
Laconia, when the Helot prisoners were told to sing something of Terpander's or
Alcman's or Spendo the Laconian's, they begged to be excused, on the ground that their
Spartan masters would not like it.'
Plutarch: Life of Lycurgus, ch. xxviii. Cf. eundem, Instituta Laconica, No. 30. For
Spartan institutions, see further Part III. A, vol. iii, pp. 50–79, below.
[5] Murdoch, op. cit., vol. cit., p. 618.

reopening of Japan to Western commercial enterprise on normal conditions in the middle of the nineteenth century of the Christian Era, have their analogy in the relations between the ancient Greeks and Egyptians from the time when the Egyptian King Amasis (*regnabat circa* 569-525 B.C.) confined the Greek residents in Egypt to the 'treaty-port' of Naucratis in the middle of the sixth century B.C. down to the time when the Greeks were made masters of Egypt by Alexander the Great. During those two centuries the ancient Greeks in Egypt, like the modern Dutch in Japan, accepted the social humiliations of a pariah status in order to earn its commercial profits, as appears plainly from the following account of the Egyptian ritual of sacrifice in the fifth century B.C. from the hand of a contemporary Greek observer.

'When the Egyptians have slaughtered the sacrificial victim, they cut off its head. Thereupon, they flay the carcase and make a fearful imprecation over the head, which they then proceed to get rid of. Where they have a market with resident Greek traders, they simply get rid of it in the market by sale; but where there are no Greeks on the spot, they get rid of the head by throwing it into the river. The formula of imprecation which is recited over the head runs thus: "If any evil is impending over us who are making this sacrifice or over the whole Land of Egypt, into this head let it go!" '[1]

The situation here depicted is a prosaic version, 'in real life', of the phantasy which Robert Louis Stevenson has played with in 'The Bottle Imp'. The sacrificial victim's head is an object charged with evil which the pious and sensitive Egyptian peasant is as anxious to get rid of as the unsophisticated Polynesian islander is anxious to get rid of the haunted bottle. The Greek trader, who is willing to take the unclean head off his Egyptian neighbour's hands any day for the sake of a pennyworth of profit, is a sordid counterpart of Stevenson's sailor-man, who cheerfully carries off the bottle for the sake of a dram and so disappears from the story. The light which this throws upon the status of the Greeks in Egypt in Herodotus's day is highly illuminating.

The Jews, Parsees, Nestorians, Monophysites, and Monotheletes

We have still to take note of the results of religious discrimination in the third of our three situations: that is, where the adherents of the penalized denomination represent a civilization which only survives as a 'fossil'. This situation need not be surveyed in great detail, since the phenomena are well known in themselves and do not differ in essence from those which we have observed in the two situations which we have examined already.

Let us glance at the various 'fossils' of the Syriac Society which

[1] Herodotus, Bk. II, ch. 39.

have been deposited, in successive social strata, during the much-interrupted and long-drawn-out course of Syriac history.[1] In the oldest stratum there are the Jews and the Parsees, who are relics of the Syriac Society as it was in its universal state, under the Achaemenian régime, before the Hellenic intrusion. In an intermediate stratum there are the Nestorians and the Monophysites, who are relics of two abortive attempts on the part of the Syriac Society to expel the intrusive Hellenism from its body social, and there are the Monotheletes, who are relics of an equally abortive attempt, on the part of the Hellenic Society *in extremis*, to retain its hold over a remnant of the Syriac World. In the most recent stratum there are the Shī'īs, who are the relics of a fissure in the Syriac World which was one of the consequences of the Hellenic intrusion[2] and which left its scar upon the Syriac body social even after the expulsion of Hellenism and the re-unification of the Syriac World had been successfully achieved, on the whole, in the 'resumption' of the Syriac universal state under the 'Abbasid régime and in the establishment of a 'totalitarian' Syriac universal church in the shape of Islam. The medium in which all these Syriac 'fossils' have been preserved is a religious medium; their religious idiosyncrasies, which have safeguarded their identities and perpetuated their existence in their fossil state, have also exposed them to religious discrimination at the hands of the alien societies in the midst of which they have managed to survive; this penalization has taken the usual form of exclusion from certain walks of life; and it has evoked the usual reaction in its victims. They have learnt to hold their own in any human environment in which they are allowed to exist on sufferance by excelling in those trades and handicrafts to which their activities have been compulsorily confined.[3]

---

[1] See I. C (i) (*b*), vol. i, pp. 90–2, above, and II. D (vii), pp. 285–8, below.

[2] For the partition of the Syriac World, over a span of some seven centuries, into an eastern section which had liberated itself and a western section which had failed to liberate itself from the Hellenic domination, see I. C (i) (*b*), vol. i, pp. 75–7, above.

[3] In general, the reaction evoked by religious penalization among the representatives of a 'fossil' civilization seems to be more thoroughgoing than the reaction which the same challenge evokes among members of a civilization which is still a 'going concern'. The 'fossils' are apt to learn how to hold their own, under penalization, in any number of human environments successively or simultaneously, whereas the range of penalized religious minorities whose civilizations are still 'going concerns' is apt to remain within the ambit of some single society. Yet this broad distinction is by no means absolute. For example, the Levantines and the Greeks and the Gujeratis, who are members of the Western and the Orthodox Christian and the Hindu Society respectively, have shown themselves as versatile as the 'fossil' Jews and Parsees and Armenians and Nestorians and Maronites. Having served their apprenticeship in penalization under an Islamic régime —the Levantines and Greeks under the Ottoman Empire and the Gujeratis under the Muslim rāj in India—they have each extended their range into other environments: the Greeks into Western Europe and America; the Gujeratis into the colonial domains of the Western peoples in East and South Africa; the Levantines into Russia and India and the Far East. Conversely, the 'fossil' Copts have not made themselves at home outside Egypt any more than 'the Old Believers' have made themselves at home outside the Russian Empire or the Quakers outside the English-speaking World.

The Jews, for example, have overcome the social handicap which their religious idiosyncrasy entails by holding their own successfully, as traders and financiers, in a great variety of human environments. They have found a place for themselves first in the Syriac and Hellenic worlds and then in the Arabic and Iranic and Western worlds; and during the last few centuries they have kept pace with the expansion of Western Christendom until nowadays their activities and interests extend, as widely as those of our modern Western Society itself, over all the habitable lands and navigable seas on the face of the planet. The Parsees, for their part, have played the same role in the Hindu World as the Jews have played elsewhere; and they have shown the same elasticity and initiative as the Jews in using their special skill and experience to good effect in a variety of circumstances. Having acquired their expertise in trade and finance in a Hindu economic environment, they have managed to turn it to account in the utterly different economic environment which has been created in India by the impact of our Western Civilization; and their response to the challenge of this impact has been so much more effective than the response of the Hindus and Muslims among whom they live that they have profited by the ordeal of 'Westernization' to increase the economic ascendancy over their Indian neighbours which they already possessed before the challenge from the West was presented.

The Armenian Gregorian Monophysites have shown the same ability and adaptability in the same lines of activity as the Parsees and the Jews, until, at the present day, the Armenian merchant, like the Jewish financier, has become ubiquitous. In a narrower field, the Syrian Jacobite Monophysites have reacted like their Armenian co-religionists, while the Coptic Monophysites have held their own by acquiring a virtual monopoly of the local but lucrative business of farming the land-tax in their native Egypt.

The Monophysites started their career by holding out under the religious persecution which they had to suffer at the hands of an Orthodox Christian régime in the Roman Empire.[1] The Nestorians, for whom life in the Roman Empire was made impossible, transferred their head-quarters to 'Irāq and Iran, and held their own there, not only as men of business but as physicians, under the comparatively tolerant Sasanid and Umayyad and 'Abbasid régimes; and they did not perish in the social cataclysm which overwhelmed

---

[1] The Monophysites called their Orthodox Christian oppressors 'Melchites', that is to say 'Imperialists'—Orthodox Christianity (from which the Catholic Christianity of the West had not yet differentiated itself) being the established religion of the Roman Imperial régime under which the Monophysites had to live from the year 451, when the schism came to an open breach, down to the Arab conquest of the Roman provinces in Syria and Egypt towards the middle of the seventh century.

these regions at the break-up of the 'Abbasid Caliphate, when Baghdad was sacked, and the irrigation-system of 'Irāq put out of action, by the Mongols.

Before this catastrophe overtook their base of operations in the Syriac World, the Nestorians had already learnt to make themselves at home in other human environments at the ends of the Earth. In one direction, they made their way by sea along the west coast of India, beyond the farthest point to which the Parsee sphere of influence extended, and established a sphere of their own at the extremity of the Indian Peninsula, where their descendants or converts survive to this day as 'Saint Thomas's Christians' in Travancore. In another direction, they ventured out overland, beyond the farthest outposts of the Syriac World in Transoxania, into the heart of the great Eurasian Steppe, and made their way, from oasis to oasis, across the whole breadth of the wilderness until they emerged on the other side in China. These continental Nestorian pioneers who once won a footing in Central Asia and in the Far East have left no survivors. Yet, although in this sense they have been less successful than their co-religionists who followed the maritime route to India,[1] they have succeeded in making a greater mark upon the history of Mankind during their briefer day.

In the Far East the Nestorians were an active element in Society in the age of the T'ang (*imperabant* A.D. 618–907); and in the oases of the Eurasian Steppe they succeeded in converting the sedentary Turkish Uighurs and came near to establishing a distinctive Far Eastern Christian Civilization in the midst of the supremely adverse human environment of Nomadism.[2] It is true that this *tour de force* was abortive. The prospect was compromised in A.D. 737–41, when the oases of Transoxania, which had been the 'jumping-off ground' of the Nestorians in their overland venture, were permanently incorporated into the Arab Empire and were thereby transferred from the sphere of Nestorian Christendom to the sphere of Islam. The *coup de grâce* was delivered in A.D. 1203–6, when the semi-Nestorianized Nomads of the high steppe—the Karāyits[3] and the more powerful and progressive Naimans—were successively defeated by the pagan chief of the Mongols, Chingis Khan. The Basin of the Orkhon, over which the Karāyits and the Naimans ranged at the time, was a key-position; and the conquest of its

---

[1] Even in India, Nestorianism has now lost its heritage; for, in the third quarter of the seventeenth century, the allegiance of Saint Thomas's Christians was usurped, under false pretences, by the Jacobite Monophysite Patriarch of Antioch. (See above, I. B (iii), vol. i, footnote 3 on p. 35.)

[2] This abortive Far Eastern Christian Civilization is discussed further in II. D (vii), on pp. 369–85, below.

[3] Wang Khan, the prince of the Karāyits, was perhaps the historic original of the legendary 'Prester John'.

contemporary occupants was the first decisive step in Chingis' career. It is interesting to speculate what the future of Nestorian Christendom might have been if Wang Khan the Karāyit and not Chingis Khan the Mongol had won the day in A.D. 1203, or again if Tayan Khan the Naiman had won in 1206.

Even as it was, the Nestorian pioneers in the Nomadic World were able, thanks to their local monopoly of the elements of a higher culture, to hold their own after the overthrow of their Karāyit and Naiman patrons; and the Mongol conqueror took them into his service as scribes and accountants and recorders. For the best part of a century, while the centre of gravity of the Mongol Empire still remained on the Steppe and its seat of government in 'Prester John's' country at Qaraqorum, on the head-waters of the Orkhon, the archives of the Great Khan's Court were kept by Nestorian Christian secretaries in a Uighur Turkish dialect conveyed in a Syriac Alphabet. The Nestorians even made some distinguished Mongol converts. Hulāgū Khan, who sacked Baghdad and devastated 'Irāq (the original point of departure of the Nestorian Dispersion) in A.D. 1258, had a Nestorian wife; and Hulāgū's advance-guard, which captured Damascus in A.D. 1260, was commanded by a Nestorian general. It will be seen that the history of these Nestorian Christian Turkish Uighurs bears a certain resemblance to the history of the Orthodox Christian Greek Phanariots. They just missed their 'manifest destiny'; yet, in response to the challenge of penalization, they had developed certain special accomplishments which so enhanced their social value in the human environment in which they lived that they were virtually taken into partnership by the rulers of a great empire.[1]

As for the Maronite Monotheletes, they have served an apprenticeship as clerks and traders in the Arabic World—especially in the fat land of Egypt which lies on the threshold of their own lean Lebanese fastness—and they have known, like the Jews and the Parsees and the Armenians, how to profit by the recent economic expansion of the Western Society over the face of the planet. The original field of Maronite commercial enterprise in Egypt now counts for less in the Maronite economy than the larger and more lucrative fields which the Maronites have found for themselves in the United States, in Latin America, and in the French Colonial Empire in West Africa. Similarly, the Ismā'īlī Shī'īs (*alias* Assassins *alias* Khwājas) have served an apprenticeship in India and have profited by 'the opening-up of Africa', where they have found a

---

[1] For the role played by the Nestorians in the Mongol Empire, see Vladimirtsov, B. Y.: *The Life of Chingis Khan* (English translation: London 1930, Routledge); and Barthold, W.: *Turkestan down to the Mongol Invasion* (English translation: London 1928, Luzac), pp. 386–92.

new field of enterprise in the British protectorates and colonies and mandated territories along the East-African seaboard of the Indian Ocean. At the opposite extremity of the Arabic World, the 'Ibādī Kharijites have held their own in a Sunnī environment as a mercantile class in the Maghrib.[1]

So much for the reactions to the challenge of religious discrimination which can be observed among the 'fossils' of the Syriac Society. If we turn from these to the 'fossils' of the Indic Society, we can observe at least one reaction of the same nature to the same challenge among the Jains in India, who, together with the Hinayanian Buddhists in Ceylon, are relics of the Indic Society as it was before the Hellenic intrusion and who thus correspond in stratum to the Jews and the Parsees.[2] In Bengal and Assam at the present day, retail trade is a perquisite of Jain shop-keepers from the State of Marwar in Rājputāna.[3]

[1] For the 'Ibādīs, see Gautier, E. F.: *Les Siècles Obscurs du Maghreb* (Paris 1927, Payot), pp. 303–4:

'Les Mzabites actuels sont assurément les descendants des ibadites rostémides, mais ils ont beaucoup changé en mille ans. Ils ont subi une transformation qui est fréquente dans la société orientale. Comme les Arméniens, comme les Parsis, comme les Juifs, qui sont l'exemple le plus éclatant, les Mzabites depuis l'écroulement de l'empire sont devenus une sorte de tribu, ou plutôt de nation constituée par des siècles d'intermariage et spécialisée dans le maniement de l'argent, où, par développement atavique progressif, ils ont passé maître. Malgré l'éparpillement des individus dans toutes les villes de l'Algérie, partout où il y a un mouvement d'affaires possible, la cohésion de la nation mzabite, qui est incroyablement forte, son patriotisme hargneux et profondément méprisant, sont assurés uniquement par le lien réligieux. Cette croûte protectrice religieuse s'est incessamment épaissie de siècle en siècle, elle s'est consolidée d'une armature compliquée de subtilités théologiques et de pratiques cultuelles minutieuses.'

[2] For the 'fossils' of the Indic Society and their stratification, see I. B (iii), vol. i, p. 35, and I. C (i) (b), vol. i, pp. 90–2, above.

[3] The remarkable resemblance, in êthos and occupation, between the Marwaris on the one hand and the Jews, Parsees, Armenians, and Maronites on the other is apparent in the following series of concordant testimonies from a number of independent authorities:

'Of the four well-known castes of India, viz., the *Brahmana*, the *Kshatriya*, the *Vaishya*, and the *Sudra*, the principal caste engaged in banking is the *Vaishya*. Among the *Vaishyas* are included the *Jainas*, *Marwaris* and *Chettis* who are the most important bankers in India.... The *Marwaris*, who are either *Jainas* or *Vaishnavites*, come from the Marwar State of Rājputāna and Central India. The majority are settled as permanent residents in Central India, but some of them travel from one place to another in search of business. Quite a number of *Marwari* merchants and bankers have migrated to trade centres like Bombay and Calcutta, whence they return home either when trade is slack or to perform religious ceremonies.... Very few of them are educated on Western lines and fewer still are acquainted with English commercial practice, but the way in which they conduct their business is remarkable. Gifted with a natural knack for trade, the *Marwari* boys quickly learn their arithmetic and accounting and start work in their family shops, where they soon pick up the necessary technique. To give an instance of their efficiency, while an English-educated graduate of an Indian university may take five minutes to work out on a piece of paper the compound interest on a given sum, the *Marwari* boy will get an answer correct to the nearest pie mentally, without the aid of pen and paper, in less than half a minute. Of course they are unfamiliar with the modern progress in their craft which is taking place in foreign countries, but, in their own sphere, they are by no means wanting in capacity.' (Jain, L. C.: *Indigenous Banking in India* (London 1929, Macmillan).)

'Almost every province has its peculiar trade-castes. The Mawaris of Rājputāna are, however, found almost everywhere, and in Assam they are of more importance than the natives of the province.' (Anstey, Vera: *The Economic Development of India* (London 1929, Longmans Green), quoting from the *Imperial Gazetteer*.)

'The Marwaris, whose home is in the Marwar State of Rājputāna, have an evil repute as usurers and skinflints. They are found in all the great trading cities, and much of the

The Ashkenazim, Sephardim, Dönme, and Marranos

Having now made some survey of the stimulating effects of religious discrimination over a wide field, we may pause, before proceeding to the next point in our study, in order to test the potency of this stimulus by our usual comparative method. The test can be applied here in two ways. We can compare the êthos displayed by members of a religious denomination when they are being penalized on account of their religion with the êthos of the same people, or their co-religionists, when the penalization has been partly or wholly remitted. We can also compare their êthos with the êthos of co-religionists to whom the stimulus of penalization has never been administered.

To start with the first of these two comparative tests, we can observe a series of gradations in the present êthos of diverse communities of Jews who are subject to penalization in different degrees of rigour or laxity.

At the present time, the Jews who display most conspicuously the well-known êthos which is commonly called 'Jewish', and which in Gentile minds is popularly assumed to be the hall-mark of Judaism always and everywhere, are the Ashkenazi Jews of Eastern Europe who, in Rumania and in the adjoining territories which used to be included in the so-called 'Jewish Pale' of the *ci-devant* Russian Empire, are still being kept morally, if not juridically, in the ghetto by the backward Christian nations among whom their lot is cast. The 'Jewish' êthos is already less conspicuous among the 'emancipated' Jews of Holland, France, Great Britain, and the United States; and when we consider how short a time has passed since the legal emancipation of the Jews took place, and how far from being complete their moral emancipation still is, even in the enlightened countries of the West, we shall not underrate the significance of the change of êthos which is already apparent here.

We may also observe that, among the emancipated Jews of the West, those of Ashkenazi origin, who have come from 'the Jewish Pale', still appear distinctly more 'Jewish' in êthos than the rarer

---

economic difficulties of the peasantry may be laid to their charge.' (Crooke, D.: *Natives of Northern India* (London 1907, Constable).)

'Marwari, literally a native of Malwa or Marwar. Most of the Marwaris found in Bengal are bankers and traders, usually Jains. The name gives no definite indication of caste. . . . In fact all traders from Rājputāna and the neighbouring districts are commonly called Marwaris.' (Risley, H. H.: *The Tribes and Castes of Bengal* (Calcutta 1891, Secretariat Press).)

'Marvari—a territorial name, meaning a native of Marwar. At times of census, Marvaris have been returned as a caste of Jains, i.e., Marvaris who are Jains by religion. The Marvaris are enterprising traders, who have settled in various parts of Southern India, and are, in the city of Madras, money lenders.' (Thurston, E.: *Castes and Tribes of Southern India* (Madras 1909, Government Press).)

See also the Report of the Calcutta University Commission (London 1917, H.M. Stationery Office, 3 vols.), vol. i, p. 25.

Sephardim in our midst, who have come originally from Dār-al-Islām; and we shall account for this difference by reminding ourselves of the diversity in the history of those two Jewish communities.

The Ashkenazim are descended from Jews who took advantage of the opening-up of Europe by the Romans and made a Jewish perquisite of the retail trade in the semi-barbarous Transalpine provinces. Since the conversion and break-up of the Roman Empire, these Ashkenazim have had to suffer doubly from the fanaticism of the Christian Church and from the resentment of the barbarians. A barbarian cannot bear to see a resident alien living a life apart and making a profit by transacting business which the barbarian lacks the skill to transact for himself; and the barbarian neophytes of Western Christendom have been humiliated by the superior ability and filled with envy by the superior prosperity of the indispensable Ashkenazi Jew. Acting on these feelings, they have penalized the Jew as long as he has remained indispensable to them, and have expelled him as soon as they have become capable of doing without him; and accordingly the rise and expansion of the Western Civilization since the days of Charlemagne and Otto I[1] have been accompanied by an eastward drift of the Ashkenazim from the ancient marches of the Roman Empire in the Rhineland to the modern marches of Western Christendom in 'the Pale'. In the expanding interior of Western Christendom, the Jews have been evicted from one country after another as successive Western peoples have attained a certain level of economic efficiency, while, in the advancing continental fringe, these Jewish exiles from the interior have been admitted and even invited into one country after another, in the initial stages of 'Westernization', as commercial pioneers, only to be penalized and eventually evicted once again as soon as they have once again ceased to be indispensable in their latest transitory asylum.

In 'the Pale' and in Rumania, this long trek of the Ashkenazi Jews from west to east across the Continent of Europe has been brought to a halt and their martyrdom has reached its climax; for here, at the meeting-point of Western Christendom with Russian Orthodox Christendom, the Jews have been caught and ground between the upper and the nether millstone. In the fullness of time, the local barbarian converts to Western Christianity on this extreme eastern verge of Western Christendom have acted after their kind. As they have gradually improved their own economic capacities, they have progressively penalized the Jews in their midst and have eventually begun to cast them out. This time,

[1] See II. D (v), pp. 166–74, above.

however, the evicted Ashkenazim have been unable to find a fresh asylum by trekking still farther eastward. Beyond the eastern boundary of 'the Pale', 'Holy Russia' has barred their way.

For the Jews, Russian soil has been forbidden ground from the time when Western and Russian Christendom originally made contact with one another on the Continent in the fourteenth century of the Christian Era right down to the Russian Communist Revolution of A.D. 1917. This barrier did not fall when Russia opened her doors to the Western Civilization in the generation of Peter the Great; and it did not fall thereafter when the eastern marches of Western Christendom were incorporated politically into the Russian Empire. The old frontier between Muscovy and the United Kingdom of Poland-Lithuania, which the Partition of Poland obliterated for the Christian subjects of the Czar, remained in force for the Jew as an eastern limit which he was absolutely forbidden to pass. It was fortunate indeed for the Ashkenazim that by this time the leading nations of the West, which had been the first to evict the Jews in the Middle Ages, had risen to a height of economic efficiency at which they were no longer afraid of exposing themselves to Jewish economic competition in a free field with no favour. The emancipation of the Jews in the West came just in time to give the Ashkenazim of 'the Pale' a new western outlet when their old eastward drift was brought up short against the blank wall of 'Holy Russia'. During the past century, the tide of Ashkenazi migration has been ebbing back from east to west: from 'the Pale' and Rumania into England and the United States. It is not to be wondered at that, with these antecedents, the Ashkenazim whom this ebb-tide has deposited among us should display the so-called 'Jewish' êthos more conspicuously than their Sephardi co-religionists whose 'lines' have 'fallen'[1] in comparatively pleasant places.

To the author of this Study, the spiritual and political duress under which the Ashkenazim have had to live their life in 'the Pale' was brought home by the following two anecdotes which were recounted to him in 1919, during the Peace Conference of Paris, by Dr. Chaim Weizmann in order to explain why this great statesman and scientist—the most distinguished member of the Ashkenazi community in his generation—had become a convert to Zionism.

The first anecdote was this. In Dr. Weizmann's boyhood, at Vilna, there was a young Jewish sculptor of great promise who was expected to become one of the historic exponents of the Jewish culture. The young man's promise was fulfilled, but Jewry's hope was disappointed; for the *chef d'œuvre* in which this Jewish artist eventually gave expression to his genius was a statue of the Russian

[1] Psalm xvi. 6.

Orthodox Christian Czar Ivan the Terrible! Under the duress of 'the Pale', Jewish genius had been perverted to the glorification of Jewry's oppressors. It was as if the *chef d'œuvre* of Jewish literature in the second century B.C. had not been the Book of Ecclesiastes or the Psalms but some panegyric, in the Isocratean manner, upon Antiochus Epiphanes. Truly, that statue of a Russian Czar by the hand of a Vilna Jew was as great an eyesore for Jewish eyes as the statue of Zeus which the Seleucid once set up in the Temple of Yahweh at Jerusalem: an 'abomination of desolation standing where it ought not'.[1]

Dr. Weizmann's second anecdote was an incident which had happened to himself as a grown man before his migration from Vilna to Manchester. A piece of urgent business made it indispensable for him to break the Russian law then in force, under the Czardom, by trespassing beyond the eastern boundary of 'the Pale' in order to have a personal meeting with a friend in Moscow. As a precaution against the vigilance of the Russian police, it was arranged beforehand that Dr. Weizmann should travel from Vilna to Moscow in a train arriving at nightfall, do his business in his friend's house during the night, and return to Vilna by a train leaving Moscow before dawn; but this arrangement fell through. For some reason, the friend whom Dr. Weizmann had come to see was unable to keep the appointment; and Dr. Weizmann found on inquiry that there was no return-train to Vilna earlier than the train which he had been intending to take. How should he pass the night hours? To engage a room in a hotel would be tantamount to delivering himself up to the police. Dr. Weizmann solved the problem by hiring a cab and driving round and round the streets of Moscow until the hour of his train's departure. 'And that', he concluded, 'was how I had to pass my time on my one and only visit to the capital of the Empire of which I was supposed to be a citizen!'

Such anecdotes as these sufficiently explain the êthos of the Ashkenazi immigrants from 'the Pale' into the more enlightened countries of the modern Western World; and the less highly accentuated 'Jewishness' of the êthos which we observe among the Sephardi immigrants from Spain and Portugal is explained by the antecedents of the Sephardim in Dār-al-Islām.

The representatives of the Jewish Dispersion in the dominions of the Sasanidae and in those provinces of the Roman Empire which ultimately fell to the Arabs and not to the North European barbarians found themselves in a happy position compared with their unfortunate co-religionists in the Rhineland. Their status under the régime of the 'Abbasid Caliphate was certainly not less favourable

[1] Mark xiii. 14; Matthew xxiv. 15; Luke xxi. 20; Daniel ix. 27.

than the status of Jews to-day in those Western countries where the Jews have been 'emancipated'; and it did not become intolerable when the Caliphate broke up and the Syriac Society finally dissolved in the interregnum from which the 'affiliated' Arabic and Iranic societies subsequently emerged. The historic calamity of the Sephardim was the transfer of the Iberian Peninsula from the domain of the Syriac to the domain of the Western Civilization: a transfer which began towards the close of the tenth century of the Christian Era and was consummated, some five centuries later, in the conquest of Granada by Ferdinand and Isabella. The change of régime was effected, from beginning to end, by force of arms;[1] and the local calamity which this violent social change entailed for the Sephardim, in common with the Muslimīn among whom they lived, was extreme in its severity. The Muslims and the Jews who came under Christian rule in the Iberian Peninsula were not offered the choice of retaining their old religion and culture under the new régime at the price of penalization, as the Ashkenazim were permitted to live under Western Christian domination on the other side of the Pyrenees or the Orthodox Christians and the Levantines under Muslim domination in the Ottoman Empire. In the Iberian Peninsula, the conquered communities had to choose between the three alternatives of annihilation, expulsion, and conversion. In Spain, the choice was presented to the Jews during the century which began with the great persecution of A.D. 1391 and ended with Ferdinand and Isabella's edict of expulsion in 1492. Let us glance at the latter state of those Peninsular Sephardim who saved their lives in one of the two alternative ways and whose posterity therefore survives down to this day.

Peninsular Sephardim who preferred to go into exile rather than to be received into the Roman Catholic Church—or rather than to remain forced and insincere converts to the Roman Catholic faith—found asylum among the enemies of Catholic Portugal and Spain: the Portuguese Sephardim in Protestant Holland, the Castilian Sephardim in Muslim Turkey, and members of both communities in tolerant Tuscany.[2] The 'Osmanlis gave asylum to the Jewish refugees from Castile for several reasons. They felt the normal

---

[1] For the effect of this warfare upon the Iberian Christians, see II. D (v), pp. 203–6, above.

[2] For the eventual dispersion abroad of the descendants of the Sephardi Jews who were forcibly converted in Castile in A.D. 1391 and in Portugal in A.D. 1497, see Roth, C.: *A History of the Marranos* (London 1932, Routledge), especially chapters viii–xi. The history of the Peninsular Sephardi community which was founded at Leghorn in A.D. 1593 (see op. cit., pp. 214–19) by Spanish and Portuguese crypto-Jewish refugees who were able to return openly to their ancestral faith under the Tuscan Government's protection, may be compared with the history of the autonomous Greek community which was founded in the last quarter of the eighteenth century at Ayvalyq under the aegis of the Ottoman Pādishāh. (See II. D (ii), p. 40, footnote 1, above.)

human sympathy for the victims of their enemies (and the United Kingdom of Castile and Aragon was the principal enemy of the Ottoman Power in the Mediterranean); they inherited the normal Muslim tradition of liberality towards Jews; and they had a special *raison d'état* for welcoming Jewish immigration into their dominions at this juncture.

While the Castilians had been rounding off their conquests and confirming their supremacy in the Iberian Peninsula, the 'Osmanlis had been rounding off their own conquests in the Balkan Peninsula and Anatolia and were anxious to confirm their supremacy likewise in their own domain. They were not, however, at liberty to confirm it by cutting the Gordian Knot in the Occidental fashion; for, in the eyes of the Islamic Law, Jews and Christians as well as Muslims had certain fundamental and inalienable rights in virtue of their common belief in the One True God. The recipients of the Torah and the Bible, as well as the recipients of the Qur'ān, were 'People of the Book'; and to non-Muslim 'People of the Book' who had succumbed to Muslim arms the Muslim conqueror was instructed to offer a less cruel choice than the three alternatives which were offered to vanquished Muslims and Jews by the Christian Church Militant in Spain. His Catholic Majesty cut the knot by giving any vanquished miscreants who did not conveniently dispose of themselves by fighting to the death a choice between conversion and expulsion. The Muslim conqueror must give them the choice between conversion and toleration—the condition of toleration being the acceptance of a status of inferiority and the payment of a special super-tax. In other words, the Muslim conqueror was bound by the Islamic Law to face the problem of having permanently under his rule an alien population which was subject to penalization but not devoid of rights. This problem was a severe test of statesmanship in a situation in which the *dhimmīs* were the majority and the Muslims the minority; and this was the situation in which the Ottoman Pādishāh found himself after the Ottoman Empire had been rounded off by Ferdinand and Isabella's older contemporary Mehmed the Conqueror. Ottoman statesmanship sought to find a solution for its problem by giving the Castilian Jewish refugees asylum and taking them into partnership.

The 'Osmanlis were confident of their own ability to fill the roles of rulers and soldiers and peasants, in which the immigrant Castilian Jews would have neither the power nor the inclination to compete with them. On the other hand, they knew themselves to be incompetent to supplant the conquered Greek Orthodox and Levantine Catholic Christians in the field of handicraft and trade; and at the same time they were afraid that these tolerated but unreconciled

native subjects might remain too strong for the safety of the Ottoman Commonwealth if even in this limited field they were permitted
to retain a monopoly. Accordingly, the Ottoman Government not
only gave the Castilian Jews asylum in its dominions but carefully
planted them in the chief commercial centres—Salonica, Adrianople,
and Constantinople itself—with the intention that these Jews should
take the lion's share in the one field of social activity which the
'Osmanlis themselves were unable to occupy. This intention was
fulfilled. The Sephardim, whose ancestors had made themselves
past-masters in this field some fifteen or twenty centuries before the
Christian subjects of the 'Osmanlis were confined to it, were easily
able, with the Ottoman Government's political support, to draw the
main threads of Near Eastern commerce into their own hands.
Under the Ottoman régime, they prospered commercially in the
Near East as they had once prospered commercially in the Iberian
Peninsula. At the same time—and this is the significant point for
our present purpose—they developed under the Ottoman régime
a quite different êthos from the Jewish êthos as we know it in the
West, because the treatment which they received at the 'Osmanlis'
hands was quite different from the treatment which Jews have
customarily received at the hands of Westerners.

The psychological effect of four centuries of the Ottoman régime
upon the descendants in the Near East of these Sephardi refugees
from Castile was once brought home to the writer of this Study by
an incident which came under his personal observation.

One day in August 1921, some eight years and more after Salonica,
with its Sephardi population of eighty thousand souls, had passed
by conquest out of Ottoman jurisdiction into Greek, I found myself
travelling by train from Salonica to Vodena in the same carriage
with three Sephardi school-teachers going on a holiday and one
Greek officer going to rejoin his regiment. The holiday-makers—
two girls and a man—were in high spirits, and they gave vent to
their mood by breaking into song. They sang in French: the 'culture language' in which the modern Near Eastern Jew has found
the necessary supplement to his hereditary Castilian vernacular.
After they had been singing for some time, the Greek lieutenant
broke his own silence. 'Won't you sing in Greek for a change?' he
said. 'This country is part of Greece now, and you are Greek
citizens.' But his intervention had no effect. 'We prefer French'
the Jews answered, politely but firmly, and fell to singing lustily in
French again, while the Greek lieutenant subsided. There was one
person in the carriage, however, who was even more surprised at
the Jewish teachers' reply to the Greek officer than the Greek himself, and that was the Frankish spectator. Seldom, he reflected,

would a Jew have shown such spirit in such circumstances in France or England or America. The incident bore witness to the relative humanity with which the Jews in the Ottoman Empire had been treated by the 'Osmanlis; and it also had a wider and more interesting significance. It was evidence that the Jewish êthos was not something ineradicably implanted by Race or something indelibly ingrained by Religion but was a psychic variable which was apt to vary in response to variations in Gentile behaviour in different times and places.

This inference is supported by other varieties of Jewish êthos within the Sephardi community itself. For instance, there is the Dönme:[1] a fraction of the immigrant Castilian Jewish community in the Near East which has been in communion with Islam for some two and a half centuries.[2] These *ci-devant* Jews have parted company with their former co-religionists without wholly merging themselves in the fraternity of Islam. They have remained in some degree 'a peculiar people', neither fish, flesh, nor fowl. Nevertheless, their *rapprochement*, so far as it has gone, towards the ruling element in the society in which they live has been accompanied by a visible diminution of the distinctively 'Jewish' element in their êthos. *A fortiori*, in the Marranos—that is, the descendants of those Peninsular Sephardim who were induced or compelled some four or five centuries ago to be received into the Roman Catholic Church rather than go into exile[3]—the distinctive Jewish characteristics have been attenuated to vanishing point.

There is reason to believe that in Spain and Portugal to-day there is a strong tincture of the blood of these Jewish converts in Christian veins, especially in the upper and middle class. Yet the most acute psycho-analyst might find it difficult, if samples of living upper and middle class Spaniards and Portuguese were presented to him for examination, to distinguish those who had from those who had not a Jewish strain in their physical race. Indeed, in most cases our psycho-analyst would have no psychic data here to go upon in attempting to separate the sheep from the goats; for in most cases he would be unable to detect in his subjects any sense, either conscious or sub-conscious, of their Jewish antecedents, even where

---

[1] 'Dönme' is a Turkish verbal noun meaning 'conversion'.

[2] The Dönme community consists of the descendants of those ex-Castilian Ottoman Jews who followed Sabbatai Zevi: a Smyrniot Jew who proclaimed himself Messiah in A.D. 1648. In 1666, the year in which the Smyrniot Messiah was to enter into his kingdom, the Ottoman Government, which had left him completely at liberty to propagate his claims for eighteen years, at last took the precaution of interning him; and thereafter Sabbatai obtained his release by making a *volte face* and proclaiming his conversion to Islam, in which his example was followed by his disciples. For Sabbatai Zevi's career, see Kastein, J.: *The Messiah of Ismir: Sabbatai Zevi* (London 1931, Lane).

[3] A genuine choice between conversion and expulsion was offered to the Castilian Jews between A.D. 1391 and A.D. 1492. On the other hand, in A.D. 1497, the Portuguese Jews were coerced into apostasy wholesale. (See Roth, op. cit., pp. 55–62.)

the Jewish physical strain was actually present. The forced converts themselves and the first few generations of their descendants
may have remained crypto-Jews; the next few generations may have
preserved some memory of their ancestors having only been Gentiles and Catholics in outward form; but, when once the traditional
social barriers had been broken down by the formal act of conversion, the perpetual intercourse and repeated intermarriage between the posterity of the converts and the hereditary members
of the society into which their forefathers' act had initiated them
must gradually have produced its full psychological effect among
the great majority of the *ci-devant*-Jewish families. With the passage
of time, a generation must have arrived in which the Jewish consciousness and the Jewish êthos were totally extinct.[1]

Thus, in Jewry, we find a graded sequence of types—Ashkenazi,
Sephardi, Dönme, crypto-Jew, and *ci-devant*-Jewish Catholic—in
which the Jewish êthos varies in intensity through all the degrees
from maximum to vanishing point; and we observe that these
variations in the intensity of the Jewish êthos correspond to variations in the severity of the penalization to which Jewry has been
subjected by the Gentiles. The distinctive êthos of the penalized
religious denomination becomes less and less sharply accentuated
as the penalization is progressively remitted; and this social law is
not valid only for the Jews. Its operation can be illustrated from the
history of other penalized sects whose reactions we have examined
above.

Nabobs and Sahibs

Examples are afforded by the history of those Western Christian
traders who have lived the ghetto-life, under alien régimes, in the

[1] This final extinction of the Jewish consciousness and êthos in the Marranos is of
surprisingly recent date—to judge by a remarkable passage in chapter xi of George
Borrow's *The Bible in Spain*. For the author arrived off the coast of the Peninsula on the
10th November, 1835, and wrote the preface to his book on the 26th November, 1842,
so that the incident recorded in chapter xi must have occurred between these two dates—
that is to say, if the tale is to be taken literally as the record of an actual experience and
is not to be interpreted as a literary artifice for conveying the 'feel' of a crypto-Jew's
existence as Borrow had reconstructed this in imagination from a book-study of the
history of the Marranos in earlier centuries. Be that as it may, Borrow's description of
his alleged encounter and conversation with the mysterious Abarbenel on the road to
Talavera is eminently worth reading; and, since the passage is far too long to quote in full,
and far too fine a piece of literary art to be quoted at all except *verbatim*, the writer of
this Study must be content to refer his readers to it and urge them to re-read it for themselves. The authenticity of Borrow's alleged encounter with a living Marrano in Spain
appears by no means incredible in the light of the well-authenticated fact that, in Portugal, a rural population of Marranos has come to notice, and has even begun to return
publicly to its ancestral faith, since the overthrow of the Monarchy and establishment of
the Republic in A.D. 1910. (See Roth, op. cit., Epilogue.) The survival of crypto-Jewish
communities in the Iberian Peninsula over a span of more than four centuries is amazing;
and our amazement will be increased when we consider that, throughout the sixteenth
and seventeenth centuries of the Christian Era, this subterranean Jewish community was
being weakened all the time by a steady drain of its more active and enterprising members,
who lost no opportunity of emigrating in order to return publicly to their ancestral
religion in a Dutch or Tuscan or Ottoman asylum.

Ottoman Empire and Russia and India and the Far East. These formerly penalized Western Christian residents in Oriental countries have all been 'emancipated' from their ghettos successively in the course of the last two and a half centuries: the 'Niemci' from the Muscovite 'Svoboda' in the time of Peter the Great; the French and English from their 'factories' on the coasts of India after the death of Awrangzīb; the Franks from their segregated quarters in the Échelles du Levant after Bonaparte's landing in Egypt in A.D. 1798; the 'South Sea Barbarians' from their 'factories' at Canton after the Anglo-Chinese 'Opium War' of A.D. 1839–42; the Dutch from Deshima after the visit of Admiral Perry's squadron to Yedo Bay in A.D. 1853. The nature and manner and extent of the 'emancipation' have been different in each case; but there is one thing that can be said of all these cases with equal truth. In all the cases, a more or less uniform 'Jewish' êthos, which these Western residents under an alien régime had developed in response to a more or less uniform penalization, has faded or vanished altogether as the social conditions conducive to it have been mitigated.

The most astonishing case is that of the servants of the English East India Company in India. In this case, the reversal of fortune was rapid and extreme. Within the span of less than a century, the Company's servants rose from being for the most part clerks and salesmen who were allowed to do their business on sufferance on the fringe of 'the Great Mogul's' dominions until they found themselves the undisputed masters of India and acknowledged heirs of 'the Great Mogul' himself, who only retained a shadow of his hereditary sovereignty as the Company's protégé and pensioner. The change of êthos which the English in India underwent in the course of this century was fully commensurate with their change in status. The 'Nabob' of the eighteenth century became the 'Sahib'[1] of the nineteenth. In the character of Jos Sedley, Thackeray has simply given a touch of caricature to a life-like portrait of the 'Anglo-Indian'[2] as he continued to be until after the turn of the century. Yet already the revolutionary change of circumstances in India had made Thackeray's picture an anachronism. The Battle of Waterloo, which is signalized in fiction by Jos Sedley's headlong flight, was won as a matter of historical fact by a 'sepoy general'; and in the

---

[1] This title 'Sahib', which has come to be applied to the Englishman in India, is an Arabic word which, in its classical usage, means 'a companion of the Prophet Muhammad'. The application of a title with this connotation to the infidel son of a shopkeeper shows how completely 'the nation of shopkeepers' was transfigured in the Indian imagination when it succeeded the Mughals in the role of being the ruling race; and this, in turn, shows how profound a change must have taken place in the êthos of the English in India themselves, since it is evident that the Indians have always taken us approximately at our own valuation.

[2] 'Anglo-Indian' in the original sense of English resident in India, and not in the latter-day usage of the name as a euphemism for 'Eurasian'.

decade of the Sikh Wars, when Thackeray was writing *Vanity Fair*,[1] the typical servant of the East India Company was no longer a chicken-livered Jos nor even a ruffianly Clive, but an evangelical soldier or administrator of heroic build: a John Lawrence or a John Nicholson.

Emancipated Nonconformists

Another illustration of our point is offered by the history of the Huguenots. In France down to this day the Huguenots continue to display the distinctive êthos of a penalized religious denomination, in spite of the fact that they have been 'emancipated' officially since the time of the Revolution. In their native land, they still tend to hold aloof from public life and to devote themselves with conspicuous success to private business. On the other hand, the descendants of those Huguenots who emigrated at the close of the seventeenth century from France to the Protestant countries have been subject to no such inhibition; and in the annals of modern England and Germany and South Africa the descendants of Huguenot refugees have distinguished themselves in every walk of life, not only in business but in the army and in the civil service and in politics. Lasalle and Ledebour, Joubert and Dufour-Féronce are examples of Huguenot names which have made a mark in German and South African history.

In England, the êthos of the non-Anglican Protestant denominations shows signs of a corresponding modification—not, in this case, in response to more favourable conditions which have been secured by migration into an alien environment, but in response to an improvement of conditions at home. 'The Nonconformist Conscience' has lost some of its sharpness since Nonconformity has ceased to be incompatible with membership in the English Governing Class, while on the other hand the Quaker Conscience has led the members of the Society of Friends to pursue their old ideals in a wider field of social action as the religious disqualifications which once circumscribed their activities have been removed. In both these otherwise dissimilar cases, the remission of a previous penalization has had one common effect. It has resulted in both the Quakers and the Nonconformists ceasing to be 'peculiar peoples'. It has led both to come out of their shells in order to live—for good or not for good, as the case may be—the ordinary life of the world around them.[2]

---

[1] *Vanity Fair* was written during the years 1846–8.

[2] This tendency, which was at work all through the nineteenth century, was brought to a head by the General War of 1914–18, in which the Nonconformists on the whole identified themselves with the policy and outlook of the Governing Class while the Quakers found themselves moved to uphold their own unchanged ideals in public action

Emancipated Raʿīyeh

In the Orthodox Christian World, the same point is illustrated by the diversity of êthos, in post-war Greece, between two sections of the population: on the one hand, the indigenous inhabitants of 'the Old Kingdom', within the frontiers as they stood before the wars of 1912–22; and, on the other hand, the new citizens whom the present Greek Republic has acquired partly through the transfer of Macedonia and Western Thrace, with their Greek inhabitants, to Greek from Ottoman sovereignty, and partly through the influx into Greece of Greek refugees from Eastern Thrace and Western Anatolia after the failure of the Greek Government to wrest these latter territories from Turkish hands. At the time of writing, some ten years after the Peace Settlement of Lausanne, the contrast between these two elements in the population of Greece is still conspicuous. It is, in fact, the most important feature of diversity in the social and political life of the country.

The old citizens and the new citizens of the Greek Republic are conscious, on both sides, of a certain *mésintelligence* with one another. Yet the differentiation of êthos out of which this tendency towards misunderstanding arises cannot be much more than a century old; for, little more than a century ago, before the Greek Revolutionary War of 1821–9, the whole of the present territory of Greece, with the insignificant exception of the Ionian Islands, was still embraced within the Ottoman Empire, so that in that generation the influence of the Ottoman environment was operative upon the ancestors of the present old citizens and new citizens of Greece alike. The present difference of êthos is to be explained by the fact that the new citizens have remained under the Ottoman régime down to the present generation, while the old citizens have been exempt from the Ottoman régime for some three or four generations past. Instead of remaining members of a penalized religious denomination under an alien ascendancy, they have been living, during these last three or four generations, as citizens of a Greek national state on the Western pattern. In this new environment, they have lost much of the êthos of the old-fashioned Ottoman raʿīyeh and have acquired something of the êthos of the modern Occidental. Though the time has been short, the psychological change which has been induced by the new conditions of the human environment has been sufficiently great to establish a perceptible psychological barrier between the two sections of the Greek people now that they have been

on a grand scale. The blunting of 'the Nonconformist Conscience' is reflected in the post-war decay of the Liberal Party. The entry of the Quakers into public life is proclaimed by the mighty works of philanthropy which have been performed in every part of the World by the Society of Friends since 1914. In these works, the Inner Light has made itself outwardly manifest. *Si monumentum requiris, circumspice.*

reunited in a single commonwealth after little more than a century of segregation.

Assimilationists and Zionists

This effect of citizenship in a Greek national state upon the descendants of the Greek ra'īyeh of the old Ottoman Empire has a bearing on a modern movement in Jewry: the movement called Zionism.

The ultimate aim of the Zionists is to liberate the Jewish people from the peculiar psychological complex induced by the penalization to which they have been subject for centuries in the Gentile World. In this ultimate aim, the Zionists are at one with the Assimilationist School among the 'emancipated' Jews in the enlightened countries of the West. They agree with the Assimilationists in wishing to cure the Jews of being 'a peculiar people'. They part company with them, however, in their estimate of the Assimilationist prescription, which the Zionists reject as inadequate for coping with the malady.

The ideal of the Assimilationists is that the Jew in Holland, France, England, or America should become a Dutchman, Frenchman, Englishman, or American, as the case may be, 'of Jewish religion'. They argue that there is no reason why a Jewish citizen of any of these enlightened countries should fail to be a completely satisfied and satisfactory member of Society just because he happens to go to synagogue on Saturday instead of going to church on Sunday. To this argument, the Zionists have two replies. In the first place, they point out that, even if the Assimilationist prescription were capable of producing the result which its advocates claim for it, it is only applicable in the enlightened countries in which the Jews have been granted 'emancipation'. It offers no solution for the Jewish problem in Eastern Europe, where the régime of the ghetto still virtually prevails and where bona fide 'emancipation' is not in prospect.[1] In the second place—and this is the more trenchant of the two Zionist attacks upon the Assimilationist position—the Zionists contend that, even in the most enlightened Gentile community in the World, the Jewish problem cannot be solved by a Gentile-Jewish 'social contract' under which the Gentile 'emancipates' the Jew and the Jew 'assimilates' himself to the Gentile. This attempt at a contractual solution is vitiated, in the Zionists' view, by the false

---

[1] This passage was written before the 'Aryan' outbreak against the Jews in Germany which accompanied the German National-Socialist Revolution of 1933. This appalling recrudescence of militant anti-Semitism in one of the leading countries of the Western World still further strengthens the already strong Zionist case. For the German outbreak of 1933 can only be compared—in its brutality, its hysteria, and its thoroughness—with the Castilian outbreak of A.D. 1391. If this could happen in the present age in a country in which the Jews had long since been emancipated, then where in the World can the Jewish Diasporà feel itself really secure?

premise which vitiates the classical 'social contract' theory of Rousseau. It presupposes that human beings are social atoms and that a human society is an aggregate of these atoms which is held together by a legal nexus between the individuals as, in the physical universe, an aggregation of physical atoms is held together by the laws of Physics according to the 'classical' physical science of the nineteenth century. The Zionist, arguing *ad hominem*, insists that the Jew, at any rate, is not in fact an autonomous individual who can make and unmake his social relations as he pleases. To be a Jew is to be a human being whose social environment is Jewry. It is an essential part of the Jew's individuality that he is a member of the living Jewish community and an heir to the ancient Jewish tradition. He cannot cut off his Jewishness and cast it from him without self-mutilation; and thus, for the Jew, an emancipation-assimilation contract with a Gentile nation has the same kind of consequence as the legal instrument which turns a free man into a slave. It 'deprives him of half of his manhood'.[1] A Jew who, by process of emancipation and assimilation, attempts, in a social contract with his Gentile neighbours, to turn himself into a Dutchman or a Frenchman or an Englishman or an American 'of Jewish religion' is simply mutilating his Jewish personality without having any prospect at all of acquiring the full personality of a Dutchman or whatever the Gentile nationality of his choice may be.

Thus, in the Zionist view, the emancipation and assimilation of the Jew as an individual is a wrong method of pursuing a right aim. Genuine assimilation is indeed the true solution for the Jewish problem and ought therefore to be the ultimate goal of Jewish endeavours; but the Jews can never escape from being 'a peculiar people' by masquerading as Englishmen or Frenchmen. If they are to succeed in becoming 'like all the nations',[2] they must seek assimilation on a national and not on an individual basis. Instead of trying to assimilate individual Jews to individual Englishmen or Frenchmen, they must try to assimilate Jewry itself to England and France. Jewry must become a nation in effective possession of a national home, and this on the ground from which the historic roots of Judaism have sprung. When a new generation of Jews has grown up in Palestine in a Jewish national environment, then, and not till then, the Jewish problem will be solved by the reappearance in the World of a type of Jew which has been almost non-existent for the past two thousand years: a Jew who has genuinely ceased to be 'not as other men are'.[3]

Though the Zionist Movement as a practical undertaking is only

---

[1] See the ancient Greek proverb quoted in the present section on p. 214, above.
[2] 1 Samuel viii. 5 and 20.　　　　　　　　　　　　　　　　　[3] Luke xviii. 11.

half a century old, its social philosophy has already been justified by results. In the Jewish agricultural settlements that have been founded in Palestine within the last fifty years, the children of the ghetto have been transformed out of all recognition into a pioneering peasantry which displays many of the characteristics of the Gentile European colonial type in the New World. The Zionists have made no miscalculation in their forecast of the effect which the establishment of a Jewish national home in Palestine would have upon Jewry itself. The tragic misfortune into which they have fallen, in company with the Mandatory Power, is their inability to arrive at an understanding with the existing Arab population of the country: prior claimants and possessors who have been roused to resistance by the very spirit of Western Nationalism which has been the inspiration of Zionism itself.

Ismāʿīlīs and Imāmīs

Lastly, we may take note of the difference between the Ismāʿīlī Shīʿīs of India, who display to-day, as strongly as ever, the distinctive characteristics of penalized religious denominations, and the Imāmī Shīʿīs of Persia, whose êthos at the present day is at the opposite extreme of the psychological gamut. In the modern Western World, the antithesis to the characteristic êthos of penalized religious denominations is the spirit of Nationalism; and the closest indigenous analogue of Western Nationalism which Western observers have detected in the modern Islamic World is the spirit of the Imāmī Shīʿī Persians.[1] Indeed, the modern Persians may be called a nation and modern Persia a national state without any flagrant misapplication of our Western terminology. In other words, the spirit of Imāmī Shiʿism, which is the established religion of modern Persia, differs at the present day from the spirit of Ismāʿīlī Shiʿism about as widely as the spirit of France or England or any of the other territorial nations of the West differs from the spirit of Jewry. Yet, as a matter of historical fact, the present differentiation of the Imāmī êthos in Persia from the Ismāʿīlī in India is of recent date, like the differentiation in êthos between the Jewish agricultural colonist in Palestine and the Ghetto-Jew of 'the Pale' or between the Greek citizen of Greece and the Greek raʿīyeh of the Ottoman Empire.

[1] In recent times, of course, the Islamic Society has become infected with the virus of Western Nationalism itself, and this infection has not attacked the Persians as violently as it has attacked certain other Islamic peoples: for instance, the Egyptians and, above all, the ʿOsmanlis. This Western type of Nationalism in the Islamic World is, however, something exotic; and if we search for a counterpart of Western Nationalism in the Islamic Society as that society was before the process of 'Westernization' began, then we shall find this counterpart among the Muslims of Persia and not among those of the Ottoman Empire. This point has been touched upon already in I. C (i) (b), Annex I, vol. i, p. 393 with footnote 1, above.

Little more than four centuries ago, the Imāmīs, like the other sects of the Shī'ah, were 'dispersed abroad' among a Sunnī majority in Persia, Bahrayn, Hasā, Syria, and elsewhere,[1] and in this situation they duly displayed, like other Shī'īs, those characteristics of a penalized religious denomination with which we have now become familiar. The situation of the Imāmī sect was revolutionized at the beginning of the sixteenth century of the Christian Era, within the short span of a single generation, by the life-work of one man: Ismā'īl Shāh Safawī. This militant apostle of Imāmī Shi'ism changed the destinies of his faith by the victories of his sword. Imāmī Shi'ism, as Shāh Ismā'īl found it, was the persuasion of a scattered and persecuted sect; as he left it, it was the established church, and very nearly the exclusive religion, of an empire which embraced the whole of Persia.[2] In modern Persia, from Shāh Ismā'īl's time onwards, the Imāmīs have ceased to be the 'peculiar people' which the Ismā'īlīs have continued to be in India. While these other Shī'īs have remained what they always were, the Imāmīs in Persia have become *the* people of a great country. They have become the Persian nation, which is master in its own house and is free to practise its national religion without being penalized by any man. In the course of four centuries, this profound change of circumstance has produced the profound change of êthos to which we have drawn attention above. There were, however, certain Imāmī communities —for example, those in Syria and in Hasā—whose homes were too distant from Shāh Ismā'īl's base of operations to be included in the empire which he carved out; and these Imāmī Shī'īs beyond the borders of Persia have never ceased to display the êthos which all Imāmīs formerly displayed in common with the Ismā'īlīs.[3]

Fossils in Fastnesses

So much for the evidence that the êthos and aptitudes which are characteristic of penalized religious denominations tend to disappear if, and when, and in proportion as the penalization is remitted.

[1] See I. C (i) (*b*), Annex I, vol. i, pp. 358–65, above.
[2] For Shāh Ismā'īl's work, see I. C (i) (*b*), vol. i, pp. 69–70, with Annex I, above.
[3] The Imāmī Shī'īs of 'Irāq are a special case; for 'Irāq is a former province of Shāh Ismā'īl's empire which was eventually conquered from the Safawis by the 'Osmanlis after having changed hands several times in a series of wars which lasted more than a century (A.D. 1534–1639). The Imāmī Shī'īs of 'Irāq are in the same situation as their co-religionists in Syria and in Hasā, inasmuch as they have been subject to the political ascendancy of a Sunnī majority. They are in a different situation, inasmuch as their subjection has not been unbroken. For a brief interval, the Imāmī Shī'īs of 'Irāq were masters in their own house, as their more fortunate co-religionists in Iran have continued to be ever since the day when Shāh Ismā'īl released the Imāmīs from the house of bondage in Iran and 'Irāq alike. In consonance with this peculiar history, the êthos of the Shī'īs in 'Irāq has become something intermediate between their êthos in Persia and their êthos in those places where they have always been under Sunnī domination. In our Western political terminology, 'Irāq is a Persian *terra irredenta* and the 'Irāqī Shī'īs, though mostly Arabs by language, may be regarded almost as a Persian minority under alien rule.

This evidence seems to indicate that the characteristics in question are not innate and ineradicable qualities, but rather symptoms of a particular response to a particular challenge—symptoms which have no greater permanence than the challenge and the response out of which they arise. We shall find this indication confirmed if we now compare the êthos of penalized denominations with that of co-religionists to whom the stimulus of penalization has never been administered. We shall observe that those who have never undergone tribulation resemble those who have come out of tribulation in being free from the distinctive and unmistakable characteristics which those who are actually suffering tribulation almost invariably display.

The 'Osmanlis draw a sharp distinction between the 'fresh-water' French, English, and so on, and their 'salt-water' namesakes. The 'fresh-water' Franks are those who have been born and bred in Turkey in the Levantine atmosphere and have duly responded by developing the Levantine character. The 'salt-water' Franks are those who have been born and bred at home in Frankland and have come out to Turkey as adults at an age when their character has already been formed. The Turks have been intrigued to find that the great psychological gulf which divides them from the 'fresh-water' Franks does not intervene when they have to deal with the Franks from beyond the sea. The Franks who are geographically their compatriots are psychologically aliens; the Franks who come from a far country turn out to be men of like passions with the Turks themselves. This apparent paradox has a simple explanation. The Turk and the 'salt-water' Frank are able to understand one another because there is a broad similarity between their respective social backgrounds. They have each grown up in a social environment in which they have been masters in their own house. On the other hand, they both find difficulty in placing themselves en rapport with the 'fresh-water' Frank because the 'fresh-water' Frank has a social background which is equally foreign to both of them. The 'fresh-water' Frank—the Frank brought up in Turkey—is not a son of the house but a child of the ghetto; and this peculiar social environment has induced in him an êthos from which the Frank brought up in Frankland and the Turk brought up in Turkey have both remained free.

This Turkish dichotomy between the 'fresh-water' and the 'salt-water' Frank, within the body social of a civilization which is still 'a going concern', has an analogue in the sociology of those remnants of extinct civilizations which survive in the form of 'fossils'; for the 'fossils' of which we have knowledge are preserved in one or other of two alternative situations which are entirely dissimilar. In the present chapter up to this point, we have confined our attention to

'fossils' which have been preserved in the shape of penalized religious denominations 'dispersed abroad among the Gentiles'; and
we have seen that 'fossils' in this situation, if they survive at all,
succeed in holding their own by learning to excel in the narrow
field of social activity to which their Gentile neighbours and masters
are apt to confine them. There is, however, another situation in
which 'fossils' can and do maintain themselves in existence on easier
terms. Instead of working their way through the fabric of some
Gentile body social until they find a precarious lodgement in its
crevices, like flints in chalk, they may segregate themselves into
some fastness where they can be sure of being left in peace by the
Gentiles round about; and most of the 'fossils' of which we have
hitherto taken account have in fact been preserved partly in such
fastnesses and not solely in dispersion. We can substantiate this by
a cursory survey.

For example, the Jewish 'Diasporà'[1]—in the variant forms of
Ashkenazim and Sephardim and Dönme and crypto-Jews—is not
the only shape in which the Jewish 'fossil' of the extinct Syriac
Civilization survives to-day. Side by side with the conspicuous
majority of Jewry which has held its own by learning to endure the
life of the ghetto, there are other Jews—less numerous and less
notorious but not less interesting to the student of history—who
have held their own by withdrawing into mountains and deserts
where they have converted the primitive inhabitants to Judaism and
have themselves reverted more or less to the primitive way of life.
Such are the Jewish peasantry and artisans in the highlands of the
Yaman, in the south-western corner of Arabia; the Jewish highlanders called the Falasha in Abyssinia; the Jewish highlanders
in the Caucasus; and the Krimchaks of the Crimea—a Turkish-
speaking Jewish community that is believed to be descended from
the Khazar Nomads who were converted to Judaism in the eighth
century of the Christian Era at a time when they were ranging over
the Don-and-Volga section of the Eurasian Steppe.[2]

Similarly, the Nestorian 'fossil' of the Syriac Civilization is not
represented solely by craftsmen in the cities of 'Irāq, or by 'Saint
Thomas's Christians' in Travancore, who are the Nestorian 'Diasporà'. There is also a Nestorian peasantry in the secluded uplands
along the western shore of Lake Urmia, in North-West Persia; and
there are (or were till yesterday) Nestorian 'wild highlanders' in the

---

[1] Διασπορά is an ancient Greek word meaning 'dispersion' which was adopted by the
Jews as a name for that section of Jewry which came to be dispersed abroad among the
Gentiles of the Hellenic World after the intrusion of Hellenism upon the Syriac World
through the destruction of the Achaemenian Empire by the action of Alexander the
Great.

[2] For further information about these Jews in fastnesses, see the Annex to the present
chapter on pp. 402–12, below.

Hakkiari highlands of Kurdistan. It is the same among the Mono-physites. The Armenian 'Diasporà' has its foil in the Armenian peasantry which used to cultivate the uplands round the shores of Lake Van and the Armenian 'wild highlanders' who used to live their own life in the fastness of Sasūn, on the watershed between the headwaters of Tigris and Euphrates, and in the fastnesses of Hajjīn and Zeytūn in the Cilician Taurus. The Coptic 'Diasporà' of Cairo and the Delta has its foil in the Coptic peasantry of the Sa'īd, and also in the Christian 'wild highlanders' of Abyssinia, who are adherents of the Coptic Monophysite Church and whose local prelate ('Abunā') is an appointee of the Coptic Patriarch of Alexan-dria. The Jacobite 'Diasporà' in Syria has its foil in the Jacobite highlanders of the Tūr 'Abdīn: a fastness on the watershed between Tigris and Khabur near the meeting-point of the post-war frontiers between Syria, 'Irāq, and Turkey. Among the Monothelete Le-banese we can make the same dichotomy between the Lebanese emigrant who sets up shop in Egypt or West Africa or America and his brother who stays at home to cultivate the terraced flanks of 'the Mountain'.

In the Shī'ah, we find that the Ismā'īlī 'Diasporà' in India and East Africa likewise has its foil in the Ismā'īlī highlanders of the Jabal Ansarīyah in Northern Syria: an untamed Ismā'īlī community which is descended from a garrison once established in this Syrian fastness by 'the Old Man of the Mountain' in the militant phase of the sect, in the age of the Crusades. The Shī'ah has also thrown off the religious community of the Druses: a 'fossil' which now survives in fastnesses only and is no longer to be found in dispersion at all.[1]

---

[1] 'The Druses were the adherents of an esoteric non-proselytizing religion founded in the eleventh century after Christ by the Fatimid Caliph Al-Hākim bi'amri'llāh, and they took their name from Al-Hākim's apostle Ad-Darazī. In matters of religion the Druse community was divided into a hierarchy of initiation-classes. There was the "spiritual section" (qism-ar-Rūhānī), subdivided into the chiefs (ar-Ru'asā), the intelligent (al-'uqalā), and the excellent (al-ajāwid); and the "corporeal section", subdivided into the lords (al-umarā) and the ignorant (al-juhhāl). Initiation was open to women as well as men. Like many other small and peculiar sects which have managed to survive, the Druses tended to withdraw into mountain fastnesses. At the date when the French and British mandates were introduced there were four main Druse strongholds—one in the Lebanon east of Bayrut, the second in the extreme south-west of the Lebanon, the third on the western slopes of Mount Hermon, and the fourth in the Jabal-ad-Durūz—an isolated mass of rugged and ill-watered mountains which rose abruptly between the fertile corn-lands of the Hawrān to the west and the Hamād steppe to the east. The central shrine of the Druse religion, Khalwat-al-Biyād, lay in the Mount Hermon district, while the chief political focus of the Druse community had formerly lain in the Lebanon; but during the past two centuries—and especially after the migration which followed the French military intervention in 1860 and the organization of the autonomous sanjāq of the Lebanon in 1861–4—the political centre of gravity had shifted to the most remote and militarily strongest of the Druse fastnesses: the Jabal-ad-Durūz (as it came to be called par excellence). During the period under review the mandatory authorities estimated that there were 48,000 Druses in the Jabal (out of a total population of about 60,000), 40,000 in the Lebanon east of Bayrūt, 2,000 in the south-west, 7,000 in the Mount Hermon district, and 7,028 in the British mandated territory.' (Toynbee, A. J.: Survey of International affairs, 1925, vol. i (London 1927, Milford), pp. 406–8.) See, in general, Hitti, P. K.: The Origins of the Druze People and Religion (New York 1928, Columbia University Press).

On the other hand, the antithesis between 'fastness' and 'dispersion' presents itself, once again, among the Greek Orthodox Christian ra'īyeh of the old Ottoman Empire, in the striking contrast between the two sections which took up arms simultaneously in A.D. 1821, at opposite extremities of the Ottoman dominions, with incompatible aspirations and diverse fortunes: the merchants and administrators of the Phanar and the 'wild highlanders' of the Mani.[1]

This brief survey of the dichotomy between 'fossils in dispersion' and 'fossils in fastnesses' yields a uniform result. The 'fossils' preserved in fastnesses, where they have never been subject to penalization, display no symptoms of the êthos which is characteristic of the same 'fossils' where they are found in dispersion in the shape of penalized and specialized minorities. The Jewish peasant in the Yaman has much more in common with his Muslim fellow-worker on the land than with his Jewish co-religionist in the ghetto; the Jewish tribesman in Abyssinia or the Caucasus has much more in common with the Christian or Muslim tribesmen round about who lead the same turbulent and predatory life in the same highlands.

VII. THE GOLDEN MEAN

The Law of Compensations

We have now reached a point at which we can bring our present argument to a head. We have ascertained that civilizations come to birth in environments that are unusually difficult and not unusually easy; and this has led us on to inquire whether or not this is an instance of some social law which may be expressed in the formula: 'the greater the challenge, the greater the stimulus.' We have pursued this inquiry by our customary empirical method. We have made a survey of the responses which are evoked by five types of challenge—the challenges of hard countries, new ground, blows, pressures, and penalization—and in all five fields the upshot of our survey appears to attest the validity of the law which we have formulated above. We have still, however, to determine whether its validity is absolute or limited. If we increase the severity of the challenge *ad infinitum*, do we thereby ensure an infinite intensification of the stimulus and, by the same token, an infinite increase of energy

[1] See the present chapter, pp. 226–7, above, and II. D (vii), p. 262, below. It is one of the curiosities of History that the Mani, which became a fastness of Orthodox Christendom under the Ottoman régime, had previously served as the last fastness of Hellenism. The fact is recorded by the learned East Roman Emperor Constantine Porphyrogenitus (*imperabat* A.D. 912–59):
'The inhabitants of the fastness of Mani are not of the same stock as the [Moreot] Slavs but are descended from the ancient Romans; and down to this day they are locally called Hellenes because once upon a time, long ago, they were idolators who bowed down to idols like the ancient Hellenes. These people were baptized in the reign of Basil of glorious memory [*imperabat* A.D. 866–86], and they have been Christians ever since.' (Constantine Porphyrogenitus: *De Imperio Administrando*, ch. 50.)

in the response which the stimulus evokes when the challenge is responded to successfully? Or do we reach a point beyond which an increase in severity brings in diminishing returns? And if we go beyond this point, do we reach a further point at which the challenge becomes so severe that the possibility of responding to it successfully is eliminated altogether? If the former of these two alternatives proves to be the truth, then we shall be able to lay down the law of 'the greater the challenge the greater the stimulus' without qualification. In the other event, we shall have to enter the *caveat* that some challenges may be excessive, and we shall then have to qualify the law of 'the greater the challenge the greater the stimulus' by formulating an overriding law to the effect that 'the most stimulating challenge is to be found in a mean between a deficiency of severity and an excess of it'.

Where does the ultimate truth lie? At first thoughts, we may incline to the view that 'the greater the challenge the greater the stimulus' is a law which knows no limits to its validity. We have not stumbled upon any palpable limits at any point in our empirical survey so far; and there are several celebrated extreme cases of the operation of the law which we have hitherto held in reserve.

We have not yet cited the example of Venice—a city built on piles driven into the barren mud-banks of a salt lagoon which has surpassed in wealth and power and glory all the cities built on terra firma in the fertile plains of the Po and the Adige. Nor have we cited the example of Holland—a country which has actually been salvaged from the sea and which has to be protected in perpetuity by dykes against submergence under the encircling waters that stand high above the level of the land. Yet Holland has distinguished herself in history far above any parcel of ground of equal area in all the rest of the great North European plain which stretches away— safe above sea-level—from the eastern margin of the Polders to the western foot-hills of the Urals.

Holland is assuredly the original, 'in real life', of that imaginary land which Goethe's Faust redeems from the waters of the Baltic when he is working out the redemption of his own soul from the toils of Mephistopheles. In this land, as Faust describes his work,

> Eröffn' ich Räume vielen Millionen,
> Nicht sicher zwar, doch tätig-frei zu wohnen;
> Grün das Gefilde, fruchtbar; Mensch und Herde
> Sogleich behaglich auf der neusten Erde,
> Gleich angesiedelt an des Hügels Kraft,
> Den aufgewälzt kühn-emsige Völkerschaft;
> Im inneren hier ein paradiesisch Land—
> Da rase draussen Flut bis auf zum Rand,

Und wie sie nascht, gewaltsam einzuschiessen,
Gemeindrang eilt, die Lücke zu verschliessen.
Ja! diesem Sinne bin ich ganz ergeben,
Das ist der Weisheit letzter Schluss:
Nur der verdient sich Freiheit wie das Leben,
Der täglich sie erobern muss.[1]

What challenge could be more extreme than the challenge presented by the sea to Holland and to Venice? What more extreme, again, than the challenge presented by the Alps to Switzerland? And what responses could be more magnificent than those which Holland, Venice, and Switzerland have made? The three hardest pieces of country in Western Europe have stimulated their inhabitants to attain the highest levels of social achievement that have yet been attained by any of the peoples of Western Christendom.

A less well-known but not less impressive example of a heroic response to an extreme challenge from Physical Nature is offered by a survey of the places which were the historical nuclei of Modern Greece. One political nucleus was the Phanar: a remote corner of Stamboul which the Ottoman Pādishāh had assigned to the Greeks as a kind of Christian ghetto. The Phanariots responded by becoming adepts in the Western art of diplomacy.[2] One cultural and economic nucleus was Ayvalyq: a rocky peninsula on the Anatolian coast which seemed so barren that the Ottoman Pādishāh was content to grant his Greek subjects an exclusive right of occupancy. The Greek settlers made the barren rock bear olives and imported Western culture into their commonwealth as the return-cargo for their exports of olive-oil.[3] Another economic nucleus was Ambelakia: a village perched high on the flank of Mount Ossa, overlooking the defile of Tempe, which made a livelihood by spinning and dyeing cotton for the Western market.[4] Another was the Macedonian village of Shátishta which stands marooned among the stony hills that flank the upper valley of the Haliacmon over against Pindus. In the eighteenth century, after the Danubian Hapsburg Monarchy, in its counter-offensive against the Ottoman Power, had pushed its south-eastern outposts deep into the Balkan Peninsula, the Greeks of Shátishta made a livelihood by organizing an overland caravan-traffic for exchanging the dyed cotton goods of Ambelakia and other products of the Ottoman Empire for the products of the

---

[1] Goethe: *Faust*, ll. 11563-76. The last two lines here quoted have been quoted already in vol. i, p. 277 and in the present volume, p. 17, above.
[2] See II. D (vi), pp. 222-5, above.
[3] See II. D (ii), footnote on p. 40, above.
[4] See the interesting account of Ambelakia which is given by Clarke, E. D.: *Travels*, Part II, section iii, ch. 9, pp. 285 sqq. (London 1816, Cadell and Davies.) Dr. Clarke visited Ambelakia on the 23rd-24th December, 1801. The red dye used by the Ambelakiots was a local product obtained from the Valona oak.

West. The commercial houses of this out-of-the-way Macedonian village had their branches in Budapest and Vienna and Leipzig and Dresden.[1] As for the maritime nuclei, Hydhra and Petses and Psarà and Kasos are uncultivable limestone islands; Trikéri is a rocky peninsula; Galaxídhi is a tiny harbour on the least inviting stretch of the coastline of the Gulf of Itéa. Yet these six maritime communities, between them, built up a thriving Greek merchant marine; and when their seamen diverted their energies from trading to fighting at the outbreak of the Greek War of Independence, their light craft swept the Ottoman Navy off the seas as effectively as the light craft of Elizabethan England dealt with the Spanish Armada. As for the places which distinguished themselves during the War of Independence in the fighting on land, the Mani, whose warriors struck the first blow,[2] is a peninsula which is almost entirely occupied by a lofty mountain-range and is almost entirely destitute of both soil and water. The soil is so meagre that it will grow neither cereals nor vines nor even olives, but only prickly pears. The water is so scarce that there are only three springs in the whole country, which has to depend for the rest of its supply upon rain-water collected in cisterns.[3] Similarly Suli, which played its part in a preliminary duel with 'Alī of Yánnina, is ensconced in the wildest and barrenest highlands of Epirus, while Mesolonghi, which is celebrated for the siege in which Byron died, is a fishing-village on a mud-bank in a lagoon: an embryonic Greek counterpart of Venice.

Venice and Holland and Switzerland, Mesolonghi and Mani and Hydhra: do they not all testify with one accord that our law of 'the greater the challenge the greater the response' holds good absolutely, without limitation? At first thoughts, the answer to this question appears to be plainly in the affirmative; yet certain cautionary second thoughts are suggested by a closer comparative study of these particularly telling illustrations which we have just assembled.

It is quite true that in all these places the challenges to which the inhabitants have responded so magnificently have been severe to an extreme degree; but it is also a fact that these superlative challenges have one feature in common which mitigates their severity considerably. Extreme though they are in degree, they are limited in range to one only out of the two realms which together constitute the total environment of any human society. These challenges are,

---

[1] When the writer of this Study visited Shátishta in the summer of 1921, he was shown portraits of ancestors—all dressed up in wigs and powder and patches and crinolines—which had been painted during their residence in the commercial centres of the West and had been brought home to Shátishta to be preserved as memorials.

[2] See II. D (vi), pp. 226–7 and 259, above.

[3] The writer tested the rigours of the Mani for himself in the spring of 1912, when he walked down to the tip of the peninsula on his own feet and returned, *hors de combat*, on mule-back.

all alike, challenges in the realm of the physical environment, and in that realm only. Before, therefore, we can properly assess the severity of the total challenge with which the inhabitants of these places have been presented by their environment as a whole, we have to examine the human environment as well, and to ascertain what challenge, if any, has been presented here. As soon, however, as we follow this line of inquiry up, we observe that in all these places the exceptional severity of the challenge from the local physical environment has carried with it an exceptional immunity from certain specific, and possibly not less formidable, challenges from the human environment which have actually been presented to the inhabitants of the regions round about. The very barrenness or inaccessibility, in which the exceptional severity of the physical challenge has consisted, has served as a shield and buckler against those human challenges inasmuch as these physical drawbacks have deterred or frustrated certain potential human aggressors.

This secondary and compensatory effect of the physical challenge is no mere matter of speculation. It is manifest in the histories of all three places in Western Europe and thirteen places in Greece.

For example, the superlative physical challenges from the sea which have been presented to Venice and Holland have not only administered to them a physical stimulus which their neighbours have lacked, but have incidentally served to shield them from a human ordeal to which their neighbours have been exposed. Venice on her mud-banks, insulated from the continent by her lagoons, was exempt from foreign military occupation for little short of a thousand years: from the day when the Franks evacuated her in A.D. 810 to the day when the French took possession of her in A.D. 1797. Holland, likewise, within her girdle of canals, was saved from foreign military occupation for the best part of two centuries—from her armistice with Spain in A.D. 1609 until she was overrun by the French revolutionary armies in 1794–5.[1] As a Dutch statesman once remarked in a famous conversation with a king of Prussia, these Dutch canals were comfortably deeper than the height of a Pomeranian grenadier; and they could be made to flood the country far and wide at a few hours' notice.[2] What a contrast to the histories of Lombardy and Flanders—the respective neighbours of Venice and Holland on terra firma—which notoriously have been the two habitual battle-fields of Europe. It will be seen that, in Dutch and Venetian history, the sea has played a dual role—the sheltering role

[1] The stimulus derived by the Dutch from their responses to human challenges represented by interludes of Spanish, French, and German domination is, of course, a factor in Dutch history which has to be kept distinct from the divers effects of the physical environment with which we are concerned here.

[2] When the French invaded Holland in 1794–5, 'General Winter', who was to defeat them in Russia eighteen years later, was fighting on their side. Holland's girdle of protecting waters was frozen hard, and the Dutch fleet itself, fast bound in the ice, was captured by the French cavalry—an incident that is perhaps unique in naval and military history.

of a guardian angel as well as the stimulating role of a Satan or a Mephistopheles—and so it has been in Swiss history with the Alps. The mountains have not only stimulated the Swiss to earn by dairy-farming and watch-making and other ingenuities the livelihood which Alpine agriculture could not afford them. The Alps have also served the Swiss in a simpler and more direct way by helping to drive out and keep out the Hapsburgs and the Burgundians and a whole series of human aggressors.

The thirteen nuclei of Modern Greece which we have passed in review reveal the same phenomenon of compensation in the sphere of the human environment for a challenge in the sphere of Physical Nature. In all these cases, the physical challenges of remoteness and stoniness and waterlessness and mountainousness were un-questionably stimulating in themselves, but they also had a protec-tive value in the human sphere which was of first-rate historical importance.

It is a well-known social law that when and where the Govern-ment is incompetent or corrupt or high-handed or malevolent, or is vicious in all these ways, or in several of them, at once, the subject's chance of prosperity depends on his escaping the Government's notice or failing to excite the Government's cupidity. In these adverse social circumstances, the normal values of the physical en-vironment are inverted. When the Government is immoderately rapacious in 'taking up that' which it 'laid not down and reaping that' which it 'did not sow',[1] the fertile field actually yields less sustenance to the cultivator than some patch of stony ground which is beneath the notice of the tax-farmer; and a situation on the brink of a fine harbour or on the route of the king's highway is actually less remunerative to the merchant and the craftsman than a fastness in the hills where he is out of sight and reach of the king's armies and officials and couriers, who make their way by commandeering food and lodging and ships and carts and horses and coolies from the local inhabitants of the harbourside and the roadside. Such circumstances came to prevail in the Ottoman Empire during the two centuries and a half that elapsed between the death of Sultan Suleymān the Magnificent in A.D. 1565 and the outbreak of the Greek War of Independence in A.D. 1821; and the sites of the places which have been the historical nuclei of Modern Greece are all in conformity with the social law which we have just formulated.

Why did the Pādishāh leave the Phanar to the Greek Orthodox Christian inhabitants of Constantinople when he expelled them from all the rest of Stamboul? Why did he grant the Albanian Orthodox Christian colonists of Hydra the privileges of complete

[1] Luke xix. 22.

local self-government and almost complete immunity from Imperial taxation? Why did he confer on the Greek colonists of Ayvalyq, in addition to the privilege of local self-government, the even more remarkable and precious concession that no Muslim should retain the right of residence within their parochial boundaries? Simply because he regarded the Phanar as an uninhabitable hole in a corner, and Hydhra and Ayvalyq as uncultivable wastes. He was not taking the children's bread and casting it to dogs. He was merely allowing the Christian dogs to eat of the crumbs which had fallen from their Muslim masters' table.[1] Why, again, were the Ambelakiots allowed to spin and dye and make money unmolested? Because Ambelakia was perched on the flank of Ossa at a safe altitude, or, in other words, at such a height that when the village caught the Ottoman extortioner's eye as he rode, far below, through the vale of Tempe, his laziness got the better of his greed, with the consequence that he rode on sullenly to plunder some poorer village within easier reach.[2] And why were the Christian Greeks of Shátishta allowed to make fortunes out of their caravan-traffic? Because their Muslim Greek neighbours had done them a double service when they drove them out of the fertile valley-bottom into the barren uplands. They had not only compelled them—at a profitable moment—to turn their attention to commerce instead of agriculture, but they had also jostled them into a cranny in the hills where they could accumulate wealth unnoticed. Why, lastly, did the Maniots and the Suliots retain their autonomy and their arms and their warlike spirit? Because it had not been worth the Pādishāh's while to follow them up into their barren highland fastnesses, as it was eminently worth his while to take and hold the orangegroves of Sparta and the currant-plantations of Elis and the masticvillages of Chios and the harbours of Patras and Nauplia and the dome of Aya Sofia and the gardens of the Seraglio. It is evident that the sites of our thirteen nuclei of Modern Greece cannot be

[1] Matthew xv. 26–7.

[2] 'This Empire, as vast and large as it is, is yet dispeopled, the villages abandoned, and whole provinces as pleasant and fruitfull as Tempe or Thessaly uncultivate and turned into a desart or wilderness—all which desolation and ruine proceeds from the tyranny and rapine of the *Beglerbegs* and *Pashaws*; who either in their journies to the possession of their Government, or return from thence, expose the poor inhabitants to violence and injury of their attendants, as if they had entred the confines of an enemy or the dominions of a conquered people. In like manner, the insolence of the horse and foot is unsupportable; for, in their marches from one countrey to another, parties of 20 or 30 are permitted to make excursions into divers parts of their own dominions, where they not onely live upon free quarter but extort money and cloaths from the poor vassals, taking their children to sell for slaves, . . . so that, rather than be exposed to such misery, and licence of the soldiery, the poor people choose to abandon their dwellings and wander into other cities, or seek for refuge in the mountains or woods of the countrey.' (Rycaut, Sir Paul: *The Present State of the Ottoman Empire* (London 1668, Starkey and Brome), p. 170.)

For the break-down of the Ottoman system, to which these evils were due, see Part III. A, vol. iii, pp. 44–50, below.

accounted for completely until the exceptional local mildness of the human environment as well as the exceptional local rigour of the physical environment is taken into the reckoning.

We have evidently to reckon with the same combination of factors in interpreting the contrast, which we have noticed in a previous passage,[1] between the respective achievements of two modern communities in Syria—the Lebanese and the Nusayrīs—who have been fellow-sufferers with the modern Greeks from the misgovernment of the Ottoman Empire in its period of decline. In seeking to account for the prowess of the Lebanese, we must take into account the political seclusion as well as the physical rigour of their forbidding mountain fastness. And conversely, in seeking to account for the stagnation of their neighbours the Nusayrīs, we must bear in mind the political disadvantages which the relative openness and agreeableness of the Jabal Ansarīyah has entailed.

'Leurs montagnes sont communément moins escarpées que celles du Liban; elles sont en conséquence plus propres à la culture; mais aussi elles sont plus ouvertes aux Turks; et c'est par cette raison, sans doute, qu'avec une plus grande fécondité en grain, en tabac à fumer, en vignes et en olives, elles sont cependant moins peuplées que celles de leurs voisins les Maronites et les Druzes.'[2]

Having caught this glimpse of 'compensations' in the human environment in the course of surveying certain superlative challenges from the physical environment which we had not examined before, let us now glance once again at some of those other illustrations of Challenge-and-Response which we have passed in review in earlier chapters of the present Part. When we thus extend our horizon, we shall find evidence of a 'compensatory' interaction between the physical and the human environments which is operative in both directions. There are not only challenges from the physical environment but also challenges from the human environment which have demonstrably tempered their own severity by producing an incidental compensatory effect in the complementary field. Let us first complete our survey of compensations accruing in the human sphere from challenges encountered in the physical, and then go on to consider the instances in which the compensation is physical and the challenge human.

The severity of a challenge in the physical sphere may be compensated in the human sphere in several alternative ways, as is already apparent from the illustrations which we have just been examining. A site which presents unusual physical difficulties to

---

[1] In II. D (ii), on pp. 55-7, above.
[2] Volney, C. F.: *Voyage en Syrie et en Égypte pendant les Années 1783, 1784 et 1785*, 2nd ed. (Paris 1787, Desenne et Volland, 2 vols.), vol. ii, pp. 7-8.

its occupants may secure them at the same time an unusual freedom
from human molestation because the site is either unattractive or
inaccessible to outsiders or because it is forbidding in both senses
at once.

We have seen that, in Orthodox Christendom in the latter days
of the Ottoman Empire, the Greek 'squatters' in the Phanar and in
Ayvalyq were compensated for an 'ineligible location' and for a
stony soil by the very fact that these physical blemishes made both
sites unattractive to the 'Osmanlis. Similarly, in Ancient Greece, at
the dawn of Hellenic history, the stoniness of Attica not only stimulated the Athenians by its challenge[1] but also brought them compensation by proving unattractive to the immigrant 'Dorians'. In
Ancient Syria, likewise, at the dawn of Syriac history, the Israelite
'squatters' were compensated as well as stimulated by the stoniness
of the Hill Country of Ephraim—a physical blemish thanks to
which these highlands overlooking the highway between Egypt and
Shinar had been preserved as an untenanted no-man's-land from
time immemorial until the Israelitish infiltration.[2] Thus, too, in
the Hindu World, when it was being visited by the calamity of
Muslim invasion, the deserts and forests of Rājputāna not only
stimulated those Hindus who responded to their physical challenge,
but also brought them compensation by offering little or no attraction to the Muslim invaders. The Muslims, descending upon India
from the Iranian Plateau, did not rest till they had conquered the
whole of the Indus Valley down to the coast of the Indian Ocean
and the whole of the Ganges Valley down to the coast of the Bay of
Bengal; but they were content to leave the Rājputs their independence in the 'bad lands' that occupied the angle between the two
river-systems, notwithstanding the fact that Rājputāna skirts the
banks of the Sutlej and the Jumna as closely as the Hill Country of
Ephraim overhangs the lowlands of Philistia and the Vale of Esdraelon. If we extend our survey to the Andean World, we may also
conjecture that the builders of Tiahuanaco were compensated for
the bleakness of the upland basin of Lake Titicaca[3] by immunity
from molestation on the part of their powerful neighbours in the
maritime plain.

In a later age, after the Titicaca Basin had been broken in by the
efforts of the ancient pioneers, its latter-day inhabitants, the Collas,
were compensated for the lesser effort of keeping the bleak uplands
under cultivation by being shielded against molestation from another
quarter. The domineering snow-peaks, which sent down chilly
winds and raging blizzards to blight their crops, also served the

---

[1] See II. D (ii), pp. 37–42, above.   [2] See II. D (ii), pp. 52–5, above.
[3] See II. C (ii) (b) 2, vol. i, p. 322, and II. D (v), in the present volume, p.208, above.

Collas as a rampart against the warlike savages of the tropical Amazonian forest, who were effectively kept at a distance by their inability to cross the snow-line.[1] These Amazonian savages would have found the Collao attractive enough if the mountains had not rendered it inaccessible to them; and thus, from the Collas' standpoint, the mountains had a twofold aspect. Though physically oppressive they were humanly protective. In fact, the Andean snows have played here the same dual role as the high altitudes of Shátishta and Ambelakia or the depression of Holland below the level of the sea. In each of these instances, a physical blemish has not only acted as a stimulus but has also brought its own compensation with it in the human sphere by conferring the boon of inaccessibility.

We may observe that a similar compensation is apt to be conferred by the physical ordeal of transmarine migration. The emigrants from the zone of post-glacial desiccation in North Africa who became the fathers of the Minoan Civilization in Crete by responding to the challenge of the sea[2] were compensated in the human sphere for the physical perils of navigation. We may read the same tale in the history of England. In the Völkerwanderung which accompanied the break-up of the Roman Empire, those continental North-European barbarians who took to the sea in order to invade the Roman island of Britain chose a harder path than their comrades who drifted into the Roman provinces on the mainland. On the other hand, throughout the whole course of Western history, from the first emergence of our Western Civilization until the recent inventions of the submarine and the aeroplane, the descendants of the seafaring Jutes and Angles have been enjoying the compensation that has accrued from their forefathers' ordeal. They have been reaping the profits of an insularity which has been the perpetual envy of their continental neighbours—the descendants of the land-loping Saxons and Franks and Sueves and Lombards.

In the modern age of Western history, the same ordeal of migration across the sea has brought a similar compensation to all those victims of religious persecution in Europe who have found freedom of worship in the New World.

> Where the remote Bermudas ride
> In the ocean's bosom unespied,
> From a small boat that row'd along,
> The listening winds received this song:
>   'What should we do but sing His praise
> That led us through the watery maze
> Unto an isle so long unknown
> And yet far kinder than our own?

---

[1] See II. D (v), p. 208, above.   [2] See II. C (ii) (b) 2, vol. i, pp. 323–30, above.

Where He the huge sea-monsters wracks,
That lift the deep upon their backs,
He lands us on a grassy stage,
Safe from the storm's and prelate's rage;

.   .   .   .   .

And in these rocks for us did frame
A temple where to sound His name.
Oh! Let our voice His praise exalt
Till it arrive at Heaven's vault,
Which thence (perhaps) rebounding may
Echo beyond the Mexique bay!'
   Thus sung they in the English boat
A holy and a cheerful note;
And all the way, to guide their chime,
With falling oars they kept the time.

The English seafarers in whose mouth this song of thanksgiving
has been placed by a seventeenth-century poet were Presbyterian
emigrants who had been rewarded for braving the perils of the
Atlantic by being led to an earthly paradise in the Antilles. Their
compensation was, indeed, in both kinds; and the physical delights
of a tropical island—which are depicted by Andrew Marvell in the
loveliest lines of his poem[1]—had the same enervating effect upon
these English navigators that we have seen them have upon Polynesian navigators on the other side of the planet.[2] To-day the song
sounds only faintly off the coast of the Bermudas; yet the singers'
pious hope has been fulfilled; for their voice has indeed rebounded
from 'Heaven's vault' till it echoes now 'beyond the Mexique bay'
in stentorian reverberations. The song of these English Presbyterian seafarers who found freedom of worship in an earthly paradise
in the Bermudas has become the song of their kinsmen and co-
religionists who have likewise crossed the Atlantic to find the same
religious freedom in a prosaic eldorado on the North American
Continent. And voices from every quarter of the overseas world
are singing in chorus: the voice of French Huguenots who have
found freedom of worship in South Africa, and the voice of Irish
Catholics who have found it in Australia and in Spanish America as
well as in the United States.

We still have to glance at certain instances in which a site that
presents unusual physical difficulties to its occupants is not only
inaccessible to outsiders but is unattractive to them as well. Where
the physical features of a site thus make it doubly forbidding, the
compensation in the human sphere accrues in double measure.
This has been the good fortune of Venice and of Hydhra: a

---

[1] These lines have been omitted in the quotation above.
[2] See II. D (i), pp. 13–15, above.

mud-bank and a rock-reef which have both been protected from molestation by the twin safeguards of insularity and barrenness. The same double compensation has accrued to the inhabitants of other barren islands in the histories of other societies besides Western and Orthodox Christendom: to the Icelanders, for example, in Scandinavian history[1] and to the Tyrians and Aradians in Syriac history[2] and to the Aeginetans in Hellenic history[3] and to the first human occupants of the Cyclades, who share with the Eteocretans the honour of being the fathers of the Minoan Civilization.[4]

The fathers of all the other 'unrelated' civilizations may likewise have enjoyed this double protection against their neighbours in compensation for the severity of the physical challenges to which they have courageously responded. At least, we may conjecture that when the fathers of the Egyptiac and Sumeric and Sinic civilizations had plunged into those jungle-swamps which they transformed in course of time into fields and cities, they did not find themselves compelled, like the Jews when they were rebuilding the walls of Jerusalem, to do their work with one hand while they held a weapon in the other.[5] It seems more probable that these primeval Egyptiac and Sumeric and Sinic pioneers, unlike Nehemiah's Jewish contemporaries, were left in peace by their fellow men to wage and win their titanic war against Physical Nature. They may have had to suffer from human molestation at an earlier stage, when they were still living in the open. Some such human pressure—accentuated, in the Egyptiac and the Sumeric case, by the gradual desiccation of the Afrasian Steppe in the post-glacial age—may even have been the proximate cause of their taking their momentous plunge into a howling wilderness which no human being had ever attempted to penetrate before them. When once, however, they had descended into their terrestrial hell, we may suppose that their former neighbours were both unable and unwilling to follow in pursuit of them. The fathers of the Mayan Civilization may have secured a similar immunity from molestation by plunging into the tropical forest, and the fathers of the Andean Civilization by settling on the arid coastal plain and mounting on to the bleak plateau in its hinterland.

Again, those 'fossil' remnants of extinct civilizations that have survived in fastnesses[6] all owe their preservation to the same double safeguard. A combination of unattractiveness with inaccessibility is the common characteristic of the Jewish fastnesses in the Caucasus and in the Yaman, the Jewish and Monophysite fastnesses in Abyssinia, the Nestorian fastness in Hakkiari, and the Monothelete fastness in

---

[1] See II. D (iii), pp. 86–100, above.   [2] See II. D (ii), pp. 51–2, above.
[3] See II. D (ii), pp. 48–9, above.   [4] See II. C (ii) (b) 2, vol. i, pp. 328–30, above.
[5] See the Book of Nehemiah, ch. iv.
[6] See II. D (vi), pp. 256–9, above, with the Annex.

the Lebanon. We have already taken note of two instances of this type in glancing at the Greek Orthodox fastnesses of the Mani and Suli in the old Ottoman Empire. It was a combination of unattractiveness with inaccessibility that saved both Suli and the Mani from ever feeling the full weight of the Ottoman oppression which crushed the life out of the Greek ra'īyeh in the neighbouring vales of Yánnina and Sparta. Hence the Suliots and the Maniots—protected as well as stimulated by the physical hardness of their highland strongholds—were able to play active and decisive parts in the creation of Modern Greece. The same twofold compensation in the human sphere has accrued to the New Englanders from the physical hardness of Town Hill, Connecticut, and to the Mormons from the diverse but not less formidable physical hardness of Utah. It is not only because these new-found fastnesses in the North American wilderness have been stimulating to their occupants, but also because they have been at the same time unattractive and inaccessible to outsiders, that they have served their occupants so well and have assisted them to make the marks which they have succeeded in making on our Western history.

Let us now examine the inverse case in which the challenge is delivered in the human sphere while the compensation accrues in the physical.

The experience of the 'fossils in fastnesses', which we have been examining just above, is precisely inverted in the experience of the 'fossils in dispersion'. The Jews, for example, who survive in the fastnesses of the Caucasus and Abyssinia have responded successfully to a challenge from the physical environment and have been compensated by immunity from penalization at Gentile hands. These Jewish 'wild highlanders' are as free, and as upstanding, as their Monophysite and Muslim counterparts. Inversely, the Jews of the 'Diasporà' have successfully responded to the human challenge of religious penalization and have been compensated for their Babylonish captivity among the Gentiles by the presence of those flesh pots to which their ancestors used to look back with such regret after Moses had led them forth into the wilderness out of the fat land of Egypt.[1] The exercise of holding their own in a hostile human environment has not only stimulated the Jews of the Dispersion to activity. It has also enabled them, in diverse Gentile societies in successive ages, to keep their footing in the market-place and their seat in the counting-house and to take their tribute from the golden stream of commerce and finance, instead of having to put up with the poverty-stricken life of the wilderness that has been led by their Abyssinian and Caucasian co-religionists.

[1] See II. D (i), pp. 24–5, above.

There is a somewhat similar relation between the diverse experiences through which the fathers of the 'unrelated' and the 'related' civilizations have passed. The fathers of the 'unrelated' civilizations, like the 'fossils in fastnesses', have responded to a physical challenge and have been compensated by immunity from human molestation. Inversely, the fathers of the 'related' civilizations, like the 'fossils in dispersion', have been compensated in physical values for responding to a human challenge. The dynamic act by which a 'related' civilization is generated is the secession of a proletariat from a dominant minority; and this is a human, not a physical, ordeal. The insurgent proletariat which initiates a new civilization by passing through this ordeal successfully is compensated by inheriting a physical habitat, ready made, from its predecessors instead of finding itself compelled to create a new physical habitat for itself out of the virgin wilderness; and this compensation is not in human currency but in physical. It takes the form of a reprieve from physical hardship in place of that reprieve from human molestation which is granted to the pioneer who initiates a new civilization by wrestling with Physical Nature in the virgin wilderness.

This same phenomenon of physical compensation for successful response to a human challenge may be illustrated by other examples. We have just observed that the 'fossils in dispersion' are compensated for their endurance in holding their ground in a hostile religious environment by the golden opportunities for economic gain which this ground, so hardly held, affords them. There is an analogy to this in the experience of those emigrants from lean countries to fat countries who find their ordeal, not in holding their ground in spite of persecution, but in changing their ground under pressure of poverty.[1] The resulting situation is substantially the same. The Hadramī in Java, the Scotsman in England, and the French-Canadian in the United States are all responding, like the Jew in the Gentile World, to the challenge of an alien human environment; and, like the Jewish 'Diasporà' again, they are being compensated for their endurance of this human ordeal by 'reaping where' they have 'not sown', inasmuch as they are participating in the material prosperity which has been built up by the work of other men's hands in a country which is not the immigrants' home.

We can see our 'law of compensation' likewise at work in certain otherwise very diverse historical situations.

For example, the militant pioneers who extended the bounds of the Far Eastern Civilization in Japan by carrying on a frontier-warfare against the indigenous barbarian inhabitants of the Kwanto,[2]

---

[1] See II. D (vi), pp. 212–13, above.   [2] See II. D (v), pp. 158–9, above.

were compensated in the economic field for their military exertions. Their strenuous life in the marches not only gave them a stimulus which was conspicuously lacking in the interior at the court of 'the Cloistered Emperors' in Yamato; it also brought them a direct material reward; for the soil of the Kwanto, where they were carving out new fiefs for themselves at the barbarians' expense, was considerably more productive than the soil of Yamato: the region which was the original home of the Far Eastern Civilization in Japan and in which the Japanese Imperial patrimony was situate. In weighing the causes of the momentous revolution in which the preponderance passed from Yamato to the Kwanto in the course of the twelfth century of the Christian Era, we must give due weight to this economic factor. We must recognize that the wardens of the marches did not owe their triumph solely to the superiority in *moral* which their military training had given them over their unwarlike peers at the Court. They also owed it in part to the superiority in wealth which had accrued to them incidentally as their compensation in the economic field for their exertions in the military field.

The 'law of compensation' has also to be reckoned with in accounting for the rise of the cities of Paris and London in and after the ninth century of the Christian Era. In an earlier passage of this Part,[1] we have noticed the stimulus which was administered to these two cities of Western Christendom by pressure from Scandinavia. We have now to observe that the rivers which Paris and London respectively commanded had a twofold social function. They served as waterways not only for Viking raids but for international commerce; and the commanding situations of the two cities, athwart the courses of the Seine and the Thames, had more than one effect upon their civic fortunes. Standing where they stood, London and Paris were marked out, as we have already observed, to bear the brunt of the sea-raiders' attacks upon England and France; but, by the same token, they were also marked out to draw to themselves the lion's share of the two kingdoms' waterborne commerce. In other words, the ordeals of ninth-century London and Paris carried with them their own prospective compensation; and in this respect the history of the Londoners and the Parisians is not incomparable to the history of the Jews dispersed abroad among the Gentiles. In both cases, we have the spectacle of a community holding its ground tenaciously against intense hostile pressure; and in both cases, again, we find that it is rewarded doubly for its tenacity. It not only gains a moral stimulus from its act of resistance, but it also obtains a material compensation for its moral ordeal in virtue of the fact that the position from which it

[1] See II. D (v), pp. 198–9, above, and also the Annex to that chapter on pp. 400–1, below.

refuses to be driven out—by persecution or by force of arms, as the case may be—is a position of unique commercial profitableness.

The existence of this 'law of compensation' and the wide range of its operation, of which we have now perhaps satisfied ourselves, may give us warning not to press to extremes our other law of 'the greater the challenge the greater the stimulus'. Before we allow ourselves to be convinced, on evidence, that this other law holds good without limitations, we must make sure that our evidence will stand the test of the supplementary 'law of compensation' which has now come to light. When we are confronted with a triumphant response to some challenge from the environment which is apparently superlative in its severity, we must not accept this evidence at its face value until we have made sure that the total environment has been taken into consideration. We must always bear in mind that the environment is twofold—a physical environment and a human—and that a challenge which is delivered in either one of these two realms and which appears superlatively severe at first sight, may prove on closer inspection to be tempered and attenuated by some compensation which it carries with it in the complementary realm, whichever of the two that may be. This is what we actually found when we examined the most extreme examples of Challenge-and-Response in the physical realm which we could call to mind: the examples of Venice and Holland and Switzerland and the thirteen historical nuclei of Modern Greece. Thereafter, when we extended our horizon, we again found our 'law of compensation' at work in the most extreme example of Challenge-and-Response in the human realm that can well be imagined: the example of the Jewish 'Diasporà'. We have not, however, come across any example of a triumphant response to a challenge which has presented itself with uniformly superlative severity in the physical and in the human realm simultaneously. This *argumentum ex silentio* does not, of course, go very far; but it goes far enough to suggest a doubt as to whether our law of 'the greater the challenge the greater the response' does retain its validity when the challenge is at once extreme in degree and relentless in presenting itself over the whole range of the total environment, instead of unobtrusively offering compensation in one of the two realms for the conspicuous severity of its incidence in the other.

How is a challenge proved excessive?

Are we, then, to conclude that the validity of this law is not absolute but limited? We can hardly draw that conclusion from the negative fact that no instance of a triumphant response to an unmitigatedly superlative challenge has actually come to our notice.

If we are to establish a convincing proof, it must be founded on positive evidence. We must be able to present unequivocal instances in which a challenge has proved to be excessive; and the excessiveness of a challenge will not be conclusively demonstrated by the mere fact that a particular party has failed to respond to the challenge in question on a particular occasion.

This will prove nothing in itself, because almost every challenge that has eventually evoked a victorious response turns out, on inquiry, to have baffled or broken one respondent after another before the moment when, at the hundredth or perhaps the thousandth summons, the victor has entered the lists at last. This is the notorious 'prodigality of Nature'; and, in the field of the histories of civilizations, a host of examples spring to mind.

For instance, the physical challenge of the North European forest effectually baffled Primitive Man. Unequipped, as he was, with implements for felling the forest trees, and ignorant of how to turn the rich underlying soil to account by cultivation, even if he had been capable of clearing it of its sylvan encumbrance, Primitive Man in Northern Europe simply avoided the forest and squatted on sand-dunes and chalk-downs which his successors afterwards scornfully rejected as 'bad lands' when the forest was falling at last under the blows of their axes. For Primitive Man, the challenge of the temperate forest was actually more formidable than the challenge of the frozen Tundras; and in North America his line of least resistance eventually led him Pole-ward beyond the forest's northern fringe to find his destiny in creating the Eskimo Civilization[1] in response to the challenge of the Arctic Circle. Yet Primitive Man's experience does not prove that the challenge of the North European forest was excessive in the sense of being altogether beyond human power of effective response; for where Primitive Man was baffled, the barbarians who followed at his heels were able to make some impression with the aid of tools and technique acquired from the rising civilizations with which they were in touch, until, in the fullness of time, the pioneers of two latter-day civilizations came and saw and conquered. Before the close of the fourteenth century of the Christian Era, the Northern forest had been effectively taken in hand and mastered—by Western Christian pioneers in Europe and by Orthodox Christian pioneers in Russia—all the way from the coast of the Atlantic to the foot-hills of the Urals.

Some fifteen centuries before that, in the second century B.C., the southern vanguard of the North European forest in the Basin of the Po had been subdued by the Roman pioneers of the Hellenic Civilization after having baffled the Romans' barbarous and primitive

[1] For the arrested civilization of the Esquimaux, see III. A, vol. iii, pp. 4–7, below.

predecessors from time immemorial. The Greek historian Polybius, who visited this country immediately after it had been opened up and been turned to account by Roman enterprise, has put on record his personal observations. He draws a striking contrast between the inefficient and poverty-stricken life of the Romans' Gallic predecessors, whose last survivors were still living this life in the backwoods at the foot of the Alps,[1] and the cheapness and plenty that prevailed in the adjoining districts which the Roman colonists had taken in hand.[2] It could never have occurred to Polybius, with this contrast before his eyes, to imagine that the Padane forest was invincible simply because the miserable remnant of the Gauls survived as a specimen of one community which had failed to respond to the forest's challenge. In Polybius's day, the testimony of the forest-bound Gallic kraals was given the lie by the opposing testimony of a thriving Roman country-side which now held the field, a stone's throw off, on ground which the forest had still been holding victoriously against Mankind a few years before. But suppose that an earlier Greek historian—let us say, a Herodotus—had been able to anticipate Polybius's visit to the Po Basin by some three centuries. He would have arrived on the scene at a moment when the Gallic avalanche had just descended from the Alps and was overwhelming the Etruscan prospectors who had ventured out north of the Apennines. After watching the discouraging spectacle of barbarism evicting the forerunners of civilization from a country which the barbarian was patently incapable of turning to account for himself, our Herodotus might well have returned to Hellas to report that the Padane forest was invincible and that the Etruscans, who had lightly taken up its challenge, had paid the inevitable penalty for their presumption by incurring the Envy of the Gods. The moral of this imaginary story may be expressed in the words of Solon's warning to Croesus: 'Respice finem.'[3] The suggested inevitability of the Etruscans' failure was disproved within three centuries by the Romans' success. It is evident that a challenge is not proved unanswerable by the fact that some attempts to answer it have failed. It has first to be shown that the series of failures has been unbroken from beginning to end of the story.

Polybius's sketch of the Basin of the Po in the latter part of the second century B.C. bears a curious resemblance to the picture of the Basin of the Mississippi at the turn of the eighteenth and nineteenth centuries of the Christian Era which has been drawn for us in detail by a host of modern Western travellers. The contrast

---

[1] Polybius, Bk. II, ch. 17.   [2] Polybius, Bk. II, ch. 15.
[3] The Greek original of the Latin proverb is placed in Solon's mouth by Herodotus (Bk. I, ch. 32).

between the last of the Gauls still starving within reach of plenty and the Roman pioneers who have compelled the primeval forest to yield up its hidden wealth at the summons of their axe and spade has been reproduced on another continent, at an interval of some two thousand years, in the modern contrast between the last of the Redskins and the American pioneers in the primeval forest of Kentucky or Ohio.

The Americans have responded victoriously to a sylvan challenge by which their Red Indian predecessors were baffled.[1] Indeed, they have increased the productivity of the soil and subsoil which they have conquered from the trees to such a degree that to-day, when the territory of the United States is occupied by 120 million people of European origin with a conspicuously higher standard of living than is enjoyed by their kinsmen and contemporaries who have not left their European homes, it is calculated that the present Red Indian population of the United States is not less numerous and possibly more numerous than the Red Indian population of the same territory some three centuries ago, before the first progenitor of the 120 million European intruders ever set foot on this American soil.[2] In other words, practically the whole of the present national income of the United States is derived from wealth that has been extracted direct from Physical Nature by the in-comers, and little or none of it is derived from wealth which has been robbed from the indigenous occupants (as the Inca's gold and silver was robbed from him by the Spanish conquistadores of Peru). On this showing, the present national wealth of the United States gives a fair economic measure of the difference between the ineffectual Red Indian response and the triumphant American response to the physical challenge of the North American forest. The monument

[1] By the seventeenth century of the Christian Era, when the English and French colonists of North America appeared on the scene, the Red Indian occupants of the vast area which is now covered by Canada and the United States had not begun to master the North American forest, though they did not lack an incentive for mastering it since they had already acquired the art of maize cultivation from the adjoining Mexic World. (See II. C (ii) (a) 2, vol. i, p. 265, above.) For the question whether an indigenous civilization, 'affiliated' to the Mexic, would or would not have emerged eventually in North America if the European Civilization of Western Christendom had not intervened, see the footnote on pp. 265–6 in II. C (ii) (a) 2, vol. i, above.

[2] If this calculation is correct, it bears eloquent testimony to the extent of the difference in degree between American and Red Indian economic efficiency, but it does not, of course, justify any retrospective condonation of the treatment which the Red Indians have received at American hands. (See II. C (ii) (a) 1, vol. i, pp. 211–14, above.) A statistical result, however interesting and remarkable, is impotent to undo crimes that have been committed and cruelties that have been suffered in real life. Though the present Red Indian population of the United States may be neither less numerous nor less well off than the Red Indian population of the same territory three centuries ago, the present representatives of the indigenous race are confined to an insignificant fraction of the area over which their predecessors once ranged, and they are descended from only a minority of the tribes which the European intruders found in existence on their arrival. The suffering and the wrong involved in the extermination of the majority of the Red Indian tribes and the alienation of the greater part of the territory over which they used to roam are hard facts which no figures can explain away.

of the American pioneer's victory over the forest is the present aspect
of the United States; and, in face of the forest's ultimate defeat by
Man, which this aspect now proclaims to the World, it is patent that
the different aspect which the same territory wore three centuries
ago, in an age when the North American forest was still dominant
over the local representatives of the Human Race, afforded no valid
evidence at all of the forest's invincibility. An Aztec explorer, visiting the Far North before A.D. 1600, would have been in grievous
error if he had returned home to report that the Northern forest
was invincible after observing the ineffectual efforts of the Algon-
quin and the Iroquois to plant their maize between the serried tree-
stems. For, by A.D. 1600, the formidable conquerors of the North
European forest were already girding up their loins to cross the
North Atlantic and repeat their exploit in a New World.

The story of Man and the Forest is reproduced in the stories of
Man and Mineral Oil and Man and the Air.

Like the forests of Europe and North America, the oil-fields of
Azerbaijan have challenged one human society after another to
master them for human ends before the challenge has eventually
been answered. The Nomads, who are the earliest recorded tenants
of the Azerbaijani Steppe, appear to have made no use whatever of
the mineral wealth which was oozing out and welling up from below
the surface of their cattle-pastures. The Syriac Society, which supplanted the Nomads in Azerbaijan in the early part of the sixth
century B.C., when the Medes overcame the Scyths,[1] was not unaware of the peculiar natural phenomenon which was native to this
remote border province on the outer edge of the Syriac World; yet,
under the Syriac dispensation, the oil of Azerbaijan was harnessed
solely for a religious purpose, without ever being turned to economic
account. A few conspicuous natural gushers were imprisoned in
towers in order that the rising jet might minister to the Zoroastrian
cult of Fire by feeding a perpetual flame at the summit; and even
this ritual use of the mineral only lasted as long as the local preva-
lence of the Zoroastrian religion. When Zoroastrianism gave way to
Islam and the Syriac Civilization was superseded, in due course, by
the 'affiliated' Iranic Civilization, these perpetual flames ceased to
burn and the sole use which Man had so far made of Mineral Oil
became obsolete. Yet the Azerbaijani oil-field was not destined to
elude economic exploitation to the end of Time. The economic
potentialities of this unexploited mineral resource did not escape
the attention of Peter the Great when he passed that way in A.D.
1723 *en route* for the conquest of the Caspian provinces of Persia;[2]

1 See II. D (v), pp. 136–8, above.
2 See Brückner, A.: *Peter der Grosse* (Berlin 1879, Grote), pp. 480 and 518.

and although in this, as in other things, the intuitive genius of this Russian changeling anticipated the laborious discoveries of *Homo Economicus* in the West by the best part of two centuries, Peter's economic reconnaissance of the Azerbaijani oil-field was a true portent of things to come. At the beginning of the nineteenth century of the Christian Era, Baku was conquered again, and this time permanently, by a Russia which still retained the impetus towards economic Westernization that Peter had communicated to her; and, in the course of the same century, Baku Oil became one of the staple commodities of a Western economic system which had come to embrace the whole World and all Mankind. Indeed, at the present day, the mastery of Man over Oil has become so complete that it looks as though he might substitute oil for coal—as he has already once substituted coal for wood—to be his ordinary fuel and standard generator of light and heat and mechanical power. Thus the successive failures of the Nomadic and Syriac and Iranic civilizations to respond to the challenge of the Azerbaijani oil-field were not, after all, good evidence that this challenge was inherently insuperable.

As for the challenge of the Air, the myths of human Icarus and human Phaethon, who fell to destruction when they presumed to imitate the flights of their superhuman sires, convey a profound conviction that the Air—unlike the Forest or the Jungle-Swamp or the Desert or the Sea—is for ever destined to defeat the utmost efforts of human daring and ingenuity. Nor has this conviction of the Air's invincibility been limited to those Hellenic minds which have given it its classic expression in Mythology. It has been taken for granted by all men in all ages; and even in our own Western Society, which has triumphantly conquered the Air in our day, the older generation now alive in this year 1935 has grown up in the old assumption. The writer of this Study well remembers how, when he was a schoolboy, at the turn of the nineteenth and twentieth centuries, the possibility of effective flight by aircraft heavier than air was still a theme for tales of mystery and imagination in the vein of Jules Verne or Edgar Allan Poe.

When we turn from the physical to the human environment, we find the same. A challenge which has defeated one respondent is afterwards proved by a victorious response on the part of some later competitor to be not insuperable.

Let us reconsider, for example, the relation between the Hellenic Society and the North European barbarians. In a previous passage of this Part, we have already examined the effect of the pressure from the barbarians upon the Hellenic World;[1] but the pressure

[1] See II. D (v), pp. 160–6, above.

was reciprocal, and there was a counter-effect of Hellenic pressure upon the barbarians which has a bearing upon our present subject of inquiry. As the Hellenic Civilization radiated deeper and deeper into the continental European hinterland of the Mediterranean, one layer of barbarians after another was confronted with a question of life and death. Was it going to succumb to the impact of this potent alien social force and suffer a disintegration of its own social fabric in order to become raw material for assimilation into the tissues of the Hellenic body social? Or was it going to hold its own and resist assimilation and be enrolled, in virtue of its resistance, in the re-calcitrant external proletariat of the Hellenic Society instead of merging its identity in that of the Hellenic Society itself? This challenge was presented by the Hellenic Civilization successively to the Celts and to the Teutons. In the earlier of these two ordeals, the Celts eventually broke down; but in the second ordeal the Teutons proved that the Hellenic challenge was not insuperable by responding to it victoriously now that their turn had come.

The break-down of the Celts was impressive, because the Celts had had a good start and had taken spectacular advantage of it to begin with. The Celts were given their opportunity by an error of tactics on the part of the Etruscan settlers along the west coast of Italy. These overseas converts to Hellenism were not content with securing their foothold on the Italian coastline nor even with ex-panding inland up to the foot of the Apennines. The Etruscan pioneers rashly crossed the Apennine watershed and scattered far and wide over the Basin of the Po right up to the foot of the Alps.[1] In expanding on this scale, they were vastly overtaxing their strength; and the consequence was as auspicious for the Celts—who happened to be the layer of barbarians immediately affected—as it was disas-trous for the Etruscans themselves. The sudden initial access of Etruscan pressure had stimulated the Celts to react against the aggressors;[2] and now an equally sudden relaxation of the pressure tempted the barbarians to pass over to the offensive. The result was a *furor Celticus* which was sustained for some two centuries.

Before the end of the fifth century B.C., a Celtic avalanche, descending from the Alps, overwhelmed the weak Etruscan outposts in the Po Basin. In the early decades of the fourth century, the invigorated barbarians were sweeping across the Apennines and sacking the walled cities of Italy, including Rome itself,[3] and were

[1] See II. D (iii), pp. 85–6, and the present chapter, p. 276, above.
[2] The length of the time during which the Celts had been in contact with the Etruscans before their reaction took a violent form in the fifth century B.C. is emphasized by H. Hubert in *Les Celtes et l'Expansion Celtique jusqu'à l'Époque de la Tène* (Paris 1932, Renaissance du Livre), p. 331.
[3] For Rome's recovery from the *Clades Alliensis* of 390 B.C., see II. D (iv), pp. 101–2, above.

sending out flying columns of raiders right to the extremity of the
Italian Peninsula. A century later, they were playing the same
havoc in Peninsular Greece. In 279 B.C. they burst through the
northern bounds of Macedonia and remained masters for four years
(279–276 B.C.) of a country which had just imposed its hegemony
on all the other states of Greece and overthrown the Achaemenian
Empire.[1] Their range of action was immense. One wing of the
horde which had descended the Danube to fall upon the heart of the
Hellenic World swerved eastward and crossed the Dardanelles instead
of heading for Pella and Delphi; and these Celts made a permanent
settlement—an Asiatic 'Galatia'—on the Anatolian Plateau. Other
Celtic hordes, bursting out in the opposite direction, descended the
Rhine and the Seine and the Loire to the shores of the Ocean and
swept on—taking seas and mountains in their stride—some across
the Channel into the British Isles and some across the Bay of Biscay
or the Pyrenees into the Iberian Peninsula. Nor were these Celtic
migrants mere marauders. Inept though they were in material
technique—as they showed in their inability to master the forest[2]—
the Celts nevertheless succeeded, under the stimulus which came to
them from Etruria and Macedon and Marseilles, in developing a
style of their own[3] which is sufficiently distinctive to enable our
modern Western archaeologists to plot out the course and extent of
these Celtic migrations on the basis of the remains of the Celtic
culture which have come to light.

During those two centuries of Celtic exuberance (*circa* 425–225
B.C.), it looked as though the Celts might actually overwhelm the
Hellenic World by breaking into its citadels in Italy and Greece and
enveloping its flanks in Spain and Anatolia simultaneously; and
then, when this Celtic terror was at its height, the barbarians missed
their chance. They were driven out and kept out of the Italian
Peninsula by the Romans and out of the Greek Peninsula by the
Antigonids. In Anatolia, the scourge of their marauding expedi-
tions stimulated the local 'successor-states' of the Achaemenian
Empire to co-operate to the extent of confining the obnoxious Celtic

---

[1] In the fourth century B.C., the Macedonians had committed the same error of tactics
on their own continental European frontier that the Etruscans had committed on theirs
a century earlier. King Philip Amyntou, the Macedonian counterpart of Peter the Great,
had stimulated the Celts by extending his rule into the interior of the Balkan Peninsula;
and thereafter Philip's son and successor Alexander the Great, and Alexander's general
and local successor Lysimachus, had both diverted the energies of Macedonia from
Europe to Asia, leaving the continental European frontier invitingly open for barbarian
reprisals.
[2] See pp. 275–6, above.
[3] The type of culture which, in the technical terminology of our archaeologists, is
known as 'La Tène', after the site, at the outflow from the Lake of Neuchâtel, on which
the first striking examples of this culture were unearthed. The five phases into which
the la Tène culture is analysed by the archaeologists on the strength of its material
remains are believed to cover, in all, a span of five centuries, from the fifth century to the
last century B.C. See Hubert, op. cit., and the *Cambridge Ancient History*, vol. vii, ch. ii.

intruders within narrow bounds in the least desirable part of the
country. In the Balkan Peninsula, in the basins of the Maritsa and
the Danube, the Celts were exterminated by the indigenous representatives of European barbarism—Thracians and Illyrians and the
like—as soon as these had recovered from the first shock of the
Celtic onslaught. In the Iberian Peninsula, they were rolled back
by the North African barbarians who gave the Peninsula its Iberian name. The last hope for the Celts lay in Hannibal's brilliant
attempt, in his passage of the Alps, to set the Celtic avalanche in
motion again at its original starting-point;[1] and this hope was forlorn,
since the hour of Hannibal's intervention was not the eleventh but
the thirteenth. The definitive defeat of Hannibal by Rome in the
last year of the third century B.C. spelled the doom of Hannibal's
Celtic allies. It was thenceforth inevitable that the encounter between the Celtic barbarism and the Hellenic Civilization should end
in a Celtic defeat, and that this defeat should be inflicted by Roman
hands. Within little more than two centuries after the close of the
Hannibalic War, the Celts had been absorbed into the Hellenic
body social through being incorporated into the Roman Empire
from the banks of the Po to the banks of the Rhine and the Danube
and from Celtiberia to Gallograecia. They had been followed up
by Roman Imperialism from the Continent on to the island of
Britain and from the British mainland on to their last sanctuary on
the Isle of Mona. Their discomfiture was complete.[2]

This disintegration of the Celtic layer of European barbarism by
the radiation of Hellenism exposed the Teutonic layer, which lay
next behind the Celtic, to the action of the same formidable disintegrating force. How must the prospects of the Teutons have
appeared to a Hellenic historian—a Diodorus of Agyrium or a
Strabo of Amaseia—who had lived to see Caesar conquer Gaul[3] or
to hear Caesar's successors debating whether it were worth their
while to conquer Britain?[4] With the Celtic débâcle in his mind, our

---

[1] See II. D (v), pp. 161–2, above.

[2] Hubert, in op. cit., on pp. 155–6, writes the epitaph of the Celts in the following
terms:
'La Civilisation de la Tène commence avec l'âge d'or de la civilisation grecque. Ce
sont les innovations de celle-ci qui ont provoqué les innovations qui caractérisent celle-
là. Les surfaces de contact se sont depuis lors régulièrement accrues et, malgré quelques
apparences contraires, l'influence des Méditerranéens et la masse des importations—
jusqu'à l'assimilation de la civilisation de la Tène par la civilisation romaine. . . .
'Mais ce que les hommes de la Tène ont emprunté, ils l'ont généralement adapté et
transformé de la façon la plus originale. Jamais encore, dans la série des emprunts faits
par les civilisations de l'Europe Centrale aux civilisations plus avancées du Midi, pareille
originalité ne s'était révélée.'

[3] The narrative of Diodorus's *A Library of Universal History* stops at Caesar's invasion
of Gaul in the year 58 B.C.; but certain later events are mentioned by Diodorus incidentally: e.g. Caesar's crossing of the Rhine and invasion of Britain, as well as his death and
apotheosis.

[4] 'Caesar the God [i.e. Divus Julius] landed on the island [of Britain] on two occasions,
but each time he withdrew again in a hurry without accomplishing anything much or

historian—quite rationally forecasting the future in the light of the past—would assuredly have been inclined to pronounce that, for the barbarians of Europe, the challenge of Hellenism was insuperable and that, however lustily the Teutons might storm and rage, as the Celts had once stormed and raged, at the first encounter with the pioneers of the conquering civilization, the Teutons, like the Celts, were bound to be discomfited in the long run.

An observer who had watched Caesar throw Teutonic Ariovistus, neck and crop, out of Gaul or Augustus push the Roman frontier forward from the Rhine to the Elbe, right into the Teutonic domain, would hardly have guessed that the boundaries of the Roman Empire on the European Continent were destined to relapse to the line of the Rhine and remain at the line of the Danube instead of continuing to advance, at the Teutonic barbarians' expense, until they reached a 'natural frontier' at the neck of the European Peninsula, along the lines of the Vistula and the Dniestr. Yet, in despite of the historical precedents, this was what actually happened. The Teutonic resistance to Roman expansion succeeded in compelling Roman statesmanship to accept the Rhine-Danube line—the longest line that it is possible to draw across the face of Europe—as the permanent European frontier of the Roman Empire; and, when once this was decided, the game was in the Teutons' hands and their ultimate victory was only a matter of time.

On a stationary military frontier between a civilization and a barbarism, time always works in the barbarians' favour;[1] and, besides this, the barbarians' advantage increases (to borrow Malthus's famous mathematical metaphor) in geometrical progression at each arithmetical addition to the length of the line which the defenders of the civilization have to hold. The unsubdued Teutonic tribesmen pressed ever harder upon the fine-drawn line of the Roman frontier along the Rhine and the Danube; and they were so far from being threatened by the fate of the Celts that they soon began to assume a threatening aspect themselves in Roman minds as the most for-

---

penetrating far into the interior. . . . Lately, however, some of the local chiefs have entered into friendly relations with the Government of Caesar Augustus by sending embassies and paying other attentions; and they have gone so far as to dedicate monuments on the Capitol and to place the whole island virtually at the Romans' disposal. There would be no advantage, however, in a military occupation of the island in view of the heaviness of the duties which the Britons are compelled, as it is, to pay to the Imperial Treasury on all imports from Britain into Gaul and exports from Gaul into Britain. (These exports consist of ivory bracelets and necklaces and amber beads and glass-ware and other rubbish.) A military occupation would not pay, because it would require at least one legion, with some cavalry, to extract revenue from the islanders by direct taxation, and the cost of this force would swallow up the net increase in receipts (allowing for the fact that direct taxation could not be imposed without a simultaneous reduction in the customs tariff). Nor could force be employed without a certain amount of risk.' (Strabo: *Geographica*, Bk. IV, ch. v. 3, pp. 200–1.)

[1] This law of the barbarian frontiers of civilizations is examined further in Part VIII, below.

midable contingent in the recalcitrant external proletariat by which
the now stationary frontiers of the Empire had come to be encircled.
The Teutons, unlike the Celts, were proof against the assaults of
Hellenic culture, whether these were delivered by soldiers or by
traders or by missionaries. Even when they succumbed, on the eve
of their final military triumph, to the spiritual assault of the Syriac
religion which had just conquered the Hellenic Society itself, they
made their Christianity their own by opting for Arianism instead of
adopting the Catholicism which became prevalent on the Roman
side of the now fast-crumbling military front. And when the Roman
Empire finally collapsed, and the Hellenic Society went into dissolution with it, the Teutons were in at the death. It was these
representatives of continental European barbarism, rather than the
Sarmatians and the Huns of the Eurasian Steppe or the Arabs and
the Berbers of Afrasia, who delivered the *coup de grâce*. A Greek
historian of the fifth century of the Christian Era—a Priscus or a
Zosimus—would have been in no danger of making that mistake
which might so easily have been made by a Diodorus or a Strabo
some four centuries earlier. In an age when Visigoths and Vandals
were harrying the Peloponnese and holding Rome to ransom and
occupying Gaul and Spain and Africa and seizing the command of
the Mediterranean, it had long ceased to be possible to argue that
the challenge of Hellenic culture and Roman arms was insuperable
for the barbarians of Europe, just because this challenge had once
defeated the Celts. The Teutonic victory robbed the Celtic defeat,
in retrospect, of the apparent historical significance which it had
seemed to possess at the time when it had been consummated.

There are other obvious illustrations of the same theme in
the realm of the human environment which we may cite more
briefly.

For example, the spiritual poverty of the indigenous Roman
religion presented a standing challenge to foreign religions when
once Rome's military career had brought her into cultural contact
with foreign communities. Was some alien religion to respond to
this challenge victoriously by filling the awful void in Roman souls
which had yawned open during the seismic convulsions of the
Hannibalic War? The Roman *numina* knew no magic formula for
closing this spiritual breach.[1] Would some foreign divinity close it
by leaping in, as the mythical Curtius once upon a time had closed
a physical abyss in the Roman forum? The Hellenic Dionysus
leapt into the breach straightway and was straightway swallowed up
without constraining the gulf to close over his head. Yet the sum-

---

[1] On this point, see Warde-Fowler, W.: *The Religious Experience of the Roman People*
(London 1911, Macmillan), Lectures xiv and xv.

mary suppression of the Dionysiac propaganda in Roman Italy by the Roman authorities in the second century B.C. was after all no proof that this challenge of the Roman spiritual void was insuperable; for, where the Hellenic Dionysus suffered defeat, the Syriac Christ descended into hell and re-ascended as a victor. Five centuries after the suppression of the Bacchanalia by the Roman Senate in the year 186 B.C.,[1] the Roman Government itself acknowledged the victory of Christianity in the conversion of the Emperor Constantine the Great.

Again, the intrusion of Hellenism upon the Syriac World in the train of Alexander the Great presented a standing challenge to the Syriac Society. Was it, or was it not, to rise up against the intrusive civilization and cast it out? Confronted with this challenge, the Syriac Society made a number of attempts to respond; and all these attempts had one common feature. In every instance, the anti-Hellenic reaction took a religious movement for its vehicle.[2] Nevertheless, there was a fundamental difference between the first four of these reactions and the last one. The Zoroastrian and Jewish reactions were failures; the Nestorian and Monophysite reactions were failures; the Islamic reaction was a success.

The Zoroastrian and Jewish reactions were attempts to combat the ascendancy of Hellenism by bringing into action two religions which had both been rife already in the Syriac World before the calamity of the Hellenic intrusion befell it. In the strength of Zoroastrianism, the Iranians, who had been the political masters of the Syriac World before Alexander overthrew the Achaemenian Empire, rose up against Hellenism and expelled it, within two centuries of the conqueror's death, from all the region east of the Euphrates. At the line of the Euphrates, however, the Zoroastrian reaction reached its limit. The remnant of Alexander's conquests was salvaged for Hellenism by the intervention of Rome; and in A.D. 628, after the Arsacids and the Sasanids had been beating upon this Roman frontier for nearly 700 years, it actually stood perceptibly farther east than the line along which Pompey had first drawn it in 64 B.C.[3] Thus the Zoroastrian reaction never succeeded in dislodging the intrusive alien civilization from the Syriac *terra irredenta*. Nor did the Jewish reaction succeed in its more audacious attempt to liberate the homeland of the Syriac Civilization from the Hellenic incubus by an uprising from within. The Jewish people was too weak in arms and numbers and Syria lay too near to the reservoirs of Hellenic energy for the Jewish reaction to be able to achieve even that measure of

---

[1] See II. D (vi), pp. 215–16, above.
[2] See I. C (i) (b), vol. i, pp. 90–2, and II. D (vi), pp. 234–6, above.
[3] See I. C (i) (b), vol. i, pp. 75–6, above.

success which was achieved by the Zoroastrian reaction; and the momentary triumph of the Maccabees over the Seleucids was effaced by an overwhelming disaster when the Romans intervened. In the great Romano-Jewish War of A.D. 66–70, the Jewish community in Palestine was ground to powder; and the Abomination of Desolation, which the Maccabees had once cast out from the Holy of Holies, came back to stay when Hadrian planted on the site of Jerusalem the Roman colony of Aelia Capitolina. The debris of this devoted Syriac people which took up the Hellenic challenge so gallantly and was shattered so remorselessly by the impact of Rome is drifting about in the World down to this day, as the ash-dust once floated in the atmosphere, and tinged the colours of the sunset on the other side of the planet, for weeks after the great eruption of Krakatoa. This pulverized social ash is familiar to us as the Jewish 'Diaspora'. The scattered survivors of Jewry are left with the cold consolation of remembering that their forefathers volunteered on a forlorn hope and went down to destruction in a splendid failure.

As for the Nestorian and Monophysite reactions, they were two alternative attempts at turning against Hellenism a weapon which the intrusive civilization had forged for itself from a blend of Hellenic and Syriac metal. In the syncretistic religion of Primitive Christianity, the essence of the Syriac religious spirit had been Hellenized to a degree that rendered it congenial to Hellenic souls;[1] and, for the Syriac underworld, this was perhaps the bitterest fruit of the Hellenic ascendancy. The Hellenic dominant minority had discovered the pearl of great price that lay buried in the field of Syriac culture, and now the hated intruder was actually carrying this precious Syriac heirloom away. The Nestorian and Monophysite reactions were attempts to snatch Christianity out of those sacrilegious Hellenic hands and to save it for the Syriac heirs of the Heavenly Kingdom. They were attempts to de-Hellenize Christianity and thereby to restore it to a pristine Syriac purity. Yet the Nestorian and Monophysite reactions failed in their turn; and they both really failed in the same way, in spite of the diversity of their theological tenets and their political fortunes. It made little difference that their theological divergences from the middle path of the Catholic Faith were in diametrically opposite directions to one another. It made little difference that Nestorianism was ignominiously driven out beyond the bounds of the Roman Empire to consort with Zoroastrianism in the limbo east of Euphrates, whereas Monophysitism held its ground in Syria and Egypt and Armenia, and defied the Melchite hierarchy, without being blasted—as Judaism had

---

[1] Mithraism, which was Christianity's contemporary and its most formidable rival in the competition for the spiritual conquest of the Roman Empire, was of a corresponding alloy. It was a Hellenized version, not of Judaism, but of Zoroastrianism.

been blasted in an earlier encounter—by the Roman thunderbolt. The fundamental reason why Nestorians and Monophysites both alike failed was that both were attempting an impossible feat of spiritual alchemy. The Hellenic alloy which both were seeking to eliminate from Christianity was really indispensable. Christianity was a syncretism or nothing; and although either one of the two blended elements might be reduced to a minimum by the alchemist's art, it could never be reduced to zero. By reducing the Hellenic element in Christianity as far as they could, the Nestorians and Monophysites were merely impoverishing Christianity without being able to rid it completely of the foreign alloy which, on a Syriac valuation, was so much intractable dross. The Nestorians and Monophysites were not so much defeated by the resistance of the Melchites as they were paralysed by an irreconcilable contradiction in their own souls. A religion which contained an irreducible residuum of Hellenism in itself could never inspire a whole-hearted anti-Hellenic crusade.

A Greek contemporary of the Emperor Heraclius, who had witnessed the ultimate victory of the Roman Empire in its last trial of strength with the Sasanidae and the ultimate victory of the Melchite hierarchy in its last trial of strength with the Nestorian and Monophysite heretics, might have been betrayed, about the year 630 of the Christian Era, into giving thanks to God for having made the Earthly Trinity of Rome and Catholicism and Hellenism invincible. First Zoroastrianism and Judaism, and then Nestorianism and Monophysitism, had taken up the Hellenic challenge, and now all these Syriac reactions had failed to achieve their common aim. Surely these four failures were conclusive proof that the challenge presented by the ever dominant Hellenism to the ever prostrate Syriac Society was insuperable?

In the year 630, this conclusion would have forced itself upon the reason of almost any intelligent citizen of the Catholic Graeco-Roman Commonwealth, to whichever side his personal sympathies might happen to incline. And yet, at that very moment, the fifth Syriac reaction against Hellenism was impending; and this fifth reaction was to give the lie to the apparent significance of the other four by succeeding triumphantly where they had all failed alike. The Emperor Heraclius himself, who had spent his life in vindicating the work of Alexander and Pompey, was condemned by a malicious Destiny not to taste of death until he had seen 'Umar the Successor of Muhammad the Prophet coming into his kingdom to undo Alexander's work and Pompey's work and Heraclius's own work—and this utterly and for ever. For Islam accomplished everything which Judaism and Zoroastrianism and Nestorianism and

Monophysitism had severally and successively attempted in vain. It completed the eviction of Hellenism from the Syriac World. It reintegrated, in the shape of the 'Abbasid Caliphate, the Syriac universal state which Alexander had ruthlessly cut short, before its term had run out or its mission been fulfilled, when he overthrew the Achaemenidae. Finally, Islam endowed the Syriac Society, at last, with an indigenous universal church and thereby enabled it, after centuries of suspended animation, to give up the ghost in the assurance that it would not now pass away without leaving offspring. When the 'Abbasid Caliphate broke up and the Syriac Society went into a tardy dissolution, the Islamic Church became the chrysalis out of which the new Arabic and Iranic civilizations, 'affiliated' to the Syriac Civilization, were to emerge in due course at the end of a post-Syriac interregnum.[1]

We may also reconsider, from our present standpoint, the challenge which was presented to Western Christendom by the impact of the Ottoman Power. During the fourteenth century of the Christian Era, the 'Osmanlis had succeeded in imposing the Pax Ottomanica upon the warring communities of Orthodox Christendom in the Balkan Peninsula. By the turn of the fourteenth and fifteenth centuries the issue between Orthodox Christendom and the 'Osmanlis was closed, and a new issue was presented. Were the warring communities of Western Christendom to have peace imposed on them now, as it had been imposed on the warring communities of Orthodox Christendom already, by the drastic discipline of an Ottoman conquest? Or would the Western Society succeed in effectually countering this danger by evolving from its own body social some kind of carapace which would be sufficiently broad and thick and tough to be impervious to Ottoman blows?

In the fifteenth century this protective function was assumed by the Kingdom of Hungary and, after a century-long ordeal, it proved to be beyond Hungary's permanent capacity. Hungary's failure was dramatically proclaimed in her crushing defeat at the hands of Sultan Suleymān in the Battle of Mohacz; and we may imagine some Venetian observer who had escaped from the battle-field alive reporting home that the 'Osmanlis were invincible and advising the Government of the Republic to agree with their Ottoman adversary quickly whiles they were in the way with him, before his cavalry had time to cross the Julian Alps and descend upon the Venetian possessions on the Italian mainland. On the morrow of the Battle of Mohacz, it might indeed have appeared to the shrewdest judge of public affairs that the Ottoman challenge to Western Christendom was unanswerable. Yet this judgement was invalidated, before

---

[1] See I. C (i) (b), vol. i, pp. 72–7, above.

the calendar year was out, by the establishment of the Danubian Hapsburg Monarchy.

This 'ramshackle empire' must indeed have appeared, at the moment of its improvisation, to be a house built on the sands, which was bound to fall as soon as ever 'the rain descended and the floods came and the winds blew and beat upon' it.[1] How could this jerry-built structure be expected to stand when the house of Hungary had fallen? Hungary had been a historic kingdom with a tradition and an *esprit de corps*. The Danubian Hapsburg Monarchy was a pile of rubble thrown together out of the nearest materials that came to hand: an incongruous amalgam of Hungarian debris, salvaged from Ottoman clutches, with a miscellaneous backing of half a dozen contiguous kingdoms and lands: the marches of Styria and Austria, the duchies of Carinthia and Tyrol, the Kingdom of Bohemia. Surely this new Danubian Hapsburg Monarchy could not succeed where the old Kingdom of Hungary had failed? Surely it must fall, with a greater fall than that of Hungary, when the Ottoman conqueror resumed his offensive? Such expectations, which assuredly were prevalent in rational minds in A.D. 1526, were nevertheless destined to be falsified in 1529 and refuted for ever in 1683. In the first siege of Vienna, the Danubian Hapsburg Monarchy survived the impact of the force to which Hungary had succumbed on the field of Mohacz. In the second siege of Vienna, the Ottoman Power was thrown into a recoil from which it never rallied. Thus the outcome of the Battle of Mohacz was not, after all, a proof that the Ottoman challenge was unanswerable for the Western World. So far from that, the shattering of the first anti-Ottoman carapace of Western Christendom actually stimulated the threatened society to provide itself with a new carapace of sufficient massiveness to withstand the blows under which the original carapace had given way.

The foregoing examples indicate that we have not yet found the right method for dealing with the problem now before us. We are concerned at the moment to lay hands on unequivocal instances—if such are to be found—in which a challenge has proved to be excessive, and we have now ascertained empirically that we cannot reach our goal by the process of demonstrating that some challenge has been too much for a particular respondent on a particular occasion or even for a succession of respondents on a series of occasions. However long the catalogue, the demonstration is bound to be incomplete because we cannot here apply the method of exhaustion. The inference suggested by a thousand successive failures may be invalidated, at the thousand-and-first encounter,

[1] Matthew vii. 25.

by a single anomalous and quite unpredictable success. This method of inquiry, therefore, is a false route, and we must make for our goal along some other line of approach.

Comparisons in Three Terms

Can we see some alternative method of research that promises better results? Let us try the effect of starting our inquiry from the opposite end. We have made no progress when we have started from instances in which a challenge has defeated a respondent. Let us now start from instances in which a challenge has administered an effective stimulus and has evoked a successful response. In previous chapters of the present Part, we have had occasion to examine many instances of this kind, and in many of these cases we have conducted our examination comparatively. We have compared the example of a successful response to a challenge with some other historical situation in which the same party (or a comparable party) has responded with less success to the same challenge (or to a comparable challenge) when the challenge has been less severe. Let us now reconsider some of these comparisons between two terms and see whether we cannot increase our two terms of comparison to three.

Let us look in each case for some third historical situation in which the challenge has been not less severe but more severe than in the situation from which we have started. If we succeed in finding a third term of this kind, then the situation from which we have started—a situation in which it is already established, by empirical observation, that our challenge does evoke a successful response— becomes a middle term between two extremes. At these two extremes, the severity of the challenge is respectively less and greater than it is at the mean. And what about the success of the response? In the situation in which the severity of the challenge is less than the mean degree, we know that the success of the response is likewise apt to be less than it is in the middle term. We have still to ascertain what kind of response is evoked in our third situation: the situation in which the severity of the challenge is above the mean and not below it. Here, where the severity of the challenge is at its highest, shall we find that the success of the response is at its highest also? Suppose that we find, on examination, that an enhancement of the severity of the challenge above the mean degree is not accompanied by any corresponding increase in the success of the response but that, on the contrary, the response actually falls off, just as it falls off when the severity of the challenge is not enhanced but diminished? If this proves to be the outcome of our inquiry, we shall have discovered that the interaction of Challenge-and-Response is subject to the well-known 'law of diminish-ing returns'. We shall conclude that there is a mean range of severity at which the stimulus of a challenge is at its highest; and—assuming that the height of the stimulus is our criterion of value —we shall call this degree of severity the optimum. On this stan-dard, we shall pronounce certain presentations of a given challenge to be 'defective', and certain other presentations of the same chal-lenge to be 'excessive', on the common ground that both alike are apt to evoke less successful responses than those which are evoked by the challenge at the optimum degree at which its effect upon respondents is the most stimulating. Having sketched this new line of inquiry, let us follow it out in order to discover experimentally whether it does lead us to the goal for which we are making.

Norway—Iceland—Greenland

For example, let us reconsider the stimulating effect which was produced upon the Norsemen by their transmarine migration from Scandinavia to Iceland. The effect is indisputable. It was in Ice-land and not in Norway or in Sweden or in Denmark that the abortive Scandinavian Civilization achieved its greatest triumphs both in literature and in politics.[1] And what were the conditions of the stimulus that evoked this supremely brilliant response? There are two conditions which are conspicuous: the transmarine migra-tion across arctic seas and the exchange of a bleak and barren country-side in Norway for an Icelandic country-side which was bleaker and barrener. As far as we can judge, these two conditions together constituted the Icelandic challenge which stimulated the Scandinavian Society to surpass itself. Now, suppose that the same challenge had been repeated with redoubled severity; suppose that the Norsemen had been challenged by their physical environment to traverse twice the width of arctic waters that separates Iceland from Scandinavia, and to settle on the farther shore in a country-side which was as much bleaker and barrener than Iceland as Iceland itself is bleaker and barrener than Norway. Would this repetition of the same challenge with twice its Icelandic severity have resulted in a repetition of the Scandinavian response with twice its Icelandic brilliance? Would this Thule beyond Thule have bred a Scandinavian community whose literature had twice the literary merit of the Icelandic Saga and their polity twice the political genius of the Icelandic Commonwealth? This question is not hypothetical; for the conditions which we have postulated were actually fulfilled when the Scandinavian seafarers pushed on from Iceland to Green-land. And the answer to the question is not uncertain; for the

[1] See II. D (iii), pp. 86–100, above.

brilliance which the Scandinavian culture had attained in Iceland was nowhere and never surpassed. Though Greenland supplanted Iceland as the Ultima Thule of the Scandinavian World, it did not supplant it as the focus of Scandinavian culture. The height to which that culture had risen in Iceland remained its zenith.

As it turned out, the conditions of enhanced severity, which had evoked so brilliant a response from the Norsemen who migrated from Norway to Iceland, brought in diminishing returns when they were imposed upon the emigrants to Greenland in double measure. The Greenlanders made hardly any contribution to Norse literature;[1] they did not distinguish themselves in politics; and they betrayed a most un-Scandinavian-like lack of drive in failing to follow up and clinch the great geographical discovery—the discovery of America—which was within their grasp.

By the time when they had reached Greenland, the Scandinavian explorers had attained the threshold of the New World. They had already put behind them the longest and most formidable stage of the journey. The relatively clement south-west coast of Greenland, which they had chosen for the site of their settlements, faces the north-east coast of Labrador across waters that are scarcely wider than the North Sea; and this side of Greenland is not more distant from the Gulf of St. Lawrence than it is from Iceland. Within the forty years immediately following the Norse colonization of Greenland in A.D. 985–6, there were no less than five separate occasions on which Norse voyagers, sailing for Greenland or from Greenland, accidentally or deliberately made the North American coast.[2] It is remarkable that these Scandinavian voyages to America all occurred during the first four decades of an occupation of the adjacent coast of Greenland which lasted altogether for more than four centuries; and the failure to follow these reconnaissances up appears all the more extraordinary when we bear in mind the usually high standard of adventurousness and hardihood which prevailed among the Scandinavian seafarers in general in the Viking Age. Moreover, in this instance, the Scandinavian settlers in Greenland had a special incentive for indulging in the traditional Viking diversion and exercising the traditional Viking virtue. Over a span of little less than half a millennium, the Greenlanders were being slowly worsted in a tragic losing battle against a physical environment which was too severe for even the Scandinavian spirit to endure permanently the ordeal of keeping alive in it. During all this time, there was knowledge in Greenland of a temperate country to the south—a land of vines—which had been proved to be within sailing distance

---

[1] They are credited with the so-called 'Greenlandic Atli Lay' in the Poetic Edda.
[2] See Gathorne-Hardy, G. M.: *The Norse Discoverers of America* (Oxford 1921, Milford); and Kendrick, T. D.: *A History of the Vikings* (London 1930, Methuen), ch. xv.

of Greenland by the voyages of the Greenlanders' own ancestors. Yet the descendants of the Scandinavian heroes who had made their way across the Arctic Ocean to Greenland as a work of super-erogation, almost for the sport of braving the elements, were not spurred on by the imminent danger of extinction in their Green-landic settlements to save their souls alive by making the easier transit to Vinland. They did not follow in the wake of their inquisitive ancestors in order to find new homes in a temperate clime where they and their descendants could look forward to living in perpetuity a life of reasonable ease.[1]

What are we to make of this strange and melancholy story? Its meaning surely is that the challenge of Greenland was excessive, and that the reason why the abortive Scandinavian Civilization actually attained its zenith neither in Greenland nor in Norway but in Iceland was that in Iceland the challenge to which the Scan-dinavian Civilization was the response happened to be presented in the optimum degree of severity—a degree which was a mean between the lesser and the greater degree of severity in which the same challenge was presented in Norway and in Greenland respectively.

Dixie—Massachusetts—Maine

The Vinland on which the Scandinavian seafarers had failed to secure a foothold at the turn of the tenth and eleventh centuries of the Christian Era was successfully colonized, rather more than six centuries later, by English maritime pioneers of Western Christen-dom who boldly steered straight across the open Atlantic instead of skirting the great Oceanic void and following the Scandinavian route through arctic waters where Iceland and Greenland offer themselves as stepping-stones. This bold Western seamanship had its reward; for New England—as Vinland was christened by Eng-lish colonists who made themselves at home there in the seven-teenth century—presented a physical challenge which had a potent stimulating effect. We have studied this physical challenge on the site of Town Hill, Connecticut;[2] and we have traced the steps by which the New Englanders were led on to the mastery of the whole North American Continent through their successful response to the severe conditions of the New England environment.[3] We have seen how, in the last round of the struggle between the diverse com-munities which had been established by European colonists along the Atlantic seaboard of North America, the New Englanders 'knocked out' their Southern kinsmen whose ancestors had likewise braved the perils of the passage from England across the open

---

[1] For traces of abortive attempts at later dates, see Gathorne-Hardy, op. cit., pp. 282–97.   [2] See II. D (i), pp. 15–16, above.   [3] See II. D (ii), pp. 65–70, above.

Atlantic in the seventeenth century, but had settled in the treacherously genial clime of Virginia and the Carolinas. After two and a half centuries of exposure, in their respective settlements overseas, to the relaxing climate of the South and to the stimulating climate of New England, these two offsprings of a single English stock had been differentiated to a degree of which the measure is given by the outcome of the American Civil War. Evidently the challenge of the physical environment, which has evoked such a triumphant response at the degree of severity in which it is presented in New England, remains stimulating at the somewhat milder degree in which it is presented in New York State and New Jersey and Pennsylvania, but becomes distinctly relaxing at the lower degrees to which it falls on the southern side of the Mason and Dixon Line. In geographical terms, we may say that, along the North American Atlantic seaboard, the Mason and Dixon Line marks the southward limit of the optimum climatic area—in the sense of the area in which the challenge of the physical environment evokes the most effective human response. We have now to ask ourselves whether this area of highest climatic stimulus has another limit on the northern side; and, as soon as we have framed this question, we are aware that the answer is in the affirmative.

The northern limit of the optimum climatic area actually partitions New England; for New England, small as it is compared to the whole range of the North American seaboard from Florida to Labrador, is by no means homogeneous within itself. When we speak of New England and the part which it has played in North American history, we are really thinking of three New England States out of the five: of Massachusetts and Connecticut and Rhode Island rather than New Hampshire or Maine; though the two latter states have just as good a title to the family name of New England as their three more distinguished sisters.[1] Historically, Maine is a mere offshoot of Massachusetts; and she only acquired her separate statehood in the year 1820, at a date when the Commonwealth of Massachusetts, with Maine as its annex, had already been in existence for the best part of two centuries. Thus the tie between Maine and Massachusetts is perhaps as close as that between any two other states in the Union.[2] The combined influences of geographical propinquity and common racial stock and common tradition and long-maintained common government have been at work to hold these two New England States together. And yet the

---

[1] This cannot be said for the state of Vermont, which falls into the same group as New Hampshire and Maine sociologically, but is historically an offshoot of New York State and therefore not strictly a part of New England by origin.

[2] It is certainly closer than the tie between Virginia and West Virginia or between North and South Carolina.

diversity of their history up to date and of their character at the present time is extreme.

Massachusetts has always been one of the leading English-speaking communities on the North American Continent. She has succeeded in maintaining this position in spite of the immense political and economic changes which, in the course of the last hundred and fifty years, have accompanied and followed the establishment of the Union and the expansion of the United States across the continent from Atlantic to Pacific. On the other hand, Maine has always been unimportant and obscure, not only before but since her erection into a separate State. Massachusetts to-day is still one of the principal seats of North American industrial and intellectual activity, while Maine survives as a kind of 'museum piece'—a relic of seventeenth-century New England, a land of woods and lakes which is still inhabited by woodmen and watermen and hunters. These children of a hard country now eke out their scanty livelihood by serving as 'guides' for the pleasure-seekers who come from far and wide out of the North American cities to spend their holidays in this Arcadian State, just because Maine is still what she was at a time when many of these great cities had not yet begun to arise out of the virgin wilderness. Maine to-day is at once one of the longest-settled regions within the frontiers of the Union and one of the least urbanized and least sophisticated.

How is this contrast between Maine and Massachusetts to be explained? It would appear that the hardness of the New England environment, which stands at its optimum in Massachusetts, is accentuated in Maine to a degree at which it brings in diminishing returns of human response to its challenge. In other words, the optimum climatic area along the North American Atlantic seaboard has a northern limit at the northern boundary of Massachusetts which corresponds to its southern limit at the more celebrated Mason and Dixon Line. If it is a fact that, beyond the southern boundary of Pennsylvania, the challenge of the physical environment becomes deficient in severity and therefore positively relaxing in its effect upon human energies, it is also a fact that, beyond the northern boundary of Massachusetts, the same challenge becomes excessive in severity and therefore repressive. And, in terms of the human response, the effects of repression and of relaxation are identical. In areas in which either of these two conditions prevails, the human respondent to the challenge is not stimulated to respond with as great effect as in the optimum area in which the highest physical stimulus is administered by a challenge of mean severity between the relaxing and the repressive extreme.

The operation of 'the law of diminishing returns', which begins to reveal itself in the contrast between Maine and Massachusetts comes out much more clearly if we extend our survey farther north-wards to the rest of the English-speaking communities along the Atlantic seaboard of North America. New Brunswick and Nova Scotia, which occupy the mainland between Maine and the Gulf of St. Lawrence, are the least prosperous or progressive provinces of the Dominion of Canada with the exception of their north-eastern neigh-bour, Prince Edward Island. On the northern side of Cabot Strait, the Island of Newfoundland is the least reputable of all the self-govern-ing communities of the British Commonwealth of Nations.[1] On the northern side of the Strait of Belle Isle, the English-speaking fisher-folk along the bleak and barren north-east coast of Labrador are fighting, at this day, the same tragic losing battle against over-whelming physical odds that was once fought out to the death, on the opposite side of Davis Strait, along the south-west coast of Greenland, by those forlorn Scandinavian pioneers whose last survivors perished some five centuries ago.

Brazil—la Plata—Patagonia

If we turn our attention to the Atlantic seaboard of South America, we shall observe the same phenomena there *mutatis mutandis*. In Brazil, for example, the greater part of the national wealth and equipment and population and energy is concentrated in the region lying south of the 20th degree of southern latitude and east of the River Paranà. This region is only a small fraction of the vast territories of the Republic, yet in social importance it far outweighs the much larger fraction that extends along the Atlantic coast from the 20th parallel up to the point where this coast strikes the Equator at the mouth of the Amazon (not to speak of the vast hinterland, which includes almost the whole of the Amazon Basin). Moreover, Southern Brazil itself is inferior in civilization to the adjoining regions that lie still farther south: the Republic of Uru-guay and the Argentinian State of Buenos Aires. It is evident that, along the South American Atlantic seaboard, the equatorial sector is not stimulating but positively relaxing, and that the optimum climatic area—in the sense of the area in which the challenge of the physical environment evokes the most effective human response—begins south of the 20th parallel (south) and is nearer to its best in the neighbourhood of the Rio de la Plata than in the neighbourhood of the Tropic of Capricorn.

Where, then, is 'the high light' of this optimum area to be found?

[1] This passage was written before the suspension of the constitution of Newfoundland, and the reassumption of a certain measure of local financial and administrative responsi-bility and control on the part of the Government of the United Kingdom, at the end of A.D. 1933.

The city of Buenos Aires has the advantage over the city of Rio de Janeiro by some dozen degrees of latitude. If we follow the coast farther southward through another dozen degrees of latitude beyond Buenos Aires, shall we find ourselves in a region which is as much superior in civilization to Central Argentina as Central Argentina is to Southern Brazil? The answer is in the negative. We shall actually find the vigour and effectiveness of the human response to the physical environment beginning to fall off before we have rounded the bight of Bahia Blanca and reached Parallel Forty. Farther south than that, we shall find ourselves traversing the bleak plateau of Patagonia which is still tenanted by a stalwart but sparse and primitive population of vagrant hunters. If we push on still farther south again and cross the Strait of Magellan, we shall find ourselves among the numbed and starved savages who just manage to keep alive among the frosts and snows of Tierra del Fuego. Thus in the Southern, as in the Northern, Hemisphere the Atlantic seaboard of America contains an optimum climatic area which has limits in both directions. In either hemisphere, this area in which the physical environment evokes the most effective human response passes over on the one side into an area in which the challenge is not of sufficiently stimulating severity and on the other side into another area in which the challenge is so severe that its excessive stimulus brings in diminishing returns.

The Pacific Seaboard of South America

Let us next re-examine the Pacific seaboard of South America, which has engaged our attention before. We have observed[1] that the original home of the Andean Civilization on this seaboard lay, not in Valparaiso or in any of the other green valleys which open out upon the Central Chilean sector of the coast south of the 30th parallel, but among the oases which hold their own against the coastal desert along the North Peruvian coast, from the Tumbez Valley on the north to the Nazca Valley on the south inclusive. We have also observed that, in Valparaiso, the physical environment does not present that challenge which is presented in the valleys of Tumbez and Chimu and Rimac and Nazca: a challenge which once evoked the Andean Civilization as the human response to it. The North Peruvian Coast has given birth to an indigenous civilization because of its relative severity, and the Central Chilean coast has failed to do the like because of its relative geniality. Are we to infer that other sectors of the South American Pacific coast would have evoked still more vigorous and effective human responses than the North Peruvian coast, supposing that the physical challenges which

[1] See II. C ii) (b) 2, vol. i, pp. 322–3, above.

they presented to Man had only been still more severe? The answer is in the negative; for any such fancy is ruled out by the fact that two coasts of this very character are actually to be found in immediate proximity to the North Peruvian coast, on either side of it, and that neither of these still more forbidding stretches of coast has been any more successful than the less forbidding coast of Central Chile in emulating the unique cultural achievement which the North Peruvian coast has to its credit. Certainly the Andean Civilization did not emerge in the Earthly Paradise of Central Chile; but neither did it emerge in the unmitigated desert which dominates the seaboard of Northern Chile and Southern Peru between the 30th parallel and the 15th; nor again did it emerge in the tropical forest which smothers the seaboard of Ecuador.

On these two latter stretches of coast, the challenge of the physical environment was presented with an excess of severity which is well brought out in the following descriptions by an expert hand:

'Along the Ecuadorian coast, conditions prevail which accord with the usual conception of the tropical environment; for in that part of the Andean area there exist tangled forests crowded with unkempt trees draped in trailing mosses: forests wherein Man must combat warm, humid, and enervating air and a too-luxuriant vegetation, not to mention vast stretches of marsh or of spongy, unwholesome soil. . . . The island of Puna, at the mouth of the Guayas River, presents a delightful park-like aspect, embellished by sightly trees that raise graceful heads above the general expanse of grass and low shrubs. But even this comparatively charming part of the coast is replete with swamps, formerly the abode of yellow-fever mosquitoes. . . . Coastland Ecuador . . . varies . . . within itself to a marked degree, some of it being, seemingly, almost incapable of supporting human society, the rest of it being, apparently, not unpropitious to Mankind. Yet in no part of it, so far as we now know, was any well-balanced culture produced and set upon a rational career. True, manifestations of advanced material culture—stone-carving, pottery-making, &c.—have been discovered there by archaeologists; but . . . they are almost certainly the product, in every case, of cultural influences from outside the region. Thus, as a whole, the Ecuadorian coast is one of those habitats wherein Man was unable to progress without help from outside—or at any rate did not—but wherein, once advanced culture was introduced, it could be carried on.'[1]

As for the Peruvian coastal desert, it

'is not uniform throughout its length; for in the northern half of the Peruvian coast it is low—some three or four hundred feet, at most, above the valley floors—and it slopes perceptibly towards the sea. . . . In the southern part of the coast, on the other hand, the desert plain lies at an altitude of two or three thousand feet above the sea, and the river itself,

[1] Means, P. A.: *Ancient Civilisations of the Andes* (New York 1931, Scribner), pp. 6–7.

at a distance of only twenty miles from its mouth, is, as in the case of the Majes River, at an altitude of a thousand feet or more and is hemmed in inexorably by the adjacent but even higher desert plains. It is little to be wondered at, therefore, that in valleys of this type—let us say, from that of Lomas southwards into Northern Chile—no great cultural advances were ever made save as the result of outside influences.'[1]

Thus the stimulating desert of the North Peruvian coast is succeeded, farther south, by a repressive desert which reaches its acme of oppressiveness in the Nitrate Coast: a howling wilderness which has only become a bone of contention between three Latin-American Republics in these latter days when its chemical deposits have acquired a commercial value.

'There is in Northern Chile none of the scenic beauty that marks the change from bleak mountains to the warm, green valleys of the coastal desert of Peru. In the latter case, the streams reach the sea, and the valley walls enclose cultivated fields that fill the valley floor. In Peru the picture is generally touched with color—a yellow, haze-covered horizon on the bare desert above, brown lava-flows on the brink of the valley, grey-brown cliffs, and greens ranging from the dull shade of *algarrobo*, olive and fig trees to the brightness of freshly irrigated alfalfa meadows. In Northern Chile there is no hint of water until one reaches the foothills of the Andes far beyond the Coast Range and across the intervening desert. Where water occurs it is so small in volume that its effects are almost completely hidden in the depths of steep-walled ravines, so that in many places one may look for miles along the Andes without seeing a single trace of vegetation or human life.'[2]

It will be seen that, in point of severity, the Pacific seaboard of South America from the 5th to the 15th parallel (south) presents a challenge which is a mean between two extremes, like the Atlantic seaboard of the same continent from the 20th to the 40th parallel or the Atlantic seaboard of North America from the 39th to the 43rd parallel (north), or again like Iceland. In Iceland, the challenge of the physical environment is a mean between extremes in Norway and in Greenland; in Massachusetts it is a mean between extremes in South Carolina and in Labrador; in Uruguay it is a mean between extremes in Amazonia and in Tierra del Fuego. Similarly, on the North Peruvian seaboard of South America, which has given birth to the Andean Civilization, the challenge of the physical environment is a mean of optimum severity between the excessive geniality of Central Chile and the excessive severity which is displayed, in diverse ways, by both the Nitrate Coast and the seaboard of Ecuador.

This Andean illustration is perhaps more illuminating than the

[1] Op. cit., pp. 12–13.
[2] Bowman, I.: *Desert Trails of Atacama* = American Geographical Society Special Publication No. 5 (New York 1924, American Geographical Society), pp. 11–12.

others, just because its geographical and climatic expression works out less simply than theirs. In all the other instances above cited, the mean or optimum challenge is presented in an area which happens to be situated geographically in between the two areas in which the challenge is respectively insufficient and excessive. In the two other American instances, again, the mean challenge coincides with a climatic mean of relative temperateness between two climatic extremes which verge respectively towards tropical and towards arctic conditions. In the Andean instance, on the other hand, the excessive challenge is presented alike by two areas which are situated on opposite sides of the optimum area and which have nothing in common with one another in their climates—one being a humid region smothered under a tropical forest and the other an arid region where inorganic chemical deposits coat an otherwise naked desert. The insufficient challenge, again, is here presented in an area which is not sub-tropical but temperate in climate, and which is separated geographically from the area of optimum challenge by one of the two areas in which the challenge is excessive. In this Andean instance, therefore, the 'mean' which we are studying cannot be mistaken for anything but what it really is. Here, clearly, it has nothing to do with a geographical 'mean' in the sense of a central location, or again with a climatic mean in the sense of a climate that is relatively temperate. It reveals itself unmistakably as a 'mean' between a greater and a lesser degree of severity in a challenge presented to Man by his Environment—a 'mean' which is also an 'optimum' because, at this mean degree of severity, the challenge evokes a more vigorous and more effective human response than is evoked by it either when its severity is greater (for whatever reason) and therefore 'excessive' or again when it is less and therefore 'insufficient' from the standpoint of the human respondent.

In the light of this Andean illustration, we can now pursue our survey with clearer insight.

Votyaks—Magyars—Lapps

Another illustration of the working of this law is offered by the migrations of the Finnish-speaking peoples. From their original habitat at the east end of the North European forest, astride the Urals, where some of these peoples have never ceased to live their old life in its old environment, other peoples of the same family have migrated into one or other of the two regions of entirely different physique which adjoin the forest-belt on the north and on the south. The ancestors of the Lapps, migrating northwards, have exposed themselves to the challenge of the Tundras, while the ancestors of the Magyars, migrating southwards, have exposed themselves to the challenge of the Eurasian Steppe. The social consequence of the change in physical environment has been very different in these two cases.

'The consanguineity of the Hungarians and Laplanders would display the powerful energy of climate on the children of a common parent; the lively contrast between the bold adventurers who are intoxicated with the wines of the Danube and the wretched fugitives who are immersed beneath the snows of the polar circle. Arms and freedom have ever been the ruling, though too often the unsuccessful, passion of the Hungarians, who are endowed by Nature with a vigorous constitution of soul and body. Extreme cold has diminished the stature and congealed the faculties of the Laplanders; and the Arctic tribes, alone among the sons of men, are ignorant of war and unconscious of human blood: an happy ignorance, if reason and virtue were the guardians of their peace!'[1]

The Lapps on their Tundras have sunk considerably below the level of their sylvan ancestors; the Magyars on the Hungarian Alföld have risen far above it. It is evident that the ordeal of exchanging the life of the forests for the life of the Steppes is sufficiently severe to be stimulating, whereas the change from forest to Tundra is so inordinately severe that its effect on those who have endured it has been, not stimulating at all, but positively repressive.

Reactions to Changes of Climate

Let us next consider the effect of migration from countries with a damp, cloudy, foggy, heavy climate—the climate which prevails in England and along the adjoining continental coasts of the North Sea from Flanders to Jutland—to countries with climates that are drier, sunnier, clearer, and lighter. In the course of our Western history, a change of climate in this direction has been made by the medieval emigrants from the original Duchy of Saxony to the new marches wrested from the Slavs beyond the Elbe.[2] In modern times, a similar change has been made by the Dutch emigrants to the Transvaal and by the English emigrants to New England. In each of these three cases the change of climate has produced on those who have made it a stimulating effect which can be measured at the present day in the difference of êthos between the Brandenburger and the Hanoverian or between the Afrikander and the Hollander or between the Yankee and the Englishman. In regard to this stimulus, however, a distinguished American climatologist strikes a warning note:

'The people of the Eastern and Central United States are more nervous and active than those of Europe—but not necessarily more efficient. . . . They are alternately stimulated and relaxed by frequent

---

[1] Gibbon, Edward: *The History of the Decline and Fall of the Roman Empire*, ch. lv.
[2] See II. D (v), pp. 168–9, above.

changes from day to day, and in this are like horses that are well driven. In the spring and autumn, however, the combined effect of ideal temperature and highly invigorating daily changes spurs them to an astonishing degree of effort. Then comes the hot summer or the cold winter, either of which is debilitating. People do not diminish their activity at once, especially in the winter. They draw on their nervous energy, and thus exhaust themselves. They are like horses which pull on the bit and, when urged a little, break into a run, straining themselves by their extreme speed. Then they are pulled up so suddenly that they are thrown back on their haunches and injured. In Germany somewhat the same conditions prevail, although not to so great an extent. England apparently comes nearer to the ideal than almost any other place. The climate is stimulating at all times, both by reason of abundant storms and because of a moderate seasonal range. It never, however, reaches such extremes as to induce the nervous tension which prevails so largely in the United States.'[1]

Is this warning justified? When we are comparing the climatic influences of England and Holland and Hanover with those of New England and the Transvaal and Brandenburg, the question cannot be answered off-hand. The points on either side are so evenly matched that, when we try to strike a balance, it seems equally reasonable to pronounce, with Dr. Ellsworth Huntington, that England, after all, 'apparently comes nearer to the climatic ideal than any other place', or to make out that, on the whole, the more violent stimulus of New England is apt to evoke a more effective response. But suppose that we raise the violence of the stimulus to a still higher degree. Suppose that we substitute California on the Pacific coast of North America for New England on the Atlantic coast, and the African highlands of Kenya Colony on the Equator for the African highlands of the Transvaal on the Tropic of Capricorn, and the Polish or the Russian section of the North European plain for the Prussian section. Suppose that we make these substitutions, which all have the effect of heightening the violence of the stimulus, and then repeat our previous question in these alternative terms. On the whole and in the long run, does the climate evoke the more effective response in England or in California? In Holland or in Kenya Colony? In Berlin or in Warsaw or Moscow? When the question is framed in these alternative and sharper terms, the answer is not in doubt; for it is evident in every case that when the violence of the climatic stimulus is increased to that degree it brings in diminishing returns of human response.

As for California, Dr. Ellsworth Huntington's verdict in this case will be accepted without hesitation.

¹ Huntington, Ellsworth: *Civilisation and Climate*, 3rd ed. (New Haven 1924, Yale University Press), pp. 225–6. Compare pp. 403–4.

'The chief defect of the climate of the California coast is that it is too uniformly stimulating. Perhaps the constant activity which it incites may be a factor in causing nervous disorders. . . . The people of California may perhaps be likened to horses which are urged to the limit so that some of them become unduly tired and break down.'[1]

As for the Kenya highlands, we may take note of the widely different estimates that are current to-day among competent observers in regard to the prospects of the White Race in Kenya Colony and in the Transvaal respectively. To-day, no serious person doubts that the White Race has already proved its ability to make itself at home in the Transvaal and even to increase and multiply there. On the other hand, no serious person to-day is yet convinced that the White settlers in Kenya Colony will prove able to bring up their children in the country, or that a native-bred generation of Whites, even if it is actually reared in the Kenya highlands by a *tour de force*, will display the physical and psychic stamina of its European-bred parents.

As for the climatic stimulus of the North European plain, which rises in violence at each farther remove from the moderating influence of the Atlantic, it may be an open question whether it attains its optimum degree on this side or on that side of the Elbe. At any rate, that is a burning question of modern German politics—a perpetual source of friction between the Rhinelander or the Westphalian and the true-blue *ost-elbisch* Prussian; and, in this German family quarrel, a foreigner will be chary of taking sides. He will not readily commit himself on the question whether the *ost-elbisch* Prussian dominion over the western half of North Germany and the Prussian hegemony over Germany as a whole is or is not an inevitable political outcome of Prussian pre-eminence in vigour and efficiency. He will be content to agree that the optimum climatic area on the North European plain is to be found in the neighbourhood of the Elbe, on whichever side of the Elbe it may be. On the other hand, he will hardly hesitate to pronounce that this optimum climatic area, which begins at least as far west as the Elbe, does not extend as far east as the Vistula; for, whatever may be the respective merits of Hanoverian phlegm and Prussian alertness, 'the law of diminishing returns' quite manifestly comes into play where Prussian alertness froths over into Polish effervescence and Polish effervescence evaporates into Russian exaltation.

The successive rise and fall in the curve of the human response to a steadily rising climatic stimulus reveals itself to the eye of any traveller who passes by train through Hanover and Berlin and Posen and Warsaw *en route* for Moscow. From Berlin eastwards, the

[1] Huntington, op. cit., p. 225.

curve unmistakably declines, and at each stage farther eastwards the decline becomes progressively steeper. If the traveller varies his route, and proceeds from Berlin east-north-eastward through Königsberg to Kovno, the same impression of a cultural fall succeeding a cultural rise in the course of his journey will be borne in upon him more forcibly; for, on this route, instead of feeling himself descending a cultural slope all the way, he will have at a certain point the sensation of falling headlong over a cultural precipice. At the frontier between East Prussia and Lithuania, as he is transported over the few yards of permanent way that link the German railway station of Eydtkühnen with the Lithuanian station of Wirballen, he will experience instantaneously as great a cultural transition as he would experience in the course of travelling the whole distance from Frankfurt-on-Oder to Brest-Litovsk. In the experience of the writer of this Study, this is the most precipitous cultural frontier that he has ever crossed—not excepting the passage of the Save between Semlin and Belgrade or the passage of the Ohio between Cincinnati and Kentucky.

Up to this point in our examination of the comparative effects of challenges from the physical environment which differ in the degree of their severity, we have been considering situations in which a challenge is presented in different degrees simultaneously in two or more separate geographical areas. Let us next consider the case in which the challenge rises or falls from one degree to another, through some process of climatic or other environmental change, in one identic area successively.

Let us examine, for example, the tropical sylvan environment—occupying the northern part of Guatemala and the western part of Honduras—in which the Mayan Civilization once emerged. We have noticed that this low-lying tropical forest presents a much severer challenge than the adjacent highlands overlooking the Pacific Coast; and we have concluded that the Mayan Civilization emerged, as it did, in the forest and not on the highlands just because the greater severity of the sylvan challenge evoked a more vigorous and effective human response.[1] But suppose that, some time after the Mayas had responded to the challenge of the forest by transforming the forest into fields, the climate of Central America had undergone some change which accentuated the challenge presented by the local physical environment to Man. Suppose that there had been a considerable increase in humidity. Might not this have rendered the challenge of the tropical forest prohibitively severe, and at the same time have rendered the challenge of the highlands adequately stimulating? As a matter of fact, at the present day, the sites of the

[1] See II. C (ii) (b) 2, vol. i, p. 321, above.

Mayan cities lie derelict, untenanted by Man and overwhelmed by the resurgent forest,[1] while the highlands are the seat of the local variety —such as it is—of the Latin-American version of our own Civilization.[2] Is it not possible that this undoubted interchange of social roles between forest and highlands may be due to some climatic change in the sense which we have suggested? One of the foremost living climatologists has advocated this hypothesis persuasively.

'The most surprising thing about the Mayas is that they developed their high civilisation in what are now the hot, damp, malarial lowlands where agriculture is practically impossible. A hundred miles away, on the coasts of Yucatan or in the Guatemalan highlands, far more favourable conditions now prevail. There, agriculture is comparatively easy; the climate, while not bracing, is at least good for the torrid zone; and malarial fevers are rare. To-day, the main cities lie in these more favourable regions; the energetic part of the population is there, and the interior lowlands are hated and shunned by all except a degraded handful. In the past, the more favourable localities were occupied by people close akin to the Mayas, yet civilisation never rose to any great height. Ruins are found there, but they are as far behind those of the lowlands as the cities of Yucatan are to-day behind those of the United States.[3]

'In explanation of these peculiar conditions, several possibilities suggest themselves. First, we may suppose that the Mayas were the most remarkable people who ever lived.... A second possibility is that, in the time of the Mayas, tropical diseases were less harmful than at present.... It may be ... that a fairly satisfactory explanation will be found if the two preceding possibilities are joined with a third, namely, a climatic change such that the dry conditions which prevail a little farther north prevailed in the Maya region when these people attained eminence. Such a shifting of zones would increase the length of the dry season which now comes in February and March. This would diminish the amount of vegetation and cause scrub to take the place of dense forest. Under such conditions, agriculture would become comparatively easy. Fevers would also greatly diminish, for in the drier parts of Yucatan they are to-day relatively mild; and the lowland plain would be the natural site of the chief development of civilisation, just as is the case in other countries.'[4]

The hypothesis expounded in the foregoing passage might be accepted in principle without our necessarily following Dr. Huntington in his estimate of the degree of the climatic change involved. If the climate of Mayaland at the time of the genesis of the Mayan Civilization really differed from the climate of the same area at the present day to the same extent and in the same sense as the present climate of Yucatan, then the fathers of the Mayan Civilization were

---

[1] See II. D (i), pp. 3-4, above.   [2] See II. D (ii), p. 35, above.
[3] On this point, see the present Study, Part II. D (ii), p. 34, above, with the references there made to Dr. Ellsworth Huntington's works.—A.J.T.
[4] Huntington, op. cit., pp. 330-2.

not confronted with the sylvan challenge at all, and we should have to regard their achievement as a response to some other challenge which is now beyond our knowledge. It is not necessary, however, to press Dr. Huntington's hypothesis thus far. It seems more reasonable to suppose that the Mayan Civilization was actually evoked by the challenge of the tropical forest, as we have already seen reason to believe, and that this particular interplay of Challenge-and-Response does explain why the civilization emerged where it did instead of emerging either on the Yucatan Peninsula or in the highlands. At the same time, we may follow Dr. Huntington so far as to conjecture that, at the time when the challenge of the forest evoked the Mayan response, the challenge was presented in a degree of severity which was stimulating, and that the subsequent abandonment of the Mayan cities to the resurgent forest may have been due, at least in part, to some climatic change which accentuated the sylvan challenge to a degree of severity that was prohibitive.[1]

Dr. Huntington's hypothesis may also have a bearing on the genesis of other 'unrelated' civilizations besides the Mayan. We have found reason for thinking that the Egyptiac and Sumeric civilizations, for example, were generated in response to a climatic change which is supposed to have overtaken Afrasia after the passing of the 'Pluvial Age' (the Afrasian variant of the European 'Ice Age'). We have suggested that the fathers of these two civilizations performed their feat of mastering the valleys of the Lower Nile and the Lower Tigris and Euphrates in response to the challenge presented by the desiccation of the Afrasian Steppe. They took their plunge into the forbidding jungle-swamps because their former habitat in the neighbourhood was beginning to turn from a genial savannah into an inhospitable desert. The ordeal of transition to the difficult environment of the un-reclaimed river-valleys from the easy environment which the savannah had provided before desiccation set in was the dynamic event by which, in our view, the fluvial civilizations were brought to birth.[2] We may now observe that the wilderness of the river-valleys, formidable though it was at the time when the fathers of the fluvial civilizations came to grips with it, was nevertheless not quite so formidable then as it must have been in the preceding period.

If we are right in conjecturing that the desiccation of Afrasia in the 'post-pluvial' age was the challenge which impelled the fathers of

---

[1] For the extent to which it is possible to accept Dr. Ellsworth Huntington's explanation of the rise and fall of the Mayan Civilization in Northern Guatemala—and likewise his complementary explanation of the vicissitudes of the Syriac Civilization at Palmyra—see II. D (vii), Annex I, below. For alternative explanations of the abandonment of the Mayan cities of 'the Old Empire', see I. C (i) (b), vol. i, footnote 2 on p. 126, above.

[2] See II. C (ii) (b) 2, vol. i, pp. 304-6, above.

the fluvial civilizations to descend into the river-valleys out of their former habitat on the surrounding savannah, then, *ex hypothesi*, the new environment which they were entering must have been tending to become easier at the same moment, and for the same reason, that the old environment which they were abandoning was becoming more difficult. For the process of desiccation which Afrasia was undergoing in this 'post-pluvial' age was part and parcel of a widespread climatic change which was simultaneously melting the ice-cap in Europe, and therefore, *a fortiori*, it must have been at work ubiquitously throughout Afrasia itself—on the savannah and in the river-valleys alike. At the same time, this uniform physical change would evidently produce diverse and even contrary social consequences in these two different Afrasian environments. A process of desiccation which was actually making the Afrasian savannah less easily habitable than it had been during the preceding 'pluvial' age by reducing the local quantum of humidity from the optimum quantity to an insufficiency, must have been making it less difficult for Man to cope with the Nilotic and Euphratean jungle-swamps, which had previously been kept uninhabited by an excess of humidity. We know, from the sequel, that the ordeal to which the fathers of the Egyptiac and the Sumeric Civilization exposed themselves, when they eventually plunged into the jungle-swamps under these changing conditions, administered a stimulus which evoked, in both instances, a brilliantly successful response. Must we not suppose that if, for some reason, they had been moved to attempt the conquest of these same jungle-swamps at an earlier time, before the pluvial conditions had begun to abate, the ordeal would have proved so inordinately severe that its effect, instead of being stimulating, would have been repressive? In that event, the Nilotic and Euphratean pioneers, instead of being rewarded for their hardihood by becoming the fathers of two great civilizations, might have been punished for their audacity by becoming the slaves of their new environment and not its masters: the fate which has actually overtaken the miserable 'Web-Feet' in a subsequently deposited section of the Tigris-Euphrates delta.[1]

If the foregoing argument is sound, we have reached the conclusion that the physical challenge by which the Egyptiac and Sumeric civilizations were evoked was a mean between two extremes. On the one hand, the conditions of life on the Afrasian savannah in the pluvial age were not sufficiently severe to bring any civilizations to birth; on the other hand, the severity of the conditions in the lower valleys of the Nile and the Euphrates in the pluvial age was excessive. The necessary conditions of 'mean' or

[1] See II. C (ii) (b) 2, vol. i, pp. 316–18, above.

'optimum' severity were realized in the Afrasian region for the first time when the post-pluvial climatic change from exuberant humidity towards desiccation came to mitigate the previously excessive challenge of the river valleys to a degree at which it ceased to be impossible for Man to respond with success. It was in these circumstances that the Egyptiac and Sumeric civilizations were born.

The same conclusion applies to the physical challenge by which our own Western Civilization and the Russian offshoot of the Orthodox Christian Civilization have been evoked in a different environment at a later date. The physical environment in which these two civilizations have eventually come to birth is Northern Europe; and during the pluvial-glacial age, when the Nilotic and Euphratean jungle-swamps were prohibitively water-logged, the birth of any civilizations in Northern Europe was prohibited, just as decisively, by the incubus of the ice-cap. The ice-cap then still covered with its dead weight the whole region which in this present post-glacial age has been conquered successively from the ice by the forest and from the forest by Mankind. Let us now ask ourselves what would have happened if the fathers of our Western Civilization and the fathers of the Russian Orthodox Christian Civilization had been moved for some reason to attempt the conquest of Northern Europe before the ice-cap had receded. The answer undoubtedly is that in that event, instead of becoming the fathers of two great civilizations, they would have suffered the same kind of fate as we have imagined the fathers of the Egyptiac and the Sumeric Civilization suffering in punishment for a premature attempt to conquer the Nilotic and Euphratean jungle-swamps. If importunate pluvial pioneers would have been punished by being depressed to the social level of the modern 'Web-Feet' in the Basra-'Amārah-Nāsirīyah triangle, importunate glacial pioneers would probably have been punished in a corresponding way by being depressed to the social level of the modern Lapps on the frozen tundras.[1]

If this analogy holds, then the physical challenge which has helped to evoke the Western Civilization in Northern Europe and the Orthodox Christian Civilization in Russia is likewise to be viewed as a fruitful mean between two extremes which have both been sterile. In Northern Europe and Russia, as in the lower valleys of the Euphrates and the Nile, the severity of the conditions was excessive in the glacial-pluvial age, in common contrast to its insufficiency in the same age on the Afrasian savannah. In Northern Europe and Russia, the necessary conditions of 'mean' or 'optimum'

---

[1] See the quotation from Gibbon on p. 301, above.

severity were realized for the first time when the post-glacial climatic change melted the ice-cap and conjured up the North European forest in its place. It is under these new conditions of 'mean'
severity that a region which was formerly inimical to Life has given
hospitality to two great civilizations in the fullness of Time.

Scotland—Ulster—Appalachia

Let us next consider an instance in which the challenge has been
not exclusively physical but partly physical and partly human.

At the present day, there is a notorious contrast between Ulster
and the rest of Ireland. While Southern Ireland is a rather old-
fashioned agricultural country, Ulster is one of the busiest work-
shops in the modern Western World. The city of Belfast ranks in
the same company as Glasgow or Newcastle or Hamburg or Detroit;
and the modern Ulsterman has as great a reputation for being efficient
as he has for being unaccommodating.

In response to what challenge has the Ulsterman made himself
what he now is? He has responded to the dual challenge of migrating to Ulster across the sea from Scotland and contending, after his
arrival in Ulster, with the native Irish inhabitants whom he found
in possession and proceeded to dispossess. This twofold ordeal
has had a stimulating effect which may be measured by comparing
the power and wealth of Ulster at the present day with the relatively
modest circumstances of those districts on the Scottish side of the
border between Scotland and England and along the Lowland fringe
of 'the Highland Line' from which the original Scottish settlers in
Ulster were recruited some three centuries ago by King James I/VI.
The comparison reveals that, in the course of the intervening centuries, the dual challenge presented by Ulster has administered a
noteworthy stimulus to those descendants of the original Scottish
settlers who have remained on the Irish soil on which King James
once planted their ancestors.

The modern Ulstermen, however, are not the only living representatives of this stock; for the migratory habit, once acquired, is
apt to persist; and the Scottish pioneers who migrated to Ulster in
the seventeenth century begot 'Scotch-Irish' children and grandchildren who re-emigrated in the eighteenth century from Ulster to
North America. At the present day, the twice-transplanted offspring of these 'Scotch-Irish' emigrants to the New World survive,
far away from their kinsmen in Ireland and their kinsmen in Scotland, in the fastnesses of the Appalachian Mountains: a highland
zone which runs through half a dozen states of the North American
Union from Pennsylvania to Georgia.

What has been the effect of this second transplantation upon the

Scotch-Irish stock? In the seventeenth century King James's colonists crossed the sea from Scotland to Ulster and took to fighting 'the Wild Irish' instead of 'the Wild Highlanders'. In the eighteenth century, their grandchildren crossed the sea again to become 'Indian fighters' in the North American backwoods. Obviously this American challenge has been more formidable than the Irish challenge, and this in both its aspects. In the human sphere, the 'Red Indian' heathen was of course a more savage adversary than the 'Wild Irish' Catholic (however wilfully the difference may have been ignored by the Scotch-Irish frontiersman in his Protestant fanaticism).[1] In the physical sphere, the Appalachian Mountains are wilder in scenery and vaster in scale than any landscape in Scotland or in Ulster, with the consequence that the Scotch-Irish immigrants who have forced their way into these natural fastnesses have come to be isolated and segregated here from the rest of the World to a much greater extent than their ancestors ever were, or than their cousins ever have been, in their Irish and Scottish habitats. In terms of the total environment, the severity of the challenge has been enhanced in the transition from Ulster to Appalachia to such a degree that 'the law of diminishing returns' has come into operation with unmistakable force.

If the modern citizen of industrial Belfast has in some respects outstripped his Scottish cousin who has never migrated from the rural neighbourhoods of 'the Highland Line' and the English Border, he has certainly not been outstripped in his turn by his American cousin who has migrated for the second time from Ulster to the Appalachian fastnesses. On the contrary, the stimulus which was once administered by the migration from Scotland to Ireland, so far from being reinforced by the subsequent migration from Ireland to America, has been more than counteracted—as we shall find if we now compare the Ulsterman and the Appalachian as they each are to-day, some two centuries since the date when they parted company.

Let us compare them, for example, on the point of their respective proneness to bloodshed: a point on which Ulster has by no means a good record. The old war to the knife between intrusive Protestants and indigenous Catholics is still carried on by gunmen from the windows of Belfast; and at this day the toll of political murders is heavier in the capital of Ulster than in any other great city of Western Europe.[2] Yet even in Ulster, where this political bloodshed still persists, there is no longer any survival of the family

---

[1] See II. C (ii) (a) 1, Annex, vol. i, pp. 465–7, above.
[2] These lines were written before the National-Socialist Revolution in Germany at the beginning of the year 1933.

blood-feud which has remained one of the regular social institutions of 'the Mountain People' of Appalachia. The Ulsterman, again, is unlikely to forget the sea, considering that one of his principal industries is shipbuilding, whereas the Appalachian, whose ancestors actually crossed the Atlantic five or six generations ago, has lost touch with the sea so completely that he no longer attaches any clear meaning to the word itself—which is preserved in his vocabulary solely through its occurrence in his folk-songs. In the third place, the Ulsterman has retained the traditional Protestant standard of education, whereas the Appalachian has relapsed into illiteracy and into all the superstitions for which illiteracy opens the door. His agricultural calendar is governed by the phases of the Moon; his personal life is darkened by the fear, and by the practice, of witchcraft. He lives in poverty and squalor and ill-health. In particular, he is a victim of Hook-Worm: a scourge which lowers the general level of vitality in Appalachia just as it does in India and for just the same reason. (The children persist in going about barefoot, and their parents either cannot afford to give them shoes, or will not take the trouble to insist upon their wearing them, or are too ignorant to be aware that Hook-Worm gains entry into human bodies through sores in naked soles.)

In fact, the Appalachian 'Mountain People' at this day are no better than barbarians. They are the American counterparts of the latter-day White barbarians of the Old World: the Rīfīs and Kabyles and Tuareg, the Albanians and Caucasians, the Kurds and the Pathans and the Hairy Ainu.[1] These White barbarians of America, however, differ in one respect from those of Europe and Asia. The latter are simply the rare and belated survivals of an ancient barbarism which has now passed away all around them; and it is evident that their days, too, are numbered. Through one or other of several alternative processes—extermination or subjection or assimilation[2]—these last lingering survivals will assuredly disappear within the next few generations, as other survivals of White barbarism have disappeared in other parts of the Old World at earlier dates: in the Scottish Highlands in the eighteenth century[3] and in Lithuania in the fourteenth.[4] It is possible, of course, that barbarism will disappear in Appalachia likewise. Indeed, the process of assimilation is already at work among a considerable number of Appalachians who have descended from their mountains and changed their way of life in order to earn wages in the North Carolinian cotton-mills. In this case, however, there is no

[1] See II. C (ii) (a) 1, vol. i, p. 236, above.
[2] For these processes, see further V. C (i) (c) 2 and 3, passim, in vol. v, as well as Part VIII, below.
[3] See II. C (ii) (a) 1, vol. i, p. 237, above.   [4] See II. D (v), pp. 172-4, above.

corresponding assurance; for the White barbarism of the New World differs from that of the Old World in being not a survival but a reversion.

The 'Mountain People' of Appalachia are *ci-devant* heirs of the Western Civilization who have relapsed into barbarism under the depressing effect of a challenge which has been inordinately severe; and their neo-barbarism is derived from two sources. In part, they have taken the impress of the local Red Indians whom they have exterminated.[1] Indeed, this impress of Red Indian savagery upon the White victors in this grim frontier-warfare is the only social trace that has been left behind by these vanquished and vanished Redskins. For the rest, the neo-barbarism of Appalachia may be traced back to a ruthless tradition of frontier-warfare along the border between Western Christendom and 'the Celtic Fringe' which had never died out among their ancestors in the British Isles and which has been revived, among these Scotch-Irish settlers in North America, by the barbarizing severity of their Appalachian environment.[2] On the whole, the nearest social analogues of the Appalachian 'Mountain People' of the present day are certain 'fossils' of extinct civilizations which have survived in fastnesses and have likewise relapsed into barbarism there: such 'fossils' as the Jewish 'wild highlanders' of Abyssinia and the Caucasus or the Nestorian 'wild highlanders' of Hakkiari.[3]

It will be seen that industrial Ulster is a social 'optimum' between rural Scotland on the one hand and barbarian Appalachia on the other; and that this 'optimum' is the product of a response to a challenge which, in point of severity, presents itself as a 'mean' between two extremes. The challenge to which King James's colonists were exposed in Ulster was distinctly more severe than the challenge that had been faced by their ancestors along the English Border or 'the Highland Line'. On the other hand, it was very much less severe than the challenge which afterwards presented itself to their Scotch-Irish descendants when these migrated from Ulster to North America in order to become 'Indian-fighters' in the Appalachian hills. The contrast between rural Scotland and industrial Ulster bears out, as far as it goes, the law of 'the greater the

---

[1] 'The wilderness masters the colonist. It finds him a European in dress, industries, tools, modes of travel, and thought. It takes him from the railroad car and puts him in the birch canoe. It strips off the garments of civilization and arrays him in the hunting shirt and the moccasin. It puts him in the log cabin of the Cherokee and Iroquois and runs an Indian palisade around him. Before long he has gone to planting Indian corn and plowing with a sharp stick; he shouts the war-cry and takes the scalp in orthodox Indian fashion. In short, at the frontier the environment is at first too strong for the man.' (Turner, F. J.: *The Frontier in American History* (New York 1921, Holt), p. 4.)

[2] See II. C (ii) (*a*) 1, Annex, vol. i, on pp. 465-7, above.

[3] See II. D (vi), pp. 256-9, above, and the Annex dealing with Jews in fastnesses, on pp. 402-12, below.

challenge the greater the response'; but in the sharper contrast between industrial Ulster and barbarian Appalachia we see this particular law overridden by the general 'law of diminishing returns': a law which, in any situation, infallibly comes into operation at some point or other when things are pushed to extremes.

In this sequence 'Scotland—Ulster—Appalachia', the challenge is on the borderline between the physical sphere and the human; but the operation of 'the law of diminishing returns' appears quite as clearly in other instances in which the challenge is presented in the human sphere exclusively.

Reactions to the Ravages of War

Let us reconsider, for example, the effects of the challenge of devastation. We have observed above[1] how the Athenians responded to the devastation of Attica at Persian hands in 480–479 B.C. and the French to the devastation of France at German hands in A.D. 1914–18. We have seen that, in both these instances, a great calamity has acted as a potent stimulus; and we have also seen that, in one instance at least, this stimulus has been worth the price, when we have compared the achievements of the Athenians in the post-war period with those of the Thebans. Thebes escaped devastation—and thereby missed the stimulus of devastation—in the Persian War; and in the sequel Thebes was outstripped by her neighbour who had come out of great tribulation. Thus the contrast between the fortunes of Athens and Thebes in this historic case bears out the law of 'the greater the challenge the greater the response'; but again it only bears it out so far as it goes. Let us now add a third term to this series and compare the sequels to the devastation of Attica in 480–479 B.C. and of France in A.D. 1914–18 with the sequel to the devastation of Italy by Hannibal in 218–201 B.C. Hannibal succeeded in inflicting deeper wounds on Italy than the Persians inflicted on Attica or the Germans on France. Did this greater calamity act as a stimulus likewise? And, if it did, was the potency of the stimulus proportionately higher? The answer to both parts of this question is decidedly in the negative. The devastation of Italy, unlike that of France or Attica, did not turn out to have been a blessing in disguise. On the contrary, the devastated area in the South became the seat of a social cancer which ate into the vitals of the Roman Commonwealth until the whole fabric of Roman economic and political life was destroyed. In post-war Roman Italy, there was no genuine parallel to the renovation of agriculture in post-war Attica and of industry in post-war France. In Italy the devastation administered an economic stimulus which proved transitory and

[1] See II. D (iv), pp. 107–11, above.

evoked a social response which proved all too difficult to revoke after its ill effects had become apparent.

What happened is well known. The devastated arable lands of Southern Italy were transformed partly into pasture-lands and partly into vineyards and olive orchards, according to the local degree of the devastation and the local nature of the terrain; and the new rural economy, planting and stock-breeding alike, was worked by slave-labour, in place of the free peasantry which had once tilled this soil before Hannibal's soldiery burnt the peasant's cottage and before the weeds and briars invaded his deserted fields. This revolutionary change from 'subsistence-farming' to 'cash-crop-farming' and from husbandry to the application of a servile 'man-power' undoubtedly increased for a time the monetary value of the produce of the land; but the social value of this temporary increase in the aggregate amount of the national income was offset by a concurrent increase in the inequality of its distribution and was more than counteracted by the attendant social evils: the depopula-tion of the country-side and the congregation of a pauper proletariat of *ci-devant* peasants in the towns. The attempt to arrest these evils through legislation, which was made by the Gracchi in the third generation after Hannibal's evacuation of Italy, only aggravated the distemper of the Roman Commonwealth by precipitating a political revolution without bringing the economic revolution to a halt; political strife became inflamed into civil war; and, a century after the tribunate of Tiberius Gracchus, the Romans acquiesced in the establishment of a permanent dictatorship by Augustus as a drastic remedy for a desperate state of affairs. Thus the devastation of Italy by Hannibal, so far from stimulating the Roman people as Xerxes' devastation of Attica had once stimulated the Athenians, actually gave them a shock from which they never recovered: a shock which revealed its demoralizing and debilitating effects in the political collapse of the Roman Republic and in the economic decay of Roman Italy and ultimately in the decline and fall of the Roman Empire.

In this sequence, again, we see the law of 'the greater the chal-lenge the greater the response' first of all borne out and then over-ridden. It is borne out in the contrast between the fortunes of Athens and the fortunes of Thebes in and after the War of 480–479 B.C. It is overridden by 'the law of diminishing returns' in the con-trast between the fortunes of Athens in and after that war, when Xerxes had chastised her with whips, and the fortunes of Rome in and after the War of 218–201 B.C., when Hannibal had chastised Rome with scorpions. The chastisement of devastation, which is stimulating when it is administered with Persian vigour, becomes deadly when it is inflicted with Punic intensity.

Chinese Reactions to the Challenge of Emigration

Let us reconsider, again, the effects of the challenge of emigration upon the modern Chinese. We have seen above[1] that when the Chinese coolie emigrates to Malaya or Indonesia, he is apt to reap a reward for his enterprise. By facing the social ordeal of leaving his familiar home and entering an alien social environment, he exchanges an economic environment which is congested and poverty-stricken for one in which he has a chance of bettering himself, and not infrequently he profits by this chance to the extent of making his fortune. Suppose, however, that we intensify the social ordeal which is the price of economic opportunity. Suppose that, instead of sending our Chinese emigrant to Malaya or Indonesia we send him to Australia or California. In these 'White Man's countries' our enterprising coolie, if he gains admission at all, will undergo an ordeal of vastly greater severity. Instead of merely finding himself a stranger in a strange land, he will have to endure deliberate and sometimes malignant penalization, in which the Law itself will discriminate against him instead of coming to his aid as it aids him in British Malaya, where an official 'Protector of Chinese' is appointed by a benevolent Colonial Administration. Does this severer social ordeal evoke an economic response of proportionately greater vigour? This question is answered in the negative when we compare the levels of prosperity which are in fact attained by the Chinese 'Diaspora' in California and Australia with the levels attained in the Philippines and Malaya. The comparison shows conclusively that the social ordeal to which the Chinese are everywhere subject abroad brings in diminishing returns when it is intensified from the Malayan to the Australian or from the Philippine to the Californian degree.

Slavs—Achaeans—Teutons—Celts

Let us next reconsider the challenge which a civilization presents to a barbarism: a challenge that has been presented in Europe to successive layers of barbarians, in successive ages, by the radiation of various civilizations into the interior of this once dark continent. When we study this drama in its European setting, our attention is caught by one instance in which the challenge has evoked a response of extraordinary brilliance. The Hellenic Civilization is perhaps the finest flower of the species that has ever yet come to bloom; and this Hellenic Civilization was generated, in response to a challenge from the Minoan Civilization, by the European Barbarism. When the maritime Minoan Civilization which had arisen in the Aegean Archipelago established a footing on the European

[1] In II. D (vi), on pp. 217–18.

continent, along the seaboard of the Greek Peninsula, the Achaean barbarians of the European hinterland were neither exterminated nor subjected nor assimilated. Instead, they managed to retain their identity as an 'external proletariat' of the Minoan 'thalassocracy' without failing to learn the arts of the civilization which they were holding at bay. In due course, these *ci-devant* continental barbarians took to the sea. Eventually they overcame the Cretan 'thalassocrats' on their own element.[1] And the Achaeans were the true fathers of the Hellenic Civilization which emerged, in its turn, in the Aegean area after the Minoan Civilization had been swamped by the Achaean Völkerwanderung.

The Achaean claim to the paternity of Hellenism is vindicated, as we have seen, by a religious test; for the Gods of the Olympian Pantheon, who were the paramount and universal objects of Hellenic worship, display manifestly in their lineaments their derivation from these Achaean barbarians who had constituted the 'external proletariat' of the Minoan World,[2] while any vestiges of a universal church derived from the Minoan 'internal proletariat' are only to be found, if at all, in the side-chapels and the crypts of the temple of Hellenic religion: in certain local cults and subterranean mysteries and esoteric creeds.[3] This reaction of the Hellenic Society to the religious test is strikingly different from the reaction of our own Western Society, in which a universal church derived from the 'internal proletariat' of an antecedent civilization has served as the chrysalis of the new civilization and has never ceased to be its most important institution. On the other hand, in the religious history of Western Christendom, the religion of the antecedent civilization's European 'external proletariat'—the primitive Teutonic heathenism and the Arianism by which this heathenism was superseded on the eve of the Teutonic Völkerwanderung—has left even less trace than has been left by the religion of the Minoan 'internal proletariat' in the religious history of Hellenism. These diverse results of the religious test plainly give us warrant for ascribing the paternity of the Hellenic Civilization to the Achaeans, and for seeing in this great feat of creation the response of these European barbarians to a challenge which the radiation of the Minoan Civilization had presented to them.

The measure of the stimulus in this instance is given by the brilliance of Hellenism, which still outshines every other civilization that has ever come into existence up to the present. And we can also measure the stimulus which was received from the Minoan Civilization by the Achaeans in another way. We can make a direct

---

[1] See I. C (i) (*b*), vol. i, pp. 92–3, and II. D (v), p. 160, above.
[2] See I. C (i) (*b*), vol. i, pp. 95–7, above.
[3] See I. C (i) (*b*), vol. i, pp. 97–100, above.

comparison between the fortunes of this Achaean layer of European barbarians and the fortunes of another layer which happened to be so remote and so effectively sheltered that it remained virtually immune from the radiation of any civilization whatsoever for some two thousand years after the Achaeans had received the Minoan challenge and had made their brilliant response. These inviolate barbarians were the Slavs, who had ensconced themselves in the Pripet Marshes when these dregs of the Continent had been yielded up to Man by the retreating ice-cap. In this fenny fastness, which offered little temptation to trespassers, the Slavs went on living the primitive life of the European Barbarism for century after century, while the history of the Hellenic Civilization, which had been begotten by their Achaean kinsmen, played itself out from start to finish. When the wheel of Hellenic destiny came round full circle, and the Teutonic Völkerwanderung ended the long drama which the Achaean Völkerwanderung had begun, the sluggard Slavs were still where they had been and what they had been some two thousand years earlier.

It was only when the Teutonic Völkerwanderung itself was approaching the end of its course that the Slavs were at last routed out of their ancient fastness by the Avar Nomads, who had been tempted to stray beyond the limits of their native Eurasian Steppe in order to take a hand in the Teutons' game of pillaging the wreckage of the Roman Empire. In the strange environment of an agricultural world, these lost children of the Steppe sought to adapt their old manner of life to their new circumstances. On the Steppe, the Avars had made their living as herdsmen of cattle; in the cultivated lands on to which they had now trespassed, these herdsmen found that the appropriate local live-stock was a human peasantry, and they therefore set themselves, rationally enough, to become herdsmen of human beings.[1] Just as they would have raided their Nomadic neighbours' cattle in order to stock some newly conquered pasture-land, so they now looked round for human cattle to re-stock the depopulated and derelict provinces of the Roman Empire which had fallen into their hands. Ranging the interior of the European Continent on this quest, the Avars found

---

[1] In sedentary societies, it is often cast up as a reproach against Nomads who have strayed off the Steppe *in partes agricolarum* that they tend to treat their sedentary subjects as 'human cattle'. Yet a sedentary and not a Nomadic society created the religion which conceives of its Lord as 'the Good Shepherd', and which represents him as enlisting fishermen in his service with the invitation 'Follow me, and I will make you fishers of men' (Matt. iv. 19). The metaphor of the shepherd (*rā'ī*) and his flock (*ra'īyah*) was no doubt derived by the Christian Church, at second or third remove, from the Nomads of the Afrasian Steppe, and it ill becomes us to foul our own nest by blaspheming against the source of one of the most pregnant similes in the imagery of the Christian Religion. For a critique of Nomadism, on and off the Steppes, as one of the 'arrested' civilizations, see Part III. A, vol. iii, pp. 7-22, below.

what they wanted in the Slavs. They forced their way into the Slavonic fastness; they herded off its helpless denizens in droves; and they stationed these captive droves of Slavonic human cattle in a vast circle round about the outlying enclave of the Eurasian Steppe in the Hungarian Alföld where the Avars had pitched their own camp. This, it appears, was the process by which the Slavs made their belated and humiliating début in History;[1] and the last of the Hellenic historians has been moved by a faint stirring of the old Herodotean curiosity to record the impression which was made on the senile Hellenic mind, towards the latter end of the sixth century of the Christian Era, by the first appearance of these Slavonic innocents abroad, when they came wandering all unarmed, out of the back of beyond, across the stricken field of the secular conflict between Teutons and Romans. Here is the passage in the annals of A.D. 591 :[2]

'Three men of Slav race without weapons or military equipment were captured by the Imperial Body-Guard. Their only baggage consisted of harps, and they carried nothing else with them. The Emperor cross-examined them regarding their nationality, their habitat, and their reasons for trespassing upon Roman territory. They explained that they were Slavs by nationality and that their homes were on the boundary of the Western Ocean. The Khaqan [of the Avars] had sent emissaries to their countrymen with a view to raising military forces and had lavished generous presents upon their chieftains. The latter had accepted the gifts but rejected the proposed alliance, on the plea of being disheartened by the length of the journey, but they had followed this up by dispatching the individuals just captured to the Khaqan on a mission of apology. It had taken them fifteen months to accomplish this journey. Forgetful of the privileges of ambassadors, the Khaqan had determined to prevent their departure; whereupon the three emissaries, who had heard of the really extraordinary reputation of the Roman People for wealth and hospitality, had procured an opportunity to withdraw to Thrace. They carried harps because they were not trained to bear arms. Their country was ignorant of iron, and this accounted for their peaceful and harmonious life. They strummed on stringed instruments because they did not know how to speak with the voice of trumpets. They were people among whom war was unheard-of; and it was only natural that there should be a bucolic note in their musical technique.

'This story inspired the Emperor with such respect for the tribe that he determined to offer hospitality to these visitors from the back of beyond, whose gigantic build and huge limbs extorted his admiration. He sent them under escort to Heraclea.'

These amiable but unpractical representatives of the European

---

[1] See Peisker, J.: *Die älteren Beziehungen der Slawen zu Turko-Tataren und Germanen* (Berlin 1905, Kohlhammer); and *The Expansion of the Slavs = Cambridge Medieval History*, vol. ii (Cambridge 1913, University Press), ch. xiv.
[2] Theophylactus Simocatta: *A Universal History*, Bk. VI, section ii, §§ 10–16.

Barbarism in its most secluded fastness were obviously the worse
for the age-long immunity from human stimulus which they and
their ancestors had enjoyed. It was assuredly better for them
when, a few years later, the Khaqan of the Avars—losing patience
with their lack of spirit—turned from blandishments to violence and
dragged the Slavs out of their seclusion by main force. The shock
administered by this Avar *coup de main* was the making of the Slavs
and the beginning of Slavonic history. It would have been better
still for these victims of Avar ruthlessness if they had been aroused
by some less brutal human stimulus at an earlier date, as once, some
two thousand years before, the radiation of the Minoan Civilization
had awakened a response in the Achaeans. The Achaeans did not
lack skill with the harp. Indeed, there is no Slavonic minstrel,
historic or legendary, who has won the fame of a Phemius or a
Demodocus or a Homer. But Achaean hands had not neglected
other arts. In their intercourse with the Minoans, the Achaeans
had made themselves masters not only of the harp but of the sword
and of the oar, and thereby masters of their environment and their
fate. This contrast between the Achaeans and the Slavs shows two
things. It shows that, for a primitive society, complete immunity
from the challenge of encounters with civilizations is a very serious
handicap. It also shows that this challenge has a stimulating effect
when its severity is of a certain degree. There is a third point,
however, which we still have to determine. Suppose that we
accentuate the challenge; suppose that we raise the degree of the
energy with which the Minoan Civilization irradiated the Achaean
Barbarism to higher and higher potencies: shall we thereby elicit
a more and more brilliant response on the barbarians' part? Or
shall we reach a degree at which 'the law of diminishing returns'
comes into play and the potency of the action ceases to be stimulating and becomes destructive? Let us make the experiment by
applying our empirical method of inquiry. Between the Achaeans
and the Slavs, there have lain several other layers of European
barbarians who have been exposed to the radiation of various civilizations in diverse degrees. What experiences have these other
barbarians had?

One instance in which European barbarians have succumbed to
a radiation of destructive intensity has come to our notice already.
We have seen how the Celts were eventually exterminated or subjected or assimilated by an overpowering radiation of Hellenism in
a Roman medium, after a transitory outburst of Celtic energy in
response to an earlier stimulus which the Celts had received from
Hellenism through the medium of the Etruscans.[1] We have

---

[1] See the present chapter, pp. 279–82, above.

contrasted the ultimate failure of the Celts with the relative success of the Teutons in holding their own against the Hellenic impact. We have noted that the Teutonic layer of European barbarians, unlike the Celtic layer, resisted the disintegrating action of Hellenism to such effect that the Teutons were able to take their place in the 'external proletariat' of the Hellenic World and to dispatch the Hellenic Society in its death-agonies with a *coup de grâce*. By comparison with the Celtic *débâcle*, this Teutonic reaction to Hellenism was a success; but as soon as we compare the Teutonic achievement with the Achaean, we are reminded that the Teutons gained nothing better than a Pyrrhic victory.[1]

The Teutons came in at the death of the Hellenic Civilization only to receive their own death-blow, on the spot, from the rival proletarian heirs of the defunct society. The victor on this field was not the Teutonic war-band but the Roman Catholic Church into which the 'internal proletariat' of the Hellenic Society had incorporated itself; and this victory of the Church over the barbarians was complete before the end of the social interregnum which the break-up of the Roman Empire had brought with it. Before the close of the seventh century of the Christian Era, every one of those Arian or heathen Teutonic war-bands that had ventured to trespass on Roman ground had been either converted to Catholicism or wiped out of existence; and, as converts to Catholicism, the surviving barbarian intruders renounced the pretension to bequeath to the future any positive contribution of their own except a racial strain of uncertain social value. The new civilization, 'affiliated' to the Hellenic Civilization, which emerged in the West when the post-Hellenic interregnum came to an end, was related to the antecedent civilization through the 'internal proletariat' and not through the 'external proletariat'. Western Christendom was essentially the creation of the Catholic Church—in contrast to Hellenism, which was essentially the creation of the Achaean barbarians. Thus the Teutons showed themselves unequal to the situation at the crucial point at which their Achaean counterparts had consummated their own brilliant achievement. The Teutons made the great refusal which Esau made when he sold his birthright to Jacob.[2] They had

[1] See I. C (i) (*a*), vol. i, pp. 58–62, above.

[2] For the replacement of pagan by Christian themes in the English version of the Teutonic Epic, see I. C (iii) (*e*), Annex, vol. i, p. 449, footnote 2, above. This compromise, however, did not save the Teutonic Epic from a premature death; for the abandonment of the pagan poetic themes was soon followed by an abandonment of the pagan poetic forms as well. For a striking account of the Teutons' repudiation of their own heritage in the domain of literature, see Ker, W. P.: *Epic and Romance* (London 1922, Macmillan), pp. 45–7. 'In mediaeval literature, whatever there is of the Homeric kind has an utterly different relation to popular standards of appreciation from that of the Homeric poems in Greece. . . . English epic is not first, but one of the least, among the intellectual and literary interests of King Alfred.'

not the spirit to compete with the Catholic Church for the paternity of a new civilization.

Let us now arrange our series of the challenges delivered by various civilizations to successive layers of the European Barbarism in the order of an ascending scale of severity. The Slavs were long immune from the challenge altogether and were patently the worse for being without the stimulus. The Achaeans were presented with the challenge of the Minoan Civilization and made the brilliant response of becoming the fathers of Hellenism. The Teutons held their own against the challenge of the Hellenic Civilization but were discomfited thereafter by the challenge of Catholicism: a universal church which first took shape as an embodiment of the Hellenic 'internal proletariat' and which eventually made itself into the chrysalis of a new civilization—the Western Christendom into which the progeny of the Teutonic war-bands was incorporated. The Celts were discomfited by the antecedent challenge of the Hellenic Civilization, against which the Teutons managed to hold their own. It is evident that the radiation from the Minoan Civilization to which the Achaeans were exposed was of the 'optimum' degree, and that this degree represents a mean between the insipid immunity of the Slavs and the overwhelming bombardment of Hellenic radiation to which the Celts succumbed. It is further evident that 'the law of diminishing returns' comes into operation, in this particular field of Challenge-and-Response, when the severity of the challenge is raised to some point between the degree at which the challenge of the Minoan Civilization stimulated the Achaeans and the higher degree at which the challenge of the Catholic Church proved too much for the Teutons.

Does our empirical method enable us to define more closely this point at which 'the law of diminishing returns' is here brought into play? Yes, it does; for the encounter in which the Teutonic trespassers on Roman ground succumbed to the Catholic Church was not the only conflict in which the Church was compelled to engage with European barbarians. Before it succeeded in bringing our Western Civilization to birth and ensuring that the child should live, the Church had to fight for her own life against two separate rear-guards of the 'external proletariat' of the Hellenic World which had not been drawn into the post-Hellenic Völkerwanderung when the Teutonic advance-guard swept over the derelict provinces of the Roman Empire *circa* A.D. 375–675. These two rear-guards were the Celts of 'the Celtic Fringe' that had remained beyond the range of effective Roman rule in the British Isles, and the Teutons of Scandinavia: a region which had lain beyond the zone of Roman border warfare on the European Continent. It was these Far Western Celts and Far Northern Teutons who proved themselves the Church's most formidable adversaries. The reckless Teutonic advance-guard, exposing itself all unprepared to the Church's counter-attack on a battle-field ill suited to barbarian weapons and barbarian tactics, was defeated by the Church without much difficulty. The prudent Celtic and Teutonic rear-guards of the European Barbarism held themselves in reserve and sought to beget new civilizations of their own in place of Hellenism, as Hellenism itself had once been begotten, in place of the antecedent Minoan Civilization, by the barbarian Achaeans. These high ambitions brought first the Far Western Celts and then the Far Northern Teutons into conflict with the Catholic Church, since in Western Europe there was not room for several separate civilizations—all related to Hellenism in different fashions and degrees—to grow up side by side simultaneously. In both these conflicts the Church eventually won the day and the ambitious barbarians were forced, after a hard struggle, to accept defeat. Yet these Celts and these Teutons of the rear-guard, unlike their Teutonic kinsmen who perished before them in the van, came very near to achieving the same success as their Achaean predecessors. They both did succeed in begetting new civilizations before they severally succumbed; and though these two embryonic civilizations were abortive, they did not pass into limbo before they had each taken a recognizable shape which can be given a name. We may call them the abortive Far Western Christian Civilization and the abortive Scandinavian Civilization. Let us take a glance at each of them.

The Abortive Far Western Christian Civilization

The distinctive feature of the Far Western Christian Civilization of 'the Celtic Fringe' was its attitude towards Christianity. Unlike the Gothic converts to Arianism or the English converts to Catholicism, the Celtic barbarians who survived to accept Christianity did not take the alien religion as they happened to find it. They moulded it to fit their own barbarian social heritage, instead of allowing it to break up their native tradition and instal itself uncompromisingly in the vacuum. In modern scientific terms, the Christianization of the Celtic rear-guard was not revolutionary but evolutionary.

'No other race showed such originality in its way of taking Christianity. . . . The Church felt no obligation to be severe towards the caprices of the [Celtic] religious imagination; it gave free play to popular instinct; and the outcome was a cult which was perhaps the most thoroughly steeped in Mythology and the most closely analogous to the Mysteries of Hellenic Antiquity of any cult recorded in the annals of Christianity.'[1]

[1] Renan, E.: *Essais de Morale et de Critique* (Paris 1859, Lévy), pp. 437–8 and 442, quoted by Gougaud, L., in *Les Chrétientés Celtiques* (Paris 1911, Gabalda), p. 58. In the

This originality showed itself even among the Celts of Britain, whose native genius had been subjected, under the Roman régime, to the standardizing impress of a latter-day cosmopolitan Hellenism. The relatively short span of perhaps not more than two centuries that intervened between the spread of Christianity through the Roman Island and the invasion of the English barbarians sufficed to produce, in Pelagius, a British 'heresiarch' who caused a stir throughout the Christian World of his day. The nascent Far Western Christendom, however, was to find its focus not in Roman Britain but in barbarian Ireland. Pelagius himself was possibly of Irish origin; but while Pelagius's work was ephemeral, both in Britain and on the Continent, the work of his British contemporary Patrick, who evangelized Ireland, was of enduring importance. If certain scholars are right in supposing that the historical home of this triumphant British apostle of Ireland lay in a neighbourhood that is the traditional home of the British hero King Arthur,[1] whose name is associated in legend with the leadership of a forlorn hope, the coincidence may be taken as symbolic. For virtue was going out of Britain into Ireland at the very time when the spearhead of the English Völkerwanderung was piercing Britain's opposite flank. In the course of the fifth and sixth centuries of the Christian Era, Ireland increased and Britain decreased until the centre of gravity of the insular Celtic World passed over decisively from the 'Roman' to the 'barbarian' island.

The English transmarine Völkerwanderung, which dealt the British Celts a crushing blow, made the Irish Celts' fortune. While the Britons bore the brunt of the English invasion, the Irish were not only immune from English attack themselves but actually emulated the English in harrying their unhappy British kinsmen. When the Roman defences of Britain broke down, the Irish raided the west coast of the derelict Roman insular dominion as the English were raiding the east coast; and it was as a captive, carried away on one of these Irish raids, that Patrick first set foot in Ireland. These

English translation of the last-mentioned work, which has been published by Dom L. Gougaud after an interval of twenty-one years under the title *Christianity in Celtic Lands* (London 1931, Sheed and Ward), the author criticizes, as overdrawn, the picture of Celtic idealism which is given by Renan in the essay entitled 'La Poésie des Races Celtiques', in which the above-quoted passage occurs. (See Gougaud: *Christianity in Celtic Lands*, p. 19.)

[1] On this location of the obscure Bannaventa, see Bury, J. B.: *The Life of Saint Patrick* (London 1905, Macmillan), pp. 17 and 322–5. The most convincing alternative location is Dumbarton on the Clyde; and this is preferred by Gougaud (see *Christianity in Celtic Lands*, p. 32) and by J. A. Duke (in *The Columban Church* (Oxford 1932, University Press), Appendix IV, pp. 145–50). But the thoroughly Roman touches in Patrick's own description of his family background make it difficult, *a priori*, to suppose that he can have been born and brought up in a district of North Britain which had only just been included within the frontiers of the Roman Empire, even at the time of the Empire's farthest extension in this quarter, and which had almost certainly been abandoned to barbarism again thereafter some time before the date of Patrick's birth.

fifth-century Irish raiders likewise emulated the English in making permanent settlements on British soil; and though these were not comparable with the English settlements in scale, one of them—planted by raiders from Dalriada, in the north-east corner of Ireland, on the opposite British coast, at the point where the intervening seas are narrowest—was destined to become the nucleus of one of the two enduring kingdoms into which the petty and ephemer⌐ successor-states of the Roman Empire in Britain were eventually consolidated.[1] The most valuable boon, however, which the Irish obtained from the English Völkerwanderung into Britain was not this opportunity of taking a modest share of the British spoils. The main effect of the English Völkerwanderung upon Irish fortunes was to segregate Ireland—immediately after the seeds of Christianity had been sown there—from those *ci-devant* Roman territories in the western part of the European Continent in which a new Christian Civilization, oriented towards Rome, began to emerge during the post-Hellenic interregnum. It was this segregation, at the most formative stage of early growth, that made it possible for the embryo of a separate and distinctive 'Far Western Christian Civilization', with its nucleus in Ireland, to emerge simultaneously with the emergence of the nascent Continental Western Christendom.

'The Irish culture differed considerably from the general European-Roman Civilisation. . . . It is true, Christianity had penetrated to this westernmost land of Europe; but in countless other respects Ireland had remained outside the spread of civilisation, so that the peculiarly Celtic culture had had time to develop in its richest and most unique form. . . . Christianity had taken root very early and had produced small hermit-like monastic settlements which were the leading force in the Irish Church. They were in a sense the heirs of the struggle waged by the ancient Druids on evil spirits with the aid of conjuring, and were at the same time consecrated to an inner religious life and an external missionary activity. A curious adventurous asceticism drove hermit societies—twelve monks and an abbot, corresponding in number to the Redeemer and His disciples—to the outermost islands, in one case even to distant Iceland, before any other human foot had stepped upon the island.'[2]

The originality of the Far Western Christian Civilization, as it emerged in Ireland, is manifest alike in its ecclesiastical organization, in its ritual and hagiography, and in its literature and art.

In Ireland conspicuously, and to some extent also in Wales and in

---

[1] For the origin of this new Dalriada on British soil, see II. D (iii), p. 86, and II. D (v), p. 194, above. It is one of the well-known curiosities of history that the Scottish name, which originally belonged to the Irish Celts and was carried from the old to the new Dalriada by Irish settlers, should have lost its association with Ireland and have become exclusively associated with a kingdom that is situated in Britain and with a language that is not Celtic but Teutonic.

[2] Olrik, A.: *Viking Civilisation* (English translation: London 1930, Allen and Unwin), pp. 107–8.

Brittany, the life of the Celtic Church was 'cellular'—in the literal as well as the metaphorical sense. It resided in the monasteries, which were sometimes federated in clusters (*familiae*) round some mother-foundation—the most famous example being the *Familia Columbae* which clustered round Iona.[1] A monastic cell or cluster of this kind was apt to be established, as a nucleus of the embryonic civilization, in each of the cantons into which barbarian Ireland was politically articulated. The initiative seems usually to have been taken by the local chieftain; and the cells and clusters thus established were governed by abbots—sometimes spiritual, sometimes temporal—who in many places were required to be of the founder's kin. The Irish called their monasteries in Latin *civitates*—the Latin name for the city-states of the Hellenic World which had become bishops' sees after the advent of Christianity. The Irish *civitates* resembled their continental European namesakes in being the seats of bishops; but here the resemblance ceased; for the Irish *civitates* were monasteries and not towns;[2] the episcopal office in an Irish monastic *civitas* was sometimes held by the hereditary abbot himself[3] and sometimes by a tame bishop living in the monastery under the abbot's control;[4] and these Irish cloistral bishops had no mutually exclusive territorial jurisdictions. There were even bishops who had no connexion with a monastery and therefore no fixed point of residence or zone of jurisdiction at all. Conversely, there were non-episcopal monasteries which were independent, *de facto*, of episcopal control.[5]

This monastic organization of the Celtic Church was an extreme development of a tendency which had declared itself to some extent in Early Christian Egypt;[6] but, on the whole, it is less reminiscent of Christian than of Buddhist or Manichaean ecclesiastical institu-

[1] See Duke, J. A.: *The Columban Church* (Oxford 1932, University Press).

[2] Perhaps the closest parallel to this Irish Society with its monastic nuclei is the outpost of the Orthodox Christian Society which was established in Calabria by means of Basilian monastic foundations in the ninth and tenth centuries of the Christian Era. These monastic foundations in Calabria provided rallying-points for the settlement of Orthodox Christian refugees from Sicily. (See Gay, Jules: *L'Italie Méridionale et l'Empire Byzantin*: A.D. 867–1071 (Paris 1904, Fontemoing.)

[3] 'The titles "bishop" and "abbot" are used almost indiscriminately for the rulers of Armagh during the 6th and 7th centuries, justification for this usage being that every ruler held in fact the two (almost equally distinguished) offices.' (Ryan, J.: *Irish Monasticism: Origins and Early Development* (London 1931, Longmans, Green and Co.), p. 171.) At Armagh the two offices were divorced between A.D. 750 and A.D. 790 (op. cit., p. 172).

[4] In this event, the abbot monopolized the administration, while the bishop devoted himself to sanctity and learning (Ryan, op. cit., p. 172)—so much so that in Ireland the word abbot became synonymous with executive authority of any kind, spiritual or secular (Gougaud: *Christianity in Celtic Lands*, p. 83). For examples of tame bishops, see Ryan, op. cit., pp. 180 and 301–2.

[5] Ryan, op. cit., p. 178. The most famous case of the kind is the constitution of the *Familia Columbae*, of which the Abbot of Iona was the head. For the Abbot of Iona was always only a presbyter, though the abbots of the affiliated monasteries were often bishops. (Duke, op. cit., p. 120; Gougaud: *Christianity in Celtic Lands*, p. 136.)

[6] For the ancestry of Irish monasticism, see Ryan, op. cit., p. 407.

tions. As for the Irish itinerant bishops, there are parallels in the history of the Nestorian Church after its dispersion abroad among the oases of the Eurasian Steppe;[1] but the very notion of a bishop without a diocese was repugnant to the Orthodox and Roman churches, whose conceptions of ecclesiastical organization were thoroughly territorial owing to the fact that these churches had grown up within the framework of the Roman Empire and had taken for granted its systematic territorial articulation into municipalities and provinces.[2]

As for ritual, the Celtic Church became doubly differentiated from the Roman Church by its conservative attitude towards Roman innovations and its proneness to innovations of its own. It did not adopt the innovations which were made by the Roman Church during the period of segregation (circa A.D. 450–600) in the method of reckoning the date of Easter.[3] On the other hand, it did adopt—possibly from the Druids—a peculiar form of tonsure;[4] and it developed a hagiography of its own in which the Celtic Saints eclipsed, or at any rate attained an equal eminence with, the most exalted figures in the Old and the New Testament. Saint Patrick, for instance, was equated with Moses and Saint Bridget with the Virgin Mary herself.[5]

The literary studies which Christian liturgical requirements kept alive everywhere during the post-Hellenic interregnum bore fruit in Ireland in a greater mastery of the Latin Classics than was retained by the Christian Church in the ci-devant Roman provinces on the Continent where Latin remained the vernacular language. More remarkable still, the Irish ecclesiastical scholars contrived to

---

[1] See II. D (vi), pp. 237–38, above.
[2] For Irish monasteries and bishops, see Bury, J. B.: The Life of Saint Patrick (London 1905, Macmillan), pp. 174–84 and 375–9; Gougaud: Les Chrétientés Celtiques, pp. 215–19 and 232–4; Gougaud: Christianity in Celtic Lands, pp. 66–75; Ryan, S. J., the Rev. J.: Irish Monasticism: Origins and Early Development (London 1931, Longmans, Green and Co.). According to Ryan, Saint Patrick's organization was clerical rather than monastic, though Patrick approved of monasticism (pp. 92–3). The ecclesiastical centres (civitates) established by Patrick resembled monasteries (pp. 94 and 88–9). 'The place of monasticism in the church founded by Saint Patrick was important but secondary' (p. 96). However, 'the clerical community at Armagh was reorganized and reconstituted on a formally monastic basis' before the end of the fifth century (p. 101). In the early sixth century, Irish monasticism received an impulsion from Britain (pp. 114–16). And about the middle of the sixth century, under the British influence of Gildas, the Irish sees were transformed into monasteries (pp. 165–6). The influence of three Britons—St. David, St. Cadoc, and Gildas—upon Irish monasticism is also emphasized by Duke in op. cit., on p. 50.
[3] According to Bury (in op. cit., pp. 371–4), the method of reckoning which prevailed in Ireland in the sixth and seventh centuries was a method which had been discarded by the Roman Church as early as A.D. 343. In other words, the Irish method was pre-Patrician; and Bury conjectures that it had been introduced into Ireland before Patrick's arrival—probably from Britain.
[4] Bury, op. cit., pp. 142–4 and 183 and 239–43; Gougaud: Christianity in Celtic Lands, p. 204.
[5] Gougaud: Les Chrétientés Celtiques, pp. 260–6; Christianity in Celtic Lands, pp. 271–2.

recapture a command of the Greek language and literature, at a time when the knowledge of Greek was extinct in Latin Christian countries that were much less remote geographically than Ireland was from the living reservoir of Greek that survived in the East Roman Empire.[1] At the same time, the ardour of the Irish in studying the culture of the Hellenic Society from which their own embryonic culture had received its impetus did not prevent them from developing a vernacular literature of their own in the line of their pagan Celtic tradition.[2] And they showed their independence in the technical domain by working out a specifically Irish adaptation of the Latin Alphabet.[3]

The new style of art which emerged, during the post-Hellenic interregnum, in the nascent Far Western Christian World 'drew its inspiration from many seemingly incongruous sources . . . and welded their several elements together into a singularly harmonious unity'.[4] There were elements from the Early Central European Iron

[1] The channel through which the Irish acquired their knowledge of Greek remains a mystery. Gougaud suggests Theodore of Tarsus, who taught Greek to a number of English pupils on the testimony of Bede (*Historia Ecclesiastica*, iv. 2, and v. 20 and 23). But this seems hardly likely, considering that Theodore arrived in England just after the conflict between the Roman and the Celtic Church had come to a head at the Synod of Whitby, and considering further that this Greek Archbishop of Canterbury took a strongly anti-Celtic line himself (*Christianity in Celtic Lands*, p. 423). Gougaud points out (in *Les Chrétientés Celtiques*, pp. 247–9) that the Irish mastery of Greek is non-proven for the period of Irish scholarship anterior to the ninth century of the Christian Era. On the other hand, the genuineness of the ninth-century Irish Hellenists (e.g. Johannes Scotus Erigena) is beyond question. (For details of John Scotus's proficiency in Greek, see Gougaud, op. cit., loc. cit., and Sandys, J. E.: *A History of Classical Scholarship* (Cambridge 1903, University Press), pp. 473–8. In *Christianity in Celtic Lands*, on p. 309, Gougaud cites the warm testimony given to John Scotus by his contemporary, the papal librarian Anastasius, for his feat in making a Latin translation of the Greek Pseudo-Dionysius Areopagita.) In *Christianity in Celtic Lands*, on p. 308, Gougaud comes to the conclusion that 'in the second half of [the ninth] century a limited number of Irish emigrants on the Continent gave proof of some acquaintance with the [Greek] language'. But he finds no proof of Greek studies in the Irish schools in Ireland (op. cit., p. 248). It was on the Continent that the Irish acquired their unusual learning, the evidence for which is all to be found in Continental manuscripts (op. cit., pp. 250 and 309).

[2] 'Noteworthy . . . is the apparently matter-of-fact way in which zeal for studies, the higher as well as the lower, is worked into the Irish system. . . . Its explanation in Ireland is probably to be sought in the native schools of druids, fáthi, filid, bards, which preceded Christianity. The monks were felt to be the successors of the two orders first mentioned of these, and thus were expected to apply themselves not only to religion, but also to the cultivation of the intellect. When they likewise took up the study of the native language and literature, their extraordinary position in the life of the country was assured.' (Ryan, op. cit., p. 408.) The pre-Christian bardic schools, instead of being abolished when the monastic schools were instituted, were simply reorganized (apparently in A.D. 573, under the inspiration of Saint Columba, who had received a bardic education himself). Thereafter, the two systems of education flourished in Ireland side by side, performing complementary functions and mutually influencing one another (Graham, H.: *The Early Irish Monastic Schools* (Dublin 1923, Talbot Press), pp. 71–8). 'The union of the two cultures in the monastic schools probably began about A.D. 600' (Ryan, op. cit., p. 377). The Latin orthography of the Irish language was definitely fixed before the end of the seventh century (Ryan, op. cit., loc. cit.).

[3] On this Irish script, see Gougaud: *Les Chrétientés Celtiques*, pp. 333–5; *Christianity in Celtic Lands*, p. 368; Ryan, op. cit., p. 380.

[4] Macalister, R. A. S.: *The Archaeology of Ireland* (London 1928, Methuen), p. 264. Vide ch. vi, 'The Principles of Irish Christian Art', and ch. vii, 'The Expression of Decorative Christian Art in Ireland', *passim*.

Age culture of La Tène—the culture of the pagan Celts at the time of their impact upon the Hellenic World in the fifth to third centuries B.C.[1] There were elements from the art of the Eurasian Steppe, which had been brought into Western Europe by the Sarmatian Nomads who broke through the Roman frontier, in company with the vanguard of the Teutonic trans-frontier barbarians, in the post-Hellenic Völkerwanderung.[2] There were elements from Hellenic art, and from the Syriac art which had eventually dominated and permeated and transformed Hellenic art from end to end of the Roman Empire. This new art was not confined to Ireland or even to 'the Celtic Fringe' as a whole. It was a common possession of the whole North European external proletariat of the Roman Empire.[3] It was in Ireland, however, that it attained its zenith—particularly in the illumination of parchment manuscripts and in the carving of stone crosses—and the influence of this Irish art radiated into England and Scandinavia,[4] and impressed itself upon the kindred art there, besides making itself felt in Continental Western Christendom.

Within a century of Saint Patrick's mission in Ireland (*Patricius in Hibernia Fidem propagabat circa* A.D. 432–61), the embryonic Far Western Christian Civilization, derived from the germs which he had planted, had not only developed on its own distinctive lines but had actually shot ahead of the nascent Western Christian Civilization on the Continent. This initial superiority of the Insular over the Continental culture was due in part to the positive cause which we have considered already—the creative reaction of an indigenous Celtic Barbarism to an intrusive Christianity during a century and a half of segregation—and partly perhaps to the negative advantage which Ireland enjoyed during the post-Hellenic interregnum in being immune from the Frankish and Lombard invasions which devastated Gaul and Italy only less cruelly than the English invasion devastated Britain.[5] But, however the superiority is to be explained, the fact is manifest. It was doubly proved, when the period of segregation came to an end towards the close of the sixth century of the Christian Era, by the warmth of the welcome which Irish missionary monks and scholars received in Britain and on the Continent, and by the eagerness with which English and Continental students sought out the Irish monastic schools, where foreigners were generously furnished with food and lodging and books and

---

[1] For this impact and its repulse, see pp. 279–82 and 319, above.
[2] The distinctive contributions of this Eurasian art were' the Animal Style' and 'Polychromy' (see Rostovtzeff, M.: *Iranians and Greeks in South Russia* (Oxford 1922, Clarendon Press)). [3] Macalister, op. cit., p. 264.
[4] For the influence of Irish on Scandinavian art, see Olrik, op. cit., pp. 117–18, and Macalister, op. cit., pp. 340–3.
[5] For the heaviness of the yoke which the Lombards imposed upon Italy, see II. D (iii), Annex, pp. 395–9, below.

teaching gratis.[1] The period of Irish cultural superiority over the Continent and over Britain may be conventionally dated from the foundation of the monastic university of Clonmacnois in Ireland in A.D. 548[2] to the foundation of the Irish monastery of St. James at Ratisbon *circa* A.D. 1090. Throughout those five and a half centuries, it was the Irish who imparted culture and the English and the Continentals who received it. But this transmission of culture was not the only social consequence of the renewal of contact between the Insular and the Continental Christendom of the West. Another consequence was a contest for power. In this conflict, the issue at stake was whether the future civilization which was to emerge in Western Europe should derive from an Irish or from a Roman embryo; and the Irish were defeated in this trial of strength long before they lost their cultural ascendancy.

The issue was raised by the great movement of missionary expansion to which the Irish monks were inspired, by their peculiar spirit of 'adventurous asceticism',[3] in the latter part of the sixth century of the Christian Era. In this manifestation of youthful energy, monastic Ireland anticipated papal Rome. While Pope Gregory the Great's emissary Augustine did not cross the sea from the Continent to Britain, on his mission of converting the pagan English, until A.D. 597, St. Columba had already crossed the sea from Ireland to Britain *circa* 563 to found a Christian cell on the Island of Iona among the Scots whose forefathers had migrated thither from Ireland a century or so before;[4] while, *circa* 590, St. Columbanus had crossed from Ireland to Britain and from Britain to the Continent itself. Columbanus reached the Lake of Constance in 610 and crossed the Alps in 613; and the simultaneous settlement, in the latter year, of Columbanus himself at Bobbio and of his companion Gallus at the spot where his name was afterwards commemorated in the monastery of St. Gall,[5] anticipated

---

[1] Bede: *Historia Ecclesiastica*, iii. 47. For a list of distinguished foreign students who studied in the Irish monastic schools, see Graham, H.: *The Early Irish Monastic Schools* (Dublin 1923, Talbot Press), pp. 84–90. The list includes Welsh, English, and Frankish names—among them, the name of Willibrord, the apostle of the Frisians (Gougaud: *Christianity in Celtic Lands*, pp. 257–8). The Northumbrian English refugees who studied in Ireland learnt to speak Gaelic and even to write in it (op. cit., p. 248). There are Irish verses which are attributed to the Northumbrian King Aldfrid (*regnabat* A.D. 686–705), the son of the King Oswiu who presided, with such momentous results, at the Synod of Whitby (see pp. 334–6, below). On the question of English and Continental students in Ireland in the seventh and subsequent centuries, see also Gougaud: *Les Chrétientés Celtiques*, pp. 251–2.

[2] The earliest of all the Irish monasteries seems to have been Cell Enda, on the largest of the Arran Islands, whose eponymous founder died in A.D. 530. (Gougaud: *Christianity in Celtic Lands*, p. 67.)   [3] See the quotation from Ölrik on p. 324, above.

[4] Duke points out (in op. cit., on p. 12) that Columba died in the year of Augustine's arrival.

[5] Gougaud points out (in *Christianity in Celtic Lands* on pp. 143 and 158) that a regularly organized monastery was not established at St. Gall till nearly a century after the eponym's death on that spot.

by twelve years the arrival of the Roman missionary Paulinus in York.

Pressing boldly into the interior of the Continent, Columbanus founded his first Continental cluster of cells in the heart of the Frankish dominions, on the borders of Burgundy, Swabia, and Austrasia, at Annegray, Luxeuil, and Fontaines; and the choice of these sites testifies to the founder's strategic intuition. It is no accident that Luxeuil lies within a hundred miles of Metz—the point of intersection of the two co-ordinate lines in the eventual structure of Western Christendom[1]—and within less than a hundred miles of La Tène, which lies in the heart of the region from which the Celtic barbarians had expanded a thousand years earlier in their counter-attack upon the Hellenic World in the fifth to third centuries B.C.[2] At Luxeuil the pioneer Celtic monk Columbanus and his companions, like their prototypes the pioneer Celtic barbarians at La Tène, commanded an ideal base for operations in all quarters of the Continent. While La Tène lies at the outlet of the Lake of Neuchâtel in the upper basin of the Aar, in the gap between the Jura and the Alps, Luxeuil stands by the head-waters of the Saône, in the gap between the Jura and the Vosges. From either base, it is equally easy to descend upon the basin of the Rhône and the basin of the Rhine and hardly less easy to reach the basins of the Seine and the Danube. The Celtic war-band at La Tène and the Celtic fraternity at Luxeuil each, in their day, took full advantage of the commanding strategic position in which they found themselves. Their expansions over the face of the Continent from these two neighbouring starting-points followed identic routes and were pursued with an equal energy.

The likenesses and the differences between the first and the last of the Celtic expansions cannot fail to exercise a historian's imagination. The very closeness of the physical points of resemblance brings into relief the sharpness of the spiritual contrast. The first Celtic expansion was a warlike Völkerwanderung, the last an ascetic pilgrimage; and while the legendary barbarian war-lord Bellovesus came to destroy the Hellenic culture, the historical Christian missionary Columbanus trod in Bellovesus's footsteps in order to re-sow the seeds of culture in lands where Bellovesus's Teutonic barbarian successors had trampled the harvest of Hellenism into the mire. At Luxeuil, Celtic monks reoccupied a derelict Roman watering-place,[3] as a Celtic war-band had once occupied a derelict Etruscan

[1] See I. B (iv), vol. i, pp. 37–9, above.
[2] See pp. 279–82 and 319, above, for this Celtic counter-attack upon the Hellenic World and its failure.
[3] Gougaud points out (in *Christianity in Celtic Lands* on p. 83) that Celtic monasteries were in the nature of pioneer settlements, and that deserted sites were favourite locations for them.

city at Milan; but the difference in the circumstances was all-important; for Etruscan Milan had been laid desolate by the Celtic invaders themselves, whereas the Irish reoccupants of Luxeuil re-inhabited a Roman site which had been desolated by others, and dedicated it to a nobler service than its original use. At Bobbio, Columbanus founded a Celtic monastery in an Apennine valley which the Celtic invaders of Italy in the fifth century B.C. had never reached;[1] and this latter-day Celtic stronghold in Liguria, commanding a passage across the Apennines from Northern Europe to Rome, was not an outpost of barbarism but a light of freshly kindled civilization shining in the darkness of a barbarized Italy. The sister foundation of St. Gall—a still more famous daughter of Luxeuil—occupied an equally commanding position on the high road leading out of Western Europe into the Danube valley, where it radiated a light of equal brilliance upon the darkness of a still pagan Bavaria.

There is, however, one point of likeness between the two Celtic expansions on the Continent which is of the highest historical importance. In the seventh century of the Christian Era, as in the fourth century B.C., the expanding Celts came into collision with Rome; and in the second of these encounters they were defeated as decisively as they had been defeated a thousand years earlier.

The conflict between the Irish and the Roman Church in the seventh century was perhaps the inevitable result of a profound difference of êthos which had arisen during the century and a half of segregation, and which declared itself as soon as the Irish missionary expansion brought the two parties into contact again. Under the stress of the breakdown of the Hellenic Society and the break-up of the Roman Empire, the Roman Church had sought to save the situation by salvaging, and making its own, those traditions of discipline and unity for which the defunct secular Roman order had formerly stood, whereas the Irish Church, in its peculiar isolation and security, had indulged, if not cultivated, a libertarian genius. When these two thus sharply differentiated churches met, it was the Irish Church that bridged the physical gulf and the Roman Church that took the human offensive.

The temporary segregation of the Irish Church had been involuntary and not deliberate;[2] and when the Irish pioneer-missionaries eventually landed on the Continent and thereby re-established contact with Continental Christendom, they were evidently uncon-scious of having drifted away from Roman practice themselves and unaware that Roman practice had parted company with theirs.

[1] There is, however, some shadow of evidence for Celtic settlements in the north-western Apennines as early as the seventh and sixth centuries B.C. (See Hubert, op. cit., pp. 322–32.)   [2] On this point, see Bury, op. cit., pp. 213–15.

They simply continued on their own course, on the assumption that their native Irish Christianity was the Christianity of the Catholic Church;[1] and in their intercourse with their Continental co-religionists, including the Pope himself, they exhibited the freedom and the self-confidence to which they were accustomed in their dealings among themselves.

Columbanus, for example, appears to have established his cluster of monasteries in Burgundy without consulting the local Burgundian ecclesiastical authorities; he certainly introduced his own Irish monastic rule;[2] and he celebrated Easter according to a method of reckoning, still employed in Ireland, which had been discarded on the Continent since A.D. 343.[3] When he was taken to task on this last account by the representatives of the Gallican Church, he counter-attacked by upbraiding the Pope himself, in an open letter, for adhering to the newfangled Continental system. The particular Pope whom Columbanus thus roundly threatened in A.D. 600 with the penalty of being 'looked upon as a heretic and rejected with scorn by the Churches of the West' was none other than Gregory the Great himself: the very incarnation of the new Roman ecclesiastical imperialism! Columbanus wrote with equal frankness to the Gallican synod at Châlon-sur-Saône before which he was arraigned in A.D. 603; and he addressed a third letter on the Paschal Controversy to one of Gregory's successors on the Papal throne.[4] His independent attitude towards the authorities of the Continental Western Church on this question of ecclesiastical practice, and his equal independence in denouncing the political and personal crimes of the Frankish Queen Brynhild,[5] eventually led to his being evicted from Gaul in A.D. 610—whereupon the Irish saint followed the example of Saint Paul and turned his back upon his co-religionists in order to preach to the Gentiles. He travelled on from Christian Burgundy into pagan Bavaria, and it was thus that he reached Lake Constance;[6] but this was not the end of his pilgrimage. For in A.D. 612 he left the shores of Lake Constance and descended, from

1 This assumption seems to underlie the concluding passage in St. Columbanus's letter to the synod at Châlon-sur-Saône before which he was arraigned in A.D. 603. (See below.)

2 The attractiveness of the Irish Christian culture to the Continental Christians of the day is illustrated by the fact that 'the rule of Saint Columbanus soon became the object of such veneration that, towards the middle of the seventh century, many Gallic cloiste adopted it simultaneously with the rule of St. Benedict'. (Gougaud, Les Chré:..ntés Celtiques, p. 146; cp. Christianity in Celtic Lands, p. 141.)

3 See p. 326, above.

4 For Columbanus's three letters on the Paschal Controversy, see Gougaud: Les Chrétientés Celtiques, pp. 180–3; and Kerr, W. S.: The Independence of the Celtic Church in Ireland (London 1931, S.P.C.K.), ch. v. An attempt to explain away the conflict between Columbanus and the Papacy in particular, and between the Irish Church and the Roman Church in general, is made by Ryan in op. cit., on pp. 302–5; but this exposition is not convincing. Duke points out (in op. cit., on p. 131) that, in Adamnan's Life of St. Columba, the Papacy is never mentioned.

5 For details, see Ryan, op. cit., pp. 308–12.   6 See p. 329, above.

this unexpected quarter, upon Italy; and his spirit was so far from being broken by his experiences in the Paschal Controversy that, between his settlement at Bobbio in 613 and his death two years later, he found time to engage in another controversy with another pontiff![1]

This independent spirit of Irish Christendom, which Columbanus displayed in the seventh century, was still alive in the ninth.

On the moral plane, the spirit reveals itself in a gloss written by an Irish hand and in the Irish language on the margin of a ninth-century manuscript of the Epistles of St. Paul:[2]

'To go to Rome is great labour and little profit. Thou wilt not find the King that thou goest to seek there unless thou bring Him with thee. It is folly, frenzy, insanity, unreason—since thou goest out to meet certain death—that thou shouldest call down upon thee the wrath of the Son of Mary.'

With the moral insight of this ninth-century Irish gloss, which conveys in two sentences the theme of Tolstoy's fable of the Two Pilgrims, we may equate the intellectual vigour and originality of the ninth-century Irish Hellenist, philosopher, and theologian, Johannes Scotus Erigena: the giant of the Carolingian Renaissance, whose like was not seen again in Western Christendom until the Italian Renaissance of the fifteenth century. In his magnum opus *De Divisione Naturae* (*scriptum circa* A.D. 867), Erigena dared to present Philosophy as an independent discipline on an equal footing with Theology, and to declare that where philosophic reason and theological authority conflict, reason and not authority must prevail.[3]

The struggle for power which was perhaps rendered inevitable by this striking difference in êthos between the libertarianism of Ireland and the authoritarianism of Rome was brought to a head by a competition for the conversion of the still pagan barbarians of

---

[1] For Columbanus's letter to Pope Boniface IV on the Controversy of 'the Three Chapters', see Kerr, op. cit., ch. xii.

[2] The Codex Boernerianus in the Royal Library at Dresden. Translations of the gloss are given in Gougaud: *Les Chrétientés Celtiques*, pp. 158–9; and in Zimmer, H.: *The Irish Element in Mediaeval Culture* (English translation: New York 1891, Putnam), p. 126. For a critical examination of this gloss, see Gougaud: *Christianity in Celtic Lands*, p. 169.

[3] For Johannes Scotus see Gougaud: *Les Chrétientés Celtiques*, ch. viii, especially pp. 280–1; *Christianity in Celtic Lands*, pp. 288–9; Zimmer, op. cit., pp. 57–60; Sandys, J. E.: *A History of Classical Scholarship* (Cambridge 1903, University Press), pp. 473–8. Erigena's independence of mind showed itself not only in the domain of Philosophy but also in that of Physical Science. For example, he believed in the existence of the Antipodes. In this belief he had perhaps been anticipated by an eighth-century Irish missionary scholar, Virgil, bishop of Salzburg (*episcopabatur* A.D. 767–84), who was denounced on this account to Pope Zacharias by the English missionary Boniface. The pope gave orders that if Virgil really did believe in the Antipodes, he was to be excommunicated and unfrocked. In this controversy, the Irishman appears to have got the better of the Englishman; for, after holding the see of Salzburg against Boniface since A.D. 745 as a mere presbyter, Virgil became a bishop after Boniface had become a martyr. (For this Irish Virgil, see Gougaud: *Les Chrétientés Celtiques*, pp. 242–3; *Christianity in Celtic Lands*, p. 151; Sandys, op. cit., p. 448; Hodgkin, T.: *Italy and her Invaders*, vol. vii (Oxford 1899, Clarendon Press), pp. 122–3. Some scepticism in regard to Virgil's supposed views is exhibited by Gougaud in *Christianity in Celtic Lands* on p. 256.)

Northern Europe on the Continent and in Britain. It was manifest that—in a region where there was no room for two separate civilizations to come to birth and grow up side by side—the unitary Western Christendom of the future would spring from whichever of the two embryonic societies that were now emerging at opposite extremities of this region should succeed in capturing the barbarian hinterland. The battle between the Irish and the Roman competitors for the privilege of becoming the creators of our Western Civilization was fought out, between the years 625 and 664, in the northernmost English successor-state of the Roman Empire, Northumbria, and was decided in the latter year at the Synod of Whitby.

The race between the Roman and the Irish Church for the prize of Northumbria was closely run. The Roman missionary Paulinus reached York in A.D. 625, and in 627 he converted the Northumbrian prince Edwin—the founder of Edinburgh[1]—who had asserted a political hegemony over the larger part of Britain. In 633, however, Edwin lost both his dominion and his life in battle with the pagan Penda of Mercia; and Christianity was reintroduced into Northumbria by Edwin's successor Oswald: the representative of a rival dynasty who had repaired in exile to Iona and had been converted to Christianity there. The new ruler of Northumbria naturally sought missionaries for his subjects in the sanctuary where he had found his own faith. He addressed himself to Iona and not to Rome; and the monks of Iona, who had already converted the Picts, in the northern extremity of Britain, from their islet-cell off the west coast, now established a new cell off the east coast of Britain on the islet of Lindisfarne (Holy Island) as a base of operations for evangelizing Oswald's Northumbrians in the first instance and the rest of the English in due course.

In the middle of the seventh century, when Northumbria was under this Irish ecclesiastical ascendancy, the prospects of the Far Western Christendom in Britain seemed promising. The Irish Christians were not alienated from the English by the implacable hatred that animated the British Christians of Wales and West Wales and Strathclyde; for, during the recent Völkerwanderung, the Irish and the English had never crossed one another's path, since their common victims, the Britons, whom they had assailed simultaneously from opposite sides, had always interposed a human 'buffer' between them. The English barbarians, on their part, were even more susceptible to the attractions of the superior Irish culture which was offered to them by the Ionan missionary Aidan than the somewhat less barbarous peoples who had recently welcomed the advent of Columbanus on the Continent. Moreover, the North-

[1] See II. D (v), p. 191, above.

umbrian principality, which was Aidan's immediate field of work, recovered momentarily in 655, under Oswald's brother and successor Oswiu, the hegemony which it had already won and lost under Oswald's predecessor Edwin. Thus a number of social and political factors were working together for the cultural union of the Teutonic with the Celtic peoples of the British Isles under the aegis of a common Far Western Christendom. In these circumstances, Northumbria was unexpectedly recaptured for the Roman Church by the influence of Eanfled, Oswiu's queen, who had been brought up in the Roman practice, and by the energy of Wilfrid, a native Northumbrian cleric who had become an ardent Romanizer. At the Synod of Whitby, where the issue was decided in A.D. 664, the rival claims of Rome and Iona were nominally debated on the merits of the Paschal Controversy; but this trivial point of ritual was merely the test question in a trial of strength between two ecclesiastical powers, and King Oswiu gave his allegiance to Rome because he came to the conclusion that Peter was stronger than Columba.[1]

The consequences of Oswiu's decision were momentous. The immediate external effect was the restoration of a uniformity of practice in the Western Church. The Picts, the Irish, the Welsh, and the Bretons successively accepted the Roman Easter and the Roman tonsure in the course of the eighth century; and Iona itself submitted as early as the year 716. Yet even this half-century's delay deprived the Ionan missionaries of all the ground which they had won by a century of effort in Britain. They had to evacuate Northumbria on the morrow of Oswiu's decision in 664,[2] and all Pictland east of the Grampians on the morrow of an identic decision which was taken by the Pictish King Nectan in 710. Moreover, in making this formal act of submission to Rome, Celtic Christendom publicly renounced its independence without obtaining any countervailing material benefits; for the questions of Easter and the tonsure, which had been taken as the test questions in the struggle for power, were by no means the only points on which the Celtic Churches had become peculiar. The residue of the Celtic peculiari-

[1] Wilfrid convinced Oswiu by quoting the text: 'Thou art Peter; and upon this rock I will build my Church; and the gates of Hell shall not prevail against it. And I will give unto thee the keys of the Kingdom of Heaven; and whatsoever thou shalt bind on Earth shall be bound in Heaven; and whatsoever thou shalt loose on Earth shall be loosed in Heaven.' Turning to Colman, the Ionan Abbot of Lindisfarne, who was the spokesman of the Ionan party at the synod, Oswiu asked him (i) whether the text quoted by Wilfrid was genuine, and (ii) whether Colman could quote any text showing that equivalent powers had been granted to Columba. When Colman answered the first of these two questions in the affirmative and the second in the negative, Oswiu closed the debate by opting for allegiance to Rome, 'lest, when I come to the gates of the Kingdom of Heaven, there should be none to open them, he being my adversary who is proved to have the keys'.

[2] They still held out in the Northumbrian monasteries—particularly at Lindisfarne, which appears to have clung to the Ionan practice for another half-century (Duke, op. cit., pp. 102–6).

ties was still sufficient to incline the rest of Western Christendom to regard the Celtic Christians as remaining in some sense beyond the Catholic Pale; and these Celtic ecclesiastical peculiarities did not entirely disappear—either in Wales or in Brittany or in Scotland or in Ireland—until the close of the twelfth century.

Thus, from the date of the Synod of Whitby onwards, the embryonic Christendom of the Far West was thrust back again into the state of isolation from which it had been released for a moment by the missionary efforts of a Columba and a Columbanus. But the last state of this abortive Far Western Christendom was worse than the first. For the iron which had entered into the soul of the Welsh with the agonies which they had suffered during the English Völkerwanderung now entered into the soul of the Irish likewise with the humiliation of their rebuff from Northumbria. The whole of the Celtic Fringe was thus now alienated from England; and at the same time the English had become much more formidable than before to the surviving insular Celts as an aggressive hostile force. Instead of being a swarm of pagan barbarians who were as abhorrent to the Continental Christians as to the British Christians themselves, the English had now become the obedient humble servants of the new ecclesiastical empire of Rome—fighting the Papacy's battles and receiving in return the Papacy's support.

From the latter part of the seventh century onwards the pressure of England upon the Celtic fringe had the whole weight of Continental Western Christendom behind it; and this weight gave the subsequent English drives against the Irish an irresistible impetus. The first of these new drives was made, not in the British Isles but on the Continent, where, in the early decades of the eighth century, the outer fringe of the Continental Teutonic countries under Frankish political suzerainty—Frisia, Hesse, Thuringia, Bavaria—was won for the Roman Church by the English missionary Boniface (*baptizatus* Wynfrith) not so much from a primitive paganism as from the Far Western Christianity of the pioneer Irish missionaries whom Boniface found already at work in this field. The English champion of Rome deliberately ousted these Irish pioneers who had blazed the trail for him, in order that on the Continent, as in Britain itself, the Roman Church might enter into the Celtic Church's missionary labours.[1] In the British Isles, more than four centuries

---

[1] For Boniface's devotion to the Papacy and warfare against his own Irish predecessors in the Central European mission field, see Gougaud, *Les Chrétientés Celtiques*, pp. 153–5, and Hodgkin, T.: *Italy and her Invaders*, vol. vii (Oxford 1899, Clarendon Press), pp. 81–4. Zimmer points out (in op. cit., p. 32) that Boniface's immediate forerunner, Willibrord, the apostle of Frisia, was Irish-trained. (See p. 329, footnote 1, above.) For the measures taken by the Continental ecclesiastical authorities to restrain the Insular *vagantes*, from the second quarter of the eighth century onwards, see Gougaud: *Christianity in Celtic Lands*, pp. 165–7.

later, the Anglo-Roman alliance against the Celts was still in operation. King Henry II's raid in A.D. 1171, which completed the first
step in the long-drawn-out English conquest of Ireland itself, was
made on the authority of a Papal Bull.[1]

Henry II's expedition to Ireland opened the third act of a tragedy
in which the first act had been closed by the Synod of Whitby. The
intervening second act was the Irish reaction to the ordeal of the
Scandinavian Völkerwanderung. In contrast to the foregoing Teutonic Völkerwanderung which had accompanied the break-up of
the Roman Empire, the Scandinavian outbreak did not spare Ireland; and the Far Western island which had been immune from
the storms of the fifth to seventh centuries was harried in the ninth
to eleventh centuries as cruelly as Britain or the Continent. The
Vikings first completed the eradication of Irish influence from
Britain by sacking Lindisfarne in A.D. 793 and Iona in A.D. 802;[2]
and thereafter they dealt such heavy blows to the nascent Far
Western Christian culture in Ireland itself that not a single Irish
monastery escaped,[3] and, as far as is known, not a single work in
Latin was written in Ireland during the ninth century of the
Christian Era (the century in which the scholarship of the Irish
refugees on the Continent stood at its zenith).[4] The Irish did not
yield any more tamely to their Scandinavian assailants than the
English or the French; and in the end the physical progress of
Scandinavian conquest in Ireland was arrested definitively by the
Irish victory in which Brian Boru met his death at Clontarf. Yet
the same Scandinavian challenge that was literally the making of
England and France, because it stimulated the French and English
peoples to the optimum degree,[5] presented itself to Ireland, in her
renewed isolation, with such excessive severity that she could win
no more than a Pyrrhic victory.

The repulse of the physical assaults of Scandinavian raiders on
France and England was followed by a spiritual counter-offensive
on the part of Continental Western Christendom; and the outcome
was a rapid and thorough-going cultural conquest of the Scandi-

[1] The Bull *Laudabiliter*, addressed to King Henry II of England by Pope Hadrian IV
in A.D. 1155, was the response to a request which the King had made for Papal approval
of his projected enterprise. The Pope acceded to the King's request on the ground that
an English conquest of Ireland would enlarge the bounds of the Church and bring
knowledge of the Truth to ignorant and barbarous peoples. The authenticity of this Bull
has been disputed without, apparently, being effectively impugned. (See Gougaud: *Les
Chrétientés Celtiques*, p. 367; *Christianity in Celtic Lands*, p. 408; and Kerr, op. cit.,
pp. 151–2.) The history of the three-cornered relation between Rome, England, and
Ireland is discussed further in Annex II, below.
[2] Gougaud: *Christianity in Celtic Lands*, p. 391. At Iona, the monks were massacred
in the subsequent visitations of A.D. 806 and 825.
[3] Gougaud: *Christianity in Celtic Lands*, p. 392.
[4] Gougaud: *Les Chrétientés Celtiques*, p. 358.
[5] For the victorious response of the French and English to the challenge from the
Scandinavians, see II. D (v), pp. 198–202, above.

navian intruders who had secured a physical lodgement on French
and English soil. In three or four generations the descendants of
the Norse assailants of Western Christendom became her Norman
champions;[1] and a filibustering band of freelance Norman knights,
which crossed St. George's Channel in A.D. 1169, was the advance-
guard of King Henry II's expedition to Ireland. On the other hand,
the victory of Clontarf, which was 'the crowning mercy' in the long
Irish struggle against the same Norsemen, was not followed by any
corresponding conversion of the Scandinavian intruders who still
managed to keep their footing on the coasts of Ireland to the culture
of the Irish hinterland. Notwithstanding the manifest attractiveness and assimilative power of the Irish culture, and the profound
cultural interactions which did in fact take place between Ireland
and Scandinavia, the 'Ostmen', in their five surviving city-states on
Irish soil,[2] remained a people apart; and on a minor scale they
played the same role towards Ireland as the English. In the first
phase of the Scandinavian Völkerwanderung, before the conversion
of the intruders to Christianity, the Viking masters of the Irish
coasts and seas isolated the Irish people from the main body of
Western Christendom as effectively as they had been isolated by
the lodgement of the pagan English in Britain during the first phase
of the Teutonic Völkerwanderung of the fifth and sixth centuries.
In the second phase, the converted Ostmen, like the converted
English, stole a march upon the Irish by entering into more intimate
relations than the Irish themselves had established with Continental
Western Christendom. In the twelfth century, when Ireland succumbed successively to the ecclesiastical authority of Rome and the
political authority of England, the Ostmen lent themselves readily
(though ultimately to their own undoing) as instruments in both
these deadly assaults upon Ireland's independence.

Thus the embryo of a Far Western Christian Civilization, which
showed such promise of life towards the close of the post-Hellenic
interregnum, was ultimately rendered abortive by the strain of
having to respond to a series of challenges which were excessive in
their severity. It was a forlorn hope for the Celtic abbot Colman,
in his islet off the coasts of Ultima Thule, to emulate the prowess
of the Oecumenical Patriarch of Constantinople by trying conclusions with the successor of the Apostle at Rome; and it was a
forlorn hope for the Irish to emulate the prowess of the English
and the French in resisting the onslaught of the Norsemen. The
gallantry of the Irish in facing these fearful odds did not enable
them to survive in a human environment which was insuperably

[1] On this point see II. D (v), p. 201, above.
[2] For these five Scandinavian city-states on the coasts of Ireland, see II. D (iii), p. 98, above.

adverse; and instead of creating a new civilization of their own it was their fate to be laid under contribution by the very competitors who were robbing them of their birthright of independent creation. Irish scholarship was made to minister to the progress of the Continental Western Christian Civilization when Irish scholars, fleeing from Ireland as refugees from Scandinavian onslaughts, were enlisted in the service of the Carolingian Renaissance;[1] and Irish art and literature served to inspire the art and literature of the Scandinavian aggressors themselves[2] and thus likewise helped to enrich the culture of Continental Western Christendom indirectly, through a side channel, when the abortive Scandinavian Civilization succumbed in its turn to a rival which proved more than a match for the Teutonic as well as the Celtic rear-guard of the North European Barbarism.[3]

These Irish contributions to the life of a Western Civilization of non-Irish origin were not even the most conspicuous contributions which medieval Western Christendom levied from the vanquished and discarded peoples of 'the Celtic Fringe'. In spite—or possibly just because—of the predominant part which the Irish had played among the Celtic Christian peoples in inspiring the embryonic Far Western Christian Civilization with its abortive vitality, the Latin (unlike the Scandinavian) genius was not attracted by the exuberant Irish imagination. In the twelfth century, when the possibilities of the French Epic had been exhausted and when French poets were on the look-out for some exotic inspiration, they found what they wanted not in Ireland—the Celtic island which had almost wrested from the Latin Continent the role of creating the new Western Civilization—but in Britain: a Celtic island which had fallen out of the running before the race between the Irish and the Latins had begun. It was no 'matter of Ireland' but 'the matter of Britain' that appealed to a Chrétien de Troyes; and if the Celtic imagination is a living force in the World to-day, it lives in the legend of the heroic failure of Arthur, and not in the history of Columba's or Columbanus's heroic success.

The measure of the difference in êthos between the Irish vein of the Celtic imagination, which left the Latin mind cold, and the Welsh vein, which took the Latin mind by storm, is given by a significant dissimilarity in the treatment of a mythical Celtic theme which the Welsh and the Irish had each cultivated in their respective manners. The peoples of 'the Celtic Fringe', with the Atlantic at their backs and a host of formidable aggressors ever bearing down upon them from the Continent, were naturally inspired to seek imaginative relief from the pressure of an adverse human

---

[1] Gougaud: *Christianity in Celtic Lands*, p. 311.   [2] See p. 328, above.
[3] See pp. 340–60, below.

environment by dreaming of an Elysium hidden in the bosom of the Ocean: a magic island which a Celtic hero might reach under the guidance of superhuman powers who would never give right of way to the hero's alien adversaries. This Elysium is the common dream of the Far Western Celtic peoples; it is the bourne alike of King Arthur and of Saint Brendan; but, in the British and the Irish heroic cycles, the hero's magic westward voyage is made in utterly different circumstances. The vanquished British warrior is wafted away to Avalon in order to find an asylum where he may depart this weary life in peace; the adventurous Irish Saint bends his sails towards the island of his dreams in order to lead a new life on this Earth in a land of hope. The fantasy of Avalon consoled the grief of the Britons when the waters of the English conquest were going over their souls; the fantasy of Saint Brendan's Isle inspired—or reflected—the feat of the Irish when they were anticipating the Norsemen in the discovery of the Faroes and of Iceland.[1]

The Abortive Scandinavian Civilization

It will be seen that, in the hard-fought contest between Rome and Ireland for the privilege of becoming the creator of a new Western Civilization, Rome only just succeeded in gaining the upper hand. And when the nascent Western Christendom which was thus enabled to develop from a Roman embryo was still in its infancy, it had to engage, after the briefest breathing-space, in a second struggle for the same prize—this time in conflict with the Teutonic rear-guard of the North European Barbarism which had been holding itself in reserve in Scandinavia.

In this conflict between the Scandinavians and Western Christendom, the issue was as doubtful as it had been in the foregoing conflict between the Irish and the Roman Church, while the circumstances were more formidable. On this occasion, the trial of strength was made on the military as well as on the cultural plane; the contest was on a far larger material scale; and the two contending parties were severally stronger, and also more alien from one another, at the time of decision in the ninth century, than the rival Irish and Roman embryos of Western Christendom had been at the decisive moment in their antecedent contest, some two centuries earlier. On the one hand, the superiority in strength of ninth-century Western Christendom over its seventh-century Roman embryo is conspicuous. The measure of the difference is given by the political and cultural vitality of the eighth-century Western Christian Civilization as this was manifested in the lives and works of its great protagonists: a Bede and a Boniface, a Liutprand and a

[1] For the Irish monks who preceded the Norsemen in Iceland, see Gougaud: *Christianity in Celtic Lands*, pp. 131-2.

Charles Martel, and, above all, a Charlemagne. On the other hand, the Scandinavian adversaries of the Carolingians surpassed the Irish rivals of Pope Gregory the Great or Bishop Wilfrid in weight of numbers and power of action at least as conspicuously as ninth-century Western Christendom surpassed seventh-century Western Christendom in the same respects.

The history of the Scandinavians in and after the post-Hellenic Völkerwanderung of the fifth, sixth, and seventh centuries of the Christian Era was in some ways like the contemporary history of the Irish and in some ways different from it.

To consider the points of likeness first: the Scandinavians, as well as the Irish, had been drawn within the ambit of the Hellenic external proletariat before the break-up of the Roman Empire; and in Scandinavia, as in Ireland, the effect of the ensuing Völkerwanderung was to insulate this portion of the barbarian hinterland, rather abruptly, from the cultural radiation, proceeding out of the body social of the moribund Hellenic World, to which it had latterly been exposed.

Just as Ireland was isolated from Roman Christendom before the end of the fifth century by the interposition of the pagan English invaders who had crossed the North Sea and made a lodgement in the Roman island of Britain, so Scandinavia was isolated from Roman Christendom before the end of the sixth century by the interposition of the pagan Slavs, who drifted overland along the southern shores of the Baltic, from the line of the Niemen or the Vistula to the line of the Elbe and the Saale, into the vacuum left by the emigration of the Goths, Vandals, Heruli, Warni, Lombards, and other Teutonic barbarians who had evacuated this region because they had been implicated in the post-Hellenic Völkerwanderung and had been lured away by its spell to inflict and suffer destruction in the derelict provinces of the Roman Empire, while the Scandinavians, in 'the back of beyond', had stayed at home. Thus, before the close of the post-Hellenic interregnum, the Scandinavians found themselves isolated from their fellow Teutons, as the Irish were isolated from their fellow Christians, by a wedge of more barbarous interlopers.[1]

[1] 'The conditions for a separate Scandinavian development were not created until the Migration of Nations, which definitely broke the bonds uniting the northern Teutonic tribes with their southern neighbours. The Angles and Saxons travelled to England; the Svevi and Goths moved southward. The lands along the Baltic were for a time deserted, but were slowly filled with a new population. Slavic tribes trickled in from the east, settling the shores of the Baltic as far west as Holstein. . . .
'Thus sharp boundaries of language had been drawn around the North, and at the same time the unrest in Central Europe had cut off the ancient connexions with the South. There had once been physical contact with the Romano-Germanic Civilization; now the bridge had been broken, and the North was thrown on its own resources.' (Olrik, op. cit., p. 8.)

There was, however, one difference between the Scandinavian and the Irish situation which was of fundamental importance and lasting effect. While the previous cultural radiation out of the Roman Empire into Ireland had just succeeded in kindling a spark of Christianity in Ireland before the interposition of the English, the feebler incidence of the same radiation upon Scandinavia had failed to produce the same effect there before the interposition of the Slavs. While the Irish barbarians were converted in the fifth century and the vanguard of the Teutonic barbarians who overran the Continental provinces of the Roman Empire were converted as early as the fourth century,[1] the rear-guard of the Teutons in Scandinavia were still pagans in the sixth century when segregation overtook them; and they therefore remained pagans so long as the segregation lasted and emerged as pagans when it came to an end. Thus the cultural histories of Ireland and of Scandinavia during their respective segregation-periods were markedly different. In Ireland, in this age, there was a mingling of the old wine of North European Barbarism with the new wine of Christianity; and this mingling had produced a creative fermentation—the potential genesis of a new civilization—before the segregation-period had reached its close.[2] In Scandinavia, during the corresponding age, the indigenous North European Barbarism 'stewed in its own juice'; and though the old wine did notably improve by keeping (as it had improved under the same treatment in the same region on other occasions before),[3] it was not, as in Ireland, miraculously changed, by a fresh infusion, into a new vintage.

[1] With the exception of the Franks, who were not converted until A.D. 496. This retardation in the conversion of the Franks is noteworthy, but its effect was mitigated by the fact that the Franks had already settled on Roman ground, where they were exposed to all the influences of the Roman Christian culture. Moreover, the Franks were converted to Catholic Christianity direct, instead of passing from paganism to Catholicism through an intermediate stage of Arianism, like the Goths, Vandals, and Lombards.

[2] For a sketch of this embryonic Far Western Christian Civilization which emerged in Ireland during the segregation period, see pp. 324–8, above.

[3] Before the abortive attempt at creating a Scandinavian Civilization, and the consequent absorption of Scandinavia into Western Christendom, between the eighth and the eleventh century of the Christian Era, the North European Barbarism had had a long history in Scandinavia; and there is one feature in its history here which is distinctive and recurrent because it arises from the permanent geographical relation of Scandinavia to the Continent. On a sociological view, Scandinavia has always been virtually an island, since the cultural radiation to which it has been subject has always travelled to Scandinavia across Continental Europe and thence, in the last stage of the journey, over the Baltic or the North Sea; and this sociological insularity has made Scandinavia particularly prone to segregation. Accordingly, during the long age of Barbarism, during which the Primitive Savagery of Northern Europe was being irradiated by the several contemporary or successive influences of the Egyptiac and Minoan and Sumeric and Hittite and Hellenic and Syriac civilizations, it frequently happened that some particular element or aspect or phase or emanation of one or other of these incoming cultures remained in being, within the secluded area of Scandinavia, and underwent new local developments there, long after it had become obsolete, not only in the focus of the civilization which had originally created it, but even in the intermediate zones of barbarism across which the cultural radiation had passed *en route* to Scandinavia from its point of origin. This peculiarity of Scandinavian cultural history in the age of barbarism becomes apparent at

'The Northman, cut off from association with the outside world, turned his attention inward. . . . In certain respects he became a barbarian again. The stately chieftain in his Romanized garb was transformed back into a long-bearded viking; his Damascene blade was replaced by a heavy sword of iron or a 'troll' of a battle-axe; he wished not to be buried in a coffin in the Southern fashion, but again piled up a mound of earth over the dead, as did his ancient forefathers. He was like the legendary hero Sinfjötli, who when ten years old was sent out into the forest to live as a wolf in order that he might be hardened for the great deed that awaited him. In the same manner the Northman was thrown back upon his own rude nature. He tried his strength against the sea, hunted seals and whales, caught small fish and large fish, went up on the mountain heights after reindeer or after Lapp tribute, or cleared his forest —and dreamed his long heavy winter dream.'[1]

There was a deep difference here, in life and in outlook, between Scandinavia and Ireland in the segregation-period; and this difference, at this stage, produced a further differentiation between the courses of Scandinavian and of Irish history in the following stage, when the Irish and the Scandinavians successively re-entered into contact with Continental Roman Christendom. This subsequent and consequent differentiation was threefold. In the first place, the Scandinavians did not begin to develop a positive civilization of their own until after they had re-established contact with Roman Christendom, whereas the emergence of an embryonic Far Western Christian Civilization in Ireland had preceded the re-establishment of contact between the Irish and the Roman Church. In the second place, the re-establishment of contact between the Scandinavians and Roman Christendom was made on Frankish and not on Scandinavian initiative. Charlemagne's thirty years' war of attrition against the Continental Saxons (A.D. 772–804), in which the Continental frontier of Roman Christendom against the North European Barbarism was carried forward overland from the Ruhr to the Eider, both anticipated[2] and precipitated[3] the Scandinavian sea-raids upon

a glance to any one who visits the Museum of National Antiquities in Stockholm. The visitor cannot fail to observe that the Swedish relics, here displayed, of the North European 'Stone Age' and 'Bronze Age' and 'Iron Age' are the finest local relics of these successive phases of the North European Barbarism that are anywhere to be seen. At first thoughts, it seems paradoxical that the finest products of a culture should have been produced on the outermost fringe of the culture's geographical range; but second thoughts discern that the geographical remoteness of Scandinavia is precisely the explanation of its technological pre-eminence, when the factors of segregation and 'time-lag' are taken into account. The barbarians of Scandinavia eventually carried the techniques of 'the Stone Age' and 'the Bronze Age' to higher degrees of excellence than were ever achieved in either technique by the barbarians of the Continent for the simple reason that the Scandinavians, segregated in their *alter orbis*, were continuing to work in stone for many centuries after the Continentals had abandoned stone for bronze and thereafter to work in bronze (when once they had adopted it) after the Continentals had taken to iron.

[1] Olrik, op. cit., pp. 9–10.
[2] The earliest recorded Scandinavian sea-raids upon Western Christendom took place some time between the years 786 and 793. (Kendrick, T. D.: *A History of the Vikings* (London 1930, Methuen), pp. 3–4.)   [3] See II. D (iii), pp. 86–7, above.

the coasts of Gaul and the British Isles. On the other hand, in the re-establishment of contact, two centuries earlier, between the Irish and the Roman Church, Roman Augustine's landing in Britain had at least been forestalled, even if it cannot be shown to have been inspired, by Irish Columbanus's landing on the Continent. The third line of differentiation between Scandinavian and Irish history, which is inherent in the other two, is perhaps the most important. The collision between the Irish and the Roman Church was pacific; the collision between the Scandinavians and Western Christendom was a clash of arms.

The Scandinavian Völkerwanderung, like other Völkerwanderungen, was the reaction of a barbarian society to the impact of a civilization.[1] The post-Hellenic Völkerwanderung, which had drawn the Scandinavians' Continental Teutonic kinsmen into its vortex and had left the Scandinavian rear-guard stranded, had been a long-term reaction to the Transalpine expansion of the Roman Empire. The Scandinavian Völkerwanderung which followed in course of time, some four centuries later, was a short-term reaction to the abortive evocation of a ghost of the Roman Empire by Charlemagne and the Carolingian epigoni.[2] The Carolingian Empire was a fiasco because it was both grandiose and premature. It was an ambitious political super-structure piled up recklessly upon rudimentary social and economic foundations;[3] and the arch-instance of its unsoundness was the *tour de force* of Charlemagne's conquest of Saxony, which brought the Carolingian Empire and Scandinavia into direct contact with one another.

During the two preceding centuries, when Scandinavia had been segregated from Roman Christendom, Continental Saxony had acted as a kind of buffer or middle term between the Scandinavian peoples and the Frankish 'successor-state' of the Roman Empire. The people of Saxony, during this period, had certain affinities with the peoples both north and south of them. They were related equally to Franks and to Scandinavians inasmuch as all three peoples were Teutons. At the same time, the people of Saxony were especially akin to the Scandinavians inasmuch as the ruling elements among them had originally come from the North during the post-Hellenic Völkerwanderung, when they had turned their faces towards the Continent and had conquered their fellow barbarians between the Eider and the Ruhr, instead of turning their faces towards the sea like their kinsmen and namesakes who conquered Britain. Like the Scandinavians, again, these Continental

---

[1] The nature and geneses of Völkerwanderungen are examined further in Part VIII, below.

[2] See II. D (iii), pp. 86–7, above.

[3] The weakness of the Carolingian Empire is examined further in Part X, below.

Saxon conquerors and their indigenous Teutonic subjects had remained faithful to their primitive Teutonic paganism when both the Franks and the transmarine Saxons had become converts to Roman Christianity. On the other hand, the subject element in Saxony was partly Frankish in origin and spoke a kindred Teutonic dialect which the Saxon conquerors themselves adopted. Thus Saxony, before Charlemagne's war, was a potential bridge between Roman Christendom and Scandinavia: a bridge over which some successor of Boniface might have led the Scandinavians into the fold of Roman Christendom by the great missionary's pacific methods. Charlemagne's militancy ruled out this possibility.

When Charlemagne set out in A.D. 772 to bring Saxony within the fold of Roman Christendom by force of arms, he was making a disastrous breach with the policy of peaceful penetration—conducted by Irish and English missionaries on the Continent for a century past—which had effectively extended the borders of Continental Christendom at the expense of the Continental Barbarism by achieving the conversion of the Bavarians and Thuringians and Hessians and Frisians.[1] And this change of policy was not only morally retrograde; it was even militarily disastrous; for though the *tour de force* of a Frankish conquest of Saxony was eventually achieved, it was a Pyrrhic victory. The ordeal of the Franco-Saxon Thirty Years' War overtaxed the limited resources of the Carolingian Empire and overstrained the weak tissues of the nascent Western Society which had been burdened with this ponderous unitary political régime. By the time when the Carolingian offensive had been carried to the line of the Eider, its force was spent; the rash advance stopped dead; and it was inevitably and immediately followed by a counter-attack in which the Scandinavians —awaking, full of vigour, from their 'heavy winter dream'—avenged upon the exhausted Franks the wrongs of the prostrated Saxons. In fact, the convulsive expansion of the Frankish Power over the basins of the Weser and the Elbe, which came to this abrupt halt at the neck of the Danish Peninsula, aroused in the souls of the Scandinavians the same demoniac *furor barbaricus*—the notorious Berserker[2] rage—that had once been awakened in the souls of the Celts when the ambitious expansion of the Etruscan Power over the Basin of the Po had come to a halt at the foot of the Alps.[3]

[1] See p. 336, above.

[2] Berserkers, i.e. warriors who went into battle without defensive armour, were an institution of the North European Barbarism which was not confined to the Scandinavian Barbarism of the Viking Age. There were Celtic Berserkers in Transalpine Gaul in the third century B.C. The Transalpine Celtic mercenaries (Gaesatae) whom the Cisalpine Celts enlisted when they made their supreme effort to break the power of Rome, fought naked at the Battle of Telamon in 225 B.C. (See Polybius, Bk. II, chs. 22, 28, and 30.)

[3] For the relation between the Etruscan expansion and the Celtic avalanche, see pp. 276 and 280, above.

'In its origin and driving force, the' Scandinavian, like the Celtic, 'movement was a tremendous expansion of the life-force of the race';[1] and the Scandinavian expansion in the eighth to eleventh centuries of the Christian Era surpassed the Celtic expansion of the fifth to third centuries B.C. both in extension and in intensity: in the impetus of its attack; in the sweep of its geographical range; in the narrowness of the margin by which it just failed to overwhelm the civilization against which it was directed; and in the brilliance of the embryonic civilization which it created on its own account. The abortive envelopment of the Hellenic World by the Celts, which had carried the right wing of the North European barbarian assailants of Hellenism into the heart of Spain and their left into the heart of Asia Minor,[2] was dwarfed in geographical scale by the operations of the Vikings, who threatened to envelop Orthodox as well as Western Christendom by extending their left wing into Russia and their right into North America. Again, the two Christian civilizations which were assaulted by the Scandinavians were in greater jeopardy when the Vikings were attempting to force the passages of the Seine and the Thames and the Bosphorus past Paris and London[3] and Constantinople, than the jeopardy in which the Hellenic Civilization found itself at the moments when the Celtic war-bands were actually masters of Rome and of Macedonia.[4] In a still higher degree, the abortive Scandinavian Civilization which began to unfold itself in Iceland before its chill beauty melted into formlessness under the warm breath of Christianity, surpassed in both achievement and in promise the rudimentary Celtic culture of La Tène.[5]

We have already observed that the short bloom of the Scandinavian Civilization in Iceland was evoked by the same stimulus as the long bloom of the Hellenic Civilization in Ionia: the peculiar stimulus which is given to barbarians by a Völkerwanderung which carries them overseas. We have taken a comparative view of the Icelandic and the Ionian achievements in the two fields of political organization and literary art;[6] and it would be superfluous at this point to enlarge upon the character of the abortive Scandinavian Civilization, and its resemblance to the successful Hellenic Civilization, any farther.[7] We may likewise absolve ourselves from recapitulating the account which we have already given of the Scandinavian assault upon Western Christendom and its ultimate failure.[8]

---

[1] Olrik, op. cit., p. 97.
[2] See pp. 280–1, above.
[3] See II. D (v), pp. 198–9, above.
[4] See pp. 280–1, above.
[5] For the La Tène culture, see p. 281, above.
[6] See II. D (iii), pp. 86–100, above.
[7] On this question, see further pp. 356–7, as well as Annex V, below.
[8] For these events, see II. D (v), pp. 196–202, above.

We may pass on at once to consider the successive consequences of this failure as far as they concern Scandinavia.

The first of these consequences was that the Scandinavian invaders who had made a forcible lodgement on the soil of Western Christendom, in the Danelaw and in Normandy, were at once lost to the Scandinavian Society, as irrevocably as if they had been annihilated, through their rapid conversion to the religion and culture of their invincible Western Christian adversaries. The enlistment of the converted Normans as knights errant in Western Christendom's service was the first signal piece of evidence which showed that, in this encounter, Western Christendom and not Scandinavia was the victor. We have noticed this metamorphosis of the Normans already;[1] but this was only the first stage in the Christian counter-attack. In the second and final stage, both the Western and the Orthodox Christian Society carried the war, which they had already won on their own ground, into the enemy's country, and rendered the nascent Scandinavian Civilization abortive by conquering the whole vast extent of the New World in the North which Scandinavian enterprise had called into existence.[2]

It is noteworthy that these successive triumphs of Western Christendom over Scandinavia were obtained by a reversion to the tactics which Charlemagne had discarded. The self-defence of Western Christendom against the Vikings' assaults had been conducted, perforce, on the militant lines on which Charlemagne had rashly embarked and on which the Scandinavians had followed Charlemagne's lead with a vengeance. But as soon as a militant Western defensive had brought the militant Scandinavian offensive to a halt, the Westerners resumed the peaceful tactics of Augustine and Boniface, which Charlemagne had abandoned with such disastrous consequences. One hundred and seven years after the end of Charlemagne's Great Saxon War, a Charles who was nicknamed 'the Simple' was able at last to set bounds to the mischief which had been done by Charles 'the Great' by making another new departure in policy—this time in exactly the opposite direction from that which had been taken by his more famous namesake and ancestor. In the treaty concluded in A.D. 911 between the Carolingian Charles the Simple and the Viking Rollo, the barbarian intruder was permitted to retain in peace his conquests on Frankish soil—from which the lawful Frankish sovereign would scarcely have been able to eject him by force—on condition that he enrolled himself as a citizen of the Western *Respublica Christiana*; and the sequel proved that the Carolingian statesman who made this compact had been right in believing that he was getting the best of the

---

[1] In II. D (v), on p. 201, above.   [2] See II. D (v), pp. 201–2, above.

bargain. This resumption of the policy of peaceful penetration in place of the policy of force in dealing with the Northern barbarians was accountable for all the subsequent successes of Western Christendom in the encounter between the two societies. By peaceful penetration, Western Christendom converted not only the impulsive Normans, who had forced an entry and made a lodgement as formidable strangers within her gates, but also the warier Northmen who had remained ensconced on their own ground in the North European hinterland beyond the pale at which the frontier of the Carolingian Empire had been fixed by Charlemagne's Saxon campaigns.

The tactics of peaceful penetration proved particularly effective in dealing with the Scandinavians because the Scandinavians were peculiarly receptive. The Scandinavians had already shown themselves susceptible to the influence of the embryonic Far Western Christian Civilization of Ireland[1] at a time when their relations with Roman Christendom and with the Carolingian Empire were still exclusively hostile. This Irish influence enriched and did not sterilize the native vein of the Scandinavian genius, because the embryonic Irish and Scandinavian civilizations had an identic source in the common reservoir of the traditional North European Barbarism, while the new Christian element, of which the nascent Scandinavian Civilization received its first infusion through this Irish channel, had already been blended harmoniously with a North European tincture in the course of its percolation through Irish soil.[2] Thus, when the Vikings overwhelmed Ireland, they plundered the spiritual as well as the material riches of their Irish victims with impunity.[3] On the other hand, when they descended upon Roman Christendom and eventually succumbed to the spell of a civilization which had succeeded in holding them at bay, they ate the bread and drank the cup of the Christian mysteries without that saving self-examination which Paul had recommended to the Corinthians and which the Delphic Apollo, long before Paul's day, had enjoined upon all Hellenes who presumed to approach a shrine

---

[1] For Irish influence on the Scandinavian Civilization see Olrik, op. cit., pp. 107–20; and Macalister, R. A. S.: *The Archaeology of Ireland* (London 1928, Methuen), pp. 340–3.

[2] For this harmonious adaptation of Christianity in Ireland to the temper of the pre-existing local culture, see pp. 322 and 324–8, above.

[3] The effect of the Irish influence upon Scandinavian culture is summed up by Olrik (in op. cit., p. 120) as follows:

'Considered as a whole, this Irish element in Scandinavian culture is a phenomenon in itself, which does not coincide with the principal current of the Christian movement as it passes over Europe. It appears more as an enrichment and expansion of the native North European stage of Civilization than as a part of the new trend accompanying the introduction of Christianity. In so far as it swept away a portion of the ancient heritage, this tendency might have made a breach for the entrance of the new main current; and furthermore certain Christian impulses did emanate from Ireland. But in at least equal measure this Irish influence contributed to the production of a special civilization which somewhat impeded the rapid absorption of the North into Christian Europe.'

once consecrated to older Minoan divinities whom the intrusive Olympian had supplanted. In thus swallowing Roman Christianity whole, the Scandinavians were eating and drinking damnation to themselves.[1] The strong wine of the South tainted and sterilized the elixir of Scandinavian culture and burst the bottles of the North European Barbarism within which this elixir was being gradually distilled.

The encounter between the Scandinavians and Orthodox Christendom followed a parallel course; for, although Orthodox Christendom had borne no share in the responsibility for evoking the Scandinavian outbreak, it suffered incidentally from the consequences of the militant Western Christian offensive against the North European Barbarism in the generation of Charlemagne. The Scandinavian movement of expansion threatened to overwhelm both the Roman and the Orthodox Christian World simultaneously. While the Vikings who had taken to the North Sea sailed up the Thames to sack London in A.D. 842 and up the Seine to sack Paris in 845, other Vikings, who had taken to the Baltic and had threaded their way, by river and portage, across the whole breadth of Russia until they emerged on the Black Sea, sailed down the Bosphorus in A.D. 860 to sack Constantinople and only just failed to take the Imperial City by surprise. Thereafter, Constantinople, like Paris and London, endured and survived the ordeal of successive Scandinavian assaults;[2] and in the great war of A.D. 967–72 the East Roman Government first incited the Scandinavian prince of Russia, Svyatoslav, to invade the rival Orthodox Christian Empire of Bulgaria overland, and finally drove the formidable barbarian intruder out again, without being forced to concede to him, on Orthodox Christian soil, the equivalent of a Danelaw or a Normandy. The sequel to the treaty which Svyatoslav found himself compelled to conclude with the East Roman Emperor John Zimisces at Drstra in A.D. 972 was the same as the sequel to Guthrum's treaty with Alfred in A.D. 878 and to Rollo's with Charles in A.D. 911, except that the discomfiture of the Scandinavian aggressor was more signal on the Orthodox Christian front and his subsequent conversion more rapid.

Thus, when the Vikings made their pacts with the Christian Powers—a Wessex and a France and an East Roman Empire—after having been flung back from the walls of Constantinople and Paris and London, the nascent Scandinavian Civilization was doomed; for nothing but the ferocity of the Northmen could save them from the fate to which their receptivity exposed them. In the collision

---

[1] 1 Corinthians xii. 29.
For the ordeal of Paris and London, see II. D (v), Annex, on pp. 400–1, below.

between the Scandinavian Völkerwanderung and Christendom, there were only two possible alternative outcomes: either Christendom must be annihilated or the nascent Scandinavian Civilization must be rendered abortive by the conversion of its makers. When the former alternative was renounced, the second inevitably came to pass. The frail fabric of the native Scandinavian culture was now disintegrated by a foreign radiation which penetrated it, layer by layer, first on the economic plane and then on the political and finally on the cultural. On the political plane, Charlemagne the heir of Augustus ultimately exercised a more profound effect upon Scandinavian minds than Charlemagne the slayer of the Saxons. On the cultural plane, the process of peaceful penetration was completed when the Northmen accepted the very religion of the Southerners.

'It was the wealth of the South that lured the Viking. . . . But the Northman was an apt pupil; he not only stole; he also imitated. He learnt to build fortresses and form a *testudo*, to imitate the high-prowed warships, the galleys of the South, in his own dragon ships; he learned to plan cities and order a state. A new goal for the ruler's power arose . . . the figure of Charlemagne: "Carolus Magnus". Even during his lifetime, in the families of Northern kings in the West, men began to call their sons Karlus or Magnus; whenever a Magnus subsequently succeeds to one of the Northern royal seats, this is a victory of the Carolus Magnus ideal. A kingship with external power, internal peace and order, and moral elevation, stands as the highest goal of princely ambition.

'As the viking king moves in the direction of the Carolus Magnus ideal, the viking ships are transformed into merchant ships. At the beginning of the Viking Age, they set forth on bloody expeditions; at the end of the Viking Age, Scandinavian merchant towns have arisen along all the coasts of Northern Europe from Novgorod to Bristol, Limerick, and Dublin. The Atlantic Ocean, the North Sea, and the Baltic Sea, formerly bare of ships, have now been absorbed into the realm of world trade. . . . Consciously or unconsciously, the Scandinavians acquire the handicrafts and art of foreign peoples. They adopt a metal currency. . . .

'The acceptance of Christianity was for many persons rather an assimilation of European life than an expression of religious enthusiasm.'[1]

The receptivity of the Northmen was indeed as sensitive on the cultural plane as on the economic or political; and here it was not merely imitative but also creative.

'The old idea of the Vikings as sweeping like a storm across the lands they touched, destroying the wealth they found and leaving themselves as poor as ever, has in our time had to give way to a breathless wonder at their craving for enrichment. The gold they found has disappeared. But we have learnt now that there was gathered together in the

[1] Olrik, op. cit., pp. 104–7.

North a treasury of knowledge and thought, poetry and dreams, that must have been brought home from abroad, despite the fact that such spiritual values are far more difficult to find and steal and carry safely home than precious stones or precious metals. The Northmen seem to have been insatiable in the matter of such spiritual treasures. . . . [And] they had not only a passionate craving to convert the elements of foreign culture to their own enrichment, but they had also a mysterious power of stirring up culture and forcing it to yield what lay beneath its surface. Even this thirst for knowledge, however, is not the most surprising thing about them. That they did learn and copy to a great extent is plain to see; but . . . there exists no magic formula whereby the culture of Viking times, as a whole, can be resolved into its original component parts. So thoroughly have they refashioned what they took, until its thought and spirit are their own.'[1]

The audacious attempt to re-cast the Christian culture in a Scandinavian mould was manifestly a forlorn hope. Yet a society which could summon up the spirit and exercise the imagination to essay this *tour de force* would not readily confess itself outmatched. And, although this spiritual encounter could have no other outcome than the assimilation of the weaker spiritual force by the stronger, the nascent Scandinavian Civilization did not reconcile itself to this spiritual discomfiture without a struggle. The spell of quiescence which had given free play to the Scandinavian faculty of receptivity at the turn of the ninth and tenth centuries was broken, before the latter century closed, by a fresh outburst of the *furor barbaricus*; this new fit of Berserker rage was provoked by a recognition of the strange and monstrous fact that the meek were fast inheriting the Scandinavian Earth; and the spirit of militant reaction was embodied, by the Northern poetic imagination of the day, in the heroic figure of Starkad the Old:[2] a mighty man of valour who, with a fervour worthy of a Syriac prophet, inspires the king his lord to cleanse his household from foreign abominations. In creating the image of this pagan zealot, the Scandinavian Society of the Viking Age was painting a portrait of itself. As he first appears upon the scene, Starkad victoriously repels the formidable oncoming tide of Christian influence; but as the poetic cycle of which Starkad is the hero develops, a tragic *motif* creeps in. In the latest version of the plot, the zealot himself is corrupted by the foreign abominations which he has denounced. For lust of foreign gold, Starkad betrays his master; and when we translate this poetry into prose, the upshot is that the tenth-century reaction was foredoomed to failure, and that the victory of the Christian over the

[1] Grönbech, V.: *The Culture of the Teutons* (London 1931, Milford, 3 parts in 2 vols.), Part I, pp. 11–12.
[2] For an analysis and interpretation of the Starkad Cycle, see Olrik, op. cit., pp. 120–7.

Scandinavian Civilization was really assured before the tenth century was over.

In the Scandinavian kingdoms of Russia, Denmark, and Norway, the formal outward act of conversion was imposed upon the people wholesale by the arbitrary will of three contemporary princes: Vladímir the Great (*regnabat* A.D. 980–1015), Harald Gormsson (*regnabat circa* A.D. 940–86), and Olaf Tryggvason (*regnabat* A.D. 995–1000). In Norway, strenuous resistance was offered to a royal command which was ostensibly actuated by nothing more reasonable than the determination of a masterful ruler to gratify a personal whim; and in Denmark and in Russia, where the royal commands were passively accepted by the princes' subjects, the princes themselves appeared to be acting on immediate considerations of political expediency. Harald imposed Christianity on Denmark in A.D. 974 as part of the purchase-price of peace from the Saxon emperor Otto II, who had invaded Denmark in force in reprisal for Danish raids on Saxony.[1] Vladímir imposed Christianity on Russia in A.D. 989 in order to win the hand of a Christian princess, the sister of the East Roman Emperor Basil II, and to obtain as her dowry a diplomatic ratification of his seizure of the East Roman fortress of Cherson in the Crimea.[2]

'At his despotic command, Peroun, the god of thunder, whom he had so long adored, was dragged through the streets of Kiow; and twelve sturdy barbarians battered with clubs the misshapen image, which was indignantly cast into the waters of the Borysthenes. The edict of Wolodomir had proclaimed that all who should refuse the rites of baptism would be treated as the enemies of God and their prince; and the rivers were instantly filled with many thousands of obedient Russians, who acquiesced in the truth and excellence of a doctrine which had been embraced by the great duke and his boyars.'[3]

Vladímir's fiat may conceivably account for the mass-conversion of the docile Slavs on whom the Scandinavian pioneers in Russia had imposed their dominion. Yet the personal opportunism or caprice of a ruler seldom or never avails to bring about a wholesale and permanent revolution in the religion of his subjects unless the religious change which the ruler enjoins is in accord with the prevalent social tendencies of the place and the time.[4] This truth is eminently true in a turbulent and individualistic society such as the

---

[1] Kendrick, T. D.: *A History of the Vikings* (London 1930, Methuen), p. 103.
[2] Kendrick, op. cit., pp. 164–5.
[3] Gibbon, Edward: *The History of the Decline and Fall of the Roman Empire*, ch. lv.
[4] The history of civilizations up to date furnishes a number of instances of signal failures in cases where rulers have attempted to use their political power for the purpose of enforcing religious changes against the spirit of the place and time. Examples of such failures (e.g., in the cases of Ikhnaton, Ptolemy Soter, Açoka, Julian, Leo Syrus, and Akbar) are examined in V. C (i) (d) 6 (δ), Annex, in vol. v, below.

Scandinavian Society was in the Viking Age. The phenomenon
that requires to be explained is not the conversion of Vladímir's
pagan Slav subjects but rather the conversion of 'his boyars': that is
to say, his pagan Swedish war-band; and the readiness of the head-
strong Vikings to abandon their primitive paganism for alien religions towards the end of the tenth century of the Christian Era,
after kicking, Starkad-wise, against the pricks, was evidently the
outcome of a deep and gradual psychological mass-movement with
a long rhythm: a movement which statecraft might bring to a head,
but which it could not have initiated and could not arrest. The
ripeness of the Russian Vikings for conversion in Vladímir's day
was not only apparent to Vladímir himself but was also the main-
spring of his religious policy, if there is any truth in the story that,
before he finally opted for Orthodox Christianity, he investigated
and compared the respective merits of Orthodoxy, Romanism,
Judaism, and Islam.[1] And the Russian prince's ultimate choice of
Orthodox Christianity can probably be accounted for by the fact
that, when once the Russian Vikings had failed to take Orthodox
Christendom by storm, and when this failure had been followed by
a substitution of peaceful for warlike relations between the discomfited barbarians and the civilization which had successfully
repelled their assaults, then the attractiveness and prestige of Orthodox Christendom prevailed, in Russian imaginations, over the
fainter impressions made upon them by the Roman Christian West
or by the Islamic 'Abbasid Caliphate or by Jewish Khazaria.[2]

'The ambassadors or merchants of Russia compared the idolatry of the
woods with the elegant superstition of Constantinople. They had gazed
with admiration on the dome of St. Sophia: the lively pictures of saints
and martyrs, the riches of the altar, the number and vestments of the
priests, the pomp and order of the ceremonies; they were edified by the
alternate succession of devout silence and harmonious song; nor was it
difficult to persuade them that a choir of angels descended each day from
heaven to join in the devotion of the Christians.'[3]

In general,

'the conversion of the North was accomplished by voluntary means. Of
course, we must not assume that compulsion was never used against any
individual; the conditions of the times would forbid any such assumption. But no Scandinavian tribe was forced as a body to assume the new
law. What happened was that leading men of the tribe appeared in
considerable numbers as its advocates, drawing the stragglers in their
wake. Behind the many decisions of the *thing* meetings in which the
acceptance of Christianity was voted, we cannot always assume the

[1] Kendrick, op. cit., p. 164.
[2] For the Judaism of the Khazars see II. D (vi), Annex, p. 410, below.
[3] Gibbon, op. cit., loc. cit.

presence of a majority, but surely [always] that of a very important minority. And, once the choice had been made, it was never rescinded; we do not encounter any pagan reaction of real moment.'[1]

The most illuminating instance of all was the conversion of Iceland, and this for several reasons. In the first place, the Scandinavian community in Iceland was particularly remote from Christendom geographically. In the second place, its political constitution and political tradition were both peculiarly individualistic, so that in Iceland it was even less easy than in other Scandinavian countries to impose conversion upon the body-politic by the arbitrary fiat of an individual or even of a strong minority. In the third place, the Icelanders had been so powerfully stimulated by the challenge of migration overseas to a country still harder than their Norwegian homeland that they had raised the Scandinavian culture which they brought with them to higher degrees of aesthetic and intellectual intensity than were ever attained in any other part of the Scandinavian World,[2] so that, in abandoning paganism for Christianity, they were sacrificing a more precious and more highly appreciated social heritage than any of the other Scandinavian converts (Russians or Swedes or Danes or other Norwegians) were called upon to give up. Yet, in spite of these special obstacles which the Christian propaganda had to overcome in Iceland, the Icelanders' own records of their conversion show plainly that the process was voluntary here as well as in other Scandinavian lands—if the word 'voluntary' may fairly be used to describe a realistic recognition and unenthusiastic acceptance of a social and psychological necessity. The history of the momentous decision which was taken at the *Althing* in the June of A.D. 1000 is recounted as follows in the *Njals Saga*:[3]

'Both sides went to the Hill of Laws, and each, the Christian men as well as the heathen, took witness, and declared themselves out of the other's laws, and then there was such an uproar on the Hill of Laws that no man could hear the other's voice.

'After that men went away, and all thought things looked like the greatest entanglement. The Christian men chose as their Speaker Hall of the Side, but Hall went to Thorgeir, the priest of Lightwater, who was the old Speaker of the law, and gave him three marks of silver to utter what the law should be, but still that was most hazardous counsel, since he was an heathen.

'Thorgeir lay all that day on the ground, and spread a cloak over his head, so that no man spoke with him; but the day after men went to the

[1] Olrik, op. cit., p. 140.
[2] On this point, see II. D (iii), pp. 86–100, above.
[3] *The Story of Burnt Njal*, translated from the Icelandic of the *Njals Saga* by Dasent, G. W. (Edinburgh 1861, Edmonton and Douglas), vol. ii, pp. 78–80. See further Kendrick, op. cit., pp. 346–53.

Hill of Laws, and then Thorgeir bade them be silent and listen, and spoke thus—

' "It seems to me as though our matters were come to a deadlock if we are not all to have one and the same law; for if there be a sundering of the laws, then there will be a sundering of the peace, and we shall never be able to live in the land. Now, I will ask both Christian man and heathen whether they will hold to those laws which I utter?"

'They all said they would.

'He said he wished to take an oath of them, and pledges that they would hold to them, and they all said "yea" to that, and so he took pledges from them.

' "This is the beginning of our laws", he said, "that all men shall be Christian here in the land, and believe in one God, the Father, the Son, and the Holy Ghost, but leave off all idol-worship, not expose children to perish and not eat horseflesh. It shall be outlawry if such things are proved openly against any man; but if these things are done by stealth, then it shall be blameless."

'But all this heathendom was all done away with within a few years' space, so that those things were not allowed to be done either by stealth or openly.

'Thorgeir then uttered the law as to keeping the Lord's day and fast days, Yuletide and Easter, and all the greatest highdays and holidays.

'The heathen men thought they had been greatly cheated; but still the True Faith was brought into the law, and so all men became Christian here in the land.'

It was here in Iceland, where the act of conversion was influenced by external pressure to a lesser extent than anywhere else in the Scandinavian World, that the cultural consequences of conversion were most manifestly devastating. This spiritual devastation is conspicuous in this case for the reason, mentioned above, that the Icelanders, before their conversion, had raised the abortive Scandinavian Civilization to its highest level of achievement, and for the further reason that the Scandinavian culture, as maintained in Iceland at this high pitch, differed markedly in many respects, and in most of these respects to its own advantage, from the contemporary culture of Roman Christendom.

While the Roman, like the Orthodox Christian, Civilization was affiliated through the Christian Church to an antecedent civilization, and was only less potently dominated by the Hellenic past than was Orthodox Christendom itself, the relation of the abortive Scandinavian Civilization to the defunct and contemporary civilizations of the South resembled rather the less intimate relation that had once subsisted between the Hellenic Civilization and the Minoan. The barbarian Vikings, like the barbarian Achaeans, were at first stimulated by their contact with the Southern cultures to create an original culture of their own rather than to bow down and worship the established civilizations which they encountered; and this similarity between the Scandinavian and the Achaean reaction to alien societies goes far towards accounting for the similarity in êthos between the abortive Scandinavian and the successful Hellenic Civilization: a family likeness which is recognized on all hands and is indeed unmistakable.[1]

The Scandinavian êthos of the Viking and the post-Viking Age, as it is reflected in the Eddic and Skaldic poetry and in the Sagas, resembles the Hellenic êthos of the Heroic and the Early Classical Age, as it is reflected in the Homeric Epic and in the prose of Herodotus. Both these young civilizations are distinguished by a freedom from the incubus of tradition, which gives them a precocious freshness and originality, and by a freedom from the incubus of superstition, which gives them a precocious clarity and rationalism. Their members are fully aware both of the extent of their human powers and of these powers' limitations; and this ever-present dual consciousness results in a combination of self-confidence with pessimism and of exaltation with melancholy, which is often puzzling, and always intriguing, to observers who have grown up in other spiritual environments.

In the Viking Movement, as in the Achaean Völkerwanderung, the

'presupposition was a people not only acquainted with maritime affairs, but possessing courage to venture forth, ability to make far-reaching plans, and a gift for keen observation, always ready to find the adversary's weak points. These powers seemed to grow with the increase of their tasks and the broadening of their horizon. Taken together, they produced a feeling of superiority and invincibility. The compass of the World was multiplied many times. The shut-in valley-dweller had felt the world of trolls and monsters, whom Man might not tempt, to be close at hand. The boundaries of this world now widened immensely, and the viking pursued his horizon, directing his course over the sea though the keel of his boat might break the back of a mermaid, or ascending to the Cave of the Giants in the farthest north to see whether this adventure was really so dangerous. It is true, the ancient terror remained in his soul, imparting the proper tension for the audacious venture; but at the same time his inborn self-assurance and matter-of-factness grew into a conscious emphasis on the tangible and reasonable, into that "faith in their own power and strength" which the vikings professed—in spite of all gods and trolls and mighty realms.'[2]

This êthos which was tempered in adventurous action found expression in literary art.

'The Sagas are partly indebted to a spirit of negative criticism and

[1] See Annex V, below, for the resemblance in the field of religion.
[2] Olrik, op. cit., pp. 97–8.

restraint: a tendency not purely literary—corresponding, at any rate, to a similar tendency in practical life. The energy, the passion, the lamentation of the Northern poetry, the love of all the wonders of Mythology, went along with practical and intellectual clearness of vision in matters that required cool judgement. The ironical correction of sentiment, the tone of the *advocatus diaboli*, is habitual with many of the Icelandic writers, and many of their heroes. "To see things as they really are", so that no incantation could transform them, was one of the gifts of an Icelandic hero, and appears to have been shared by his countrymen when they set themselves to compose the Sagas. The tone of the Sagas is generally kept as near as may be to that of the recital of true history. Nothing is allowed any preponderance over the story and the speeches in it. It is the kind of story furthest removed from the common pathetic fallacies of the Middle Ages. The rationalist mind has cleared away all the sentimental and most of the superstitious encumbrances and hindrances of strong narrative.'[1]

This original Scandinavian êthos, which attained its highest tension and finest harmony in Iceland, was relaxed and confused and eventually annihilated in consequence of the conversion of the Icelanders to Christianity.

It is true that the abortive Scandinavian Civilization did not perish without a struggle on this remote island which had been the theatre of its greatest achievements. Indeed, the Icelandic scholars who committed the Sagas to writing and collected the Eddic poems and made the classic digests of Scandinavian Mythology and Genealogy and Law, were all possessed of a Christian as well as a Northern cultural background and education; and the century during which they flourished (*circa* A.D. 1150–1250) was some hundred and fifty to two hundred and fifty years posterior to the date of the conversion.[2] Yet this backward-looking scholarship was the last achievement of the Icelandic genius; and it is significant that, although the Sagas acquired their final literary form in 'the age of peace' (which intervened between the act of conversion and the age of faction and scholarship), nevertheless 'the age of the Sagas', in the sense of the age from which the historical plots and historical characters of the Sagas were exclusively drawn, did not extend beyond about A.D. 1030: that is to say, beyond the deaths of the generation which was already in its prime by the time when the conversion to Christianity took place. Lives that had come to their maturity in the pre-Christian social environment and atmosphere were apparently the only stuff out of which Icelandic sagas

---

[1] Ker, W. P.: *Epic and Romance* (London 1922, Macmillan), p. 212.

[2] On the political plane, this last century of Icelandic intellectual activity was also the last century of the free Icelandic Commonwealth. Snorri Sturlason, the prince of Icelandic scholars, who lived from A.D. 1178 to A.D. 1241, was also a politician who met a violent death in the last political convulsions of the Commonwealth, which ended in the submission of the Icelanders to the Norwegian Crown in A.D. 1262.

could be made. Icelanders who had sucked in the Christian tradition with their mothers' milk might be the collectors or even the composers, but they could never be the heroes, of these essentially pagan works of art. For the heroic Northern self-confidence could not dwell harmoniously in the same heart with the Christian conviction of sin, nor the stoical Northern rationalism in the same mind with Christian sentiment and Christian superstition.

As the alien civilization to which the Icelanders had capitulated in A.D. 1000 gradually establishes its dominion over their hearts and minds,

'a mysterious fantasy, pregnant with disaster, comes into being and carries off the victory over the ancient worldly wisdom and the poet's sense of proportion. In the bitter years of the Sturlung conflicts, about the middle of the thirteenth century, the fear in people's souls expresses itself constantly in visions and dreams. Elements that had once been subject to poetic domination now gradually gain the upper hand. The downfall of the Icelandic Free State brings about also a cessation of the national Saga literature. Preference is shown for the romantic saga, to which the cultivated aesthetic sense is now turned; its fantastic elements become stronger and stronger and digress farther and farther from reality. The nation that once had so sharp an eye for the world of reality falls into slumber—politically, aesthetically, economically—and sleeps its sleep of centuries, full of disturbing dreams, while the elves shriek their shrill laughter from all the cliffs and the giants from all the rocky caves, while the Earth quakes, and the fire-mountains shine, and souls fly about the crater of Hekla like black birds.'[1]

By the fourteenth century of the Christian Era, the Icelandic *Kulturkampf* is over and the paralysis of the Icelandic genius is complete. The clear light of the pale Northern sunshine has now been refracted through the exotic medium of a stained-glass window; and the Icelandic mental landscape, thus weirdly illuminated, has become stupefyingly outlandish.

'Hauk Erlendsson, an Icelander of distinction in the fourteenth century, made a collection of treatises in one volume for his own amusement and behoof. It contains the *Volospá*, the most famous of all the Northern mythical poems, the Sibyl's song of the doom of the gods; it contains also the *Landnámabók*, the history of the colonization of Iceland; *Kristni Saga*, the history of the conversion to Christianity; the history of *Eric the Red*, and *Fóstbrǽðra Saga*, the story of the two sworn brethren, Thorgeir and Thormod the poet. Besides these records of the history and the family traditions of Iceland and Greenland there are some mythical stories of later date, dealing with old mythical themes, such as the life of Ragnar Lodbrok. In one of them, the *Heidreks Saga*, are embedded some of the most memorable verses, after *Volospá*, in the old style of Northern poetry—the poem of the *Waking of Angantyr*. The other contents of the book are as follows: geographical, physical, and theological pieces; extracts from St. Augustine; the *History of the Cross*; the *Description of Jerusalem*; the *Debate of Body and Soul*; *Algorismus* (by Hauk himself, who was an arithmetician); a version of the *Brut* and of *Merlin's Prophecy*; *Lucidarium*, the most popular medieval handbook of popular science. This is the collection, to which all the ends of the Earth have contributed, and it is in strange and far-fetched company like this that the Northern documents are found. In Greece, whatever early transactions there may have been with the wisdom of Egypt or Phoenicia, there is no such medley as this.'[1]

The century in which Hauk Erlendsson's mental vision was confounded, and his mental abilities paralysed, by this criss-cross of broken intellectual lights was the tenth century since the Scandinavian rear-guard of the Teutonic line (in the embattled army of the North European Barbarism) had struck out on an independent course of its own by parting company with the Teutonic van-guard at a moment when Goths and Vandals and Angles and Lombards had allowed themselves to be drawn, to their own eventual undoing, into the social vacuum produced by the break-up of the Roman Empire. During this millennium, the whole drama of an abortive Scandinavian Civilization had been played out from the first act to the last. After cultivating their native barbarism in their native fastness for some four centuries after their kinsmen and former neighbours had struck their tents and moved off westward and southward, the Scandinavians had been stimulated at last, by Charlemagne's challenge, to break out in their turn; and then, in their Viking Age, they had made a supreme effort to overwhelm the civilizations of the South which they encountered on their warpath, and to establish in their stead a new Scandinavian Civilization erected on barbarian foundations and unencumbered by reminiscences of a traditional style or by traces of a traditional groundplan. By the fourteenth century of the Christian Era—the century in which Hauk Erlendsson lived—this ambitious Scandinavian enterprise had lamentably miscarried. That century saw the extirpation of the North European Barbarism finally consummated by the establishment of continuous contact between the Western Christian and the Orthodox Christian Civilization along a line stretching across the whole breadth of the European Continent from the coast of the Adriatic Sea to the coast of the Arctic Ocean;[2] and this new line of demarcation cut sheer across the domain which the abortive Scandinavian Civilization had once staked out for itself. By the fourteenth century, the *ci-devant* Scandinavian dominion in

[1] Ker, W. P.: *Epic and Romance* (London 1922, Macmillan), pp. 47–8.
[2] See II. D (v), pp. 168–9, above.

Russia had become incorporated into Orthodox Christendom, while Western Christendom had annexed Scandinavia itself with its over-seas outposts in the Orkneys and Shetlands and Hebrides and Faroes and Ireland and Iceland and Greenland. The partition of the Scandinavian World between two alien civilizations was thus complete.

We are now in a position to arrange the encounters between the North European Barbarism and the Southern Civilizations in a series, and to embrace them all in a single comparative survey.

In the Achaean achievement, the North European Barbarism successfully performed the feat of begetting a new civilization on the site of a pre-existent civilization which had incorporated a layer of the barbarians into its 'external proletariat'. In the Scandinavian and the Irish endeavours, the same barbarism just fell short of repeating the same performance because the challenge from Roman Christendom was just too severe. The excessive severity of the challenge which defeated the Scandinavian and Irish endeavours—and the earlier endeavours of the Teutonic and Celtic van-guards *a fortiori*—proved inimical to success, no less than the deficiency of stimulus which handicapped the secluded Slavs. Thus our sequence of encounters between the North European Barbarism and the several Southern civilizations does display the operation of 'the law of diminishing returns' in the movement of Challenge-and-Response in an instance in which the challenge is presented in the human sphere and not in the physical sphere. Moreover, our examination of the abortive Scandinavian and Far Western Christian civilizations has enabled us to define within quite narrow limits the locus of the point at which 'the law of diminishing returns' comes into play in this sequence of comparable encounters. The point has been located in the narrow interval between the severity of the challenge presented by the Minoan Civilization to the Achaeans—a challenge which is proved, by the resulting genesis of Hellenism, to have been of the optimum degree—and the slightly enhanced severity of the challenge presented by Roman Christendom to the Irish and the Scandinavians: a challenge which is proved to have been excessive by the consequent abortion in which the embryonic Far Western Christian and Scandinavian civilizations both met their fate.

The Impact of Islam upon the Christendoms

Another sequence of challenges in the human sphere in which we can locate with some precision the point at which 'the law of diminishing returns' comes into play is offered by a series of en-counters between the Islamic wave of Syriac religion and the preceding Christian wave, which had been emitted some six hundred years earlier from approximately the same geographical point of departure. Each of these two successive waves travelled outwards in all directions in a circle with an ever expanding circumference but with a constant and identic centre;[1] and the younger Islamic wave, travelling at a six hundred years' time-interval in the older Christian wave's wake, caught up and collided with different portions of the Christian wave in different sectors of the circumference of their common circular field at different moments and with different degrees of violence and with different results.

If we take a comparative view of the several collisions between these two waves in the several sectors of their circular line of contact, we shall at once observe one instance in which a portion of the older Christian wave responded to the challenge of the younger Islamic wave's impact with conspicuous success. When the Islamic wave impinged upon the Roman portion of the Christian wave in the western sector of their common circumference, it was Western Christendom and not Islam that ultimately profited by the encounter.[2]

The Primitive Muslim Arab conquerors, who burst the bounds of Arabia in A.D. 632, took just a century to push their conquests, round the southern and western shores of the Mediterranean, from the former Arabian frontier of the Roman Empire to the southern bank of the Loire. As early as A.D. 647 they made the first movement to recapture for the Syriac Civilization (whose unconscious and unintentional champions they were) the colonial area in North-West Africa and in the Iberian Peninsula which had been first won from barbarism by Phoenician enterprise and then annexed by Hellenism as the spoils of Rome's victory over Carthage. By A.D. 713, the year which saw the completion of the Arab conquest of the Visigothic 'successor-state' of the Roman Empire in the Peninsula and in Septimania, the Arabs had not only recovered the whole of the former colonial domain of the Syriac Society in the Western Mediterranean but were penetrating into territory which had been originally won from barbarism not by Syriac Tyre and Carthage but by Hellenic Marseilles and Rome; and when 'Abd-ar-Rahmān marched from the Pyrenees to the Loire in A.D. 732, he was breaking ground which Hannibal himself had never trodden.[3]

---

[1] For this refraction of Syriac religion, through the impact of Hellenism, into a series of waves emanating successively from an identic geographical centre, see II. D (vi), pp. 234–6, and II. D (vii), pp. 285–8, above, and II. D (vi), Annex, pp. 402–3, below, as well as Part IX.

[2] For the reaction of Western Christendom to the pressure of the Syriac Civilization, represented by the Primitive Arab Muslim conquerors and the subsequent Arab Caliphates and their 'successor-states', see II. D (v), pp. 202–6, above.

[3] See II. D (v), p. 203, above.

The only Syriac conqueror that had preceded the Muslim soldier in his invasion of Gaul was the Christian Church; and in this sector of the expanding circumference of the wave-field of Syriac religion, by the time when the Christian wave was here overtaken by the Islamic, the Christian wave, as we have observed above, had already differentiated itself locally into a specifically Roman Christendom which was struggling to become the chrysalis of a new Western Civilization 'affiliated' to the Hellenic Civilization. The Arab invasion of Gaul in A.D. 732 struck this nascent Roman Christendom at a critical moment, when it had just emerged victorious from its struggle with the Far Western Christendom of 'the Celtic Fringe'[1] and was on the verge of a still more formidable struggle with the Teutonic rear-guard of the North European Barbarism in Scandinavia.[2] The challenge presented to Roman Christendom by the impact of Islam at this juncture was more severe than any challenge from the North European barbarians that it had to face either before or after.[3] Yet, severe though this Islamic challenge to Roman Christendom was, the sequel showed that it was not excessive; for the actual effect of this collision of the Islamic wave with the western portion of the Christian wave was to stimulate Western Christendom over a long period and to a high degree.

The strength of this stimulus is displayed in a whole series of responses. In this year A.D. 732 itself, 'Abd-ar-Rahmān's attack upon the Continental European homeland of Western Christendom was repelled once and for all by Charles Martel. By the turn of the eighth and ninth centuries of the Christian Era, the Continental European border between Western Christendom and Dār-al-Islām had been pushed back from the northern to the southern foot of the Pyrenees.[4] At the turn of the tenth and eleventh centuries, the Western Christians assumed the offensive against Dār-al-Islām along the whole Mediterranean front, from the Iberian Peninsula to Syria, in the great movement of political and economic expansion which is known as 'the Crusades':[5] a movement which eventually engulfed Orthodox Christendom as well as Dār-al-Islām. At its furthest extent, this movement carried Western Christian arms down the whole length of the Peninsula and across the Straits of

---

[1] See pp. 329–40, above.   [2] See pp. 344–60, above.
[3] See II. D (v), p. 202, above.
[4] Pepin conquered Septimania from the Arabs in A.D. 755. Charlemagne crossed the Pyrenees in A.D. 778 and succeeded, before his death, in enlarging his Empire by the addition of a Spanish march which included both Barcelona and Pampelona. Thereby a direct contact was established, south of the Pyrenees, between the Carolingian Empire and the remnant of the Visigothic Power which had survived in isolation, for the best part of a century, in the mountain-fastness of Asturia. For the probable fate of the Asturians if the Franks had not delivered their counter-attack against the Arabs, see Annex VIII, p. 447, footnote 4, below.
[5] In the Western Mediterranean, this movement began a century before the date of 'the First Crusade' in the technical sense of the term.

Gibraltar to Ceuta,[1] and from Italy over the stepping-stone of Sicily to the coasts of Tunisia and Tripoli,[2] and from Europe *outre mer* to Syria, and from Syria across the Euphrates to Edessa and across the Jordan to Kerak and even to the head of the Gulf of 'Aqabah—not to speak of 'the Latin Empire' of Constantinople and the cluster of petty principalities which a host of French and Venetian and Genoese and Catalan adventurers carved out for themselves in the Aegean as a sequel to 'the Fourth Crusade'. On its economic side, the same movement carried Western trade much farther: from the Levant across Egypt to India and from the Black Sea across the Eurasian Steppe to the Far East.[3] It is true that most of these deliberate economic and political conquests were ephemeral; but even this ephemeral contact with Dār-al-Islām and with Orthodox Christendom on the economic and political planes was sufficiently intimate to produce cultural effects upon Western life which were not only fruitful but enduring.[4]

Moreover, a portion of the political as well as the cultural conquests was permanent. While the medieval Western principalities and colonies in the Levant were all eventually wrested away out of Western hands and gathered up into the Ottoman Empire, Calabria and Sicily and the Iberian Peninsula were permanently incorporated into Western Christendom; and the incorporation of the Iberian Peninsula had momentous consequences, which we have reviewed already, in the histories of the West and of the World. The Atlantic sea-front of the Peninsula from Lisbon to Cadiz, which the Western Christians conquered from Dār-al-Islām between the middle of the twelfth and the middle of the thirteenth century of the Christian Era, became 'the jumping-off ground' from which the Portuguese and Castilian pioneers of Western overseas expansion launched the Western Civilization upon the open Atlantic and thereby extended its potential domain, at one stroke, from the narrow bounds of Western Europe to all the navigable seas and habitable lands on the face of the globe. It was the spirit aroused in these Western Christian frontiersmen by their triumphant response to Muslim pressure that nerved them to hazard their lives on the apparently illimitable ocean; and it was the impetus acquired in their victorious counter-attack that carried them not only out into the great deep but right across it into new worlds beyond.[5]

Thus the challenge presented to Western Christendom by the

---

[1] Conquered by the Portuguese in A.D. 1471.
[2] A number of places on these North African coasts, from Bona to Tripoli inclusive, were held by the Norman Kings of Sicily for a few years in the middle of the twelfth century. [3] See I. B (iv), vol. i, p. 38, above.
[4] The cultural effects of the contact of Western Christendom with Orthodox Christendom and with Dār-al-Islām in 'the Crusades' are examined in Part IX, below.
[5] See II. D (v), p. 204, above.

impact of Islam is manifestly proved, by the outcome of the encounter, to have been highly stimulating, which is as much as to say that in this local encounter the challenge was presented in the optimum degree of severity. The west, however, was only one of several sectors of the concentric Christian and Islamic circles in which a collision between the two waves occurred. While Islam was colliding with Roman Christendom on the west, it was also colliding with Orthodox Christendom on the north and with Monophysite Christendom on the south and with Nestorian Christendom on the east. These several portions of Christendom, which were already alienated from one another spiritually before the Islamic wave welled up in the midst of them, were thenceforth also isolated from one another geographically as the Islamic wave, expanding in their wakes, drove them all outwards and asunder. In consequence, each of these fragmentary Christendoms responded to the Islamic challenge separately and independently on its own account, and these several responses to different presentations of an identic challenge can be compared with one another.

If Western Christendom responded to the challenge of Islam with success, that is the only instance of a successful response which this series of encounters will discover to us. In each of the three other encounters between Islam and a local Christendom, the Christian response was a failure; and when we investigate these failures we shall find that they were not all due to one and the same cause. The encounter between Islam and Monophysitism offers an example of a response which failed because the local presentation of the challenge was not sufficiently severe. In the encounters between Islam and Orthodoxy and between Islam and Nestorianism, the responses were failures because the severity of the challenge was excessive.

The Monophysite failure is Abyssinia: a Monophysite Christian community which has survived in its African fastness, on the southern periphery of the *ci-devant* Syriac World,[1] to become one of the social curiosities of a latter-day Great Society. This Abyssinian Monophysite Christendom is a curiosity nowadays on two accounts: in the first place on account of its sheer survival here, in almost complete isolation from other Christian communities, during the thirteen centuries that have elapsed since the Primitive Muslim Arabs conquered Egypt in A.D. 639–41;[2] in the second place on account of its extraordinarily low cultural level. 'The common

[1] For this Abyssinian fastness, see II. D (vi), p. 258, above, and II. D (vi), Annex, pp. 403–7, below.
[2] The antecedent conversion of Abyssinia to a still undifferentiated Christianity had taken place in the fourth century of the Christian Era; the conversion to the Monophysite differentiation of Christianity dates from the latter part of the fifth and early part of the sixth century.

Christianity' of Abyssinia and the West, in a world which the radiation of our Western Christian Civilization has now unified upon a Western basis, is a theme for satire to which only a Voltaire or a Gibbon could do justice. Though Christian Abyssinia has been admitted, with some heart-searching and hesitation, to membership in the League of Nations,[1] she is a byword for disorder and barbarity: the disorder of feudal and tribal anarchy and the barbarity of the slave-trade. In fact, the spectacle presented by the one indigenous African state that has succeeded in retaining its complete independence is perhaps the best justification that can be found for the partition of the rest of Africa among the European Powers.[2]

Consideration shows that the peculiarities of modern Abyssinia —the survival of her political independence in the midst of an Africa under European dominion, the survival of her Monophysite Christianity in the borderland between Islam and paganism, the survival of her Semitic language between the Hamitic and Nilotic language-areas, and the stagnation of her culture at a level which is really not much higher than the level of the adjacent Tropical African Barbarism—are all peculiarities which derive from the same cause: that is, from the virtual impregnability of the highland-fastness in which this Monophysite fossil is ensconced.

This is the explanation of Abyssinian survival-power. Each casual piece of jetsam that has been left stranded on this rock by the passage of successive waves of civilization has remained high and dry beyond the reach of the waves that have followed.[3] A Semitic language has mounted the plateau without succeeding in extinguishing the Hamitic languages which preceded it; a Monophysite Christianity has mounted without succeeding in extinguishing the antecedent Judaism.[4] The wave of Islam, and the mightier wave of our modern Western Civilization, have washed round the foot of the escarpment without submerging the summit.

The occasions on which these later waves have swept up on to the highlands have been few and brief; and they are the exceptions which prove the prevailing rule of Abyssinian immunity. Abyssinia was in danger of Muslim conquest during the first half of the sixteenth century of the Christian Era when the Muslim inhabitants of the adjoining lowlands along the coasts of the Red Sea and the

[1] For the circumstances of her admission, see Toynbee, A. J.: *A Survey of International Affairs in 1920–3* (London 1925, Milford), pp. 393–6.
[2] The only other completely sovereign and independent state in Africa besides Abyssinia in the year 1933 was Liberia: a republic in which a helpless aboriginal Negro majority was being mishandled by a repatriated American Negro minority with an almost Abyssinian brutality. [3] See II. D (vi), Annex, pp. 403–7, below.
[4] For the Jewish fossil (the Falasha) which is ensconced, in the heart of the Monophysite fossil, among the recesses of Semyen, see II. D (vi), p. 257, above, and Annex, pp. 406–7, below.

Gulf of Aden forestalled the Abyssinians in the acquisition of fire-arms; but the newfangled weapons which the Somalis had acquired from the 'Osmanlis were acquired by the Abyssinians from the Portuguese a quarter of a century later, just in time to save Abyssinia from destruction.[1] Thereafter, when the Portuguese had served their turn and had begun to make themselves a nuisance by attempting to convert Abyssinian Christendom from Monophysitism to Roman Catholicism, the Western version of Christianity was suppressed and all Westerners—priests and laymen alike—were expelled in the 'thirties' of the seventeenth century, at the moment when the same policy was being carried out against the same intrusive forces in Japan.[2]

Like contemporary Japan, Abyssinia then retired into a deliberate isolation, which lasted until it was eventually broken by the British military expedition to Magdala in 1868. This was a portent of recurring danger from abroad which corresponded in Abyssinian history to the appearance of Commodore Perry's squadron in Yedo Bay in 1853. For the subsequent 'opening-up of Africa' by European Powers whose weapons had just achieved another sudden advance in deadliness—this time in consequence of the Industrial Revolution—exposed Abyssinia once more, towards the close of the nineteenth century, to the menace of foreign conquest which she had had to face in the sixteenth century. This time the formidably armed invaders were not the local Muslims from the Somali coast but a European nation from overseas, the Italians; but once again Abyssinia was saved from destruction by receiving in the nick of time, from friendly hands, a consignment of the deadly weapons that were being used against her. In 'the eighteen-nineties', the Negus Menelik was supplied with breech-loading rifles by the French, as in 'the sixteen-forties' his predecessor Claudius had been supplied by the Portuguese with matchlocks; and in consequence the Italians suffered as signal and decisive a defeat at Abyssinian hands at Adowa in 1896 as the Muslims had suffered at Woina Dega in 1543.

Thus the only two serious foreign attacks which Abyssinia has had to face during the fifteen or sixteen centuries that have elapsed since her conversion were both repelled too quickly and too decisively to serve as stimulating ordeals. The conversion itself has been both the first and the last stirring event in Abyssinian history;

---

[1] See Alvarez, Father Fr.: *Narrative of the Portuguese Embassy to Abyssinia*, A.D. 1520-7: English translation = Hakluyt Society Publication, 1st series, No. 64 (London 1881, Hakluyt Society); Castanhoso, M. de, and Bermudez, J.: *The Portuguese Expedition to Abyssinia in 1541*: English translation = Hakluyt Society Publication, 2nd series, No. 10 (London 1902, Hakluyt Society).

[2] The expulsion of the Portuguese and Spaniards and the suppression of Roman Catholicism were accomplished in Japan between A.D. 1614 and A.D. 1638.

both before and after, uneventfulness has been the rule; and there is a remarkable contrast between the profound and enduring effect that was made on Japanese minds by the naval demonstration of Commodore Perry and the apparent indifference of the Abyssinians to the military operations of Lord Napier of Magdala. If the Abyssinians have reacted so much less vigorously than the Japanese to our modern Western pressure, that is because the stimulus of the human environment is robbed of half its effect on Abyssinian minds by a knowledge, born of long experience, that the physical environment can be relied upon to relieve the inhabitants of the Abyssinian highlands from most of the onus of self-preservation.

This persistent lack of stimulus fully accounts for the lowness of the cultural level at which Abyssinian Christendom stands to-day. This sheltered Christian society could afford to let the salt of Christianity lose its savour—to relapse almost to the pre-Christian level and to remain at that low level in perpetuity—because its survival was almost automatically secured by the impregnability of the physical fastness in which it had barricaded itself. In fact, the backwardness of Monophysite Christendom on the Abyssinian Plateau is due to precisely the same cause as the failure of Primitive Man to create any indigenous civilization in the adjacent forests and savannahs of Tropical Africa.[1]

Thus the response of Abyssinian Monophysitism to the challenge of Islam was a failure because this challenge, like all the challenges with which the Abyssinians have ever been confronted, was mitigated, to a point far below the optimum degree of severity, by the impregnability of the local physical environment. On the other hand, the responses of Anatolian Orthodoxy and Transoxanian Nestorianism to the Islamic challenge were failures for just the opposite reason.

While the wave of Islamic expansion impinged upon Western Christendom in Gaul with stimulating vigour and washed ineffectively round the impregnable fastness of Monophysitism in Abyssinia, it broke upon Orthodox Christendom in Anatolia with almost overwhelming force. Whereas Transpyrenaean Europe was almost out of range of the Muslim Arab Power with its capital at Damascus and its reservoir of soldiers in Arabia,[2] Transtauric Asia Minor was within easy striking distance; and for some three centuries, from the launching of the original Arab offensive in A.D. 632 until the break-up of the 'Abbasid Caliphate in the tenth century of the Christian Era, the Arab military efforts which were concentrated

---

[1] For the non-emergence, up to date, of any indigenous civilization in Tropical Africa, see II. C (ii) (a) 1, vol. i, pp. 233–8, and II. C (ii) (b) 2, vol. i, pp. 312–15, above.
[2] See Annex IV, below.

upon this Anatolian front were considerably greater than the contemporary efforts which resulted in more spectacular conquests on
other fronts. In the first phase, the Arabs sought to put 'Rūm' out
of action and to overwhelm Orthodox Christendom altogether by
striking, right across Anatolia, at the Imperial City itself; and they
came within an ace of attaining this ambitious objective when they
besieged Constantinople in A.D. 673–7 and again in A.D. 717–18.
Even after the failure of the second siege, when the frontier between
Rūm and Dār-al-Islām settled down along a more or less stable line
coinciding with the physical barrier of the Taurus Range, the surviving Anatolian domain of Orthodox Christendom was regularly
raided by the Muslims twice a year, in spring and in autumn, from
their *place d'armes* in the Cilician plain at Tarsus.[1]

Thus Orthodox Christendom had to resist a pressure from Islam
which was distinctly more severe than the pressure from the same
force to which Western Christendom was exposed, and infinitely
more severe than any Islamic pressure upon Monophysite Abyssinia. The Orthodox Christians responded to this pressure by a
political expedient; and this response was successful inasmuch as it
availed to keep the Arabs at bay. On the other hand, it was unsuccessful inasmuch as the expedient adopted for this specific purpose
had far-reaching effects, which were almost wholly pernicious, upon
the inward life and growth of the Orthodox Christian Society:
effects which caused the Orthodox Christian Civilization, after a
brief spell of illusory power and prosperity, to break down and go
into disintegration in the latter part of the tenth century of the
Christian Era, just at the time when the sister civilization of Western
Christendom was surmounting its early difficulties and entering
upon that course of almost uninterrupted progress which has carried
it to the pinnacle on which it stands to-day.

The political expedient which Arab Muslim pressure impelled
Orthodox Christendom to adopt was the evocation of a 'ghost' of
the Roman Empire: a feat which was achieved effectively, and
therefore disastrously, in the Orthodox Christian World by Leo
the Syrian about two generations before it was attempted unsuc-
cessfully, and therefore innocuously, in Western Christendom by
Charlemagne. The disastrous effects of this Orthodox Christian
tour de force have been mentioned in passing already[2] and are
examined in greater detail below.[3] In this place it is sufficient to take
note of two of these effects, one general and the other particular.

---

[1] For these periodic raids, see Le Strange, G.: *The Lands of the Eastern Caliphate*
(Cambridge 1905, University Press), pp. 132–9; Brooks, E. W.: 'The Struggle with
the Saracens (717–867)', in *The Cambridge Medieval History*, vol. iv (Cambridge 1923,
University Press), ch. v.
[2] See Part I. C (i) (*b*), vol. i, pp. 65 and 67, above.
[3] In IV. C (iii) (*c*) 2 (β), vol. iv, pp. 320–405, below.

The general effect was a premature and excessive aggrandizement of the State in Orthodox Christian social life at the expense of all other institutions. The particular effect was the special consequence of the aggrandizement of the Orthodox Christian State at the expense of the Orthodox Christian Church. In Orthodox Christendom in the eighth century the Church suffered a fate which it escaped in Western Christendom until the sixteenth century, and which it only suffered then, immediately and completely, in those Western Christian countries that turned Protestant. In the eighth century, the Orthodox Christian Church was relegated to the position of a department of state; and thus, instead of serving as an institutional embodiment of the unity of Society, as the Roman Church served during the Western 'middle ages', the Orthodox Church served from the outset, like the 'established' churches of Protestant states in the modern age of Western history, to accentuate and aggravate the division and the strife which were produced in the bosom of Society by its articulation into sovereign independent states. The ultimate consequence was an internecine hundred years' war between an East Roman Empire and Patriarchate on the one side and a Bulgarian Empire and Patriarchate on the other which ended in a 'knock-out blow'; and this self-inflicted wound was the death of the Orthodox Christian Society.[1]

It will be seen that the premature breakdown of the Orthodox Christian Civilization was the penalty of malformation due to overstrain, and that this overstrain was imposed upon the Orthodox Christian social fabric by the necessity of resisting the Islamic impact. In other words, the severity of the challenge which this Islamic impact presented to Orthodox Christendom was excessive.

The Abortive Far Eastern Christian Civilization

If we now turn our attention, in conclusion, to the eastern sector of the circular line of contact between the Christendoms and Islam, and examine the effects of the Islamic impact upon Nestorian Christendom, we shall find that the severity of the challenge here was greater still. An ordeal which condemned the Orthodox Christian Civilization to die a premature death actually prevented a 'Far Eastern Christian Civilization' from being born.

This embryonic Far Eastern Christian Civilization in a Nestorian chrysalis, which the Islamic impact rendered abortive, was germinating in the Oxus-Jaxartes Basin; and the blow that robbed it of its chance of coming to life was the permanent annexation of the

[1] For the Ottoman sequel to this 'time of troubles' in Orthodox Christendom, see Part III. A, vol. iii, pp. 26–7, below.

Oxus-Jaxartes Basin to the Arab Empire in A.D. 737-41.[1] The Arab Empire was a resumption or reintegration of the Syriac universal state which had originally been embodied in the Achaemenian Empire before the premature overthrow of the Achaemenidae by Alexander; and the Arab conquest of Transoxania re-extended the limits of the Syriac universal state, over against the Eurasian Steppe, to the line at which these limits had stood during the Achaemenian régime.[2] This restoration, however, was by no means a foregone conclusion; for, by the time when it was at last achieved by the Arab commanders Asad and Nasr, the Oxus-Jaxartes Basin had been politically divorced from the rest of the Syriac World for the best part of nine centuries;[3] and this political divorce had been followed by a cultural estrangement.

The frontier drawn across the ancient Syriac domain from the highlands of Afghanistan down the basin of the Murghab and out on to the Transcaspian Steppe, which the Arab conquest of the Oxus-Jaxartes Basin obliterated in A.D. 737-41, was as old, and as deeply scored, as the more famous frontier—running from the Armenian highlands down the Euphrates Basin and out on to the North Arabian Steppe—which the Arabs had obliterated in A.D. 632-41, when they had conquered the Sasanian Empire with one hand and the Syriac provinces of the Roman Empire with the other. Moreover, the conquest of Transoxania, which was relatively remote from the Arabs' base of operations, instead of lying at the threshold of Arabia like Syria and 'Irāq, was only undertaken after a long delay and was only carried through to a successful conclusion after strenuous exertions. The Arabs had completed the conquest of the Sasanian dominions, up to the line of the Murghab, by A.D. 651; they did not seriously attempt the conquest of the Oxus-Jaxartes Basin till more than fifty years later, in A.D. 705; and their successive attempts, which began in that year, all failed to achieve more than a transitory success until in A.D. 736 the Arab commander Asad, like the Macedonian Alexander before him,[4] supplemented an ineffective policy of force by a masterly policy of conciliation.[5] Even so, the definitive Arab conquest of Transoxania, which followed in A.D. 737-41, was not confirmed until the Chinese, who had been supporting the Transoxanians in their resistance, were defeated by the Arabs on the banks of the River Talas in A.D. 751, just a century after the Arabs had reached the banks of the Murghab.

---

[1] See II. D (v), p. 141, with footnotes 2 and 3; and II. D (vi), p. 237, above.
[2] See II. D (v), p. 142, above.   [3] See p. 141, footnote 2, above.
[4] See II. D (v), p. 140, above.
[5] For Asad's policy see Gibb, H. A. R.: *The Arab Conquests in Central Asia* (London 1923, The Royal Asiatic Society), pp. 80-1.

The embryonic civilization which was germinating in the Oxus-Jaxartes Basin at the time of the Arab conquest, and which resisted the annihilating impact so obstinately, though ultimately in vain, was the product of Central Asian history during those eight or nine preceding centuries during which the Oxus-Jaxartes Basin had been living a life of its own with special functions and special experiences.

The intrusion of Hellenism into the Syriac World at the heels of Alexander the Great affected the Oxus-Jaxartes Basin as profoundly as any other part of the Syriac domain, notwithstanding the fact that Transoxania lay at the opposite extremity of the Syriac World to the point at which Hellenism had made its entry. In spite of this geographical remoteness, the Bactrian and Sogdian oases received a greater infusion of Greek colonists—and therewith a stronger tincture of Hellenic culture—than many regions which lay nearer to the Aegean: the reason, no doubt, being the intrinsic importance of Transoxania as the march over against the Nomads of the Eurasian Steppe.[1] The process of Hellenization was even intensified, for a time, when the Greek settlers in Central Asia severed their political connexion with the Seleucid Macedonian 'successor-state' of the Achaemenian Empire in the middle of the third century B.C. and set up a Bactrian Greek Empire of their own; but there were other sequels to this Central Asian Greek secession which were of greater historical moment.

In the first place, the hostility between the Bactrian Greek Power and the Seleucid Power set up a barrier between the Oxus-Jaxartes Basin and the rest of the Syriac World—a barrier that was quickly broadened when, in the adjoining province of Khurāsān, a community of Nomad origin followed the Bactrian Greeks' example and founded a principality which began as a buffer state between the Bactrian Greek and the Seleucid Greek Power and ended as the so-called Parthian Empire.[2] In the second place, the Bactrian Greeks turned their arms against India and thereby opened the way for the intrusion of Hellenism upon the Indic World: an intrusion which is to be dated from the passage of the Hindu Kush by the Bactrian Greek prince Demetrius about 190 B.C., and not from Alexander's brilliant but ephemeral Indian campaign of 326–

---

[1] For this function of the Oxus-Jaxartes Basin, see II. D (v), pp. 138–50, above.

[2] The founders of 'the Parthian Empire' were Parni; and the Parni were one of the three semi-Nomadic hordes of the Dahae, who had been deposited in Transcaspia by the same eruption out of the Steppes that had carried their neighbours and kinsmen, the Massagetae, to the Jaxartes, and the Cimmerians and Scythians as far west as the shores of the Black Sea and the Mediterranean. The particular war-band of Parni who founded 'the Parthian Empire' appear to have drifted out of Transcaspia on to the northern rim of the Iranian Plateau *circa* 250 B.C.; and since their new home lay in the old Achaemenian province of Parthia, the Parthian name came to be applied both to the new arrivals themselves and to the empire which they eventually built up round this territorial nucleus.

325 B.C.[1] In the third place, the Greek Power in Bactria, alienated as it was from the Seleucidae and cut off from the main body of the Hellenic World by the rise of the Parthians in Khurāsān, proved unequal to the task of holding the Eurasian border of the Hellenized Syriac World against Nomad pressure.

In the last quarter of the second century B.C., the Nomads broke through the Bactrian frontier defences in two successive waves—Sakas[2] and 'Indo-Parthians' in the van, Yuechi or Kushans in the rear—submerged the oases of the Oxus-Jaxartes Basin and flooded on round, or over, the Hindu Kush into India in the footsteps of the antecedent Bactrian Greek conquerors. This barbarian Völkerwanderung put an end to Greek rule in Central Asia and in India. It did not, however, extinguish Hellenic culture in the regions on either side of the Hindu Kush which the Bactrian Greek princes had united under their sceptre. These Eurasian barbarians were Philhellenes;[3] and under their aegis Hellenism survived to be an effective cultural force in the Kushan Empire, which was brought into existence in the first century of the Christian Era by the reunion of all the *ci-devant* Bactrian Greek dominions under the rule of an ex-Nomad dynasty. The effect of the Nomad influx was unfavourable not to Hellenism but rather to the Syriac Civilization in Central Asia. The cumulative effect of all the events that have been recited was temporarily to disconnect the Oxus-Jaxartes Basin from the Syriac World and to connect it up with the Indic World instead. The north-eastern escarpment of the Iranian Plateau became a cultural and political barrier, whereas the statesmanship of local Greek and Kushan empire-builders temporarily 'abolished the Hindu Kush' as Louis XIV boasted himself to have 'abolished the Pyrenees'.

During the four hundred years or so—from the second century B.C. to the third century of the Christian Era—during which Central Asia and North-Western India were clamped together first under Greek and then under Kushan rule, this temporary political union had a momentous and enduring cultural result which was parallel, *mutatis mutandis*, to the cultural result that followed from the clamping together of Syria and the Hellenic World for an approximately equal length of time under the Roman Empire. In either case, the

---

[1] On this point, see I. C (i) (*b*), vol. i, p. 86, above.
[2] These Sakas appear to have been identical with the (Massa-)getae who had ranged the Steppes immediately adjoining the Oxus-Jaxartes Basin in the Achaemenian Age. They are probably represented by the modern Jāts of the Panjab (compare Annex V, below), and their companions or pursuers the Tochari by the Doghras.
[3] Hellenism had previously proved attractive to the Scyths: a Nomadic people who had been carried out of the interior of Eurasia on to the steppes adjoining the north coast of the Black Sea in the preceding period of disturbance in Eurasia (*circa* 825–525 B.C.), and who had thus come into contact with the Greek movement of maritime expansion. (See the story of Scyles in Herodotus, Book IV, chs. 78–80.)

political union of heterogeneous cultural elements generated a great syncretistic religion: in the one case the Syro-Hellenic religion of Catholic Christianity, in the other case the Indo-Hellenic religion of Mahayanian Buddhism. The Mahayana grew up within the framework of the Kushan Empire as the Catholic Church grew up within the framework of the Roman Empire; but in Central Asia the situation was complicated by further factors.

One new factor was that, under the Kushan régime, the Oxus-Jaxartes Basin ceased to be a march between a civilization and a barbarism and became, instead, a corridor along which three different civilizations entered into communication with one another. In the last quarter of the second century B.C., immediately after the exodus of the Sakas and the Yuechi from the Central Asian Steppe, the Sinic Society, which at that time was living, under the Han Dynasty, through its universal state, expanded its spheres of exploration and influence westward, beyond the western extremity of the Great Wall, along the line of oases in the Tarim Basin, and thereby established contact with the Hellenic and the Indic Civilization which were then beginning, under the auspices of the Bactrian Greek Empire, to blend with one another in the Basin of the Jaxartes and the Oxus. The resultant commerce of cultures along this Central Asian corridor became more active at the turn of the first and second centuries of the Christian Era, when the dust of the Nomad Völkerwanderung was subsiding. The Han Empire and the Kushan Empire marched with one another in Central Asia for at least a century (circa A.D. 75–175); in the wars between them, the oases of the Tarim Basin were bandied to and fro between the one Power and the other; and thus the seeds of the Mahayana which were sown in the Tarim Basin during the periods when it was under Kushan rule were able to propagate themselves in the Far East during the periods when the Tarim Basin was united politically with China. In consequence, the Mahayana did not remain confined to the Kushan Empire in which it had originated. After issuing out of India across the North-West Frontier, it passed on in a curving orbit—skirting Tibet on three sides—through the Oxus-Jaxartes Basin and the Tarim Basin into the Far East;[1] and, like Catholic Christianity, it was destined to receive more honour in a new world than in its own birthplace. At the present day, the Mahayana is a mighty power in China and Korea and Japan while it is extinct in both India and Central Asia.

The extinction of Mahayanian Buddhism in India through the rise of a 'totalitarian' Indic religion in the shape of Hinduism does

---

[1] On the route by which the Mahayana reached the Far East, see II. D (vi), Annex, p. 405, footnote 1, below.

not here concern us.[1] Its extinction in Central Asia—where, as in India, this was a gradual process—was due to a resurgence of the Syriac Civilization which made itself felt in all parts of the buried, but not dead, Syriac body social. From the third century of the Christian Era onwards, this Syriac risorgimento manifested itself, as we have noticed in another connexion,[2] in the waves of religion which were periodically emitted by the Syriac internal proletariat. While Judaism had only defied Hellenism as a forlorn hope and Catholic Christianity had not defied Hellenism at all but had found its field of action in the Hellenic World as a Syro-Hellenic syncretism, most of the subsequent Syriac religious movements were deliberate and successful anti-Hellenic reactions.[3] In the third century of the Christian Era, a Zoroastrian Church Militant constituted itself the established church of a Sasanian state whose mission was to fight Hellenism with temporal weapons by wresting back all ex-Achaemenian territories from the Roman Empire. In the fifth century, the Nestorian and Monophysite movements sought to wrest back Christianity itself from the Hellenizers by recovering the Syriac gold in the Christian syncretism from its Hellenic alloy; and both these anti-Hellenic Christian movements managed to survive: Nestorianism outside and Monophysitism actually inside the Roman frontiers.

The frontier between the Roman and Sasanian Empires was the line along which these battles were fought; but the forces there brought into action soon began to make themselves felt, as well, on the opposite frontier of the Sasanian Empire, where it marched with other ex-Achaemenian territories in the Oxus-Jaxartes Basin. The Kushan Empire broke up about the time when the Sasanian Empire came into existence; but the Sasanidae were no more successful on the north-east than they were on the west in their long efforts to restore the lost unity of the Syriac World by force of arms. The political heirs of the Kushans were not the Sasanidae but two fresh hordes of Nomad invaders who were carried out of the Steppes in this direction in the ensuing period of disturbance in Eurasia (circa A.D. 375–675). The Huns overran the ci-devant Kushan dominions in both Central Asia and India in the fourth and fifth centuries of the Christian Era; and the White Huns or Ephthalites, who had fastened upon the Oxus-Jaxartes Basin, were supplanted

---

[1] On this matter, see I. C (i) (b), vol. i, pp. 85 and 87, above, and II D (vi), Annex, in the present volume, p. 405, footnote 1, and V. C (i) (c) 2, vol. v, pp. 136–9, as well as Part IX, below.

[2] On pp. 234–6, and 285–8, above.

[3] Manichaeism may be regarded as a partial exception. At any rate, it took pains, like Catholic Christianity before it, to propagate itself in the Hellenic World. Both Manichaeism and Mazdakism were directed, in the first instance, not against Hellenism so much as against the Zoroastrian established church of the Sasanian Empire. (See further V. C (i) (c) 2, Annex I, vol. v, pp. 575–80, below.)

there by the Turks in A.D. 563–8. Thus the political divorce of the Oxus-Jaxartes Basin from the rest of the Syriac World was still maintained. On the other hand, the Syriac Civilization began to recapture its lost Central Asian provinces not by force of arms but by the peaceful penetration of religious propaganda.

In this north-eastward expansion of Syriac religion, Zoroastrianism might have been expected to play the leading part in virtue of the geographical proximity of its base of operations on the Iranian Plateau; but it actually failed to play this part because it was handicapped by its status as the established religion of the Sasanian Empire, with which the rulers of Central Asia were at enmity. The Syriac religions which did successfully penetrate the Oxus-Jaxartes Basin under the Ephthalite and the Turkish régime were those which had been subjected to persecution in the empires in which they had first raised their heads; for their adherents were driven by *force majeure* to seek asylum abroad and were readily received by the Powers which were at enmity with the persecuting Governments, since the persecuted refugees could fall under no suspicion of intending to act as the secret agents of Governments before whose face they had fled. Thus Manichaeism, which was proscribed and persecuted in the Sasanian Empire in the third century of the Christian Era, and Mazdakism, which had the same experience in the Sasanian Empire in the fifth century, and Nestorianism, which was proscribed and persecuted in the fifth century in the Roman Empire and was therefore granted free passage into and across the Sasanian dominions, all in turn passed on into the Central Asian corridor and made their way through it into the Far East.[1] This new north-eastward radiation of Syriac culture in the form of religious waves was so vigorous that the Nestorian Christian wave, which was the latest in the series, had already reached the capital of the T'ang Empire, Si Ngan, in A.D. 636,[2] only just over two hundred years after the outcome of the Council of Ephesus had made life impossible for the Nestorians within the frontiers of the Roman Empire in A.D. 431. Contemporaneously, the Mahayana appears to have decreased in Central Asia as the Syriac religions increased. In the Oxus-Jaxartes Basin, it was evidently in decline by the time when the Chinese Buddhist pilgrim Hiuen Tsiang (Yuan Chwang) traversed the Central Asian corridor from east to west *circa* A.D. 629, *en route* from China to India.[3]

This was the situation in Central Asia at the moment when the Primitive Muslim Arab conquerors of the Sasanian Empire completed their conquest by reaching the Sasanids' north-east frontier along the River Murghab in A.D. 651.[1] Their advent raised a momentous issue. Would the new Islamic wave of Syriac religion roll on in the wake of the preceding Nestorian and Mazdakite and Manichaean waves until it broke, in its turn, upon the western borders of the Far Eastern World?[2] Or would the Nestorian Christendom which had forestalled Islam in Central Asia succeed in resisting and repelling the Islamic impact? In other terms, was the embryo of a new 'Far Eastern Christian Civilization' in the Oxus-Jaxartes Basin to succeed or to fail in coming to birth?

In the middle of the seventh century of the Christian Era, all the local conditions in the Oxus-Jaxartes Basin appear to have been in favour of the genesis of a new civilization there. There had been a long and thorough local intermingling of cultures: Syriac and Hellenic and Indic. There had been an equally long and thorough local intermingling of races: an indigenous Iranian peasantry overlaid by a deposit of Iranian-speaking Nomads in the second century B.C. and by a further layer of Turkish-speaking Nomads (Ephthalites and Turks) in the fifth and sixth centuries of the Christian Era. And this fruitful diversity of the human element was preserved and accentuated by the character of the physical environment. The concentration of the sedentary inhabitants into a number of separate fortified oases (working together, it may be, with a lingering memory of the Hellenic social tradition which had been imported by Alexander and his successors) had resulted in the social articulation of the country into a number of politically independent but economically and culturally inter-connected city-states; and the princes and merchants of these city-states were on good terms with their Ephthalite and Turkish Nomad overlords, who were enlightened enough to understand that their own true advantage lay in fostering the prosperity of their sedentary vassals and not in killing the goose that laid the golden egg.

'The golden egg' of seventh-century Central Asia was the transit-trade along the corridor between the still surviving Roman Empire and the 'ghost' of the Sinic universal state which had just been revived in the Far East under the dynasties of the Suei and the T'ang.[3] Under the aegis of the Ephthalite and Turkish khans, this trans-steppe commerce (which resembled maritime rather than overland trade) was being conducted, with profit to all parties concerned, by the merchants of the Transoxanian cities; and this

---

[1] See the masterly description in Gibb, op. cit., pp. 1–11.
[2] This, of course, has been the actual outcome. The Syriac religion which has a footing in North-Western China at the present day is neither Manichaeism nor Nestorianism but Islam.
[3] For the role of the T'ang Empire as a 'ghost' of the Han Empire, see Part X, below.

commerce was opening up, for the embryonic new civilization of the communities that were conducting it, the vast hinterland of the Eurasian Steppe. Transoxania possesses greater natural advantages as a 'jumping-off ground' for the conquest of the Steppe by a sedentary society than any of the other settled regions by which the coasts of the great Eurasian Steppe are bounded; and we have observed already[1] that even in the actual event, when Nestorianism had been robbed of its Central Asian base of operations through the Muslim conquest of Transoxania in A.D. 737–41, it very nearly succeeded in permanently converting the whole of the Eurasian Nomadic Society.

Thus, in the middle of the seventh century of the Christian Era, the new embryonic civilization in Central Asia had fair prospects in every quarter except the south-west, where the wave of Islam was welling up and menacingly raising its crest. If that menacing tide had been successfully stemmed, we must suppose that the embryo would have come to birth, and we can even conjecture to some extent the physiognomy which this civilization would have assumed if it had not been abortive.

The 'Far Eastern Christian Civilization' of Central Asia would probably have displayed a certain resemblance to the 'Far Western Christian Civilization' of Ireland.[2] The introduction of the germ of Christianity into Central Asia by Nestorian missionaries, just before Central Asia was isolated from the other Christendoms by the welling up of the Islamic wave in the midst of them, was analogous to the introduction of the germ of Christianity into Ireland by Saint Patrick just before Ireland was isolated from the other Christendoms by the settlement of the pagan English barbarians in Britain. In these circumstances, we have observed how, in Ireland, Christianity blended harmoniously with the indigenous culture of the island to create a new civilization with a high vitality and a distinctive character. If Nestorian Christianity in Central Asia had been able to repel the Islamic assault, or had been screened from its incidence as Ireland was screened from the incidence of the English assault by a Welsh buffer, we may conjecture that in those circumstances Nestorian Christianity would have followed the same course in the Far East that Patrician Christianity actually followed in the Far West. We can imagine Central Asian Nestorianism coming to some permanent local understanding with the Mahayana—and perhaps even with the remnants of Zoroastrianism as well; for the Zoroastrians, who maintained their independence in a fastness between the Elbruz Mountains and the Caspian for two or three hundred years after the Arab conquest of the rest of the Sasanian

[1] In II. D (vi), on pp. 237–8, above.   [2] See pp. 322–8, above.

Empire, had been chastened by adversity. In their new predicament they would assuredly have abandoned their traditional exclusiveness and intolerance (which had lost their *raison d'être* after
the overthrow of the empire in which Zoroastrianism had been the
established church); and we can imagine them making common
cause with any forces in Central Asia which could offer them a
point d'appui for that resistance to Islam which had become their
absorbing occupation. We have, then, to conceive of the unrealized
'Far Eastern Christian Civilization' as based upon an entente between Nestorianism on the one hand and Buddhism and Zoroastrianism on the other: an entente which might have taken the
alternative forms of coalescence (like the coalescence between
Christianity and the Celtic Paganism in Ireland) or of eclecticism
(like the abortive Neoplatonic Church of the Emperor Julian or the
successful eclectic religion of Hinduism)[1] or of 'tri-religionism' (like
the simultaneous practice of the Mahayana with Confucianism and
Taoism by Buddhists in latter-day China, and with Confucianism
and Shintoism by Buddhists in latter-day Japan).[2] On any of these
alternative bases, we can imagine the rise of a great creative 'Far
Eastern Christian Civilization' and picture it spreading from the
oases of the Oxus-Jaxartes Basin over the Eurasian Steppe, and
from Eurasia into the other regions round about.

Why did this potential 'Far Eastern Christian Civilization' fail to
materialize? Or, in concrete terms, why did the Nestorian Christendom of the Oxus-Jaxartes Basin fail to resist the impact of the Arab
Muslim conquerors during the critical century A.D. 651–751? The
problem can be stated in this way: In (let us say) A.D. 721, the
strategic position of the Arabs *vis-à-vis* the Oxus-Jaxartes Basin
was not unlike their position at the same moment *vis-à-vis* Gaul.
On both their Central Asian and their European front, at that
moment, the Arabs were standing just on the farther side of a well-
defined physical boundary at the threshold of a new world which
they might or might not proceed to conquer. As early as A.D. 713,
Musa had quietly occupied Septimania,[3] while Qutaybah's more
ambitious Central Asian campaigns of A.D. 705–15 had evoked a
more vigorous riposte, with the result that, by the year 721, the

---

[1] For the nature of Hinduism and Neoplatonism, see further V. C (i) (*c*), 2 vol. v,
pp. 136–9; V. C (i) (*d*) 6 (δ), vol. v, pp. 565–7; V. C (i) (*d*) 6 (δ), Annex, vol. v, pp. 680–3;
and V. C (ii) (*a*), vol. vi, pp. 222–3, below.

[2] In the thirteenth century of the Christian Era, in Uiguria, Nestorianism and
Buddhism were actually living cheek by jowl on a *modus vivendi* of mutual toleration.
This relation between these two religions at that time and place has been put on record
by the Western travellers who passed that way *en route* for the Court of the Mongol
Great Khan. These Western travellers were naturally impressed by finding two would-
be universal churches at peace with one another, in contrast to the perpetual state of
'Holy War' which was the contemporary relation between Western Christendom and
Islam. (See Barthold, W.: *Turkestan down to the Mongol Invasion* (2nd ed. *Anglicè,*
translated and edited by Gibb, H. A. R.: Oxford 1928, University Press), pp. 389–90.)

[3] See p. 361, above.

Arabs' holdings in Tukharistan and Transoxania, beyond the north-eastern foot of the Iranian Plateau, were no larger than their con-temporary holdings in Gaul, beyond the northern foot of the Pyrenees.[1] By the year 732, after another dozen years of campaign-ing on either front, the respective positions were still apparently the same. By the beginning of the year 732, in consequence of the disas-trous Battle of the Pass in 731, the Arabs had lost all but three posts beyond the Oxus, and all but one or two in Tukharistan; while at the same date, owing to the (less serious) reverse at Tours, they had retreated again to the Septimanian extremity of Gaul. Ultimate success was not in either case out of the question, but experience seemed to show that in both areas it could only be purchased at the price of great and sustained military efforts. In both areas, how-ever, the sequel failed to bear out the natural expectations. The Battle of Tours was accepted as final, and from that time onwards the Arabs often lost, but practically never gained, ground on their north-western frontier. On the other hand, the seemingly not less serious situation on the north-east was so dramatically reversed during the next nine years that by A.D. 741 the whole of the Oxus-Jaxartes Basin had been incorporated definitively into the Arab Empire at a relatively small cost in the shape of fresh military operations.

How are we to account for the remarkable difference between Arab military fortunes in these two war-zones? Why did the Arabs fail to conquer Gaul and succeed in conquering Transoxania? One obvious explanation is to be found in the very much greater distance of the European war-zone from the Arab base of operations. We have already had occasion[2] to remark upon the inordinate length of 'Abd-ar-Raḥmān's line of communications in A.D. 732 by the time when he had reached the Loire. The distance overland[3] (and the Arabs did not command the Mediterranean) from the Umay-yads' capital at Damascus to Narbonne, their advanced base on the threshold of Gaul, is approximately twice as great as the distance from Damascus to Merv, their advanced base on the threshold of the Oxus-Jaxartes Basin. This difference in distance explains much; yet the whole explanation of the difference between the outcomes of the two encounters can hardly lie here; for, while sheer distance told in favour of Western Christendom in its resistance to the Islamic impact, there were other factors—including certain geo-

[1] Qutaybah had penetrated far beyond the bounds of Khurāsān into Khwārizm and Farghana. It has been shown, however, by Mr. H. A. R. Gibb (in op. cit., pp. 29–87) that Qutaybah's campaigns in the Oxus-Jaxartes Basin, though brilliant and extensive, were superficial, and that the results were almost entirely lost, within six years of his death (op. cit., p. 55), by a Central Asian counterstroke.

[2] On pp. 203 and 361, above. On this point see further II. D (vii), Annex IV, pp. 428–9, below.   [3] Via North Africa and the Straits of Gibraltar.

graphical factors—in which Far Eastern Christendom had the advantage.

For example, the Pyrenees were not nearly so formidable a political and cultural barrier in the first half of the eighth century of the Christian Era as the north-eastern escarpment of the Iranian Plateau. By that date the Oxus-Jaxartes Basin had been divorced politically, and to a large extent also culturally, from Iran for close upon nine hundred years; and there was a profound cleavage in tradition and êthos between the two regions. On the other hand, eighth-century Aquitaine had a stronger sense of affinity with the Iberian Peninsula—a country with which Aquitaine had been united politically not only under the Roman Empire but also for a time thereafter under the Visigothic 'successor-state'—than she had with Northern Gaul: an ex-Roman territory that had been barbarized by the immigration of the Franks.[1] Although, by the year 732, Aquitaine had been subject to Frankish political domination for more than two centuries—ever since Frankish Clovis had won his victory over Gothic Alaric at Vouillé in A.D. 507[2]—the Aquitanians had never become reconciled to Frankish rule; and if 'Abd-ar-Rahmān had won a victory over Charles Martel in A.D. 732, or had even subsequently retrieved his defeat, the Aquitanians would assuredly have been well content to exchange a Frankish for an Arab master. In this important matter of local political sentiment, the conditions were certainly less unfavourable to the Arabs in Gaul than they were in Transoxania.

As compared with Gaul, again, Transoxania possessed other assets as well. From the military point of view the Empire of the T'ang may have proved a broken reed, but the diplomatic support against the Arabs which the independent states of Transoxania and Tukharistan were constantly receiving from the Court of Si Ngan was at any rate an effective moral weapon, especially since, to the Arabs, its value long remained imponderable and therefore subject to over-estimation. The Aquitanians, Neustrians, and Austrasians, in the crisis of A.D. 713–32, do not appear to have received either naval assistance in the Mediterranean or diplomatic support at Damascus from the Court of Constantinople, so that both the fighting and the bluffing had all to be their own. In matters of topography and climate, moreover, Transoxania was a more difficult country than Gaul for the invader. The cultivated areas were not continuous, but were separated by stretches of steppe and desert; the rivers, being mightier streams than the Garonne, the Loire, or the Seine, offered correspondingly greater obstacles; and

---

[1] See II. D (vii), Annex IV, p. 428, below.
[2] For the Battle of Vouillé, see II. D (v), p. 166, above.

between the crossing of the Oxus at Tirmidh and the Transoxanian metropolis of Samarqand there were formidable mountains to be traversed which had not their like at any point on the road from Narbonne to Tours. As for political unity, it was still hardly more than nominal in the Frankish dominions at this period and was of little account for the practical purpose of military co-operation, so that, even from this point of view, the Transoxanians and Tukhari-stanis were scarcely at a disadvantage as compared with the peoples of Gaul, while such disadvantage as there may have been was no doubt more than compensated by the greater vitality of local political life in the Oxus-Jaxartes Basin and the distinctly higher level of general civilization.

These further considerations have to be set off against the simple explanation of the difference between the Arabs' military success in Central Asia and their military failure in Europe in terms of the relative distance of the two theatres of war from Arabia. In fact, they diminish the force of this explanation to such a degree that we can hardly regard the problem as solved unless some supplementary explanation is forthcoming. Perhaps the higher level of general civilization that prevailed in Transoxania at the time supplies the clue.

In what, after all, did the superiority, in this respect, of Trans-oxania over contemporary Gaul consist? Undoubtedly in an im-measurably greater development of international trade, as might be expected in a region which had long been, and still was, a corridor of communication between surrounding societies, whereas the Gaul of that day was a semi-civilized region penned up in a blind alley at the ends of the Earth. That difference has an important bearing on our problem, for it means that the eighth-century population of Gaul possessed no vital commercial interests which would be damaged or promoted by possible alternative relations between them and the Arab Empire. At that date they were an agricultural society, and little more besides—such commerce as existed between Gaul and the rest of the World being then largely carried on by Italians, Syrians, and other outsiders. Transoxania, on the other hand, was a commercial community first and foremost.[1] Her numerous and well-peopled cities could not subsist upon the local oasis-cultivation, the extent of which was limited by a restricted water-supply, however scientific the methods of irrigation. For such a society, international trade was not a mere optional source of surplus profit but a necessity of existence; and each new develop-ment of the struggle with the Arabs struck a fresh blow at this staple of Transoxania's economic life.

[1] On this, see Gibb, op. cit., especially pp. 2, 5, and 88.

During the first phase of the struggle, which may be dated from Qutaybah's opening campaign in A.D. 705 down to A.D. 719 (by which year the greater part of his work had been undone through the unaided efforts of the Transoxanians and Tukharistanis themselves), the damage to trade was evidently not intolerable. The commercial classes in the Oxus-Jaxartes principalities were not yet faced by an unprecedented situation, for the Arab Empire in this quarter had simply stepped into the shoes of the Sasanian Empire, with which the Transoxanian Powers had frequently been at war. During these earlier hostilities, the Government at Ctesiphon appears, on more than one occasion, to have placed embargoes upon Transoxanian trade along routes that traversed the Sasanian dominions; but they had never succeeded in dealing that trade a mortal blow, and the Sughdi merchants had shown enterprise and ingenuity in opening up alternative lines of communication with their Mediterranean customers.[1] Even, moreover, if their trade with the Roman Empire were temporarily cut off, they still remained the monopolists of the overland route between the Far East and India, and the volume of this branch of commerce was no doubt sufficient to secure them against anything like an economic catastrophe. This was the situation down to A.D. 719; but it was altered —and, as it turned out, very much for the worse from the point of view of Transoxanian trade—when, in A.D. 720-1, the Türgesh Nomads from the heart of the Eurasian Steppe began to take a hand in the struggle between the Transoxanian city-states and the Arab Empire.

The Türgesh intervened as mandatories of the Government of Si Ngan and as auxiliaries of the Transoxanians in their war of liberation; and, as far as fighting the Arabs was concerned, they performed their task efficiently. For seventeen years they kept the Arab forces on the defensive, inflicted upon them several military disasters, and gradually forced them out of their fortresses beyond the River. The nominal beneficiaries discovered, however, that the remedy was worse than the disease. Officially, the Türgesh were the subjects and agents of China; but the Chinese authorities exercised no supervision, and the Türgesh evidently behaved as irresponsible Nomads do behave when they find themselves in military control of sedentary populations. The eastern trade-routes were cut; and, when the Türgesh actually crossed the Upper Oxus and began to push the Arabs out of Tukharistan, that must have

[1] e.g. the embassy which arrived in A.D. 568 at the Court of Constantinople from the Khaqan of the Nomad empire of the Turks included a Transoxanian prince, whose object was to open up a trade-route north of the Caspian and therefore beyond the reach of interference by the Persians. It seems probable that this embassy was sent on the initiative of the Transoxanian merchants, though it was headed by a representative of their suzerain, the Turkish Khaqan.

made matters still worse from the economic point of view, for the
insecurity was thereby extended to the routes between Transoxania and Hindustan. Meanwhile, the Chinese suzerains of the
Türgesh had already become so incensed against their unmanage-
able vassals that they took the opportunity of a victory which was
gained at last (in A.D. 737) by the Arab governor Asad over the
Türgesh Khaqan in Juzjān and Khurāsān to destroy the Türgesh
Confederacy and to disperse the horde. It is safe to conjecture that
the Transoxanian commercial classes, on whom the direct losses
had fallen, felt even more bitterly against the Türgesh than did the
Government of the T'ang, and this explains the immediate and
general success which attended the conciliatory policy that had
already been initiated by Asad and was being followed out by his
successor Nasr.

In 736 Asad appears to have come to an understanding with the
Iranian notables of Tukharistan. The national capital of Balkh,
ruined in the previous wars, was rebuilt, under Asad's auspices, by
the Tukharistanis themselves, in order to replace Merv as the seat
of the Arab provincial administration. This step was taken by Asad
the year before his victory over the Türgesh, and the succeeding
year (A.D. 738) was signalized by Nasr's declaration of amnesty and
guarantee of rights to the peoples of the Oxus-Jaxartes Basin. The
tolerance of non-Arab nationalities and non-Islamic religions, upon
strict but not unbearable conditions of inferiority, was a permanent
feature in the policy of the Arab Empire—a feature without which
that Empire could never have achieved its astonishing triumphs.
Nasr's charter, however, appears to have been exceptionally favourable; and, by granting it, he offered the Transoxanians an honourable escape from the terrible choice between political servitude and
commercial ruin. On condition of accepting Arab sovereignty on
not intolerable terms, they were given the prospect, not merely of
commercial recovery, but of perhaps unprecedented prosperity.

If once the political objections to incorporation into the Arab
Empire were surmounted, there could be no doubt of its advantages from the economic point of view; for, in place of a permanent
military front upon their south-western border, it opened up to
Transoxanian merchants a hinterland stretching from Khurāsān to
the Mediterranean and from the Mediterranean to the Atlantic.
Moreover, Arab statesmanship set itself promptly to reopen the
trade-routes leading along the Central Asian corridor to the Far
East. 'Shortly after his recapture of Samarqand' (probably in A.D.
739), Nasr 'sent an embassy to China. This was followed up in
744 by a much more elaborate embassy, obviously intended to
regulate commercial relations in the most complete manner possible,

in which the Arabs were accompanied by ambassadors not only from the Sogdian cities and Tukharistan, but even from Zabulistan' (south-east of the Hindu Kush), 'Shash, and the Türgesh. Two other Arab embassies are also recorded in 745 and 747.'[1] The inclusion of representatives from Zabulistan suggests that steps had already been taken to reopen the overland trade-route to India.

These facts[2] satisfactorily explain the ease and the permanence with which the Oxus-Jaxartes Basin was incorporated into the Arab Empire between A.D. 737 and A.D. 741. Do they not also suggest a reason for the failure of the Arabs, during the same period, in Gaul? The non-commercial Aquitanians and Neustrians were not confronted with the same dilemma as the Transoxanians in dealing with the Arabs. They had little or no foreign commerce to lose by war with the great neighbouring Power; in defending their political independence, they were at the same time defending their fields, which were the source of their prosperity as a primitive agricultural population; and by summoning their over-lords, the Austrasians, to the rescue, they were not exposing themselves to any such economic calamities as those which the Transoxanians incurred when they called in the Türgesh.

If this line of argument is correct, the superior civilization of eighth-century Transoxania—in other words, her higher commercial development—as compared with eighth-century Gaul was the principal reason why she succumbed to Arab imperialism and lost this opportunity of founding a distinctive civilization of her own, whereas Gaul preserved her liberty of self-determination and so eventually gave birth to that Western Civilization in which we ourselves still live and move and have our being.

Whatever the true explanation of the actual course of history on this occasion may be, it is evident that, in the capitulation of A.D. 737–41, the unborn Far Eastern Christendom renounced its birthright.

We can now arrange our series of collisions between Islam and the several Christendoms in a sequence. The impact of the Islamic wave upon the Monophysite Christendom of Abyssinia was so feeble that it hardly administered any perceptible stimulus. The more vigorous impact upon Western Christendom was highly stimulating, as is demonstrated by the vigour of the response. The considerably more forcible impact upon Orthodox Christendom was so severe that the social structure of Orthodox Christendom was permanently warped and its social fabric fatally overstrained by the *tour de force* of holding its ground. The impact upon Nestorian Christendom

---

[1] Gibb, op. cit., p. 92.
[2] Established and interpreted by Professor Gibb in op. cit.

caught this Christendom while it was still in embryo and dealt it a blow that rendered it abortive. It is evident that the severity of the Islamic challenge to Western Christendom was of the optimum degree; that the challenges to Abyssinian Monophysite Christendom and to Central Asian Nestorian Christendom were both equally remote in degree from the ideal mean, though this in opposite directions; and that the challenge to Orthodox Christendom, while less remote from the mean that either of these other two challenges, was still decidedly beyond the limits of the optimum, and this in the direction of excessive severity.

Miscarriages and Births of Civilizations in Syria

One further example of Challenge-and-Response in which the challenge has been presented in the human sphere may suffice to conclude this survey of serial encounters in which an identic challenge is delivered on different occasions with different degrees of severity and with resultant responses that differ by comparison with one another in the respective degrees of their failure or success.

This final instance of our present object of study is the human challenge presented to the inhabitants of Syria, on successive occasions when they have been moved to create an independent local Syriac Civilization, by the geographical proximity of the Egyptiac Civilization on one flank, and the Sumeric (followed by the Babylonic) Civilization on the other flank, as 'going concerns'. This human challenge became potential from the time when, under pressure of the desiccation of the Afrasian Savannah into the Afrasian Steppe, the fathers of the Egyptiac and Sumeric civilizations braved and mastered the physical challenge of the Nilotic and Euphratean jungle-swamps, whereas in Syria—the section of Afrasia that lies in between the Land of Egypt and the Land of Shinar—the corresponding challenge which was there presented by the Jordan Valley was left unanswered by Afrasian Man.[1] Thenceforward, any movement to create an independent civilization in Syria was exposed to a challenge from the presence of the civilizations that were now already established in close proximity on either side; and this challenge continued to be presented in some degree until the extinction without issue of the Babylonic Civilization in the Lower Tigris-Euphrates Valley in the last century B.C. was followed, in the fifth century of the Christian Era, by the extinction without issue of the Egyptiac Civilization in the Lower Nile Valley.

Within this long period of some four thousand years during which the challenge now under consideration was operative, there

[1] See II. C (ii) (a) 2, vol. i, pp. 256-7, above, especially the quotation from Eduard Meyer on p. 257.

is one conspicuous occasion on which it was taken up successfully. The Syriac Civilization which came to birth towards the end of the second millennium B.C. is perhaps the most brilliant and most original representative of the species, next to the contemporary Hellenic Civilization, that has appeared up to date within the period of some six thousand years during which this species of societies has so far been in existence. This Syriac Civilization, as we have remarked at other points in this Study, has three great feats to its credit.[1] It invented an alphabetic system of writing; it discovered the Atlantic Ocean; and it arrived at a particular conception of God as a personal and moral and unique and omnipotent being. And it performed these great works of creation independently of the two imposing civilizations which overlooked its tiny original domain from either side.

The Syriac Civilization, arising in an interstice between the Egyptiac Society and the Babylonic, was neither beholden to, nor impeded by, either of them;[2] and, so far as it was related to any antecedent civilization at all, its affinity was not with a society whose roots were in the soil of Egypt or Shinar but with the relatively distant Minoan Civilization of the Aegean. In virtue of this affinity, the Syriac Civilization was not only the contemporary of the Hellenic Civilization but its sister; and it revealed its common descent from the Minoan Civilization in a common taste for long-distance deep-sea navigation: a taste which made the Phoenicians and the Greeks, between them, the masters of the entire basin of the Mediterranean by the middle of the last millennium B.C. Even, however, in its relation to the sister Hellenic Civilization and to the antecedent Minoan Civilization, the Syriac Civilization maintained its

---

[1] See I. C (i) (b), vol. i, pp. 82 and 102; and II. D (ii), p. 50, above.
[2] It used to be assumed—on rather slender evidence—that the Phoenicians were beholden to the Egyptiac Society for the Alphabet. The subsequent discovery of the several Minoan scripts has evoked the counter-conjecture that the Alphabet may be of Minoan origin. (See I. C (i) (b), vol. i, p. 102, footnote 3, above.) Pending a settlement of this controversy, we may say at once that, even if the earlier view of the Egyptiac origin of the letters of the Alphabet were eventually to be confirmed, this would not deprive the Phoenicians of the credit of having invented the Alphabet; for the essence of the invention lies not in the equation of particular signs with particular sounds, but in the analysis of the sounds of human speech into a minimum number of simple elements. Both the Egyptiac and the Sumeric script, in so far as they were phonetic at all and not ideographic, were content to represent whole syllables, without pushing the analysis further. The further analysis of syllables into their consonantal elements was the new Syriac invention which gave birth to the Alphabet; and the invention is just as great an invention if the inventors happen to have used Egyptiac or Babylonic syllable-signs to represent the consonants as if they had coined brand-new signs to represent the new elements of sound which they had succeeded in isolating by analysis. As a matter of fact, the post-war researches of Western archaeologists in Syria have brought to light, in the north, an alphabetic script employing signs which are quite different from those of the historic Alphabet and which seem to be borrowed from the signs of the Babylonic Syllabary. This discovery indicates that the Syriac inventors of the Alphabet were experimenting simultaneously with different traditional materials. (The question of the origin of the Alphabet has been touched upon already above in I. C (i) (b), vol. i, p. 102, footnote 2, and in II. D (ii), pp. 50-1.)

independence. For the greatest creative achievement of the Syriac
Society was neither its discovery of the Atlantic nor its discovery
of the Alphabet but its discovery of God; and the particular conception of God at which the Syriac Society arrived—a conception
which is common to Judaism and Zoroastrianism and Christianity
and Islam—is alien (as we have seen) not only from Babylonic
religious thought and Egyptiac religious thought (apart from the
flash of illumination in the single soul of Ikhnaton) but also from
Hellenic religion and from Minoan (as far as the êthos of Minoan
religion is known to us).

Thus the historical Syriac Civilization proclaims, in its magnificent creative originality, the triumphant success of its response to
the challenge which the proximity of the Egyptiac and Babylonic
civilizations presented to it. Yet, without disparaging the Syriac
achievement, we may notice that this successful Syriac Civilization
came to birth at a juncture when the social pressure exerted upon
Syria from Egypt on the one side and from Shinar on the other was
at less than its average strength.[1] The post-Minoan interregnum,
during which the Philistine wave of Minoan refugees broke upon
Syria from the Eastern Mediterranean and the Hebrew wave of
Afrasian Nomads from the North Arabian Steppe, may be dated, in
round figures, between 1425 and 1125 B.C.; and during these three
centuries, in which the Syriac Civilization actually emerged, both
the Egyptiac and the Babylonic Society were in a low state of
vitality. The Egyptiac World was then wholly on the defensive.
Its energies were being absorbed in the effort of self-preservation
amid the formidable social convulsions which the dissolution of the
Minoan Civilization was producing in the Levant; and so long as
'the New Empire' succeeded in saving the homelands of the Egyptiac
Civilization in the Nile Valley from being overwhelmed, it was
content to leave Syria to take care of itself. On the other flank of
Syria, in the same age, the Babylonic Civilization, which had
recently taken the place of the Sumeric Civilization, was equally
passive; for Babylonia was still torpid under the feeble rule of the
last epigoni of her Kassite barbarian conquerors, while Assyria
had not yet started upon her career of militarism.[2] As for the sister
civilization which the Hittites had created in Anatolia, this had
been shattered, in the course of the post-Minoan Völkerwanderung,
by the impact of the great migration at the beginning of the
twelfth century B.C.: an impact which the Egyptiac Civilization

[1] This point is noticed by Eduard Meyer in his 'Zur Theorie und Methodik der Geschichte' (*Kleine Schriften* (Halle 1910, Niemeyer), p. 56).
[2] The Third (Kassite) Dynasty of Babylon 'petered out' *circa* 1173 B.C.; Tiglath-
Pileser I of Assyria, who made the first tentative essay in Assyrian militarism, *regnabat*
circa 1115-1089 B.C.

just managed to resist by the expenditure of its last remaining reserves of vitality.[1]

Thus, in observing that the historical Syriac Civilization responded to the challenge of Egyptiac and Babylonic proximity with conspicuous success, we have also to observe that it made this successful response at a time when the challenge was presented in less than its normal degree of severity; and in order to appraise this success we must compare it with a previous failure. For the creation of a Syriac Civilization was not achieved at the first attempt. The successful attempt which resulted in the historical Syriac Civilization had been preceded on the same Syrian soil, some four or five centuries earlier, by a similar attempt which was abortive.

We have come across this earlier Abortive Syriac Civilization already in other connexions.[2] We have seen that when 'the Empire of Sumer and Akkad', which was the Sumeric universal state, broke up, and the Sumeric Civilization itself went into dissolution, after the death of Hammurabi at the end of the twentieth century B.C., the former domain of the Empire was overrun by Aryan Nomadic invaders from the Eurasian Steppe; and that one horde of these invaders—the people who afterwards became known in the Egyptiac World as the Hyksos—migrated right across the breadth of the Sumeric World from north-east to south-west and came to a halt at the furthest extremity of that world, in Syria.

At that time Syria was a kind of debatable border or no-man's-land or limbo between the Sumeric World and the Egyptiac World. The rift-valley of the Jordan—having failed to evoke from Man the response which had given birth to civilizations in the valleys of Euphrates and Nile—remained desolate and uninhabited; and the Hill Country of Ephraim was still uninhabited likewise.[3] On either side of these physical barriers, the Sumeric and Egyptiac civilizations had respectively acquired footholds on Syrian soil and had staked out spheres of interest. The Egyptiac Civilization had radiated up the coast of Syria as far as Byblos soon after, or possibly some time before, the foundation of the Egyptiac United Kingdom circa 3200 B.C.; and Byblos, which was its farthest bourne, was also its firmest point d'appui in this quarter. From the other side, the interior of Northern Syria was raided as far as the Jabal Ansarīyah and the Lebanon, and even occasionally as far as the Mediterranean coast, by the Sumerian militarist Lugalzaggisi of Uruk (Erech) and Umma (regnabat circa 2677–2653 B.C.) and his

---

[1] See I. C (i) (b), vol. i, pp. 93 and 101, above.
[2] See I. C (i) (b), vol. i, pp. 105-7; and I. C (ii), vol. i, p. 139, footnote 1, and p. 144, above.
[3] See the present Study, II. C (ii) (a) 2, vol. i, p. 257, and II. D (ii), in the present volume, p. 53, above, as well as Meyer, E.: Geschichte des Altertums, vol. ii (i), 2nd ed. (Stuttgart and Berlin 1928, Cotta), p. 96.

Akkadian supplanters and emulators Sargon (*regnabat circa* 2652–2597) and Naramsin (*regnabat circa* 2572–2517);[1] and the seeds of Sumeric culture which were scattered in the west by these passing whirlwinds of military conquest took permanent root among the Amorites: a Semitic-speaking Nomadic people who appear to have drifted off the North Arabian Steppe and silted up against the eastern flank of Lebanon about the middle of the third millenium B.C.,[2] as their fellow-Semites and fellow-Nomads, the Aramaeans, drifted from the same starting-point to the same resting-place some twelve centuries later.[3]

The Amorite settlers in the interior of Syria became incorporated into the Sumeric body social, worked their way towards the heart of the Sumeric World, and eventually founded the First Dynasty of Babylon, which was also the last dynasty to rule and maintain the Empire of Sumer and Akkad. Thus, by the time when the Empire finally broke up after the death of Hammurabi, the greatest of the latter-day Amorite emperors, the interior of Syria had long formed an integral part of the Sumeric World; and when, in the ensuing Völkerwanderung, Syria was overrun by a horde of barbarians who had broken into the Sumeric World from the Eurasian Steppe, it might have been expected that the local outcome would have been similar to the outcome in Babylonia and in Cappadocia. In both these other *ci-devant* provinces of the defunct Sumeric universal state, the interregnum occupied by the post-Sumeric Völkerwanderung was followed by the emergence of new civilizations, closely related to the Sumeric, which were built up by the joint efforts of the ex-provincials and the immigrant barbarians.[4] In Babylonia, the new Babylonic Civilization emerged after the irruption and settlement of the Kassites; in Cappadocia, the new Hittite Civilization emerged after the irruption and settlement of the 'Kanisians' and the 'Luvians'.[5] Why was it that, in contemporary Syria, a new Syriac Civilization did not emerge simultaneously after the irruption and settlement of the Hyksos? In other words, why was it that the potential Syriac Civilization of this age miscarried and never came to birth?

The explanation of this miscarriage seems to be that the Aryan Nomadic invaders of the Empire of Sumer and Akkad who settled in its Syrian province overshot the boundaries of the Sumeric

---

[1] For these militarists and their role in Sumeric history, see I. C (i) (*b*), vol. i, p. 109, above.
[2] For the Amorites see Meyer, E.: op. cit., vol. ii (i), 2nd ed., pp. 18 and 100.
[3] For the Aramaeans, see II. D (v), pp. 134–5, above.
[4] See I. C (i) (*b*), vol. i, pp. 110–12, above.
[5] For these barbarians, who spoke Indo-European languages of 'the Centum-group' and who had presumably descended upon the Sumeric World from South-Eastern Europe, see I. C (i) (*b*), vol. i, p. 113, footnote 3, above.

World, impinged upon the Egyptiac World, and became implicated, to their own undoing, in the course of Egyptiac history. The settlement of the Hyksos in Syria, which may be dated between the death of Hammurabi *circa* 1905 B.C. and the foundation of the Kassite 'successor-state' of Hammurabi's Empire in Babylonia *circa* 1749 B.C.,[1] would normally have been followed by a long period of local stagnation and quiescence; but in Syria, unlike Babylonia and Cappadocia, this normal sequel to a Völkerwanderung did not follow, and therefore, on this occasion, the promise of a new Syriac Civilization did not come to fruition; for, without a spell of quiescence and recuperation after the tumult in which it has been conceived, an embryonic civilization can never be brought to birth.

The reason why the Hyksos were unable to settle down after their arrival in Syria was because the province of the defunct Empire of Sumer and Akkad into which Fate had carried them happened to be in immediate proximity to the Egyptiac World.

The site at the southern extremity of the Syrian coast, which the Hyksos selected for the capital of their 'successor-state',[2] actually lay within the Egyptiac and not within the Sumeric sphere; and soon after the beginning of the seventeenth century B.C., perhaps not more than a century after the Hyksos had made their headquarters here, an event occurred in the Egyptiac World which could not leave the Hyksos indifferent. The Egyptiac universal state (the so-called 'Middle Kingdom', which lasted from *circa* 2075 to *circa* 1675 B.C.) broke down;[3] an interregnum ensued in the Egyptiac World which was comparable to the Sumeric interregnum that had set in after the death of Hammurabi some two centuries earlier; and, once again, the Hyksos were drawn into the vacuum. Instead of settling down to collaborate with the Canaanites in the gradual building up of a local Syriac Civilization, they struck the tents which they had so lately pitched and marched on into Egypt, as they had once marched across Shinar into Syria, in their old role of barbarian invaders.

The consequences of this diversion of the Hyksos' energies from Syria to Egypt were disastrous to all parties; but they were disastrous first and foremost to the Hyksos themselves; for the tincture of Sumeric culture which the Hyksos had acquired *en route* made them unassimilable by, and therefore abominable to, their Egyptiac subjects.[4] Thus the first effect of the Hyksos' conquest of the Egyptiac World was to evoke a militant Egyptiac reaction; and this

---

[1] See I. C (i) (*b*), vol. i, p. 111, footnote 1, above.
[2] For the archaeological excavations on this site, in 1931, see a letter from Sir Flinders Petrie in *The Times*, 31st May, 1931.   [3] See I. C (ii), vol. i, p. 137, above.
[4] See I. C (ii), vol. i, pp. 139, footnote 1, and 144, above.

reaction was victorious. The Hyksos were driven out of Egypt
again, within a century of their original entry, by a restored Egyptiac
universal state;[1] and 'the New Empire' was not content to bring its
successful counter-offensive to a halt at the Syrian border. It
followed up the discomfited Hyksos in their retreat and annexed
the Syrian territories which the Hyksos had previously taken over
from the Empire of Sumer and Akkad, right up to the Euphrates.
The Aryan personal names of certain Syrian princes which are preserved in 'the New Empire's' official records testify that the Hyksos
survived in Syria for some centuries longer as a people;[2] but they
only survived under Egyptiac dominion; their political power was
at an end; and, more than that, their chance of creating a Syriac
Civilization had vanished.[3] In yielding to the temptation of invading a prostrate Egypt, the Hyksos had thrown away their Syrian
birthright. The distracting proximity of Egypt to Syria thus explains why, in the first half of the second millennium B.C., the
promise of a Syriac Civilization, related to the Sumeric Civilization,
came to nothing, while a Hittite and a Babylonic Civilization were
successfully brought to birth. In Syria, this miscarriage was followed by a period of frustration which lasted until 'the New Empire'
of Egypt had run its course and until the post-Minoan Völkerwanderung supervened to offer a new opportunity for creation: an
opportunity which was seized this time, as we have seen, with
brilliant success.

Thus the challenge to which the historical Syriac Civilization
responded triumphantly had proved excessive when it had been
presented on an earlier occasion with greater severity; but there
was another occasion on which a civilization that had been conceived and duly born on Syrian soil was manifestly starved of
stimulus because this very challenge of Egyptiac and Babylonic
proximity had ceased to operate.

By the time when the Arabic Civilization emerged in Syria after
the post-Syriac interregnum (circa A.D. 975–1275), both the Egyptiac
and the Babylonic Civilization had long been extinct. Their extinction had been accomplished by the society to which the nascent
Arabic Civilization was 'apparented': that is to say, by the historical
Syriac Civilization itself. For the Syriac Civilization—acting as
though it were conscious of the Egyptiac and Babylonic menace—
had set itself, from the moment of its own birth, to devour its two
venerable neighbours and to absorb their tissues into its own body
social. The process began with the peaceful penetration of Egypt

[1] See I. C (ii), vol. i, pp. 138 and 144; and II. D (v), p. 112, above.
[2] See I. C (i) (b), vol. i, p. 105, footnotes 4, 5, and 6 above.
[3] For the lack of originality in the local culture of Syria in that age, see Meyer, E.:
Geschichte des Altertums, vol. i, part (ii), 3rd ed. (Stuttgart and Berlin 1913, Cotta), p. 682.

and Assyria by Phoenician and Aramaean traders; it was completed by the successive conversions of the Egyptiac and Babylonic worlds to a series of Syriac missionary religions: Primitive Christianity and Nestorianism and Monophysitism and Islam. By the time when the Syriac Civilization died at last—after a life that had been unnaturally interrupted but also unnaturally prolonged by a Hellenic intrusion—the work of assimilation had been performed so thoroughly that Egypt on the one side and 'Irāq on the other were now just as Syriac as Syria herself.

Thus, when the Arabic Civilization was in embryo, it was not confronted with the challenge which had proved so stimulating to the historical Syriac Civilization and so upsetting to its abortive predecessor. While the Syriacized land of 'Irāq lay derelict on the morrow of the Mongol devastation, the Syriacized land of Egypt offered the embryonic Arabic Civilization a safe citadel in which its birth could be accomplished. The ancient challenge of Egyptiac and Babylonic proximity to Syria had entirely ceased to operate. Yet, if we are justified in concluding that, in the first half of the second millennium B.C., the severity of that challenge was excessive, we are also bound to conclude that the entire cessation of the challenge by the time when the Arabic Civilization was in gestation, at the turn of the first and second millennia of the Christian Era, was an untoward circumstance. For the Arabic Civilization which had this easy birth did not have a distinguished career.[1] Its possession of a citadel in Egypt gave it no substantial security; for its independence was prematurely brought to an end by the masterful intervention of a sister society—the Iranic—which had been nurtured in a harder environment. Yet, before this misfortune overtook it in the early decades of the sixteenth century of the Christian Era, the Arabic Society had been granted two centuries' grace in which to prove its mettle; and the time was long enough to show that no great creative forces were gathering in its bosom. If the Arabic Civilization had not had such an easy start but had been confronted at the beginning by the challenge which Egyptiac and Babylonic proximity had presented to its Syriac predecessor, it would assuredly have acquitted itself with greater distinction than it actually achieved.

It will be seen that this Syrian series of encounters has presented us with a sequence once again. The brilliantly successful response of the historical Syriac Civilization to the challenge of Egyptiac and Babylonic proximity proves to be a middle term between two extremes. On the one hand, the greater severity with which the same

---

[1] For the career of the Arabic Civilization, see I. C (i) (b), vol. i, pp. 70–2, with Annex I, above.

challenge was presented in the first half of the second millennium
B.C. rendered a first attempt at creating a Syriac Civilization abortive. On the other hand, the complete absence of this challenge in
the history of the subsequent Arabic Civilization—a younger local
civilization which was 'affiliated' to the Syriac—had an untoward
effect upon this latter-day civilization's career. In this sequence,
the historical Syriac Civilization, to which the identic challenge was
presented in a mean degree of severity, stands out as the conspicuous
instance of success against a double background of failure: failure
from an excess of stimulus and failure from a lack of it.

Perhaps we are now in a position to answer the question which
originally drew us into our present inquiry. After finding, by our
empirical methods of study, that, in diverse instances and variations
of the movement of Challenge-and-Response, 'the greater the challenge the greater the response' appeared to be a working 'law', we
then set out to discover whether this 'law' which we had traced
inductively were valid absolutely, or whether it were subject, like
so many other particular laws, to the general 'law of diminishing
returns'. The inquiry which we have just concluded indicates that
'the law of diminishing returns' does hold good in this connexion.
In the language of Mythology, the encounter between two superhuman personalities, which is the dynamic force in human affairs
and the key to the plots of the great tragic works of art, does not
result *semper et ubique et omnibus* in the denouement which is given
to the play in the Book of Job and in Goethe's *Faust*. A wager
between God and the Devil in which the Devil cannot be the winner
nor God the loser is not, after all, the course which the action of
this universal drama invariably follows. It turns out that this is
only one possible rendering of the plot—a rendering which depends
upon the terms in which the bet is offered and taken; and there is
another alternative rendering in which the denouement is that of
Euripides' *Hippolytus*. There are challenges of a salutary severity
that stimulates the human subject of the ordeal to a creative response; but there are also challenges of an overwhelming severity
to which the human victim succumbs. In scientific terminology,
'the most stimulating challenge is to be found in a mean between
a deficiency of severity and an excess of it.'[1]

The meaning of this proposition has gradually unfolded itself in
the long empirical process of proof. There is, however, at least one
word in the formula that remains ambiguous, and this is the word
'stimulating'; for a stimulus evokes a reaction, and a reaction implies a movement in some definite direction after the stimulus has
been received. What, then, is the movement towards which a

[1] For this formula see p. 260, above.

nascent civilization is stimulated by the challenge that brings it to birth? Presumably the nascent civilization is stimulated to fulfil its nature. And what is it in the nature of a new-born babe to do? When the babe has come to birth, it is in its nature to grow in wisdom and stature. Growth is what birth implies; and if our study of the geneses of civilizations has now at last reached its term, the study of the growths of civilizations still lies before us.

IS 'OLD GROUND' LESS FERTILE THAN 'NEW GROUND' INTRINSICALLY OR BY ACCIDENT?

IN one passage of a foregoing chapter[1] we have examined the histories of seven civilizations of the 'related' class, each of which has comprised some 'old ground' and some 'new ground' in its domain. The upshot of this survey is that 'old ground' is apt to make a less fertile field than 'new ground' for human culture; and we have interpreted this result of empirical observation as a confirmation of the doctrine—implicit in the myths of the Exodus and the Expulsion—that the ordeal of breaking 'new ground' has an intrinsic stimulating effect. This interpretation of our empirical evidence rests on the assumption that the reason why 'old ground' is relatively sterile is because it presents a less formidable challenge to its occupants than the challenge presented by 'new ground', and therefore exerts a proportionately less powerful stimulus.[2] Some readers, however, may contest this explanation of the facts and may discount accordingly the value which we have placed upon this empirical evidence in our argument. Even assuming that the facts, as we have set them out in our survey, are correctly stated, our critics may submit that these facts are to be explained in another way. The explanation, they may represent, lies not in any subtle influence of the physical environment upon the behaviour of its human occupants, but in certain obvious external misfortunes which happen to have afflicted the inhabitants of certain regions in certain ages. In terms of our metaphor, the poorness of the crop in these particular fields is accounted for (according to our critics' contention) by the ravages of blight and mildew, and is therefore no evidence of any intrinsic lack of fertility in the soil. This

---

[1] On pp. 74–84, above.

[2] This assumption is borne out by two instances that have already come to our attention—one in Ceylon and the other in Central America—which stand out as exceptions to our law; for they both turn out to be exceptions that prove the underlying rule. In both Ceylon and Central America, the modern Western planters or colonists have occupied 'new ground' which had been left virgin by the pioneers of the foregoing indigenous civilizations; yet in both cases the new-comers on the 'new ground' have achieved nothing that can compare with the respective achievements of the Sinhalese and the Mayas. (For the Ceylonese case see II. D (i), pp. 6–7, above; for the Central American case see II. C (ii) (a) 2, vol. i, p. 267; and II. D (ii), pp. 35–6, above.) When we look closer, however, we observe that, in both cases, the mere 'newness' of the 'new ground' was not such a formidable—and therefore presumably not such a stimulating—factor as the inherent and perpetual challenge of Physical Nature which the 'old ground' presented. In Central America, it was less difficult for the Spanish colonists to open up the relatively dry highlands than for the Mayas to keep the jungle at bay in the rain-sodden lowlands. And in Ceylon it has been less difficult for the Scottish and English planters to clear the rain-smitten highlands than for the Sinhalese to keep the parched plains supplied with water by irrigation.

criticism deserves consideration. Let us see what our critics have to say, and what we have to say to them in reply.

Our critics are likely to open their attack by pointing out that, in several of the instances which we have brought forward, the 'old ground' which has proved sterile is ground which happens to have been overlaid by a peculiarly barbarous deposit of barbarians in the Völkerwanderung antecedent to the birth of the particular 'related' civilization in question. For example, at the birth of the Babylonic Civilization, Babylonia was overrun by the barbarous Kassites, while Assyria was surrounded but never quite engulfed by the Mitannians. At the birth of the Arabic Civilization, Syria was harried by the incurably barbarous Crusaders and Mongols, while the Kurdish and Turkish and Caucasian barbarians who fell upon Egypt were human wolves who proved capable of transforming themselves into human watch-dogs: the Mamlūks. At the birth of the Iranic Civilization, Transoxania and Iran were blighted by the Mongols, while the 'new ground' occupied by the Iranic Civilization in Anatolia and Hindustan was as relatively fortunate as Egypt in respect of the barbarians which fell to its lot. In Anatolia and in Hindustan, the Iranic Civilization was not only first propagated by Turkish barbarians who had been converted to Islam but was afterwards protected by them—as Egypt was protected by the Mamlūks—against the ravages of the more barbarous Mongols who followed at the Turkish barbarians' heels. Again, at the birth of the Hellenic Civilization, Crete was saddled with the 'Dorians'—barbarians whose yoke weighed so heavily upon the local descendants of the Minoans that the very name 'Minōs', which had once denoted the ruler of the seas, became the hall-mark of serfdom in the derivative 'Mnoïtês'.[1] Naturally, it may be represented, the nascent Hellenic Civilization did not ever come to flower in this wilderness of uncivilized masters and barbarized slaves. Naturally, likewise, it did first come to flower among the descendants of those Minoan refugees who had saved themselves from enslavement by finding asylum along the Anatolian coast.

This array of facts is impressive, but it is not impregnable. To take, for instance, the contrast between the roles of Doric Crete and *ci-devant* Minoan Ionia in Hellenic history: we may retort to our critics by pointing out to them that the Cyclades, which were as free as Ionia herself from the 'Dorian' incubus, played as poor a part in Hellenic history as Doric Crete, whereas one of the first points at which Hellenism flowered in Continental European Greece was Doric Corinth. Moreover, Doric Laconia and Doric Rhodes, which flanked Doric Crete on either side, each came to play an

[1] See I. C (i) (*b*), Annex II, vol. i, above.

eminent part as the movement of Hellenic history developed. The case of Laconia is particularly striking, inasmuch as the likeness between Dorian institutions in Laconia and in Crete was notorious.[1] The same yoke weighed with the same weight upon the Laconian Helots as upon the Cretan Mnoïtae. Yet the descendants of the Dorian conquerors of Sparta rose to a greatness which was never emulated by their kinsmen in Crete. On the hypothesis that Dorian brutality accounts for the benightedness of Hellenic Crete, these further facts are inexplicable. On the other hand, they are all intelligible on our hypothesis that the occupation of 'old ground' fails to provide a stimulus which the breaking of 'new ground' does provide. This hypothesis explains the common obscurity, in Hellenic history, of Crete and the Cyclades—the two foci of the antecedent Minoan Civilization—notwithstanding the presence in Hellenic Crete and the absence in the Hellenic Cyclades of the Dorian incubus. It also explains the common eminence, in Hellenic history, of Ionic Ionia and Attica and Doric Corinth, Laconia and Rhodes; for both Ionia and Corinth appear to have lain beyond the range of the thalassocracy of Minos, while Attica, Laconia, and Rhodes came only just within its pale.

Moreover, we may suggest that, in any Völkerwanderung, each invaded district is apt to get the barbarians whom it deserves, and, having got them, to bear their yoke until it earns its liberation. For instance, was it a mere external accident that, in the post-Sumeric Völkerwanderung, Assyria kept her head above the Mitannian flood when the waters of a Kassite domination went over Babylonia's soul? Is it not more credible that Assyria managed to keep her local barbarians at bay because she offered a stouter resistance than her Babylonian neighbour; and that she offered a stouter resistance because the Assyrians had responded to some stimulus in their local environment which was not offered to the Babylonians by theirs? Again, the failure of the Mnoïtae in Crete—and, for that matter, of the Helots in Laconia—to liberate themselves from the yoke of their Dorian masters was by no means a matter of course. It was only one of two possible alternative outcomes of the Dorian conquest of Crete, as is shown by the historical parallel of the Lombard conquest of Italy.

The Lombards, at the time when they overran Italy in the last convulsion of the post-Hellenic Völkerwanderung, were more barbarous than any other barbarian conquerors of Roman provinces in the West except the English conquerors of Britain; and their treatment of the conquered population was proportionately harsh. Though the Lombards did not go to the length of exterminating

[1] On this point, see further Part III. A, vol. iii, p. 55 below.

the native Italians, they did impose upon them a much heavier yoke
than had been imposed by the Lombards' predecessors in Italy,
the Ostrogoths, or by the Franks in Gaul, or even by the Vandals in
Africa. Thus, at the dawn of our Western history, the situation in
Italy was closely comparable to the situation that existed at the
dawn of Hellenic history in Crete. An extreme reversal of fortune
had placed a once imperial people under the heel of a particularly
brutal barbarian master. Yet, though the situation was comparable,
the outcome was completely different; for, while the Cretan Mnoïtae
never recovered from the shock of their abasement and continued
to bear the Dorian yoke to the end of Hellenic history, the Italian
Aldi boldly and victoriously took their savage Lombard conquerors
captive.[1] They converted the Lombards from their Arian heresy to
the Catholic Faith; they taught them to discard their Teutonic
vernacular for the Italian language; and by such means they succeeded, within four or five centuries of the Lombard conquest, in
transforming an unsocial aggregation of serfs and masters into a
single people, abounding in energy and morally fit to take the leading part in the next act of the drama of Western history. This
evidence proves that a calamity like the Lombard conquest of Italy
or the Dorian conquest of Crete is by no means bound to blight for
ever the prospects of the region upon which it descends. While the
history of Dorian Crete shows that this may be the effect, the history of Lombard Italy shows not less clearly that the effect may
equally well be just the opposite.

Finally we can refute our critics by joining issue with them on
the field of Orthodox Christian history; for here it is impossible to
adduce any evidence for a special extraneous calamity, exclusively
afflicting the 'old ground' in the Orthodox Christian domain, which
might be held to account for this 'old ground's' relative sterility.
It is true that, in the domain of Orthodox Christendom, the 'old
ground'—that is, the Aegean area—was visited by the twin calamity
of Slav invasions overland and Arab raids by sea; but the same
visitations fell much more severely upon the two pieces of 'new
ground' in which Orthodox Christendom successively found its
centre of gravity. The brunt of the Arab offensive was borne by
Eastern and Central Anatolia, from the Taurus to Amorium; the
brunt of the Slav invasions was borne by the interior of the Balkan
Peninsula from the Danube to Salonica. The bands of Slavonic
invaders that penetrated beyond Salonica into Peninsular Greece
were forlorn hopes; the Arab sea-raids were 'side shows' compared
to the Arab land operations. Thus it will be seen that, in Orthodox
Christendom, the 'old ground' was afflicted not more but less

[1] Horace: *Epistolae*, II, Ep. i, l. 156.

grievously than the 'new ground' by these barbarian blights; yet in Orthodox Christian history—just as in Babylonic and Hindu and Arabic and Iranic and Hellenic and Sinic history—the 'old ground' has proved less fertile than the new.

Perhaps our thesis that 'old ground' is less fertile than 'new ground' intrinsically and not by accident has now been sufficiently vindicated against the criticism to which it might seem, at first sight, to be exposed.

HISTORIC SIEGES AND THEIR AFTER-EFFECTS

CITIES, like ships, are readily personified by the human imagination; and their greatness depends, not merely upon immediate practical values which can be expressed statistically, but also always to some extent, and often to a far greater extent, upon an imponderable prestige which is created and sustained by an emotional consciousness of their historic trials and triumphs. In many cases it is possible to trace the origin of this prestige to certain particular outstanding ordeals; and the prestige of Vienna is a case in point. It is manifestly founded upon the successful resistance of Vienna to the Ottoman assaults of A.D. 1529 and A.D. 1682–3.

A city's resistance, however, need not be successful in order to win the reverence and affection of later generations. For example, the prestige of Moscow is founded upon the passive endurance of the city on two occasions when she has fallen, without serious military resistance, under the heel of a Western invader: a Polish invader in 1610–12 and a French in 1812. On the other hand, the prestige of Constantinople in Orthodox Christendom, like that of Vienna in the Western World, is founded on a series of successful resistances: to the Persians and Avars in A.D. 626 (a supreme crisis which is commemorated, down to this day, in the Liturgy of the Orthodox Church, in the Ἀκάθιστος Ὕμνος); to the Arabs in A.D. 673–7; and to the Arabs again in A.D. 717–18. The prestige of Constantinople, like that of Vienna and unlike that of Moscow, is bound up with the concept of inviolability; and it has suffered from the Latin conquest of A.D. 1204 and the Ottoman conquest of 1453, as the prestige of Vienna has suffered from the French occupations of 1805 and 1809. In contrast to Constantinople and Vienna, Rome and Paris and London, all three, owe their present eminence, as the respective capitals of Italy, France, and England, to prestige gained by them in ordeals in which they have made an heroic resistance but have not remained inviolate.

How was it that Rome achieved the *tour de force* of becoming the capital of the new Kingdom of Italy in preference to Turin, a city which enjoyed the practical advantage of being the capital of the particular Italian State that was the instrument of national unification, and likewise in preference to Milan, a city which enjoyed the practical advantage of being the industrial centre of the Italian Peninsula? These practical considerations telling in favour of Milan or Turin would hardly have been overridden, in favour of

Rome, on the strength of historical sentiment pure and simple, if Rome had not identified herself, in the hearts and minds of the Italian people, with the Risorgimento of Italy by standing siege from the French in 1849. So far from Rome suffering any loss of prestige through the fact that her resistance to her besiegers on this occasion was unsuccessful, she gained her prestige in 1849 in virtue of the very fact that her resistance was a forlorn hope. She rejected the summons to capitulate with the clear foreknowledge that her fall was inevitable; for by that time the Italian national uprising of 1848 had already suffered defeat in almost every other quarter; the reaction was in the ascendant all over the European Continent; and the reactionary forces which were being concentrated upon Rome were overwhelming. Rome's heroic gesture in making this last and hopeless stand against overwhelming odds in 1849 was just what appealed to the Italian national imagination.

As for the prestige of Paris and London, which was won a thousand years earlier than the prestige of modern Rome in the utterly different ordeal of the Scandinavian Völkerwanderung, inviolability was not of its essence either. In fact, at the first encounter with the Vikings, both London and Paris were ignominiously taken by assault and pillaged: London in A.D. 842; Paris in 845. London was actually ceded to the invaders by Alfred under the Treaty of Wedmore in A.D. 878 and remained for seven years in their hands. The two cities emerged from their ordeal with a new and enduring prestige not because they never fell but because they fell only to rise again and oppose a firmer resistance to the invader. As the ordeal continued, this resistance became indefatigable. The Vikings never succeeded in forcing their way above Paris up the Seine or above London up the Thames; and either city crowned its long endurance with a final feat of arms which made a permanent impress upon the national imagination: Paris with her successful resistance to the great siege of A.D. 885–6; London with her successful barrage of the Thames in A.D. 895.

JEWS IN FASTNESSES

IN the relevant chapter,[1] we have drawn attention to the fact that the fossils of extinct civilizations are found in two distinct situations—in 'dispersion' and in 'fastnesses'—and we have observed that these situations are not only different but are in sharp contrast with one another. The most familiar example of a fossil in dispersion is the Jewish 'Diasporà'. On the other hand, it is perhaps not so well known that there are other Jewish communities that have survived in fastnesses down to the present day. The contrast between the êthos of these Jews in fastnesses and the êthos of the Jewish 'Diasporà' is extreme; and some description, in greater detail, of extant 'Jews in fastnesses' may therefore be of interest.

In this connexion it may be recalled that Judaism is a fossil of the extinct Syriac Civilization, and that the successive religions which the Syriac Civilization begot in the course of its history all arose, in turn, in the heart of the Syriac World, and all radiated out from the centre, in every direction, towards the circumference. The result has been not unlike what happens when a child throws one stone after another into the middle of a pond. When several stones have been thrown in succession, the surface of the pond displays a pattern of several concentric circular waves which are all travelling outwards from the centre towards the circumference simultaneously. The outermost of these expanding circles is the product of the first stone thrown in; the wave raised by the second stone forms the second circle which is expanding in the first circle's wake; and so on—each wave that has travelled a shorter distance from the centre being the product of a stone which has been thrown into the pond at a later moment of time. On this pattern, the religions successively begotten by the Syriac Civilization have expanded in concentric circles from the heart of the Syriac World: Jewry and Christianity and Islam from Syria and the Hijāz; Zoroastrianism and Shi'ism from Iran. The Jewish-Zoroastrian wave, being the earliest, is the outermost; the Christian wave has followed in its wake; the Islamic wave is the innermost and the latest.[2]

Of course, at the present day, some thirteen centuries after the date when even the youngest of these waves was originally launched,

---

[1] See II. D (vi), pp. 256–9, above.

[2] This refraction of Syriac religion into a series of successive waves is a consequence of the impact of Hellenism upon the Syriac World. (See II. D (vi), pp. 234–5, and II. D (vii), pp. 285–8, above, and Part IX, below.) The boy who threw the first stone of Hellenism into the Syriac pond was Alexander of Macedon.

the pattern of concentric circles has lost its regularity. The Jewish-Zoroastrian wave has mostly dissolved into spray which has scattered itself all over the World in the form of a diasporà. As for the Christian wave, certain sectors of its circle—e.g. the Orthodox sector and the Western (now broken up into a Catholic fraction and a Protestant)—have swollen to unexpected dimensions, while other sectors—e.g. the Nestorian and the Monophysite—have shared the fate of the Jewish-Zoroastrian wave ahead of them. Only the Islamic wave still clearly retains its original formation. It needs the discerning eye of a historical geographer to reconstruct the original pattern of the whole series of waves from the present state of the map; and the materials for reconstruction would have been altogether insufficient but for the existence of certain rocks and reefs on which the waves, in breaking, have thrown up fragments of jetsam which have provided a permanent record of their passage. These rocks are the fastnesses in which fossils have been preserved in a state of fixity thanks to their isolation from the moving and changing world outside.

On the periphery of the Syriac World, there are two notable fastnesses of the kind: on the south, Abyssinia with its outwork the Yaman; on the north, the Caucasus with its annex the Crimea.[1] If we examine the present human fauna of either of these fastnesses, we shall find in either place a Jewish fossil still preserved in the inmost recesses and a more recently deposited Christian fossil surrounding the Jewish fossil and embedding it. In either place, again, we shall see the Islamic wave—the youngest and innermost wave of the three—washing round the foot of the rock, occasionally beating tempestuously against its flanks, and ever seeking to submerge it from base to pinnacle.

In Abyssinia, the local Jewish fossil—the Jewish community known as the Falasha—occupies the central district of Semyen: the highest highlands of the Abyssinian Plateau. The Jewish highlanders of Semyen are entirely surrounded by Abyssinian Monophysite Christians, who occupy all the rest of the plateau from the bounds of Semyen to the edge of the escarpment. The lowlands adjoining the plateau on the north and on the east are inhabited by Muslims—the foot of the Abyssinian escarpment constituting the limit of the Islamic domain in this direction.[2]

Similarly, in the Caucasus, the habitat of the local Jewish fossil—the so-called 'Mountain Jews'—is Daghestan (i.e. 'the Highlands'

---

[1] For a former Jewish fastness on the west, in the Maghrib, which held out till A.D. 1492, see Gautier, E. F.: *Les Siècles Obscurs du Maghreb* (Paris 1927, Payot), p. 200. Cf. op. cit., 415–16.

[2] See the map on p. 111 of *A Handbook of Abyssinia*, vol. 1: General (London 1917, H.M. Stationery Office).

par excellence), a district which may be regarded as the innermost recess of all Caucasia. The local Christian fossils—Georgian Orthodox Christians in the basins of the Rion and the Kur, and Armenian Monophysites on the plateau south of Georgia—occupy more exposed positions. As for the Muslims, they have penetrated into the Caucasus more deeply than they have succeeded in penetrating into Abyssinia up to the present, so that the Mountain Jews of the Caucasus find themselves embedded to-day in a non-Jewish population which is not Christian but Muslim.

As regards the outwork of Abyssinia in the Yaman and the annex of the Caucasus in the Crimea, it is noteworthy that in both places Jewish fossils have survived, while the more recently deposited Christian fossils, which were once to be found there, are now no longer extant. The Nestorian Christendom of the Yaman did not survive the first impact of Islam; and the indigenous Orthodox Christendom of the Crimea[1] is extinct to-day, though it was extant no longer ago than the sixteenth century of the Christian Era.[2] On

[1] As distinct from the Russian Orthodox Christendom which has been introduced into the Crimea, by Russian colonization, since the annexation of the Crimea to the Russian Empire in A.D. 1783.

[2] The indigenous Orthodox Christendom of the Crimea was originally represented by two communities: the Greeks of Cherson, on the site now occupied by the modern Russian foundation of Sebastopol near the southern corner of the peninsula; and the Crimean and Tetraxite Goths, who occupied respectively the eastern end of the Crimean mountains and the western end of the Caucasus Range, on opposite sides of the Straits of Kertch. These Goths were jetsam from the Völkerwanderung which had carried the main body of their kinsmen not only from the shores of the Baltic to the shores of the Black Sea, but on and beyond from the shores of the Black Sea to the shores of the Mediterranean and the Atlantic. The Crimean and Tetraxite Goths had been left behind at the first halting-place on the long trek which the Visigoths and the Ostrogoths continued to the bitter end. When the main body went west and was straightway consumed in the holocaust of the Roman Empire like a moth that flies into a candle-flame, the lost Gothic rear-guard in the Crimea lived on in obscurity in this fastness for another millennium. The last descendants of these Crimean Goths were found surviving by the Flemish scholar and traveller Busbecq in the middle of the sixteenth century, when he was the Ambassador of the Hapsburg Monarchy at the Sublime Porte. In the fourth and last of his famous Turkish Letters, he describes an interview with two envoys from these Crimean Goths who had come on official business to the Ottoman Imperial Government at Constantinople, and he gives a short vocabulary of their language, which he recognizes to be Teutonic. As for Cherson, it was not only a representative of Orthodox Christendom but a fossil of the Hellenic Society in its pristine state. Cherson was the last survivor of the hundreds of sovereign independent city-states into which the Hellenic World had been articulated before it was unified politically in the Roman Empire. Cherson, alone, had become an ally of Rome without ever losing its autonomy, and it also survived the post-Hellenic Völkerwanderung in which the Roman Empire broke up. In fact, Cherson lived on as a sovereign city-state on the old Hellenic pattern until the East Roman Empire —a resuscitation of the Roman Empire in the Orthodox Christian World—annexed Cherson outright in the ninth century of the Christian Era. Thus the mountainous southern portion of the Crimea has provided fastnesses not only for Orthodox Christendom and Jewry but for the North European external proletariat of the Hellenic Society as represented by the rear-guard of the Goths, and the Hellenic city-state as represented by Cherson. At the same time, the flat and lowlying northern portion of the Crimea has repeatedly provided an asylum for Nomadic peoples who have been driven off the Great Eurasian Steppe by more powerful hordes of their own kind, but have managed to hold their own on the miniature Crimean Steppe to the south of the Isthmus of Perekop. The Thracian-speaking Taurians, the Iranian-speaking Scyths, and the Turkish-speaking Khazars and Tatars are examples of *ci-devant* masters of the Eurasian Steppe who managed to survive in the Crimea for some centuries after they had been trampled out of

the other hand, the Yamanī Jews have managed—under great and apparently increasing pressure from the local Muslims who have occupied the place of the former local Christians and pagans since the seventh century—to maintain themselves in existence down to the present day, when the remnant is gradually being evacuated from the Yaman to Palestine by Zionist enterprise. As for the Jewish fossil in the Crimea, it is represented—and this likewise down to the present day—by two separate Jewish communities: the Krimchaks, who are Talmudists, and the anti-Talmudist Qara'im.

Thus the original pattern of concentric Jewish and Christian and Islamic waves is preserved by the Jewish and Christian jetsam that has remained stranded in the fastnesses of Abyssinia and the Yaman and the Caucasus and the Crimea, while the tide of Islam has filled the vast intervening area and has flooded round the bases and up into the gateways of the fastnesses themselves.[1]

existence everywhere else. The Khazars who survived in the Crimea after the destruction of the Khazar Empire on the Eurasian Steppe in the eleventh century of the Christian Era are believed to be the ancestors of the Krimchak Jews.

[1] This pattern of concentric waves, representing the expansion, from a common centre, of successive religious movements, is not a unique and peculiar product of the Syriac Civilization. We have observed already (on pp. 234-5 and 285-8, above) that the refraction of Syriac religion into separate and successive and sometimes conflicting waves is an outcome of the collision between the Syriac Civilization and the Hellenic Civilization. We have also observed (vol. i, on pp. 85-6 and 91-2, in I. C (i) (b), above) that the Syriac Civilization was not the only civilization which the impact of the Hellenic Society deflected from its natural course. This experience of the Syriac Civilization was shared by the Indic Civilization; and if we now glance at the historical geography of the religious movements that have emanated from the ancient Indic World, we shall find analogous traces of an identical pattern of successive concentric waves.

In this Indic pattern, the oldest and outermost wave—corresponding to the Jewish-Zoroastrian wave in the Syriac pattern—is represented by the Primitive or Hinayanian Buddhism which survives down to the present day on what used to be the southern sector of the periphery of the ancient Indic World in Ceylon and Burma and Siam, and which was once to be found likewise on the northern sector of the same periphery, in the Tarim Basin. This first wave is likewise represented by Jainism, which still survives in dispersion nearer the heart of the ancient Indic World, in continental India. This Jainism and Hinayanian Buddhism are fossils of Indic religion as it was before the Hellenic impact, just as Zoroastrianism and Judaism are fossils of Syriac religion as it was before the Hellenic impact. The next wave in the Indic pattern—corresponding to the Christian wave in the Syriac pattern—is represented by the Later or Mahayanian Buddhism, which, like Christianity, is a syncretism between the indigenous culture and the intrusive Hellenism; and this Mahayanian wave, like the Christian wave, again, has developed a marked irregularity of form. What was originally its north-western sector has completely disappeared in Afghanistan and in the Oxus-Jaxartes Basin, which were the first stages on its course of expansion; and it has also disappeared in the Tarim Basin, where it followed and effaced the Primitive Buddhism of the Hinayana. On the other hand, this north-western sector of the Mahayanian Buddhist wave has swollen to unexpected proportions in its final resting-place in the Far East, which it has reached at the end of a journey that has carried it, in a sharply curving track, round the southern and western and northern foot of the Tibetan Plateau. As for the north-eastern sector of the Mahayanian wave, which is constituted by the Tantric or Lamaistic variety of Mahayanian Buddhism, this has spread from Bengal to Tibet and thence to Mongolia—Tibet and Mongolia being the places where it survives to-day. It will be seen that the Lamaistic Mahayanian Buddhism corresponds to the Monophysite-Nestorian sector of the Christian wave, and the Far Eastern Mahayanian Buddhism to the Western sector. Finally, while the Mahayanian Buddhism, in its two extant varieties, constitutes the middle wave in the Indic pattern, the latest and innermost wave is represented here by Hinduism, which—like Islam in the Syriac pattern—now occupies the central position and still clearly retains its original formation. It will be seen that Hinduism also resembles Islam in

If we now concentrate our attention upon the Jews in fastnesses, who have been deposited there by the expansion of the oldest and outermost of the three concentric waves, we shall find that in physique and language and culture these Jews have far more in common with the pagans and Christians and Muslims with whom they share their asylum than they have in common with Jews elsewhere. It is to be inferred that Judaism, like its successors Christianity and Islam, has propagated itself by the process of conversion as well as by the process of migration. At any rate among the Jews in fastnesses, the predominant element in the life and in the blood of the community seems to be the contribution of the indigenous proselytes.

In Abyssinia, for instance, 'the Falasha are Hamites by race and Jews only by religion'.[1] They 'are in general darker and more corpulent than the Amharas, among whom they live. Their hair is shorter and often curly; their eyes are smaller and their faces not so long.'[2] They 'have no language of their own, but speak various Agau dialects'.[3] 'They are ignorant of Hebrew, but possess in Ge'ez the canonical and apocryphal books of the Old Testament' and various other religious works.[4] 'They know nothing of the Babylonian and Jerusalem Talmud, composed during and after the Captivity respectively, and do not observe the feast of Purim, i.e. the dedication of the post-Exilic Temple.'[5] 'Their Judaism does not exclude a very strong tincture of paganism. . . . Especially curious is their worship of Sanbat, the Goddess of Sabbath.'[6]

From its origins down to the end of the eighteenth century of the Christian Era, this Falasha Jewish community seems to have lived a life of warlike independence in its highland fastness of Semyen. This community 'consolidated itself into an independent Kingdom in Semyen at the time of the conversion of Abyssinia [to Monophysite Christianity]. In [A.D.] 937 Judith, queen of Semyen in her own right, murdered the whole [Christian] royal family of Axum, with the exception of one child who was conveyed to Shoa, and usurped the throne. In 977 she was succeeded by her daughter, who was deposed a few months later by a prince of the house of

---

standing for the ultimate victorious reaction by which the indigenous culture eventually drove the intrusive Hellenism out. If we may venture to pursue our parallel still farther, we may also perceive Indic analogues of the Syriac fastnesses. The Plateau of Tibet, which gives asylum to the Lamaistic Mahayanian Buddhism, plays the part of the Caucasus; the highlands of Ceylon, which give asylum to the Hinayanian Buddhism, play the part of Abyssinia. (The historical geography of the Indic and the Syriac religions is examined at greater length in Part IX, below, apropos of the contacts between civilizations in Space.)

[1] *British Admiralty Handbook of Abyssinia* (cited on p. 403, above), p. 107.
[2] *The Jewish Encyclopaedia* (New York and London 1901–6, Funk and Wagnall), s.v. 'Falasha'.
[3] *British Admiralty Handbook of Abyssinia*, p. 109.
[4] Op. cit., p. 120.　　　[5] Op. cit., pag. cit.　　　[6] Op. cit., pp. 120–1.

Zagwe. The dynasty founded by this prince was at first perhaps Jewish but later Christian.'[1] Thereafter, in Semyen, the Falasha maintained their independence in periodic warfare with the surrounding Christians; but 'their line of kings became extinct about 1800, when the Falasha became subject to Tigre'.[2]

During the last century and a half, under the new conditions of subjection of Christian rule, the Falasha seem to have entered on a process of transformation from a fossil in a fastness into a fossil in dispersion. They still 'live mostly in Semyen in villages of their own',[3] and 'agriculture is' still 'their chief occupation'.[4] At the same time, members of the Falasha community are now dispersed abroad in other parts of Abyssinia, and in this situation they are already displaying the characteristic traits of a penalized religious minority. 'If resident in a Christian or Muhammadan town', they 'occupy a separate quarter. They do not mix with the Abyssinians; indeed, they are forbidden to enter the house of a Christian and never marry the women of other religions. Polygamy is unknown; early marriages are rare; and the moral standard is superior to that of the Abyssinians.'[5] 'They are fanatical in observing the Sabbath, the circumcision of both sexes, certain fasts, and several festivals, annual and monthly. They are scrupulous in following the laws of purification by means of baths and ablutions.'[6] Moreover, 'they excel in all trades. In their eyes work is not, as it is, for example, in the eyes of the Shoans, the attribute of serfs and slaves. They are cultivators, smiths, masons, architects, ebony-workers, weavers, potters, and so on. We have seen them, in the course of this history [of Abyssinia], forming regular centres of almost constant rebellion. For more than a century past, however, they have no longer made themselves notorious. Their skill in manual work leads to their being exploited by the chiefs and even maltreated—treated, in fact, as an inferior race.'[7] Evidently the Falasha who are now dispersed abroad in Abyssinia beyond the confines of their native fastness in Semyen are rapidly approximating towards the well-known type of the Jewish 'Diasporà'. As yet, however, the approximation is imperfect; for although they 'ply the trades' and 'make the articles necessary for the home or the field', they still 'reject commerce'.[8]

The modern history of the neighbouring Jewish community in the Yaman has run a parallel course. 'At the beginning of the 19th century, the condition of the Jews of Yaman was miserable. . . . They were prohibited . . . from engaging in money transactions and

---

[1] Op. cit., p. 218.   [2] Op. cit., p. 122.   [3] Op. cit., pag. cit.
[4] The Jewish Encyclopaedia, s.v. 'Falasha'.   [5] British Admiralty Handbook, p. 122.
[6] Colbeaux, J.-B.: Histoire Politique et Religieuse d'Abyssinie (Paris 1929, Geuthner), vol. ii, pp. 399–401.
[7] Op. cit., loc. cit.   [8] The Jewish Encyclopaedia, s.v. 'Falasha'.

were all mechanics, being employed chiefly as carpenters, masons, and smiths. . . . The chief industry of the Jews of Yaman is the making of pottery, which is found in all their settlements and which has rendered them famous throughout the East.'[1]

If we turn now to the Caucasus, we shall find the same phenomena as in Abyssinia. In physical race, the 'Mountain Jews' of Daghestan, like the Falasha of Semyen, are of one blood with the non-Jewish peoples round about them. Socially, they are an agricultural community which is just beginning to migrate into the towns and to take up some of the occupations which are characteristic, elsewhere, of the Jewish 'Diasporà'—though in the Caucasus this tendency does not seem to have gone so far as in Abyssinia up to the present.

The racial character of the Caucasian Jews is clearly described by a Jewish authority in the following passage:[2]

'The Jews of the Caucasus are very interesting. Historically it has been proven that they have been there for more than two thousand years. They claim that they are the descendants of those ubiquitous Ten Lost Tribes, and many missionaries are inclined to believe them. The most curious, both from an anthropological and ethnological standpoint, are the Mountain Jews of Daghestan. They have diverged completely from the ethnic type of the Jews in every other country. According to the measurements obtained recently by Kurdoff, they are tall, averaging 166·0 cm. in height, and 57 per cent. of them were above the average height. Very few blonds are met with among them, 87 per cent. have both dark hair and eyes. Their head-form is hyperbrachycephalic, the average cephalic index being 86·35, and not one dolichocephalic individual was found among 160 measured by Kurdoff. Their face is broad, the forehead straight, the aperture of the eye horizontal; the cheek-bone being somewhat protruding, the nose straight and of medium size; only thirty per cent. have "Semitic" noses. The mouth is broad, the lips thick, and the ears large. That author concludes that the Daghestan mountain Jews are physically far removed from all other Jews, and have nothing in common with them. They are a product of mixture of the mountain tribes of Daghestan on the one hand, and some other races, especially the Kirghiz Mongolians, on the other.[3] Their language, dress, and manners are the same as those of the other mountaineers among whom they live. All who have observed these Jews agree that they are of a totally different type from the one generally known as "Jewish". It is impossible to distinguish them from the Tats, Lesghians, and Circassians, among whom they live, says one who has studied the races of the Caucasus,[4] and most other ethnologists agree with this view.'

[1] Op. cit., s.v. 'Yemen'.
[2] Fishberg, M.: The Jews: A Study of Race and Environment (New York and Melbourne 1911, The Walter Scott Publishing Company), pp. 130–1.
[3] K. Kurdoff, 'Gorskie Yevrei Dagestana' (Russian Anthropological Journal, 1905, Nos. 3–4, pp. 57–87).
[4] Hahn, C.: Aus dem Kaukasus (Leipzig 1892, Duncker and Humblot), pp. 161 and 232.

As for the social life of the Caucasian Jews—their occupations and institutions and êthos—it will be sufficient to quote a passage from one of the leading modern Western authorities on the Caucasian peoples:[1]

'One principal reason for the incompleteness of earlier works about the Mountain Jews of the Caucasus is to be found in the fanaticism and exclusiveness which these Jews display towards other Jews. They have a mass of religious usages and articles of faith which to European Jews are entirely unknown; above all, they are zealous adherents of the Talmud. Their hatred of other Jews was still further accentuated by the fact that, after the conquest of the Caucasus, the Jewish soldiers from Russia, who were hospitably received by the Mountain Jews as co-religionists, chose to nickname their hosts "oxen"—a nickname which persists down to this day—on account of the roughness and grossness of their manners. The extent of the enmity between the two is best shown by a saying current among the Mountain Jews: "Don't kill an Ashkenazi by cutting his throat; stab him in the neck to prolong the agony." There have been a number of bloody encounters between these two Jewish races. . . .

'The Mountain Jews are mostly dispersed up and down Daghestan and the Terek District; and, in consonance with their principal occupations, their settlements are located on the alps or in the gorges or on the slopes of the mountains. Their auls are in some cases dispersed among the auls of other tribes, in some cases segregated from them, while there are places where they live cheek by jowl with the natives. In general, with few exceptions, they live in a good understanding with the natives. It is not uncommon for a Jew to contract a close friendship with a Musulman and to become, after the exchange of the kiss of friendship, his life-long *kardash* [brother]. In this rite the parties exchange weapons and contract a solemn mutual obligation to stand by one another, in time of stress, till they have shed their last drop of blood in their comrade's defence. . . .

'A considerable section of the Mountain Jews live in the towns and devote themselves to trade and business. Those who live in the auls are predominantly agriculturists. They cultivate wheat, barley, rice, tobacco, fruit, and vines, as well as vegetables. A small section are artisans and make morocco leather. . . .

'The attitude of the Mountain Jews towards European education is very hostile; and so it is no wonder that in the auls one often finds hardly two or three people who can read and write. The reason for this is fanaticism. There is a fear that those who acquire some learning may become apostates. It is only lately that the children are being sent to school, and the number of illiterates has already come down to something like 85 per cent. On the other hand, the number of those who attend the higher schools in order to acquire a rabbi's diploma amounts to only 1 per cent. The Mountain Jew mostly lives by the work of his

---

[1] Hahn, C.: op. cit., ch. vi: 'Die Juden in den Kaukasischen Bergen'.

own hands, and he needs his children's help, so that the children have
no time for school. . . .

'When we come to the physiognomy of the Mountain Jews, we have to
observe that the Semitic type has been substantially modified by mixture
with the native peoples of the Caucasus. . . . The Mountain Jew resembles the Lesghian, Chechen, and Circassian, and even the Armenian,
much more than he resembles the European Jew. . . .

'The character and occupation of the Mountain Jew is profoundly
influenced by his physical environment. Here we see him, armed *cap-à-
pie*, riding past us on a handsome charger; there we see him, in old ragged
clothes, clambering up the mountain-track in order to hew stumps or
dig up the roots of trees and bushes to be carried home on bended back;
here again we see him digging the ground, ploughing, making wine,
gathering in his fruit crop or perhaps standing in a tub by the spring and
stamping out raw hides. . . .'

The two Jewish communities in the Crimea differ from one
another in their theology and also, apparently, in their racial origin.
The 'Krimchaks', who are Talmudists, are believed to be descended
from the Khazars: a Turkish-speaking Nomadic people who erupted
from the depths of the Eurasian Steppe in the latter part of the
sixth century of the Christian Era; found themselves new pastures
between the Lower Volga and the Lower Don; made themselves
the dominant power between the Caucasus and the Urals and the
Russian forest and the Black Sea; and eventually became converts
to Judaism—probably in the eighth century of the Christian Era,
more than two hundred years before the White Bulgars on the
Middle Volga were converted to Islam or the Russians on the Upper
Dniepr to Orthodox Christianity. The Krimchaks are believed to
be descendants of a remnant of the Khazars who found asylum in
the Crimea[1] after they had been driven off the main steppe in the
eleventh century, partly by the Russians and partly by a fresh
eruption of kindred Turkish-speaking Nomadic tribes (Ghuzz and
Cuman or Qipchāq) from the heart of Eurasia.[2]

'Krimchaks: the so-called "Turkish Jews", inhabitants of the Crimea,
whose centre of population is Qara-Su-Bazar, one of the most densely
populated districts of Taurida. They differ from the other Jews of
Russia in that the Semitic and Tatar elements are in them intimately
blended. In their mode of life, they greatly resemble their Tatar neighbours, but in religion they adhere strictly to the Jewish faith, even to
Talmudic Judaism. Their dress is identical with that of the Tatars. . . .
The men are almost all of tall stature and slenderly built, and are marked
by the reddish-golden colour of their hair, a tint which is uncommon
among Semitic tribes. The women have retained more tenaciously the

---

[1] 'Many intermingled in the Crimea with the local Jews; the Krimchaki are probably
their descendants' (*The Jewish Encyclopaedia*, s.v. 'Chazars').
[2] See the second footnote on p. 404, above.

characteristically Jewish type. . . . The houses of the Krimchaks are built in the usual Tatar style. . . . The Krimchaks employ a pure Tatar language, but use the Hebrew Alphabet in writing.'[1]

The other Jewish community in the Crimea are the anti-Talmudist Karaites (Qara'im: i.e. readers of the Law and the Prophets as opposed to the commentaries upon them). The Karaite Sect appears to have arisen somewhere near the centre of the Syriac World —perhaps in Northern Persia—in the eighth century of the Christian Era, after the reintegration and resumption of the Syriac universal state in the Arab-Caliphate.[2] In its Syriac homelands, the Karaite Movement attained its zenith in the tenth and eleventh centuries of the Christian Era. Thereafter, in the Syriac World, and in the new Arabic and Iranic worlds which arose on its ruins, Talmudic orthodoxy began to regain its ascendancy among the local Jewry, and the Karaites went out in search of new worlds to conquer. In the twelfth and thirteenth centuries, they were able to offset their losses among the Jews of Dār-al-Islām by gaining ground among the Jews in the main body of the Orthodox Christian World and the Jews in the Crimea and on the adjoining stretches of the main body of the Eurasian Steppe. Of the Karaites who established themselves on the north side of the Black Sea, some were transplanted to Troki in Lithuania by the Lithuanian conqueror Witold the Great (regnabat A.D. 1392–1430).[3] Others remained in their Crimean fastness, which is described in the following passage from the work of one of the earliest travellers with a Western scientific outlook that visited the Crimea on the morrow of the modern Russian conquest of the peninsula:[4]

'At three versts' distance, as the crow flies, from the upper part of Baghcheserai, at the entry of the gorge where the Juruk-su[5] rises, one reaches the fastness of the Jews: Jufut-Qal'eh. It is situated at the junction of the gorge with another valley, on a high limestone mountain which juts out between the two ravines. . . . One climbs up to the fortress by a path used for carrying water on donkey-back (in little barrels, slung pannier-wise, at a charge of ten kopeks). Outside the town, at the entry of the valley, one sees the cemetery of the Jews, shaded by magnificent trees and covered with rows of tombs. . . . The Jews have such veneration for this Valley of Jehoshaphat that at one time, whenever the Khans wanted to make a levy on the Jews, they were sure of obtaining from them whatever sum they demanded by the threat of felling the trees surrounding

---

[1] *The Jewish Encyclopaedia*, s.v. 'Krimchaks'.
[2] See I. C (i) (*b*), vol. i, pp. 76–7, above.
[3] For the expansion of the Lithuanians to the shores of the Black Sea under the stimulus exerted by the pressure of the Teutonic Knights from the Baltic, see II. D (v), p. 172, above.
[4] Pallas, Professor: *Voyages entrepris dans les Gouvernemens Méridionaux de l'Empire de Russie dans les Années 1793 et 1794* (French translation from the German: Paris 1805), vol. ii, pp. 34–6.   [5] Choraq-su?

the Jewish cemetery, on the pretext that they needed the timber. The Jewish town is situated on the narrowest part of the salient of the mountain and is fenced in by walls and by houses. It has two outer gates, which are shut every evening: one at the peak of the crag; the other at the point where the ridge spreads out into a plateau. The streets are narrow and tortuous but very clean. The rock itself serves for paving, but the principal streets have side-walks for the convenience of the inhabitants. In the centre of the town one sees a third gate which indicates the limit of the town's original area and gives a measure of the extent to which it has grown. One observes in the vicinity the mausoleum of a daughter of Toqatmysh Khan. . . . The Synagogue, which is a fine piece of architecture, possesses a little garden which serves for the Feast of Tabernacles. All the courtyards are surrounded, in the Tatar fashion, with high walls built of undressed limestone and clay. The houses, which are built in continuous blocks number about two hundred and are inhabited by twelve hundred persons of both sexes, who are all Karaïtes. These Jews still use the name Qara'im among themselves, and do not admit the orthodoxy of any other Jews except the Polish Karaïtes who agree with them in rejecting the Talmud. They also import their bibles from Poland; but they have almost entirely adopted the ancient costume and language of the Tatars, because they have been living under the domination of that people from time immemorial, from the produce of their commerce, manufactures and trades.'

This brief survey may give some notion of the great gulf in race, occupation, and êthos which divides the little-known Jews in fastnesses from the well-known Jews in dispersion.

DR. ELLSWORTH HUNTINGTON'S APPLICATION OF HIS CLIMATE-AND-CIVILIZATION THEORY TO THE HISTORIES OF THE MAYAN AND YUCATEC CIVILIZATIONS IN CENTRAL AMERICA AND TO THE HISTORY OF THE SYRIAC CIVILIZATION IN THE OASES OF THE NORTH ARABIAN STEPPE

IT will be evident to any reader of this Study that the writer of it has the greatest admiration for Dr. Ellsworth Huntington and his work; and it is with considerable diffidence that the writer now ventures upon a criticism of Dr. Huntington's views on one particular point. He therefore wishes to preface this criticism by noting that the point in question does not touch the substance of Dr. Huntington's theory: the theory, that is to say, that the fluctuations jn the fortunes of civilizations are in some cases and to some extent connected with variations in climate arising from a periodic shifting of climatic zones. The criticism refers to two only out of a very large number of applications of this theory which Dr. Huntington has made; and the present critic will seek to show that, in these two particular applications, Dr. Huntington is (no doubt, unintentionally) departing from his own theory in effect, instead of supporting it.

With Dr. Huntington's main positions, as he understands them, the writer of this Study profoundly agrees.

He recognizes that Dr. Huntington—with the just sense of proportion which is characteristic of big minds—avoids the mental pitfall of ascribing exclusive or even paramount efficacy to the particular factors which happen to have been the object of the scholar's own researches. Dr. Huntington perceives and declares that, in human affairs, the efficacy of spiritual factors is primary and the efficacy of climatic and other physical factors secondary.[1] And, in the sphere of application which he assigns to the climatic factor, he generally portrays this factor as acting upon human life, not in a mechanical, *a priori*, necessitarian way, but in the form of a stimulus. Indeed, a sentence in which Dr. Huntington sums up this view of the relation between climate and civilization has been quoted in an earlier passage of this Study as one in a series of illustrations of the action of Challenge-and-Response. 'A relatively high degree of storminess and a relatively long duration of the season of cyclonic

---

[1] See, for example, his *The Climatic Factor as illustrated in Arid America* (Washington 1914, Carnegie Institution of Washington, Publication No. 192), p. 226.

storms have apparently been characteristic of the places where civilization has risen to high levels both in the past and at present.'[1]

Moreover, in the present Study, Dr. Huntington's special climatic theory of the periodic shifting of climatic zones has been accepted as supplying the key to the geneses of three civilizations—the Nomadic, Egyptiac, and Sumeric—on the assumption that a desiccation of the former Afrasian Savannah into the present Afrasian Steppe has presented the human inhabitants of this region with a common challenge that has evoked several alternative responses.[2]

Dr. Huntington goes on, however, to apply this same special theory of the shifting of climatic zones to explain the rises and falls of the Mayan and Yucatec civilizations in Central America and the Syriac Civilization in the oases of the North Arabian Steppe; and it is in regard to these two applications that the writer of this Study finds himself unable to see eye to eye with Dr. Huntington altogether.

Stated briefly, the theory of the shifting of climatic zones supposes that two things are constant from age to age—in the first place, the amount of water existing on the surface of the planet, and in the second place the nature and relative position of the successive zones of climate that encircle the globe latitudinally—while one thing varies periodically, this variable being the absolute positions of the boundaries between the same three successive zones as measured by their respective distances, at different times, from the Equator on the one hand and from the Pole on the other. This periodic variation in the absolute positions of the zones is ascribed to a periodic shifting of the track of the cyclonic storms, these storms being the climatic agency (as distinct from the astronomical factors involved) to which the differentiation of the face of the planet into this series of climatic zones is ultimately due.

In order to grasp the application of this meteorological theory to human affairs, we must remind ourselves of the respective characteristics of the successive climatic zones which always retain their relative positions but periodically change their absolute positions on this view. Proceeding from the Equator towards the Pole, the first zone is a tropical zone of drenching rain and rank vegetation; the second is a sub-tropical zone of drought and barrenness; the third is a temperate zone of moderate humidity and moderate fertility (the succeeding sub-arctic and arctic zones do not concern us here). From the human standpoint, the temperate zone offers Mankind the climatic and vegetational golden mean; the sub-

---

[1] Huntington, E.: *Civilization and Climate*, 3rd ed. (New Haven 1924, Yale University Press), p. 12, quoted above in II. C (ii) (*b*) 1, vol. i, on p. 278.
[2] See II. C (ii) (*b*) 2, vol. i, pp. 304–6, above.

tropical zone challenges Man by offering him less moisture and less vegetation than he requires; and the tropical zone challenges him equally severely by offering him an *embarras de richesse* in both these commodities.

Assuming the truth of the hypothesis that the absolute positions of these three zones periodically shift, it is obvious that there are two sets of regions—one along the borderline between the tropical and the sub-tropical zone, and the other along the borderline between the sub-tropical and the temperate zone—which must be periodically changing their climate in an alternation between one of two different climates and the other. And this periodic alternation of climates in any given area will obviously affect the character of this area as a physical environment for human life. Confining our attention, for present purposes, to the Northern Hemisphere, we shall observe that, when the whole series of latitudinally parallel zones shifts southward, certain areas on the borderline between the temperate and the sub-tropical zone will now become easier for human beings to live in because they will now be turning temperate instead of sub-tropical and will thereby be making good their previous deficiency in moisture and vegetation; and concurrently certain areas on the borderline between the sub-tropical and the tropical zone will also now become easier for human beings to live in because they will now be turning sub-tropical instead of tropical and will thereby be getting rid of their previous excess of moisture and vegetation. Conversely, when the whole series of latitudinally parallel zones shifts northwards, the same two sets of areas in the Northern Hemisphere will both now simultaneously become harder for human beings to live in: on the margin between the tropical and the sub-tropical zone owing to the northward advance of the zone of excessive moisture and vegetation, and on the margin between the sub-tropical and the temperate zone owing to the simultaneous northward advance of the zone of insufficient moisture and vegetation.

Now, on the assumption that civilizations arise as responses to challenges, and that their birth-places are therefore regions in which life is relatively hard, and not regions in which life is relatively easy, we have found no difficulty in explaining the geneses of the Nomadic, Egyptiac, and Sumeric civilizations as responses to the challenge of a particular northward shift on the margin of oscillation between the sub-tropical zone and the temperate zone. On the same showing, the rise of the Syriac Civilization on the same margin—for example, in the oasis of Palmyra[1]—ought to be the result (in so far as it is due to the climatic factor at all) of a similar

---

[1] For Palmyra, see II. D (i), pp. 9–12, above.

northward shift presenting a similar challenge of increasing aridity and barrenness. *Mutatis mutandis*, on the margin of oscillation between the sub-tropical zone and the tropical zone, the rise of the Mayan Civilization in Guatemala[1] ought also to be the result of a northward shift: a shift which, on this other margin, presents the antithetical but equally severe challenge of an increasingly excessive rainfall and an increasingly rank growth of vegetation.

It is here that Dr. Ellsworth Huntington appears to abandon, in detail, the view—which he shares with the writer of this Study in general and in principle—that civilizations arise as responses to challenges, whether these challenges be human or physical. For, in a passage already quoted in this Study,[2] Dr. Huntington suggests that the Mayan Civilization arose in Guatemala when the local climate was relatively dry and therefore relatively easy, and that its eventual decline was due to a local increase in moisture and vegetation which made the homeland of the Mayan Civilization a relatively difficult place to live in. Similarly, in another place,[3] he suggests that the age in which Palmyra rose to eminence was an age in which the North Arabian Desert was relatively moist and fertile, and that the decline of Palmyra was the consequence of desiccation. In putting forward these two suggestions, Dr. Huntington appears to depart from his own general view that civilizations flourish on challenges and decay in their absence, and to range himself, for the moment, with the vulgar view that civilizations flourish on ease and wilt under difficulties.

With regard to Palmyra, the climatological evidence is scanty; and we shall simply observe that Dr. Huntington, in assuming a deterioration of the local climate in the age of Palmyra's decline, has to resort to the argument by exhaustion and that in arguing, on this line, that we must assume a climatic cause for lack of a social cause, he gravely underestimates the strength of the social factors by which the decline of Palmyra can actually be accounted for.[4]

With regard to Central America, Dr. Huntington has at his disposal the far more precise and detailed evidence that is afforded by a study of the growth-rings on cross-sections of the trunks of specimens of the Californian giant pine (*Sequoia*).[5] On the basis of this evidence, he has compiled a remarkable table of dates[6] purporting to show a chronological correspondence between 'inferred

---

[1] For the Mayan Civilization, see I. C (i) (*b*), vol i, pp. 125–7; II. C (ii) (*a*) 2, vol. i, pp. 260–1; II. C (ii) (*b*) 2, vol. i, p. 321; II. D (i), pp. 3–4; II. D (vii), pp. 304–6.
[2] Huntington, E.: *Civilization and Climate*, 3rd ed., pp. 330–2, quoted in II. D (vii) on p. 305, above.
[3] Huntington, E.: *Palestine and its Transformation* (London 1911, Constable), ch. xv.
[4] See, in particular, his *Palestine and its Transformation*, p. 335.
[5] See *The Climatic Factor as illustrated in Arid America*, especially ch. xiv.
[6] Huntington, op. cit., Table 12 on p. 231.

climatic conditions in Mayaland' and 'historical conditions in Mayaland'. And, on the strength of the correspondence which he believes
that he has established, he proceeds to argue[1] that, in the ages in
which the Mayas created and maintained their civilization in the
lowlands of Guatemala, this homeland of the Mayan Civilization
was not covered by a rain-sodden tropical forest, as it is to-day, but
then enjoyed the drier climate and less overwhelmingly luxuriant
vegetation that are to be found to-day on the Pacific Highlands of
Central America on the one hand and in the Mexican Province of
Yucatan in the tip of the Yucatan Peninsula on the other hand—
these being the regions which are comparatively populous and
prosperous at the present time, when the rain-sodden forest that
covers the former homeland of the Mayan Civilization is almost
uninhabited.

In other words, Dr. Huntington suggests that, while the climatic
zones have shifted to and fro in the course of the last two or three
thousand years, the relation between Man and his Physical Environment has remained constant. As none of the present inhabitants of
Central America are masters of the tropical forest, so, he suggests,
it must always have been with their predecessors. The fathers of
the Mayan Civilization must have made themselves at home in
Guatemala in an age when the boundary between the climatic
zones ran relatively far south and when accordingly, in Guatemala,
the tropical forest was not in possession. Their descendants must
have been evicted from Guatemala by the irresistible might of
Physical Nature when the climatic zones shifted northward again
and in consequence the tropical forest returned upon Guatemala to
reclaim the country for its own. Indeed, Dr. Huntington goes so
far as to maintain that the true tropical forest (as distinct from the
jungle through which it tails off into the sub-tropical bush) has
never yet been mastered by any human society at any time or in
any place.[2]

In putting forward this view, Dr. Huntington believes that he is
elucidating both the rise and the fall of the Mayan Civilization;
but, to leave its fall out of the question for the moment, its rise, on
this showing, surely becomes more difficult, and not more easy, to
account for. Dr. Huntington asks us to believe that the Mayas have
never faced the challenge of the tropical forest at all, but have lived,
throughout the successive histories of the Mayan and Yucatec
civilizations, in no other physical environment but that of the sub-
tropical bush in which their descendants in north-western Yucatan

---

[1] In op. cit., ch. xvii: 'Guatemala and the Highest Native American Civilization',
and ch. xviii: 'Climatic Changes and Maya History'.
[2] See op. cit., pp. 180, 186, and 187.

are living to-day. If that supposition is accepted as the truth, we
are left without an answer to the question of what the challenge was
that did evoke the Mayan Civilization. It was not, on Dr. Huntington's hypothesis, the challenge of the tropical forest; and at the
same time we can cite the testimony of Dr. Huntington himself to
show that no equivalent challenge, and indeed no challenge of any
sort, is presented by the sub-tropical bush in which, according to
Dr. Huntington, the Maya have lived and moved and had their
physical being at all times in the history of the race and in all parts
of Central America in which the race has ever at any time established
itself.   In describing the life and êthos of the present-day Maya
in the bush of north-western Yucatan, Dr. Huntington draws a
picture that bears an amazing resemblance to a description of
primitive life in Tropical Africa which we have quoted already in
another connexion.[1]

'The pure Indian is a quiet, slow being, inoffensive and retiring unless
abused. He seems never to work unless compelled. As for storing up
anything for the future, the thought seems scarcely to enter his head.
If he has enough to eat, he simply sits still and enjoys life until hunger
again arouses him to activity. His wants are few and easily supplied.
His agriculture begins by cutting the small growths of the bush, or
jungle, girdling the larger trees, leaving the bush to dry during the
season of little rain, and finally burning it off. Then he goes around
with a pointed stick, making holes into which he drops corn, pumpkin
seed, beans, and the seeds of one or two other vegetables. The corn is
his chief reliance. When the corn is ripe, he has no thought of gathering
it all at once and storing it away safely, perhaps in the form of flour or at
least shelled. His method is to go out to the field in the early part of
the dry season after the corn is well ripe, and half break each stalk in the
middle so that it is bent over and the ears point downward. Little by
little, he picks what ears he needs for daily use, caring nothing that
insects, birds, and beasts are also eating what they need. He knows that
a quarter or a third of the ears may be spoiled; but, so long as there are
some for him, he cares little. The only thing that ultimately stirs him up
to gather the remainder of the crop is the end of the dry season. Before
the rains come he knows that he must harvest his crop and plant more
seed or else he will starve. Therefore he arouses himself for the one
period of effort during the year. He is hardly to be blamed for his
apparent laziness. He certainly is lazy according to our standards; but he
has little to stimulate him, and it is easy to get a living without much
work.'[2]

One has only to compare this passage with the description, referred to above, of primitive life in Nyasaland in order to realize

[1] Drummond, H.: *Tropical Africa* (London 1888, Hodder and Stoughton), pp. 58–9,
quoted in II. D (i) on pp. 26–7, above.
[2] Huntington, Ellsworth: *The Climatic Factor as illustrated in Arid America* (Washington 1914, Carnegie Institution of Washington, Publication No. 192), p. 180.

that, in the un-exacting, and therefore un-stimulating, environment of the sub-tropical bush, the descendants of the people who created and maintained the Mayan and Yucatec civilizations have relapsed right back to the primitive level. And, in the light of this fact, it is surely more difficult to imagine how, once upon a time, this self-same environment can have stimulated earlier representatives of the self-same race to build Copan and Uxmal or to think out the Mayan calendar than it is to suppose that these immense achievements were evoked by the tremendous challenge that is presented—not by the sub-tropical bush, but by the tropical forest.

So much for the attempt to ascribe the birth of the Mayan Civilization in Northern Guatemala or the blossoming of the Syriac Civilization at Palmyra to a state of physical ease arising from a shift in the absolute position of the tropical and sub-tropical and temperate climatic zones. At the same time, there is no objection to supposing that, not only in these two cases but also in several others which have been cited in this Study,[1] a physical alleviation, produced in this way, may have played a secondary 'permissive' or 'enabling' part in the genesis of a civilization, not by introducing a condition of physical ease, but by tempering a physical challenge of previously prohibitive severity to a lesser degree at which the severity has ceased to be prohibitive and has become, instead, a potent stimulus. And, conversely, we may legitimately suppose that, in a case where a civilization is already in decline through other causes, an accentuation in the severity of the climatic challenge may have the effect of making the decline irretrievable and hurrying it towards a final fall.

We may also suppose that, in a case where a civilization is in an exact, and therefore static, equilibrium with its environment,[2] a change in the physical environment, arising from a shift of the climatic zones, may act upon the society in question in a mechanical way instead of through the vital give-and-take of Challenge-and-Response. This is to be expected, because a society that is 'arrested' in static equilibrium is inhibited, *ex hypothesi*, from exercising the vital mobility and free will and initiative which the movement of 'Challenge-and-Response' involves. In this condition, a society must either remain unaffected by the impact of an external force or else react to this impact in a merely mechanical fashion. A case in point is the reaction of the 'arrested' Nomadic Civilization of the Afrasian and Eurasian steppes to climatic changes arising from the periodic shifting of the climatic zones in this area. In periods of increasing humidity, the Nomads are apt to yield ground to the

---

[1] See II. D (vii), pp. 306–9, above.
[2] For such 'arrested' civilizations see Part III. A, below.

encroachments of their agricultural neighbours in the borderland between the Desert and the Sown. Conversely, in periods of increasing aridity, the Nomads are apt to burst the bounds of the Steppe and to pour out, in eruptions of volcanic violence, over the domains of their sedentary neighbours. The connexion between these eruptions of the Nomads and the pulsatory variations in the climate of the Steppes is examined further in Part III. A, Appendix II, in Volume III, below.

THE THREE-CORNERED RELATION BETWEEN THE ROMAN CHURCH, ENGLAND, AND IRELAND

SINCE the first encounter between the English and Irish peoples and the Roman Church, the relations between the three parties have passed through almost every possible permutation and combination. From the seventh century to the twelfth, the English were apt to be the faithful servants of the Roman See, while the Irish were disinclined from the Roman practice and recalcitrant towards the Roman authority. Since the sixteenth century, on the other hand, the Irish have been devoted adherents of Rome, while the English have been Protestants. It is noteworthy, however, that, although the changes which the three-cornered relation has undergone in the course of nearly thirteen centuries have been kaleidoscopic, the English have always contrived, in each successive situation, to retain the superior position which they secured in the seventh century and to keep the Irish at a disadvantage.

It might have been supposed, for example, that the English would have forfeited their advantage in the twelfth century when, nearly five hundred years after the Synod of Whitby, the Irish at length followed the English into the Papal fold. The incorporation of the Irish Christendom into the Roman Church was formally completed in A.D. 1152, when Cardinal Paparo, the first Papal Legate in Ireland, convened the Synod of Kells and reorganized the Irish dioceses. Yet it was only three years after this that a successor of the Pope who had dispatched the legate addressed to a King of England the Bull *Laudabiliter*,[1] which gave approval to the project of an English conquest of Ireland on the ground that this would have the effect of enlarging the bounds of the Church (just as though the Irish had not already come within the Roman fold of their own accord). Thereafter, the English conquerors arrogated to themselves—again, apparently, with Papal approval—a virtual monopoly of all high ecclesiastical offices in Ireland, from which the Irish came to be excluded generically. Thus their tardy reconciliation with Rome in the twelfth century profited the Irish nothing.

Again, it might have been supposed that the Irish would at least have profited by their loyalty to Rome in and after the sixteenth century, when the English turned Protestant; for now, at least, the Roman Church was bound to treat Ireland as her child when her former spoilt child, England, had shown herself so unfilial. Would

[1] See p. 337, footnote 1, above.

not Ireland be strengthened now, as England had been strengthened during the past nine centuries, by having the weight of the Continental Roman Church behind her in her everlasting struggle with her insular enemy? Unfortunately for Ireland, England has always had sufficient command of the sea since the sixteenth century to isolate Ireland from the Catholic countries of the Continent and to deal with her *tête-à-tête*.

But was not this situation, in which Ireland was isolated from the Continent by an English barrier, precisely the situation in which the abortive Far Western Christian Civilization had flourished so remarkably in the fifth and sixth centuries?[1] Unfortunately, again, for Ireland, the situation since the sixteenth century has differed from the situation in the fifth and sixth centuries in two important respects. In the first place, the English in the modern age, instead of being isolated and backward pagans, have been converts to Protestantism: a revised version of Western Christianity which has been adopted, not by the English alone, but by half the nations of the Western World, including some of the most energetic and progressive and successful members of the Western Society. The second difference in the situation is that, in the fifth and sixth centuries, the English had not yet attempted to invade and conquer Ireland and would not have been strong enough to succeed in the attempt even if they had made it. By the sixteenth century, on the other hand, the English conquest of Ireland was already half completed; and the new religious gulf which opened between the English and the Irish peoples, when the former turned against Rome and the latter remained loyal to her, inclined the English more than ever to treat the Irish as 'Natives' who were 'beyond the Pale' (an expression which is actually derived from conditions which prevailed in Ireland during the first phase of the English conquest). In the seventeenth century, the English 'planted' Catholic Ireland with Protestant settlers as ruthlessly as they were 'planting' pagan North America.[2] In consequence, after the Reformation, as before it, the Irish had to suffer from an English ecclesiastical tyranny which remained identical in substance in spite of its change in form. From the twelfth century to the sixteenth, when there was nominally one single church in Ireland to which Irish and English alike belonged, the English (as has been mentioned) assumed in this Church a monopoly of high ecclesiastical offices. Since the sixteenth century there have been two Churches in Ire-

---

[1] In those centuries, no doubt, Ireland had still maintained some communication, round the corner, with the coasts of Gaul and Spain. The ship on board which St. Patrick, in his youth, made good his escape from his slavery in Ireland was bound for a Gallic port.

[2] On this point see II. C (ii) (*a*) 1, Annex, vol. i, pp. 465–7, above.

land, and the Catholic Church has been in the hands of the Irish themselves. But from the moment when the Catholic Church in Ireland was thus thrown back into Irish hands as an incidental consequence of the English secession from Rome, this local native Irish Roman Church became a penalized institution with an alien Protestant Church in a dominant position over it. Thus the effect of the English Reformation upon the ecclesiastical position of the Irish was simply to confirm and accentuate the inferiority of their ecclesiastical status—an injustice which was only remedied by the combined effect of two nineteenth-century acts of the Parliament of the United Kingdom at Westminster: the Catholic Emancipation Act of 1829 and the Episcopalian Church of Ireland Disestablishment and Disendowment Act of 1869.

It will be seen that the history of the three-cornered relation between Ireland, England, and the Roman See from A.D. 664 to A.D. 1869 aptly illustrates the aphorism that *plus ça change, plus c'est la même chose.*

THE EXTINCTION OF THE FAR WESTERN
CHRISTIAN CULTURE IN IRELAND

THE discomfiture of the Far Western Church by the Roman Church at the Synod of Whitby in A.D. 664 was the beginning of the end of the distinctive Far Western Christian culture in 'the Celtic Fringe' as a whole and in Ireland in particular, but the process of extinction was long-drawn-out.

In Ireland, this process was completed at different dates in different spheres of social life. In the ecclesiastical sphere, it was completed in the twelfth century, with the thoroughgoing incorporation of the Irish Christendom into the Roman Church.[1] In the political and literary spheres, it was completed in the seventeenth century, when Ireland was systematically 'planted' and subjected by the successive efforts of James I/VI and Cromwell and William III, and when the traditional art of the vernacular Irish literature fell into decay. This tradition, which went back without a break to the pre-Christian age, and which had been quickened into new life by the conversion of Ireland to Christianity and the development of a peculiar Far Western Christian Civilization, was not broken by the subjection of the Irish Christendom to Rome and of Ireland herself to England in the twelfth century; but the tribulations of the seventeenth century were fatal to it. Finally, in the linguistic sphere, the Irish Celtic vernacular language itself died out (except in a few remote and secluded districts in the west) in the course of the nineteenth century, partly owing to the spread of elementary education imparted in the English language, and partly through the retroaction upon Ireland of the Irish community in America, who became English-speaking instead of Irish-speaking as a result of crossing the Atlantic and settling in a New World where English was the *lingua franca*.

The fact that, by the twentieth century, English had become the real national language of Ireland was brought out in an amusing incident that occurred during the negotiations which preceded the conclusion of the Anglo-Irish Agreement of 1921. During these negotiations, the Irish representatives had been making a point, in the presence of the British representatives, of talking Irish with one another and signing their names in Irish characters; and it had become evident that they did not speak and write this Irish without a certain difficulty. Thereafter, there came a moment when the

[1] See II. D (vii), Annex II, above.

principal British negotiator, who was none other than the then Prime Minister of the United Kingdom, Mr. David Lloyd George, had occasion to hold a confidential conversation with his private secretary, Mr. Thomas Jones. Instead of taking the trouble to withdraw from the room where the negotiations were taking place, the two British representatives simply ceased talking English and began to talk to one another in Welsh, which was the native language of both of them. It then became evident to the Irish representatives in the room that, whereas their own real native language was English, there were at least two British representatives negotiating with them whose real native language was Welsh: a Celtic language to which these champions of England resorted for the sake of privacy because they could be certain that it would not be understood by any representative of Celtic Ireland!

The last stage in the long-drawn-out process of the obliteration of a distinctive Far Western Christian culture in Ireland has been the establishment of the Irish Free State, in which the negotiations of 1921 have happily resulted. Among the Irish themselves, this happy event has been widely regarded as a great act of restoration— a liberation of the Irish genius from the shackles placed upon it by the successive acts of foreign aggression which have followed one another since the seventh century. This is surely an amiable illusion; for, when the nature of modern Irish nationalism is analysed, it proves, like Zionism, to be really a radical form of 'Assimilationism'.[1] Nationalism (whatever nation's nationalism it may happen to be) is the characteristic and fundamental political creed of our modern Western Society; and 'to go nationalist' is the most infallible of all the symptoms of 'Westernization'. The captivation of the Irish by Nationalism, like the captivation of the Jews by Zionism, signifies the final renunciation of a great but tragic past in the hope of securing in exchange a more modest but perhaps less uncomfortable future. If Jewish Zionism and Irish Nationalism succeed in achieving their aims, then Jewry and Irishry will each fit into its own tiny niche in the colossal structure of the modern Western World as one among sixty or seventy national communities all organized on the standard Western pattern. In this posture, the Irish and the Jews may find life in a Western environment somewhat easier than they have found it under the previous conditions when each of them still represented, not just a commonplace national articulation of an overgrown Western body social, but the relic of an independent society of the same species and order as the whole of Western Christendom.

Thus the establishment of the Irish Free State is a prosaic rather

[1] See the critique of Zionism in II. D (vi), on pp. 252-4, above.

than a romantic event. In fact, it signifies that the romance of Ancient Ireland has at last come to an end, and that Modern Ireland has made up her mind, in our generation, to find her level as a willing inmate in our workaday Western World. The romantic trappings of the Free State, which catch (and are no doubt intended to catch) the English eye, are superficial and perfunctory. While the new Irish Parliament and political parties, and the Free State itself, have been decked out with arresting Irish styles and titles, Irish civil servants and school-teachers are rebelling against the demand that the qualifications required of them shall be made to include an effective knowledge of the Irish language (a non-utilitarian accomplishment, inasmuch as Irish is no longer a living language except among the peasantry of a few districts in the west of the island). It is also significant that there has been no movement in Ireland for changing the seat of government: a costly and inconvenient proceeding which is almost common form at the foundation of 'successor-states'. Tara, the deserted capital of the Ancient Irish High Kings, has been left at the disposal of the archaeologists, while the Government of the Irish Free State has installed itself in Dublin: a city originally founded by Scandinavian interlopers and afterwards taken over from them by the English conquerors to become the head-quarters of the foreign garrison by which Ireland has been dominated for more than seven centuries. Yet, in spite of this historic association with an alien ascendancy, Dublin has been accepted as the inevitable capital of a new Irish national state for the substantial reason that Dublin is the geographical point of contact between little Ireland and the great circumambient modern Western World in which Ireland has now resolved to merge herself.

THE FORFEITED BIRTHRIGHT OF THE ABORTIVE FAR WESTERN CHRISTIAN CIVILIZATION

Now that the issue between Iona and Rome has been settled conclusively and irrevocably, it needs a vigorous effort of the historical
imagination to conceive that, in the seventh century of the Christian
Era, the embryonic Celtic and the embryonic Roman Church contended with one another for the prize of becoming the chrysalis of
the new society which was to emerge in the West. The actual
emergence of our modern Western Civilization from a Roman
ecclesiastical chrysalis is such a prominent and important fact in
our Western history as it has happened to take shape, that it is
difficult to persuade oneself that this historic outcome was not
inevitable but was merely one of two possible alternatives. Yet this
now barely credible proposition is the manifest truth. During the
post-Hellenic interregnum there was a real possibility of an Irish
victory and a Roman defeat; and this alternative outcome—which
would have given the whole of our Western history quite a different
turn from that which it has actually taken—might have been realized
in the seventh century, or even in the eighth, if, in certain stub-
bornly contested battles between certain well-matched forces, the
victory had remained with the side which actually accepted defeat.

It may be suggested, without extravagance, that our modern
Western Civilization would probably have been derived from an
Irish instead of a Roman embryo *either* if Colman instead of Wilfrid
had won the Synod of Whitby in A.D. 664 *or* again if 'Abd-ar-Rahmān instead of Charles Martel had won the Battle of Tours in
A.D. 732. And we may confidently promote this probability into a
certainty if we allow ourselves the historical licence of imagining
that in *both* these 'decisive battles of the World' the Fortune of
War had fallen out otherwise than it did.

The course which European history seemed likely to take, at the
moment when 'Abd-ar-Rahmān, carrying all before him, was bearing down upon Charles Martel, has been imagined by Gibbon in a
famous *tour de force* of historical speculation:

'A victorious line of march had been prolonged above a thousand
miles from the Rock of Gibraltar to the banks of the Loire; the repetition
of an equal space would have carried the Saracens to the confines of
Poland and the Highlands of Scotland: the Rhine is not more impassable
than the Nile or Euphrates, and the Arabian fleet might have sailed
without a naval combat into the mouth of the Thames. Perhaps the

interpretation of the Koran would now be taught in the schools of Oxford, and her pulpits might demonstrate to a circumcised people the sanctity and truth of the revelation of Mahomet.'[1]

We should rather be inclined to speculate that 'Abd-ar-Rahmān's victory—had he overthrown Charles Martel in A.D. 732—would have proved of less advantage to the Arabs and Islam than to the Celts and Far Western Christendom.

An Arab victory at Tours might conceivably have had the effect of adding the Gallic territories south of the Loire and west of the Alps to the permanent dominions of the Arab Caliphate. The *ci-devant* Roman citizens of Aquitaine and Provence had already been linked once before with their fellow-Latins in the Iberian Peninsula under the rule of the Visigoths: the Teutonic barbarians who had set up the first 'successor-state' of the Roman Empire in this quarter. The Visigoths had been driven back from the Loire to the Pyrenees by their Frankish kinsmen and rivals in A.D. 507–8;[2] yet, until the Arabs superseded them in the possession of their remaining dominions, the Goths had always retained a foothold on the Gallic side of the Pyrenees in Septimania; and, though more than two centuries had passed between Clovis' march to the Pyrenees and 'Abd-ar-Rahmān's march to the Loire, the Aquitanians had never become reconciled to the rule of the Franks, whose little finger was thicker than the Visigoths' loins.[3] No doubt the Latins of Aquitaine would have been at least as well content as the Latins of the Iberian Peninsula were to exchange a Teutonic for an Arab master. And we can therefore readily imagine an Arab victory at Tours being followed by a permanent annexation of Aquitaine and Provence, as well as Spain and Septimania, to the Arab Caliphate.

On the other hand, it is not so easy to follow Gibbon's flight of imagination in fancying that the troops of 'Abd-ar-Rahmān might have doubled their thousand-mile march from Gibraltar to the Loire by marching on from the line of the Loire to the line of the Caledonian Canal or the line of the Oder. For even if 'Abd-ar-Rahmān had scattered the Franks to the winds and had found himself, on the morrow of a decisive victory at Tours, left master of the situation, with no organized military power any longer in existence anywhere in Northern Europe to contest his advance, it seems probable that the further advance which Gibbon imagines, and which no human obstacle would then have hindered, would have been prohibited—as inexorably as Alexander's ruefully abandoned

---

[1] Gibbon, Edward: *The History of the Decline and Fall of the Roman Empire*, ch. lii. The passage has been cited in this Study already, by anticipation, in I. B (iii), vol. i, on p. 30, footnote 1, above.
[2] For Clovis' victory at Vouillé in A.D. 507 see II. D (v), p. 166, above.
[3] 2 Chronicles x. 10.

advance beyond the Ganges—by the physical impossibility of lengthening any further an already stupendously long line of communications. From their capital at Damascus and their reservoir of soldiers in the Arabian hinterland, the Umayyad Caliphs were unable to send reinforcements and supplies by sea from the Mediterranean ports of Syria and Egypt to those of Spain and Gaul, because the naval command of the Mediterranean had been retained by the East Roman Empire.[1] They thus had no short and easy alternative to the land-route across the whole breadth of North Africa from the Isthmus of Suez to the Straits of Gibraltar; and this route was not only long and round-about but was also beset with obstacles, both physical and human: the difficulty of crossing the desert and the danger of being set upon by the Berbers. Accordingly it seems wise, on this point, to differ (with great deference) from Gibbon; and to imagine that an Arab victory at Tours in A.D. 732 would have carried the North-West frontier of the Arab Caliphate up to the Loire and the Alps but (in all probability) not beyond them.

What would have been the probable effect of an expansion of the Caliphate, up to but not beyond these limits, upon the history of Europe?

The first effect would have been once again to isolate the Far Western Christendom of the British Isles from the Roman Church —as it had been isolated once before, three centuries earlier—by the interposition of an alien society. In this respect, the Muslim Arabs in Southern Gaul would have performed the same function as the pagan English in Eastern Britain; only, this time, the barrier would have been drawn along a line which would have given a much greater geographical advantage to the Far Western embryo of a nascent Western Civilization than to its Roman competitor. In the first place, the Far Western Church would assuredly have retrieved the defeat which it had suffered at Whitby half a century earlier, and would have drawn the English, as well as the Irish and the Welsh and the Bretons, into its fold. In the second place, the Far Western Church would then almost certainly have captured from the Roman Church the whole existing and surviving extent of Continental North European Christendom. The country between the Loire and the Rhine was already honeycombed with Irish monastic cells;[2] and in A.D. 732 the Irish missionaries in the Continental pagan marches of the day—Frisia and Hesse and Thuringia and Bavaria—had not yet been suppressed by the English Romanizing

---

[1] See J. B. Bury's *editio minor* of Edward Gibbon's *The History of the Decline and Fall of the Roman Empire*, vol. vi, Appendix 5: 'The Byzantine Navy.'

[2] See the map illustrating 'Les Expansions Irlandaises' in Gougaud, *Les Chrétientés Celtiques* (Paris 19:1, Gabalda), ad fin.

interloper Boniface. We may even conjecture that Boniface himself would have found it impossible thereafter to carry on his own missionary work in Central Europe without transferring his ecclesiastical allegiance from Rome to Iona. In our mind's eye we begin to perceive the outlines of a picture—never committed to canvas by the Artist of human destiny—in which a Far Western Church, with its centre and source of energy in Ireland and its southern frontier along the Loire, consolidates its dominion over the British Isles and the adjacent portions of the European Continent and then gradually extends its domain north-eastwards—by converting the Saxons and the Scandinavians—until its advance in this direction is eventually barred by a collision with the Orthodox Christian Church, as the actual advance of the Roman Church in the same direction was eventually barred by the same barrier in the fourteenth century.

In studying this actual historical process we have had occasion to notice that when Roman and Orthodox Christendom did collide in Northern Europe, after the elimination of the last of the pagan North European barbarians, the eventual line along which the two Christian civilizations established their contact ran south and north from the shores of the Adriatic to the shores of the Arctic Ocean.[1] Where are we to draw our imaginary boundary between the Orthodox and the Celtic Christendom in our hypothetical reconstruction of our Western history? We may assume, to begin with, that if 'Abd-ar-Rahmān had won the Battle of Tours in A.D. 732 and had carried the permanent frontier of the Caliphate to the foot of the Alps as well as to the banks of the Loire, the whole of Italy, including Rome itself, would then have clung to the skirts of Orthodox Christendom as the only valid protection against this Arab menace.

The moment when the Arabs and the Franks were fighting their decisive battle at Tours was also a turning-point in the relations of the Roman See with Orthodox Christendom and of Italy with the East Roman Empire. At this moment, the iconoclastic policy of the Imperial Government at Constantinople—a policy which the Emperor Leo the Syrian had promulgated in A.D. 726[2]—was driving a wedge between these two portions of a hitherto undivided Catholic Christendom.[3] The Pope was refusing to accept the proscription of image-worship by Imperial decree; the enclaves of Imperial territory in Central Italy which had hitherto held out against the

[1] See II. D (v), pp. 168–9, above.
[2] This policy of Iconoclasm was launched by Leo as soon as he had succeeded in restoring the East Roman Empire (a ghost of the Roman Empire) in the homelands of Orthodox Christendom. (For Leo's role in Orthodox Christian history see I. C (i) (b), vol. i, p. 64, footnote 3, above, and Part X, below. For Leo's personal history see III. C (ii) (b), vol. iii, pp. 274–6, below.)
[3] For the progressive alienation of the Roman from the Orthodox branch of Catholic Christendom see I. C (i) (b), vol. i, pp. 66–7, above.

Lombard barbarian intruders were renouncing their allegiance to the Empire; and the Lombards themselves were preparing to round off their uncompleted conquest of the peninsula by attacking and conquering piecemeal these long-recalcitrant enclaves which had now at last rendered themselves defenceless by deliberately repudiating the East Roman Government's support. At the news of an Arab victory over the Franks at Tours we may conjecture that all these incipient movements in Italy would have been arrested forthwith and reversed.

The Pope and the Romagnols would have hastened to make their peace with the Emperor at Constantinople in order to make sure of Imperial protection against an agile Arab aggressor who had shown himself far more formidable than the heavy-footed Lombard. The Franks—defeated at Tours and now cut off from Italy by the new dominion of the Arab Caliphate in Southern Gaul—would never have suggested themselves to the minds of Papal statesmen as possible alternative protectors of the Roman See, in lieu of the East Roman Emperors. The Lombards would have ceased to cast covetous eyes upon the surviving East Roman possessions in Italy, and would rather have offered their own allegiance to the East Roman Empire in order to save themselves from suffering, at Arab hands, the fate which had already overtaken their own Teutonic kinsmen the Visigoths and the Franks. Thus Justinian's 'great idea' of reuniting the Italian with the Balkan and the Anatolian Peninsula in a reconstituted Roman Empire—a feat which had actually been accomplished in the sixth century, only to be undone forthwith by the Lombard invasion—would have been realized definitively in the eighth century of the Christian Era, thanks to the masterful intervention of the Arabs in Gaul.

In that event we may conjecture that, a century later, the Orthodox Christian missionaries Cyril and Methodius would have been successful in winning the field of their labours—Moravia and Bohemia—for an Orthodox Christendom which would have embraced both the Patriarchate of Constantinople and the Patriarchate of Rome.[1] In these circumstances it is probable that, in the partition of barbarian Europe between the Orthodox and the Celtic Christendom, the Orthodox Church would have gathered into its fold the whole vast family of the Slavs, and that the ecclesiastical boundary between the two Christian societies would have run through Central Europe, south and north, from the Alps to the Baltic, along the line of the contemporary linguistic boundary

[1] The geographical conditions resulting from the historical schism between the Patriarchates of Constantinople and Rome in the eighth century actually rendered Cyril and Methodius's work for Orthodox Christendom in Central Europe abortive. (See I. C (i) (b), vol. i, p. 65, above.)

between the Slavonic and the Teutonic vernaculars. The new Western Society derived from an Irish embryo would then have been confined on the European Continent to a modest enclave between the Loire and the Alps and the Böhmer Wald and the Elbe, and its centre of gravity would have rested overseas: in the British Isles or perhaps eventually in Scandinavia. As for the rival Roman embryo, its attempt to arrogate to itself the function of becoming the chrysalis of a new Western Civilization would have been written off by latter-day historians as an effort which was not uninteresting in spite of its having been abortive, just as the Irish attempt is written off now.

On this showing we may perhaps partly attenuate and partly embroider Gibbon's fantasy. We have already represented the Celtic pioneer Columbanus to ourselves as a second Bellovesus.[1] Let us think of the Syriac conqueror 'Abd-ar-Rahmān as a second Hannibal;[2] and let us imagine him—after a decisive victory over the Franks at Tours—taking up again the brilliant policy, which the Carthaginian statesman and strategist had conceived a thousand years before, of an anti-Roman coalition, on West European ground, between the Syriac Society and the Celts.[3] Let us further suppose that the Arab—rendered more prudent than the Carthaginian by the greater distance at which, in Gaul, he finds himself from his base— is content to clip the wings of Rome by excluding her from Transalpine Europe, and that he does not follow the path of his Carthaginian predecessor in the hazardous enterprise of crossing the mountains and seeking out his enemy in Italy itself. In that event, the picture which we have already drawn will materialize. While Italy and the Slavinias gravitate towards Orthodox Christendom, the Arab victor at Tours, who is too prudent to attempt the passage of the Alps, is equally firm in declining to march on, another thousand miles, into the heart of an unknown and barbarous continent until he arrives at the western confines of Slavdom or at the northern extremity of Britain. Instead of embarking on any such crackbrained military adventure, he insures the exclusion of Roman and East Roman influence from North-Western Europe by making friends, beyond the Loire, with the Bretons and the other Far Western Christians who follow the Celtic Rite, and who are just as ready as the Far Eastern Christian Nestorians and Monophysites to escape the yoke of a Catholic-Orthodox Christendom by placing themselves under the aegis of Islam.

On this reckoning we need not push our flight of fancy so far as to imagine the interpretation of the Qur'ān being taught in the

---

[1] See II. D (vii), pp. 330–1, above.
[2] This analogy had already been suggested in II. D (v), on p. 203, above.
[3] For Hannibal's policy see II. D (v), pp. 161–2, above.

schools of modern Oxford. We may paint, instead, the rather less sensational picture of a Celtic Easter being celebrated in the University Church by monks exhibiting the Celtic tonsure and belonging to the Ionan Order of Saint Columba. And we may imagine Irish scholars, with their lively intellectual curiosity and their restless *Wanderlust*, resorting to the seats of Arabic learning—not merely to Cordova but to distant Baghdad and Samarqand—and bringing back a knowledge of Aristotle, not to Oxford or to Paris but to Clonmacnois: the metropolitan university of a Western World which looks for intellectual light to Ireland.[1] Assuredly these active and brilliant Irishmen would have acquired this precious knowledge from the Arabs at least three centuries earlier than the date at which it was actually conveyed from Toledo to Paris by the stolid descendants of Charles Martel's Franks who have deflected the course of our Western history for ever, but perhaps not for good, by refusing to accept defeat at Tours at the hands of ʿAbd-ar-Rahmān's Arabs!

So near did the Celtic rear-guard of the North European Barbarism come to wresting from the Roman Church the privilege of creating a new Western Civilization. In this conflict, Rome only just succeeded in gaining the upper hand over Ireland.

[1] A certain affinity between the Irish and the Saracenic genius appears to reveal itself in the realm of art; for the Irish art of the now extinct Far Western Christendom is on a par with the Saracenic art in its love for, and mastery of, geometrical design, while its weakness lies in the delineation of living creatures, which, for Muslim artists, is *tabu*. (For these characteristics of Irish art, see Gougaud: *Christianity in Celtic Lands*, pp. 371 and 374.)

THE RESEMBLANCE BETWEEN THE ABORTIVE SCANDI-NAVIAN CIVILIZATION AND THE HELLENIC CIVILI-ZATION

THE resemblance of the abortive Scandinavian Civilization to the successful Hellenic Civilization is not of course confined to the fields of literary art and political organization;[1] it reveals itself likewise in the fields of religion and of êthos. The resemblance in êthos, which consists in the combination of a precocious originality with a precocious rationalism, is touched upon on pp. 355–7, above. The resemblance in religion is twofold. In the first place, the Pantheon of Asgard resembles the Pantheon of Olympus in being a society of divinities conceived in the likeness of human beings, and this not only in their physical form but in their heart and mind and experience and fortune. In the second place the mythology of which this pantheon is the subject is strangely divorced from worship. The Gods and Goddesses who are most prominent in the myths are not invariably the objects of the most popular or the most hallowed cults; and, conversely, some of the *numina* which are the objects of these outstanding cults play quite an obscure part, or no part at all, in the mythological drama. This divorce between myth and cult is brought out in the case of the Hellenic religion by Miss J. E. Harrison in her *Prolegomena to the Study of Greek Religion*,[2] and in the case of the Scandinavian religion by Professor H. M. Chadwick in *The Cult of Othin*.[3]

These resemblances in religion and in êthos between the Scandinavian and the Hellenic Civilization cannot be explained, like the political and artistic resemblances, as outcomes of the identic experience of transmarine migration which was common to the Greek settlers in Ionia and to the Norse settlers in Iceland. On the other hand, they seem too close to be fortuitous. Can we then account for them otherwise?

A generation or so ago scholars would have confidently attributed all these resemblances alike to 'the common Indo-European origin' of the Teutonic-speaking and Greek-speaking layers of North European barbarians by whom the Scandinavian Civilization and the Hellenic Civilization were respectively created, but this explanation no longer satisfies us; for we have now realized that a genetic relationship between two languages is no evidence for the existence of any racial relationship between peoples speaking

---

[1] For the resemblance in these two fields, see II. D (iii), pp. 86–100, above.
[2] 2nd ed., Cambridge 1908, University Press.   [3] London 1899, Clay.

those languages, and also that a racial relationship, even if effectively demonstrated by direct anthropometric measurements, is no evidence for any community of êthos or tradition between peoples that prove to be racially akin to one another. In fact the old hypotheses of 'an Indo-European race', 'an Indo-European êthos', and 'an Indo-European religion' have been exploded; and explanations of actual resemblances between different peoples of Indo-European speech have therefore to be sought elsewhere.

The resemblances in certain religious phenomena between the Scandinavian rear-guard of the Teutons and the post-Minoan Greeks do extend to at least one other people speaking an Indo-European language: namely, the Aryan-speaking Nomads from Eurasia who created the Indic Civilization on the site of the foregoing 'Indus Culture'. On the other hand there are other Indo-European-speaking peoples—for example, the Italici—who display no trace of these particular religious phenomena. The Italici do not appear to have conceived their divinities in human likeness; they had little or no mythology; and their cults were crude magic. Yet the Italici were 'Indo-European' in just the same sense (whatever the sense may be) as the Teutons and the Greeks and the Aryas. Thus these particular religious phenomena are palpably something less than the universal heritage of 'an Indo-European family' of peoples. Yet, even if the old concept of 'an Indo-European family' is abandoned, this does not exclude the possibility of a common origin for certain particular Indo-European tribes which are geographically far removed from one another at the time when they first emerge into the light of History. It may not be fantastic to conjecture that the Teutonic-speaking Goths and Gauts of Scandinavia may have been descended from a fragment of the same Indo-European-speaking tribe as the homonymous Getae and Thyssagetae and Massagetae of the Eurasian Steppe who are represented to-day by the Jāts of the Panjab.[1] A similar connexion may be postulated between the Aryan-speaking Bhrigus of India and their Thraco-Phrygian-speaking homonyms the Brigoi of the Balkan

[1] If the European Getae in the Lower Danube Basin were a fragment of the same Nomad horde as the Thyssagetae between the Volga and Emba and the Massagetae on the Lower Jaxartes, then it is natural to postulate the same relation between the Davi or Daci, who were the historical neighbours of the European Getae in Transylvania, and the Dahae, who were the historical neighbours of the Thyssagetae and Massagetae in Transcaspia. Since the Dacians, at any rate, were regarded as a Thracian people by the time when they emerged into the full light of history in consequence of their collision with Rome, it might seem at first sight as though the tribal names Getae and Davi were both common to the Iranian-speaking and the Thracian-speaking branches of the Indo-European linguistic family. It is, however, perhaps more likely that the European Getae and Davi, like their homonyms east of the Volga, were a pair of originally Iranian-speaking hordes who gradually became assimilated to the sedentary Thracian-speaking populations whom they had conquered. Since the founders of 'the Parthian Empire' appear to have been Dahae (see p. 371, footnote 2, above), it would follow that the Roman Emperor Trajan's Transeuphratean and Transdanubian adversaries were blood brothers.

Peninsula and the Bebryces and Phryges of Anatolia; and again between the Kašyapas who were the historical neighbours of the Bhrigus and the Cassiopaei who were the historical neighbours of the Brigoi. The same postulate may be extended to another series of tribal homonyms: the Illyrian-speaking Veneti (Enetoi) of Venetia, the presumably Thraco-Phrygian-speaking Enetoi on the Black Sea coast of Anatolia, the Slavonic-speaking Venedi (Wends) in the Pripet Marshes, and the Celtic-speaking Veneti on the Atlantic coast of Gaul, whose tribal name has survived as Vannes. Is there any evidence of the same kind for a common origin of the Teutonic-speaking and Greek-speaking tribes who respectively created the Scandinavian and the Hellenic Pantheon? In a recent study of the Greek language[1] it is pointed out that 'there was a Germanic tribe called Ingaev-ones, a name that apart from the suffix corresponds exactly phonetically to the name Akhaiw-oi'. And when we ask which particular Teutonic peoples these Ingaevones were, we find that 'by native tradition—assuredly the most trustworthy class of evidence which we possess in such matters—the name Ingaevones is connected with the peoples of the Baltic and with them alone'.[2]

Then can we explain the common features of the Scandinavian and Hellenic religions as the common heritage of a single Indo-European-speaking tribe, the Ingaevones-Akhaiwoi, which had broken into fragments and come to be dispersed, in the course of history, from the Baltic to the Aegean? We may go on, if we choose, to fortify—or weaken—this equation between the Teutonic Ingaevones and the Greek Akhaiwoi by adding an equation of our own between the Teutonic Istaevones and the Greek Histiaioi; and at first sight this modified version of the 'common Indo-European origin' hypothesis looks attractive. Yet, before accepting it, we may pause to take account of two considerations: first, that it is notoriously hazardous to build historical hypotheses upon resemblances in nomenclature which may be accidental; and second that, in this particular case, the 'tribal identity' hypothesis which explains the resemblance between early Scandinavian religion and early Hellenic religion does not explain their common resemblance to early Indic religion as it is conveyed in the Vedas.

A more convincing explanation will be found in a common experience and achievement of the Norsemen and the Achaeans and the Aryas which has nothing whatever to do with the 'Indo-European' family-relationship between their respective languages. All three peoples alike were barbarians who happened—each in their

[1] Atkinson, B. F. C.: *The Greek Language* (London 1932, Faber & Faber), p. 14, footnote 1.
[2] Chadwick, H. M.: *The Origin of the English Nation* (reprint: Cambridge 1924, University Press), ch. ix: 'The Classification of the Germani', p. 219.

own time and place—to become 'external proletariats' of declining civilizations, and who each succeeded, or very nearly succeeded, thereafter, in becoming the creators of new civilizations on the sites of the antecedent civilizations whose domains they overran in their Völkerwanderungen. At previous points in this Study[1] we have already attributed the idiosyncrasy of the Hellenic religion to the barbarian origin of the Hellenic Society. We have derived the Olympian Pantheon from the barbarian war-band, and have explained the divorce between Hellenic mythology and Hellenic worship as a vestige of the unbridged cultural gulf between barbarian intruders who fashioned a new civilization out of their own social heritage and the heirs of an antecedent civilization who had failed to assimilate the intrusive barbarians. If this explanation of the Hellenic religion is right, then we can account in the same way for the features which the Hellenic religion shares with the Indic and the Scandinavian; since these are precisely the features that derive from the barbarian origin which the successful Hellenic and Indic and the abortive Scandinavian Civilization have in common.

[1] e.g. in I. C (i) (a), vol. i, on pp. 95–100, and in II. D (vii) on p. 316.

THE FORFEITED BIRTHRIGHT OF THE ABORTIVE SCANDINAVIAN CIVILIZATION

HAVING observed the narrowness of the margin by which the abortive Scandinavian Civilization failed to achieve its manifest destiny, let us now imagine to ourselves that the historic encounter between the Vikings and the Civilizations of the South had ended, not as it actually did, but in the other of the two possible alternative outcomes. Let us imagine, that is to say, that the Teutonic rear-guard, instead of being eventually discomfited like the Teutonic van-guard, had eventually triumphed over Roman and Orthodox Christendom, as the Achaean barbarians had once actually triumphed over the Minoan Civilization and the Hittite Civilization. Owing to the accident that, in the Scandinavian case, history has happened to take the other of the two equally possible alternative courses, the unfulfilled consequences of the unachieved victory of the Scandinavian barbarians are as difficult to apprehend in our latter-day imaginations as the unfulfilled consequences of the unachieved victory of the Far Western Christians of Ireland.[1] Yet, if we glance again at the critical events in the history of the Viking Age, we shall recognize that the Scandinavian Vikings, like the Irish missionaries, came within an ace of succeeding in their gigantic enterprise.

Let us suppose that they had just succeeded, instead of just failing, to capture Constantinople in A.D. 860[2] and Paris in A.D. 885–6 and London in A.D. 895;[3] let us suppose that Rollo had not been converted by Charles the Simple in A.D. 911[4] nor Svyatoslav defeated by John Zimisces in A.D. 972;[5] let us suppose that, at the turn of the tenth and eleventh centuries of the Christian Era, the Scandinavian settlers in Greenland had just managed, instead of just failing, to gain a footing on the North American Continent;[6] and let us suppose that the Scandinavian settlers in Russia, having actually made themselves masters of the Dniepr and the Volga waterways, had proceeded to make use of these key-positions not merely for occasional raids upon the Caspian provinces of the 'Abbasid Caliphate[7] but for the exploration and mastery of the whole network of waterways that gives access to the Far East across the face of Eurasia. None of these seven suppositions are at all far-fetched or fantastic; and if we allow ourselves to postulate all

[1] See Annex IV, above.   [2] See p. 349, above.
[3] See II. D (v), p. 199, II. D (v) Annex, pp. 400–1, and II. D (vii), p. 349, above.
[4] See pp. 347–8, above.   [5] See p. 349, above.   [6] See pp. 291–3, above.
[7] For these occasional Viking raids in the Caspian, see Kendrick, op. cit., pp. 158–63.

of them, or even a majority of them, in imagination, we shall obtain a reconstruction of the course of history which will perhaps surprise us.

We shall see the Vikings trampling the nascent civilizations of Roman and Orthodox Christendom out of existence as thoroughly as the Achaeans actually crushed the decadent Minoan and the rising Hittite Society: so thoroughly, in fact, that the two annihilated civilizations do not leave any spiritual children, affiliated to them through a universal church, behind, but vanish, bag and baggage, from the face of the Earth to leave the field free for a new Scandinavian structure on barbarian foundations.[1] We shall then see this new Scandinavian Civilization reigning supreme in Europe in Christendom's stead and marching with the Arabic Civilization across the Mediterranean, and with the Iranic Civilization across the Caspian, as the Hellenic Civilization, once created on new barbarian foundations by the Achaeans, actually marched with the Egyptiac and Babylonic civilizations in the place of the Minoan and Hittite civilizations, when these had been so utterly overthrown that their place did not know them any more.[2] And, after this, we shall watch the Scandinavians turning their energies to the extension of their domain into the barbarian hinterlands on either flank.

The Scandinavians, in their day, were assuredly as efficient in the art of exploration and commerce and conquest and colonization along the channel of inland waterways as the latter-day Cossack pioneers of the Old World or the latter-day French and English pioneers of the New World. The Cossacks, who made themselves masters of the waterway of the Lower Dniepr some five or six hundred years later than the Vikings, conducted their north-eastward operations from this base with such effect that, within two or three centuries, they had threaded their way across the vast expanse of river-shot continent that stretches away from the left bank of the Dniepr to the coast of the Sea of Okhotsk.[3] Is it credible that the Dniepr-Vikings and the Volga-Vikings would have failed to anticipate the achievement of the Cossacks if they had applied their thoughts and energies seriously to this task?[4] Again, the French

[1] For this unfulfilled possibility, see I. C (i) (b), vol. i, p. 99, above.
[2] Job vii. 10.
[3] For the achievement of the Cossacks, and the stimulus of alien pressure to which this achievement was a reaction, see II. D (v), pp. 154–7, above.
[4] The Vikings were actually better placed than the Cossacks for penetrating and mastering the Great North-East, since they were already masters of the Volga—a waterway of unique importance over which the Cossacks never obtained control (the Cossacks were anticipated by the Muscovites on the Lower Volga and therefore had to make the leap from the Don to the Yaik). The Vikings reached the Volga partly direct from the Baltic (the portage to the Volga Basin from the Volkhov Basin is shorter, though less level, than the portage to the Dniepr Basin from the Volkhov Basin) and partly by a roundabout route down the Dniepr into the Black Sea and out of the Black Sea into the Sea of Azov and up the River Don and across the portage between the Don and the Volga at the point where the courses of the two rivers approach nearest to one another. (See Kendrick, op. cit., pp. 158–63.)

and English mariners who eventually made themselves masters of the St. Lawrence and the Hudson, some six centuries after the Greenland Vikings had just failed to master these two North American waterways, pushed westward, inland, up-stream, and on into the Basin of the Mississippi with such effect that, within two centuries, the victorious Western pioneers had reached the coast of the Pacific. Is it credible that the Vinland-Vikings (if Vinland had actually become, as it so nearly became, a Scandinavian colony) would have failed to anticipate the achievement of the French *coureurs* and the English backwoodsmen? The estuary of the St. Lawrence, which offers itself invitingly to any seafarer approaching North America from the direction of Greenland, inducts the explorer, through the chain of the Great Lakes, into the heart of the Continent; and here, at the head of the Lakes, lie vast tracts of country with a soil and a climate in which the Viking pioneer would have found a larger and more genial reproduction of his native Scandinavia.

The peculiar suitability of this region for Scandinavian agricultural settlement is demonstrated by the strength of the modern Scandinavian contribution to the population of the present States of Wisconsin and Iowa and Minnesota; but the Swedish and Norwegian farmers who have been attracted to the American North-West and have 'made good' in these new surroundings within the last half-century have not been pioneers themselves. They have waited for French and English pioneers to lead the way into an American land of promise which these modern Scandinavian settlers' Viking forefathers were on the verge of discovering for themselves at the turn of the tenth and eleventh centuries of the Christian Era. If a few more Viking ships had made the passage from Greenland to Vinland in that age, or if the ship's companies that did make the passage had not shown something less than the usual Viking determination and enterprise in failing to push on beyond the fringe of the great new world upon which they had stumbled, we must surely suppose that, by Hauk Erlendsson's time, some three centuries later, the Scandinavian World would have extended to the Pacific coast of North America[1] as well as to the Pacific coast of Northern Asia. Perhaps the fourteenth century of the Christian Era, which actually saw the completion of the partition of the *ci-devant* Scandinavian domain between Western and Orthodox Christendom, would have seen, instead, a Scandinavian encirclement of the globe, when

[1] There is one alleged piece of material evidence—a Runic inscription, bearing the date A.D. 1362, which came to light at Kensington, Minnesota, in 1898—which opens up the possibility that, in Hauk Erlendsson's age, one band of Norse explorers from Greenland may have penetrated thus deep, at any rate, into the interior of the North American Continent. (See Holand, H. R.: *The Kensington Stone* (privately printed: Wisconsin 1932, Ephraim).)

Viking pioneers who had made their way across the breadth of the
North Atlantic Ocean and the breadth of the North American
Continent to Alaska[1] joined hands at last, across the Behring
Straits, with other Vikings who, in starting out from Scandinavia,
had turned their faces in the opposite direction and had crossed the
Baltic in order to make their way across the breadth of Eurasia to
Kamchatka.[2]

What would have been Iceland's rank and role in Hauk Erlendsson's day in a world in which Western Christendom and Orthodox
Christendom were both extinct, and in which a triumphant Scandinavian Civilization, that had overrun Europe and encircled the
globe, now found itself marching with the Arabic Civilization across
the Mediterranean and with the Iranic across the Caspian and with
the Far Eastern along the Amur and perhaps even with the Mexic
Civilization along the Rio Grande? In this unrealized and therefore unfamiliar but by no means impossible world, it is evident that
Iceland would long since have ceased to be a Scandinavian Ultima
Thule and would have become, instead, the centre-point of the
Scandinavian World: the inevitable stepping-stone, in mid-ocean,
between the European and the American half of the gigantically
expanded domain of a living and growing Scandinavian Society.
And what would then have been the state of Icelandic culture?
Would this brilliant culture, which actually wilted away under the
transforming touch of Christianity before it had attained its prime,
have been able to fulfil its early promise by going on steadily from
strength to strength if a successful Viking conquest of Europe had
extirpated Roman Christianity on its native soil before ever the
alien religion had acquired an opportunity of exerting its corrosive
influence upon Icelandic life? And if the Icelandic culture really
had continued to develop, what special colour would it have taken
and what special lines would it have followed?

From its actual development, before its life was cut short, we
can surmise with some confidence that its aesthetic sensibility
and intellectual penetration would have been of a rare quality and
that its religious temperature would have been sub-normal.[3] The

---

[1] This Arctic route from Europe to North America, which the Scandinavian mariners
just failed to open up in the eleventh century of the Christian Era, is perhaps destined to
be opened in the twentieth century by Western airmen. 'On the British Arctic Air
Expedition [of 1930–1] we spent a year in Greenland investigating the possibilities of an
air route between Europe and America. The advantages of the Arctic route are many.
There are no long sea-crossings; the weather in most parts of the Arctic is more stable
than in Europe; and, lastly, owing to the shape of the World, the Arctic route is the
shortest between England and Central North America.' Mr. H. G. Watkins in *The
Times*, 30th June, 1932.

[2] See Annex VII, below, for a comparison of the lost opportunities of the Scandinavians with those of the 'Osmanlis.

[3] For an imaginary reconstruction of the religious history of medieval and modern
Europe on the supposition that Christendom had succumbed to Viking assaults instead
of beating them back, see I. C (i) (*b*), vol. i, p. 99, above.

two tendencies are interdependent, for both spring equally from the specific êthos of the Scandinavian Civilization which we have attempted to appraise above.[1] This êthos, as we have observed, bears an unmistakable resemblance to the Hellenic; and if we wish to conjecture what the Scandinavian genius might have achieved by the fourteenth century of the Christian Era —supposing that it had enjoyed the Hellenic immunity from a sterilizing contamination—we cannot do better than to remind ourselves of what had actually been achieved by the more fortunate Hellenic genius in its most brilliant early focus at a corresponding date.

What is the corresponding century in Hellenic history to Hauk Erlendsson's in Scandinavian? Hauk Erlendsson actually lived, and was no doubt highly conscious of living, in the fourteenth century of the Christian Era; but if Scandinavian history had taken the alternative course that we have allowed ourselves to imagine, Christianity would have been virtually extinct and the Christian Era therefore presumably obsolete by Hauk's time. In that case Hauk might have been conscious rather of living in the tenth century since the moment when his Scandinavian forefathers had struck out that independent course of their own which had eventually led their descendants to unforeseen heights of achievement. He might have reckoned his chronology from the beginning of the post-Hellenic Völkerwanderung (*circa* A.D. 375), when the Teutonic van-guard went off to the wars and the Teutonic rear-guard made its momentous choice of staying four centuries longer at home. And if we take the corresponding starting-point for Hellenic history, and measure off the centuries from the beginning of the post-Minoan Völkerwanderung, when the Achaeans made a Vandal choice and won Scandinavian laurels, what is the tenth century of the Hellenic Era on this computation? Simple arithmetic informs us that the Hellenic century which corresponds to Hauk Erlendsson's century in Scandinavian chronology is the fifth century B.C. (*circa* 525–425 B.C.). And if we contemplate the historic cultural achievement, in that famous century, of Ionia, the Hellenic Iceland, we may begin to imagine what might have been achieved, at an equivalent date, by Iceland, the Scandinavian Ionia, if Fortune had permitted the Icelanders, as she graciously permitted the Ionians, to work out their own high destinies undisturbed. In that contingency the Icelandic culture in Hauk Erlendsson's day might have reached and even passed its zenith, and Iceland might then have been in the act of handing the torch of Scandinavian Civilization to Norway and to Vinland, as Ionia, in the fifth century B.C., did

[1] See pp. 355–7, as well as Annex V, above.

hand the torch of Hellenic Civilization to Athens and to Magna Graecia.

So near did the Scandinavians come, when they responded to the challenge of Roman Christendom, to achieving the same success as the Achaeans achieved when they responded to the challenge of the Minoan Civilization.

THE LOST OPPORTUNITIES OF THE SCANDINAVIANS AND THE 'OSMANLIS

IN the narrowness of the margin by which the achievement of success was missed on a number of crucial occasions, and in the vastness of the difference in the course that would have been taken by History if some or all of these enterprises had succeeded, the history of the Vikings bears a curious resemblance to the history of the 'Osmanlis.

For example, the fate of Western Christendom was at stake in the Ottoman siege of Vienna in A.D. 1529, as it was at stake in the Norse sieges of Paris in A.D. 885–6 and of London in A.D. 895. Again, the 'Osmanlis, like the Vikings, just missed a number of opportunities for expansion which other peoples took.

The 'Osmanlis' acquisition of Algeria in A.D. 1512–19 came just too late, and fell just too far short, to enable them to cut off, at its base, the Oceanic enterprise of the Castilians and the Portuguese. If Ottoman sea-power had been able to make itself felt at the western end of the Mediterranean some thirty years earlier, it might have come to the rescue of the last Moorish enclave in the Iberian Peninsula and have compelled the Castilians to fight for the retention of Andalusia at the moment when Ferdinand and Isabella were actually rounding off their Peninsular dominions by the conquest of Granada. In that event, the Spanish sovereigns might have lacked the leisure and the means for patronizing Christopher Columbus; and Columbus himself might have found it impossible, in A.D. 1492, to set sail across the Atlantic from Palos. (The 'Osmanlis did take sufficient interest in the discovery of the New World to execute a careful copy of a very early map of the Americas which they found on board a Spanish prize that was captured by an Ottoman squadron in the Western Mediterranean.)[1] Again, if the 'Osmanlis had followed up their acquisition of Algeria by making themselves also masters of Morocco, they might have brought Henry the Navigator's work to naught by closing the Portuguese route round Africa to India and the Far East. The Portuguese circumnavigators of Africa who were scarcely hampered in their enterprise by the activities of the Moorish pirates of Salee might have found themselves paralysed if the Atlantic coast of Morocco

---

[1] See Kahle, P.: *Die verschollene Columbus-Karte von 1498 in einer türkischen Weltkarte von 1513* (Berlin and Leipzig 1933, de Gruyter).

had given harbour to Ottoman fleets with the whole power of the Ottoman Empire behind them.

Similarly, the Ottoman conquest of Egypt in A.D. 1517 and of 'Irāq in A.D. 1534 came just too late to forestall the arrival of the Portuguese mariners in the Indian Ocean; and although the acquisition of seaboards on the Red Sea and on the Persian Gulf, in addition to their seaboard on the Mediterranean, gave the 'Osmanlis the great strategic advantage of holding the interior lines, this geographical asset did not make up for lost time. When an Ottoman naval squadron attacked the Portuguese at Diu in A.D. 1538, and Ottoman matchlockmen fought Portuguese matchlockmen in Abyssinia in A.D. 1542–3, these Ottoman operations were unsuccessful and they were never followed up.

Again, after the Ottoman victory over the Türkmen prince Uzun Hasan at Baiburt in A.D. 1473, there was nothing at the moment to stop the expansion of the Ottoman Empire overland into the central and eastern sections of the domain of the Iranic Civilization; and the 'Osmanlis would assuredly have been called in to the rescue by the Transoxanians and the Khurāsānīs at the beginning of the sixteenth century of the Christian Era, when the Eurasian frontier of the Iranic World was attacked by a new Nomadic invader in the shape of the Uzbegs, if this avenue for Ottoman expansion had not been closed, at that very moment, by the meteoric rise of Ismā'īl Shāh Safawī.[1]

Finally, we may note that the Grand Vizir Mehmed Sököllü's project of cutting a canal from the Don to the Volga, and so securing for the Ottoman Empire the command of the great Eurasian network of waterways, miscarried when it was actually attempted, in A.D. 1568–70, because the Muscovites had just anticipated the 'Osmanlis in securing command of the Volga by taking Qāzān in A.D. 1552 and Āstrakhān in A.D. 1554. This Ottoman project might well have succeeded if it had been put in hand in or immediately after A.D. 1475: the year in which the necessary base of operations had actually been secured by the conquest of Caffa and Tana and by the establishment of Ottoman suzerainty over the Crimean Tatars. In A.D. 1475 Muscovy had not yet doubled her power by the annexation of Novgovod, nor the Cossacks strengthened their hold on the Steppes by advancing from the line of the Dniepr to the lines of the Don and the Yaik.

These Ottoman lost opportunities are a remarkable analogue of the Scandinavian lost opportunities which we have reviewed in Annex VI.

---

[1] See I. C (i) (b), vol. i, pp. 69–70, with Annex I, above.

THE FORFEITED BIRTHRIGHT OF THE ABORTIVE FAR EASTERN CHRISTIAN CIVILIZATION

WE have found reason for believing that the capitulation of the embryonic Far Eastern Christendom to Islam in A.D. 737–41 was an event of historic importance. We may measure its importance by allowing ourselves to conjecture what might have happened if the Umayyads had left unretrieved their great defeat of A.D. 731 in the Pass between Kish and Samarqand, as they were content to leave the defeat which they suffered the year after at Tours. In that event, it is scarcely credible that the situation on the north-eastern front of the Arab Empire would have stabilized itself on the *status quo*. If the Arab frontier had not been carried forward, after A.D. 731, from the Murghab to the Jaxartes, it is improbable that the Arabs would have retained their hold upon Khurāsān. Within the next half-century, the independent principalities in Sughd and Tukharistan (reinforced by Türgesh and other adventurous Nomads off the Steppe) might have driven the Arabs back south-westward through Damaghan and the Caspian Gates, and have made the Dasht-i-Lūt the boundary between Far Eastern Christendom and Dār-al-Islām for the time being. But if the frontier had once moved back to that point, a comparison with the actual course of events on the north-western front of the Arab Empire, where the frontier actually did recede after the failure to retrieve the Battle of Tours, indicates plainly that the ebb of the Islamic wave in this quarter would eventually have gone very much farther than the Caspian Gates.

The strategic circumstances of the European and Central Asian fronts were curiously similar to one another. While the ultimate base of the Umayyad Power lay in Syria, it possessed two secondary bases, nearer to the respective fronts, in two rich lowlands—Andalusia in the one case and 'Irāq in the other—from which armies could draw abundant supplies. Beyond these friendly lowlands the Arab lines of communication had to traverse two comparatively arid and inhospitable plateaux—the Plateau of Castile in Europe, and the Plateau of Iran in Asia—and, on either plateau, the Arab lines were dangerously flanked to the left by a long, narrow strip of unconquered territory. The previous Western Christian masters of the Iberian Peninsula were still holding out in the narrow zone between the crest-line of the Asturian Mountains and the southern coast-line of the Bay of Biscay. The previous Zoroastrian masters of Iran were likewise still holding out in the almost equally narrow (though much longer and altogether more extensive) zone between the crest-line of the Elbruz Mountains and the southern coast-line of the Caspian Sea.[1] In both cases these unconquered enclaves of hostile territory were dangerous—partly because they threatened a long and exposed flank; partly because they were natural fastnesses which it would be extremely difficult to occupy and subdue effectively in the teeth of a hostile population; but, most of all, because both enclaves were hemmed in by the Arab dominions on the landward side only, and were saved from the moral and material handicap of geographical isolation by the fact that they were in contact, by sea,[2] with more powerful opponents of the Arabs in still unconquered hinterlands.

The actual course of history in the north-west indicates what might have happened in the north-east had Qutaybah's work not been performed over again—and, this time, conclusively—by Asad and Nasr. Because, in A.D. 732, the Arabs lacked the will-power to complete the conquest of Aquitaine, the Austrasian Franks were able to join hands with the Asturians and to ensure that Asturia should be an advanced base for future Western counter-offensives against the Muslims. This was one of the objectives of Charlemagne's campaign which ended in A.D. 778 at Roncesvalles; and, in spite of that discomfiture, the objective had been achieved by A.D. 801, when Charlemagne's Spanish march was pushed forward beyond Barcelona.[3] From that date onwards, the local Asturian front became part of a united front of Western Christendom; the ascendancy on the Iberian border had definitely passed from the Muslims to the Westerners; and there is nothing surprising in the developments of the next four centuries, which were consummated in A.D. 1235 by the conquest of Cordova and which resulted in the extinction of Muslim rule in every part of the Peninsula except the enclave of Granada.[4]

---

[1] In climate and vegetation the Elbruz range may be considered as being a detached and remote enclave of Northern Europe, and the sub-tropical coastal belt between the Elbruz and the Caspian as a similar enclave of India. We may compare with this the equally curious enclave of the Mediterranean climate along the eastern part of the south coast of the Black Sea, which also, of course, faces northward.

[2] At that time the main stream of the Oxus may possibly have flowed into the Caspian, and this would have afforded water transport all the way from Daylam to Sughd via Khwārizm. But, in any case, there was always a caravan-route between Khwārizm and the eastern coast of the Caspian. (For the variations in the course of the River Oxus, see Huntington, Ellsworth: *The Pulse of Asia* (London 1907, Constable), ch. xvii. The only period for which a discharge of part of the waters of the Oxus into the Caspian instead of into the Sea of Aral is satisfactorily attested is the period A.D. 1221–*circa* A.D. 1550 (op. cit., p. 350).)   [3] See p. 362, above.

[4] Conversely, what actually happened in the north-east enables us to reconstruct, with some confidence and even in some detail, the first stages of what would presumably have happened in the north-west had the fate of Aquitaine, like that of Transoxania, been redecided between A.D. 732 and 741. With the Arab Empire permanently established in

On this showing, it is surely clear that, if the Far Eastern Christendom of Central Asia had survived the Islamic impact, the boundary between Dār-al-Islām and the new Central Asian World which would then have taken substance would not have stood permanently at the Caspian Gates. For while that narrow passage between desert and mountain is admirably protected by the no-man's-land of the Dasht-i-Lūt on the south, it is outflanked on the north by the fastnesses of Tabaristan and Daylam; and we have suggested already[1] that the Zoroastrians who were holding out in these fastnesses against the Arabs would have made common cause with the Nestorians and Manichaeans and Buddhists of Central Asia if the Central Asians had succeeded in turning back the tide of Arab conquest in the eighth century of the Christian Era. Even as it was, the Tabaris and Daylamis resisted conversion to Islam until the ninth and tenth centuries, and even then they only accepted their Arab enemies' religion in the unorthodox version of the Shī'ah. Had a previous turn of the tide encouraged them to hold out only a few years longer than they actually did, then, upon the break-up of the 'Abbasid Caliphate, the Buwayhids would duly have descended upon the Iranian Plateau from Daylam, but as Zoroastrians and not as Muslims and as conquerors of fresh territory for the nascent Central Asian Civilization at the expense of Islam, instead of their passage being a mere domestic incident in the last phase of Syriac history.

The progress of Central Asia at the expense of Dār-al-Islām would, no doubt, have gone steadily forward. Even if the Sunnīs had made more effective efforts to save 'Irāq, or, at least, Baghdad itself, from the hand of a Buwayhid unbeliever than they actually made when the Caliph fell into the power of a Buwayhid sectarian, the Buwayhid's work would have been finished by a Zoroastrian or a Nestorian Saljūq; for, in the meantime, the Far Eastern Christen-

their rear, as well as in front of them, and with their co-religionists in Aquitaine aposta-sizing in increasing numbers to Islam, the Christians of the Asturian enclave could no more have resisted assimilation than the Zoroastrians of the Caspian Provinces found themselves able to resist it after the Arab conquest of Transoxania. The Asturians, like the Daylamites, Tabaris, and Jurjanis, would almost inevitably have been converted to Islam in the course of the ninth and tenth centuries of the Christian Era. It is true that such conversion, had it taken place, would not have prevented the Asturian mountaineers, in the course of the tenth century and thereafter, from issuing out of their fastnesses and beginning to push down across the Castilian Plateau towards the lowlands of Andalusia, as they actually did. That historical movement was a consequence of the growing social and political weakness, at that time, of the Arab Empire through its whole extent, both under Umayyad sovereignty in the Peninsula and under 'Abbasid sovereignty elsewhere. It was not affected by the religious factor, and the converted Daylamites therefore took the offensive in Iran simultaneously with the unconverted Asturians in the Peninsula. In the sequel, however, the religious factor made a world of difference. The Buwayhids, descending as Muslims (though as Muslims of the Shī'i persuasion), were not, by their conquests, diminishing the territories of Dār-al-Islām. For this reason, these conquests were not so fiercely opposed as those of the Christian Asturians, and were therefore not only more rapid in their extension, but also more superficial and transitory in their effects.

[1] On pp. 377-8, above.

dom would have become solidly established in between Dār-al-
Islām and the Eurasian Steppe, and the Nomadic peoples who
broke upon the Transoxanian coasts of the Steppe in the eruption
of A.D. 975–1275 would therefore have been converted to Nestorianism and would have come, not as reinforcements, but as alien and
destructive enemies to Islam. As it was, the Saljūqs, meeting Islam
and succumbing to it in the Oxus-Jaxartes Basin, travelled on westward as Muslims and discharged their thunder upon Orthodox
Christendom in Anatolia. If we may imagine them converted, in
Transoxania, to Nestorianism instead, and meting out to a Muslim
'Irāq and Syria the treatment which they actually meted out to an
Orthodox Christian Anatolia, we can estimate how disastrous the
effect would have been for the destinies of Islam.

This, again, is not a fantastic conjecture, for, in the last phase
of the post-Syriac Völkerwanderung, a catastrophe of this very kind
actually did bring Islam to within an ace of destruction. The post-
Syriac Völkerwanderung was contemporaneous with a period of
effervescence on the Steppes; and on the Eurasian Steppe, in this
period, the convulsions reached their maximum degree of intensity
immediately before the disturbance died down altogether.[1] As the
disorder worked up towards its climax, successive hordes of Eurasian
Nomads were upheaved and discharged outwards from deeper and
deeper recesses of Eurasia. The first elements discharged upon
Dār-al-Islām were the occupants of the peripheral or 'in-shore'
zone of the Steppe, of whom the Saljūqs may be taken as the leading example. Since, for a considerable period before their upheaval,
these peripheral Nomads had been in contact with, and under the
influence of, the religion then prevalent in Transoxania, and since,
furthermore, that religion happened, owing to the decision of A.D.
741, to be not an unconquered Nestorian Christianity but the conquering religion of Islam, the Saljūqs had themselves become
Muslims before the Völkerwanderung hurled them upon Muslim
lands, and it has just been remarked how this previous assimilation
rendered their invasion comparatively harmless to the invaded
society. In the final and most convulsive phase of the eruption,
however, the circumstances were not equally favourable from the
Islamic point of view; for, in this phase, Dār-al-Islām was assailed
by Nomadic invaders from the innermost depths of the Steppe—
depths to which Islam, in spite of having conquered Transoxania,
had not had time to penetrate during the five centuries which had
since elapsed.

These depths, however (which lay in what are now Mongolia and
Zungaria), had not been left unevangelized. In conquering the

[1] On this point, see further Part III. A, Annex II, below.

Oxus-Jaxartes Basin, Islam had, indeed, effectively prevented that region from becoming the centre of a new Far Eastern Christian Civilization based on an entente between all Islam's local rivals—Nestorianism and Buddhism and Manichaeism and Zoroastrianism—but she could not prevent these rival religions, whose future in Central Asia she had destroyed for any effective purpose of social construction, from drifting eastwards along the Central Asian corridor and establishing a curious, transitory, and abortive ascendancy over the minds of Uighurs and Naimans.[1] Indeed, it is possible that Muslim aggression against Sughd and Farghana hastened the conversion of the Far North-East to Manichaeism and Nestorianism[2] by causing a dispersion of Transoxanian refugees abroad among Nomad Gentiles.[3] If so, the unborn civilization of Central Asia at any rate left a ghost in the shape of 'Prester John', and that ghost very nearly succeeded in taking its revenge upon the remote successors of those Muslim conquerors who, five centuries before, had cheated it of life in the flesh. It is doubtful whether there were any Buddhist or Nestorian elements in the original nucleus of Chingis Khan's Nomadic confederacy; and, even among the tribes on the pasture-lands immediately to the west of his, these elements were probably very small in numbers. They possessed, however, something like a local monopoly of technique and knowledge; the communities among whom they were found were incorporated into the Mongol community on terms more nearly approaching equality than any terms granted to remoter and more alien populations that were subsequently conquered; moreover, their incorporation occurred at a moment when Chingis' empire was assuming proportions which made the introduction of some kind of civil order a necessity—and thus it was that these few and scattered survivors of an abortive civilization were paradoxically raised to places of honour and influence round a throne which bade fair to dominate two continents.

Had this suddenly evoked spectre of the abortive Far Eastern Christendom succeeded in grasping the hand of the Western Christendom which (owing to the faint-heartedness of Arab empire-builders after A.D. 732) was by this time a creature of flesh and blood in all the aggressive lustiness of early manhood, it is hardly

[1] See II. D (vi), pp. 237–8, above.
[2] Buddhism, which travelled eastward and south-eastward to the Far Eastern World along the corridor of the Oxus-Jaxartes Basin and the Tarim Basin, does not appear to have penetrated the steppe-country to the north.
[3] The ruling house of the Uighurs was converted to Manichaeism in A.D. 762–3: that is to say, twenty-one years after the definitive incorporation of the whole of Transoxania into the Arab Empire. In this case, however, the immediate source of radiation seems to have been the Manichaean Church which by this time had been established for a century in the Far East, and not the Manichaean Church in Transoxania. (See Cordier, H.: Histoire Générale de la Chine (Paris 1920–1, Geuthner, 3 vols.), vol. i, p. 500.)

possible to believe that Islam could have survived; and it is sometimes forgotten how very near to accomplishment this dramatic
reunion of co-religionists, long sundered by the barrier of Islam,
was several times brought, through overtures from both sides, in
the course of the thirteenth century after Christ. The overthrow
of the Khwārizm Shah in A.D. 1220 seemed at first sight to have
cancelled, at one stroke, five centuries of Islamic effort in the Oxus-
Jaxartes Basin; and the sack of Baghdad and the irreparable devastation of 'Irāq in A.D. 1258 by Hulāgū Khan were like mortal
blows at the political and economic heart of the Islamic commonwealth. Now the project of Hulāgū's expedition appears to have
been suggested to the mind of Hulāgū's overlord, the Khaqan
Mangu, by the Uniate-Catholic King Hayton of Little Armenia;
and it may have been Hulāgū's Nestorian wife who inspired him,
in turn, to send his advance-guard across the Euphrates, in order to
attack the Muslims in their last citadel of Egypt, under the command of the Nestorian general, Kit-Bugha.[1] In A.D. 1260, when
Kit-Bugha captured Damascus and momentarily gave the local
Monophysite and Orthodox Christians the dominion over their
Muslim neighbours, the Western Crusaders were still clinging to
Acre and a few other strongholds on the Syrian coast, and they were
not blind to the possibilities which 'Prester John's' miraculous
intervention might offer. Already Friar Giovanni di Piano Carpini
had been sent to the Khaqan's court at Qaraqorum by Pope Innocent IV in A.D. 1246 and Friar William of Rubruck by St. Louis in
A.D. 1253. Between 1260 and 1269 Marco Polo's father and uncle
made their way to the same destination as private merchants, and
returned as bearers of a letter to the Pope from the Khaqan. In
1271 they set out, this time from Acre, to make the journey to
Qaraqorum again, bearing an answer from the Pope, and accompanied by Marco, and it was not till 1295 that they returned to
Venice via the Indian Ocean. Meanwhile, a letter (still preserved)
had been sent in 1295 by the Il-Khan Arghun to the Court of
France, to be followed by another in 1305 from his son Uljaytu.
Thus, during the latter half of the thirteenth century, the two
deadly enemies of Islam came within measurable distance of co-
operation. It was not till after the fall of Acre in 1291 and the
successive failure of the second and third Mongol invasions of
Syria in 1281 and 1303 that this possibility disappeared.

Such were the straits to which Islam was reduced in the last phase
of the Nomad eruption and post-Syriac Völkerwanderung of A.D.
975–1275, and this although, as recently as A.D. 1220, Islam had
been the dominant cultural and political force as far north-eastward

1 See II. D (vi), p. 238, above.

as the Oxus-Jaxartes Basin. Supposing, however, that, five centuries earlier, that region had resisted assimilation and had developed an independent and aggressive civilization in the meantime on the lines suggested above, the eventuality which, in actual fact, only passed in a flash across the page of History as a picturesque possibility, would almost certainly have taken shape as a historical event of permanent importance. Supposing that, by A.D. 1220, Islam had already been driven west of the Euphrates, and that a new Far Eastern Christian Civilization had already extended its domain from that river on the south-west to the border of Chingis Khan's homelands in the opposite quarter, it is probable that the Buddhist-Nestorian culture, which exercised so marked an influence upon the twelfth- and thirteenth-century Mongols even in its dim and shadowy residue, would have captured them heart and soul, and that they would have made themselves its apostles as they went forth, conquering and to conquer, to the ends of the Earth. In that case the western bank of the Euphrates would have been Islam's first and last line of defence, and it is hardly conceivable that a single line would not have been broken. Had that breach occurred, Islam in the thirteenth century of the Christian Era would have suffered the fate of Orthodox Christendom in the eleventh. The Eastern and the Western Christian enemy would have united to storm her Egyptian citadel.[1] She would have become a submerged society, and by the twentieth century of the Christian Era she might only have been represented by such 'fossils' as now actually survive of the Gregorian and Jacobite Monophysites or of the Nestorians themselves.

---

[1] Just as in the eleventh century the Saljūqs and the Normans broke simultaneously upon the Orthodox Christian World from opposite quarters of the compass.

GALAXY BOOKS